Using

UNIX

Second Edition

Steve Moritsugu (DTR Business Systems)

James Edwards

Sanjiv Guha

David Horvath

Gordon Marler

Jesper Pedersen

David Pitts

Dan Wilson

que

A Division of Macmillan Computer Publishing, USA
201 W. 103rd Street
Indianapolis, Indiana 46290

Contents at a Glance

Using UNIX, Second Edition

International Standard Book Number: 0-7897-1632-1

Library of Congress Catalog Card Number: 98-84201

Printed in the United States of America

First Printing: *July 1998*

00 99 98   4 3 2 1

Trademarks

Executive Editor
Jeff Koch

Acquisitions Editor
Tracy Williams

Development Editor
Fran Hatton

Managing Editor
Sarah Kearns

Project Editor
Tom Dinse

Copy Editor
Keith Cline

Indexer
Ginny Bess

Technical Editors
Stan Spink
Billy Barron

Production
Laura A. Knox
Pamela Woolf

Contents

About the Authors

DTR Business Systems (the company authoring this book) has sold, integrated, installed, configured, and currently supports thousands of UNIX systems across the continent.

Steve "Mor" Moritsugu (the actual writer) got his B.S. at Caltech, and for over 20 years has specialized in computer operating systems. He is a senior software engineer and is the support supervisor at DTR. He has been a featured speaker at computer conferences world-wide and has written articles for various computer magazines. In addition, Mr. "Mor" also teaches UNIX Operating System, System Administration, and Shell Script Programming at Santa Ana College in Southern California. He has tried a number of UNIX books as the textbook of his classes and therefore has a unique perspective on what is needed to make an effective book on UNIX.

James Edwards is an IT professional experienced in data communications, network integration, and systems design in both North America and Europe. He holds an M.S. in information technology from the University of London, and a B.A. (Hons) from Middlesex University, both in the United Kingdom. James currently resides in Toronto, Canada, where he is employed as a manager with the Deloitte & Touche Consulting Group. His spare time is taken up with his girls, Denise, Lauren, and Poppy.

Sanjiv Guha has 15 years of experience managing and developing financial, banking, and other application systems. He specializes in Visual C++, C, and COBOL development on various hardware platforms, including RISC 60000 AIX, IBM ES9000 MVS, VAX 3400, and Windows 95. He has coauthored a couple of other UNIX books. He is in the process of developing his Java and Windows NT skills. Sanjiv holds a Master of Technology Degree from the Indian Institute of Technology, New Delhi, India. He currently resides in Delaware with his wife, Misty, and four-year-old son, Saptarsi.

David B. Horvath, CCP, is a senior consultant in the Philadelphia, Pennsylvania area. He has been a consultant for over 12 years and is also a part-time adjunct professor at local colleges, teaching topics that include C Programming, UNIX, and Database Techniques. He is currently pursuing an M.S. degree in Dynamics of Organization at the University of Pennsylvania. He has provided seminars and workshops to professional societies and corporations on an international basis. David is the author of *UNIX for the Mainframer* (Prentice-Hall/PTR), contributing author to *UNIX Unleashed, Second Edition: System Administration Edition and Internet Edition* volumes (with cover credit), contributing author to *Red Hat Linux, Second Edition*, and he has written numerous magazine articles. When not at the keyboard, he can be found working in the garden or soaking in the hot-tub. He has been married for over 10 years and has several dogs and cats. If you have questions for David about this book, he can be reached at usu@cobs.com. (No spam, please!)

T. Gordon Marler started playing with UNIX on a DECStation running Ultrix in 1987 and hasn't stopped since. He graduated from the Louisiana School for Math, Science, and the Arts, and has a B.S. in Computer Science Engineering from the University of Texas at Arlington. His first large UNIX system administration job was with the Superconducting Super Collider particle accelerator lab as a member of a group of six who were responsible for approximately 750 workstations and the servers to support them. Gordon works for AT&T Wireless as Lead Unix System Administrator in Redmond, Washington. He can be reached at gordon.marler@attws.com.

In September, 1998, **Jesper Kjær Pedersen** will complete his master's thesis in computer science at Odense University, Denmark. He considers that the most important thing he has done to this point is developing The Dotfile Generator. He has also written articles for Linux Journal, given talks about UNIX, and worked on the UNIX system at Odense University. When he has finished his Master's thesis, he would like to go abroad (to England or the United States) for a few years, to try to conquer the world. In his spare time he does jiu-jitsu, and enjoys life with his lovely girlfriend, Anne Helene.

David Pitts is a senior consultant with BEST Consulting, one of the premier consulting companies west of the Mississippi, with over 1,400 highly trained consultants. Currently on assignment with The Boeing Company, David is a system administrator, programmer, Webmaster, and author. He lives in Everett, Washington, with his wonderful wife, Dana. Everett, he explains, is like living in a postcard, with the Puget Sound 10 minutes to the west and the year-around snow-capped Cascade Mountains to the east David's favorite quote comes from Saint Francis of Assisi: "Preach the Gospel, and, if necessary, use words." He can be reached at dpitts@mk.net or dpitts@bestnet.com.

Daniel Wilson is a principal consultant with Oracle Corporation with the Indianapolis practice. His background includes UNIX Systems Administration and Oracle Database Administration in both SMP and Clustered environments. He has programmed in 'C', 'C++', COBOL, and SQL. He graduated from Ball State University, in Muncie, Indiana in 1984. He currently lives just outside Indianapolis with his wife, Angela, and their two children, Tim and Emily.

Acknowledgments

I would like to thank...

my co-workers and management at DTR for making time and resources available for me to work on this book, DTR's customers for a steady stream of questions and technical challenges, my students at Santa Ana college for their feedback and help with this book, my friends and family for love and understanding, and most of all, to all the UNIX experts who help me when I get stuck.

—Steve "Mor" Moritsugu

Tell Us What You Think!

As the reader of this book, you are our most important critic and commentator. We value your opinion and want to know what we're doing right, what we could do better, what areas you'd like to see us publish in, and any other words of wisdom you're willing to pass our way.

As the executive editor for the operating systems team at Macmillan Computer Publishing, I welcome your comments. You can fax, email, or write me directly to let me know what you did or didn't like about this book—as well as what we can do to make our books stronger.

Please note that I cannot help you with technical problems related to the topic of this book, and that due to the high volume of mail I receive, I might not be able to reply to every message.

When you write, please be sure to include this book's title and author as well as your name and phone or fax number. I will carefully review your comments and share them with the author and editors who worked on the book.

Fax: 317-581-4663

Email: opsys@mcp.com

Mail: Executive Editor
Operating Systems
Macmillan Computer Publishing
201 West 103rd Street
Indianapolis, IN 46290 USA

Welcome to UNIX. UNIX systems are valued because of their great reliability. Often they run for months or years without any system problems or crashes. UNIX systems usually offer the best performance, most throughput, and support for the most concurrent users of any computer configuration. UNIX offers unparalleled scalability, allowing a computer system to serve as a single-user workstation or as a server supporting hundreds of concurrent users accessing a common database. UNIX offers a wealth of utilities, networking and programming tools, and custom applications for almost every business and industry. UNIX rewards the time and effort that you put into it by giving you shortcuts to make you more productive and by revealing its secrets so you can get in "under the hood" to find and fix things that go wrong and to customize the system for your preferences. As new CPU chips are developed, the great portability of UNIX will allow you to retain your software investment as you migrate to newer, faster machines.

UNIX commands have names like ls, mv, awk, grep, and sed, and with them, UNIX experts can do almost magical things to accomplish in a few lines what might otherwise take hours of work or special programming. In fact, Microsoft has just announced a Windows NT Services for UNIX Add-On Pack, which, among other things, allows more than 25 UNIX commands and the Korn shell to run under Windows NT.

On the other hand, there are people who don't like UNIX or its commands. They find them to be cryptic, terse, and unfriendly. UNIX assumes you know what you are doing and usually does not give any warning if you enter a command that makes no sense or can overwrite your files. UNIX error messages often give no clue as to what you are doing wrong, and beginners may not even realize that their commands have failed. Beginners often get their port hung up and have to ask for help to get going again. Each UNIX command can be like a separate kingdom with its own language, customs, procedures, and lore. These kingdoms reward the explorer with new capabilities, but at first it is no fun being a stranger in so many strange lands.

Who This Book is For

If you are new to UNIX, this book can guide your exploration. It will help you with the underlying concepts to most of the UNIX rules and commands so they will make more sense and you will remember them better. It will help you avoid the pitfalls and traps most beginners fall into. You do not have to be a programmer or a Windows user. If you are familiar with MS-DOS, you will find some things in UNIX that are similar, but a background in MS-DOS is not required.

If you have used UNIX for several years and are now ready to improve your mastery of it, this book will help you. The book is grounded in the years I have spent supporting UNIX and teaching an on-going sequence of three full-semester classes on UNIX at Santa Ana College in Southern California. In particular, Chapter 9 (on generating file lists) and Chapters 15 and 16 (on regular expressions) illustrate difficult subjects that I have organized into a series of concepts that build layer-by-layer to over-all mastery.

If you are a Linux user, there is a book in this series called *Using Linux* where you will find more specific information on using and setting up Linux than you will find in this book. However, because so much of any Linux book covers installation and setting up users, disks, printers, modems, networks, ppp, tcp/ip, web servers, DNS, and so on, you will probably find that the coverage of the standard UNIX concepts and commands available under Linux is not as extensive as you will find in this book.

If you use UNIX on a particular type of computer, you may wonder if this book will be useful for that computer. The answer is yes. Traditional UNIX documentation is usually divided into user manuals, programming manuals, and system administration manuals. This book concentrates on user documentation and script programming documentation, which tend to be uniform for all types of UNIX systems, and thus this book will be useful to you (even if you are running UNIX commands from the Windows command line). While there are some topics in this book covering user and system level administration, this is not a system administration book. Topics such as system installation and setting up users, disks, printers, modems, networks, tcp/ip, web servers, DNS, and so on, vary widely depending on the type of UNIX system. For installation and setup, consult a book that specializes in your type of computer or in system administration.

Contacting the Lead Author

Several authors have written chapters for this book to help us meet the publishing deadlines and I much appreciate their help. As the lead author, I would enjoy hearing from readers with comments or questions about this book. My email address is mori@dtrbus.com

I plan to compile a list of corrections and revisions for this book in hopes that it will do well enough to warrant a second edition. I am also talking to the publisher about producing a workbook of exercises and answers to accompany this book. Please let me know if readers would purchase such a workbook.

The company I work for, DTR Business Systems, has provided my services as lead author for this book. DTR supports a network of UNIX Value Added Resellers across the country. I regret that I cannot provide free UNIX support by email, but I'm sure that we can refer you if you need commercial UNIX products or services.

What's in This Book

Part I: What Is UNIX?

Chapter 1, "Introduction to UNIX and the Shell," discusses what UNIX is, its history, and why it comes in so many different flavors. It brings the history up-to-date with the recent release of the 64 bit SVR5. It covers some basic but essential UNIX concepts that you will need throughout the rest of the book.

Chapter 2, "UNIX Directories and Pathnames," shows how to access UNIX directories and files. This chapter covers absolute versus relative pathnames, which is of critical importance in forming UNIX file commands.

Chapter 3, "Displaying Information about the System," shows commands that you can run when you log into a new system, to give you information about your login and station, other users, the system, and its filesystems and processes.

Chapter 4, "Rules for Entering UNIX Commands," explains command syntax so you'll know which spaces are required and which are illegal. It describes the man command, which enables you to look up command usage and options. It shows common errors made on the command line and how to interpret common UNIX responses. It describes what to do if your station is hung up. It tells you how to save the output or errors from a command in a file.

Chapter 5, "The UNIX Graphical User Interface (GUI)," describes the X Window system, which enables you to use a mouse and graphical icons under UNIX. It uses Solaris as a specific example. It covers the Common Desktop Environment that is found on numerous types of UNIX systems and that includes such graphical applications as a text editor, file manager, and email handler.

Part II: Working with UNIX Files

Chapter 6, "Listing, Finding, Displaying, or Printing Files," covers listing files using ls, finding files using find, displaying files using cat, pg, more, less, nl, od, strings, banner, and col. It also covers printing files, checking the queue, canceling a print job, moving print jobs, and formatting output using pr.

Chapter 7, "Copying, Moving, Renaming, or Deleting Files," covers how to do these actions with simple examples and strategies and when different directories are involved. It also covers creating multiple names for the same file using hard and soft (symbolic) links.

Chapter 8, "Modifying, Combining, and Splitting Files," covers how to sort files; how to display just the beginning or the end of a file; and encrypting, compressing, and encoding a file to a printable text form. It covers how to combine files using sort, cat, paste, and join. It covers how to split files using split and csplit.

Chapter 9, "Generating and Using File Lists," covers how to use filename generation wildcards to generate a list of desired files for those UNIX commands that can operate on multiple files. It also describes how backquotes and xargs can be used to process lists of files, particularly when there are too many matching files for wildcards to handle.

Chapter 10, "Comparing Files by Date, Size, or Contents," shows how to use the ls command to list files in order of last access, last modification, or file size. It shows how to use find to list files modified or accessed within a given time span or of a certain size. It shows how and when to compare the contents of files using diff, sdiff, diff3, comm, cmp, and sum.

Part III: User and System Administration

Chapter 11, "File Permissions and System Security," discusses login and password security, and how users and groups can be set up under UNIX to share some files and directories while others are restricted. It covers file and directory permissions and the chmod command in both numeric and symbolic mode. It covers how umask affects permissions assigned to new files and directories. It discusses the security implications of the SUID and SGID bits.

Chapter 12, "Startup, Shutdown, and Managing Jobs," covers how to start up and shut down a UNIX system. It discusses how both users and the system administrator can automate jobs at system startup, on login, and at predefined times or periodic intervals. It covers job priorities and how these can be set and changed. It discusses job control and how to suspend, resume, and kill background jobs.

Chapter 13, "Saving and Restoring Files Using tar and cpio," covers UNIX device names, in particular for tape and diskette. It covers how to use tar to back up a directory or selected files, list the contents of a backup, and strategies and precautions for restoring files. It then covers the same material for cpio.

Chapter 14, "Managing System Resources," covers filesystems and disk quotas.

Part IV: UNIX Text Processing

Chapter 15, "Searching for Lines in a File or Pipeline," describes how to use grep to display lines that contain a pattern. It covers regular expressions, an extremely important but difficult topic, broken down into a series of layered lessons. It covers extended regular expressions in egrep. It covers using perl and awk from the command line to provide additional capabilities to search for patterns.

Chapter 16, "Replacing or Removing Text from a File or Pipeline," describes how to use sed to modify lines using the power of regular expressions. It covers using perl and awk from the command line to provide additional capabilities for replacing and removing text. It also covers cut, tr, and uniq to modify or remove lines or characters.

Chapter 17, "Using vi to Edit a Text File," shows the first 10 vi commands to learn that enable you to do all basic editing. It then covers the next eight commands to learn. It lists various vi commands for inserting text and moving the cursor, introducing the concept of separated words versus contained words and non-words. It lists vi commands for deleting and changing text.

Chapter 18, "Letting the vi Editor Work for You," shows the power of vi in zipping through any repetitive editing chores. Rather than learn separate vi built-in commands, it shows how to invoke sed and awk for search and replace operations, sort for sorting, grep -v for selectively deleting lines, encrypting sections, inserting a banner, printing a section, and counting lines in a section. It shows how to cut and paste and set desired vi options.

Chapter 19, "Command-Line Editing in the Korn Shell," shows how to recall previous commands, modify, and execute them. The simplicity of this chapter belies its usefulness since it enables the UNIX expert to build up elegant command line structures in layered stages.

Chapter 20, "Introducing the emacs Editor," describes another UNIX editor that has great power and flexibility. Many users prefer this alternative to vi.

Part V: Communicating with Other Users and Systems

Chapter 21, "Accessing Other UNIX Systems by Modem," describes how to use write and talk to have an on-line conversation with another user. It covers how to send email to another user and read any pending email. It mentions wall and rwall to broadcast to all users.

Chapter 22, "Accessing Other UNIX Systems on the Network or Internet," covers the basics of TCP/IP, how to use telnet and rlogin to login to another system in the network, how to use ftp and rcp to transfer files, and how to execute commands using rsh (called rcmd on some UNIX systems).

Chapter 23, "Accessing UNIX from Windows," shows how to set up TCP/IP on Windows, how to use Windows ftp to transfer files both to and from UNIX, how to use Windows telnet to login to UNIX, how to connect your Windows to the Internet, where you can then use telnet and ftp to connect to any UNIX server on the Internet. It also covers how to use a modem on Windows, and how to use Netscape to read your UNIX mail and send replies.

Chapter 24, "UNIX and the Internet," shows how to surf the Internet from UNIX; how to download software using your Web browser; how to download and use Lynx, a character base Web browser useful on UNIX terminals for Internet browsing; how to use make to compile the software; how to access UNIX vendors and get help on the Internet (for example, year 2000 patches needed for UNIX); how to access security bulletins; and how to read the Network News on UNIX.

Part VI: Shell Programming

Chapter 25, "Writing Bourne Shell Scripts," covers writing programs in the Bourne shell scripting language. It describes shell variables, prompts, input from the user, command-line arguments, if tests, checking command results, calculations, special variables, usage errors, looping through command-line arguments, debugging, looping to process a group of files, and the case statement.

Chapter 26, "Writing awk Scripts," covers programming using the awk language, which is similar to the C programming syntax. It includes variables, strings, operators, built-in functions, arrays, array functions, if statements, looping, getline to get input, printf to format output, user defined functions, and the system command to execute UNIX commands.

Chapter 27, "Writing Perl Programs," covers programming in perl, which is commonly used both on UNIX and Windows to look up and display information on Web sites. This chapter covers built-in variables, if statements, loops, functions, arrays, file access, hashed arrays, strings, and debugging. It does not cover CGI Web programming, but all the elements in this chapter are useful in CGI Web programming.

What Is UNIX?

Introduction to UNIX and the Shell

By Steve "Mor" Moritsugu

UNIX Is an Operating System

To explain what UNIX is, I am going to first cover some very basic terms dealing with computer hardware and software, and applications versus operating systems. If you already know all this, be my guest and skip these next two sections on computer hardware and software generalities.

Computer Hardware in General

Computer hardware refers to physical elements that make up the computer—things you can touch. Most computers have a keyboard where you type, for example, and a monitor or screen where you view the computer's output. The box where the computer is housed (its chassis) will contain more hardware elements such as one or more hard-disk drives that enable you to store data. You may have heard of disk drives with capacities as large as 500 megabytes or 2 gigabytes. Mega means one million, and giga means one billion. Byte is a unit of computer storage equivalent to one character in a document. Therefore a 500MB disk drive could hold 500 documents that each contain one million characters. A 2GB disk can hold four times as much data as a 500MB disk.

Another hardware component is memory or RAM (random access memory). Often the amount of memory is a power of 2, such as 32MB (megabytes) or 256MB. Some very powerful (and expensive) computers have gigabytes of memory. Memory is the computer's workspace, so having more memory allows the computer to work faster.

The CPU (central processing unit) is an essential hardware element. This is the brain of the computer that allows it to follow a set of program instructions to do computations and process information stored in memory or on the disk drives. You have probably heard of Intel processors such as the Pentium chip, but there are also other types of CPUs that are not like Intel processors at all—RISC processors (reduced instruction set computer)—for example, like the PowerPC. Some computers have multiple CPUs to improve performance.

A computer can also contain other system components such as one or more tape drives, floppy-disk drives, or CD-ROM drives. These components may also be called peripheral devices and auxiliary devices, but these terms are often reserved for attached devices such as terminals, printers, and modems.

Computer Software in General

A set of instructions for the computer is a called a program. Programs reside on the hard disk, run from RAM, control the CPUs, and use the peripheral devices. To distinguish this programming from the hardware pieces of the computer, it is referred to as software. Computer software can be grouped into these categories:

Applications

Languages

Operating system

Utilities

Applications are programs designed to provide a particular set of capabilities to a user. A word processing application program, for example, enables the user to key in and modify documents and print them out. Application programs are available for almost every aspect of business such as accounting, payroll, inventory, point of sale, and scheduling appointments. Application programs also can be found for scientific or financial calculations, personal and home use, and games. The person who uses the application program is called the end user.

Computer languages are software programs that enable people called programmers to create computer programs. Computer languages such as BASIC, FORTRAN, and COBOL have been around for a number of years and are still used today. New computer languages are developed to give programmers better tools for writing programs. Visual BASIC provides graphics tools, for example, to write programs to run under Windows. Java provides graphics tools for applications that run on the World Wide Web. The C programming language is an older, multipurpose, highly efficient language that is still very much in demand today along with C++, a revised version of C that supports newer object-oriented programming methods that make it easier to write complex programs.

An operating system is the central controlling program for the entire computer, controlling the jobs that are run. It also organizes the hard disk into files, where a file is a collection of disk blocks that store information that we want to keep together. The operating system allows each file to be given a name, called a filename, to make it easy for a human to tell the computer which disk blocks to access. Files can be grouped into directories that in turn can be grouped into larger, more inclusive directories.

An operating system enables a user to run application programs and perform system functions such as creating directories and copying files. An operating system schedules and runs all the jobs on the computer. It enables users to log on and use the system. It controls all the system resources such as memory, files on disk, tape drives, CD-ROM drives, modems, printers, terminals, and the network connection. UNIX, MS-DOS, Windows 95, Windows NT, and Apple Macintosh are all examples of different operating systems that are commonly in use today. UNIX is an operating system, not an application—so don't expect to find it as a program on a Windows system.

Many users are more aware of available applications than available operating systems and what they do. When you first power on the system, the operating system must be started before you can run any application programs. This process of starting the operating system is called "bringing up" the system; it is also called "booting up" the system. During this boot up process, the operating system initializes all the devices, meaning it sends them any needed instructions so that they will be ready for use. After the system is up, the operating system has full control over most or all the system hardware—especially the disk drives. When application programs want to access or create files on the disk drive, they don't do this directly. Instead, they ask the operating system to do this for them. Several application programs can access different files at the same time. The operating system keeps track of which programs are using which files. If several programs all request a disk access at the same time, the operating system decides which request to service first. The operating system also determines whether a user has permission to access a file and can block access if not.

Utilities are smaller, independent programs that are usually narrow in scope, providing a single capability or a single area of functionality such as a backup utility. Utilities may be strongly coupled with the operating system or an application, meaning that they are an essential, indispensable part. Utilities may also be loosely coupled as in the cases where the utility is optional, is extra cost, is shareware or freeware, or must be downloaded from the Internet, or is sold by a different company than the one that provides the operating system or application.

The History of UNIX

UNIX is an operating system that was developed at AT&T's Bell Laboratories in the early 1970s by Ken Thompson, Dennis Ritchie, and others. In those days, interaction with a computer was much different than it is today. A computer user was usually also a programmer who would write a program and then punch each line onto a computer card. The user would also put the data to process onto these punch cards. The user would assemble these cards into a deck and pray that he didn't accidentally drop them, because trying to put a large deck back together again in the right order could take hours. The deck would be submitted to the computer operators who would feed each deck into the computer, which would run the program, process the data, and print out the results. The operators would then put the deck and printouts into public bins. Users would have to check these bins periodically to see whether their job was done. If the computer was very busy, the job might not be done until the next day. If your program had any errors, you would have to analyze your listing and printout, repunch the incorrect cards, resubmit the whole job, and wait for the new results. The middle of the night was often a good time to submit jobs because the results would come back quickly and you could change and resubmit the job several times with a minimum of waiting. This style of computer usage is called batch operation because the computer runs only one job at a time. It does not run the next job until the current job has totally completed.

In the late 1960s, a new way of using computers was being developed called time-sharing. Under time-sharing, the computer can run several jobs simultaneously by switching from job to job and giving each job a small, limited piece of time to run until it is time to switch to the next job. Time-sharing enabled multiple users to interact directly with the computer. The computer could immediately show them any errors in their programs and they could correct the errors and rerun the job without the large delays that occur in batch processing. Bell Laboratories, along with GE and MIT, was working on a time-sharing system called Multics. In 1969, however, it was canceled because Multics was too complex and difficult. Thompson, Ritchie, and other Bell Laboratory people continued to work on their own time-sharing system. They called it UNIX because it was a simpler, more efficient operating system than Multics.

Many other computer operating systems were being developed at this time. New computers, faster and more powerful, were being developed. And in those days, each new computer had its own unique operating system. Whenever a computer manufacturer developed a new computer, it would also have to provide an operating system to run on that computer. It would also provide new utilities and applications to run on that new operating system. These were called proprietary systems because the computer manufacturer owned the only operating system that would run on this computer. Users were locked into that vendor to supply the basic and necessary software for that machine.

A key part of the UNIX story is the fact that, at this time, AT&T could not branch out into the computer business because of legal restrictions. Therefore AT&T did not develop and sell its own computer systems. It purchased computers from other companies. Because they were using UNIX on more and more of their computers, they wanted to find a way to easily move it to run on different computers that they might purchase.

Most operating systems, including early UNIX, were written in assembly language. Assembly language is called a low-level computer language because each instruction is a basic operation of the computer hardware. Low-level languages work with the registers and memory accesses that form the basic operation of the computer. Hence an assembly language programmer can code very tight efficient loops—this is essential for operating system code used over and over. High-level languages such as BASIC, FORTRAN, and COBOL are far removed from the machine level. They provide programming tools and concepts that make it much easier to write programs, but the code produced is not as efficient as assembly language coding.

Thompson and the others realized that it was important to be able to port UNIX to run on new computers as they became available. They also realized that if they continued to write UNIX in assembly language, it would take far too much effort to port the whole system to new computers. Thompson developed a language called B, and Ritchie improved it and called it C. By 1973, they had rewritten almost all of UNIX in this new high-level C programming language that was still very efficient for writing operating system code. They could now provide the same operating system on several different types of computers. They continued to add new functionality to UNIX, wrote papers on UNIX internals, and made it available to universities who were intrigued by the design concepts and the fact that it would run on many computers. New features and variants of UNIX were offered by universities and other computer companies who started to use UNIX and extend it for their own needs.

I first encountered UNIX in the mid 1980s. I was part of an operating system group that wrote and supported a proprietary operating system for the Point 4 minicomputer. In those days, our whole proprietary operating system and all the user data could fit in a 20MB disk drive. It could run with only 128KB of memory. UNIX was not a threat to the proprietary systems of those days because UNIX required much more disk space, memory, and CPU power; therefore it was not as cost-effective. All the computer manufacturers offered their own highly optimized proprietary operating systems that could run with a minimum size disk and with minimum memory. These proprietary time-sharing systems still locked computer users into the computer products from one company. This resulted in higher prices because the one company had to do all the program development; therefore there was little competition.

By 1990, the computer landscape had changed considerably. UNIX had won the battle against the proprietary systems. The hardware costs of memory and disk had gone down so much that the extra memory and disk required by UNIX was no longer a major consideration. The big selling point of UNIX was that it was an open system, meaning that users would no longer be locked into a proprietary system. Because UNIX was written in a higher-level language, it could be easily ported to other types of computers and all the application software that ran on the old computer could be easily ported to the new computer. Prices on open UNIX systems were much more competitive than on proprietary systems. At the same time, UNIX had an extremely rich set of utilities and capabilities as a result of the combined efforts of Bell Laboratories, universities such as Berkeley, and companies such as Sun Microsystems. As UNIX gained momentum, companies writing new software applications would choose to write for the UNIX platform so that their software could run on a variety of hardware, which again hastened the demise of the proprietary systems. Although some computer vendors still offer or support a proprietary operating system, they also usually offer an alternative UNIX product line.

How UNIX Built the Internet

The Internet began as a Defense Department project (DARPA) to connect government, military, and university computers. As the number of host systems in the network grew, they needed an efficient method of sending information in packets from one system, through other systems and routers in the network, to a desired destination. As the network grew larger, they needed dynamic routing to bypass down computers or bad connections. The packet routing protocol that was developed is called TCP/IP, first implemented in UNIX at the University of

California at Berkeley. UNIX and TCP/IP became the backbone of the Internet, tying thousands and then millions of computers together. UNIX and other servers on the Internet make vast amounts of data, research, news, current events, business, and human interest information available via the World Wide Web. In this way, millions of people use UNIX systems and are not even aware of it.

The Diversity of UNIX

As computer vendors ported UNIX to their own machines, they often gave it a unique name. The following section provides a partial list, in no special order, of some computer companies that sell UNIX systems.

What Types of UNIX Systems Are There?

This list shows whether the vendor has given UNIX a special name and whether they have given the system they sell a special name.

TABLE 1.1   Some companies that sell UNIX

Computer Company	UNIX o/s
AT&T	UNIX SVR3
AT&T	UNIX SVR4
Sun Microsystems/SunSoft	SunOS (which is a component of Solaris)
Sun Microsystems/SunSoft	Interactive UNIX
Hewlett-Packard (HP)	HP-UX
Data General (DG)	DG-UX
Novell	UnixWare (early version)
Santa Cruz Operation (SCO)	UnixWare
Santa Cruz Operation (SCO)	OpenServer
Santa Cruz Operation (SCO)	XENIX

continues…

TABLE 1.1   **Continued**

Computer Company	UNIX o/s
Microsoft	XENIX (early version)
IBM	AIX
SiliconGraphics (SGI)	IRIX
Digital Equipment Corp (DEC)	ULTRIX
Digital Equipment Corp (DEC)	Digital UNIX
NCR	NCR UNIX
Siemens Nixdorf (SNI)	Reliant UNIX
Caldera	Caldera OpenLinux
RedHat Software	RedHat Linux
Noncommercial sources	**UNIX o/s**
UC Berkeley	BSD (Berkeley Software Distribution)
FreeBSD Project	FreeBSD
Free Software Foundation	GNU/Linux
Linus Torvalds	Linux kernel
Debian	Debian GNU/Linux

This list is by no means complete. Other companies such as Bull and Motorola, for example, sell computer systems using the AIX operating system. Unisys sells computers running UnixWare. Other well-respected companies sell UNIX and Linux systems. Some of the products listed may be old products that have been superseded by newer ones. Some of the listed companies may no longer sell the particular UNIX product listed.

Non-AT&T UNIX

If you watch a UNIX system as it is first powered on, you may see a long series of copyright notices acknowledging the various companies and organizations that have contributed software to UNIX over the years. One of the copyright notices you might see is from the Regents of the University of California for the considerable work done at Berkeley on UNIX. The UNIX produced at this university is called BSD—for Berkeley Software

Distribution. Many of the BSD utilities have become standard in all UNIX packages. FreeBSD is an extension of BSD where the copyrighted AT&T UNIX code has been removed or rewritten so that it can be distributed without the usual UNIX royalties and source code restrictions. For more complete information, see www.freebsd.org on the World Wide Web.

Linus Torvalds wrote his own UNIX kernel that is the main executable part of the operating system. He called this kernel Linux; and although it emulates the main features of UNIX, it does not use any restricted source code. His kernel is distributed with utilities from the Free Software Foundation's GNU project— which stands for "GNU's not UNIX." The goal of this project was to create a free UNIX system. It had created many significant free software utilities such as the GNU C Compiler and the GNU emacs text editor. Combining the Linux kernel with the GNU utilities at last created a complete UNIX-like system that was free of AT&T UNIX copyrights and royalties. This version of UNIX can be used for commercial purposes. It is governed by a special license called the GPL, which prevents the operating system source code from being restricted or copyrighted. For more complete information, see www.gnu.org and www.linux.org.

Commercial UNIX systems usually run on expensive computers that support a large number of users. They are usually maintained by a computer operations staff. The average user never even sees the UNIX machine, just terminals that are attached to it. All system administration functions are done by the computer staff. The average user cannot even view most of the system configuration files. These free non-AT&T UNIX systems, on the other hand, have allowed UNIX to be loaded on a home computer. Users can install and administer their own personal UNIX systems. In fact, they usually have no choice because private homes rarely have their own data processing departments. These free UNIX systems can be connected to the Internet as a Web server, email handler, or DNS server.

Dedicated volunteers add new modules to the free UNIX so that it stays current with new hardware as it becomes available. Although some companies provide commercial support for

Linux, there is still a hesitancy to use free UNIX in large commercial enterprises. Still this free, fully functional UNIX is certainly playing an important role in the evolution of UNIX.

How UNIX Differs from MS-DOS/Windows

UNIX, MS-DOS, Windows 95, and Windows NT are different operating systems. From its beginning, UNIX was designed to be a multi-user, time-share operating system that can efficiently handle a large number of user stations running different programs simultaneously. Personal computers, or PCs, developed along a totally different path. PCs have one keyboard, one screen, and one mouse; therefore they accommodate only a single user. The same Pentium processor that supports a single user under MS-DOS or Windows might support 100 concurrent users under UNIX.

The look and feel of Windows software is quite different from traditional UNIX character-based software. If a Windows user starts a job, the processor normally has a lot a spare computing power available; therefore Windows users are used to busy screens, colorful indicators that graphically show a job progressing. In contrast, traditional UNIX software outputs few messages until the job is done. Keep in mind that UNIX may be running 100 other jobs at the same time it is running your job. Any wasted effort or output would slow down someone else's job.

Today the differences between UNIX and Windows are not so clear cut. Many UNIX systems are single-user workstations, where the user utilizes a mouse to click on icons and manipulate windows. Some Windows systems directly run jobs for other users logged on from serial ports or from another Windows PC. Some Windows NT and UNIX servers have no direct users at all. They provide services to a network such as print sharing, file sharing, email, or Internet access. Many UNIX systems can run Windows programs (for example, through WABI). Many Windows systems can run UNIX utilities such as vi, awk, and shell (through MKS tools).

One large difference between UNIX and Windows is where users get applications for their system. A wide range of general purpose utilities are available for Windows systems at the local PC store. Programs such as word processing, spreadsheet, and checkbook balancing are generally useful no matter what business you are in. On the other hand, you will rarely find any UNIX applications at the PC store. One of great strengths of UNIX is that it is an excellent platform to write custom software for a particular industry. UNIX supports many programming languages, databases, and program development tools. It is an open system, so it runs on many different hardware systems. UNIX software developers often study one industry such dental offices, lumber stores, auto parts, or flower shops. They then create a set of applications to computerize all the business functions needed by that particular business, using the jargon and special regulations, forms, and accounting needed. We can call these vertical applications: a complete set of applications for one target business, whereas PC stores often sell horizontal applications where one application is general enough for a wide range of businesses. The software developer uses UNIX to create a turn-key system—that is, the end user turns the key to power the system on and then uses just the supplied custom programming to run his business.

Today, Windows systems are being networked together to provide the multi-user capability that UNIX provides. Software developers are creating Windows graphics multi-user programs that have a jazzier look and feel than traditional UNIX character-based applications. UNIX can support graphic applications by using special X Windows stations; however, these stations cannot run Windows software from the PC store. Led by Sun Microsystems and its support of the Java language, there is an effort to capitalize on the success of the World Wide Web to provide multi-user graphics Web-based applications. Running the application through a Web browser is a way to provide the jazzier graphic look and feel that traditional UNIX character-based applications lack. These applications can run on local networks, and they can run over the Internet. They can run on low-cost network computers that are minimal computer stations specially designed to run these browser applications. The host server can be Windows or UNIX; this should be appealing for software development companies. Will browser-based applications become a new application standard? Only time will tell....

UNIX Standards and Revisions

Table 1.1 listed many companies that have modified UNIX and distribute the operating system under some name other than UNIX, such as HP-UX or SunOS. In this book, you will sometimes see two or three different ways to do one task, because some types of UNIX computers can only do it the first way, some only the second way, and some only the third. At one company, you may regularly use several different types of UNIX servers where the commands have such differences. If you connect to a wide area network such as the Internet, you will encounter even more UNIX hosts where UNIX is slightly different than what you are used to. At first you may find this variety disconcerting.

In answer to that, let me describe how UNIX is like a car radio. All car radios can play music, adjust the volume, and change the station. Radios differ considerably, however, in the placement and use of knobs, buttons, or sliders. The volume control is not always on the left. Yet if you rent a car, you can usually still get the radio to work. People are accustomed to fiddling with the controls until they get it to do what they want. In the same way, there is no need to panic when you work on a UNIX system where the commands are slightly different than the UNIX you are used to. After you know the major varieties, if a command does not work one way, you just try the other standard methods.

Efforts to standardize UNIX abound, attempting to make the commands uniform across different hardware and vendor platforms. POSIX is a standard from an organization called IEEE that many types of UNIX adhere to. The international X/Open organization provides UNIX standards called XPG3, XPG4, and Spec 1170. Many companies—such as IBM, HP, Sun, and

SCO—have adopted the common desktop environment (CDE) to provide a common look and feel for graphic UNIX. SVID (System V Interface Definition) is another standard to help keep UNIX more uniform.

It helps to see how UNIX evolved to anticipate what command variations to expect on an unknown UNIX system. In the beginning, UNIX was developed at AT&T Bell Laboratories, who gave these names to successive revisions of AT&T UNIX:

Sixth edition

Seventh edition

System III

(They skipped System IV.)

System V   (That is, Roman numeral five)

System V, Release 2   (Abbreviated as SVR2)

System V, Release 3   (SVR3)

System V, Release 4   (SVR4)

SVID describes a standard for UNIX based on AT&T's System V UNIX.

While this AT&T development was occurring, an early version of UNIX was being modified at the University of California at Berkeley. Their version of UNIX is called BSD, standing for Berkeley Software Distribution. BSD added many important capabilities to UNIX, but some of these overlapped new features added by AT&T.

Today, all UNIX systems can be classified by the extent to which they are based on System V UNIX versus BSD UNIX. The presence of the directory /etc/rc2.d denotes System V-based UNIX, whereas the absence of this directory usually indicates a BSD-based UNIX. Here are some specific examples of how some specific commands differ between System V and BSD:

System V	**BSD**
shutdown -g3 -i0 -y	shutdown -h +3
lp -dlaser2 -n2 acme	lpr -Plaser2 -#2 acme

If your system does not support the System V lp command for printing, it probably uses the BSD lpr command. Some systems support both printer commands. SunOS rev 4, for example, was a BSD UNIX variant. The next major release, SunOS rev 5, switched over from BSD to SVR4, which combined features from (System V) SVR3, XENIX, BSD, and Sun. SunOS rev 5 still supports the rev 4 BSD versions of utilities as optional alternatives. Users on SunOS rev 5 can customize their UNIX session to use System V, BSD, or XPG4 versions of utilities by default. (This is done by changing the PATH variable.)

SEE ALSO

➤ *For more information on the* PATH *variable, see page* 97

UNIX After AT&T

Initially AT&T developed and licensed UNIX, controlled the restricted source code, and collected royalties from other companies who sold UNIX. Around 1991, AT&T created a company called UNIX System Laboratories to do this. Around 1993, Novell purchased UNIX from AT&T. Novell integrated some of their NetWare technology and created UnixWare, which is based on SVR4. Novell transferred the UNIX trademark to the X/Open Company Ltd. , which publishes standards and certifies whether a version of UNIX meets the standard. Novell retained the right to license UNIX System V source code. Around 1995, the Santa Cruz Operation (SCO) purchased UNIX from Novell. SCO then had two major lines of UNIX it supported: its own OpenServer and UnixWare. This year (1998) SCO, in conjunction with a number of major UNIX vendors, is releasing UnixWare 7, which contains the next major release of UNIX: SVR5, a 64-bit UNIX operating system. This is not the only 64-bit UNIX operating system, so there is still healthy competition in the UNIX marketplace.

Important UNIX Concepts You Must Know First

The following sections cover the basic features of the UNIX operating system you need to understand.

The UNIX Kernel

In Figure 1.1, you can see the UNIX operating system represented as three concentric circles. The innermost circle is called the kernel, which refers to the nucleus or core of the operating system. The kernel is the most hidden part of the operating system. It contains code called drivers; these allow the system to control all the system hardware, the disk drives, the peripherals, and so on.

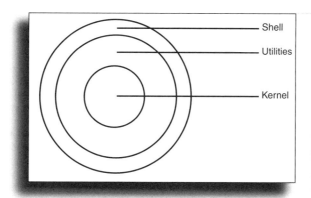

FIGURE 1.1
UNIX kernel, utilities, and shell.

The next circle represents the system utilities and commands. When you run a command such as vi, it uses routines within the kernel to display output on your screen, get input from the keyboard, and save files on the disk.

The UNIX Shell

The outermost circle represents the UNIX shell. The shell is a program that accepts commands from a user and starts the requested commands. The shell is all that the user sees of the UNIX operating system—just as when you view an egg or a nut, all you see is the outermost shell layer and none of the complexity inside.

The shell does more than just pass on the commands you type in. The shell enables the user to run commands in the background; this means that the user's station is not tied up while the command runs. The shell enables the user to use wildcards to indicate which files should be processed. The shell in fact supports a complete programming language that allows conditional execution of commands based on the results of other commands and loops to repeat sequences of commands.

A number of shell programs are actually available on UNIX, and different users can be using their preferred, different shells at the same time. The first three shells in the following table are usually available on most commercial UNIX systems today.

TABLE 1.2   Available UNIX shells

Shell Name	Command	Description
Bourne shell	`sh`	Available on all UNIX systems
C shell	`csh`	C programming-like syntax
Korn shell	`ksh`	Superset of the Bourne shell
Bash shell	`bash`	Contains both C and Korn shell features
tcsh shell	`tcsh`	Like the C shell

Because each shell is a system utility, you can start using a particular shell just by entering the command shown in Table 1.2.

The Bourne shell is the oldest shell. It is an adequate programming environment, but it is weak in user conveniences; its offers no way to repeat or re-edit previous commands and no way to control background jobs. Some older systems did not have the C shell or the Korn shell. Therefore many programmers today still write programs (called scripts) primarily for the Bourne shell, even though they use other shells when they are typing in commands.

Although the C shell was an improvement in user convenience over the Bourne shell, some of its syntax is not compatible with the Bourne shell. Because Bourne shells scripts are common, C shell users must learn the syntax for both shells and avoid confusing them.

The Korn shell offers similar user conveniences as the C shell. It has a powerful command-line editing capability, not available in the C shell, using either `vi` or `emacs` editing commands that enable you to retrieve previous commands, edit, and execute them. The Korn shell is a superset of the Bourne shell, so there are no syntax conflicts between them. The Korn shell offers more powerful programming constructs than the Bourne shell. These should be avoided, however, if you need to run your programs on older UNIX systems that did not offer the Korn shell.

The Shell Prompt

To use a UNIX system, the system administrator (called "root") must create an account for you to use. The start of a UNIX session will look something like this:

```
acme login: fred
Password:
TERM = (vt100)
$ _
```

At the logon prompt, you must identify yourself and enter your password (which will not display as you type it for security). The dollar sign ($) is the shell prompt that shows that UNIX is ready for you to enter commands. The underline character (_) following the dollar sign ($) represents the cursor waiting for commands to be input. Here are the standard shell prompts:

```
 Bourne shell or Korn shell:    $
                   C shell:    %
root login regardless of shell:    #
```

The shell prompt can be customized to contain your system name, your current directory, or other characters. Here are some shell prompts you might encounter:

```
acme$ _
/usr/fred> _
[acme] _
```

You must be at the shell prompt before you can enter UNIX commands. You can also use UNIX through a graphical user interface (GUI) as described in Chapter 5.

Warning

The root logon is the all-powerful system administrator. If you are a beginner, stay away from the root logon. If you make mistakes as root, you can crash or corrupt your UNIX system.

Shell Variables

The shell supports variables. Words, phrases, and other information can be saved in a named variable and used later. Some variables have special meaning to the shell and control how the system operates. The TERM variable, for example, should be set to the type of terminal you are using; otherwise, your screen output may contain garbage. Many shell variables have names in all uppercase to avoid confusion with UNIX commands (which are usually in lowercase).

Standard Output, Standard Error, Standard Input

Programs under UNIX usually do not display messages directly to your screen. Instead they call a special output routine called Standard Output (or stdout, for short). stdout is normally set up to go to your screen, but stdout can be easily redirected to go to a device such as a printer or to a disk file. This is one of the elements of UNIX that is truly elegant. Programs and utilities do their output to stdout so that they have no idea where the output is really going. The shell can easily redirect stdout to a device or file as desired.

```
$ cal
$ cal > /dev/lp0
$ cal > /usr/fred/year
```

The preceding three examples use the UNIX cal command, which outputs a calendar of the current month to stdout. In the first example, stdout has not been redirected; therefore the output goes to your screen. In the second example, the greater than sign (>) redirects stdout to a printer device (/dev/lp0) so that the output appears on that printer. In the third example, stdout has been redirected to a disk file so that the output is saved on disk.

There is also a special routine to use to display error messages. This is called Standard Error (or stderr, for short). stderr usually goes to your screen so that you can see any error messages. But again, the shell can easily redirect stderr to a device or file, totally independently of stdout. Therefore stdout can be saved in a separate file from stderr.

A special routine to do input is available. This is called Standard Input (or stdin, for short). If a program gets its input from stdin, the shell can provide this input by redirecting it from a device or disk file. If a utility always asks three questions before it starts to run, for example, you could put the answers to those three questions into a disk file and then redirect that disk file to provide the input so that you don't have to type the input yourself.

Piping and Filters

stdout from one command can be redirected as stdin to another command, creating a direct pipeline from one command to another. We call this operation *piping*, and we use the vertical bar (|) as the pipe sign character.

```
$ ls ¦ pg
```

In the preceding example, ls is the UNIX command to list the current files. If you run ls by itself and there are more than 25 files, some names will go off the screen before you can read them. pg is a UNIX command to display output one screen at a time. It waits for user input before displaying the next screen. We can pipe the output from ls directly to pg so that we can see the filenames one screen at a time.

Some UNIX commands display so much information that the lines we are looking for get lost. grep is a UNIX command that only displays lines that contain a desired pattern, as the following example shows:

```
$ ls ¦ grep acme
```

In the preceding example, ls will output all the files. These will not go directly to your screen, but will be piped instead to grep. grep will only display those filenames that contain *acme* somewhere in their name. grep is like a coffee filter. Both the hot water and coffee grounds go into the filter. The filter removes the things we don't want (the grounds), and it passes through what we do want (the liquid coffee). In the same way, the grep filter removes the lines we don't want and passes through only the lines that contain the desired pattern. The term *filter* can be

used for any UNIX utility that can be used in a pipeline to modify the output as desired.

Users and Groups

UNIX is a multi-user system. Normally each user must log on
with a unique logon name so that the system knows who just
logged on. This system keeps track of the files and mail for this
user.

A group is a collection of users. Users can belong to more than
one group. Each group has a group name. Each file has an
owner: the user who owns the file. Each file also belongs to a
group that is usually the primary group of the user that created
the file. Chapter 11, "File Permissions and System Security," discusses users, groups, and permissions in more detail.

Getting Access to UNIX

Commercial UNIX tends to run on more expensive computers
in data processing departments. Companies and institutions
may have terminals where you can log on to a UNIX server.
However, you must be given a UNIX account before you can
use the UNIX system.

Linux/GNU, and FreeBSD are non-AT&T UNIX that are sold
in magazines, at computer swap meets, at PC stores, in technical
book stores, via mail order, and via the Internet. You can get a
free SCO UNIX license over the Internet from www.sco.com. You
can also order the installation media for a modest price. This
offer is just for educational, noncommercial purposes. Sun also
offers a low-cost, noncommercial version of their operating system for Intel computers called Solaris x86.

These UNIX systems can be loaded on a home computer.
However, this process requires an available partition and is not
for the beginner. (Linux can load into a DOS file system or run
directly from CD-ROM also.) If you have Windows on the same
computer, do not load UNIX unless you are confident that you
can restore Windows and all the files in case something goes

wrong! You will learn a lot about UNIX and computers in general if you load your own UNIX system.

Doing Things the UNIX Way

Here are some general rules to help you adjust to UNIX.

No News Is Good News

Because the output of one command is often piped as input to another UNIX command, commands do not output unnecessary messages. If a command is successful, it just goes back to the shell prompt without any other output. Don't expect a completion message or a status message. On the other hand, if any output is generated, this is cause for alarm. Study any output carefully because it could be an indication that something went wrong.

Commands Are Building Blocks

Many UNIX commands seem to be primitive or unfinished. Think of them as raw building blocks. You can create your own commands by putting a series of commands in a pipeline. Most commands do not have a print option because you can pipe the output to the printer. Most commands do not have a sort option because you can pipe the output to sort.

Minimum Keystrokes

UNIX enables the skilled user to accomplish marvels using a minimum of keystrokes. You can see this tendency to minimize keystrokes in the names of the common commands:

ls (list files)
rm (remove files)
cp (copy files)
mv (move files)
cd (change directory)
pg (page the output)

Chapter 19, "Command-Line Editing in the Korn Shell," shows how a small wildcard pattern can save typing long lists of file-names. Chapter 9, "Generating and Using File Lists," explains how the shell can facilitate keying in commands. Throughout this book, you will see cases where UNIX provides features and tools that enable you to automate situations that would normally require tedious repetitive keyboard entry.

SEE ALSO

➤ *For more information on the PATH variable, see page 97*

UNIX Directories and Pathnames

By Steve "Mor" Moritsugu

Introducing the UNIX Directory Tree Structure

UNIX stores information such as user data on one or more disk drives. Each disk drive typically has a capacity measured in megabytes (MB) where each megabyte is equivalent to one million characters. For example, a 500 MB disk drive could hold 50,000 documents, where each document has 10,000 characters of text. Some disk drive systems have capacities measured in gigabytes (1 GB = 1,000 MB = 1,000,000,000 characters) or even terabytes (1 TB = 1,000 GB = 1,000,000,000,000 characters).

Since there is so much data to keep track of, all of this information is grouped into collections of related information called files. If you write a letter to send to a relative, the text of that letter would all be stored as one file. Files can serve different functions on the system. Some files are documents, some are programs, some are data files or other types. Each file under UNIX has a number called an inode number (see glossary) that UNIX uses to access the file. To make it easier for humans to work with files, each file can also be accessed by a name.

Filenames under old versions of UNIX could only contain 14 characters. Most current UNIX systems allow much longer filenames, sometimes several hundred characters. Filenames can start with or contain any letters, digits, punctuation, or spaces but in practice, avoid putting spaces and most punctuation into filenames because that makes them difficult to use in command lines.

UNIX systems can have hundreds of thousands of files to keep track of, or more. To simplify this, files are grouped into collections of related files called directories. Think of a directory as a folder or container into which you can put related files. For example, if you wrote 20 letters to your aunt Alice, you could put all 20 of those files into a directory of aunt Alice letters. I might call the directory auntAlice since I don't want any spaces in my file or directory names. Similarly, directories can be collected together and put into larger directories. For example, I might create a directory called correspondence that contains

How fast things change

When I started in computers, my system had 10 MB of disk space. Today the specifications for a new release of UNIX called UnixWare 7 says it supports 76,800 TB of disk space. This is 7.68 billion times larger than my old 10 MB drive. Amazing!

a directory for each person, which is contained by another directory. auntAlice would be a subdirectory of the correspondence directory. The correspondence directory is said to be the parent directory of the auntAlice directory.

The Root Directory Contains All the Other Directories

In Figure 2.1, we see a pictorial representation of the way that files and directories are organized under UNIX. There is one directory or folder that contains all the other directories and files. We call it the root directory since from it grows an entire tree structure of other directories and files.

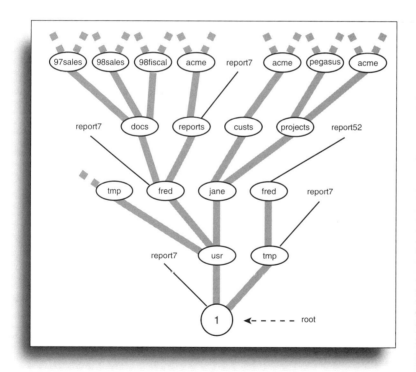

FIGURE 2.1.

UNIX Directory Tree Structure.

The root directory is always denoted by a single slash (/). Whenever you see the slash (/) symbol, picture that slash (/) as a tree root growing diagonally into the ground, anchoring our UNIX tree structure.

Finding a Path to a Name (full pathnames)

Figure 2.1 shows three files coming out of the root directory (/):

report7

usr

tmp

We say that these three files reside in the root directory. In a real UNIX system, many more files would reside in the root directory, so Figure 2.1 is just showing you a portion of an example UNIX directory tree.

The usr and tmp directories contain other directories and files as shown in Figure 2.1. Under UNIX, a directory exists on the disk as a file that keeps track of the contents of that directory. A directory then is a special type of file.

There are other types of files. For example, character and block device node files allow UNIX to access hardware devices in the system. The majority of all files on a UNIX system are called regular files, which are files that contain text, data, or programs. The next most common type of file are the directories. All the other file types, such as device node files, are rarely encountered.

In Figure 2.2, the tmp directory is shown to contain a regular file called report7. Notice that the root directory (/) also contains a regular file called report7. In fact, our tree example shows four report7 files in different directories. UNIX allows different files with different contents to have the same filename as long as they are in different directories.

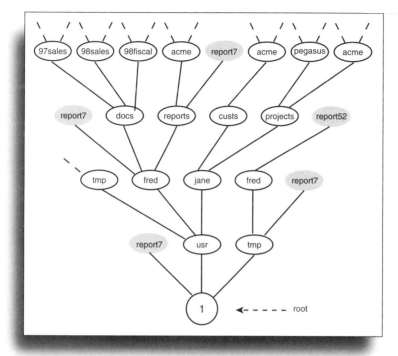

FIGURE 2.2.

The same name can exist in different directories.

Within any one directory, all filenames must be unique. This is true whether the file is a directory or not. For this reason, I could not have both a regular file called usr and a directory called usr in the root directory.

Figure 2.3 highlights one of the report7 files in our tree. The complete name for a file includes all the directory folders that you have to go through to get to the desired file. You can see that this sequence of directories, when highlighted as a chain, makes a path through the tree structure, leading to your desired file, hence we call this complete name a full pathname. With a full pathname, there is no danger that someone will mistakenly think you are referring to one of the other report7 files in the tree. A full pathname is also called an absolute pathname.

Don't confuse UNIX directory names with DOS directory names

DOS uses a similar directory tree structure, which also grows from a root directory. However DOS uses the backslash (\) symbol for the root directory and to separate directory names whereas UNIX uses the slash (/) symbol, which is also called the forward slash (/).

FIGURE 2.3.

The full pathname
/usr/fred/reports/report7.

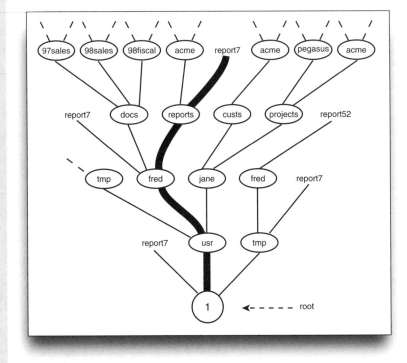

Directories in UNIX

There are some standard directory names that you will
encounter on most UNIX systems. I have already mentioned
that all UNIX systems will have a root directory (/).

Standard UNIX Directory Names

How long will files be left in /tmp?

This can vary from system to system. Often the system will delete files from /tmp or its subdirectories that have not been accessed in 7 or 14 days. Sometimes the system administrator, facing a sudden lack of disk space, will delete all files in /tmp regardless of age. Sometimes users are expected to purge their own /tmp files periodically.

The /tmp and /usr/tmp directories are used by the system to
store temporary files. Users may also store temporary files there
but beware, the system may purge (or delete) older files from
tmp directories periodically, without any warning.

/dev is a directory in root that contains the special device node
files that access hardware on the system such as tape drives and
floppy disks. These device nodes files can exist anywhere, but by
convention are put into /dev or its subdirectories to remind us
we are dealing with a device instead of a regular file.

/bin is a directory in root that holds system utility programs such as the `ls` command. bin is short for binary executable files. The term bin today may `also` be used to name other directories of executable files, whether they are binary or text files, for example /usr/fred/bin.

/usr is a directory in root that holds user files and system utilities needed to support user programs. For example, /bin holds system utilities required for essential system operation whereas /usr/bin holds system utilities needed by users and user programs. /usr/lib holds libraries of useful system tables and subroutines. /usr/spool holds spool files which are temporary copies of files queued up for printing held until they are finished printing. /usr/spool `also` holds many temporary files held by other system processes such as uucp. /usr/bin, /usr/lib, and /usr/spool are important parts of the operating system and it is often wise to dedicate /usr to system purposes and place actual user data and programs into other directories.

lost+found is a directory that exists in root and in other directories where the system will store file data if the filename has been lost due to system crashes. If you are missing important data after a system crash, you might find it here.

New directories in SVR4 (Solaris)

/home is a directory specifically for users' home directories where they can store their individual files. (See the following section on home directories.)

/sbin and /usr/sbin contain executable files specifically for system administration and system operation.

/stand is a special directory on some SVR4 systems (but not Solaris) to specifically house the UNIX kernel and boot files.

/var contains files with system variable information, that is temporary files and logs whose contents vary with time. /var replaces the older /usr/spool directory.

Changing to Another Directory

Being able to freely move around in the UNIX directory tree is a very important skill for UNIX users.

Changing to a directory and viewing its contents (*cd, ls*)

UNIX would be very difficult to use if you had to specify a full pathname every time you referenced a file. As always, UNIX has a short-cut to reduce typing. You can specify a directory to be our current directory which allows us to reference filenames in that directory without giving the full pathname. The current directory acts as a default directory since it will be used whenever you don't specify which directory to use.

Other names for the current directory are:

working directory

present directory

present working directory

default directory

Picture in your mind that we have started walking the path from the root directory through the UNIX tree structure and have decided to stop somewhere to see what you can see from that point of view. Imagine you are sitting on a branch of the tree structure. You can only sit in directories, not in regular files. The directory in which you are sitting is called your current directory.

We can change our current directory by using the UNIX cd command followed by the directory name we want to change to.

In Figure 2.1, if I execute:

```
cd /usr/fred
```

then my current directory will be /usr/fred. By changing to /usr/fred, it will be easy for you to access any files in that directory. You can list all the files in your current directory by entering the ls command at the shell prompt (shown here by a dollar sign ($)). The following example shows the output you would see if your files were the same as Figure 2.1:

```
$ cd /usr/fred
$ ls
docs
report7
reports
$
```

If report7 is a regular file in your current directory, you can simply access it as report7. You don't have to specify which report7 file in which directory since the system will assume your current directory whenever you don't specify a full pathname.

Using *basenames* and *dirnames*

A filename usually has a directory portion (which I will call the dirname) and a final base name (which I will call the basename). This basename does not include any slashes (/) and hence does not include any preceding directory names. The basename may indicate a regular file or a directory. The dirname indicates how to get to the desired basename. If the pathname is given as just a basename, then you indicate its dirname with a period (.) that you shall see later is a symbol that represents the current directory. For example:

Table 2.1. **Some example *dirnames* and *basenames***

full pathname	- - dirname	- - basename
/usr/fred/report7	- - /usr/fred	- - report7
/usr/fred/docs	- - /usr/fred	- - docs
report7	- - .	- - report7

Displaying Your Current Directory Name

To display the name of your current directory, enter:

pwd

which will display the full pathname of your current directory. To remember pwd, think: print working directory.

Changing to Your Home Directory

On most UNIX systems, every user of the system is given a special directory called a home directory to hold the files that they create and to hold the special system files to customize system and utility operations for their preferences. When you first login to the UNIX system, your current directory is usually set automatically to your home directory (but not necessarily).

To change to your home directory, enter cd

When you use the cd command without specifying a directory, it takes you to your home directory, that is your home directory becomes your current directory.

The name of your home directory can vary from system to system but it will normally contain your login name. For example, if you login as user jane, your home directory on one UNIX system might be /usr/jane. It might be /home/jane on a different UNIX system esp. SVR4 (for example Solaris) or even something else. To display the name of your home directory, enter:

```
$ cd
$ pwd
/home/fred
$
```

The cd command takes you to your home directory, even if you don't know its name. The pwd command then tells you where you ended up, that is the name of your home directory. In the above example, /home/fred is this user's home directory.

Changing to an Absolute Directory

As we have seen before, we can set our current directory by using the cd command with an absolute (that is full) pathname.

If you don't know the exact spelling of the full pathname, use the procedure described later on in the section "Changing to a Directory in Little Steps." If you know the exact spelling, you can change to that directory in one cd command. Make sure that you start your directory with a leading slash (/).

For example, to change to directory /usr/fred/reports, enter:

```
cd /usr/fred/reports
```

To change the root directory, enter:

```
cd /
```

Changing to a Subdirectory of the Current Directory (relative)

If we want to change to a subdirectory of the current directory, we have another short-cut we can use. We can specify a relative pathname which shows how to get from where we are to where we want to be. For example, in Figure 2.1, assume the following is true:

/usr/fred is our current directory

/usr/fred/docs/98sales is the directory to which we want to change

We could get there by using a full pathname:

```
cd /usr/fred/docs/98sales
```

However, since /usr/fred is the current directory, it would be easier to use a relative pathname as follows:

```
cd docs/98sales
```

Notice that relative pathnames do not begin with a slash (/) since they do not indicate the path all the way back to root. For that reason, relative pathnames are also called partial pathnames. They are called relative since they are based on our current directory. For example, the following table shows how the relative pathname changes as our current directory changes:

Table 2.1. How the relative pathname to get to /usr/fred/docs/98sales changes based on your current directory

your current directory	-- cd command needed
/usr/fred/docs	-- cd 98sales
/usr/fred	-- cd docs/98sales
/usr	-- cd fred/docs/98sales
/	-- cd usr/fred/docs/98sales

Tip: A starting slash (/) always means start at root (/)

Learn to pay attention to the very first character of a pathname. If it begins with a slash (/), then it is an absolute pathname and it includes all directories back to root (/).

Changing to a Directory in Little Steps

Sometimes you have a vague idea of your desired destination directory but don't know exactly how to get there or don't know the exact spelling of each intermediate directory. Sometimes you think you know these things but your cd command fails with the error: No such file or directory. Here is a procedure to help you:

Changing to a directory in little steps

1. Determine in your mind the first directory you have to get to on your way to the final destination. If you want to use a relative path, the first directory would be a subdirectory of your current directory. If you want to use an absolute path, then your first directory is root (/). If you are not sure, then mentally plan to start at root.

2. If you are using a relative path, skip this step and go on to step 3. Do this step 2 if you are using an absolute path or if you decided to start with the root directory. Enter:
   cd /

   Press the Enter key after this step and every step in this procedure. Now you are sitting in the root directory.

3. If you are not sure which directory to go to next, or are not sure of its spelling, enter:
   ls -CF

   Press the Enter key after this step and every step in this procedure. ls (see appendix) will show you the spelling of all the files and directories that you can get to from here. The -C option to ls will display the output in columns. The -F option to ls will add a slash (/) to the end of directory names so you can distinguish them from regular files.

   If there are so many files that the output goes off the screen, you can see the output a page at a time by entering one of these commands:
   ls -CF ¦ pg
   ls -CF ¦ more
   ls -CF ¦ less

   pg, more, and less are utilities to see the output a page at a time. If your system does not have one of these utilities, you will see an immediate error: Command not found. In that case, try one of the other alternatives shown. To go to the next page, press the Enter key or the Spacebar. To quit before the end, enter q.

4. Having determined the correct spelling of the next directory to go to, change to that directory as follows:

```
cd nextdir
```

Replace nextdir with your desired directory name. Notice you are not to enter any slashes (/) in this cd command. If this command gets a No such file error, repeat step 3 above and double-check your spelling. If you get a permission error, you may not have access rights to change to that directory.

5. If the cd command in step 4 is successful, we are now one directory closer to arriving at our desired destination. Repeat steps 3 and 4 over and over until you reach your desired directory.

SEE ALSO

➤ *For more information on listing files see page 151*

➤ *For more information on viewing output a page at a time see page 160*

Accessing the Current Directory (.)

Every directory contains two special subdirectories. One has a name which is a single period (.) and we call it the "dot" directory. The other's name is two periods (..) and we call it the "dot-dot" directory. Both of these directories are special and you should never try to delete them. A directory is considered to be empty if it only contains dot (.) and dot-dot (..). The dot (.) directory is actually a pointer to the current directory. Many UNIX commands use the dot (.) directory to determine what the current directory is.

What is the difference between these two filenames?

```
./report7
report7
```

The answer is nothing. They both reference the report7 file in the current directory.

Going Back One Directory to the Parent (..)

The dot-dot (..) directory is a pointer to the parent directory of the current directory. Thus it is correct to say that every directory contains itself as a subdirectory (.) and it contains its own parent directory as a subdirectory of itself (..).

You can use the dot-dot (..) subdirectory of your current directory to change to the parent directory. If your current directory is /usr/fred/docs/98sales/NorthAm, then after

```
cd ..
```

your current directory will be /usr/fred/docs/98sales.

You can also go to the parent directory of the parent directory. If your current directory is /usr/fred/docs/98sales/NorthAm, then after

```
cd ../..
```

your current directory will be /usr/fred/docs.

Changing to a Subdirectory of the Parent

root is the only directory that is its own parent

If your current directory is root, **cd** .. is legal and leaves you still in the root directory. **cd** ../../../.. would have the same result.

In Figure 2.1, imagine that your current directory is /usr/fred/docs/98sales. How would you change to /usr/fred/docs/97sales? You cannot just cd to 97sales since that is not a subdirectory of your current directory. You could change to that directory by either of these two commands:

```
cd ../97sales
cd /usr/fred/docs/97sales
```

In Figure 2.1, if /usr/fred/docs/98sales is again your current directory, how can you use dot-dot (..) to change to /usr/fred/reports/acme? The answer is:

```
cd ../../reports/acme
```

if you are not sure how many dot-dot's (..) to go back, use the technique of changing by little steps, for example

```
cd ..
ls -CF
cd ..
ls -CF
```

```
cd reports
ls -CF
cd acme
```

Each `ls` command lists the contents of the current directory, so you can see the available directories to go to next. Remember do not start any of the directory names with a slash in any of the little steps since that would take you all the way back to root.

Returning to the Previous Directory

The `cd` command under the Korn shell has an extra option not available in the Bourne shell:

```
cd -
```

will return you to the previous directory that you were last in. This command can also be used to easily toggle back and forth between two directories as in this example:

```
cd /data
# now do some work in /data
cd /usr/fred
# now do some work in /usr/fred
cd -
# now you are back in /data
cd -
# now you are back in /usr/fred
cd -
# now you are back in /data
# etc.
```

How to Formulate a Relative Pathname to a File

Frequently in this book, instructions will specify to enter either an absolute or relative pathname to a desired file. An absolute pathname includes all the parent directories back to the root directory. This is easy to understand but requires a lot of keyboard entry.

If your current directory is the directory that contains the desired file, you can access that file simply by its `basename` (see glossary) which is much shorter to enter than an absolute pathname. A basename is an example of a relative pathname since the path to follow to get to the indicated file starts from your current directory. Do not put a slash (/) in front of the basename since that would indicate an absolute pathname telling the system to look for that basename in the root directory, not your current directory.

To access a file in a child directory (i.e. subdirectory) of your current directory using a relative pathname, enter this relative pathname:

```
child-dir/filename
```

Replace child-dir with the name of the desired subdirectory in your current directory. Again please notice that a relative pathname must not begin with a slash (/). For example, if the current directory has a subdirectory called reports and you want to access the acme file in that directory, the relative pathname would be:

```
reports/acme
```

To access a file several subdirectories removed, enter a relative pathname like this:

```
sub-dir/its-sub-dir/its-sub-dir/filename
```

The advantage of such relative pathnames is that you don't have to specify every directory back to root.

To access a file in the parent directory of your current directory, enter this relative pathname:

```
../filename
```

dot-dot (..) indicates the parent directory as you saw earlier in this chapter.

Using multiple dot-dot (..) entries, it is possible to use a relative pathname to access any other file or directory in the whole system, for example

```
../../../usr/jane/accounts/progs/acme
```

In practice, multiple dot-dot entries are difficult to comprehend and are not found very often.

Relative pathnames are used in UNIX much more often than absolute pathnames since they reduce the amount of typing needed to enter a command. People use cd to change to a directory just so that they can use basenames or simple relative pathnames to access the desired files.

Creating New Directories (*mkdir*)

There are three ways to create a new directory:

1. Go to the parent directory and create it
2. Stay where you are and create it
3. Create all intervening directories also

Go to the parent and create the new directory

1. cd to the parent directory where you want to create to a new directory. You can specify either an absolute or relative pathname to get there.

    Enter:
    ```
    mkdir new-dir
    ```

    Replace new-dir with the name of the new directory that you want to create. Do not include any slashes (/) in new-dir. mkdir will create the desired new directory.

To remain in your current directory and create the new directory elsewhere, enter the mkdir command followed by a full or relative pathname to the new directory to be created. mkdir will fail with an error message if any of the intervening directories do not already exist.

Create a new directory and all intervening directories

1. Enter:
    ```
    mkdir -p
    ```

    (Do not press the Enter key until instructed.)

2. Enter a space and then a full or relative pathname to the new directory to be created. Then press the Enter key to complete this command. The -p option to mkdir causes it to create any parent directories which do not exist as well as the final directory in the pathname given.

Removing Existing Directories (*rmdir*)

Removing existing directories

1. Enter:

   ```
   cd dir-name
   ```

   Replace dir-name with either an absolute or relative pathname to the desired directory to be removed.

2. Enter:

   ```
   ls -aCF
   ```

   to see all the files in the current directory including files whose filename begins with a dot (.). To remove a directory, there must be no files in it except for dot (.) and dot-dot (..).

3. If a large number of files are listed in step 2 above, make sure that you really want to delete them all and the directory that contains them. If you are sure, change to the next procedure on Removing Entire Directory Subtrees. Go on to step 4 in this procedure if there are only a few files or directories shown in step 2 above.

4. The -F option to ls in step 2 causes ls to add a slash (/) following the filename to denote directories. If there are any subdirectories in the directory to be removed, they must be removed first by applying this procedure from the beginning to each subdirectory and each subdirectory of the subdirectory, and so on

5. All regular files in the directory to be removed must be deleted before the directory can be removed. To remove a file in the current directory, enter:

   ```
   rm file-name
   ```

   Replace filename with the file to be removed. rm (see appendix) is the UNIX command to remove (that is delete) a file.

6. Once the directory is empty of all regular files and subdirectories except for dot (.) and dot-dot (..), enter:

   ```
   cd ..
   ```

   to move to the parent of the directory to be removed. You cannot remove a directory while you are sitting in it.

7. Remove the directory by entering:

```
rmdir dir-name
```

Replace dir-name with a relative or absolute pathname to the empty directory to be removed. `rmdir` is the UNIX command to remove (that is delete) an empty directory.

SEE ALSO

➤ *For more information on deleting files see page 191*

Removing Entire Directory Subtrees (*rm*)

It is possible to remove a directory and all of its existing files and subdirectories (that is the whole directory subtree) in one command. However this command is very powerful and hence very dangerous and must be typed in very carefully to avoid tragedy.

Removing Entire Directory Subtrees

1. Make sure you know the exact spelling and full pathname of the directory to be removed. Use the `cd` and `ls` commands to change to that directory and list its contents and the contents of any subdirectories. Make sure that you want to remove all of these files and subdirectories. Make sure that you are deleting a directory created by a user and not a required system directory, especially if your are logged in as root.

2. Enter:

```
cd parent-name
```

Replace parent-name with either an absolute or relative pathname to the parent directory of the directory to be removed.

3. Enter:

```
pwd
```

to verify that you have arrived in the correct directory.

4. Enter:

```
ls -dF dir-name
```

Replace dir-name with the directory to be removed. This command should display the same dir-name back to you, followed by a slash (/). If you see an error message: No such

file, something is wrong. Go back to step 1 of this procedure.

5. Enter:

```
rm -rf dir-name
```

Avoid using rm -r while running as root

A mistake or typographical error in the specified dir-name, such as wrong spaces or slashes (/), could wipe out important parts of the UNIX system and make it totally inoperable. There is no undelete option. To be even safer, alias rm to "rm -i" if your shell permits this.

Replace dir-name with the directory to be removed. This
command is very dangerous. Double-check that you have
spelled everything correctly before you press the ENTER
key. The rm command normally only removes regular files
and not directories. The -r option to rm causes rm to recursively remove the specified directory and its files and all of
its subdirectories and their files and all of their subdirectories and their files, and so on. There is no undelete option.

Increasing Productivity in Accessing Directories

Switching between long directory names can become tiresome
and frustrating. Here are some UNIX techniques that can help.

Setting CDPATH for Most Accessed Directories

In the first chapter, we saw how shell variables can be set to customize how the system operates for us. The Bourne shell and
the Korn shell have a shell variable called CDPATH to allow
you to easily get to directories that you use most often as long as
they have distinctive names. Once you have set up CDPATH,
you can cd to the basename of your common directories as
though you were always sitting in the parent directories of those
directories.

Setting and using CDPATH

1. Make a list of the full pathnames of the directories that you
cd to most often. The list can be in your head, on scratch
paper, in a file, and so on. If the basenames of those directories are mostly unique, then this procedure will help you.

2. Make a new list of the full pathnames of the parent directories of the most accessed directories. I will call this the
CDPATH list.

3. Place the CDPATH list in order so that the parent directories of the directories you cd to most often come first.

4. If any directories you cd to often have the same basename, put the parent directory of the most used basename before the parent directory of the least used basename. This procedure will allow you to access only the identical basename whose parent comes first in the list. Other identical basenames in other directories must be accessed using a full or relative pathname.

5. Decide whether you want to check for the given basename in the current directory before or after you check all the directories in CDPATH. If before, then the current directory overrides or has higher priority than the CDPATH directories. If after, then CDPATH overrides or has higher priority than the current directory.

For example, assume you enter:
```
cd docs
```

and assume that a docs directory exists as a subdirectory of your current directory and also as a subdirectory of one of the directories in CDPATH. We can control whether the current directory has higher or lower priority than the CDPATH directories, hence we can control which docs directory we end up at.

6. Enter:
```
CDPATH=
```

Do not press the Enter key until instructed to. Do not put any spaces around the = sign.

7. If the current directory is to have higher priority than the CDPATH directories, enter:
```
.:
```

(that is period colon) and no spaces.

8. Enter all the full pathnames in your CDPATH list, using a colon (:) to separate each entry. Do not end your list with a colon (:). Do not enter any spaces.

9. If the current directory is to have lower priority than the CDPATH directories, enter:

`: .`

(that is colon period) and no spaces.

10. Press the Enter key to complete your command. Here is an example of a complete command:

`CDPATH=.:/usr/fred/reports:/data/acme`

11. Now any time you cd to a basename, the shell will search each of the directories in order in CDPATH until it finds the given basename as a subdirectory of one of these parent directories in CDPATH. It will then take you to that directory.

12. You must re-enter your whole CDPATH= line each time you log in unless you set this shell variable definition in your .profile.

SEE ALSO

➤ *For information on setting up shell variables definitions in .profile so they occur automatically each time you log in, see page 307*

➤ *For more information on the different shells see page 27*

Saving/Accessing Often Used Directory Names

Sometimes you will find that there are some directories you want to return to several times, but not often enough to warrent updating CDPATH. You can create and use your own temporary shell variables to make it easy to return to directories.

Saving/accessing often used directory names

1. cd to a directory that you know you want to return to several times.

2. Enter:

`D1=`pwd``

Make sure you enter backquotes (`` ` ``) and not apostrophes ('). Do not enter any spaces in this command. This command will save the full pathname of your current directory in shell variable D1.

3. To return to the directory in D1, enter:
```
cd  $D1
```

Notice you must precede the variable with a $ sign to use its contents but not to set its contents.

4. Following steps 1 through 3, you can set and use other variables such as D2 or D3 to remember and easily change between several directories.

5. You can choose more descriptive variable names such as:
```
CUSTS=`pwd`
REPORTS=`pwd`
```

You must be sitting in the desired directory before you issue the above command. You must not choose the name of an existing shell variable. Enter:
```
env
```

to see a list of the existing shell variables.

6. If you forget which directory is in a variable, you can display its contents using the echo command, for example
```
echo $D1
```

7. If you want to make some of these shell variables permanent so you don't have to set them up each time you log in, set them up in .profile as referenced in the above procedure on CDPATH.

Displaying Information About the System

By Dan Wilson

One of the first things you probably want to do as a new user on your UNIX system is to see what the system really looks like from the inside. The UNIX system maintains detailed information about who you are, what your current environment looks like, and what you're doing. Much of this information is available to you through simple commands or the more in-depth shell programming languages.

This chapter concentrates on using the commands that are available to you as soon as you log into the system. As your skills and confidence grow, you can learn to combine the numerous commands that UNIX provides you into sophisticated shell programs. Take comfort in the fact that even the best UNIX gurus out there had to start out the same way that you are now. UNIX is a very powerful operating system and places a lot of that computing power in the hands of the average user.

Keep in mind that numerous flavors of UNIX exist and that your output may not match exactly what you see here—be sure to check the commands you use here with your own system documentation. The good news is that after you learn these commands, you'll be able to sit down at virtually any UNIX machine and start working. Let's take a look at what you can find out about your system with several useful commands.

Displaying Information About You and Your System

Let's start out by letting UNIX tell you what it knows about your current session. This information is important because who you are in the system determines a lot of what commands and programs you are capable of executing. You see, a userid (uid) owns programs—which is what a UNIX command really is—and attaches certain permissions to those programs and commands. Now let's look at several commands that will tell you about your current login session.

The first command to explore is the whoami command.

1. At the shell prompt, type whoami.

2. Depending upon your system, you should see your userid on one line and the shell prompt below it:

```
$ whoami
  nick_humes
$
```

We can slightly alter this command to see more information by typing who am i.

1. At the shell prompt, type who am i.

2. You should see information similar to the following:

```
$ who am i
             nick_humes    ttyp1       Mar 18 12:12
         $
```

3. As you can see, this command gives you more information; it returns your username, terminal, and the initial date and time you logged into the system.

Another useful command that you will find yourself frequently using is the id command.

1. At the shell prompt, type id.

2. You should see the following information returned by the system:

```
$ id
   uid=101(nick_humes) gid=20(users)
$
```

The command returns your userid (uid) and group id (gid). This information is very useful because it tells you who you currently are in the system. You need to know this because one of the powerful features of UNIX is that you can switch to a different userid—as long as you have a valid password. You can also change your current group affiliation. These features are valuable because you may need to run programs under different user and group ids than the ones under which you logged in.

Another command you should examine is the tty command. This command tells you the terminal or, if you are logging in across the network, the pseudo-terminal with which you are connected. The term *pseudo-terminal* means that you are not directly connected to the machine through a physical connection; you are connected through the network. Let's look at an example.

1. At the shell prompt, type tty.

2. You should see something close to the following:

```
$ tty
  /dev/ttyp1
$
```

3. The system returns the device name that your terminal uses to connect to the system.

   Take note that the output /dev/ttyp1 contains a "p" before the device number. This indicates that this device is a pseudo-terminal. If you logged directly into the machine via your system console, you would see the following:

```
$ tty
  /dev/console
$
```

The $TERM environment variable tells the system the terminal type you want to emulate. Depending upon the system and terminal you are on, you can emulate either a character terminal or an X-Windows terminal. The X-Windows type terminal grants you graphics capabilities, whereas the character-based terminal does not. You can check with your systems administrator to determine your type of terminal. Chances are, he or she has already set your environment variables, which are active as soon as you log into the machine.

Take a look at how you view your $TERM setting and how you would change it if you needed to.

1. At the shell prompt, type echo $TERM.

2. The system will echo the value of TERM to the screen.

```
$ echo $TERM
  vt100
$
```

If you are in the ksh (Korn shell) or the sh (posix shell) and you want to change the value of TERM, you would perform the following steps:

1. At the shell prompt, type TERM=vt220;export $TERM.

2. To check whether TERM changed, you would type echo $TERM.

3. You would see that TERM is set to vt220.

In the csh (C shell), you perform these steps to change TERM:

1. At the shell prompt, type set term=vt220.

2. To check whether TERM changed, type set.

   ```
   % set
   ```

3. You'll see *all* your environment variable settings. In the output, you should see a line similar to this one:

   ```
   term     vt100
   ```

The stty command sets or displays the current settings of I/O options for your terminal. You use stty to set useful functions, such as your backspace or process interrupt keys. Let's look at an example of this:

1. At the prompt, type stty -a.

   ```
   $ stty -a

       speed 9600 baud; line = 0;
       rows = 0; columns = 0
       min = 4; time = 0;
       intr = ^C; quit = ^\; erase <undef>; kill = ^U
       eof = ^D; eol = ^@; eol2 <undef>; swtch <undef>
       stop = ^S; start = ^Q; susp <undef>; dsusp <undef>
       werase <undef>; lnext <undef>
       parenb -parodd cs7 -cstopb hupcl -cread -clocal
       ➥-loblk -crts
       -ignbrk brkint ignpar -parmrk -inpck istrip -inlcr
       ➥-igncr icrnl -iuclc
       ixon -ixany ixoff -imaxbel -rtsxoff -ctsxon -ienqak
       isig icanon -iexten -xcase echo echoe echok -echonl
       ➥-noflsh
       -echoctl -echoprt -echoke -flusho -pendin
       opost -olcuc onlcr -ocrnl -onocr -onlret -ofill -ofdel
       ➥-tostop
   $
   ```

2. From the preceding output, you see that there are numerous settings. For the most part, you'll have to alter only a few of

these. Notice in the output that the erase setting is unde-fined (<undef>). Set this to work for the Backspace (<Backspace>) key. (CTRL-H is the key combination of the Control key and the H key. CNTRL-H is the default value for the backspace key.) You use the stty command to tell the system to use this key sequence to perform the Backspace function.

At the shell prompt, type stty erase ^H.

```
$ stty erase ^H
```

3. Now look at the results of typing stty -a:

```
$ stty -a

    speed 9600 baud; line = 0;
    rows = 0; columns = 0
    min = 4; time = 0;
    intr = ^C; quit = ^\; erase = ^H; kill = ^U
    eof = ^D; eol = ^@; eol2 <undef>; swtch <undef>
    stop = ^S; start = ^Q; susp <undef>; dsusp <undef>
    werase = ^K; lnext <undef>
    parenb -parodd cs7 -cstopb hupcl -cread -clocal -loblk
    ➥-crts
    -ignbrk brkint ignpar -parmrk -inpck istrip -inlcr
    ➥-igncr icrnl -iuclc
    ixon -ixany ixoff -imaxbel -rtsxoff -ctsxon -ienqak
    isig icanon -iexten -xcase echo echoe echok -echonl
    ➥-noflsh
    -echoctl -echoprt -echoke -flusho -pendin
    opost -olcuc onlcr -ocrnl -onocr -onlret -ofill -ofdel
    ➥-tostop
$
```

As you can see, the Backspace key is set.

Displaying Information About Other Users

You're now ready to learn commands that tell about the other users logged into the system. Start by seeing who is logged on by using none other than the who command.

At the shell prompt, type who.

```
$ who
    Tim_Wilson              ttyp1         Mar  19  18:27
    Emily_Wilson            tty10         Mar  19  18:30
    oracle                  ttyp2         Mar  19  15:27
    Taylor_Klausner         ttypd5        Mar  19  10:20
    Marissa_Klausner        ttypd1        Mar  18  06:00
    BPierce                 ttyp7         Mar  19  19:17
    BWood                   ttyp47        Mar  19  14:00
    CSarjent                ttyp10        Mar  19  11:27
    PSingleton              ttyp19        Mar  19  08:27
    Zach_Wilson             ttyp15        Mar  19  09:27
    Travis_Wilson           ttyp17        Mar  19  12:27
    JBerglund               ttyp19        Mar  19  08:27
    Rich_Blum               tty21         Mar  19  12:12
    Ed_Lewis                tty35         Mar  19  12:13
    Tony_Amico              console       Mar  19  12:00
$
```

As you can see from the output from who, a good number of users are on the system. Notice that some of the users are directly connected (tty terminal ids), and others are connected through the network (ttyp terminal ids). Also notice that terminal ids ttypd1 and ttypd5 are different from the others. That's because these users are logged in through a modem.

You can also see that someone other than the systems administrator has logged onto the system console. This is potentially dangerous because on some systems it is easier to gain privileged access by logging into the system console. You can use this one simple command to see who is logged on, how they are coming into the system, and when they logged in.

Let's look at another use for the who command. This time you'll use the command to show some information about your UNIX machine.

At the shell prompt, type who -b.

```
$ who -b
                system boot   Oct 28 13:35
```

The above output tells us the date and time that the machine was booted (or restarted). This is useful to know if you had started a job prior to leaving work and had come in the next day and found that the computer had crashed. Any information you find out before you talk to your systems administrator will help in solving any problems you encounter.

Another command that shows you information about users and the system is the uptime command. Here's an example of its use:

At the shell prompt, type uptime.

```
$ uptime
        8:00pm   up 142 days,   6:25,   2 users,   load
        ➥average: 0.51, 0.52, 0.52
    $
```

The output tells us that the current time is 8:00 pm and that the system has been up for 142 days, 6 hours, and 25 minutes. Two users are currently logged onto the system. The load average is used by the systems administrator to help gauge the performance of the system.

Now let's take a look at how we can use the uptime command with a special option to see output identical to the w command.

At the shell prompt, type uptime -w.

```
$ uptime -w
    7:55pm  up 142 days,   6:20,   2 users,   load average:
    ➥0.51, 0.52, 0.52
    User     tty           login@  idle   JCPU   PCPU  what
    dwilson  ttyp1         6:27pm    3            uptime -w
    root     ttyp2         7:53pm                 sh
```

Now enter the w command.

At the shell prompt, type w.

```
$ w
    7:55pm  up 142 days,   6:21,   2 users,   load average:
    ➥0.51, 0.52, 0.52
```

```
User      tty         login@  idle  JCPU  PCPU  what
dwilson   ttyp1       6:27pm    3                 w
root      ttyp2       7:53pm                      sh
$
```

As you can see, both commands produced the same output. Using the w command, however, is a bit easier than remembering the options to the uptime command.

Another command you can use is the finger command. This command displays the following information:

- Login name.
- User's full name, if listed in password file.
- Terminal write status (The *write* command enables users to directly communicate with one another via their terminals).
- User's idle time.
- User's login time.
- Any plan information placed into the user's .plan file. This file resides in the user's home directory.
- Project information placed into the user's .project file. This file also resides in the user's home directory.
- The user's office information, as listed in the password file.
- The user's phone number, as listed in the password file.

You can use the finger command to display information about other users registered on the system. Keep in mind that these users don't have to be logged on for you to see information about them. In this example, the user <llaurie> is shown; substitute the user on which you want to use the finger command.

At the shell prompt, type finger llaurie.

```
$ finger llaurie

Login name: llaurie      (messages off)  In real life: Linda
➥Laurie
Bldg: Indy, Work phone: 317.555.7180
Directory: /home/llaurie                 Shell: /usr/bin/sh
On since Mar 21 14:48:10 on ttyp1 from Hydra.
```

```
Plan:
Oracle 8.1 Web Server
$
```

Notice the `"(messages off)"` phrase in the preceding output. This means that you can't interact with this user with the `write` command. The `mesg` command controls this; with the `write` command, you can enable or disable other users' ability to interact with your terminal.

Assume that `messages` is set to `y` in the following example:

1. At the shell prompt, type `mesg`.

```
$ mesg
is y
```

The command returns the current status of your terminal's capability of receiving messages from other users (the superuser can always send a message to another user). Now change this setting to `n`.

2. At the shell prompt, type `mesg n`.

```
$ mesg n
```

3. At the shell prompt, type `mesg`.

```
        $mesg
is n
```

Now to see how the finger command looks when a user is able to receive messages, let's look at the following output:

```
$ finger llaurie
Login name: llaurie        In real life: Linda Laurie
Bldg: Indy, Work phone: 317.555.7180
Directory: /home/llaurie   Shell: /usr/bin/sh
On since Mar 21 14:59:15 on ttyp1 from Hydra.
Plan:
Oracle 8.1 Web Server
```

Notice that the `(messages off)` output is no longer there. You can now interact with this user through programs such as `write`.

Displaying Information About the UNIX Password File

As with most secure systems, UNIX requires users not only to be registered with the system but also to validate their login by supplying a userid and a password. It's not completely foolproof, though, because users sometimes share their passwords with others, or someone uses another user's password.

First, take a look at the UNIX password file (passwd). The following is an example password file that resides in the /etc directory.

```
root:Thisisasecret:0:3::/:/sbin/sh
daemon:*:1:5::/:/sbin/sh
bin:*:2:2::/usr/bin:/sbin/sh
sys:*:3:3::/:
adm:*:4:4::/var/adm:/sbin/sh
uucp:*:5:3::/var/spool/uucppublic:/usr/lbin/uucp/uucico
lp:*:9:7::/var/spool/lp:/sbin/sh
nuucp:*:11:11::/var/spool/uucppublic:/usr/lbin/uucp/uucico
hpdb:*:20:1:ALLBASE:/:/sbin/sh
nobody:*:-2:-24::/:
oracle:BJXXXX3HTWSls:201:200:,,,:/home/oracle:/usr/bin/sh
cfliss:XXXXXXXXXXXXX:100:200:,,,:/home/cfliss:/usr/bin/sh
dwilson:Can'tguessme!:101:200:DanWilson,Indy,
➥317.555.5555,:/home/dwilson:/usr/bin/sh
```

Each line in the passwd file identifies a single user to the system. Each field is separated by a colon (:) .You can break down each entry as follows:

- Login name
- Encrypted password
- Numerical user identification
- Numerical group identification
- User information field
- User's home directory
- Shell program to use at sign-on

Changing user information

If you would like to change the information in the User Information Field, try the following:

1. At the shell prompt, type chfn dwilson.
```
$ chfn dwilson
Default values are
printed inside of
'[]'.

To accept the default,
type <return>.
To have a blank entry,
type the word 'none'.
Name [Dan Wilson]:
Daniel Wilson
Location (Ex: St Paul)
[Chicago]: Carmel
Office Phone (Ex:
1234) [317.555.555]:
1.800.555.5555
Home Phone (Ex:
5555555 []:
```

To see your changes, perform the following step:

2. At the shell prompt, enter grep -i dwilson /etc/passwd.
```
$ grep -i dwilson
/etc/passwd

dwilson:Can'tguessme!:101:
20:Daniel Wilson,Carmel,
➥1.800.555.5555,:/home/
dwilson:/usr/bin/sh
```

Updating user information

You use this command to update your user information without involving the system administrator. Check your systems manuals or man pages to see whether your version of UNIX supports this command.

In the preceding example of passwd, you'll notice that some accounts have an asterisk (*) in their encrypted password field. This instructs the operating system to prevent anyone from directly logging into these accounts.

Notice the root (userid 0) account. This account is the super-user account. Persons logging onto this account are usually systems administrators because this account enables them to execute any command in the system, as well as start up and shut down the machine.

Also take a look at the nobody account. Notice that its userid is -2. This account is reserved for remote root access—specifically NFS. NFS is a Network File System that enables you to mount directories (through a remote file system) onto your host machine.

Most versions of UNIX support shadow passwords. As you'll notice in the above passwd file example, you can see the encrypted password for each user who has a password (it is possible but inadvisable to have user accounts without passwords). This is somewhat of a security issue because other users can use this information to break other user's passwords. To prevent this, the UNIX vendors started implementing a shadow password system. This system places the encrypted password information into a special shadow password file located in another directory that only privileged users can access. Some systems have an /etc/shadow file that only privileged users can access. Either way, the goal is to keep ordinary users from reading the encrypted password.

Another system file worth mentioning is the group file. This file also resides in the /etc directory and maintains a list of your primary and associated groups to which you belong. Let's take a look at an example of a group file and identify the components that comprise it.

```
root::0:root
other::1:root,hpdb
bin::2:root,bin
sys::3:root,uucp
adm::4:root,adm
daemon::5:root,daemon
mail::6:root
lp::7:root,lp
tty::10:
developer::99:dwilson,ssmith,cfliss
nuucp::11:nuucp
users::20:root,dwilson,ssmith,cfliss
nogroup:*:-2:
dba::200:oracle,dwilson,ssmith,cfliss
```

Notice that a user can exist in more than one group. Your entry in the passwd file determines your primary group membership. The 'cfliss' account's primary group is 200 (dba). But she also is a member of the developer (99) and user (20) groups as well.

Now is a good time to take a look at how you can change your password with the passwd command.

At the shell prompt, type passwd.

```
$ passwd
Changing password for mschick
Old password: <Enter Old Password Here>
New password: <Enter New Password Here>
Re-enter new password: <Re-Enter New Password Here>
        $
```

The passwd command interactively steps you through changing your password.

Displaying Information About the System

The UNIX system provides numerous commands to its users that enable them to obtain information about the system. A typical user can execute a variety of commands from those that tell him the time and date to commands that provide detailed information about the current state of the UNIX system. In this section, you learn how a typical user can take advantage of the available commands to obtain information from the system.

Getting a Date (*date*)

Let's start by learning how to display the date and time from the system.

At the shell prompt, type date.

```
$ date
Sun Mar 22 10:25:28 CST 1998
$
```

You can also add formatting options that will altar how the date is displayed. Here are a few examples.

At the shell prompt, type date +%j.

```
$ date +%j
081
$
```

The preceding example printed the Julian date, which is the three-digit representation of the current day of the year.

At the shell prompt, type date +%D.

```
$ date +%D
03/22/98
$
```

The preceding example causes the date command to print the date in mm/dd/yy format.

Type $ date +%I:%M%p.

```
$ date +%I:%M%p
11:20AM
$
```

This example provides the time with either the "am" or "pm" displayed.

At the shell prompt, type date "+%A %B %e %Y.

```
$ date "+%A %B %e %Y"
Sunday March 22 1998
$
```

This example shows how to display the full weekday name, the full month name, the day of the month, and the full four-digit year.

As you can see from each of these examples, the date command with its formatting options enables the user to display the date in virtually any format.

Getting System Name Information (*uname*)

Let's now look at how you can display the system's official name. The command that performs this is the uname command.

At the shell prompt, type uname -a.

```
$ uname -a
HP-UX Hydra B.10.20 E 9000/890 7017254010 unlimited user
➥license
$
```

This output can be broken down into the following components:

- The operating system name
- The network system name by which the system is identified
- The operating system release
- The operating system version
- The machine and model number

- The machine ID number
- The operation system license

Check your system manuals for the exact break-down for your machine. If you are using a Hewlett-Packard system, the preceding example applies.

Understanding UNIX Filesystems

The UNIX environment supports what is called a hierarchical filesystem and file/directory structure. This means that your filesystem (and directories) takes on an upside-down tree appearance. People sometimes refer to this structure as a tree. This directory structure closely resembles the more familiar MS-DOS directory layout. The top of the tree is called the root directory. Beneath the root directory lies all the remaining directories.

All directories are maintained inside the UNIX filesystem. This method of file management makes it easier to partition files and users onto the disk devices. Another added benefit is that if the system were to lose a non-system disk drive, the system administrator could simply replace the drive and recover the data from a backup. The hierarchical filesystem provides for flexibility when allocating space for files by making the actual location of your data transparent to you.

As a user, you shouldn't care whether your data lies on physical drive A or B. The job of logically mapping your files and directories to a physical disk drive is entirely up to the administrator. You, as a user, may or may not be in a position to change filesystem or directory configurations.

Now let's take a look at the df command. With this command, you can see your filesystems and their sizes.

At the shell prompt type df -k.

```
/data1(/dev/vg01/lvol1        )  :   1803132 total allocated Kb
                                      162443 free allocated Kb
                                     1640689 used allocated Kb
                                      90 % allocation used
```

```
/data2(/dev/vg02/lvol1        ) :   901556 total allocated Kb
                                     387825 free allocated Kb
                                     513731 used allocated Kb
                                     56 % allocation used


/data3(/dev/vg03/lvol1        ) :   540513 total allocated Kb
                                     130087 free allocated Kb
                                     410426 used allocated Kb
                                     75 % allocation used


/data4(/dev/vg04/lvol1        ) :   901556 total allocated Kb
                                     184337 free allocated Kb
                                     717219 used allocated Kb
                                     79 % allocation used


/data5(/dev/vg01/lvol2        ) :   2704904 total allocated Kb
                                     351091 free allocated Kb
                                     2353813 used allocated Kb
                                     87 % allocation used


/data6(/dev/vg03/lvol2        ) :   2254018 total allocated Kb
                                     173082 free allocated Kb
                                     2080936 used allocated Kb
                                     92 % allocation used


/data7(/dev/vg02/lvol2        ) :   2254018 total allocated Kb
                                     2026370 free allocated Kb
                                     227648 used allocated Kb
                                     10 % allocation used


/data8(/dev/vg04/lvol2        ) :   1803132 total allocated Kb
                                     1466125 free allocated Kb
                                     337007 used allocated Kb
                                     18 % allocation used


/data9(/dev/vg04/lvol3        ) :   2704904 total allocated Kb
                                     2251531 free allocated Kb
                                     453373 used allocated Kb
                                     16 % allocation used
```

```
/home(/dev/vg00/lvol5        ) :    17874 total allocated Kb
                                    16586 free allocated Kb
                                    1288 used allocated Kb
                                    7 % allocation used

/opt (/dev/vg00/lvol6        ) :    358982 total allocated Kb
                                    5224 free allocated Kb
                                    353758 used allocated Kb
                                    98 % allocation used

/tmp (/dev/vg00/lvol7        ) :    432306 total allocated Kb
                                    428873 free allocated Kb
                                    3433 used allocated Kb
                                    0 % allocation used

/usr (/dev/vg00/lvol8        ) :    598200 total allocated Kb
                                    283706 free allocated Kb
                                    314494 used allocated Kb
                                    52 % allocation used

/var  (/dev/vg00/lvol9        ) :    259341 total allocated Kb
                                    68893 free allocated Kb
                                    190448 used allocated Kb
                                    73 % allocation used

/stand(/dev/vg00/lvol1        ) :    43046 total allocated Kb
                                    28522 free allocated Kb
                                    14524 used allocated Kb
                                    33 % allocation used

/     (/dev/vg00/lvol3        ) :    75359 total allocated Kb
                                    53928 free allocated Kb
                                    21431 used allocated Kb
                                    28 % allocation used
```

The preceding output comes from a production system. The df
-k command reports the number of free kilobytes available in the
filesystem, as well as the total kilobytes allocated to that filesystem. The output also shows the kilobytes used and the percent
of the filesystem that is used. This information is extremely useful in the sense that you can determine where the system's freespace is and how much is available for additional storage.

Keep in mind that not all of this freespace will be available to you as a standard user. UNIX requires that its filesystems and directories have enough space available to guarantee that they can grow. Your system administrator uses df quite frequently as part of his tool suite to manage the system. As a rule of thumb, when a filesystem's free space falls below 10 percent, it's time to start archiving and deleting old unused files to free up space.

The output from the df command brings up another interesting point. Notice the /dev/vgxx/lvolxx that follows the filesystem name (that is, /usr (/dev/vg00/lvol8). This indicates that the filesystem is being managed by a volume manager, more specifically Hewlett-Packard's Logical Volume Manager (LVM). Briefly, this means that when your filesystems become full, you can simply add another disk drive to the pool of disks that make up this filesystem.

Note

Again, be sure to read the documentation for your specific system; Hewlett-Packard has a better command, bdf.

UNIX Processes

This chapter ends by discussing UNIX processes. A *process* is simply a program in execution. Every command you have seen so far is really a program that somebody wrote to perform a useful function.

The UNIX system is designed to be capable of handling the execution of numerous programs being run at the same time. The idea behind this is the virtual machine. Put simply, the *virtual machine* means that each person appears to have the full power of the machine all to himself. Each user can execute commands or programs without worrying about what the other users are doing.

For the most part, this system autonomy is true. However, if another user is running a program that takes up most of the machine's resources, the rest of the users know because their programs and commands run slower than normal. This is where your system administrator steps in to provide performance tuning. The system administrator may add memory, disks, or CPUs to fix the problem. He may ask that all *hog* programs run after hours so as to not impact the other users. Regardless of the choice they make, the goal is to enable the user community to do work as efficiently and economically as possible.

Take a look at how you can see the processes that are currently running on your machine.

At the shell prompt, type ps -ef.

UID	PID	PPID	C	STIME	TTY	TIME	COMMAND
root	0	0	0	Oct 28	?	1:05	swapper
root	1	0	0	Oct 28	?	0:00	init
root	2	0	0	Oct 28	?	0:36	vhand
root	3	0	0	Oct 28	?	308:32	statdaemon
root	4	0	0	Oct 28	?	8:57	unhashdaemon
root	7	0	0	Oct 28	?	356:35	ttisr
root	70	0	0	Oct 28	?	0:00	lvmkd
root	71	0	0	Oct 28	?	0:00	lvmkd
root	72	0	0	Oct 28	?	0:00	lvmkd
root	13	0	0	Oct 28	?	26:35	vx_sched_thread
root	14	0	0	Oct 28	?	5:16	vx_iflush_thread
root	15	0	0	Oct 28	?	5:24	vx_ifree_thread
root	16	0	0	Oct 28	?	5:45	vx_inactive_cache ➥thread
root	17	0	0	Oct 28	?	1:35	vx_delxwri_thread
root	18	0	0	Oct 28	?	1:18	vx_logflush_thread
root	19	0	0	Oct 28	?	0:07	vx_attrsync_thread
root	20	0	0	Oct 28	?	0:17	vx_inactive_thread
root	21	0	0	Oct 28	?	0:18	vx_inactive_thread
oracle	25194	1	0	Feb 2	?	14:00	ora_dbwr_prototype
oracle	25192	1	0	Feb 2	?	8:28	ora_pmon_prototype
oracle	25203	1	0	Feb 2	?	0:48	ora_smon_prototype
oracle	25199	1	0	Feb 2	?	9:46	ora_lgwr_prototype
dwilson	8736	8735	1	20:08:32	ttyp2	0:00	-sh
dwilson	8765	8736	9	20:22:26	ttyp2	0:00	ps -ef

$

Now let's look at the output. You'll notice from the headings that several columns result from this output; you must understand just the columns that are significant to this discussion.

- *UID*. The userid of the process owner.
- *PID*. The process ID number of the process.
- *PPID*. The process ID number of the parent process.
- *STIME*. The starting time for the process. If greater than 24 hours, the starting date is displayed.
- *TTY*. The controlling terminal for the process.
- *TIME*. The cumulative execution time of the process.
- *COMMAND*. The command being executed.

Notice that the final entry of our abbreviated output shows the process that executed the `ps -ef` command. Also take note of the process right above it—this is the parent process of the command. By looking at a report such as this, we can see how UNIX executes the commands and programs that are running in the system at a specific point in time. If we were to execute the `ps -ef` command again, we would see a mix of both new and old processes. This is because some programs remain in the system for the entire life of the machine. These programs belong to the operating system and perform the necessary resource management to keep the system functioning.

After all this, you've only scratched the surface of what UNIX has to offer in terms of computing power. As I said in the beginning of the chapter, even the most knowledgeable UNIX experts started out similar to where you are now. The more you learn and familiarize yourself with the UNIX operating system and its utilities, the more computing power you will have at your fingertips.

Note

The `ps -ef` command reports back the systems process status. I've elected to add the `ef` option because it returns more useful information. As with all the commands you've seen, certain options that go with these commands. For this and other UNIX commands, you should check the systems manual or `man` pages to determine the command's proper syntax, as well as any options that are available to it.

Rules for Entering UNIX Commands

By Steve "Mor" Moritsugu

Recognizing the UNIX shell prompt

Understanding commands, options, and arguments and putting required spaces between them

Adding comments to commands

Getting help from the man pages

Getting help from the permuted index

Command not found errors

Setting the path to your command directories

A Review of the Shell Prompt

Let's look at what happens when I log in to a UNIX system:

```
login: mori
Password:
Last login: Fri Mar 13 17:33:22 from :0
Sun Microsystems Inc.   SunOS 5.6        Generic August 1997
$ _
```

The messages that appear upon login will differ from system to system. In the preceding example, after the login messages are complete, the system displays a dollar sign ($) and the cursor sits next to it, waiting for input. The dollar sign is called a *prompt* because it prompts the user to enter a command.

The program that generates the dollar sign prompt is the *shell*. The shell program is a command-line interpreter that allows the user to enter commands. The purpose of this chapter is to go over the rules for entering UNIX commands to the shell.

There are three main shell programs. All of them are available on most commercial UNIX systems:

Bourne shell

C shell

Korn shell

The syntax of the Korn shell is a superset of the Bourne shell, so the two are very compatible. Both the Bourne and Korn shells use the dollar sign prompt. The only exception to this rule occurs if you log in as root, the system administrator. Since the root account co-owns all files and directories, it can make changes regardless of file or directory permissions. A special shell prompt, the pound sign (#), is presented when you log in as root, to remind you that this is the all-powerful account and that you must take care not to make any mistakes or leave the terminal for anyone to access.

If you see a percent sign (%) as the shell prompt, you are probably in the C shell. The C shell uses different syntax and rules from the Bourne and Korn shells, so it presents a different prompt to the average user. If you log in as root, the C shell will use the pound sign prompt, as the Bourne and Korn shells do.

Root precautions

It's a good idea to give the system administrator a regular UNIX account to use most of the time. Then use the **su** command to become root only when necessary.

Other shells you may encounter, especially under Linux, are *tcsh*, which is like the C shell, and *bash*, the GNU Bourne-Again Shell, which incorporates useful features from both the C shell and the Korn shell.

It is possible to customize the shell prompt just for a particular user. If you are on a network, you will sometimes see that your shell prompt includes your system name. For example:

```
sparcster$ _
```

This is a useful prompt, because a network allows you to log in to various UNIX hosts, and it sometimes becomes confusing as to which system you are currently accessing. The shell prompt need not end in the usual shell prompt character, as you can see in the following example:

```
[sparcster] _
```

In the Korn shell (but not the Bourne shell), it is possible to add your current directory as part of your shell prompt. Take a look at the following example:

```
/usr/fred > cd /tmp
/tmp > cd /usr/jane/reports
/usr/jane/reports > cd acme/fiscal97/glaccounts
/usr/jane/reports/acme/fiscal97/glaccounts > ls
acme
report6
report7
/usr/jane/reports/acme/fiscal97/glaccounts > _
```

Here, the shell prompt contains the current directory and ends in a greater-than sign (>). Your current directory starts as /usr/fred. When you change to /tmp, you can see that the shell prompt automatically tracks our current directory. Notice also that the current directory can include many subdirectories and become quite lengthy, leaving you very little room to type in commands. You can still type in long commands, because the command will automatically wrap to the next line and continue to echo your input. However, this can be difficult to read when you want to look over your previous commands.

As you have seen, the shell prompt can appear in many different guises. When you first log in, take an extra moment to see how your shell prompt appears on that system so that you will recognize it later. As you will see throughout this chapter, one of the skills you must develop in order to use UNIX is to recognize when you are at the shell prompt versus when you have ended up in some unexpected situation.

SEE ALSO

➤ *For more information on the UNIX shell, see page 27*

UNIX Command-Line Options, Arguments, and Comments

At the shell prompt, you are expected to enter commands to UNIX. A UNIX command can be a simple one-word command:

```
$ exit
```

Here, the exit command allows you to end the shell and go back to a login prompt. If exit doesn't work, try the logout command or Ctrl+D instead.

```
$ date
Sun Mar 15 07:30:49 PST 1998
$
```

In this example, date is another simple one-word UNIX command. Most UNIX commands are in all-lowercase, although there are exceptions. You must use the proper case (uppercase versus lowercase) when entering commands in UNIX. Be especially wary of handwritten instructions containing UNIX commands. Many people always handwrite certain characters in uppercase or lowercase without remembering that this makes a difference under UNIX.

Some commands require *arguments* (also called *parameters*), which are words telling the command what to act on:

```
$ rm acme peagasus
```

In this example, acme and pegasus are arguments to the rm command. rm is the UNIX command to remove files, so in this instance, rm will delete the acme and pegasus files. Notice that the first word in the command line must be the UNIX command

Case-sensitivity matters

Case-senstivity—whether a word is in uppercase, lowercase, or a combination of the two—matters very much, depending on the circumstances.

you want to run. Notice also that multiple arguments are separated by spaces, not commas (,).

```
$ cd /tmp
$
```

In this example, /tmp is an argument to the cd command, which you saw in Chapter 2, "UNIX Directories and Pathnames." The cd command lets you change your current directory. Note that in UNIX, no news is good news. You know the cd command was successful in this example because the shell prompt reappears on the next line and there were no error messages.

It is very important to put a space between the command and any arguments. In this next example, you can see that some news is probably bad news:

```
$ cd/tmp
cd/tmp: not found
$
```

Here, the space was accidentally omitted after the cd command. First note that you got a message before the next shell prompt. You must read any messages carefully, because they usually mean that your command failed (or UNIX wouldn't have generated any message at all). Beginners often enter a series of commands, ignore the messages, and then wonder why things don't work.

In the previous example, you might think that the cd command failed because the system couldn't find the /tmp directory. This is not correct. Look at the error message more carefully. cd/tmp wasn't found. Most commands under UNIX are actually compiled or script utilities that reside in separate disk files. The system is telling you that cd/tmp is not a valid command—that is, there is no system utility on disk with that name.

Let me summarize the key points so far:

1. At the shell prompt, the first word you enter must be a UNIX command.

2. Most UNIX commands must be typed in lowercase (but there are exceptions).

3. If the command requires a following argument, you must type a space after the command.

4. You may then enter one or more arguments if required for that command. Multiple arguments must be separated by spaces.

5. You must enter the proper uppercase and lowercase letters for commands and arguments and all words on the command line.

SEE ALSO

➤ *For more information on the* date *command, see page 72*
➤ *For more information on the* rm *command, see page 191*
➤ *For more information on the* cd *command, see page 42*

Adding Comments to the Command Line

In some of the following examples, I will add comments to the command lines, so let me introduce you to comments now. A *comment* (also called a *remark*) contains explanatory words meant for a human reader. In the UNIX shell, any word that begins with a pound sign (#) is regarded as the beginning of a comment. The comment continues to the end of the line.

```
$ rm acmetmp      # no longer needed so free up the disk
➥space
```

In this example, the rm command is followed by a comment. The shell will ignore everything from the pound sign (#) to the end of the line. Comments are used primarily in script programming, where UNIX commands are saved in text files.

The pound sign must be preceded by a space if you want it to begin a comment. Otherwise, it is just a normal character (although I recommend that you avoid using it in filenames).

Entering Options to Commands

Most UNIX commands allow options to be specified on the command line that modify how the command operates. Look at the following example:

```
% ls -l /tmp
```

White-space separators

UNIX allows any combination of one or more spaces or tabs to separate commands, options, and arguments. These separators are called *white spaces* for short.

Filenames that start with the pound sign (#)

Some system files start with a pound sign on purpose so that you must pause and think before handling the file. The shell can't access #acme because that is a comment, but it can access ./#acme.

Here, ls is a command you have seen earlier to list the files in a directory. -1 is an option to the ls command that causes it to list in long format, showing details about the file as well as the file-name. Notice that there is a space after the command, as required. Notice that a dash (-) is used to denote options from arguments. In this example, -1 is an option that modifies how ls operates. /tmp is an argument to the ls command that tells ls which directory to list. Options must follow the command and come before any arguments to the command. Also notice that we are in the C shell, since we have a percent sign (%) shell prompt.

```
$ ls -l -a /tmp       # case 1
$ ls -a -l /tmp       # case 2
$ ls -la /tmp         # case 3
$ ls -al /tmp         # case 4
```

In these examples, you can see that UNIX allows great flexibility when entering multiple (simple) options. -a is another option to ls (see Appendix A, "UNIX Commands," for more information on ls if you are curious about everything it does).

All four of the preceding cases are different and valid ways to do the same thing. Notice that I used a pound sign on each line to begin a comment, as we discussed in the preceding section. The shell will ignore all text from the pound sign to the end of the line, allowing me to add explanatory words so you will know which line I am referring to.

In case 1, I specified each option, preceded by a dash. Notice that a space is required between each option and argument. In case 2, notice that the order of the options doesn't matter. In case 3, notice that simple one-letter options can be combined into a composite option, preceded by one dash. In case 4, notice that the options can be combined in any order within the composite option.

Note that options are not universal. -v to one command can mean something totally different when used with another command. You may find some commands that have the same meaning for one option, but other commands where that option letter has a totally different meaning. Also be aware that some options might not be supported on some versions of UNIX, or the option might cause a totally different result on another version of UNIX.

If options are not single letters, they can't be combined into a composite option, as follows:

```
$ find -mount -print
```

Here, the find command is called with two options, -mount and -print. These two options can't be combined into a composite option. Also, find is an example of a command where the order of the options does make a difference.

One UNIX command doesn't always use a dash before its options:

```
$ tar tv
```

t and v are options to the tar command. This is the one command that usually doesn't use the dash for historical reasons. Most modern versions of UNIX (including SCO and Solaris) allow a dash before tar options, so it doesn't have to be different from other commands in specifying options, like so:

```
$ tar -tv
```

Remember that commands must be entered in the following order, separated by spaces:

1. The name of the command.
2. Any desired command options, preceded by a dash.
3. Any desired command arguments.
4. Any desired comments. Put a space and then a pound sign at the start of the comment.

SEE ALSO

➤ *For more information on the* ls *command, see page 151*
➤ *For more information on the* find *command, see page 153*
➤ *For more information on the* tar *command, see page 340*

Entering Arguments to Options

Some options require arguments of their own:

```
$ lp -d laser4 -n 3 acme pegasus
```

lp is a command to print files to a system printer. -d is an option to lp that lets you specify which printer to use; laser4, in this example, is an argument to the -d option. It is not an argument to the command; in other words, it is not a filename to be printed. Similarly, -n is an option to lp, and 3 is an argument to that option that specifies the number of copies of each file to print. acme and pegasus are arguments to the lp command that specify which files to print.

Most commands allow or require a space between an option and the argument to that option. Some commands might not allow any spaces between the option and its argument. I usually try a space first, because the whole command is a little more legible that way. If I get an error, I retry the command without a space. Hint: Using Korn shell command-line editing makes it easy to edit and submit a previous command.

When you first learned English grammar, separating a sentence into subject, predicate, prepositions, and objects of prepositions helped you improve your reading and formulate correct sentences. In the same way, analyzing UNIX command lines into commands, options, arguments to options, and arguments to commands helps you better understand the UNIX commands you encounter, and also helps you formulate correct UNIX commands.

SEE ALSO

➤ For more information on the lp command, see page 169

Where Can You Get Help? (*man*)

There are over 100 standard UNIX commands and utilities. Each one may have options; some commands may have 15 options or more. These options are not universal, so how on earth are you supposed to remember all the options for all the commands? Luckily, you don't have to. UNIX maintains a set of online manuals with information about each command and its options.

Getting Help from the Man Pages

You use the man command to access this information:

```
$ man ls
```

This command will show you the online manual pages that describe how to use the ls command. This process is called checking the man page on ls. Most commercial UNIX systems have similar man pages. Let's take a look at the man page for ls on my Solaris system:

```
User Commands                                              ls(1)


NAME
    ls - list contents of directory

SYNOPSIS
    /usr/bin/ls [ -aAbcCdfFgilLmnopqrRstux1 ] [ file... ]
    /usr/xpg4/bin/ls [ -aAbcCdfFgilLmnopqrRstux1 ] [ file... ]
```

The SYNOPSIS section is sometimes called SYNTAX or USAGE on other systems. It shows the form required to put together this command. Items in square brackets ([]) are optional. Notice that the ls command supports a large number of command options. It also allows one or more filenames to be listed as arguments to the ls command. This example shows that Solaris supports two forms of the ls command. Later in the man page, it will point out differences between the two forms.

```
DESCRIPTION
    For each file that is a directory, ls lists the contents
    of the  directory;  for  each file that  is an  ordinary
    file,  ls repeats  its  name  and any  other information
    requested.  The  output  is  sorted  alphabetically  by
    default.  When no arguments
       ...
```

The DESCRIPTION section goes on for a while, so let me skip down and show you where the command-line options are covered:

```
OPTIONS
    The following options are supported:

    -a    List all entries, including those that begin with a
          dot (.), which are normally not listed.

    -A    List all entries, including those that begin with a
          dot (.),  with  the  exception of the working
          directory (.) and the parent directory (..).

    -b    Force printing of non-printable characters to be in
          the octal \ddd notation.
```

Since there are so many options available in `ls`, this section also goes on for a while. In fact, the man section on `ls` would be about seven pages long if you printed it.

On some UNIX systems, the man pages have so much text that it will go off your screen before you can read it all. In that case, you must pipe the output of `man` to a page utility:

```
$ man ls | pg
```

On other systems, the man pages automatically pause at the end of each page, but then you must determine which paging utility you are in and issue the correct commands to move around and end your session. I cover how to do this in Chapter 6, "Listing, Finding, Displaying, or Printing Files," in the section "Displaying Files/Pipelines a Page at a Time." Here are the basics that will get you around no matter what pager you are in:

- To get to the next page, press the Enter key or the Spacebar.
- To end your man session, press the Q key. You may also have to press the Enter key.

For more information on the `man` command itself, enter this command:

```
$ man man
```

SEE ALSO

➤ *For more information on displaying a file a page at a time, see page 160*

Setting up the man PAGER

If man on your system doesn't page
the output, or you don't like the
paging utility it invokes, set PAGER
to your favorite paging utility (for
example: **PAGER=pg**) and then
export PAGER.

Recognizing Man Pages for System Subroutines

The man pages are arranged in sections that cover commands
that users can run from the shell, commands for system administration, file formats, system subroutines available when you write
C programs under UNIX, and so on. Some commands, such as
the kill command, are also the name of C language subroutines,
as in this example:

```
System Calls                                                 kill(2)


NAME
    kill - send a signal to a process or a group of processes

SYNOPSIS
    #include <sys/types.h>
    #include <signal.h>

    int kill(pid_t 4mpidm, int 4msigm);

DESCRIPTION
    kill() sends a signal to a process or group of processes.
    The process or group of processes to which the signal is
...
```

In this example, notice that following the name kill is the man
section number in parentheses. Also note the #include statements in the SYNOPSIS section. #include always indicates that
you are looking at a C language subroutine and not a command
you can enter at the shell prompt. Do a man on man to see how
to specify the order of searching the man sections. If you never
write C language programs, you want to set up man so that it
checks the commands sections of the man pages before it checks
system subroutines.

The man command will only display the man page from the first
section it encounters. Use the -a option with man to search all
the sections. If the first man page is a system subroutine, the second man page displayed may be from the command section you

are interested in. There is usually a man option to tell it which man section you are interested in, so it will only search that section.

Finding Information in the Man Page Quickly

UNIX beginners go through man pages one page at a time, which is difficult because there is a lot of information to go through on each command. You also might miss an important reference by scanning the pages.

Intermediate UNIX users know how to use the slash (/) command to quickly move the cursor to desired information. For example, if I am checking the man page on the df command, I might want to know whether the size in blocks is based on 512-byte blocks or 1024-byte blocks. Rather than go through page by page, I might enter this command:

```
/512
```

This command tells the paging utility to advance the cursor to the next place it finds the requested string—512 in this case. To find the next occurrence of the same string, enter

```
/
```

Advanced UNIX users know that because man pages can contain special control characters that format the output, the slash command in man pages might not find a given string even though you can find that string visually a few pages down. I explain this problem and its solution in Chapter 6, in the section "Cleaning up Man Pages (col)." Here is how advanced UNIX users start the man command so that the slash command will be able to find all strings correctly:

```
$ man ls | col -bx | pg
```

You may replace pg with your favorite pager.

SEE ALSO

➤ *For more information on cleaning up man pages, see page 168*

Finding the Desired Man Page if You Don't Know the Command

To use the man command, you must give it the UNIX command, spelled correctly. But what can you do if you don't know the command? For example, assume I want to move print jobs currently in one print queue to a different printer. How can I look up the command to do this?

To find UNIX commands on a certain topic, use the -k option to man. For example:

```
$ man -k print
accept            accept (1m)      - accept or reject print
➥requests
acctcom           acctcom (1)      - search and print process
➥accounting files
asa               asa (1)          - convert FORTRAN carriage-
➥control output to printable form
cancel            cancel (1)       - cancel print request
curs_printw       curs_printw (3x)   - print formatted output
➥in curses windows
devinfo           devinfo (1m)     - print device specific
➥information
...
```

The -k option tells man to search the description of each command to see if it has anything to do with the argument given (which is print in this example). The output shown here is for my Solaris system. This output went on to show over 100 commands whose description contains the word "print."

In Chapter 15, "Searching for Lines in a File or Pipeline," you will see how to use the grep command to filter out lines you don't want and leave the lines you do want. In the following example, I use grep to find out whether any of these 100-plus lines are commands that move printer requests from one printer to another:

```
$ man -k print | grep move
lpmove            lpmove (1m)      - move print requests
lprm              lprm (1b)        - remove print requests
```

```
from the print queue
$
```

Aha! There *is* a command to move print requests, called `lpmove`. To find out more about `lpmove`, I can now issue this command:

```
$ man lpmove
```

Of course, you might not find the command you're looking for as easily as I did in this example. You often have to search for various related keywords and try different filter words before you have any success. For example, if I had looked for "transfer" instead of "move," I wouldn't have found the command I was looking for.

If your system doesn't support the `-?` option to `man`, try the `apropos` command:

```
$ apropos print
```

Sometimes the `man -k` or `apropos` command will fail, giving you an error message saying that the `whatis` database must be created before they can run. Usually the message will suggest running `catman -w` to create this database. SCO UNIX has a different command, `makewhatis`, to create this database. Refer to the man page on `man` for information that applies to your system. Root privilege is usually required to create this database.

SEE ALSO

➤ *For more information on the* grep *command, see page 380*

Using the Permuted Index

The Permuted Index is a book that ships with some UNIX systems, providing another way to look up topics of interest. To help you understand a permuted index, I have created a permuted index with just two entries: one for `lpmove` and one for `lprm`:

```
                          lpmove (1m) - move print requests
                          lprm (1b) - remove print request from the
                          ➥print queue
lpmove (1m) -             move print requests
lpmove (1m) - move        print requests
lprm (1b) - remove        print requests from the print queue
lprm (1b) -               remove print requests from the print queue
lpmove (1m) - move print  requests
```

Each entry is placed in the permuted index multiple times—once for each of the important words in that line. Note that there is a gap in the middle of all the entries. The permuted index is arranged in alphabetical order based on the word immediately following the gap. Each entry is included multiple times so that each of its keywords can be placed just after the gap. When you want to look up an entry by keyword, find the word you want in alphabetical order just after the gap. Then look at the entire entry to see if it is one you are interested in.

command not found Errors

To execute a UNIX command, utility, or shell script, simply type the command name at the shell prompt, including any options and arguments needed by the command. Some commands are built into the shell program, but most standard UNIX commands are program files stored in directories such as /bin, /usr/bin/, /etc/, /usr/local/bin, /sbin, and so on.

If you try to run a command, you might get an error like this:

```
$ myscript
myscript: not found
$ ./myscript
acme
pegasus
$
```

It's common to see this not found error when you first begin writing your own shell scripts. If the script is in your current directory, run the file as ./scriptname. This might solve the problem.

If you still get a *command* not found error, check that you have spelled the command properly, that you are using the correct case (upper, lower, or mixed), and that you have a space after the command to separate it from any options or arguments. Check the man page for that command. If the man page doesn't exist, maybe the version of UNIX on your system doesn't support that command.

Some UNIX systems offer a series of layered products (extra-cost software). In order to use certain commands, you must purchase additional packages containing that command. It is now common for the UNIX C compiler to be an extra-cost item. Therefore, you will get a *command* not found error when you try to run the cc command or the make command until you purchase that software and install it. Sometimes there are freeware alternatives that can be downloaded from the Internet to provide the same or similar functionality. Many of the Web sites for the major UNIX vendors have links to such freeware.

SEE ALSO

➤ *For more information on writing shell scripts, see Chapter 25, "Writing Bourne Shell Scripts," page 637*

Setting the Path to Your Commands

When you run commands such as ls, cp, and rm, you don't have to worry if they are in /bin versus /usr/bin. You don't have to type in the full pathname of the command. This is because the shell PATH variable makes it easy to run the standard UNIX commands.

You can display the current contents of the PATH variable using the echo command:

```
$ echo $PATH
/usr/bin:/usr/ucb:/etc:.
$
```

The dollar sign ($) before the shell variable indicates that we are referring to the contents of that variable. PATH contains a series of directory names separated by colons (:). The full pathname of each directory must be specified. The order of the directories is important, because it determines how the shell looks for commands that you type in.

The preceding example is from my Solaris 2.x system. PATH on other UNIX systems would include /bin as well as /usr/bin. On Solaris 2.x SVR4, /bin is now just a symbolic link to /usr/bin. In other words, all the system binaries have been collected into one directory, /usr/bin.

My PATH also contains /usr/ucb, which contains many BSD utilities. If I log in as root, my PATH would also contain /usr/sbin, which contains system administration commands.

Let's see what happens when you type in a UNIX command to the shell.

The shell first checks to see if the command name contains a slash (/). If the name contains a slash, the shell will use that name as a pathname and try to execute that file. Here are some examples of commands that contain a slash:

```
$ /usr/fred/bin/myscript -p acme
```

```
$ ./yourscript file1 file2
```

If the command name doesn't contain a slash, the shell will check each of the directories in PATH for an executable file with the correct name and will try to run only the first one it finds. For example, assume that PATH contains /bin:/usr/bin:/usr/local/bin.

```
$ ls /usr/fred
```

This command word is ls, which doesn't contain a slash. Therefore, the shell will check the first directory in PATH, which is /bin in our example. If /bin/ls is an executable file, the shell will try to run that program and won't check any more directories in PATH. If /bin/ls doesn't exist or isn't a regular file or isn't executable, the shell will then move to the next directory, which is /usr/bin in our example. If /usr/bin/ls is an executable file, the shell will try to run it and won't check any more directories in PATH. Once the shell has tried all the directories in PATH and has not found an executable file, it will give up with a *command not found* error.

Adding Your Current Directory to *PATH*

If your UNIX command doesn't contain a slash, only the directories in PATH will be checked. Some people also want the current directory to be checked. This is usually useful only if you write your own shell scripts and you want to be able to run them easily when you are in the directory where they reside.

To include the current directory in the PATH variable, add either the period directory or an empty directory. I prefer to add the period directory because that is the common way to indicate the current directory. However, you should be able to recognize empty directories in PATH because there are security implications (which we will cover).

Here is an example from the Bourne shell or Korn shell of adding the current directory to PATH using the period (.):

```
PATH=/bin:/usr/bin:.:/usr/local/bin
```

Here, we have set up PATH to search the current directory after /bin and /usr/bin but before /usr/local/bin. Here are some more examples using the period:

```
PATH=/bin:/usr/bin:/usr/local/bin:.        # case 1
PATH=.:/bin:/usr/bin:/usr/local/bin        # case 2
PATH=$PATH:.                               # case 3
```

In case 1, we search the current directory only if the command isn't found in the first three directories. In case 2, we search the current directory before the other three directories. In case 3, we keep the default value of PATH and specify the current directory as the last directory to search.

As a shorthand method, you can use an empty directory to indicate the current directory. An empty directory is just like using the period, but don't put in a period, just an extra colon (:). For example:

```
PATH=/bin:/usr/bin::/usr/local/bin        # case 1
PATH=:/bin:/usr/bin:/usr/local/bin        # case 2
PATH=/bin:/usr/bin:/usr/local/bin:        # case 3
PATH=$PATH:                               # case 4
```

In case 1, the current directory is searched after /usr/bin. In case 2, it is searched before the other directories. In cases 3 and 4, it is searched after the other directories in PATH.

Security Implications of *PATH*

In general, you shouldn't specify the current directory at the beginning of PATH. For security reasons, if you're going to add the current directory to PATH, add it at the end. Otherwise, a hacker could create files with common command names such as cp or ls in /tmp or other commonly used directories. If you execute that system command while sitting in the booby-trapped directory, you will run the hacker's program instead of the system command.

For the same reason, any directories in the root's PATH should not have write permission for the average user.

PATH and Add-On Packages

If you add a new software package to your system, that package might want you to add its executable directory to your PATH variable. The installation script for the package might modify PATH in /etc/profile automatically. It requires root privilege to modify /etc/profile. After you add a package as root, log in again and check your PATH variable. Make sure the order of the directories is reasonable, especially if it has been modified by adding that package.

Where Is That Command? (*type, which, whence*)

Sometimes it's useful to know the full pathname of commands you run, especially if they aren't working properly and you want to investigate why. PATH can include many directories, so it is fortunate that there are commands that will check PATH for you and tell you the full pathname of commands.

The most useful of these is the type command, which works in both the Bourne shell and the Korn shell:

```
$ type ls                       # from the Bourne shell
ls is /usr/bin/ls
$ exec ksh                      # change to the Korn shell
$ type ls
ls is a tracked alias for /usr/bin/ls
$
```

Here, type takes the command you give it and determines the command's full pathname.

If your system doesn't support the type command, use the which command or the whence command to get the full pathname of a command:

```
$ which ls
```

```
$ whence ls
```

Often the which command works only in the Bourne shell. Often the whence command works only in the Korn shell.

Common Errors Users Make When Entering UNIX Commands

UNIX can be very frustrating for beginners. At first, it can seem as if UNIX is very picky and will object to everything you type. I have listed here the common errors that beginners make to help you avoid them.

Incorrect Uppercase and Lowercase

Under UNIX, the following filenames would refer to different files:

acme	aCme	acMe	acmE
ACME	acME	aCMe	AcMe
AcmE	Acme	aCME	AcME

All of these files could be in use in a directory at the same time, because under UNIX, it matters whether the letter is in uppercase or lowercase. At first, your eyes might not even notice a mistaken uppercase letter when it should be lowercase, or vice versa.

Be wary of handwritten instructions to type in UNIX commands, because people often don't pay attention to upper- and lowercase when writing.

Incorrect Spacing

As mentioned earlier in this chapter, commands, options, and arguments must not be run together. They must be separated by a space. It is equally invalid to insert a space in the middle of a command or pathname.

Misusing the Arrow Keys, Insert, Page Up, and So On

Avoid using the special keys on the keyboard, such as the arrow keys, the Insert key, the Home key, the End key, and the Page Up and Page Down keys. Linux is the one flavor of UNIX that incorporates these keys well. For most other types of UNIX systems, use of these special keys will simply insert escape sequences into files, email, and even filenames. Once you have inserted this garbage, it can be very tricky to remove.

If you ever find garbage like this:

```
^[[A^[[B^[[C^[[D
```

in a text document, email, or filename, it resulted from the user's trying to correct some misspelling by using the arrows keys to reposition the cursor.

To display control characters in a filename, use the `ls -b` option:

```
$ ls
acme
acme
$ ls -b
acme
abm^[[0^[[0cme
$
```

Here, at first `ls` seems to show that there are two files named acme in the same directory, which we know can't be true. By adding the `-b` option to `ls`, we can see the controls within the second filename. That filename was created by a user who wanted to redirect output to acme but typed abm by mistake. He pressed the left arrow key twice and typed cme over the bm so that the command line would show acme. The user never realized he made this mistake, because everything looked normal.

Correcting Errors Using Backspace Versus Delete

How should you back up and correct typing errors? Well, it depends. There are two primary ways to back up and correct errors:

Use the Backspace key or Ctrl+H

Use the Delete key or Ctrl+?

What makes this complicated is the fact that, on some keyboards, the Delete key sends an ASCII DEL (127) character. On other keyboards, it sends an ESC sequence. The Backspace key will either send a Ctrl+H or an ASCII DEL. Sometimes Backspace is programmable, especially if you use a PC to log in to UNIX. Sometimes Backspace will send Ctrl+H, and Shift+Backspace will send DEL, or vice versa.

To clear up the confusion, enter this command:

```
$ stty -a
speed 38400 baud;
eucw 1:0:0:0, scrw 1:0:0:0
intr = ^c; quit = ^\; erase = ^?; kill = ^u;
eof = ^d; eol = <undef>; eol2 = <undef>; swtch = <undef>;
start = ^q; stop = ^s; susp = ^z; dsusp = ^y;
rprnt = ^r; flush - ^o; wcrase - ^w; lnext = ^v;
-parenb -parodd cs8 -cstopb -hupcl cread -clocal -loblk
➥-crtscts -crtsxoff -parext
-ignbrk brkint ignpar -parmrk -inpck istrip -inlcr -igncr
➥icrnl -iuclc
ixon -ixany -ixoff imaxbel
isig icanon -xcase echo echoe echok -echonl -noflsh
-tostop echoctl -echoprt echoke -defecho -flusho -pendin
➥iexten
opost -olcuc onlcr -ocrnl -onocr -onlret -ofill -ofdel tab3
$
```

The fourth line tells you how the system expects you to erase characters. You will see erase set to ^H, ^?, or DEL.

To test your erase key, enter this command:

```
$ datex
```

Erase the letter x and press the Enter key. If you see the system date and time, you used the correct key to erase the letter x. Try using Ctrl+H, Delete, Backspace, and Shift+Backspace in separate tests to see if any of these are successful in erasing the letter x. Hopefully you will find an erase character that works with your current setup.

If not, change your erase character to Ctrl+H as follows:

```
$ stty erase Ctrl+H
```

Here, enter Ctrl+H by holding down the Ctrl key and then pressing the H key. Do not press C then T then R then L then + then H. Now you should be able to use Ctrl+H to backspace and correct input. You can add this stty command to your .profile if you want to make the change permanent.

Misusing the Three Different Quote Types

UNIX uses all three different quoting characters:

" is the quotation marks key, which I call the double quote.

' is the apostrophe key, which I call the single quote.

` is the grave accent, which I call the back quote.

Each of these quote keys has different uses under UNIX, so you must use the correct one for different situations.

To include spaces in one argument, use the double or single quotes to surround the argument:

```
$ mail -s 'Meeting next week' fred jane harvey    # correct
➥way
```

Here, the mail command allows an -s option to specify a subject for the email being sent. The -s option accepts an argument to that option, which is the text of the subject. The single quotes make the phrase "Meeting next week" all one argument. Here is the wrong way:

```
$ mail -s Meeting next week fred jane harvey    # wrong way
```

Here, the single word "Meeting" is the subject of the email, and the phrase "next week" is considered part of the list of users who will receive this mail. Later you will get bounced mail with a message saying that the system can't deliver mail to users "next" and "week."

Use double quotes when you want to include shell variables:

```
$ mail -s "$PROJECT proposal" fred jane harvey    # correct way
```

Here, the subject of the mail will contain two words: the contents of the shell variable $PROJECT, and the word "proposal."

Use back quotes when you want to use shell command substitution. This allows you to take the output of one command and use it as text within another command:

```
lp `cat flist`
```

Here, the command within the back quotes will be run first, displaying the contents of file flist. That output is then substituted in the original command in place of the backquoted words. Thus, the lp command will be followed by a list of filenames as contained within the flist file. The lp command will then be executed to print those files to the default system printer.

SEE ALSO

➤ For more information on back quotes and command substitution, see page 245
➤ For more information on quoting regular expression patterns, see page 393

What Is UNIX Telling Me?

Some UNIX messages are very cryptic. This section tells you how to interpret common error indications so that you can quickly and easily correct what is wrong.

Usage Errors

One kind of error you might receive when entering UNIX commands is a usage error:

```
$ cp abc
Usage: cp [-fip] source_file target_file
       cp [-r¦-R][-fip] source_file... target_file
$
```

Remembering that no news is good news, this error means that something is wrong and your command didn't execute. In this case, the error message means all of the following:

The command didn't execute because you made an error.

You have misused this command.

Here is the correct usage (syntax) so that hopefully you will be able to re-enter it correctly.

This usage error is telling you that cp needs both a source_file and a target_file, but you didn't enter both on the command line. The usage statement also shows you valid options that are possible. Since they are shown in square brackets, they are not required (they are optional).

Usage means misusage

I have seen many UNIX beginners ignore usage messages and then wonder why things aren't working. Whenever you see a usage message, remember that it is an *error* message. You messed up the command, so it didn't run properly.

The > Sign (PS2 Prompt)

The greater-than sign (>) is called the PS2 prompt. It appears in cases like this:

```
$ mail -s "meeting tomorrow jane fred
> quit
> exit
> :q!
>
```

The PS2 prompt appears when UNIX thinks you are entering a multi-line command. The shell uses this distinctive PS2 prompt on the next line to warn you that what you type is part of the command started on the previous line. In the preceding example, notice that the closing double quote is missing from the mail command, so the command is incomplete. The PS2 prompt appears on the next line. The user in this case didn't recognize the PS2 prompt and became confused because the system had stopped responding to his commands. He couldn't quit or exit to the shell prompt or to a new login. He should abort that command using Ctrl+C or Delete and enter the whole command again.

There are cases in which the PS2 prompt is valid. For example:

```
$ lpstat -t |
> grep '^p104-' |
> awk '{print $1}' |
> while read $RR
> do
>    cancel $RR
> done
p104-143234 canceled
p104-142337 canceled
p104-142338 canceled
$
```

Here, the output from one command is being piped to another command. If one line ends in a pipe sign (|) , that signals the shell that the rest of this pipeline command will be entered on the next line. If a pipeline consists of several commands, putting each command on a separate line can improve legibility. Notice that the PS2 prompt appears, confirming that we are entering a long multi-statement command.

If you get the PS2 prompt by mistake, press Ctrl+C, Delete, Backspace, or Shift+Backspace to abort the command and get back to the shell prompt. (See the later discussion of the intr key.)

Dropping to the Next Line with No Prompt

When the system is waiting for keyboard input, the cursor will drop to the next line with no prompt, like this:

```
$ grep 'acme' | sort

_
```

The cursor is sitting on the second line. If you don't recognize the problem, you might let the command sit for a while, thinking that maybe it will complete soon. But this command will never complete. Like many UNIX commands, grep can accept a list of filenames after specifying the pattern to look for in those files. If no files are given, grep will read from standard input for lines to process. This example doesn't pipe any output to grep, so it simply waits for keyboard input of the lines to process.

When you recognize that you have this problem, press Ctrl+C, Delete, Backspace, or Shift+Backspace to abort the command and get back to the shell prompt. (See the later discussion of the intr key.)

Can't Stat Filename

The stat subroutine is one way that UNIX utilities determine information about a file or directory. If a command can't stat the filename, it can't get that information. Check to make sure that you have entered your command correctly and that you correctly spelled any filenames or directories within the command. Also check to make sure that expected files exist and are of the correct type (for example, a directory file versus a regular file).

What to Do When Your Session Seems to Be Hung

If you were in vi, it is possible that you are still in insert mode. In that case, all commands you type will echo to the screen but won't execute. Press the Esc key to terminate insert mode. See if you can now use normal vi commands to check your file, and then save and exit, or exit without saving your changes. If that doesn't solve the problem, go on to the next idea.

If you were in a pager program, input would echo to the screen but not be acted on. Press the Q key and then press the Enter key to see if that terminates the pager program and takes you back to the shell prompt. If that doesn't solve the problem, go on to the next idea.

Try aborting whatever command you're in. Press Ctrl+C, Delete, Backspace, Shift+Backspace, and Ctrl+\ to see if any of these take you back to the shell prompt. If that doesn't solve the problem, go on to the next idea.

It's possible that some of your terminal settings have been disturbed. Enter the following, but don't press the Enter key in doing so:

```
Ctrl+J
stty sane
Ctrl+J
stty sane
Ctrl+J
```

Now go back to the beginning of the list of suggestions and try the suggestions again. If that doesn't solve the problem, go on to the next idea.

If you're using a Windows PC or an X terminal to connect to UNIX over a network, it's possible that the UNIX window doesn't have focus. Click inside the window to select it. The outline of the window should be a more intense color once it is selected. After entering the preceding lines of code, go back to the beginning of the list of suggestions and try them again. If that doesn't solve the problem, go on to the next idea.

Make sure that the cable that connects you to the UNIX system is connected securely. Usually cables should be screwed in tightly to avoid connection problems. If you found a loose cable and corrected it, go back to the beginning of the list and try the suggestions again. If that doesn't solve the problem, go on to the next idea.

Your terminal or Windows PC might have lost the correct connection settings. You should record how to set up your terminal or Windows PC program and how to check whether the settings are correct. If you have never done this, check another station nearby using the same terminal or PC program and compare its settings to your own. If you found a bad setting and corrected it, go back to the beginning of the list and try the suggestions again. If that doesn't solve the problem, go on to the next idea.

Some network or device problems can take up to 10 minutes to time-out and give control back to your station. If you have been hung up only a few minutes, wait a total of 10 minutes, and then go back to the beginning of the list and try the suggestions again. If that doesn't solve the problem, go on to the next idea.

If you're connected through a terminal, try powering off the terminal, count to 20, and then power the terminal on again. This might allow you to communicate with UNIX again. Warning: Do not power off the UNIX system itself. If you are unsure of the difference, do not proceed. Ask your system administrator for help.

If you are connected through a Windows PC, start another connection to UNIX and see if you can log in. If this is successful, terminate the window that is not responding, and work in the new window.

The UNIX system itself might be down, or the network might be down. Ask other users if they are having the same problem. If so, report the situation to the system or network administrator.

As a last resort, if you are on a terminal and not a Windows station, you might have to kill your process to see if a new login prompt will let you log in using the following procedure:

How to kill your process to get a new login

1. If you're on a Windows station, close the UNIX window to end that session. Start a new UNIX window to begin another session.

2. If you're on a terminal that is hung up, go to another terminal or station and log in on the same id.

3. Enter this command, replacing `fred` with your login id:
   ```
   who -u | grep fred
   ```

   You should see output like this:
   ```
   fred    term/a    Mar 15 19:12    .    9476    (10.1.1.7)
   fred    pts/1     Mar 15 20:30    .    0302    (10.1.1.1)
   ```

4. Determine your current working UNIX port by using the `tty` command. For example:
   ```
   $ tty
   /dev/term/a
   $
   ```

5. Find the line in the `who -u` output that corresponds to the hung session. The `tty` won't match your current working session. Look for the PID number at or near the end of the

line. In the preceding example, PID 9476 is for the working session, so PID 10302 must be the hung session. If your results are unclear, get help. Do not continue.

6. If you have determined the PID of your hung session, kill that session by entering the following two kill commands, replacing 10302 with the PID for the hung session:

```
$ kill 10302
$ kill -9 10302
```

7. Go to the hung session and see if you have a new login prompt. If so, go ahead and log in. If you don't, ask your system administrator for help.

SEE ALSO

➤ *For more information on accessing UNIX from Windows, see, page 589*

➤ *For more information on X terminals, see page 120*

➤ *For more information on* ps *and processes, see page 316*

➤ *For more information on killing processes, see page 320*

Check Your Intr and Erase Keys in Advance (*stty*)

Earlier in this chapter, we discussed how to determine your erase character and how to change it if necessary. You use a similar process to test your character and change it if necessary. Enter this command:

```
$ date
```

Do not press the Enter key. Press Ctrl+C, Delete, Backspace, and Shift+Backspace to see if any of these take you back to the shell prompt. If so, enter date (but don't press the Enter key) and try that same key again. If it takes you back to the shell prompt, it is your intr key. Write down what key it is for this station as it is connected to UNIX. If none of the keys or key combinations worked, press the Enter key to get to a new shell prompt. Enter this command:

```
$ stty intr Ctrl+C
```

Enter Ctrl+C by holding down the Ctrl key and then pressing the C key. Do not enter C then T then R then L then + then C. Now you should be able to use Ctrl+C to abort commands and terminate the current job. You can add this stty command to your .profile if you want to make the change permanent.

Saving Command Output or Errors in a File

Every UNIX command has access to three system functions:

Standard input (`stdin`)

Standard output (`stdout`)

Standard error (`stderr`)

Usually all UNIX commands display their results using the standard output routine supplied by the system. Commands display any error messages using the standard error routine. These standard output and standard error routines are written in such a way that it is easy for the shell to redirect the output to a file or pipeline instead of to the screen. Commands use the standard output or standard error routines, but they have no idea if the output is really going to the screen or a file, or being piped to another UNIX command.

Not all command output goes to standard output or standard error. Some error messages go to the system console and hence don't go through standard error, so they can't be redirected or saved in a file. Similarly, some command output can go directly to a physical device, such as the user's terminal. In that case, the output can't be redirected or saved in a file. However, most command output goes to standard output, and most command errors go to standard error.

SEE ALSO

➤ *For more information on standard output or error, see page 30*

Saving Command or Pipeline Output in a File (>)

When in the Bourne shell or the Korn shell, use the greater-than sign (>) to redirect standard output to go to a file instead of the screen:

```
$ cal 1998 > thisyear
```

Here, the output of the `cal` command will be put into a file called `thisyear` and will not appear on-screen. The act of redirecting output to a file will create the file if it doesn't exist. To save the output in the current directory, use a basename as the filename. To save the output in a different directory, use an absolute or relative pathname to specify the file.

The shell sets up redirection before it actually starts the command running. The shell then removes all redirection symbols and files from the command, so the command never sees them when it runs. The following are equivalent to the `cal` command just shown:

```
$ cal > thisyear 1998
$ > thisyear cal 1998
```

Thus, it makes no difference where in the command you specify redirection.

If you are in the Bourne shell or the Korn shell, to create an empty file, enter the following:

```
$ > filename
```

If this command gives you the error `Invalid null command`, you are in the C shell, where this command won't work.

> is short for 1>. They are equivalent; hence, these two commands are equivalent:

```
$ cal 1998 > thisyear
$ cal 1998 1> thisyear
```

Standard output is channel 1, which explains the 1 in 1>.

On older UNIX systems, you had to create an empty file, as follows:

```
$ cat /dev/null > filename    # old method, no longer used
```

The shell will give no warning if you are about to overwrite an existing file. Therefore, you should make sure your destination file doesn't have important data before you redirect output to that file.

SEE ALSO

➤ *For more information on redirection, see page 30*

The *noclobber* Option in the Korn Shell

The Korn shell has an option called `noclobber` that prevents you from redirecting on top of an existing file:

```
$ date > junk              # step 1
$ date > junk              # step 2
$ set -o noclobber         # step 3
$ date > junk              # step 4
ksh: junk: file already exists
$ date >¦ junk             # step 5
$ date > junk              # step 6
ksh: junk: file already exists
$ set +o noclobber         # step 7
$ date > junk              # step 8
$
```

In step 1, we create a file called junk by redirecting the output from the `date` command to it. In step 2, we overwrite the old junk file with new information. Notice that no error message is generated. In step 3, we turn on the `noclobber` option in the Korn shell. In step 4, we try to redirect to our junk file again, but it fails, saying that the file already exists. In step 5, notice that we can use greater-than vertical bar (>|) to overwrite an existing file even with `noclobber` turned on. In step 6, notice that `noclobber` is still in force for normal redirection. In step 7, we use the +o option to set `noclobber`. In step 8, notice that we can redirect over our junk file with no errors.

An Input File Can't Also Be an Output File

Because the shell initializes the output file before the command starts running, you can't use the same file as both the source and the destination of a UNIX command or pipeline.

```
$ grep -v discontinued pricelist > pricelist  # won't work
```

In this example, we want to remove all lines of file pricelist that have the word "discontinued" and save the result to the same file. The file pricelist is initialized for output as an empty file before the grep command starts. Thus, it finds an empty source file and ends immediately, leaving the destination file empty. The same is true if you use a pipeline:

```
$ sort acme | grep -v discontinued > acme     # won't work
```

The way to accomplish this is to use a temporary intermediate file:

```
$ sort acme | grep -v discontinued > /tmp/tmp$$  # step 1
$ mv /tmp/tmp$$ acme                             # step 2
```

Here, we save the output from the pipeline or UNIX command in a temporary file, typically in /tmp if there is sufficient disk space there. I recommend you use a temporary filename ending in $$, as shown. This will append a unique number to the end of the file so that other users running at the same time and executing the same code won't interfere with us. In step 2, we take our temporary file and overwrite the original source file, completing our procedure.

Saving Errors in a File (2>)

You can save error messages totally independently of saving standard output. Since standard error is channel 2, use 2> to save standard error in a file:

```
$ anycommand 2> anycommand.err   # case 1
$ anycommand > log 2> errs        # case 2
$ anycommand 2> errs > log        # case 3
$ anycommand > log                # case 4
```

In case 1, standard output is not redirected, so it goes to your screen, while any error messages go to a file called anycommand.err and hence are not seen on-screen. In case 2, standard output goes to one file, and standard error goes to a different file. In case 3, it makes no difference if you redirect standard error before standard output or vice versa. In case 4, standard output is redirected to a file. Standard error is not redirected, so any errors will appear onscreen.

Appending Output or Errors to a File (>>)

Use the double greater-than sign (>>) to append standard output or standard error to a file. To *append* means to keep the current information in the file and add the new information to the end of the file. If the file doesn't exist, this command will create it.

```
$ anycommand >> outlog 2>> errlog
```

Since standard output and standard error are independent, you can append to one file but not the other if desired:

```
$ anycommand 2>> errlog > anycommand.out
```

Saving Both Output and Errors in One File (2>&1)

To save standard output and standard error in the same file, redirect standard error using 2>&1:

```
$ anycommand > anycommand.out 2>&1
```

You must not put any spaces within 2>&1, but there must be a space before the 2. 2>&1 must come after redirecting standard output in the command line. 2>&1 means redirect standard error to the same place that standard output is going.

Duplicating Output to a File and to the Screen (|*tee*)

The tee pipe gets its name from the image of a pipe with flowing liquid that then splits off into two pipes in a T shape, so that half of the liquid goes in one direction and half in the other. For UNIX, the tee pipe actually sends duplicate information flowing to two different places: standard output and a file:

```
$ anycommand |tee filename
```

Here, the output of anycommand is stored in the filename specified. That same information also goes to standard output, which will go to your screen since it is not being redirected.

```
$ anycommand | tee file1 | grep -v discontinued | tee file2 |
➥pg
```

This example shows that it is possible to use two tee pipes in one pipeline. The first tee pipe saves the output from anycommand in file1. The same information goes to standard output, where it is piped to grep, which removes any lines containing the word "discontinued." The output of grep is then saved in file2 and displayed on-screen one page at a time.

The -a option to the tee command allows output to be appended to the specified filename:

```
$ anycommand ¦ tee -a filename
```

The UNIX Graphical User Interface (GUI)

By Steve "Mor" Moritsugu

Using a mouse and icons under UNIX (GUI)

What is X Windows and Motif?

Solaris contains SunOS UNIX and two GUIs

A common desktop environment for UNIX systems (CDE)

How to use the CDE

Running UNIX commands from the CDE

Editing text files from the CDE

The CDE File Manager

Sending and reading email via the CDE Mailer

Introducing GUI and X Windows

UNIX can run on inexpensive character-based ASCII terminals that are usually limited to 80 columns by 24 rows of text or limited graphic characters. UNIX can also utilize more expensive bitmapped monitors that can display pictures, images, and graphics and use a mouse to interact with the user. This second method of interaction is called a GUI, or graphical user interface.

A GUI screen looks very much like a Windows screen on a PC with small pictures called icons that represent programs and functions. Like Windows, a GUI also uses a mouse to enable the user to make selections by pointing at icons and clicking or double-clicking. A UNIX GUI also usually offers scrollbars, buttons, dialog boxes, and menus. These things can make UNIX much easier to use, especially for a Windows user who only uses UNIX occasionally and therefore does not remember the commands, options, and syntax required to enter UNIX shell commands. Even for experienced UNIX users, GUI icons and graphics often give a clearer picture of what is going on. Because the GUI enables you to start a shell command-line session in a window of the screen, it offers the best of both worlds. In fact, a GUI allows multiple command-line windows to be running simultaneously, each running independently of the other. The user can use the mouse to interact with these different shell windows and even cut and paste text from one window to another.

X Windows

Most UNIX GUI implementations are based on the X Window System (also called X11) developed at MIT and further enhanced by the companies that make up the X Consortium. X11 provides a library of graphics routines that can be used to create applications that use graphics display elements and mouse input. Although many UNIX GUI implementations run on the console of the UNIX system itself, X11 also allows graphics programs to run on stations connected by ethernet to the host UNIX system. X11 software is also available to run graphics programs on Windows PCs and Macintosh systems connected to a UNIX system.

X Terminals

There are also low-cost stations called X Terminals that are minimal computer stations with a graphics monitor and mouse. They have a CPU and memory, but typically do not have a hard disk. They connect to the UNIX host over a network connection and can run X11 applications. The UNIX host computer does the higher-level program computing and the X Terminal does the lower-level graphics manipulation. This removes overhead from the UNIX host and allows graphics applications without the cost of a full PC.

The Window Manager

A Window Manager is software that utilizes the X Window System to start jobs in windows on the graphic screen, change the size of a window, minimize the window to an icon, maximize the window to the full screen, and so on. One of the most common of these is the Motif Window Manager developed by the Open Software Foundation (OSF), which is a consortium of companies.

Console GUIs

Most UNIX systems have one special station that is called the system console. Usually this is a bitmapped monitor with mouse and keyboard very near to the computer system itself. The console is where any unexpected system warnings display. The console is usually used to interact with the computer when the computer is first powered on or shut down. In large companies, the UNIX computer and its console are often locked away in the computer department, so the average users never see them. On the other hand, there are also UNIX workstations dedicated to a primary user who sits at the console and runs applications such as CAD (computer aided design) or animation.

Many UNIX systems today provide a GUI to run on the system console. On some UNIX systems, all the terminals are character based except for the GUI console, which is then the only station that can run graphics applications and display images. If your system is connected to the Internet, a UNIX GUI console may support a Web browser so that it can surf the Internet. If your system has an application such as WABI, a UNIX GUI console can run Windows applications. If your system network includes X Terminals or PCs running X11, they may also be able to run the same applications as the graphic UNIX console.

The Solaris Desktop

Solaris is an operating system from SunSoft Inc., which is a subsidiary of Sun Microsystems Inc. Underlying Solaris is Sun's version of UNIX called SunOS (currently version 5.6, which is based on SVR4). Because the previous SunOS version 4.x was based on BSD UNIX, the current SunOS still offers many BSD utilities even though it is a System V (SVR4) type of UNIX. Solaris also includes Sun's networking additions to UNIX and it includes two different GUIs that you can choose from when you log on to the system console. These are described in the following sections on OpenWindows and the CDE. Like most UNIX GUIs, they provide graphic mouse controlled applications to edit a text file, manipulate files and directories, read/send email, and perform system administration functions. In addition to these standard applications, Solaris provides a number of others. Actually Solaris provides two different versions of most applications, an OpenWindows version and a CDE version.

SEE ALSO

➤ *For more information on BSD and SVR4 UNIX, see page 19*

Solaris' Older GUI: OpenWindows

Older versions of Solaris provided only one GUI, called OpenWindows, based on the Open Look Window Manager. Figure 5.1 shows an example of two windows open on one screen in this GUI format:

1. A UNIX command-line window (called cmdtool)

2. A File Manager window

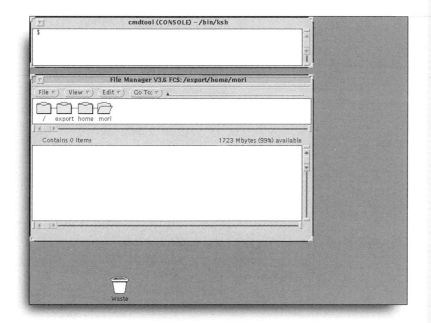

FIGURE 5.1

Solaris' older GUI:
OpenWindows.

Notice that each window has a triangle in the upper-left corner.
If you single-click on that triangle, you will see the following
options. (Double-clicking has no effect.) The words in parenthesis () are descriptions of what the options mean.

Close	(This means minimize to an icon.)
Full Size/Restore Size	(These choices toggle.)
Move	(Allow the whole window to be moved.)
Resize	(Allow the window to be changed to a different size.)
Back	(Move window in back of others.)
Refresh	
Quit	(This means terminate and close this window.)

If you move the cursor to a vacant part of the background and
click the right button, you will see these options:

Programs

Utilities

Properties   (Set color scheme.)

Workstation Info...   (System name and IP address, mem-
                          ory, versions.)

Help...

Exit...   (Log off.)

If you select Utilities, you will see these options:

Refresh

Reset Input

Function Keys

Window Controls

Save Workspace   (Customize workspace on logon.)

Lock Screen   (Enter your logon password to
                          unlock.)

Suspend

Console   (Start a command session to receive
                          system errors.)

If you select Programs rather than Utilities, you will see these
options:

File Manager   (Create dirs, copy files, rename,
                          delete, floppy.)

Power Manager   (Set autoshutdown if inactive.)

Text Editor   (Edit text files using the mouse.)

Mail Tool   (Send/receive mail.)

Calendar Manager   (Schedule appointments, meetings.)

Command Tool   (History, cut/paste between cmds and
                          files.)

Shell Tool   (Simple tty command line.)

Clock

Calculator

Performance Meter	(Monitor CPU usage, disk, and so on.)
Print Tool	(Print files and manage print queue.)
Audio Tool	(Record/play back sound files.)
Tape Tool	(Save/restore/list tape files.)
Image Tool	(View/Save GIF, JPEG, PostScript, TIFF, ...)
Snapshot	(Save GUI screen images.)
Icon Editor	(Create your own icons.)
Binder	(Connect file type to icon, application, and so on.)
AnswerBook2	(Online documents.)
Demos	(How to run various applications.)

The OpenWindows Text Editor provides a unique split screen option that enables you to edit or cut and paste between two parts of the same file. Note that this capability is not available in the Text Editor that comes with the other Solaris GUI called the CDE, described later in this chapter. However, most of these OpenWindows programs can be run from the OpenWindows section of the CDE App Manager. OpenWindows, on the other hand, cannot run the newer CDE applications.

OpenWindows has a feature to keep a desired window from disappearing after you use it. In some OpenWindows menus or windows, a little push-pin icon appears in the upper-left corner. If you click the push pin, it will pin your window or menu in place so that it does not disappear right after you make your selection. You can later make other selections from that window or menu. If you desire no more selections from that window, click the push pin to unpin it and allow it to close.

This older OpenWindows GUI is still available on current Solaris systems for those users who don't want to switch to the newer GUI called the CDE, discussed in the following section.

Common Desktop Environment (CDE)

Solaris contains a second GUI called the common desktop environment (CDE), which is based on the X Window System and the Motif Window Manager. Hewlett-Packard, IBM, and Sun jointly contributed to the development of the CDE, so this same GUI is now found on their versions of UNIX: HP-UX, AIX, and Solaris.

At the CDE logon screen, there is a button labeled Options. One of the available options is a Failsafe Session, which is useful in case you have misconfigured your video card or screen resolution. When logging on to the Solaris GUI, you can choose between the older OpenWindows and the newer CDE. On SCO UnixWare 7, you can choose between the newer CDE GUI and a Panorama GUI available on older SCO systems.

Figure 5.2 shows the main panel of the CDE on Solaris 2.x. Here is an explanation of the numbers marked in that figure:

1. Click this bar to manipulate the CDE main panel:
Move (its position)
Minimize (the main panel to an icon)
Lower (the main panel underneath any overlapping window)
Refresh
Log off

2. Shows the current time

3. Shows the current month and day

4. Click this triangle to see Folders options
Home Folder   (graphic access to your home directory)
Personal Bookmarks
Open Floppy   (graphic access to a disk)
Open CD-ROM   (graphic access to the CD-ROM)

5. Click this triangle to see Personal Applications options
Text Editor
Terminal   (UNIX command line)
Web browser   (HotJava)

6. Mailer application (send/receive email)

7. Lock this station   (prompts for UNIX password to unlock)

8. Four separate desktop areas can have windows open

SCO UNIX adopts the CDE standard

In its most recent OS release, UnixWare 7, SCO UNIX provides the CDE GUI as the default. After you learn this GUI, you will appreciate finding it on a number of UNIX platforms.

9. EXIT   (log off UNIX)

10. Flashing LED indicates the GUI is busy

11. Click this triangle to see Printers options

12. Style Manager   (Configure colors, fonts, backdrops, keyboard, mouse, beep, screen, window, startup)

13. Click this triangle to see Applications options

14. Click this triangle to see Help options (online documentation)

15. Trash Can icon   (Drag items to this icon to delete them)
Double-click this icon to see available files for:
Put Back (undelete)
Shred (permanent delete)

16. Click here to minimize the main panel.

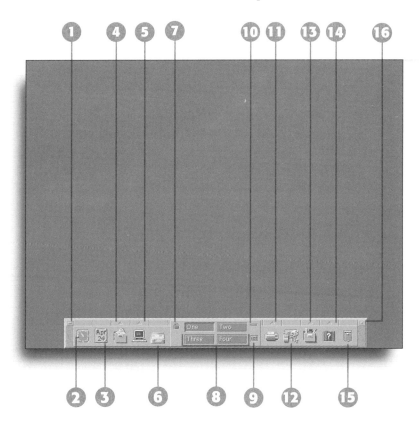

FIGURE 5.2
Main panel of the CDE.

In Figure 5.2, numbers 4, 5, 11, 13, and 14 point to triangles.
When you click on a triangle, it opens a set of options. When

the options are open, the triangle turns over and points downward as a reminder that if you click the triangle again, the choices will go away. Beneath each triangle is one icon from the choices in that section. It is a quick start icon because you can click that icon and start it directly from the main panel without having to click the triangle and open all the options.

To change the quick start icon below a triangle in the main panel, follow these steps:

1. Click on the triangle to open the choices.

2. Place the cursor on the desired icon.

3. Right-click once.

4. Select Copy to Main Panel.

5. Click on the triangle to close the choices. Now your desired icon should be in the main panel.

In Figure 5.3, we have clicked the Personal Applications triangle to open those selections. Here is an explanation of the numbers marked in that figure:

17 Click this bar for these options:
Move   (Keeps this menu on the desktop for easy access)
Lower   (put this menu underneath any overlapping window)
Close   (this menu)

18 Install Icon   (drag a program or file icon here to add it to this menu. Right click a menu item if you want to delete it from the menu.)

19 Text Editor   (click here for a graphics text editor)

20 Terminal   (click here for shell command-line window)

21 Web Browser   (click here to start the HotJava browser)

22 Menu button   (click this downward pointing triangle to close the menu. The triangle will then point upward to indicate it can be used to open the menu.)

23 Main Panel quick access icon   (This allows quick access to one of the items in the menu. In this example, it is currently set to the Terminal application, but this can be easily changed as previously described.)

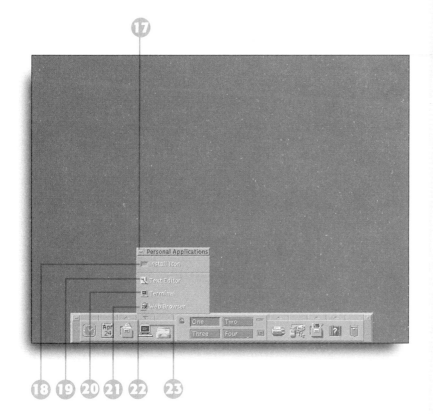

FIGURE 5.3
Personal applications.

Using Motif Windows

In Figure 5.4, we have started an application using the CDE main panel. The CDE using the Motif Window Manager and each application we start will run in its own Motif window. Figure 5.4 shows the window controls available on all Motif Window applications.

24 Click this menu button for these options:
Move   (move this window)
Size   (resize this window)
Minimize   (reduce window to an icon)
Maximize   (enlarge window to full screen Click Restore from this menu to undo this.)
Lower   (put this window underneath any overlapping window)
Close   (terminate application and close window)

Why can't rm use the Trash Can

If you delete files in the CDE, you can recover recent files from the trash can. However, you can't do this from the shell command line. Be careful using the UNIX **rm** command because there is no undelete.

Toggle Menu Bar   (remove it or restore it—see item 29 below)
Double-click this menu button as a quick way to invoke close

25 Title bar   click and drag here to drag whole window

26 Name of application running in this window

27 Minimize button   (reduce window to icon)

28 Maximize button   (enlarge window to full screen) (click this
again to undo this.)

29 Menu bar   (options depend on the application)

30 Scrollbars will appear on the right or at the bottom as needed.

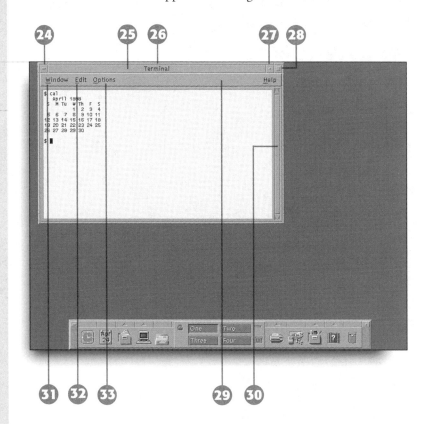

FIGURE 5.4
Window controls.

If you have started several applications, each one will have its
own window. Before you can enter text in that application, you
must first select the window by clicking anywhere inside the window. This is called making that window active or giving that
window focus. The border around the active window will

become darker in color. Selecting one window will automatically de-select the other windows. When a window is not selected, its border becomes a neutral gray color.

In the CDE Style Manager, in the Window section, you can select either:

Point in Window to Make Active

Click in Window to Make Active (the default)

Selecting Point in Window to Make Active enables you to select a window just by moving the mouse into that window. I personally don't like this setting because all the windows jump around when I have to go from one end of the screen to another, but different users can have different settings for this option.

You can change the size of a window (resize it) either through the menu button as listed before or by placing the cursor on one corner of the window and dragging it larger or smaller.

You can reposition a window on the screen (that is, move it) either through the menu button as listed before or by placing the cursor within the title bar and dragging the window to its new location.

If one window is behind another, you can lower the top window (that is, put it behind the other) through the menu button as listed before. Alternatively, you can click any visible part of the lower window to make all of it visible in the foreground.

Transferring Text Between Windows

Motif enables you to easily transfer text between two windows. The windows can be running different applications; so for example, you can transfer text from an email to a text editor, or text from a help document to a UNIX shell command. There is an easy way to transfer text once and a longer way that allows the same text to be remembered and entered multiple times.

How to transfer text once

1. Highlight the desired text by moving the cursor to that text, hold down the left mouse button, and drag the cursor to the end of the text. Then release the left button.

2. Move the mouse cursor to where you want to put the text, either in the same window or a different window. If the

window is running the UNIX vi command, use vi commands to position the vi cursor and then enter an insert or append command if you have not already done so in this window.

3. Middle click or right-click to insert the text.

How to save text and paste it one or more times

1. Highlight the desired text by moving the cursor to that text, hold down the left mouse button, and drag the cursor to the end of the text. Then release the left button. If you have a three-button mouse, you can now paste the highlighted text by moving the mouse pointer and clicking the middle button. If you have a two-button mouse, you must perform the following steps.

2. In the menu bar, click Edit and then Copy to save the highlighted text. Alternatively, if Edit also shows a Cut command, you can use it to save the text and remove it from the current application.

3. Move the mouse cursor to where you want to put the text, either in the same window or a different window. Click one time to set the text cursor. If the window is running the UNIX vi command, use vi commands to position the vi cursor and then enter an insert or append command if you have not already done so in this window.

4. In the menu bar, click Edit and then Paste to insert the saved text at the cursor. If you are in vi, now press Esc manually to end Insert mode.

What Applications Does the CDE Support?

The CDE is available on HP-UX, AIX, Solaris, UnixWare 7, and possibly more versions of UNIX. Each of these versions usually supports some basic CDE graphics applications such as the following:

File Manager   (create, copy, move, delete files and directories)

Text Editor   (to edit UNIX text files)

Terminal   (to run UNIX shell commands)

Mailer   (to send and read email)

Print Manager   (to view the UNIX print spooling)

Help   (to view online doc for this system)

Some systems, like Solaris, have added a number of other applications that can be invoked from the CDE, which you will not find on other systems. Under Solaris, you can access these extra applications by moving the cursor to an empty part of the screen, right-clicking, and then clicking on Programs.

Solaris 2.6 programs:

File Manager   (create, copy, move, delete files and directories)

Text Editor   (to edit UNIX text files)

Mailer   (to send and read email)

Calendar   (schedule appointments, meetings)

Web Browser   (HotJava)

Terminal   (to run UNIX shell commands)

Console   (like Terminal, but receives system console errors)

Clock   (graphic clock that can be put on the desktop)

Calculator   (scientific and financial graphical calculator)

Performance Meter   (graphically shows system usage over time)

Print Manager   (view UNIX print spooling)

Audio   (record and play back audio files)

Image Viewer   (View/Save GIF, JPEG, PostScript, TIFF, and so on)

Snapshot   (save GUI screen images)

Icon Editor   (create your own icons)

Style Manager   (customize look of the CDE)

App Manager   (access to more programs)

Desktop Apps   (programs and CDE program development App Builder)

Desktop Controls   (Style Manager and handicap access)

Desktop Tools   (utils to format floppy, compress file, and so forth)

Information   (Readme files and Answerbook2)

OpenWindows   (apps from the older OpenWindows GUI)

System Admin   (Admintool, Power Manager, and so on)

Help   (CDE info)

AnswerBook2   (Solaris and SunOS info)

Extensive Help in the CDE

Figure 5.5 shows some of the Help table of contents from the CDE Text Editor application. Each CDE application has helpful information about the screens and options for that application. The Help uses hypertext links (like a Web page) where under-lined phrases can be clicked to immediately go to that specific documentation. Hypertext documentation is great because it shows you an overview of each topic in a section and enables you to quickly go to the topics and related topics that you select.

FIGURE 5.5

Extensive help in the CDE.

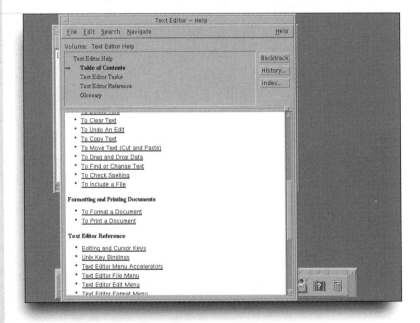

Running Shell Commands from the CDE

The Terminal application creates a CDE window where you can enter shell commands as if you were on a character-based terminal. You can run this Terminal application in more than one window, so you can run and watch several UNIX commands simultaneously. You can even cut and paste text as described in the preceding section between two UNIX Terminal sessions or between a CDE application and a UNIX Terminal session.

To start the Terminal application, click the Terminal icon as shown in Figure 5.3. Under the Solaris CDE, you can also start this application by moving to an empty part of the screen, right-clicking, selecting Programs, and then selecting Terminal.

In Figure 5.4, we have started the Terminal command line application. Here is an explanation of the numbers marked in that figure that are specific to the Terminal application:

31 Window   click here for these options:
New   start another Terminal session
Close   close/terminate this window

32 Edit   click here for these options:
Copy   save highlighted text
Paste   insert saved text

33 Options   click here for these options:
Terminal characteristics (for example, allow 132 col, allow line wrap)
Window Size
Font Size

When you start a Terminal window, you do not have to log on because you have already logged on at the start of your CDE session. If you type exit in a Terminal window, you will end that window but not your CDE session. To end your CDE session, click the word EXIT (as shown in Figure 5.2).

Editing Text Files from the CDE

The Text Editor is a CDE window application where you can create and modify UNIX text files and system files. You can also cut and paste text as described earlier between this Text Editor and other CDE applications such as a UNIX Terminal session.

To start the Text Editor application, click the Text Editor icon as shown in Figure 5.3. Under the Solaris CDE, you can also start this application by moving to an empty part of the screen, right-clicking, selecting Programs, and then selecting Text Editor.

CDE Text Editor—Open a File

From the Text Editor, you must first open any UNIX file that you want to edit. Click on File, Open. You will see a dialog box as shown in Figure 5.6. Here is an explanation of the numbers marked in that figure:

1. The Files box shows files that may be opened just by double-clicking on the filename.

2. The Filter box shows a Regular Expression wildcard pattern which is used to hide some of the names in the Files box. [^.]* is the default that hides hidden files (that is, files that start with a period).
   * would show all files (hidden and non-hidden)
   a* would show only files that start with the letter: a

3. The path or folder box shows the UNIX directory for the files displayed in the Files box. It begins as your current directory but you can change this to any desired directory. Click on the triangle to the right to get a list of previous and other directories that you can select.

4. The Folders box shows subdirectories of the directory in the path box. Double-click on any of these and the contents of that new directory will appear in the Files box. You can also click on .. to go up one level to the parent directory.

5. In the Filename box, you can enter a full pathname for the desired file without having to set any of the other boxes. Press Enter here to open that file.

6. Click OK to open the file shown in the file name box.

7. Click Update to update the contents of the Files and Folders boxes, including any recent changes.

8. Click Cancel to terminate this attempt to open a file.

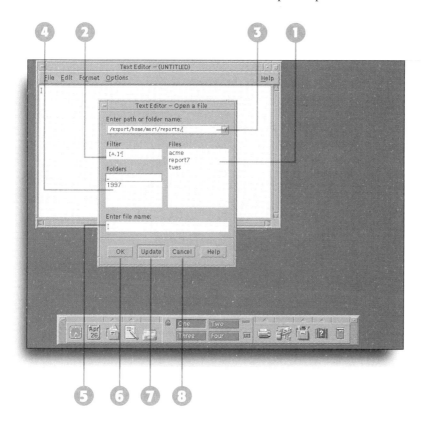

FIGURE 5.6
CDE Text Editor—Open a File.

SEE ALSO

➤ *For more information on regular expression wildcards, see page 388*

CDE Text Editor—Basic Editing

You can move around in the file using the scrollbar or the Page Up and Page Down keys. You can use the Home key to go to the start of the line, and the End key to go to the end of the line.

You have two modes for entering text. In Insert mode, the cursor will be a thin line, and any characters you type in the middle of the line will push the rest of the line to the right. You can change to Overstrike mode by pressing the Insert key or click Options and then Overstrike. The cursor will change to a block and any text you type in the middle of a line will overwrite any existing text there. You can change modes by pressing the Insert key again or by clicking Options and Overstrike again.

The Backspace key will delete the character to the left of the cursor. If the cursor is a block, the delete key will remove the character under the cursor. If the cursor is a line, delete will remove the character to the right of the cursor. You can delete a section of text by dragging over it to highlight it and then press the Delete key.

You can cut and paste or copy and paste within this text file or between windows. See the preceding section on transferring text between windows.

This is a text editor and not a word processor. There are no options for font types or font sizes.

CDE Text Editor—Check Spelling

To spell check the current file, click on Edit, Check Spelling. This will open a dialog box as shown in Figure 5.7. Here is an explanation of the numbers marked in that figure:

1. Word is the problem word found in your file.

2. Suggestion is the best alternative found by the spell checker.

3. Shows other alternatives that are valid words. You can double-click one of these to replace your word.

4. Shows how much of the file has been spell checked.

5. Change says replace Word with Suggestion once.

6. Change All says replace Word with Suggestion throughout the file.

7. Skip says ignore Word, but flag the same Word if found later.

8. Skip All says ignore this Word throughout the file.

9. Learn Word adds this word as a valid word in your personal dictionary so it will not be questioned any time you run spell check on any file.

10. Options allows you to view and remove words from your personal dictionary.

11. Stop Check stops the spelling check but leaves the spell check dialog box open so it can be easily restarted.

12. Close closes the spell check dialog box.

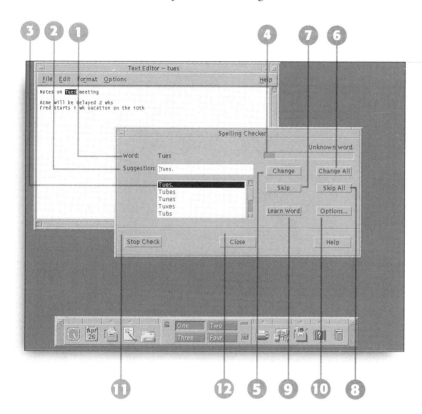

FIGURE 5.7
CDE Text Editor–check spelling.

CDE Text Editor–Format Paragraphs

In the UNIX vi command, it can be difficult to format paragraphs. This may leave you with some files that have paragraphs with some lines that are too short and some that are too long. You can use the CDE Text Editor to edit these files and format the problem paragraphs.

Start the CDE Text Editor and open the desired file. Move the cursor to the problem paragraph. Click Format, and then click Settings. You will see a dialog box as shown in Figure 5.8. In this box, set the column numbers for your left and right margin. Then choose your desired paragraph alignment: Left, Right, or Center.

You can also choose Justify to do both Left and Right alignment, which gives your paragraph a nice block look. You can then click on Paragraph to format just the current paragraph or All to format the whole document.

After you have defined your settings, the next time you want to format, click Format and then click Paragraph or All.

FIGURE 5.8
CDE Text Editor–format
paragraphs.

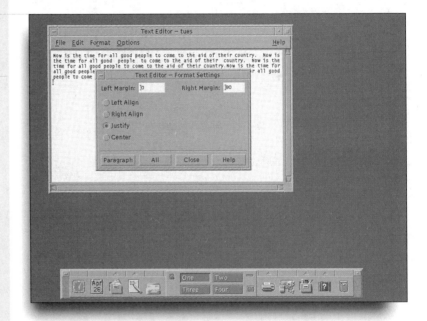

Copying and Moving Files/Directories via the CDE File Manager

Figure 5.9 shows how to start the File Manager from the CDE main panel. Click on the icon of a file drawer overflowing with files. On Solaris, it is labeled as Home Folder because it begins showing you your home directory.

Figure 5.10 shows the File Manager window. Here is an explanation of the numbers marked in that figure:

1. Shows how many directories deep your selected directory is. A pencil with a slash through it indicates a directory where you do not have write permission. You can double-click on one of these icons to change to that directory.

Copying and Moving Files/Directories via the CDE File Manager

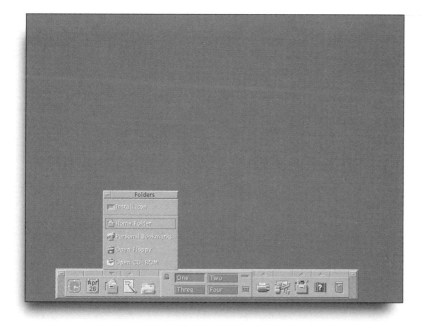

FIGURE 5.9
Starting the CDE File Manager.

2. Shows the name of each directory

3. Shows the full pathname of your selected directory. You can use your mouse to edit this and change to a different directory.

4. Shows the files and subdirectories in your selected directory. You can double-click on any of the subdirectories to change to that directory.

5. You can click on this .. directory to go up one level.

To rename a file or directory, click on it and then change or replace the name as desired.

To move file to a subdirectory, drag its icon to that directory. To copy the file, press and hold the Control key and then drag the file. To move or copy the file to a different directory, click on View, and then click on Open New View, which will start another File Manager window. Select the destination directory in that window and drag the file to that directory. To create a symbolic link, press and hold both Shift and Control and then drag the file icon.

FIGURE 5.10
CDE File Manager.

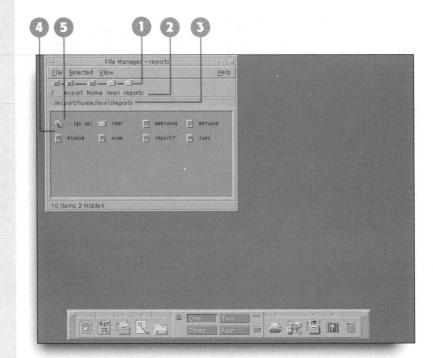

To delete a file, drag it to the Trash Can icon. To permanently delete the file (called shredding it), double-click the Trash Can, select the desired file, click File, and then click Shred. Instead of clicking Shred, you can click Put Back, which would undelete that file.

You can drag a file or folder to the desktop for easy access.

Reading/Sending Email Using the CDE Mailer

The UNIX mail and mailx utilities can be very difficult for UNIX neophytes. The graphic CDE Mailer application makes it much easier to send and receive email. It also handles attachments, which is something the UNIX mail and mailx utilities cannot handle. To start the CDE Mailer application, click on the Mail icon in the main panel (see number 6 in Figure 5.2). You will then see the Mailer window as in Figure 5.11. Here is an explanation of the numbers marked in that figure:

1. Menu bar

2. This window shows one line for each mail item in your mailbox. An N at the start of the line indicates this item has never been read. A diamond indicates the mail item contains one or more attachments.

3. This window shows the text of the currently selected mail item in window 1.

4. This window will only appear if there are attachments.

5. Delete the current mail item.

6. Go to and display the next mail item.

7. Go to and display the previous mail item.

8. Click here to Reply to sender. This automatically adds the text of the received mail in the reply.

9. Click here to Forward a copy of this mail item to another user.

10. Click here to compose and send new mail. You can also include attachments.

11. Print mail item.

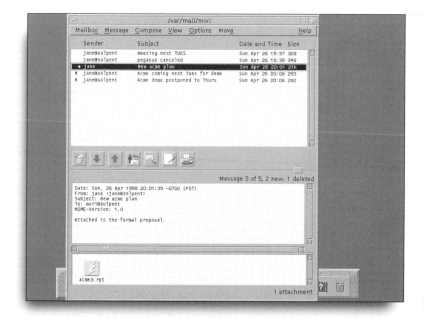

FIGURE 5.11
CDE Mailer.

The CDE Mailer enables you to set up your own mail aliases. This is useful if you frequently send mail to a consistent group of people. Click on Options, and then click on Aliases. Create an alias name for the group, such as salesteam. Enter the list of people under Addresses. Then click Add to add this alias. Now you can send one piece of mail to salesteam and a copy will go to each member of the group.

There are numerous other capabilities. You can create a signature that contains useful and personal identifying text to add to outgoing mail. You can set up a Vacation Message that is automatically sent in reply to incoming mail for the days you specify. You can check spelling when composing mail. You can create templates for mail messages. You can create other mailboxes to separate and archive correspondence by project. All these and more are covered in the Help section with hypertext links to quickly get you to the section you need.

Working with UNIX Files

CHAPTER

6

Listing, Finding, Displaying, or Printing Files

By Steve "Mor" Moritsugu

Determining the type of file and type of file contents

Listing and finding files

Displaying files one screen at a time

Adding line numbers and handling control characters

Using banner headings

Printing files and pipelines

Checking the print queue

Canceling print jobs

Formatting output for printing

Introducing UNIX Files

We already know a lot about UNIX files from Chapter 2, "UNIX Directories and Pathnames." From that chapter, we learned that UNIX accesses each file through a number called an *inode* number. Humans can access files through a filename, which can contain any letters, digits, or punctuation, and modern UNIX systems can allow as many as several hundred characters in the filename. All the files are organized into a tree-structured directory system. We can then access any file by using an *absolute* or a *relative pathname*.

How to Determine the Type of File (*ls*)

The most common type of file under UNIX is called a *regular file*. All programs, data files, documents, text files, system utilities, and system configuration tables are regular files. Application languages such as COBOL or BASIC can create sequential files under UNIX, which are read from start to end in sequence, or indexed files, which contain key fields that grant quick access to desired data. To UNIX, these are all regular files.

UNIX does not support contiguous files in which all the blocks of a contiguous file are allocated next to each other in one area of the disk. Because UNIX is a *multiuser*, *multitasking* operating system, the disk services requests from multiple users and multiple jobs and would gain little benefit by keeping all the blocks of one file close together.

Directories are the second most common type of file under UNIX. They contain a list of the filenames within that directory and the inode number for each of those files. Every directory is a UNIX file, so it also has an inode number.

Another important type of file is the *device file*, which is also called a *device node*. All access to hardware devices, such as tape drives or floppy disks, is done by accessing the device node file for that device. Two types of device nodes exist:

```
character device nodes for raw access to the device
block device nodes for non-raw ("cooked") access to the
device
```

Some devices can be accessed by both character and block device nodes. Device nodes are also called *special files*.

Another important type of file is the *symbolic link*, which is a pointer to a different file on the system.

A few other types of UNIX files are used by the system, but the average user almost never needs to know about them.

How to determine the file type

1. Enter ls -l.

   Do not press Enter until instructed. The -l option to ls will display long information for each file, including the file type.

2. Enter a space and then the file or files to be listed. You can specify either a *basename* in the current directory, or an absolute or a relative pathname to a different directory. If you enter a directory name here, ls displays information for each file in that directory.

3. Press Enter to execute your command. The leading character in each line of output tells you the UNIX file type for that file per this table:

TABLE 6.1 **File type letters used by *ls* -l**

File Type Letter	- - description
-	- - regular file
d	- - directory
l	- - symbolic or soft link
b	- - block special device node file
c	- - character special device node file
p,s,m	- - other types you might encounter

Following is an example of the previous procedure showing various file types. The ls command is a system command, passwd is a text file, fd0 is a device node for the floppy drive, tmp is a directory, and uncompress is a symbolic link to compress.

```
# ls -ld /bin/ls /etc/passwd /tmp /dev/fd0 /dev/rfd0
/usr/bin/uncompress
-r-xr-xr-t   1 bin        bin          43296 May 13   1997
/bin/ls
brw-rw-rw-   2 bin        bin          2, 64 Feb 13 10:11
/dev/fd0
crw-rw-rw-   2 bin        bin          2, 64 Feb 13 10:11
/dev/rfd0
-rw-rw-r—    1 bin        auth          3001 Feb 16 16:01
/etc/passwd
drwxrwxrwt   7 sys        sys           3072 Feb 20 11:16 /tmp
lrwxrwxrwx   1 root       root            40 Feb 13 10:02
/usr/bin/uncompress -> /usr/bin/compress
```

In the preceding example, we use the -l option to ls to produce a long listing with details about each file. We use the -d option so that ls displays information about any directories and not the contents of the directories, as is its habit.

SEE ALSO

➤ *For more information on symbolic links, see page 197*

Determining the Type of Contents of a File (*file*)

To determine the type of contents of a file, use the file command. Give the command a filename whose type you want to determine:

```
$ file /bin/ls
/bin/ls:        ELF 32-bit MSB executable SPARC Version 1,
dynamically
linked, stripped
$
```

In the preceding example, we see that the /bin/ls file is a system utility that has been compiled to produce executable code for a SPARC system running Solaris. In the next example, we use the asterisk (*) Filename Wildcard to determine the type of contents of all non-hidden files in the current directory:

```
$ file *
acmetab:    ascii text
report7:    English text
report8:    empty file
runcpio:    executable shell script
```

```
cpiofile:    ASCII cpio archive
$
```

In the preceding example, the file command makes its best guess as to the type of contents of the file, usually based on analyzing just the beginning of the file. In some cases, the command uses a "magic" number imbedded in the file that looks up the type of contents in a table of magic numbers (often found in file /etc/magic).

Listing Files (*ls*)

We can use the `ls` command to list the filenames in either the current directory or a different directory.

Using *ls* to list files

1. At the shell prompt, enter `ls`.

Do not press Enter until instructed.

2. Enter a space and then any desired options. (See the appendix entry under `ls` for a list of possible options and their meanings.) If more than one option exists, these can be entered in any order individually, as in this example:

```
ls -l -a -L
```

The options also can be combined as one set of options, as in this example:

```
ls -Lla
```

3. Enter a space, and then enter one or more directories or files to list. Enter a space between each directory or file entered. Entering a directory causes the output from `ls` to list the contents of that directory (unless the -d option has been specified). This list of files and directories can also include file lists generated by Filename Wildcard patterns. If the filename or directory is located in the current directory, enter just its basename. Otherwise, enter an absolute or a relative pathname for the file or directory.

4. If you want to see the output from `ls` one page at a time (so the lines do not go off the screen before you can read them), enter a space. Then enter this line:

```
| pg
```

> **Understanding bad magic number error**
>
> If you get this UNIX error, it means the utility is checking a special word (that is, the magic number) in a file to confirm that the file has the expected type of contents. If a file has a bad magic number, it either is corrupted or is the wrong file.

You can replace "pg" with the more command or with the less command, depending on which pager utility your UNIX system supports and what your favorite pager utility is. These are covered in more detail later in this chapter.

5. Instead of performing step 4, you also have the option to save the output from ls in a file. Enter a space and then enter this line:

```
> filename
```

Replace "filename" with the absolute or relative pathname to the file in which you want to save the results.

6. Instead of performing steps 4 or 5 above, you also have the option to accomplish both steps at once—that is, save the result in a file and see the results one page at a time. Enter a space, and then enter this line:

```
¦ tee filename ¦ pg
```

Replace "filename" with the absolute or relative pathname to the file in which you want to save the results. You can replace "pg" with the more command or with the less command, depending on which pager utility your UNIX system supports and what your favorite pager utility is. These are covered in more detail later in this chapter.

7. Press Enter to execute your command.

The following is an example ls command:

```
ls -l ¦ pg
¦  ¦  ¦ ¦
1  2  4 4
```

In the preceding example and the one that follows, below each word of the command appears the number of the procedure step that generated that word. In the preceding example, we list all non-hidden files in the current directory in long format to see details about each file. We use the pg utility to show us the results one page at a time.

This is another example of an ls command:

```
ls -aid /usr/fred/reports /usr/jane/* > ls.save
   ┊   ┊      ┊                ┊        ┊      ┊
   1   2      3                3        5      5
```

In this example, the -a option shows us both non-hidden and hidden files. The -i option shows the file *inode number* as well as its name. The -d option shows information about any directories listed instead of their contents. Next we specify which files to list. The first one is /usr/fred/reports. If this *is* a directory, we will see information about that directory (instead of the contents of that directory) due to the -d option. This file has been specified as an absolute pathname in this example.

The second file to list is /usr/jane/*, which is a Filename Wildcard pattern. The shell replaces this pattern word with a list of all non-hidden files in /usr/jane. The ls command then operates on all those filenames as if we had typed them individually instead of the Wildcard pattern. The results of this command do not go to the screen. Instead they go to file ls.save in the current directory.

SEE ALSO

➤ *For more information on redirection and piping, see page 26*

➤ *For more information on Filename Wildcards, see page 232*

Finding Files (*find*)

The UNIX directory tree can easily store tens of thousands of files or much more, depending on your total disk capacity. It is easy to lose track of a pathname, especially when you work with a number of different files every day. The find command can help you locate the pathname of a file based on various search criteria.

Finding Files Given a Filename or Part of the Name (*find*)

If you know just the basename of the file you want (for example: report27), but you don't know its pathname, you can use the find command to walk through all or part of the UNIX directory tree and show you where it finds that basename. You can even use Filename Generation Wildcard patterns (which are covered in Chapter 9, "Generating and Using File Lists") when you only know part of the file basename.

How to find a file by its name or part of its name

1. At the shell prompt, enter find.

   Do not press Enter until instructed.

2. Enter a space and then the directory in which you want to start searching. Enter the directory as if it is a subdirectory of your current directory. Otherwise, enter the directory as an absolute or relative pathname. To search the whole system, enter this line for the root directory:
   /

   To search just the current directory and its subdirectories, enter a period (.); this indicates the current directory. The find command searches all subdirectories of the starting directory (unless the -mount option is given in step 5 below).

   If many files are on the system, find can take a long time to complete. If you can specify a starting directory other than root (/) (that is, the whole system), then the find command will complete much more quickly.

3. Enter a space, and then enter -name.

4. Enter a space, and then enter the filename you are seeking. If you know only part of its name, enter that part of the name using this punctuation:
   '*partname*'

   For example, if the filename you are looking for contains acme, enter this:
   '*acme*'

   After you have read about file lists and Filename Generation Wildcards (Chapter 9), you can use any of those wildcards to specify the file you are seeking. Remember to place the Wildcard pattern within single quotes.

5. If desired, you can now enter any other search criteria in case you want to see only files of a certain size, owner, permissions, and so on. See the appendix entry on find for a list of such options. For example, you could now add the -mount option, which prevents find from following mount points into other filesystems (that is, other disk drives).

6. Enter a space, and then enter: -print.

Press Enter to complete your find command. You could also perform the more adventurous step 7 below instead of this step 6.

7. Enter a space, and then enter -exec ls -l {} \. This is an alternative to step 6 to complete our find command. This shows you the same long information about each file found that ls -l would show. You could also enter -exec followed by a different command to perform some operation on each of the files selected if desired. See the appendix entry on find for more information on -exec.

8. If you want to see the output from your find command one page at a time (so the lines do not go off the screen before you can read them), enter a space. Then enter this line:

```
¦ pg
```

You can replace "pg" with more or with less, depending on which pager utility your UNIX system supports and what your favorite pager utility is. These are covered in more detail later in this chapter.

9. Instead of performing step 8 above, you also have the option to save the results in find in a file. Enter a space, and then enter this line:

```
> filename
```

Replace "filename" with the absolute or relative pathname to the file in which you want to save the results.

10. Instead of performing steps 8 or 9, you also have the option to accomplish both things at once; that is, you can save the result in a file and view the results one page at a time. Enter a space, and then enter this line:

```
¦ tee filename ¦ pg
```

Replace "filename" with the absolute or relative pathname to the file in which you want to save the results. You can replace "pg" with the more command or with the less command, depending on which pager utility your UNIX system supports and what your favorite pager utility is. These are covered in more detail later in this chapter.

11. Press Enter to execute your command.

12. The output from your find command is a list of pathnames. Each pathname begins with the directory you specified in step 2. This is a key point: If you specify an absolute pathname in step 2, all the files generated will be absolute pathnames. If you specify a relative pathname in step 2, then all files listed will be relative pathnames.

This is an example find command from the preceding procedure. Beneath each word of the command is the step in the procedure that generated that word. This find command searches directory: /usr/fred and all of its subdirectories to display the pathname of any files whose basename is report7.

```
find  /usr/fred  -name  report7  -print
   ¦       ¦         ¦      ¦        ¦
   1       2         3      4        6
```

In the preceding example, the starting directory is an absolute pathname because it begins at root (/). Therefore, all the pathnames generated by that find command are also absolute pathnames. Following is some possible output from the above find command:

```
/usr/fred/report7
/usr/fred/acme/reports/report7
/usr/fred/pegasus/report7
```

This is another example find command, again showing the procedure steps that generated each word of the command. The starting directory for this find command is the period (.), which indicates the current directory. The command finds all file basenames in the current directory and its subdirectories that contain the partial name report27. The -user option tells find to consider only files that are owned by user Fred. The results of this find command go both to a file called /tmp/findlog and to the screen, to be displayed one page at a time.

```
find . -name '*report27*' -user fred -print ¦ tee /tmp/findlog
¦ pg
   ¦  ¦  ¦           ¦              ¦    ¦    ¦    ¦  ¦
¦        ¦  ¦
   1  2  3           4              5    5    6   10  10
10       10 10
```

The starting directory of the preceding command is a relative pathname, and the output of the command is also a relative pathname beginning with a period (.). Following is some possible output from the preceding command:

```
./casereport273a
./1998/reports/acme.report27-2-98
```

SEE ALSO

➤ *For more information on running jobs in the background, see page 319*

➤ *For more information on using* find *to find files based on last access date or last modification date, see page 153*

Using *find* Options Versus *find* Actions (*find*)

The find command has a number of options, including -name and -user, that enable us to specify conditions that a file must satisfy to be selected by our find command. The -type option is another find option that enables us to specify the file type (such as directory or regular file). Files that don't satisfy the find conditions are not selected. (See the appendix entry on find for a list of possible find options. Also see the man page on find.) These find options can be used in any combination and in any order.

After specifying all desired options, you should end your find command with one or more actions. The -print option is the most common action because it simply instructs the system to display the files found. If you forget to include an action, some systems will assume -print by default. On other systems however-er, find will take as long as it needs to locate the files, but then it will display nothing because you forgot to put in the action. It is a good habit to always specify an action.

Another useful action is `-exec`, which enables us to specify a UNIX command to run on every file found. Use {} within the command to specify where to insert the filename. The command must end with a space and then "\;".

The following is an example `find -exec` command that looks for any files with the basename of core and removes them from the system. The -f option to `rm` means don't ask for confirmation if you don't have write access to the file being removed; that is, it gives blanket confirmation to all removals.

```
find / -name core -print -exec rm -f {} \;
```

Notice in the above command that two actions take place: `-print` to display the pathname of the core files found, and `-exec` to delete them.

Following is an example `find` command that renames all regular files in the current directory and its subdirectories. This command adds .old to all the regular filenames.

```
find . -type f -exec mv {} {}.old \;
```

How to Find a File Whose Contents Contain a Word (*find,grep*)

Sometimes you don't remember anything about the filename, but you know that within the file is some distinctive word. You can find all such files as in this example:

```
find / -exec grep WORD {} /dev/null \;
```

Replace "WORD" with the word for which you want to search. You can include Regular Expression Wildcards (covered in Chapter 15, "Searching for Lines in a File or Pipeline") within WORD, but then you should enclose WORD in single quotes. In the preceding example, the `find` command calls the `grep` command to check each file in the system to see whether it contains the given word. The inclusion of a second empty file (/dev/null) causes grep to display the filename as well as the line that contains the word.

The preceding example gives you some idea of how to use `find` and `-exec`, but also be aware that this is inefficient and takes a long time to complete because it calls the grep command so many times. Here is a more efficient way to do the same thing:

```
find / -print ¦ xargs grep WORD /dev/null
```

This use of xargs is described in Chapter 9. This method is more efficient because xargs will call grep only once for each group of files to check.

SEE ALSO

➤ *For more information on xargs, see page 247*

Using Logical AND, OR, and NOT with find Options (*find*)

Any time you specify more than one find option, all must pass for the file to be selected. This is, in effect, the logical AND case.

```
find / -name acme -user fred -type d -print
```

The preceding example contains three options and one action. A file must pass all three options before the action is applied. In this case, the basename must be acme AND the owner must be fred AND it must be a directory.

The -o command can be used to indicate the logical OR, and *escaped* parentheses can be used for grouping, as in this example:

```
find / \( -name acme -o -user fred \) -type d -print
```

In the preceding example, we are looking for files that either have the basename of acme or that are owned by fred. In either case, these files must be directories if find is to select and display them. Notice there must be spaces around the escaped parentheses.

The bang (!) sign can be used to reverse or negate a condition, as in this example:

```
find / ! -user fred -print
```

In the preceding example, find displays all files except those owned by fred. Notice there must be spaces around the bang (!) sign.

Why escaped parentheses?

Generally, we use parentheses to tell the shell to run the enclosed commands in a sub-shell. We escape the parentheses (that is, put a backslash [\] in front) to tell the shell to ignore them and pass them on to the **find** command.

Displaying Files

The following section provides an overview of commands and options for displaying files in the UNIX environment.

Displaying a Small File (*cat*)

The standard way to display a small file is to use the `cat` command:

```
cat filename
```

In UNIX, the word `cat` is synonymous with *display*, so directions may ask you to *cat* a file or may refer to *catting* a file.

Displaying Files/Pipelines a Page at a Time (*pg/more/less*)

UNIX commands do not have an option to display the results one screenful (that is, one *page*) at a time. This is because you can always pipe the output to your favorite pager utility and let it display the output one page at a time. Three common pager utilities exist under UNIX:

```
pg
more
less
```

Unfortunately, you cannot just learn one these, because that one is likely to be missing on some types of UNIX systems. Each pager has a slightly different set of commands. Some utilities, such as the man pages, automatically invoke one of these pager utilities, which makes things difficult for beginners because now you must figure out which pager you are in and how to make it work.

In general, commercial UNIX systems offer `pg` and `more`. The `pg` option has the most functionality, but `more` is often the default pager. Commercial UNIX systems do not usually offer the `less` pager. Linux/GNU offers the `less` pager but typically not `pg` or `more`.

Each of these pagers can be used in two ways:

- You can specify one or more files on the command line, as in this example:
  ```
  pg file1 file2
  more file1 file2
  less file1 file2
  ```

- You can pipe (|) to any of these pagers. This example displays the output of ls -l one screen at a time:
  ```
  ls -l ¦ pg
  ls -l ¦ more
  ls -l ¦ less
  ```

If you both pipe to the pager AND give the pager a list of files, the pager displays the list of files and ignores the piped data.

```
How to recognize which pager your are in:
      If the bottom line of            Then you are
      each screen looks like           running this
      this:                            pager utility:

      :                                pg
      --More--(34%)                    more
      Filename (34%)                   more
      --More--                         more
      stdin                            more
      line 203                         less


How to go to the next page:
      pg:    press the ENTER key
      more:  press the space bar
      less:  press the space bar


How to display a help menu of available commands in the
pager:
      pg:    h
      more:  h
      less:  h
```

How to go to the previous page:

    pg: enter dash (-)

    more: enter Ctrl+B   (for back — this is often
    ➥not supported)

    less: enter Ctrl+B   (for back)

How to go forward to the next occurrence of STRING:

    pg: /STRING

    more: /STRING   (This is often not supported)

    less: /STRING

How to go to the end of the file:

    pg: $

    more: G   (This is often not supported)

    less: G

How to go back to the beginning of the file:

    pg: 1

    more: 1G   (This is often not supported)

    less: 1G

How to redisplay the current page:

    pg: .

    more: Ctrl+L

    less: Ctrl+L

How to go down a half page: (This is useful when you are interested in something at the bottom of the screen and want to see the surrounding lines)

    pg: d

    more: d

    less: d

How to exit from the pager even if not at end of file:

    pg: q

    more: q

    less: q

Comparing pg, more, and less on commercial UNIX systems

    less is usually not offered on commercial UNIX
    ➥systems. less has

        all the features of pg and is a consistent

```
    super-set of the more commands.
more is often very limited -- often there is no
➥way to skip to
    the end, or go backwards.  This is especially
    ➥true if you pipe (¦) to
    more.
pg is more useful than more because it can go
➥backward, go to
    end of file, go to start of file, etc.
    ➥Unfortunately there is
    no way to determine how far through the file you
    ➥are
    with pg.
```

Beware of using pg on a huge pipeline. When you use the pg $ sign command when displaying piped output, it can take a long time to complete because the system is saving in a temporary file all the text encountered so you can go back to the first page if desired. Some systems do not have enough temporary disk space to store huge files, and when that is exhausted, all user tasks can be disrupted and the system can crash.

The pg option has a feature that is useful when you want to locate and consider each occurrence of some word in the file. Usually this is difficult because the slash (/) command to locate a word begins its next search at the end of the current screen. If there are multiple occurrences on one screen, you might miss some of them.

Using *pg* to find all occurrences of a string

1. Use pg to view a file or pipeline.

2. While running pg, enter this line:
   /string/b

   Replace "string" with the text you want to find. Without /b, the found string would be placed on the top line of the screen. The /b tells pg to put the found line at the bottom of the screen for this and future searches.

3. To find the next occurrence of the same string, enter this line:
   /

How large is huge?

When do you have to start worrying about crashing the system by using **pg** of a pipeline? The **pg** pager usually builds its temporary file in /tmp. Use the **df** command to check how many free blocks you have in /tmp, or in root (/) if **df** does not show /tmp. That free block count is your limit, but you should not even come close to that for safety.

The system uses the previous string given. Because /b was given in step 2, the next occurrence of the string will be positioned on the bottom line. Without the /b in step 2, you might miss some occurrences of string because / assumes you have visually found all matches anywhere on the current screen, and it starts searching from the bottom line of the screen.

4. Repeat step 3 as desired or until the end of the file.

SEE ALSO

➤ *For more information on the* df *command and filesystem available blocks, see page 93*

Adding Line Numbers to File Display (*nl,cat*)

You can add line numbering to the display of a file or pipeline, using either nl (number lines) or cat -n, as in this example:

```
$ cal ¦ nl
     1        February 1998
     2     S   M Tu  W Th   F  S
     3     1   2   3   4   5   6  7
     4     8   9  10  11  12  13 14
     5    15  16  17  18  19  20 21
     6    22  23  24  25  26  27 28


$ cal ¦ cat -n
     1        February 1998
     2     S   M Tu  W Th   F  S
     3     1   2   3   4   5   6  7
     4     8   9  10  11  12  13 14
     5    15  16  17  18  19  20 21
     6    22  23  24  25  26  27 28
     7
     8
$
```

In the preceding examples, we take a calendar of the current month and pipe it so each line is numbered in the output. Notice that cat -n numbers all lines, including blank lines. The nl command does not number the blank lines. Certain options can change this behavior, however.

To number all lines, including blank lines, enter this line:

```
cat -n
nl -ba
```

To number only the non-blank lines, enter this line:

```
cat -nb
nl
```

Both cat and nl accept a list of files on the command line. If none are given, they read from standard input so that you can pipe to these commands. Some UNIX systems may not support both of these commands, so it useful to know that both are available.

Displaying Files Containing Control Characters (*cat, od, strings*)

Text files contain only printable characters, whereas binary files can contain all possible character values, including the range we call *control characters*. If you display a binary file to your screen, the control characters within the file can set undesirable modes for your station, can cause all further output to appear as garbage or gibberish, and can even make your station stop responding altogether.

Before you display an unknown file, use the file command discussed at the start of this chapter to see whether it is a text file. If it is not a text file, then it is not safe to simply display it to your screen. Some safe ways to look at the text within binary files do exist, as we shall see in this section.

The od command stands for octal dump. This command displays every word of a file or pipeline in octal (that is, using the base 8 numbering system), as in this example:

```
# od /bin/ls ¦ head -5
0000000 077505 046106 000402 000400 000000 000000 000000
➥000000
0000020 000002 000002 000000 000001 000001 007374 000000
➥000064
0000040 000000 040140 000000 000000 000064 000040 000005
➥000050
```

```
0000060 000030 000027 000000 000006 000000 000064 000001
➥000064
0000100 000000 000000 000000 000240 000000 000240 000000
➥000005
#
```

The -b option to od breaks each word into 2 bytes or characters, as in this example:

```
# od -b /bin/ls ¦ head -5
0000000 177 105 114 106 001 002 001 000 000 000 000 000 000
➥000 000 000
0000020 000 002 000 002 000 000 000 001 000 001 016 374 000
➥000 000 064
0000040 000 000 100 140 000 000 000 000 000 064 000 040 000
➥005 000 050
0000060 000 030 000 027 000 000 000 006 000 000 000 064 000
➥001 000 064
0000100 000 000 000 000 000 000 000 240 000 000 000 240 000
➥000 000 005
#
```

The -c option to od shows you any printable characters within the output, as in this example:

```
# od -c /bin/ls ¦ head -5
0000000 177   E   L   F 001 002 001  \0  \0  \0  \0  \0
➥\0  \0  \0  \0
0000020  \0 002  \0 002  \0  \0  \0 001  \0 001 016 374  \0
➥\0  \0   4
0000040  \0  \0   @   `  \0  \0  \0  \0  \0   4  \0
➥\0 005  \0   (
0000060  \0 030  \0 027  \0  \0  \0 006  \0  \0  \0   4
➥\0 001  \0   4
0000220  \0 001  \0  \0  \0  \0  \0 001  \0  \0   : 250
➥\0 002   : 250
#
```

Here, strings is the command that shows any strings of printable characters with a length of about four characters or longer. Notice in the preceding example that the printable letters ELF occur near the beginning of the file, but strings does not report it because four printable characters do not exist in that section.

```
# strings /bin/ls ¦ head -5
SUNW_OST_OSCMD
RaAdC1xmnlogrtucpFbqisfL
```

```
usage: ls -1RaAdCxmnlogrtucpFbqisfL [files]
COLUMNS
total %llu
```

You can use the `-n` option to `strings` to set the minimum length of printable string to display.

Displaying Text in Large Banner Letters (*banner*)

The `banner` command can be used to display short messages using large scale letters, as in this example:

```
# banner hello

    #      #   ######  #        #            ####
    #      #   #       #        #           #    #
    ######     #####   #        #           #    #
    #      #   #       #        #           #    #
    #      #   #       #        #           #    #
    #      #   ######  ######   ######       ####

    #
```

This technique is useful in creating separator pages between printer jobs because it generates readable text that stands out. You can redirect the output of `banner` when you want the output in a file.

The `banner` command puts separate words on separate lines. If you want these on the same line, escape any spaces between the words by preceding each space with a backslash (\), or enclose any spaces in single or double quotes, as in this example:

```
banner "Acme Corp."
```

The maximum line for `banner` is 10 characters. The command truncates any characters after that.

Displaying DOS Files (*col*)

Text files under DOS/Windows end each line with both a carriage return and a linefeed. UNIX text files end with just the linefeed, which UNIX calls the *newline character*. If you bring a DOS text file to UNIX and try to edit it with `vi`, you might see that the file looks like this:

> **Finding text clues in binary files**
>
> Finding printable text in binary programs can be useful in solving problems when the program is not working. Sometimes text error messages, usage messages, and file and directory names contained within the binary file offer just the clue needed to set up the environment so the program will start working.

```
This is a text file^M
that came from a DOS^M
system via disk or^M
download via network.^M
```

The Ctrl+M at the end of each line is the carriage return. There
are a number of ways to remove the Ctrl+M by using the col
command, which is a utility to filter control characters.

To create a UNIX text file from an existing DOS text file, enter
this line:

```
col -bx < dosfile > unixfile
```

If you are in vi and find each line ends with ^M, enter this line:

```
:%! col -bx
```

The preceding command causes vi to apply col -bx to every line
in the file, removing the ^M at the end of each line. You can
now continue your editing.

Cleaning Up Man Pages (*col*)

If you save a man page to a file, you are likely to find ^H or
backspace characters interspersed inside important words. The
^H is a directive to the printer to go back and reprint the previous character again as bold or to underline the character. The
following is an example of a saved man page showing the ^H's:

```
NAME
     ls - list contents of directory


SYNOPSIS
     /usr/bin/ls [ -aAbcCdfFgilLmnopqrRstux1 ] [
     ➥_^Hf_^Hi_^Hl_^He... ]
     /usr/xpg4/bin/ls [ -aAbcCdfFgilLmnopqrRstux1 ] [ _
     ➥^Hf_^Hi_^Hl_^He... ]


DESCRIPTION
     For each _^Hf_^Hi_^Hl_^He that is a directory, ls lists
     ➥the contents  of
     the  directory;  for  each  _^Hf_^Hi_^Hl_^He that is an
     ➥ordinary file, ls
     repeats its name and any other information  requested.
     ➥The
```

You can run `col -bx` from either the command line or in `vi`, as shown in the previous section. The following is the same man page file after `col -bx` has been run:

```
NAME
     ls - list contents of directory


SYNOPSIS
     /usr/bin/ls [ -aAbcCdfFgilLmnopqrRstux1 ] [ file...  ]
     /usr/xpg4/bin/ls [ -aAbcCdfFgilLmnopqrRstux1 ] [ file...
     ➥]


DESCRIPTION
     For each file that is a directory, ls lists the
     ➥contents  of
     the  directory;  for  each file that is an ordinary
     ➥file, ls
     repeats its name and any other information  requested.
     ➥The
```

This also explains why sometimes, in a man page, you use slash (/) to search for a string and man says it is not there—yet you find that string later in the man page. Why didn't slash (/) find it? The answer is likely to be that it is an important word, hence it contains some ^H's. You can improve your ability to search the man pages by entering your man commands like this:

```
man ls ¦ col -bx ¦ pg
```

The `col -bx` removes the ^H's from key words, which enables slash (/) to find them in searches.

SEE ALSO

➤ *For more information on man pages, see page 90*

Printing Files

Usually one or more printers exist on a UNIX system. The system administrator gives each printer a name so that users can specify the printer or group of printers to which they want their output to go. Users use the `lp` or `lpr` commands to print to the desired printer.

Introducing the UNIX Spooling System

What actually happens is that the text to be printed is saved in a system disk file, called a *spool file*. Each different print job gets its own spool file. The lp/lpr command actually completes very quickly because it does not take long to save all the text in a disk file. This process is called queuing up a printer request. A print scheduler program, which runs in the background, waits for the desired printer to become available and then prints the next job in the queue for that printer.

Spooling provides a number of benefits. With spooling, printing does not tie up your station while the printer prints your job (this can be a slow process for large print jobs). All jobs go through one printer scheduler program, so there is no danger that two users printing to the same printer at the same time will get their output interspersed with each other.

Spooling has some disadvantages. A spool job does not start printing until the spooling program has terminated. This fact offers a distinct advantage, in that the printer can always run at full speed because it does not have to wait for program computation and disk access to generate the next line of printer output. The disadvantage occurs when a job takes a long time, say six hours, to generate the output. After the six-hour job completes, the printing begins, so the user must wait even longer for the printed output.

It is possible for applications to open and output directly to a printer device. For the example in the previous paragraph, a direct printer would allow printing to be done throughout the full six hours of program time, so most of the printing would be completed with a direct printer just when a spooled printer would be starting the output.

A direct printer is also more useful when you have checks and forms on the printer and want to control the proper centering of the form from the application. Often the application will print some test forms and ask the user to check the form alignment before printing the batch of forms. A spooler cannot print a test form unless the application closes the output channel, which leaves the printer open to jobs that will waste the forms just loaded.

A direct printer has difficulty keeping users from interspersing their output. Often an application will lock the printer while it is in use, forcing all other users to wait until the job is done. Different applications often use different locking mechanisms, so output from one application can intersperse with another application. If more than one application uses the same printer, spooling is usually required to keep the output from interspersing.

Whenever UNIX documentation refers to printing, it usually means the print queuing/spooling system. The rest of this section refers to the print queuing/spooling system.

How to Determine Your System Printer Names (*lpstat*)

To get a list of the printer names on your system, enter this line:

```
lpstat -p -D
```

The lpstat command shows us the printer status. The -p option to lpstat limits the output to show the printers and their availability. The -D option to lpstat displays the description, if any, for that printer. You should see output that looks like this:

```
printer p104 is idle. enabled since Sat Aug 23 16:32:49
➡1997. available.
        Description:
printer p108 is idle. enabled since Thu Aug 21 16:28:28
➡1997. available.
        Description: Laser III by copy room
printer p206 is idle. enabled since Sat Feb 14 16:50:49
➡1998. available.
        Description: HP LaserJet in Accounting
```

The preceding example shows that three printer names are available: p104, p108, and p206. All are currently idle, which means they're not printing any jobs. None has been disabled (for example, none is out for repair). There is no way to determine where printer p104 is located in the building, though; it might be in room 104, but it might also be the printer that started in room 104 but was later moved to room 237.

UNIX spooling also works with network printers

You can use the same spooling commands in this section to print to printers on other systems in the network or to printers with their own network cards. The system administrator must first configure those printers under UNIX so they appear in lpstat. This configuration process is different for each type of UNIX.

How to Print a File or Pipeline (*lp, lpr*)

Two general commands under UNIX handle printing a file or pipeline:

```
lp  (a System V utility)
lpr (a BSD utility)
```

You should learn both styles of print commands so that you can function on a UNIX system that offers only one of them. The following procedure describes how to print one or more files or the output of a pipeline.

How to print file(s) or pipeline output

1. If you are printing one or more files, skip to step 2. Otherwise, at the shell prompt, enter the UNIX command whose output you want to print. End the command with a pipe (|) sign. Spaces are optional around the pipe (|) sign. Do not press Enter until instructed. Now go to step 3.

2. If you are printing one or more files, check them first by using the file command, as shown at the start of this chapter. Make sure these are text files. If you print a binary file by mistake, you could waste a lot of printer paper and make everyone else mad at you.

3. Enter lp or lpr.

   Enter whatever command your system supports. If you are not sure, try one. If the command you choose is not supported, you will get a command not found error when you run the command.

4. If you want to specify which printer to go to, follow these instructions:

   For lp, enter a space and then enter -d.

   For lpr, enter a space and then enter -P.

   Now enter the desired printer name.

   If you omit this step, your output will go to the default system printer, or your command will produce an error if no default system printer exists.

5. If you want to specify how many copies to print, follow these instructions:

For lp, enter a space and then enter -n.

For lpr, enter a space and then enter -#.

Now enter the number of copies to print.

6. If you want to print one or more files, enter a space and then list each file, separated by a space. If the file is in the current directory, list just its basename. Otherwise enter an absolute or a relative pathname to each file. You can also use one or more Filename Generation Wildcard patterns to generate your list of files.

7. Press Enter to execute your command and queue up the output. You should see one request id displayed for your output so you can track whether your job has printed yet and so you can abort the printing, if desired, as in this example:

```
$ ls -l ¦ lp   -n2
request id is hp-85 (standard input)
$
```

How to Check the Print Queue (*lpstat*)

On System V UNIX, you can check the requests in the print queue by entering lpstat with no options, as in this example:

```
$ lpstat
hp-85                     mori            111946    Feb 23
                                        ➡22:03 on hp
hp-86                     fred               203    Feb 23
                                        ➡22:04
$
```

Each line output by lpstat begins with the print job request id, which starts with the printer name. In the preceding example, both fred and mori queued up print jobs for printer hp at about the same time. Mori got there first, and his job is currently printing "on hp." Even though fred's job is quite small (only 203 characters), his job won't print until mori's job is done.

If lpstat is not supported on your system, try lpq to get a list of queued print jobs, as in this example:

```
lpq -P printer-name -l
```

If lpq is not on your system, try lpc. Once in lpc, useful commands are help, status, and quit.

How to Cancel a Print Job (*cancel, lprm, qcan*)

On System V UNIX, you can cancel a print job by its request id number. Use the lpstat, lpq, or lpc command as shown in the previous section to determine which current print request you want to cancel, as in this example:

```
$ lpstat
hp-85                          mori                   111946    Feb 23
                                                      ➡22:03 on hp

hp-86                          fred                      203    Feb 23
                                                      ➡22:04
$ cancel hp-85
request "hp-85" canceled
$ lpstat
hp-86                          fred                      203    Feb 23
                                                      ➡22:04 on hp

$
```

On BSD UNIX, use lprm with a job number to remove (that is, cancel) a current print request.

On AIX UNIX, use qcan to cancel a print request, as in this example:

```
qcan -P printername -x jobid
```

On all systems, non-root users can cancel only jobs they submitted; root can cancel any print job.

Moving Print Requests from a Down Printer (*lpmove*)

If a printer is broken, the system administrator (root) can move some or all pending print requests for that printer to another printer by using the lpmove command.

To move one or more specific print jobs to another printer, root can use this syntax:

```
lpmove list-of-req-ids new-printer
```

To display all pending print job request ids from all users for a given printer, root can enter this syntax:

```
lpstat -p printer-name
```

To move all print jobs from a broken printer to another printer, root can enter this syntax:

```
lpmove broken-printer new-printer
```

This will also take the broken printer out of service so that it no longer accepts new print jobs.

How to Format Output for Printing (*pr*)

If you print output on a dot matrix continuous feed printer, the most unsatisfactory part of the output will be the fact that the printing does not leave any margins at the top and bottom of each page. If you print output on a laser printer, you will notice that all the output starts at the very left margin and gives you room to bind the pages or three-hole punch them. These types of problems can be solved by processing your output through the pr command before printing it.

By default, pr puts a five-line header and trailer at the top and bottom of each page. The header includes the page number, date/time, and filename (if not piped). The pr command accepts a list of files on the command line. If no list of files is given, you can pipe your output to pr. You can then pipe the output of pr directly to the printer, as in these two examples:

```
pr file1 acme* ¦ pr ¦ lp
prog2 ¦ pr ¦ lpr -Paccting
```

The main problem in using pr is to determine the number of lines per page on your printer. Here, pr assumes 66 lines per page, which does not work on many printers—you end up with page breaks in the middle of pages. To set the number of lines per page, use the length option -l, as in this example:

```
pr -l60 file
```

Because pr does not usually send a form feed at the end of each page, you must set the length to the exact value required, or you will find page breaks in the middle of later pages of output. Previously, this chapter discussed how to number each line of output. Printing the output with line numbers will help you determine the value to use for your printer. Print at least 10 pages of output to make sure you are using the correct value.

You can tell pr to send a formfeed at the end of each page by using the -f option, as in this example:

```
pr -f file
```

This method can be useful if page breaks drift on the page on very long outputs. This will be more efficient if you are printing only a small number of lines per page on normal-size paper. If the output is going to your screen (that is, if it is not redirected) then the -f will cause a beep and wait for you to press the Enter key at the beginning of the first page. This is useful if you are running on a printing terminal so you can adjust the top of form.

If you are running on a sheet-feed terminal, use the -p option to pr so it will beep and wait for the Enter key at the start of each page.

To set a left margin for output, use the -o option to offset printing, as in this example:

```
pr -o5 file
```

In the preceding example, pr prints five spaces at the start of each line of output. The default (if no -o option is given) is offset 0.

To set your own heading at the top of each page instead of the filename, use the -h option. To include spaces in your new header, enclose the whole header in double or single quotes. Warning: You must include a space after -h, or your whole output will be garbage, as in this example:

```
pr -h "     Acme Proposal     " acmeprop ¦ lp
```

To double-space your output, use the -d option to pr.

To number each line of output, use the -n option. Follow -n with an optional number of characters to use for the line number.

The default, if no value is given, is to use five characters, as in this example:

```
pr -n file
pr -n4 file
```

Although pr will number all lines (even blank lines) in the body, it will not number the lines in the header and trailer on each page. Line numbering will start at 1 and increase constantly throughout the document—that is, it never resets back to 1.

To expand tabs in the output to the corresponding number of spaces, use the -e option. To change the default tab setting from every eight columns, follow -e with a new value, as in this example:

```
pr -e file
pr -e12 file
```

This can be useful when printing tab-separated columns that are longer than eight characters.

Then pr can display your output in columns, as in this example:

```
pr -3 file
```

In the preceding example, -3 tells pr to compose the output into three equal-size columns across the page. Note that pr does not take normal line length output and transform it into columns. You must first manually compose your output so that no one line exceeds the column size (1/3 of a page for three columns, 1/4 of a page for four columns, and so on). Any text that is longer than the column size is truncated—that is, lost.

SEE ALSO

➢ *For more information on the* df *command and filesystem available blocks, see page* 74

Copying, Moving, Renaming, or Deleting Files

By Steve "Mor" Moritsugu

Choosing the Destination

In this chapter, the concepts of *absolute* and *relative pathnames* are very important. You can review them in Chapter 2, "UNIX Directories and Pathnames," if needed. That chapter also discusses standard directories found on most UNIX systems. In that discussion, /tmp was mentioned as a directory for temporary files. This is a good directory for users to use when they want to build a few small temporary files (also called *scratch files*).

Because all users can build files in /tmp, choose a name for your file that is not likely to be used by other users—include your logon ID as part of the name, for example. I usually add the word *junk* or *tmp* to such files. Whenever I later encounter files that I created with *junk* or *tmp* in the name, I can freely delete them without having to take time to evaluate their contents.

Chapter 2 also mentioned the fact that every user has a home directory. Some systems make a group of users share the same home directory, but usually you have a home directory all to yourself. Therefore it is a good place to store files that you want to keep for a while.

It is a good idea to create subdirectories within your home directory so that you can organize your files. One of the traditional ways to organize files is by file type or function. You might create a directory for text files, for example, and another for executable programs. (Traditionally executables would be put in a bin directory.) The advantage of having one bin directory is that you can then add it to your PATH to make it easy to execute any program in that directory no matter what your current directory is.

I recommend organizing your home directory by projects. Create a directory for each project and put all files associated with that project into the one directory. You can create subdirectories if it is a complex project. The benefit of this organization is realized when you need to purge old unneeded files to clean up your disk usage. Many projects are no longer needed six months or a year later. Organizing by project enables you to easily remove all the files associated with that project.

If you need to build any huge files or create thousands of files, you should consult with your system administrator first. If you use up all the disk space or *inodes* in a filesystem, you can cause serious system problems. The df command can show you the free disk space and free inodes in each filesystem. If you need a large amount of disk space, the system administrator might create a directory in another filesystem for you to use.

SEE ALSO

➢ *For more information on absolute and relative pathnames, see page 42*

➢ *For more information on standard UNIX directories, see page 40*

➢ *For more information on home directories, see page 44*

Handling Permission-Denied Errors

To create files and subdirectories within a directory, you need write permission to that directory. If you created the directory, you normally have write permission for that directory. If the directory belongs to someone else, you may need to ask him or her to open up write permission to the directory. He or she may be hesitant to open up write permission for everybody. The traditional UNIX approach is to create a new group for users who need to share files and directories, assign those files and directories to the new group, and allow write permission for group members but not the whole world. You must then ask root (the system administrator) to add you to the group.

SEE ALSO

➢ *For more information on Permissions, see page 273*

Copying, Moving, or Renaming Files (*cp,mv*)

There are many instances when you need to rework a file's name or location, and special concerns for each action. UNIX has a number of commands and options for these procedures; the following sections detail the available commands and options.

Copying, Moving, or Renaming Within the Current Directory (*cp,mv*)

To rename a file, we use the UNIX mv command to move it to the new name. No actual blocks are transferred (unless we move it to a different filesystem). If we copy the file, we create a new file with a different name and copy all the contents of the source file to the new file.

How to copy/move/rename a file within a directory

1. Make sure you are in the desired directory. If you are not sure what directory you are in, display your current directory using this command:
pwd

2. At the shell prompt, if you want to move (that is, rename) the file, enter the following:
mv

If you want to copy the file, enter this:
cp

Do not press the Enter key until instructed. Notice that the command is only two letters and not the whole word.

3. Enter a space and then enter ·i.

This is a useful option on modern UNIX systems that is not available on older UNIX systems. This will give a warning if you are about to overwrite an existing file.

4. Some UNIX systems such as Solaris or Linux allow a ·p option to the cp command, which preserves the file owner, group, and permissions when doing the copy. (You can check this in the man page on cp for your system.) This option works best if you are running as root (the system administrator). If you want to include this option for cp, enter a space and then enter ·p.

5. Enter a space and then enter the existing filename to move or copy. Enter this as a *basename* because it is in the current directory. This file must already exist, and so it is sometimes referred to as the existing file or the sourcefile.

6. Enter a space and then enter the new filename to create. This is called the destination file. Enter this destination file as a basename. This basename cannot match any other file or subdirectory name in the current directory. Your new filename can start with and contain any upper or lowercase letters, digits, the underscore (_) sign, a dash (-), or a period (.). Older UNIX systems were limited to 14 characters, but modern UNIX systems allow over 100 characters in one basename (but please don't make them that long). Don't begin your new filename with a period unless you want it to be a hidden file, to keep it separate from your normal files.

7. Press the Enter key to execute your command.

8. If you get a Usage error, complaining that -i is not a valid option, your UNIX system does not allow that option. Re-enter the whole command without the -i option. If the -i option does not work on your system, you must manually check whether the destination already exists before doing any mv or cp commands.

9. If you get a Permission Denied type of error, you either don't have permission to read the source file or you don't have permission to write to the directory and create a new file there. See the preceding section on handling permission-denied errors.

10. If you get this message:
```
overwrite dest-file?
```

the -i option is alerting you that the destination file you selected already exists. You now have the option to enter y and overwrite the file or enter n to abort your copy or move. If you are not sure, enter **n** and then display the contents of the destination file (see the preceding chapter) to see whether you need to preserve it.

11. No news is good news.

If no message is generated and you just return to the shell prompt, your copy or move was successful.

-i Option and Automatic Headlights

Under the C shell or Korn shell, it is possible to set up an alias for your logon ID so that the -i option is automatically added to any **cp** and **mv** commands that you enter. I personally don't do this for the same reason I don't like car headlights that turn off automatically—it teaches you bad habits for driving other cars or working under other logons or on other UNIX systems.

Copying, Moving, or Renaming to a Different Directory (*cp,mv*)

This section assumes that you have read the preceding section on performing a copy or move. This section discusses how to use copy or move commands when the source file and destination file are in different directories.

If the destination filename is to be the same as the source filename, you can specify just the destination directory without specifying a filename.

Option #1 is to use absolute pathnames for both the source and destination of your copy or move. Then it does not matter what your current directory is. The drawback to this approach is that it requires so much more typing so it is rarely used.

Option #2 is to sit in the source directory when you do the command (which means it is your current directory). Then you can specify the source file as a basename. You must specify the destination file as either an absolute or relative pathname. This option is useful when you have further commands to do in the source directory.

Option #3 is to sit in the destination directory, specify the source file as either an absolute or relative pathname, and specify the destination file as a basename. This option is useful when you have further commands to do in the destination directory.

Option #4 is to sit in some nearby directory that can access both the source and destination directory conveniently. Consider this copy command, for example:

```
cp -i /usr/fred/reports/acme/report7
/usr/fred/reports/98Jan/report7
```

Notice that /usr/fred/reports is common to both the source and destination directories, so you can sit there and access the files using convenient relative pathnames as shown here:

```
cd /usr/fred/reports
cp acme/report7  98Jan/report7
```

Option #5 is to use your own shell variables when you want to copy several different files between the same two directories as described next.

Setting shell variables for two directories

1. cd to the source directory.

2. Enter: SD=`pwd`.

In the preceding command, you are taking our current directory as reported by pwd and using backquotes to save that directory name in variable SD. You can choose your own variable names. I chose SD for source directory in capital letters to avoid confusion with UNIX commands, which are usually lowercase.

3. cd to the destination directory.

4. Enter DD=`pwd`.

5. Now it is easy to copy or move files between the two directories. SD and DD contain absolute pathnames, so it does not matter what the current directory is. To copy a file from the source directory to the destination directory, enter the following:

```
cp -i $SD/filename $DD/.
```

Notice you do not have to specify the destination filename if it is to be the same as the source filename. Notice that I add slash period (/.) after the directory name as described next.

SEE ALSO

➤ *For more information on shell variables, see page 30*

Determining Where Your File Is Going (*cp,mv*)

It is not always so easy to predict what destination file will be created by cp or mv. This is because the results differ depending on whether the destination specified is an existing directory. For example,

```
mv /usr/jane/acme   /usr/fred/reports
```

if reports (in /usr/fred) is a directory, mv (or cp) will take the source file acme and move it (or copy it) into the reports directory. Therefore the resultant filename will be this:

```
/usr/fred/reports/acme
```

Notice that the *source dirname*, /usr/jane in this case, only tells us where to find the source basename. It is just the source basename that is moved or copied. None of the source dirname directories are ever brought along.

If the specified destination /usr/fred/reports does not exist, mv (or cp) will create it and put the contents of acme into it. Therefore the resultant file will be a regular file named:

```
/usr/fred/reports
```

If reports existed as a *regular file* in /usr/fred, we would get the same result. The old reports file would be lost and the contents of file acme would be put in its place. There would be no warning that the old contents of reports had been overwritten because we did not use the -i option in this example.

Whenever you copy or move a file into a directory, I recommend that you add slash period (/.) to the directory name. For example,

```
mv acme   /usr/fred/reports/.
```

The slash period (/.) tells the system that I am expecting /usr/fred/reports to be a directory and to move the acme file into that directory. If reports was not an existing directory, the command would fail with an error message and I would be alerted that something went wrong. If reports happened to be an existing filename, adding slash period (/.) in the preceding command prevents overwriting the reports file and losing its data.

Another attempt to do the same thing is to add just a slash (/). For example,

```
mv acme   /usr/fred/reports/       # can get a syntax error
```

I don't recommend just adding slash (/) because it is an illegal syntax on many UNIX systems.

Here is an example where using slash period (/.) would have prevented loss of data:

```
mv file1 /usr/fred/reports
mv file2 /usr/fred/reports
mv acme /usr/fred/reports
```

In the preceding example, the user expected that
/usr/fred/reports is an existing directory; however, this was not
true. Therefore the first command created a regular file in
/usr/fred called reports containing all the data from file1. The
second command overwrote the reports file with the contents of
file2. The contents of file1 is now totally gone from the system
and irretrievable. (Notice that the -i option would have given a
life-saving warning here.) The third command will again overwrite reports, so the contents of file2 will also be lost and irretrievable. Here is the same sequence as I recommend it be done:

```
mv -i file1 /usr/fred/reports/.
mv -i file2 /usr/fred/reports/.
mv -i acme /usr/fred/reports/.
```

The very first command will fail with an error message if
/usr/fred/reports is not a directory.

Adding slash period (/.) to destination directories also makes it
easier to understand what result to expect from mv or cp. This is
true for both written instructions and when we insert commands
in shell scripts (as covered in a later chapter).

Copying/Moving a List of Files to a Directory (*cp,mv*)

If the destination for cp or mv is a directory, the source can
include one or more regular files; that is, a list of files. For example,

```
cp -i file1 file2 file3 /data/acme/.
```

In this example, file1 and file2 and file3 will be copied to the
/data/acme directory. If there are two or more source files, the
destination file must be a directory; otherwise, you will get an
error.

In a later chapter, you will see that file lists can be created using
filename generation wildcards, which can be used with cp and mv if
the destination is a directory. For example,

```
cp -i *acme* /usr/fred/acmefiles/.
```

SEE ALSO
➤ *For more information on Filename Generation Wildcards, see page 232*

Handling Confirmation Requests

If mv or rm is about to overwrite or delete an existing file, these commands will check to see whether you have permission to write to the file. If not, it will ask for confirmation like this:

```
mv: dest-file: override protection 400 (yes/no)?
```

On some systems, the confirmation message is very terse. For example,

```
400?
```

For this confirmation message, mv is about to overwrite another user's file, and that user has not given you permission to write to or modify this file. You have administrative control over the directory, however, therefore you can override the permissions. The three permission digits for this file are XXX (400 in the preceding example). Do you want to overwrite this file anyway? Please enter y for yes or n for no.

Moving/Renaming a Directory (*mv*)

You can use the mv command to move or rename directories. In this way, directories can be removed from the UNIX directory tree structure and reattached to a different part of the tree. All the subdirectories of that directory will go along with it.

Assume this file exists on a system:

```
/usr/fred/reports/compsys/pegasus
```

Note that file pegasus is in the compsys directory. Now assume that we execute this command:

```
mv /usr/fred/reports/compsys /usr/fred
```

For both mv and cp, if the specified destination is an existing directory, the destination will be created within that directory. We know that /usr/fred does exist as a directory in this example.

From the previous part of this chapter, we know that mv (and cp) take only the source basename and place it into the existing destination directory. Therefore the new absolute pathname for compsys will be as follows:

/usr/fred/compsys

The new absolute pathname of the pegasus file will be this:

/usr/fred/compsys/pegasus

In the preceding example, the mv command removed directory compsys and all its files and subdirectories from the UNIX directory tree structure and reattached compsys and all its files and subdirectories in a new place.

Older versions of UNIX aborted with an error if you tried to move a directory into a different filesystem. Many modern UNIX systems can do this without any problems.

Copying a Whole Directory Subtree (*cpio*)

Sometimes you may want to copy a directory and all its subdirectories and files to some destination directory. Some UNIX systems offer a copy command (spelled c o p y) that can do this if you use the -r option, which means *recursively* copy subdirectories; that is, copy all the subdirectories no matter how many levels removed. Other UNIX systems may offer the -r option to cp to allow recursive copying of directories. Some UNIX systems (especially older ones), however, do not offer any recursive copy or cp options.

There is a way to recursively copy a directory subtree using the cpio command, which works on older UNIX systems as well as newer ones. You must learn only one technique for all systems, and it offers more versatility than other methods.

Copy a whole directory subtree

1. If the source directory contains files owned by several users, and if you want the destination directory to accurately mirror the ownership and permissions of the source, you must be logged on as *root* to do this procedure.

2. Determine the exact absolute pathname of the source directory. Every file and subdirectory of this source directory is to be copied to the destination.

3. Determine the exact absolute pathname of the destination directory. A copy of each subdirectory and file of the source directory (and its subdirectories) will be made in the destination directory.

4. cd to the source directory.

5. Enter pwd to make sure you are sitting in the source directory.

6. Enter:

```
find . -print ¦ cpio -pvdum dest-dir
```

Replace dest-dir with the desired destination directory. You may express the dest-dir as either an absolute or relative pathname. When you run this command, cpio will display each filename as it copies the whole directory subtree.

7. In step 6, the following cpio command options are optional, and one or more of them may be added or left out as desired:

a   means reset date/time of last access for each file to what it was before cpio accessed the file. May not be used if -m option is included.

d   means create destination directories as needed.

L   means follow soft links (see next section) so that the pointed to file is copied rather than the pointer file

m   means keep the same date/time of last modification for each destination file as in the source directory. May not be used if -a option is included.

u   means unconditionally overwrite any existing destination files else an older file will not overwrite a newer one.

v   means verbose output which lists each file as it is copied.

SEE ALSO

➤ *For more information on* cpio, *see page 355*

Deleting Files (*rm*)

There are many situations when you will have to delete files and directories, and depending on where the file is, special concerns for each action you take to do so. UNIX has a number of commands and options for these procedures. The following sections detail the available commands and options.

Deleting Files Within the Current Directory (*rm*)

How to delete files in the current directory

1. Make sure you are in the desired directory. If you are not sure what directory you are in, display your current directory using this command:
pwd

2. At the shell prompt, enter:
rm

Do not press the Enter key until instructed. To delete a file, we use the remove command. Notice that the command is only two letters and not the whole word.

3. Previously we discussed confirmation requests for rm and mv. If you want to prevent getting a confirmation request when you delete another user's file that you don't have permission to modify, enter a space and then enter the following:
-f

This option to force the delete or replacement is useful when you are deleting a group of files that you are sure you want to delete.

4. If you are deleting a group of files, you can cause rm to ask for confirmation on each one by entering a space and then entering this:
-i

tar can also copy a directory tree

I discuss how to use cpio to copy a directory tree because older versions of tar could not restore empty directories or device files or preserve directory owner, group, or permissions. If you use cpio, you don't have to worry about these old tar limitations.

This interactive option is useful when you are using a wild-card pattern to specify the list of files to delete to make sure you do not delete more files than you intended.

5. Enter a space and then enter one or more filenames to delete, separated by spaces. Enter each filename as a base-name, because it is in the current directory.

6. Double-check your command carefully because there is no undelete command if you make as mistake. Press the Enter key to execute your command.

7. No news is good news.

   If no message is generated and you just return to the shell prompt, your delete was successful.

Deleting Files in a Different Directory (*rm*)

A single rm command can delete files in many directories. In the list of files for the rm command, just include an absolute or rela-tive pathname for the desired file or files to delete. Review the previous section in this chapter on how to formulate a relative pathname.

Deleting a List of Files (*rm*)

The rm command does allow a list of files to be specified. This list can be generated by filename generation wildcards (see chap-ter 9). For example,

```
rm *acme*   /tmp/*acme*
```

Deleting a Whole Directory Subtree (*rm*)

To remove a directory, it must be entirely empty except for a dot (.) and dot-dot (..) entry. If you are sure that you want to delete a directory and all of its files and subdirectories, and all their sub-directories, there is a way to accomplish this in one simple com-mand. You must be very careful when you use this command because there is no way to bring files back if you make a mistake. The procedure to delete an entire directory and its contents was covered in the Chapter 7 (on directories) and pathnames.

SEE ALSO
➤ *For more information on deleting a whole directory tree, see page 53*

Creating Multiple Names for the Same File (*ln*)

UNIX refers to all files and directories by an inode number. This inode number is actually an entry number into an inode table. Each filesystem has its own inode table. Each inode entry in use contains information about one file in that filesystem. An inode entry contains most of the information about a file such as the owner, group, permissions, type of file, date/time of last access, date/time of last modification, and so on. You might be surprised to learn that the inode table entry contains everything about the file except for the filename.

A directory is a file under UNIX that has two purposes:

1. To keep track of the filenames and subdirectory names contained in that directory

2. To keep track of the inode number for each of those filenames

When you access a filename under UNIX, the system determines which inode table entry to use from the directory entry for that filename. UNIX allows more than one filename to reference a given inode number, which in effect allows multiple names for the same file. Because the filename is not part of the inode information, each of the names for a file are equally valid. It does not matter which name came first.

It would be incorrect to think of these names as copies of the file because there is only one inode being referenced. That means if you change the file using one name, that change will be visible when you access the file under its other names.

When you have multiple names for the same file, each name is called a hard link to the file. Allowing multiple names or hard links for a file can be useful in UNIX's hierarchical directory system when you want to put the same file into two different directories. Let's say, for example, that I have a customer directory with one file for each of my customers, which contains their name, address, phone number, and transaction history. Let's say I also have a vendor directory for companies that I purchase products from, and each file in the vendor directory has the vendor name, address, phone number, and transaction history.

Now let us say there are some companies that buy things from me, so they should be in the customer directory; but I also buy things from them, so they should be in the vendor directory. I can solve this problem by creating two hard links. That is, I can create a file in the customer directory and also put that same file in the vendor directory. By using hard links, these files are not copies of each other; they are two names for the same file. Therefore if I update the phone number for that company in the customer directory, that change is automatically reflected for that company in the vendor directory.

If I have a large file, hard links take up much less space than making copies of the file. No matter how many hard links there are, there is only one copy of the file.

SEE ALSO

➤ *For more information on UNIX directories, see page 36*

Creating Multiple Names Using Hard Links (*ln*)

Now that you have seen what hard links are and what their advantages are, here is the procedure to create an additional hard link to a file—that is, to create another name to access a particular file.

Creating a hard link to an existing file

1. Make sure you know the full pathname of the existing file and the desired name to give the new hard link to this existing file. The existing file must be a regular file, not a directory. The hard link filename must not already be in use as a file, directory, link, or so on.

2. The new hard link to create must be in the same filesystem as the existing file. If you are not sure where your filesystem boundaries are, enter this command:
   df

You might see output like this:

```
/           (/dev/root        ):     724074 blocks
➥137175 i-nodes
/stand      (/dev/boot        ):      13780 blocks        3825
➥i-nodes
/u          (/dev/u           ):     601622 blocks
➥289486 i-nodes
/data       (/dev/dsk/c0d1s2  ):   1776032 blocks      632983
➥i-nodes
/u/tmp      (/dev/dsk/c0d1s3  ):      42302 blocks       37293
➥i-nodes
```

In the preceding output from df, the left column shows the directory names for your filesystems. To determine if two absolute pathnames are in the same filesystem, match up the beginning part of the pathname to the longest matching filesystem directories from the df output. If both files match up to the same df output line, they are in the same filesystem. For example, /u/tmp/reports would be in the /u/tmp filesystem (because we take the longest match).
/u/reports/acme would be in the /u filesystem. Because they are in different filesystems, they could not be hard links to the same file. Another example, /usr/fred/reports is in the / filesystem. /acme/Jan23 is also in the / filesystem. Therefore it could be created as hard link to /usr/fred/reports.

3. At the shell prompt, enter ln.

Do not press the Enter key until instructed.

4. Enter a space, and then the name of the existing file. You may enter this as an absolute or relative pathname.

5. Enter a space and then the name of the new hard link you want to create for the existing file. You may enter the new link name as either an absolute or relative pathname.

6. Press the Enter key to complete your command.

Finding All the Hard Links to a File (*ls, find*)

To determine how many hard links there are to a file, enter the following:

```
ls -l filename
```

Here is an example output:

```
-r-xr-xr-x    3 bin        bin          15176 Jul 15   1997
➥compress
```

After the permissions, and before the owner and group, is a field called the *link count*, which has a 3 in the preceding example. This means that the compress command (which is in the /bin directory) has a total of three names to reference the same file. One of the names is compress, so there are two other names for the file that we don't know.

To determine whether there are more hard links for the file in the same directory, enter the following:

```
ls -li ¦ sort ¦ pg
```

Here is an example output:

```
5527 -r-xr-xr-x    1 bin        bin          10832 Jul 15
➥1997 col
5528 -r-xr-xr-x    1 bin        bin           6344 Jul 15
➥1997 comm
5529 -r-xr-xr-x    3 bin        bin          15176 Jul 15
➥1997 compress
5529 -r-xr-xr-x    3 bin        bin          15176 Jul 15
➥1997 uncompress
5529 -r-xr-xr-x    3 bin        bin          15176 Jul 15
➥1997 zcat
5530 -r-xr-xr-x    1 bin        bin          30596 Jul 15
➥1997 csplit
5531 -r-xr-xr-x    1 bin        bin          39916 Jul 15
➥1997 dc
```

The -i option to ls causes ls to display the inode number at the start of the line where it is in perfect position to apply the sort command so that lines that start with the same inode number will be together. Notice in the preceding example that compress, uncompress, and zcat all have the same inode number (5529), the same permissions (r-xr-xr-x), the same owner, group, size (15176), and date of last modification. Because they have the same inode number and are in the same directory, they are hard links to the same file—that is, different names for the same file.

If all the hard links are not found, some of them must exist in other directories. To find all filenames that match a given inode number, enter the following:

```
find /STARTDIR -inum INODE -print
```

Replace INODE with the inode number that you want to look up. Replace /STARTDIR with the desired filesystem directory from the df command, as you saw in step 2. For example,

```
# find / -inum 17248736 -print
/usr/fred/acme
/usr/jane/acme
/acmeproject/report7
/data7/pegasus3
#
```

In step 2 of the preceding procedure, you saw how to determine whether two pathnames were in the same filesystem. Inode numbers are re-used in other filesystems for other totally unrelated files. Filenames with the same inode number are only hard links to the same file if they are in the same filesystem. Use this knowledge to ignore files reported by Find that are not in the correct filesystem.

SEE ALSO

➤ *For more information on the* ls *command, see page 151*

➤ *For more information on filesystems, see page 72*

Deleting a Hard Link (*rm*)

If a file has multiple hard links, it has multiple names. If you use the rm command to delete one of those names, the rest of the names and the file contents are not affected, except the total link count for the file is reduced by one. If you delete a filename with a link count of one, the link count for the inode will go to zero, which means there are no names left to access this file. After the link count goes to zero, that file will be deleted from the system. After a file has been deleted, there is no way to bring it back.

Creating Pointers Using Soft/Symbolic Links (*ln*)

There is another way to create multiple names for the same file. You can create a soft link, also called a symbolic link, to an existing file. Soft links have two advantages over hard links:

1. You can create a soft link to a directory.

2. You can create a soft link to a file or directory in another filesystem.

A soft link is a small pointer file, indicated with a small arrow (->) in `ls -l` output. For example,

```
$ ls -l /usr/spool
lrwxrwxrwx   1 root      root        10 Feb 13 09:19
➥/usr/spool -> /var/spool
$
```

In the preceding example, `/usr/spool` is a soft link to directory `/var/spool`. One of the changes introduced in SVR4 was to move the spool directory from `/usr` to `/var`. SVR4 usually creates `/usr/spool` as a soft link to `/var/spool`. This enables users and programs to continue to access `/usr/spool` and the soft link will cause them to actually access `/var/spool`. In the preceding example, notice that `/usr/spool` is a file whose size is only 10 characters; that is, its only contents is `/var/spool`, which is 10 characters. Notice at the beginning of the line, the type is `l`, which indicate a soft link. Notice the permissions are `rwx` for all users. This allows all users to access the soft link. However, read/write/execute permissions are then determined by the file being pointed to.

Creating a soft/symbolic link

1. Determine the absolute pathname of the desired soft link and the file that you want it to point to. This pointed-to file does not have to exist when you create the link. The pointed-to file can be a directory and it can be in a different filesystem from the soft link. The soft link filename must not already be in use.

2. At the shell prompt, enter `ln -s`.

Do not press the Enter key until instructed.

3. Enter a space and then enter the full pathname of the pointed-to file.

4. Enter a space and then enter the soft link filename to create. This can either by an absolute or relative pathname. Usually an absolute pathname is preferred.

5. Press the Enter key to complete your command. Older UNIX systems did not support soft links. Some UNIX systems only allow root (the system administrator) to create soft links.

Determining Whether a Command Follows a Soft Link

Using hard links, every name for the file is indistinguishable from every other name for that file. On the other hand, a soft link is quite different from the file to which it refers. Most commands will follow the soft link, which means that when you ask them to access a soft link, they will instead access the file pointed to by the soft link.

If you use vi to edit a soft link, for example, it will edit instead the file pointed to by the soft link. If that file does not exist, you have a stale soft link—that is, a link that goes nowhere. In that case, vi will give a No Such File error, even though the soft link itself does exist.

Some UNIX commands will not follow the soft link, which means they operate on the soft link itself. mv and rm normally do not follow the link, for example, enabling you to rename or delete the soft link itself. Check the man pages for individual commands to see whether they follow the soft link and operate on the pointed-to file.

Here is an excerpt from man rm on a Solaris system:

```
If file is a symbolic link, the link will  be  removed,
➥but
the file  or  directory  to  which  it  refers  will
➥not be
deleted.  Users do not need write  permission  to
➥remove  a
symbolic  link,  provided they have write permissions
➥in the
directory.
```

The preceding excerpt tells us that rm does not follow the link. It operates on the soft link itself.

Avoid linking a directory to itself

A command like this can link a directory to itself:

```
ln -s dir2 dir2
```

The **cd** command on modern UNIX systems will detect this error and immediately report **Bad Directory**. In general, it is safest to use an absolute pathname for the pointed-to file.

Here is an excerpt from man ls on a Solaris system:

```
-L    If an argument is a symbolic link,  list  the
➥file  or
directory  the  link  references  rather  than  the
➥link
itself.
```

This excerpt tells us that ls normally does not follow the link. It normally gives information about the soft link itself. If we add the -L option to ls, it will follow the link and display the pointed-to file.

Here is an excerpt from man file on a Solaris system:

```
If file is a symbolic link, by default the link is
➥followed and
file tests the file to which the symbolic link refers.
```

SEE ALSO

➤ *For more information on the* man *command, see page 89*

Modifying, Combining, and Splitting Files

By Steve "Mor" Moritsugu

Sorting lines in a file, multiple files, or pipeline

Displaying just the first or last lines of a file or pipeline

Encrypting a file so only you can decrypt it

Compressing/uncompressing a file

Changing a binary file to simple text format

Sorting a group of files

Concatenating files one after the other

Pasting files so that corresponding lines are side by side

Sorting Files or Pipelines (*sort*)

Sorting means to arrange lines in alphabetical order. To sort one or more files, use the sort command, as in the following:

```
sort file1 file2 file3
```

sort will merge all the specified files into its workspace, sort the workspace, and then display the result to standard output which will go to your screen unless you redirect the output to a file or pipe it to another command.

The sort command can also be used as a typical UNIX filter in pipelines like this:

```
ls acme*  *.c | sort | uniq
```

In the preceding example, sort reads from standard input the lines generated by the ls command. sort then arranges those lines in alphabetical order and passes them on to standard output. In the preceding example, standard output from sort is being piped to the uniq command to remove any duplicate lines.

If you specify any filenames after the sort command, it will get its input from those files and not from standard input. Here is an incorrect use of sort:

```
ls acme*  *.c | sort acme* | uniq    # incorrect sort usage
```

The preceding example is incorrect because one or more filenames have been specified after the sort command, so sort will not read from standard input and will ignore the output generated by the ls command.

SEE ALSO

➤ *For more information on piping, see page 31*

➤ *For more information on Filename Generation Wildcards, see page 232*

Determining How Lines Will Be Sorted (ASCII)

sort will arrange lines based on the ASCII values of the characters within the lines. You can usually look up the ASCII sequence by entering this command:

```
man ascii
```

Why don't UNIX commands have built-in sort or paging options?

If a user wants sorted output from any UNIX command, or paged output, or sorted output one page at a time, it is expected that the user will just pipe to **sort** or pipe to **pg** or pipe to **sort** and then to **pg**. In this way, UNIX utilities don't duplicate efforts and can be more efficient.

Here is some sample output from a Solaris system:

```
|000 NUL|001 SOH|002 STX|003 ETX|004 EOT|005 ENQ|006 ACK|007
➥BEL|
|010 BS |011 HT |012 NL |013 VT |014 NP |015 CR |016 SO |017
➥SI |
|020 DLE|021 DC1|022 DC2|023 DC3|024 DC4|025 NAK|026 SYN|027
➥ETB|
|030 CAN|031 EM |032 SUB|033 ESC|034 FS |035 GS |036 RS |037
➥US |
|040 SP |041  ! |042  " |043  # |044  $ |045  % |046  &
➥|047  ' |
|050  ( |051  ) |052  * |053  + |054  , |055  - |056  .
➥|057  / |
|060  0 |061  1 |062  2 |063  3 |064  4 |065  5 |066  6
➥|067  7 |
|070  8 |071  9 |072  : |073  ; |074  < |075  = |076  >
➥|077  ? |
|100  @ |101  A |102  B |103  C |104  D |105  E |106  F
➥|107  G |
|110  H |111  I |112  J |113  K |114  L |115  M |116  N
➥|117  O |
|120  P |121  Q |122  R |123  S |124  T |125  U |126  V
➥|127  W |
|130  X |131  Y |132  Z |133  [ |134  \ |135  ] |136  ^
➥|137  _ |
|140  ` |141  a |142  b |143  c |144  d |145  e |146  f
➥|147  g |
|150  h |151  i |152  j |153  k |154  l |155  m |156  n
➥|157  o |
|160  p |161  q |162  r |163  s |164  t |165  u |166  v
➥|167  w |
|170  x |171  y |172  z |173  { |174  | |175  } |176  ~
➥|177 DEL|
```

The preceding table shows that each ASCII character has a value, often given in octal or base 8 numbering. A capital A has the value 101, for example, whereas a lowercase a has the value 141. Lines that start with capital letters will come before all lines that start with lowercase letters. Notice that the digits sort before any letters. Punctuation characters also have values; hence, lines that begin with punctuation will be sorted based on the ASCII value of the punctuation characters. Notice that the bang sign (!) has the smallest ASCII value for any printing character (except for a space). Sometimes you will find headings that begin with a bang sign (!) so that they will still be at the start of the output even if the output is sorted.

The order in which characters are sorted is called a *collation sequence*. Although ASCII is the normal sort order in the United States, other countries sometimes have special keyboards and special alphabets. Therefore, you may encounter a different collation sequence.

SEE ALSO

➤ *For more information on man pages, see page 90*

Ignoring Leading Blanks When Sorting (*sort -b*)

If lines begin with the same character, their order will be determined by the first character in the lines that is different. For example, long lines that start with many spaces will sort before long lines that start with fewer or no spaces, since a space sorts before any nonspace character based on the ASCII chart. For example:

```
$ sort tstfile
    zebra
  monkey
 apple
$
```

To ignore leading spaces in the line when sorting, use the -b option, as shown here:

```
$ sort -b tstfile
 apple
  monkey
    zebra
$
```

Sorting Numbers by Magnitude (*sort -n*)

This left-to-right principle also applies to lines that start with numbers. For example:

```
$ sort numfile
10 oranges
5 apples
66 grapes
$
```

The preceding lines are in sorted order because 1 comes before 5, which comes before 6. To sort lines based on the magnitude of numbers at the start of the lines, use the -n option, as shown in the following:

```
$ sort -n numfile
5 apples
10 oranges
66 grapes
$
```

The sort -n option handles negative numbers and decimal fractions as well. For example:

```
$ sort -n numfile3
-30 bananas
-2 pineapples
5.44 apples
5.5 apples
10 oranges
66 grapes
$
```

In the next example, the numbers are right-justified, which means the numbers may start in different columns, but they all end in the same column position.

```
$ cat numfile?
     5 pencils
  2032 crayons
   153 erasers
$
```

In the preceding case, and whenever you have lines that start with right-justified numbers, the -n is not needed because a regular sort will arrange them by magnitude, as follows:

```
$ sort numfile2
         5 pencils
       153 erasers
      2032 crayons
$
```

When the -n option is used, it ignores all leading blanks in the line as if a -b option had also been given. If any lines do not start with a number, -n will regard those lines as having a zero value and will sort them before lines that do start with a number.

Saving the Result Back in the Original File

sort outputs the sorted lines to standard output. This means that the output will go to your screen and the original file will not be affected. To save the results in a file, you can redirect standard output to a different file, as shown here:

```
sort file1 > file2
```

In the preceding command, the sorted output will be put into file2 and will not be displayed on your screen.

If you want to modify a file so that all its lines are in sorted order, use a temporary file, as follows:

```
sort acme > tmpfile$$
mv tmpfile$$ acme
```

In the first line, I save the sorted output in a temporary file called tmpfile$$. $$ is a special shell variable that gives me my current process number. I add $$ to the tmpfile name to make it unique—that is, to avoid the chance that some other user might use the name tmpfile just at the same moment I am using that filename. The second line uses mv to remove my old unsorted acme file and replace it with the sorted acme file.

Note that you must not use the same file as both an input file and an output file in a pipeline. For example:

```
sort acme > acme    # this is wrong
```

The preceding command fails because the shell will first set up the redirection to go to an empty acme file. Then the shell will start the sort process that will find that acme is empty and therefore will produce an empty output file. The contents of acme are now lost and irrecoverable.

Folding Lower/Uppercase Together (*sort -f*)

In the ASCII sequence, all lines beginning with any capital letters will sort before any lines beginning with lowercase letters. To sort ignoring upper- or lowercase, add the -f option to sort. This is called folding the upper- and lowercase letters together. For example:

```
$ sort tstfile
APPLE
Orange
banana
grape
$ sort -f tstfile
APPLE
banana
grape
Orange
$
```

Ignoring the sort -o option

The **sort** command actually has a -o option that enables you to save the sorted results on top of the original file using only one command. Other UNIX commands do not have this option, so I have shown you a method to save the sort results that also applies to any UNIX commands that write to standard output.

Sorting in Reverse Order (*sort -r*)

To sort the lines in reverse order, add the -r option to sort. This can be especially useful with the -n option to sort when you want to see the largest values first. For example, ls -s will list the files in the current directory, preceded by the size of the file in blocks. (You can review the ls command in the appendix.)

```
$ ls -s
total 660
 15 acme
625 pegasus
 20 report7
$
```

When there are a lot of files, it can be difficult to visually pick out the large files. We can pipe the output to sort and let sort arrange the files from largest to smallest.

```
$ ls -s | sort -rn
625 pegasus
 20 report7
 15 acme
total 660
$
```

In this example, notice how we combined the `-r` and `-n` options to sort. Actually the `-n` option to sort was not really needed because the numbers are right-justified. Notice that the total line comes at the end. Because it does not start with a number, `-n` sorts it as a zero value.

In the preceding example, why does 660 in the total line come at the end? Answer: `sort -n` is looking for a number at the start of the line (after any leading spaces). Any line that starts with a nonletter (like the total line) is regarded as having a zero value.

Ignoring Punctuation When Sorting (*sort -d*)

As you have seen, punctuation is scattered throughout the ASCII table and will therefore affect the sort order of lines that begin with punctuation, as in the following:

```
$ sort tstfile3
"orange"
'grape'
<apple>
melon
{banana}
$
```

To ignore punctuation and sort only on letters, digits, spaces, and tabs, use the `-d` option to sort in dictionary order, as shown here:

```
$ sort -d tstfile3
<apple>
{banana}
'grape'
melon
"orange"
$
```

The -d option to sort cannot be combined with the -n option, so there is no way, using only sort options, to sort numbers by magnitude if the lines start with punctuation.

Sorting Based on Fields Within the Line (*sort +n*)

The sort command regards any sequence of spaces or tabs as starting a new field. For example, underneath each column of the last line of the following output of ls -l, I have numbered the field that it is in. Assume we want to sort this output by field 5, which is the size of the files in bytes.

```
$ ls -l
total 3
-rw-r--r--  1 mori      users          17157 Feb   1 11:31 acme
-rw-r--r--  1 janepf    accounting      1972 Feb   1 11:31
➥report04
-rw-r--r--  1 mori      users         196484 Feb   1 11:33
➥report07
1111111111122223333344444444445555555555556666777888888999999
➥99
```

Notice that fields 4 and 5 start in different column positions for each line. To cause sort to ignore or skip some fields in the line, use the +*n* option (where *n* is the number of fields to skip).

```
$ ls -l | sort +4       # this is not what we want
total 3
-rw-r--r--  1 mori      users          17157 Feb   1 11:31 acme
-rw-r--r--  1 mori      users         196484 Feb   1 11:33
➥report07
-rw-r--r--  1 janepf    accounting      1972 Feb   1 11:31
➥report04
$
```

In the preceding example, sort +4 says to skip 4 fields and begin sorting on field 5, which is the size in bytes of the file. However, the fifth field begins with the leading spaces in that field. When you skip the first four fields, here is how the remaining lines look to sort:

```
   17157 Feb   1 11:31 acme
  196484 Feb   1 11:33 report07
1972 Feb   1 11:31 report04
```

Notice that the numbers are not right-justified when you skip the first four fields. Because we want to sort the lines by magnitude and the fifth field is not right justified, we will add the -n option to get the output we want:

```
$ ls -l | sort -n +4
total 3
-rw-r--r--   1 janepf    accounting   1972 Feb   1 11:31
➥report04
-rw-r--r--   1 mori      users        17157 Feb  1 11:31 acme
-rw-r--r--   1 mori      users       196484 Feb  1 11:33
➥report07
$
```

When using the +n option to sort to skip fields, the number of leading spaces in the field can affect the sort order. If the field we want to sort contains numbers, use the -n option to sort by magnitude and ignore the leading spaces in that field. If the field we want to sort contains text, use the -b option to sort to ignore leading spaces in that field. If the field we want to sort contains leading spaces and the text has leading punctuation to ignore, use -bd to ignore both leading spaces and leading punctuation, as shown here:

```
$ sort -bd +3 report8
```

Sorting Based on Primary and Secondary Sort Keys (*sort +m -n*)

Assume that we have a friends file that lists the first name, middle initial, last name, and city for several friends. Notice what happens if we sort by the last name:

```
$ sort +2 friends      # this is not what we want
William A.  Smith, St. Louis
James B. Nguyen, Los Angeles
Henry H. Nguyen, Yuba City
Mary K. Zornan, Cleveland
Mary A. Zornan, Pittsburgh
$
```

Notice that Smith comes first because there happens to be two spaces before Smith in that entry and space-space comes before space-letter, just as aa comes before ab. We can ignore leading spaces by adding the -b option, as shown here:

```
$ sort -b +2 friends    # this is closer to what we want
James B. Nguyen, Los Angeles
Henry H. Nguyen, Yuba City
William A.  Smith, St. Louis
Mary K. Zornan, Cleveland
Mary A. Zornan, Pittsburgh
$
```

Now notice that the two Nguyen entries are in order by city. This is understandable because we are skipping the first two fields and sorting the rest of the line. What if we want to sort first by last name, and if the last names are the same, then by the first name? We call this process using a primary and secondary sort key.

The last name field would be the primary sort key in this example. The first name and middle initial would be the secondary sort key, which is used only if two lines have the same primary sort key. You can even specify more levels of sort keys to use only if all the higher-level sort keys are the same.

You can specify to ignore leading blanks in the primary key but not the secondary. You can specify to sort the primary key field(s) in normal order but, if the primary key field(s) are the same, sort by the secondary key field(s) in reverse order. You can specify to ignore one or more characters of the primary or secondary keys. You can sort the primary key field(s) by magnitude and the secondary key field(s) as text. Here is how you can do all that.

Sorting with primary and secondary sort fields

1. If you are going to pipe to sort, enter the command line that will generate the output to sort. Follow that with the pipe sign (|). Spaces are optional around the pipe sign (|). Do not press the Enter key until instructed.

2. Enter sort.

   Do not press the Enter key until instructed.

3. If you want any sort options to apply globally to the primary, secondary, and all sort keys, enter a space and then enter a dash (-) followed by the desired options from this list:

b to ignore leading blanks
d to ignore leading punctuation (if n isn't specified)
f to fold upper- and lowercase
n to sort numbers by magnitude and ignore leading blanks
r to sort in reverse order

4. Enter a space and then enter +m.

Replace m with the number of fields to skip to get to the first field of the primary sort key.

5. If you want to ignore characters at the start of the primary sort key, enter .n.

Replace n with the number of starting characters to ignore. For example, +3.2 says to skip three fields and then skip two characters, so we would sort on field 4, starting with character 3; that is, sort on field m+1 beginning with character n+1. Because it is rare to sort on part of a field, the .n is usually omitted.

6. You can now enter one of these options to apply to this sort key:

b to ignore leading blanks
d to ignore leading punctuation (if n isn't specified)
f to fold upper- and lowercase
n to sort numbers by magnitude and ignore leading blanks
r to sort in reverse order

For example, +3.2bfr says this sort key is found by skipping three fields, then skipping two characters ignoring leading blanks, folding upper- and lowercase together, and sorting in reverse order for this sort key only.

7. Enter a space and then specify the end of the primary sort key. Use the notation: -m.nOPTS, where

m is the ending field number (not fields to skip)

n is the number of characters to include after the last character of the mth field

OPTS can be b, d, f, n, or r as described in step 6, but in practice only b is useful to define the end of the sort field. Because it is rare to end in the middle of a sort field, .nOPTS is usually omitted. If -m.nOPTS is omitted entirely, the sort key is considered to extend to the end of the line.

8. Because the preceding steps are complicated, let us stop a moment and summarize how to specify the primary sort key in normal situations:

```
sort -GGG +xOPTS -y
```

where

GGG can be sort options b, d, f, n, or r and will apply globally to the primary, secondary, and all sort keys

+x says how many fields to skip to get to the primary sort key

OPTS can be sort options b, d, f, n, or r and will apply only to primary sort key

-y says which field ends the primary sort key

For example:

```
sort -f +2b -4
```

In the preceding example, -f to fold upper- and lowercase applies to all sort keys. The start of the primary key is found by skipping two fields and ignoring leading blanks. The primary sort key ends in field 4. Therefore, fields 3 and 4 make up the primary sort key in this example.

9. Enter a space and then enter the secondary sort key in the same way you specified the primary key. For example:

```
+sort -GGG +m.nOPTS -m.nOPTS +m.nOPTS -m.nOPTS
            ppppppppppppppppppp ssssssssssssssssss
```

In the preceding format, the repeated letter p indicates where the start and end of the primary sort key are specified. The repeated letter s indicates where the start and end of the secondary sort key are specified.

Removing the less commonly used options, here is the simplified format for primary and secondary sort keys:

```
sort -GGG +xOPTS -y +xOPTS -y
            ppppppppp sssssssss
```

10. More sort keys can be added by adding more start and end specifications to your sort command. For example:

```
sort -GGG +xOPTS -y +xOPTS -y +xOPTS -y +xOPTS -y
           ppppppppp ssssssss 333333333 444444444
```

Remember that secondary sort keys are not used unless two lines have the same primary sort key contents. Tertiary, or third order, sort keys are not used unless two lines have the same primary and secondary sort key contents.

11. If you are piping to this sort command and you have entered all the sort field specifications, press the Enter key to complete your command. Otherwise, you may now enter a space and a list of one or more filenames to sort. If you list more than one filename, separate each name with a space. The list can include Filename Generation Wildcard patterns. Then press the Enter key to complete your command.

Now we can complete the example started earlier and sort the friends file by last name. If the last names are the same, sort by first name and middle initial. If that is the same, sort by city to the end of the line. Here is the sort command that accomplishes all of that:

```
$ sort -b +2 -3 +0 -2 +3 friends
Henry H. Nguyen, Yuba City
James B. Nguyen, Los Angeles
William A.  Smith, St. Louis
Mary A. Zornan, Pittsburgh
Mary K. Zornan, Cleveland
$
```

Sometimes you will encounter a -k option to sort, which allows specifying the sort keys using a newer method. Most UNIX systems today support both the newer method and the older method. We covered the older method earlier because it is supported on older and newer UNIX systems. Here is the equivalent command for the friends file, using the newer -k method:

```
sort -b -k 3,3 -k 1,2 -k 4 friends
```

Use -k to specify each sort key using this general, simplified format:

```
-k aOPTS,b
```

where

a is the starting field (not the fields to skip) for this sort key

OPTS can be b, d, f, n, or r and will apply only to this key

b is the ending field for this key

Displaying the Starting Lines of a File or Pipeline (*head, sed*)

To display just the first lines of a file, use the head command, as shown here:

```
head groceries friends
```

head does accept a list of files on the command line. When more than one file is given, head will identify the start of each one with a small banner, as follows:

```
==> groceries <==
5 apples
3 grapes
2 melons

==> friends <==
James B. Nguyen, Los Angeles
Henry H. Nguyen, Yuba City
William A.  Smith, St. Louis
Mary K. Zornan, Cleveland
Mary A. Zornan, Pittsburgh
```

head normally displays a maximum of 10 lines of output. This can be useful when you want to see some of the lines of several files. To display more or fewer lines, use the -n option to head, as follows:

```
ls -lt | head -20
```

In the preceding example, the -20 option causes the head to display a maximum of 20 lines. Also in the preceding example, you can see that if no files are specified as arguments on the command line, head will read from standard input, so you can use it in a pipeline. In the this example, ls -lt displays the files in order of most recently modified, so the entire pipeline shows the 20 files most recently modified.

If the head command is not available on your system, you can use the sed command in this way:

```
sed nq filename
```

Replace n with the number of beginning lines to display, as shown here:

```
ls -lt | sed 5q
```

This example displays only the first five lines. The preceding example also illustrates that seq will read from standard input if no files are specified on the command line, so it can also be used in pipelines. If multiple files are given on the command line, sed nq will display the first *n* lines of those files, but it will not identify the filenames as head does.

SEE ALSO

➤ *For more information on the* sed *command, see page 417*

Displaying the Ending Lines of a File or Pipeline (*tail*)

To display just the ending lines of a file, use the tail command, as shown here:

```
tail filename
```

The tail command usually only accepts one filename on the command line. tail normally displays just the last 10 lines of the file. To specify how many of the last lines to display, use the -n option to tail, as follows:

```
ls -lt | tail -20
```

This example displays only the last 20 lines from the ls command. (You can review options to the ls command in the appendix.) The preceding example also illustrates that tail will read from standard input if no filename is given and therefore can be used in pipelines.

To display the end of the file by starting at line n of the file, use tail with the +n option. For example:

```
tail +350 filename
```

The preceding example will start at line 350 of the file and display all lines until the end of the file.

To watch lines being added to a file, such as a log file, enter this:

```
tail -f filename
```

tail will first display the last 10 lines of the file. The command will not stop there. It will continue to follow the file, and as new lines are added to the end of the file, tail will display them on your screen. This will continue until you press the INTR key, which is usually Ctrl+C or Delete.

Warning: tail output is limited

On many versions of UNIX, tail -n is limited to a maximum of several hundred or several thousand lines. tail will accept larger values of −n, but it won't display that many lines.

Encrypting a File or Pipeline (*crypt*)

If you have confidential text information or data, you can use the crypt command to encrypt or scramble the information so that only someone who knows the proper password or key can decrypt—that is, unscramble the information and use it. Be aware that encryption has come a long way since the crypt command, and today there are reportedly several programs that can break this security. For better encryption, look into pgp or des, available from some UNIX vendors, technical bookstores, and via the Internet.

How to encrypt a file using *crypt*

1. Make sure you know the full pathname of the file that you want to encrypt. That file can either be a text file or a data file.

2. **cd** to the directory that contains the file to encrypt.

3. Enter crypt < EXISTING-FILE > tmpfile$$.

   Replace EXISTING-FILE with the basename of the file to encrypt. tmpfile$$ is a temporary file we will use in this procedure. Enter that name exactly as shown, but be aware that the shell will replace $$ with some digits to make the name unique so that we will not have a conflict if other users are doing this same procedure at the same time in the same directory.

4. After you enter the command in step 3, you will see this prompt:

```
Enter key:
```

Enter one or more characters or words to be the encryption key. What you type in will not echo to the screen as a security measure, so enter your key slowly and carefully.

Warning: You will need to know the exact spelling of this key to decrypt and use your file later. There is no back door around this key, so if you can't remember this key, you can't decrypt your file.

5. After you enter the key in step 4, tmpfile$$ will hold the encrypted information.

6. Test tmpfile$$ by entering this command:

```
crypt < tmpfile$$ > tmp2$$
```

Again you will see this prompt:

```
Enter key:
```

Enter the same key used to encrypt this file. Note that the same key is used to encrypt and decrypt the information.

7. Enter cmp EXISTING-FILE tmp2$$.

Replace EXISTING-FILE with the original filename we want to encrypt. This cmp command should just return to the shell prompt with no other output, indicating that the two files are the same. If not, something went wrong.

Do not proceed with this procedure. Perhaps you entered the key incorrectly. Try going back to step 6 again. If step 7 still shows the files are not the same, delete the temporary files, as follows:

```
rm tmpfile$$ tmp2$$
```

and go back to step 1 of this procedure.

8. Enter `mv tmpfile$$ EXISTING-FILE`.

Replace `EXISTING-FILE` with the original filename we want to encrypt. This will replace the original file with the encrypted version.

9. Enter `rm tmp2$$`.

This removes the other temporary file that we don't need anymore.

To decrypt the file, enter the following:

```
crypt < ENCRYPTED-FILE > DECRYPTED-FILE
```

Replace `ENCRYPTED-FILE` with the filename to decrypt. Replace `DECRYPTED-FILE` with any new name that you want to create. Make sure that that name does not already exist, because that name will be overwritten by this command. `crypt` will output this prompt message:

```
Enter key:
```

Enter the same key used to encrypt the file.

You can also supply the key on the command line. For example:

```
crypt "Mary had a little lamb" < file1 > file2
```

This can be useful when you want to use `crypt` within a shell script and you don't want to be prompted to enter the key from the keyboard. Be aware, however, that anyone who reads the shell script will see what the key is; that is, this is not very good security.

Compressing Files (*compress, gzip*)

Compressing a file means to encode its contents so that it becomes smaller in size and yet can be restored to its original size and contents later when desired. How small you can make the file depends on the data within the file. Text files with many repeated characters can be compressed to a much smaller size than binary files with random data.

Encryption software is often not included

You don't always get encryption software because the United States government has rules that prevent the export of this type of security technology to outside countries. If encryption is not on your commercial UNIX system, you may find that it is available for domestic use. Ask your UNIX vendor.

Files are usually compressed for two reasons:

- **They take up less disk space.** For example, you might compress a group of archive files that are rarely used but must be kept accessible.

- **They can be transferred to another system in a shorter amount of time.** This can be an important factor if you are downloading the file by a slow modem.

Under UNIX, you can use two commands to compress a file:

```
compress
gzip
```

compress is available on most UNIX systems. gzip usually performs better compression—that is, makes the compressed file smaller than the compress command. However, gzip is often not part of the standard UNIX distribution.

To compress a file with the compress command, enter the following:

```
compress FILENAME
```

Replace FILENAME with the file to be compressed. compress creates a compressed file with the same name ending in .Z and removes the original file. On SCO UNIX OpenServer5 only, there is a -H option to compress that causes it to use a better compression method and produce smaller files that can still be uncompressed using the standard uncompress. Solaris 2.6 does not offer this option for compress.

To compress a file using gzip, enter the following:

```
gzip FILENAME
```

Replace FILENAME with the file to be compressed. gzip creates a compressed file with the same name ending in .gz and removes the original file.

To get the best compression in gzip, add the -9 option, as shown here:

```
gzip -9 FILENAME
```

Nine options, from -1 to -9 are available. Use -1 when your main concern is to finish the compression quickly even if the file is not as small as possible. Use `-9` when your main concern is to make the result as small as possible, which will take more time to complete. Use any number in between as a trade-off between speed versus smallness. `-6` is the default if no value is given.

How to uncompress a file

1. Enter uncompress.

If the file to uncompress ends in `.Z`, enter gunzip.

If the file to uncompress ends in `.gz`, do not press the Enter key until instructed.

2. Enter a space and then enter the name of the file to uncompress, which must end in either `.Z` or `.gz`.

3. Press the Enter key to execute this command. The file will be uncompressed and the `.Z` or `.gz` ending will be removed from the filename.

Encoding Files as Transmittable Simple Text (*uuencode*)

To send information in the body of an email, it is necessary that the information be simple, printable text characters. When you use the UNIX `mailx` command from the command line, you cannot include attachments, so any binary files to be sent must be converted or encoded into a string of simple text characters. We call this process *uuencoding*, where *uu* is a standard UNIX prefix used for utilities that involve UNIX-to-UNIX transfers.

uuencoding is also useful if you are dialed in to another UNIX system using `cu` and you want to download or upload a binary file. The ~%put and ~%take commands in `cu` can only download or upload text files. Binary files can first be uuencoded into text files. These files can be transferred and then uudecoded back to their original binary form.

To uuencode a file, at the shell prompt, enter the following:

```
uuencode BINFILE DESTFILE > TEXTFILE
```

`gzip` is often downloadable

`gzip` is usually not supplied with commercial UNIX systems, but is often available through the Internet from Web sites that specialize in shareware or non-supported free utilities for the UNIX platform you are running (www.`sun`.`com`, www.`ibm`.`com`, or www.`sco`.`com`, for example) Look for downloadable operating system software.

Replace BINFILE with the binary file to encode. Replace DESTFILE with the desired filename to create on the destination system. Replace TEXTFILE with the filename to create on your system with the uuencoded text information.

To uuencode the output of another UNIX command or pipeline, enter this:

```
CMD | uuencode DESTFILE > TEXTFILE
```

Replace CMD with the desired UNIX command or pipeline to generate the output to be uuencoded.

After the TEXTFILE has been transmitted to the other UNIX system, you can restore it to its original form by entering the following:

```
uudecode TEXTFILE
```

The preceding command creates the binary file and gives it the name DESTFILE, which was specified when uuencode was run.

To determine that DESTFILE will be created before you run uudecode, enter this:

```
head TEXTFILE
```

You should see output like this:

```
begin 660 /usr/fred/acme
M?T5,1@$! 0                ( P !   <)T$"#"#        !0I@        #0 (   &
M "@ $@ 0  8    T    -( $"   #       P    4         P    /0
M               !,        !      !    -      #2 ! @      9'X
M &1^     %    "   "  "8  F #       #@)@  5$8  <      $
```

In the first line, you can see that when this file is uudecoded, it will create a file called /usr/fred/acme. You can edit the name in this file if you want to change the destination file created by uudecode. This is especially true if sending uuencoded files between UNIX and Windows. Notice that the rest of the lines begin with the letter M. A begin line followed by many M lines usually indicates a uuencoded file.

If you receive email with a uuencoded file in the middle, you can save this email and uudecode it without stripping off the mail lines that come before or after the uuencoded lines.

SEE ALSO

➤ *For more information on using* cu, *see page 252*

Combining Files

This section looks at several commands that can combine file contents together for various purposes.

Sorting Multiple Files Together (*sort*)

We looked at sort at the beginning of this chapter. If sort is called with a list of files on the command line, sort will first merge their contents and then display the combined contents in sorted order, as shown here:

```
sort file1 file2 file3 > bigsort
```

Concatenating Files One After the Other (*cat*)

To combine files one after the other, use the cat command:

```
cat file1 file2 file3 > bigfile
```

The cat command gets its name from concatenation.

Pasting Files Together Side by Side (*paste*)

The cat command combines files one after the other. The paste command combines files side by side. Line 1 of the paste output contains line 1 of file1, then a tab, then line 1 of file2, then a tab, then line 1 of file3, and so on. Similarly, line 2 contains line 2 from each of the files. To paste files together in this way, enter the following:

```
paste file1 file2 file3 ...
```

If the colors file contains one color per line and the fruits file contains one fruit per line, pasting them together would produce output like this:

```
$ paste colors fruits
```

uuencode/uudecode under Windows email

Some email programs under Windows support uuencode/uudecode. This is useful if you want to email a binary file from Windows to UNIX. Click on uuencode to insert a text version of the binary file directly into your email. It is not an attachment! If you receive uuencoded data in email on Windows, click uudecode to save the data in a file. You may have to adjust the destination filename in the uuencoded text.

```
red      grape
green    apple
blue     banana
yellow   melon
$
```

Merging Sorted Files Based on a Join Field (*join*)

The join command enables you to merge data from a line in one file with data from a corresponding line in a second file. The corresponding line is determined by finding a line with a matching *join* field. Both files must be in sorted order. You can designate which field is the join field and that field number can be different between the two files. You can designate what data will be extracted from each file. Here is an example.

A friend of mine was studying the stock market. He joined a service that would send him the average stock prices each day in a file. He wanted to put these small files together into one large history file that would show him at a glance if a particular stock value was rising or falling over time. Here is an example file for day1. It just has three made-up stocks:

```
ABC      2 1/8
DEF     24 5/8
GHI      6 3/8
```

Here is the file for day2:

```
ABC      2 3/8
BCD     12 2/8
DEF     22 7/8
GHI      6 5/8
```

Here is the file for day3:

```
ABC      2 5/8
BCD     14 3/8
DEF     22 5/8
```

You can see that in day2 we gained a new stock, BCD. In day3, we lost stock GHI. Line 3 of each file is not always the same stock; therefore, we cannot use the paste command to combine these files. This is a job for the UNIX join command. In this example, we use the stock name as the join field.

```
$ join -t'    ' -a1 -a2 day1 day2
ABC     2 1/8     2 3/8
BCD    12 2/8
DEF    24 5/8    22 7/8
GHI     6 3/8     6 5/8
$
```

In the preceding example, `-t` enables us to specify the field separator. In this case, a tab separates the stock name from its average value in each file. Therefore, a tab has been indicated after the `-t` option to `join`. `-a1` and `-a2` mean include all lines from file 1 and from file 2. Otherwise, only lines whose join field value appears in both files will be listed. In this example, stock BCD is only listed in file 2, so it would not have been included in the `join` output if `-a2` was not specified.

```
$ join -t'    ' -a1 -a2 day1 day2 | join -t'    ' -a1 -a2 -
➡day3
ABC     2 1/8     2 3/8     2 5/8
BCD    12 2/8    14 3/8
DEF    24 5/8    22 7/8    22 5/8
GHI     6 3/8     6 5/8
$
```

In the preceding example, the joined output of day1 and day2 was joined to day3. Notice how the output of one `join` command can be piped to another `join` command if that `join` command lists dash (`-`) as one of its filenames to indicate standard input.

To handle cases where the join field is not the first field on each line, add the `-j` option to `join`. Follow `-j` with the field number of the join field in each file. For example:

```
join -j 3 file1 file2
```

To handle files where the join field is not the same field number between the two files, use `-j` followed by n m, where n is 1 or 2 for files 1 or 2, and m is the field within that file to use as the join field, as shown here:

```
join -j1 2 -j2 4 file1 file2
```

In this example, the join field is field 2 in file 1, but it is field 4 in file 2.

To display only certain fields for each line of output from join, use the -o option followed by a space separated list of n.m entries, where n is 1 or 2 for file1 or file2 and .m specifies the mth field in that file, as follows:

```
join -j1 2 -j2 4 -o 1.1 2.3 2.5 file1 file2
```

The preceding example will display only three fields per line of output as controlled by the -o option:

```
1.1 means display field 1 in file1 first.
2.3 means display field 3 in file2 next.
means display field 5 in file2 next (and last).
```

How useful is join**?**

Some UNIX books imply that you can implement a whole relational database with join. Other UNIX books don't mention join at all. I find join is useful in some cases for merging data from different files. Because join is very limited, however, I would use awk or perl to query and write reports from my data files.

Splitting a File into Multiple Smaller Files

Sometimes it is useful to be able to split a file into smaller files. If a file will not fit on a disk, for example, you could split the file into smaller files that would each fit on a disk. Another example, when using cu to dial into another UNIX system, you can put and take text files between systems. Because there is no error checking, noisy phone lines can result in the destination file being corrupted. In this situation, I have had good success by splitting the file into several smaller files and then transmitting them separately. Using the cat command, it is simple to reconstitute the original file by concatenating the smaller files.

Splitting a File into Equal-Length Pieces (*split*)

How to split a file into equal-length segments

1. At the shell prompt, enter split.

   Do not press the Enter key until instructed.

2. Enter a space, and then enter -LINES.

   Replace LINES with the number of lines to put into each file segment; for example, -400 says to create smaller files, each 400 lines long. If this step is omitted, each segment will be created with 1,000 lines.

3. Enter a space, and then enter the existing file to be split. If the file is in the current directory, enter just its basename

(see the glossary). If the file is not in the current directory, enter its absolute or relative pathname. This file will not be affected by this command.

4. Enter a space, and then enter the segment prefix. The first segment will begin with the segment prefix followed by aa. The second one will be followed by ab, then ac, and so on. If the given prefix is small, for example, the existing file will be split into segments named smallaa, smallab, smallac, smallad, and so forth. If this step is omitted, the segment prefix will be x (that is, xaa, xab, xac, and so on).

5. Press the Enter key to execute this command.

To re-create the original file from the segments, you can use a Filename Generation Wildcard. For example:

```
cat small* > bigfile
```

small* will match smallaa, smallab, smallac, and so on. If other files begin with the prefix but are not segments of the large file, you can use a more specific wildcard pattern to avoid them. For example:

```
cat smalla[a-f] > bigfile
```

Splitting a File by Section Headings (*csplit*)

The csplit command enables you to split a file into segments based on the context within the file.

Splitting a file by repeated section keyword

1. Determine a keyword that appears in each section heading. For example, if each key section heading began with the word *Chapter*, *Chapter* would be the keyword. If there is no single keyword that appears in each section title, you cannot use this procedure.

2. At the shell prompt, enter csplit -k.

Do not press the Enter key until instructed.

3. Enter a space, and then enter the name of the existing file to be split.

4. Enter a space, and then enter a single quotation mark (`'`) and then a slash (`/`).

5. Enter the section keyword.

6. Enter a slash, and then enter a single quotation mark (`/'`).

7. Enter a space, and then enter `'{99}'`.

Press the Enter key to execute this command.

8. Ignore the error message:

`{99} - out of range`

We told it to create 99 segments if necessary, but usually there will be fewer than that.

9. This command creates files named `xx00`, `xx01`, `xx02`, and so on. Each segment will contain all lines up to but not including the line containing a keyword (as mentioned in step 1). If *Chapter* was the keyword, `xx00` would contain all lines up to the start of `Chapter 1`; `xx01` would contain all lines of `Chapter 1` up to but not including `Chapter 2`, and so forth.

Splitting a file based on unique keywords

1. Use this procedure when you can identify a unique word that starts each section.

2. At the shell prompt, enter `csplit`.

Do not press the Enter key until instructed.

3. Enter a space, and then enter the name of the existing file to be split.

4. Enter a space and then enter, within slashes (`/`), the keyword that ends the first segment. The line containing this keyword will start the second segment.

5. Enter a space and then enter, within slashes (`/`), the keyword that ends the second segment. The line containing this keyword will start the third segment.

6. Continue entering keywords within slashes (`/`) until all segments are defined. Press the Enter key to execute your command.

7. This command will create files named xx00, xx01, xx02, and
so on.

This is an example of the preceding procedure:

```
csplit existing-file '/INSTRUCTIONS/' '/WARNINGS/' '/APPENDIX
➥1/'
```

Four smaller segment files will be created with the preceding:
xx00, xx01, xx02, and xx03. xx00 will contain all lines up to but
not including a line that contains INSTRUCTIONS. xx01 will start
with the INSTRUCTIONS line and continue until it finds the word
WARNINGS. xx02 will start with the line that contains the word
WARNINGS. xx03 will start with a line that contains the phrase
'APPENDIX 1' and will contain all the rest of the lines of the file.

Generating and Using File Lists

By Steve "Mor" Moritsugu

Creating file lists by using filename generation wildcards (*, ?, [...])

Checking which commands allow file lists

Handling the filename wildcard error *arg list too long*

Creating file lists by using backquotes (`)

Handling the backquotes error *No Space*

Using *xargs* to process really long lists of files

Using Filename Generation Wildcards

Most of the file commands can work with one or more files. File commands can work, for example, with the following:

- Single files
- Several files
- Hundreds of files
- Tens of thousands of files (This is, of course, more difficult.)

As always, UNIX can increase productivity. In this case, UNIX increases productivity by providing a way to enter a very long series of filenames to a command by using a very short sequence of keystrokes. The user can enter within any command one or more pattern words, and the shell will replace each pattern with a list of all filenames that match that pattern. A pattern word is any word that contains one of the wildcard characters shown in Table 9.1.

TABLE 9.1   **Filename Generation Wildcard characters**

Character	Description
*	Matches zero or more of any characters
?	Matches any one character
[. . .]	Matches any one of the alternatives enclosed in brackets
[! . . .]	Matches any one char except those listed

Generating Names That Start with, End with, or Contain a Pattern (*)

We will start with the asterisk (*) wildcard because it is both the most powerful and easiest to understand of the wildcards and hence the most commonly used one. Here is an example:

```
rm report*
```

rm is the UNIX command to remove (that is, delete) one or more files. report* is a pattern word because it contains one of the three possible wildcard characters given in Table 9.1. Before the command begins to execute, the shell will recompose the command, replacing the pattern word with a list of all existing filenames that match the pattern.

From Table 9.1, you can see that asterisk (*) matches zero or more of any characters. Therefore, report* is a pattern that matches all existing filenames that begin with report and are followed by zero or more of any characters.

TABLE 9.2   **Using *rm report***

Files that would be removed by *rm report*

Report	report2	reports	1reporters
Reportacme	report.acme	report-98.01.15	

Files that would not be removed by *rm report*

Filename	Reason Pattern Does Not Apply
Report	Uppercase *R* does not match the pattern
98report	Filename does not start with the word *report*
reprot.acme	Report is misspelled in this name

Deleting all files that start with a pattern

1. Enter rm.

Do not press the Enter key until instructed. We are using rm as an example command, but the procedure will work with any commands that operate on a list of files (as rm does).

2. Enter a space and then the pattern. This pattern will define a prefix that we want to look for. Any files beginning with this prefix (that is, pattern) will be removed.

3. Enter asterisk (*), and then press the Enter key to complete the command.

4. The shell will accept your command and recompose it, replacing the wildcard pattern with a list of all existing files that match the pattern. We can call this step preprocessing. The shell will then execute the rm command, which will remove the list of files provided by the shell just as if you had typed them on the command line.

We can modify the preceding procedure slightly to remove all files that end with a pattern or that contain a pattern. To use the asterisk wildcard as shown in the following table, you should learn three useful phrases. The wording of the phrase tells you whether the asterisk (*) should come before, after, or on both sides of the pattern.

TABLE 9.3   **Asterisk (*) filename wildcard useful phrases**

Useful Phrase	Example	Description
"Start with …"	rm acme*	Removes all filenames that start with the word *acme*
"End with …"	rm *acme	Removes all filenames that end with the word *acme*
"Contain …"	rm *acme*	Removes all filenames that contain the word *acme*

Where does the term *wildcard* come from?

In some card games, such as poker, the Joker is a wildcard that you can use as if it were some other card in the deck that you need. The asterisk (*) ia an extremely powerful wildcard because it can stand for zero or more of any card (oops–I mean character). I wish I had an asterisk (*) wildcard the next time I play poker.

Checking Man Pages to See Whether File Lists and Wildcards Are Allowed

The shell will preprocess and expand all filename wildcard patterns into a list of matching files; however, not all commands can accept a list of files. For example,

```
pwd report*
```

does not make any sense because pwd just displays your current directory and does not expect any following arguments on the command line. Similarly,

```
cd report*
```

does not make any sense if several directories all start with the word *report* because you can only change to one directory at a time.

The UNIX man command (online manual) gives us extensive information on how to use each UNIX command, including syntax (that is, how to correctly put together the elements of the command). Here is the syntax for several commands to illustrate how file lists are documented in the man pages.

TABLE 9.4   **How man pages indicate file lists**

Command Syntax from Man	My Description (Not in Man Page)
head [-count] [file ...]	Displays the beginning lines of a list of files.
sort [-cmu] ... [files]	Sorts the contents of a list of files.
tail [+/-[number][lbc] [-f]] [file]	Displays the ending lines of the given single file.
tr [-cds] [string1 [string2]]	Translates characters from std input to std output.
cp file1 file2	Copies file1 to file2.
cp files directory	Copies list of files to a directory.

In the preceding table, ignore the command options such as -count or -cmu and focus for now on how filenames are specified to these commands. Notice the head and sort commands both allow a list of files to be specified; but one case uses "file ..." and the other case uses "files" to indicate that one or more files are allowed. The tail command shown only allows a single file. The tr command does not allow any filenames at all. The cp command has two modes. The first mode copies a single file to another name. The second mode shown copies a list of files to a directory. Commands can vary in this regard from one type of UNIX system to another. Therefore, check the man pages for the system you are on to see whether a particular command allows a file list, a single file, or no files at all.

SEE ALSO

➤ *For more information on man pages, see page 89*

The appendix to this book contains a capsule summary of how to use each command and where information about aspects of that command are described in the book. From the appendix, here are the first two lines of the sdiff and sort commands. Notice that sdiff does not allow a list of files, and hence we would not use wildcard patterns in an sdiff command. Notice that sort does allow a list of files which we could compose by using one or more wildcard patterns. The brackets ([...]) under sort usage tell us that the list of files is optional, meaning zero or more filenames may be supplied.

Redirection does not allow filename wildcards

The shell will not do wildcard expansion on any filename used for redirection (that is, after a >, >>, or < sign). Don't redirect output to a filename containing an asterisk, which could normally be a shortcut to a longer existing name. You will create a name containing an asterisk, even if the longer name exists.

`sdiff` - Show text file differences side by side

usage: `sdiff file1 file2`

`sort` - Sort file or datastream

usage: `sort options [list-of-files]`

Reducing Typing of Long Filenames

UNIX avoids using the word *wildcard*

Standard UNIX documentation often goes to great lengths to avoid the word *wildcard*. The documentation calls them things such as filename generation pattern characters, normal shell argument syntax, or shell pattern metacharacters. I think the term *wildcard* is apt and easier to grasp, so I use it in this book.

The asterisk (*) wildcards can be useful when you encounter very long filenames. Older versions of UNIX were often limited to 14 character filenames, but current versions of UNIX often allow filenames to be hundreds of characters long. Assume, for example, that the current directory contains these five files:

inventory-after-special-order

pricelist

reports-in-old-format

sales-Jan-1997-to-Dec-1997-adjusted-for-new-commission-structure

security.memo

If I want to remove the sales file, the asterisk (*) wildcard can save me a lot of typing, as in the following:

`rm sales*`

However, I cannot shorten the command to this:

`rm s*`

This would remove more than just the `sales` file.

Using the asterisk (*) as a shortcut

1. Find a distinctive pattern in the filename you want to access that does not exist in any other filename. The distinctive pattern can either come at the start of the filename, the end, or somewhere in the middle.

2. Enter your desired UNIX command followed by the appropriate asterisk (*) wildcard pattern to select the desired file without selecting any of the other files.

Ignore Directories in Your File List

File lists, generated by the asterisk (*) wildcard (and the other wildcards discussed in this chapter), can include regular files (see glossary), directories, device node files, and so on. All filenames that match the pattern are included in the list, regardless of the type of file. If the command cannot process that type of file, it will report an error for that file and continue processing the list.

```
$ rm abc*
rm: abcrdr: is a directory
rm: abc25: is a directory
$
```

In the preceding example, the asterisk-generated list included two directory names. rm did delete all the regular files whose filenames matched the pattern given. rm also output error messages for the two directories, indicating that it did not process them. In general, I just ignore these directory errors because I usually use wildcard patterns to process a list of text or data files. It is nice that the error messages appear, telling me what was not processed in case I want to take further action on them.

Making One File List from Multiple Patterns

One file list can be generated by more than one wildcard pattern, as shown here:

```
rm acme* report*
```

In this example, two wildcard patterns are separated by a space, making up one list of files to be removed. Any filenames that start with the word *acme* and any filenames that start with the word *report* will be in the one list to be removed.

Be aware that multiple lists may generate the same filename more than once. For example:

```
lp acme* *.c
```

In the preceding example, we are using the lp command (see appendix) to print on the system printer. We are giving it a list of files made by two wildcard patterns: all files that start with acme and all files that end in .c. Note that any files that both start with acme and end in .c will be in the lp file list twice, and hence will be printed twice. Later in this chapter, you learn how backquotes (`) can resolve this problem.

Later in this chapter, as we encounter backquotes (`) and other wildcards—such as question mark (?) and brackets ([...])—keep in mind that one file list can be made up by combining smaller lists generated by any of these techniques.

SEE ALSO

➤ *For more information on the* lp *command, see page 169*

Including Hidden Files in File Lists

Filenames that begin with a period are called "hidden" files because the ls command normally hides them (that is, ignores them) unless you add the -a option to ls to show all files. Hidden files are usually system files and are hidden so that they will not be displayed or affected when the user lists or processes data and application files.

Wildcards also follow this convention by ignoring hidden files unless they are specifically indicated in the wildcard pattern. For example:

```
rm *-sav
```

The preceding command would remove any nonhidden files that end in -sav. However, .acme-sav ends in -sav but would not be removed because a leading asterisk (*) cannot match a leading period in the filename.

To remove all hidden files that end in -sav, use this command:

```
rm .*-sav
```

This command removes only files that start with a period (.) and end in -sav. To remove both hidden and nonhidden files that end in -sav, use this command:

```
rm    *-sav    .*-sav
```

This command uses two wildcard patterns to create one list of files to be removed. I have added extra spaces just for clarity.

Generating Lists of Files in Other Directories

You have seen that the asterisk can match zero or more of any character except for a leading period. There is a second exception. The asterisk cannot match a slash (/) directory separator. This is a good rule. Otherwise commands like

rm *-sav

would comb the whole system looking for files ending in -sav to remove. Because asterisk (*) cannot match a slash (/), the list is restricted to just files in the current directory that match the pattern.

We can explicitly generate filenames in directories other than the current directory by using either absolute or relative pathnames. For example:

TABLE 9.5 **Using file lists not necessarily in current directory**

UNIX Command	Description
rm *-sav	Removes any files in the current directory ending in -sav
rm /tmp/*-sav	Removes any files in /tmp ending in -sav
rm /tmp/*/*-sav	Removes any files in any subdirectory of /tmp ending in -sav
rm /*-sav	Removes any files in the root directory ending in -sav
rm */*-sav	Removes any files in any subdirectory of the current directory ending in -sav
rm *-sav */*-sav	Removes any files in the current directory or any subdirectory of the current directory ending in -sav

Later in this chapter, as we encounter other wildcards, such as question mark (?) and brackets ([...]), keep in mind that they can generate file lists in other directories just as the asterisk (*) does.

Allowing Any Characters in Certain Pattern Positions (?)

The question mark (?) wildcard matches any single character except for a leading period (.) or a slash (/). It enables us to specify exactly how many character positions to allow before, after, or in between other pattern elements. For example:

```
rm report-?
```

This command removes any filenames that begin with `report-` and are followed by exactly one character.

TABLE 9.6   *rm report-?*

Files that would be removed by *rm report-?*

report-3

report-7

report-d

report-M

report—

Files that would not be removed by *rm report-?*

Filename	Reason Pattern Does Not Apply
report	No dash (-) after report
report-	No character after dash (-)
report-33	Too many characters after dash (-)
acme.report-4	Does not start with report

As with the asterisk (*), the ? wildcard cannot match a leading period or a slash (/).

Specifying Fixed-Length Filenames

The question mark wildcard is also useful for situations where you want to access all files whose names are an exact number of characters. For example:

```
rm x??
```

The preceding command deletes all three-character filenames that start with the letter *x*.

```
rm report??
```

This command deletes all filenames that start with the word *report* and are followed by any two character suffix.

Specifying Allowed Characters in Pattern Positions ([...])

Square brackets enable you to specify a range of alternatives for that character position within the filename, except for a leading period (.) or a slash (/). Assume, for example, that more than 20 filenames begin with report- followed by a single character, and we want to remove just the following seven files:

```
report-1  report-2  report-3  report-4  report-5  report-m
report-v
```

We can accomplish that by using the bracket wildcard ([. . .]) as in this example:

```
rm report-[1-5mv]
```

The square brackets enable us to specify the character alternatives we want to allow for this position within the filename. A dash (-) between two characters within the brackets allows all characters in that inclusive range. Do not include any spaces or commas within the brackets unless they are character alternatives in the filename itself.

What if report-3 did not exist? There is no problem, and no error message would be generated by the preceding command. These wildcard patterns select from the existing files just those filenames that match the wildcard pattern.

```
rm report-[4m51-3v]
```

The preceding example is equivalent to the previous example. It is not good practice to jumble up your alternatives in this way. It does, however, illustrate that the alternatives can be listed in any order. Ranges using dash (-) must be specified from low to high. For example, specify b-g, not g-b. Notice that 51 in the brackets in the preceding example means that both a 5 and 1 are alternatives for this character position in the filename. This pattern would *not* match report-51 because the square brackets match only a single character from the alternatives, not multiple characters.

TABLE 9.7   *rm report-[1-5mv]*

Files that would be removed by rm report-[1-5mv]

report-1

report-2

report-3

report-4

report-5

report-m

report-v

Files that would not be removed by *rm report-[1-5mv]*

Filename	Reason Pattern Does Not Apply
report	No dash (-) after report.
report-	No character after dash (-).
report-33	Too many characters after dash (-).
report-6	6 is not one of the allowed alternatives.
report-x	x is not one of the allowed alternatives.
acme.report-4	Does not start with the word report.

Asterisk (*) or question mark (?) within square brackets would not be treated as wildcards. It is not a good idea, however, to include asterisks or question marks as characters within file-names; therefore, you will usually never include them within square brackets.

If you want to include a dash (-) as one of the alternatives, include it as the first or last character within the square brackets. For example:

```
rm report-[a-g-]
```

TABLE 9.8   **More examples of *[...]* wildcard**

Wildcard Pattern	Description
report[0-9]	Matches report followed by one digit
report[0-9][0-9]	Matches report followed by two digits

Wildcard Pattern	Description
[A-Z]*	Matches all files which start with a capital letter
report[0-9][a-zA-Z]	Matches report followed by a digit followed by a letter in upper- or lowercase

As with the asterisk, the bracket wildcard cannot match a leading period or a slash.

Specifying Disallowed Characters in Pattern Positions ([!...])

If the list of characters inside the square brackets begins with an exclamation point (!), any one character will match that wildcard except for the characters within the bracket list. For example:

```
rm acme[!2-5x].c
```

The pattern in the preceding example removes any existing files that

begin with acme and ...

then contain one character that is not 2, 3, 4, 5, or x, and ...

then .c follows immediately

> **Don't be confused by the words *at least***
>
> *[a-z][a-z] selects file-names that end in at least two letters. This just means the asterisk could supply more letters just before that last two letters. Creating wildcard patterns that end in at least two letters is the easiest case (as shown). Creating patterns that end in "exactly" or "only" two letters is more difficult.

TABLE 9.9   *rm acme[!2-5x].c*

Files that would be removed by *rm acme[!2-5x].c*

acme1.c

acme6.c

acme9.c

acme-.c

acmea.c

acmeB.c

acmeX.c

continues...

TABLE 9.9   **Continued**

Files that would not be removed by *rm acme[!2-5x].c*

Filename	Reason Pattern Does Not Apply
acme.c	Needs one char after acme and before .c.
acme2.c	2 is specifically dis-allowed.
acme77.c	Only one char allowed between acme and .c.
acmex.c	x is dis-allowed, but X (uppercase) is allowed.
acmeb.m	Does not end in .c.
f-acme9.c	Does not start with acme.

Handling the Error *arg List Too Long*

The shell processes the command line in a buffer that on older UNIX systems was several hundred characters long and on newer UNIX systems is several thousand characters long or longer. If the wildcard pattern generates a file list that overflows the command-line buffer, it would be dangerous to execute this partial command or use a partial filename and so the shell aborts immediately, as in this example:

```
$ rm report*
rm: arg list too long
$
```

The UNIX standard is, "No news is good news." The message from the rm command indicates a problem. In the preceding example, too many filenames begin with report and the shell's command-line buffer has overflowed; therefore, the shell will not allow the command to start. Some users mistakenly think that maybe the rm command has removed some of the files that start with report before it got the error. They keep repeating the same command in hopes that the list will keep getting smaller and smaller until the command eventually succeeds, but it never does.

One workaround for this problem is to divide up the one command into several commands, each specifying a smaller group of files. For example:

```
rm report[a-m]*
rm report[n-z]*
rm report[!a-z]*
rm report
```

The remainder of this chapter discusses other ways of using file lists that do not use filename wildcards, and therefore can be used whenever you get the arg list too long error.

Using Backquotes (`) to Generate a List of Files

In addition to Filename Generation Wildcards, backquotes (`) are another (different) mechanism that we can use for many purposes including generating a list of files for a command to use. The backquote (`) is the "other" single quote and is more correctly called the grave accent.

Use backquotes to take the standard output of a UNIX command or command sequence and use that output as part of another command. This technique is called *command substitution*. If I have a file called flist that contains a list of files that I want to remove, for example, I can remove all of those files as follows:

```
rm `cat flist`
```

In this example, the list of files to remove is generated by the cat command (see appendix) in backquotes. It is essential that the command inside the backquotes output the list of files to standard output as cat does in the example. If the files are not in the current directory, the list should contain a proper relative or absolute pathname for each file, for example, not just a basename.

Using backquotes to generate a file list

1. Enter the UNIX command you are going to use to process the list. (Do not press the Enter key until instructed.) You can use any UNIX command that accepts a list of files such as rm, lp, sort, and so on. (The appendix shows the commands that accept a list of files.)

Finding the backquote (`) key on the keyboard.

It is usually located on the same key as the tilde (~). The backquote (`) slants from upper left down to lower right, but is not as long as a backslash (\). Don't confuse it with the single quotation mark—that is, the apostrophe ('), which slants from upper right down to lower left or sometimes has no slant at all.

2. Enter a space and then a backquote (`` ` ``).

3. Enter the UNIX command sequence that will generate on standard output all the files that you want to process. This sequence may be a series of UNIX commands in a pipeline. If the files are not all in the current directory, this command must generate a proper relative or absolute pathname for each file. Multiple filenames may be separated by a white-space or output on separate lines as the backquotes will convert each newline to a space.

4. Enter a backquote (`` ` ``) and press the Enter key to execute the command.

Backquotes can also solve the printing problem we could not solve by using wildcard patterns. Assume that you want to print all files that either start with acme or end in a .c. Using multiple wildcard patterns—for example, _lp acme* *.c—we saw that any files that started with acme *and* ended in .c would be printed twice. We can now solve that problem by using backquotes:

```
lp `echo acme* *.c ¦ sort ¦ uniq`
```

In the preceding example, the echo command generates a list of files that start with acme or end in .c. This list is then piped to sort so that any duplicates will be put on adjoining lines. That result is then piped to uniq, which ignores any lines identical to a previous line—that is, it removes the duplicate lines. The backquotes then cause that list to become part of the lp command line, and therefore the files will be printed with no duplicates.

Backquotes give us finer control over the file list generated than filename wildcards alone could do. Here is a command to remove all files that start with acme except for those acme files that end in -sav:

```
rm `echo acme* ¦ grep -v '-sav$'`
```

Let me analyze for you the parts of this command.

```
echo acme*
```

generates the list of all files that start with acme.

```
grep -v '-sav$'
```

uses regular expression syntax to display only lines that do not end in `-sav`; hence, `grep` removes any files from our file list that end in `-sav`. The backquotes then provide this generated list to the remove command.

SEE ALSO

➤ *For more information on the* `cat` *command, see page 160*

➤ *For more information on the* `grep` *command and regular expressions, see page 380*

Handling the Backquotes Error *No Space*

If the backquotes generate a file list that is too long, the command can fail with error messages such as the following:

```
sh: no stack space
```

or

```
ksh: no space
```

Newer versions of UNIX seem to be able to process much longer backquotes lists than earlier UNIX versions. If using backquotes gets this `No Space` error, your list is too long. To solve the problem, go to the following section in this chapter on `xargs`.

Using *xargs* to Process a List of Files (*xargs*)

So far in this chapter, we have used filename wildcards to generate file lists on the command line, but that technique can fail if there are too many files that match the pattern. Backquotes can be used to generate file lists from a pipeline of UNIX commands, giving us much more control over the files in the list. However, backquotes can fail if too many filenames are generated, especially on older UNIX systems.

We can use one more technique at the command-line level to process a list of files. It offers the same degree of control over the list that backquotes offer. It has no limitation on the number of files it can process. The method that accomplishes all of this is the `xargs` commands. When you have tens of thousands or millions of files to process, `xargs` can do the job.

Using *xargs* to process a list of files

1. Enter the UNIX command or pipeline that will generate on standard output the list of files that you want to process. (Do not press the Enter key until instructed.) If the files are not in the current directory, the list should contain a proper relative or absolute pathname for each file, for example, not just a basename. This command could be as simple as

    cat flist

where flist is a file that contains the filenames to process.

2. Enter the pipe sign (¦). Spaces before and after the pipe sign are optional.

3. Enter xargs.

4. Enter a space and then the desired command that will process the list of files. Follow that with any options the command requires.

5. Press the Enter key to execute this whole sequence. The command entered in step 1 will generate a list of files. The pipe sign in step 2 will feed those files as the input to xargs. xargs will construct and execute a command that begins with the command entered in step 4 and ends with a file list that is a subset of the total files that xargs is receiving from the pipeline. xargs will invoke the step 4 command a second time with the next group of files. xargs will invoke the step 4 command as many times as it takes to process all the files that it is receiving. There is no danger of the arg list being too long or running out of space, because it never tries to process the whole list at one time.

Here is an example of using xargs:

```
$ cd /usr/fred
$ chmod a+r gl*
chmod:arg list too long
$ ls | grep '^gl' | xargs chmod a+r
```

In this example, we want to add read permission for everyone to all files in directory /usr/fred that start with gl. First we try using a filename generation wildcard (gl*). Because too many files match that pattern, we get the error arg list too long. The xargs command shown accomplishes the same objective and will never get the arg list too long error.

If you get the error arg list too long when using xargs in the preceding procedure, change xargs to the following:

```
xargs -n 20
```

This forces xargs to issue multiple commands where any one command uses a maximum of 20 arguments from standard input. xargs on commercial UNIX systems usually does not need the -n option because xargs will automatically adjust the number of arguments placed on the command line so that no one command ever gets the error arg list too long.

Using *xargs* to solve *arg list too long* error

1. If you get the error arg list too long, you are using two elements in your command:

   a. A UNIX command and possibly options

   b. A list of files generated by filename wildcards

2. Enter a UNIX command that generates the same list using regular expression wildcards. (Do not press the Enter key until instructed.) For example, if you were using this filename wildcard:

   ```
   abc*
   ```

   you could generate the same list using:

   ```
   ls | grep '^abc'
   ```

   (see Table 9.11)

3. Enter the pipe sign (|), and then Enter xargs.

   Spaces are optional around the pipe sign.

4. Enter a space and then the UNIX command and options in step 1.a.

5. Press Enter to execute your command.

TABLE 9.10   **Filename wildcard to regular expression wildcard conversion**

Filename Wildcard	Equivalent Regular Expression Sequence
abc*	ls | grep '^abc'
*abc	ls | grep 'abc$'
abc	ls | grep 'abc'
abc[0-9]	ls | grep '^abc[0-9]$'
[!A-Z]??.c	ls | grep '^[^A-Z]..\.c'

SEE ALSO

➤ *For more information on piping, see page 31*

➤ *For more information on command-line arguments, see page 84*

10

Comparing Files by Date, Size, or Contents

By Steve "Mor" Moritsugu

Comparing, listing, or finding files by date of last modification or last access

Comparing, listing, or finding files by size

Many ways to display differences in text files

Comparing non-text files

Comparing files on different systems

Finding identical files under different names

Comparing Files by Date

UNIX systems contain many files, sometimes thousands or tens of thousands of files or more in just one project. With so many files, UNIX users often need to compare files in various ways. We can compare files by dates—for example, which files were modified more recently or which files have not been accessed in a long time. We can compare files by size—for example, which are the largest files using up most of the disk space. And very frequently we want to compare files by contents—for example, which files are duplicates (just wasting disk space). Sometimes we need to compare files between two different systems—for example, which system has the newest copy of a utility program, or do two systems have the same data file. If you transfer a file from one system to another, it is useful to compare their contents to make sure the transfer worked properly. These types of file comparisons are the topic of this chapter.

Comparing Files by Date Last Modified (*ls*)

To just list the files in the current directory, use the `ls` command (for more information on the `ls` command and its options, see the appendix). Here is some typical output from `ls`:

```
acme.linda
acme.sam
report.bak
report.sav
```

Looking at this output, we see there are two report files. But which one is newer? There are two acme files, but which one was used most recently?

To determine when files were last modified, use this command:

```
ls -l
```

The `-l` option to `ls` causes it to list in long format, which gives us more information about each file (including the last modification date/time). You should then see output similar to this:

```
total 4
-rw-------   1 lindap    group        552 Feb  1 08:48
➥acme.linda
```

```
-rw-------   1 samw     prog            552 Aug 13  1996
➥acme.sam
-rw-r--r--   1 stevem   group           420 Feb  1 09:07
➥report.bak
-rw-r--r--   1 stevem   group           552 Jan 31 18:48
➥report.sav
```

Now we can see that report.bak was last modified on February 1st at 09:07 a.m. We know this was in the morning because ls would have shown 9:07 p.m. as 21:07. Notice that it does not show the year. Could it be referring to February of the preceding year? The answer is no, because ls follows this rule: If the event was less than one year ago, it shows the time and not the year. If the event was over a year ago, it would show the year and not the time. See the line for acme.sam as an example of a much older date showing the year and not the time of last modification.

In this case, ls -l shows that report.bak contains newer contents than report.sav, and acme.linda is much newer than acme.sam.

One very useful way to compare files by date of last modification is to list them all from oldest to newest or vice versa.

```
ls -lt
```

The -t option causes ls to list the files in order of date/time rather than alphabetically by name. You should see the files from newest to oldest modification date/time like this:

```
ls -lt
total 4
-rw-r--r--   1 stevem   group           420 Feb  1 09:07
➥report.bak
-rw-------   1 lindap   group           552 Feb  1 08:48
➥acme.linda
-rw-r--r--   1 stevem   group           552 Jan 31 18:48
➥report.sav
-rw-------   1 samw     prog            552 Aug 13  1996
➥acme.sam
```

This can be useful if you recently changed several files and want to find them quickly.

To reverse the sort order from oldest to newest, use this command:

```
ls -ltr
```

The -r option causes ls to reverse its normal order of listing whether by date/time or alphabetic. The option letters l, t, and r can be specified in any order. You should now see output like this:

```
ls -ltr
total 4
-rw-------     1 samw      prog          552 Aug 13   1996
➥acme.sam
-rw-r--r--     1 stevem    group         552 Jan 31 18:48
➥report.sav
-rw-------     1 lindap    group         552 Feb  1 08:48
➥acme.linda
-rw-r--r--     1 stevem    group         420 Feb  1 09:07
➥report.bak
```

This can be useful to find files that have not changed in a long time.

Comparing Files by Date of Last Access (*ls*)

To determine when files were last accessed, use this command:

```
ls -lu
```

The -u option to ls changes the -l long output to show the last access date and time rather than the last modification. Access could mean that someone displayed the file, copied it, printed it, and so on—but did not modify it. You should see output similar to this:

```
total 4
-rw-------     1 lindap    group         552 Feb  1 08:48
➥acme.linda
-rw-------     1 samw      prog          552 Feb  3 10:14
➥acme.sam
-rw-r--r--     1 stevem    group         420 Feb  2 12:21
➥report.bak
-rw-r--r--     1 stevem    group         552 Jan 31 18:48
➥report.sav
```

Because no year is specified for any of these files, we know that the dates displayed are all within the past year.

As before, it is very useful to compare file access by listing the files from most recently accessed to least recently accessed. Add the -t option (ls -lut) to list the files in order of date/time rather than by name—that is, from most recently accessed to least recently accessed. Add the -r option (ls -lutr) to reverse the order so that the oldest accessed files are listed first. This can be useful when you are low on disk space and you want to archive and purge files that no one uses anymore. The option letters to the ls command can be specified in any order.

SEE ALSO

➤ *For a summary of all the* ls *options, see page* 778

Comparing and Finding Files Newer Than a Given File (*find*)

In practice, the ls command enables us to compare files that are in only one directory. We can use the find command (see appendix) to compare all files in a directory subtree (or the whole system) and list all files that were modified more recently than a given file. This is useful if we want to make sure the given file has the most up-to-date information.

The find command will search many or all directories on the system in one command. Here is the procedure to help you compose the desired find command.

Listing files modified more recently than a given file

1. Enter find.

Do not press Enter until instructed.

2. Enter a space and then the directory you want to start searching. find will also search all subdirectories of that directory. To search the whole system, enter /.

3. Enter a space, and then enter -newer.

UNIX does not keep track of the file creation date

UNIX maintains a third date and time for each file: the last inode change, which can be displayed by adding the -c option to ls -l. I have seen erroneous references to this option as showing the file creation date. The inode (see glossary) is changed when the file is created but also when you change its owner, group, or permissions.

4. Enter a space and then the given filename. When you finish typing this command, find will display all files modified more recently than this given file. If the file is in the current directory, enter only its name. If it is in a different directory from your current directory, enter its pathname.

5. If desired, you can now enter any other desired search criteria—in case you want to see only files of a certain size, owner, permissions, and so on. See the appendix entry on find for a list of such options.

6. Enter a space, and then enter -print.

Press Enter, completing your find command. find should then display a list of files modified more recently than the given file. You could also do the more adventurous step 7 rather than this step 6.

7. Enter a space, and then enter -exec ls -l {} \;.

Press Enter, completing your find command. This is an alternative to step 6 to complete the find command. This will show you the same long information about each file found that ls -l would show. You could also enter -exec followed by a different command to perform some other operation on each of the files selected if desired. See the appendix entry on find for more information on -exec.

Here is an example find command from the preceding procedure. Beneath each word of the command is the step in the procedure that generated that word. This find command will search directory /usr/fred and all its subdirectories and display the pathname of any files modified more recently than the given file. The given file is the acme file in the reports subdirectory of the current directory.

```
find  /usr/fred  -newer  reports/acme  -print
 ¦        ¦         ¦          ¦           ¦
 1        2         3          4           6
```

Here is another example find command. It will search the whole system for any files modified more recently than the acme file in the current directory. It will ignore any files unless the file owner is fred. It will display the long ls output for any files that satisfy both conditions.

```
find / -newer acme -user fred -exec ls -l {} \;
  ¦  ¦    ¦    ¦     ¦     ¦      ¦     ¦   ¦  ¦  ¦
  1  2    3    4     5     5      7     7   7  7  7
```

This -newer option to find is also useful for doing incremental backups, in which you want to backup only those files that have changed since the last backup. Your backup script should modify a dummy file when it does a backup. Use the find command to find all files that have been modified since the dummy file. Then use cpio to back up all the filenames generated by that find command.

SEE ALSO

➤ *For more information on* cpio *and backups, see page 327*

Finding Files by Last Access or Modification, Even in Different Directories (*find*)

In this chapter so far, you have seen how to compare files by dates by using the ls command to list them in order so that you can easily pick out the files accessed most recently or least recently and the files modified most or least recently. Using the ls command does not work to compare files in more than one directory by date.

The find command can access a whole directory subtree or even the entire system. find can display all files that were accessed or modified more than or less than x days ago. Here is the procedure to help you compose the desired find command.

Listing files accessed/modified more than/less than x days ago

1. Enter find.

Do not press Enter until instructed.

2. Enter a space and then the directory you want to start searching. find will also search all subdirectories of that directory. To search the whole system, enter /.

3. Enter a space, and then enter either -atime or -ctime or -mtime.

atime checks last access date/time.

mtime checks last modification date/time.

ctime checks last inode change date/time.

4. Enter a space and then a plus or minus sign, and then enter the desired number of days to check.

   -atime +90 means last accessed more than 90 days ago—that is, not accessed in the previous 90 days.

   -mtime -7 means last modified less than 7 days ago.

5. If desired, you can now enter any other desired search criteria in case you want to see only files of a certain size, owner, permissions, and so on. See the appendix entry on find for a list of such options.

6. Enter a space, and then enter -print.

   Press Enter, completing your find command. find should then display a list of files modified more recently than the given file. You could also do the more adventurous step 7 rather than this step 6.

7. Enter a space, and then enter -exec ls -l {} \;.

   Press Enter, completing your find command. This is an alternative to step 6 to complete the find command. This will show you the same long information about each file found that ls -l would show. You could also enter -exec followed by a different command to perform some other operation on each of the files selected if desired. See the appendix entry on find for more information on -exec.

Here is an example find command from the preceding procedure. It will search directory /usr/fred and all its subdirectories. It will display the pathname of any files last accessed more than 90 days ago—that is, files that have not been accessed in the previous 90 days.

```
find /usr/fred -atime +90 -print
  |      |        |      |    |
  1      2        3      4    6
```

Here is another find command. It will search the whole system for any files last modified less than 7 days ago and owned by user fred. It will display the long ls output for any files that match both conditions.

```
find / -mtime -7 -user fred -exec ls -l {} \;
     |  |      |      |          |    |    |  |  |  |  |
     1  2      3      4          5    5    7  7  7  7  7
```

To compare all files and find which were most (or least) recently accessed (or modified), it is important that you pick a good numeric value for the number of days given in the -atime, -mtime, or -ctime option in your find command. Some values may find too many files and therefore not pinpoint the extreme files you are seeking. Other values may be too extreme and find no files that match. Keep adjusting your number of days value until you get the results you want.

SEE ALSO

➤ *For more information on the* find *command, see page 770*

Comparing Files by Size

As when comparing files by date, when we compare files by size we often want to pick out the largest files. We can use the ls command to pick out the largest files in one directory. We can also use the find command to search a whole directory tree or the whole system to locate the largest or smallest files.

Determining a File's Size (*ls*)

To determine, for your current directory, the size of the files in characters, use the following command:

```
ls -l
```

The -l option to ls produces long output similar to this:

```
total 3
-rw-r--r--    1 mori      users        17157 Feb  1 11:31
➥report02
-rw-r--r--    1 mori      users         1972 Feb  1 11:31
➥report04
-rw-r--r--    1 mori      users       196484 Feb  1 11:33
➥report07
```

In the preceding example, report07 is the largest file with 196,484 characters.

Listing Files Sorted by Size

One of the best ways to compare a group of files by size is to use ls and pipe its output to the sort command. After the files are listed in order of size, it is much easier to compare them and determine the largest or smallest files quickly.

```
ls -l | sort -bn +4
```

The ¦ sign uses piping (see glossary) to take the output from ls -l and process it with the sort command (see appendix on sort). Here are the sort options used:

+4   Ignore the first four fields, so we sort on the size

-n   Sort in numeric order, not alphabetic

-b   Ignore leading blanks before the size

We will then see output like this:

```
total 3
-rw-r--r--    1 mori       users         1972 Feb  1 11:31
➥report04
-rw-r--r--    1 mori       users        17157 Feb  1 11:31
➥report02
-rw-r--r--    1 mori       users       196484 Feb  1 11:33
➥report07
```

To list the files in order from largest to smallest, use this command:

```
ls -l | sort -bnr +4
```

Adding the -r option to sort reverses the order, so files are listed from largest to smallest.

SEE ALSO

➤ *For more information on piping, see page 26*

➤ *For more information on the* sort *command, see page 202*

Finding Files by Their Size

You can also use the find command to list all files larger or smaller than a given block size. find will search many or all directories on the system in one command. Here is the procedure to help you compose the desired find command.

Listing files larger or smaller than a given size

1. Enter find.

Do not press Enter until instructed.

2. Enter a space, and then enter the directory you want to start searching. find will also search all subdirectories of that directory. To search the whole system, enter /.

3. Enter -size.

4. Enter +number or -number.

+600 means find files larger than 600 blocks. -200 means find files less than 200 blocks. Most systems assume 512 bytes (that is, characters) per block, but some systems may use 1024 bytes per block. Check the man page (see glossary) on find on your system to see how many bytes per block the -size option uses on your system.

To help you convert from MB (megabytes) to blocks, here are two rough rules of thumb:

2,000 blocks of 512 bytes = 1MB (approximately)

1,000 blocks of 1024 bytes = 1MB (approximately)

To find files of about 10MB or larger, for example, I would specify +20000 blocks of 512 bytes or +10000 blocks of 1024 bytes.

5. If desired, you can now enter any other desired search criteria in case you want to see only files of a certain size, owner, permissions, and so forth. See the appendix entry on find for a list of such options.

6. Enter -print.

Press Enter, completing your find command. You could also do the more adventurous step 7 rather than this step 6.

7. Enter -exec ls -l {} \;.

Press Enter, completing your find command. This is an alternative to step 6 to complete the find command. This will show you the same long information about each file found that ls -l would show. You could also enter -exec followed by a different command to perform some operation on each of the files selected if desired. See the appendix entry on find for more information on -exec.

Here is an example find command from the preceding procedure. Beneath each word of the command is the step in the procedure that generated that word. This find command will search directory /usr/fred and all its subdirectories and display the pathname of any files larger than 600 blocks.

```
find /usr/fred -size +600 -print
  |      |        |      |      |
  1      2        3      4      6
```

Here is another find example. It will search the whole system for files smaller than 200 blocks that are also in group acct, and will produce the same output that ls -l shows.

```
find / -size -200 -group acct -exec ls -l {} \;
  | |    |        |      |        |      | | | |
  1 2    3        4      5        5      7 7 7 7
```

Comparing Text Files

UNIX uses simple text files in a variety of important roles, including system configuration tables, C program source code, HTML Web pages, and user data. Because text files have so many important uses under UNIX, several different UNIX utilities enable us to compare text files and see their differences.

Showing Differences Between Two Files (*diff*)

To show the differences between two text files, use this command:

```
diff file1 file2
```

You should see output similar to this:

```
287c287
<          Now is the time for all good men to come to the
➥aid of
- - -
>          Now is the time for all good men to go to the aid
➥of
```

Because there is little output from `diff` in this example, the two files must be very similar. A lot of output from `diff` would indicate the files are very different. No output before the next shell prompt would indicate the files are identical.

After `diff` finds any differences between the two files, it looks ahead in both files trying to find whether any later lines in one file match later lines in the other. In this way, it can identify added lines, deleted lines, and changed lines. Output lines that begin with the < sign are from the first file. The > sign indicates lines from the second file that differ. Only lines that are different are displayed. The preceding example shows the only difference between the two files is that the word *come* in the first file has been changed to *go* in the second file.

In the preceding output, `287c287` indicates directives to change the first file into the second file. In this case, the `c` indicates that line `287` of the first file must be changed to match line `287` of the second file. Other possible directives are `a` for append line(s) and `d` for delete line(s). In practice, most UNIX users look at the line differences that are displayed and ignore the directives except for the line-number information.

Use the `-b` option to `diff` to cause it to ignore trailing spaces and tabs in the line. It will also regard any collection of consecutive spaces and tabs as one space. This can be useful if you want to compare two text files, but want to ignore the fact that one has a larger left-hand margin (that is, more leading spaces) than the other.

Showing Differences Side by Side (*sdiff*)

To show the differences between two text files side by side, use this command:

```
sdiff file1 file2
```

You should see output similar to this:

```
report02                        report02
report07                      | report05
report09                      <
```

```
report04                        report04
report03                        report03
                              > report01
```

The left column shows lines in the first file. The column on the right shows lines in the second file. The < sign shows lines that occur in the first file but not the second. The > sign shows lines that occur in the second file but not the first. The ¦ sign shows lines that are different between the two files.

sdiff works well to compare lists of short words or filenames, but can be very difficult to read with longer lines.

Showing Differences Between Three Files (*diff3*)

To show the differences between three text files, use this command:

```
diff3 file1 file2 file3
```

The contents of three example files are shown here:

TABLE 10.1   Contents of three example files

file1	file2	file3
green	green	yellow
blue	blue	blue
red	red	green
yellow	yellow	brown
blue	blue	tan
green	green	red
brown	brown	orange
pink	azure	black
red	red	gray
orange	orange	
black	black	
gray	gray	

The command:

```
diff3 file1 file2 file3
```

will produce this output:

```
====3
1:1,3c
2:1,3c
  green
  blue
  red
3:0a
====
1:8c
  pink
2:8c
  azure
3:5c
  tan
```

==== separates each section of differences found in the three files.

====n means that file *n* differs from the other two.

==== means that all three files differ in this section. Here is a commentary on the preceding output from diff3:

```
====3       means file 3 differs from the other two as
            ➥follows:
1:1,3c      means file 1, lines 1 thru 3 contains the same as
                    contents as the following file:
2:1,3c      means file 2, lines 1 thru 3 contains these 3
            ➥lines
                    as listed here:
  green
  blue
  red
3:0a        means file 3 would have to add the above 3 lines
            ➥after
                    line 0 in order to become the same as the
other
                    two files.
====        means all three files differ in this next area:
1:8c        means file 1, line 8 contains: pink
            ➥pink
```

```
2:8c          whereas file 2, line 8 contains: azure
              ➥azure
3:5c          whereas file 3, line 5 contains: tan
              ➥tan
```

Finding Common and Unique Lines in Sorted Text Files (*comm*)

If two text files are in sorted (that is, alphabetic) order, the comm command can show easily the lines common between the two files and the lines that are unique. To do this, enter the following command:

comm file1 file2

You should see output similar to this:

```
                    report21
report23
          report29
                    report33
report34
                    report35
          report37
report91
```

The leftmost column shows lines unique to the first file; therefore, report23, report34, and report91 exist only in the first file. The middle column shows lines unique to the second file; so report29 and report37 exist only in the second file. The third column shows lines common to both files. In this case, report21, report33, and report35 exist in both files.

We can add options to comm to suppress one or more of the columns, as follows:

```
comm -1 file1 file2   # suppress column 1, so we show
➥only
                      # columns 2 and 3
comm -23 file1 file2  # show only lines unique to file1
comm -13 file1 file2  # show only lines unique to file2
comm -12 file1 file2  # show only lines in common
```

Remember that the files must be in sorted order for comm to work. If you have two files to compare that are not sorted, you can use the sort command (see appendix) to create sorted versions of those files and then use the comm command on the sorted versions.

Comparing Any File Type by Contents (*cmp*)

To compare any type of files, even if they are not text files, use this command:

```
cmp file1 file2
```

You should see output similar to this:

```
file1 file2 differ: char 26, line 3
```

If cmp goes back to the shell prompt without displaying any messages, the files are identical. cmp stops after the first difference is found, so it does not tell you how similar the two files are. Use the -l option to cmp to list all the differences between the two files.

Use cmp to compare non-text files, because it does not try to output the differences. Using diff, sdiff, diff3, or comm on binary files can cause misleading output because control characters from the binary files can leave your screen in an unknown state.

Comparing Files on Different Systems (*sum*)

If you transfer a file to another system, you may want to verify that the file arrived intact. diff, sdiff, diff3, comm, and cmp can only compare files on the same system.

To compare two files that exist on different systems, use this command on each system:

```
sum -r filename
```

Don't use comm if there are leading tabs

comm uses one tab character to start lines in the middle column and two tabs to start lines in the right column. If your two files start with one or more tabs, the comm output will be incorrect.

---

cmp versus diff

If you want to know only whether two files are identical, cmp is faster than diff because it stops on the first difference. cmp works with all types of files; diff handles only text files. diff, however, shows the actual line differences. This enables us to pinpoint added or deleted characters or lines.

You should see output similar to this:

```
35424      14      filename
```

The sum command calculates a checksum (see glossary) on the full contents of the file. In the preceding output, 35424 is the checksum for the file. 14 is the size in blocks. If the checksums for the two files do not match, the two files are not identical. If the checksums match, there is a very high probability that the two files are identical. The checksum algorithm (that is, calculation) is the same on almost every type of UNIX system, allowing remote files to be compared even if the UNIX system is a different type.

Note that the size in blocks reported by sum may differ by a factor of two between two different types of UNIX systems. This is because some UNIX systems compute file size using 512 bytes per block and others use 1024 bytes per block. SunOS Version 4 (based on BSD) uses 1024 bytes per block, for example, whereas Solaris 2.x using SunOS Version 5 (based on System V) uses 512 bytes per block. Note that the block size in bytes used by the sum command may not be the internal logical block size used when adding additional blocks to the file.

The -r option to sum causes it to use a better (rotating) checksum calculation that can better detect differences in the order as well as the contents of the files. If you want to be extra sure that two files are identical, take advantage of these two different calculations, as follows:

Taking an extra step to ensure files are the same

1. On the first system, do this:
   ```
   sum filename
   sum -r filename
   ```

2. On the second system, do the same:
   ```
   sum -r filename
   sum -r filename
   ```

3. Check whether the results of the two sum calculations are the same. Check whether the results of the two sum -r calculations are the same. Note that the sum results should not match the sum -r results.

What are the odds?

sum produces a checksum that can range up to about 65,000. In general, if two files have the same checksum, there is only one chance in 65,000 that they could still have different content.

4. If the two types of checksums match, the files are the same (to a very high degree of probability).

There is a slim chance that two files can be different and still produce the same checksum, but it is extremely unlikely that two different files would match using both checksum methods.

Finding Identical Files Under Different Names (*sum*)

To quickly determine which files in a directory are identical, use this command:

```
sum -r *
```

You should see output similar to this:

```
22792    192 acme.980201
06948     21 report02
14252     15 report04
22792    192 report05
```

If the output goes off the screen, rerun the command and pipe the output to pg or more or less. In the preceding example, acme.980201 and report05 have the same checksum and size in blocks. Therefore, it is highly probable that they are identical. We could then use diff or cmp on those two files if we needed to be 100 percent certain. report02 and report04 have different checksums from the others and therefore cannot match them or each other.

You can use other wildcards than * to generate the list of files to checksum.

SEE ALSO

➤ *For more information on using wildcards to create file lists, see page 232*

User and System Administration

File Permissions and System Security

By Jesper Pedersen

Login security

Planning groups for a system

Understanding file and directory permissions

Changing permissions/owner/group

Setting default permissions for new files (*umask*)

Watching the dangerous *SUID, SGID* permissions

Login Security

When you want to log on to a UNIX system, you are queried for a login name and a password. The login name is your unique name on the given UNIX system. The password is your secret key to the account, which, when selected carefully, is your guarantee that no one else (except root) can access your personal files.

Changing your login name

Your login name can be changed by the system administrator, but this is, as stated, not advisable.

You can change your password yourself, but your login name will be the same forever. If you changed your login name, your email address would change, too, and people would not know how to contact you on the computer. You can think about your login name as your personal name and your password as the key to your home.

Delays After Invalid Login

If you mistype your password, you get a message saying that the login was invalid. After a few seconds of delay, the computer will ask you for a login name and password once again.

This delay is imposed to avoid the instance when someone may try to log into your account over and over again, with a different password each time. With a delay, a program can try only about 500 different passwords per hour. Without the delay, such a program may try above a hundred thousand passwords per hour.

Secondary Passwords

On some systems, you may encounter additional passwords when you want to use a modem, a fax, or another external device. You may also encounter passwords when you want to start a program that is licensed and thus restricted.

The reason for passwords on devices may be to restrict the devices to a certain group of people. For example, it is possible to restrict the use of a modem to only employees at a university and not the student users.

Such restrictions can be obtained by setting up a group in which the given device was located. This way only the members of this group have read/write/execute permissions to the device in question. Password restriction on the device has one major advantage over the group solution: namely, if someone guesses your login password, he or she still must guess your password to the device as well before using it. The moral of this: Do not use your login password as the same password for such secondary passwords. If you do, the security will be compromised.

Password Aging

On some systems, you may have your password for only a maximum amount of time before the system requires you to change it. This is designed to increase the level of security in the system, which occurs in two ways:

- When your password is periodically changed, the chance that someone may learn your password (over your shoulder) decreases. It may take several attempts for someone to steal the whole password, so the fact that it is changed periodically lessens the chance of a complete password theft.

- If someone has gotten his hands on the encrypted version of your password (a description of the encrypted password appears later in this chapter), he may systematically try to crack your password by encrypting words and comparing the encrypted version with the encrypted version of your password. The shorter a period you have for each password, the less the chance someone will crack your password this way as well.

In addition to restricting the maximum time you may have a password, some systems also restrict the *minimum* time you may have one. This is to ensure that you do not have one favorite password that you insist on using all the time. This prevents you from using a dummy password when the system prompts you to change your password, and then promptly returning to your favorite one.

If you use the recipes for choosing passwords described in the next section, it should not be hard to select a new password each time the system asks you to do so. Proper use of passwords increases the security that no one else can access your personal files, your email account, and so forth.

Changing Your Password

Several reasons exist as to why you may want to change your password:

- Because you suspect that someone has guessed your password or has seen you type it
- Because the system demands that you change it once in a while
- Because the initial password given to you is hard to remember, or that the password is required to be changed at first login

Different UNIX systems have different restrictions on which passwords you may choose. If you choose a password that fulfills the following recommendations, however, you should be on safe ground:

- Choose a password with at least eight characters (only the first eight characters matter, but if it is easier for you to remember a longer password, you are welcome to use more than eight characters.)
- Use lowercase and uppercase letters.
- Use characters from the keyboard that are not letters. For instance, numbers or some of the special characters such as the dollar sign, the quotation mark, or the less-than sign make good additions to a password.
- Choose a password that is not available in a dictionary, a book, or any other text that might be electronically available.

Several good rules exist for choosing a password that is easy to remember.

Password security

Technically, passwords with three to seven letters are legal, too, but hackers may try these passwords first. If they have the encrypted version of your password, it will only take a few hours to a few days to guess these passwords.

- Choose the first letter from each word of a poem, a saying, or a song, and capitalize some of the letters (maybe include a non-letter somewhere in between). An example might be the phrase "There is more to love than boy meets girl," which might give you the password `TimtlTbmg`. (Note this password is nine character long, so the final g may be omitted, but it might be easier to remember if you include it.)

- Choose two words that have something to do with each other, and combine them with a non-letter). An example might be "dog" and "capital," which might give the passwords `cApI dOg`, `DOG=capi`, or `dog&capital`. It might be easier if you choose two words that have some kind of connection for you (but which no one else knows about). Using the previous example, you might have bought a dog the weekend after you had visited someone in the capital!

After you've chosen a good password, it is time to actually change your login password. Depending on your system, you should use either `yppasswd`, `nispasswd`, or `passwd`. If you do not know which one to use, try `yppasswd` and `nispasswd` first; if the result of both commands is `command not found`, try `passwd`.

When you have invoked the appropriate command, the system asks you for your old password. (By first asking for your old password, nobody can change your password if they find a terminal where you have forgotten to log out.) Next, the system asks you for the new password. Finally, you are asked to retype your new password to make sure you have not made a typing error.

Who Can See Your Password?

To fully understand how secret (or non-secret) your password is, you need to understand how the password mechanism works. When you select a new password, it is encrypted to a text string, which is saved on the system. It is not possible to do the inverse function—that is, given an encrypted password, you cannot find the non-encrypted version. (Technically, it is possible, but it is *very* unlikely. Such a process might take thousands of years on even the fastest computers.) When you want to log on to the system, the unencrypted password (which you type to log on) is encrypted, and the result is matched against the version that was computed when you first selected the password.

If someone wants to crack your password, and if he has the encrypted version, he may take a word, encrypt it, and compare it with your encrypted password. This, however, is not as simple as it sounds because there are so many words to try. Imagine that you choose between 90 different keys on your keyboard (including capital letters) and that you use the full length of eight characters for your password. Then, it takes a computer that has the capability to test 1,000 words per second more than two hundred thousand years to try all combinations; said in another way, it will take all computers in a large city one year to crack just one password.

If, however, your password can be found in a dictionary, then it may be cracked this way within a few seconds by a powerful computer.

One conclusion you can draw from the preceding information is that not even root may see your nonencrypted password!

In older UNIX systems, the encrypted password was located in the /etc/passwd file, and this file could be read by everybody. This produced a possible security hole; a user with access to the system could crack other users' password by the method described earlier. A new method was developed, which many systems use today, called *shadow passwords*. The idea is to remove the encrypted password from the /etc/passwd file and hide it in a file that is readable only by root and the login programs (which is to say, SUID root programs).

To see whether your system uses shadow passwords, you can check the /etc/passwd file. If the second field contains 13 letters (which seem random), then it doesn't. (These 13 letters are, in fact, your encrypted password.)

Permitting Users to Become Another User or root (*su*)

Occasionally, it happens that you want to access another user's files or run a program in the name of another user. One way you can do that is to log out and let the user log in on your terminal. However, there is an easier way! Using the command su (*substitute user*), you can change the owner of the shell to another user.

Typing su username changes the owner of the shell to the user *username*. If you don't give a user name, you will change to root. After having typed the su command, you will, of course, have to give the password for the given user.

When you change the ownership of the shell using su, the shell still knows who the original user was (due to environment variables). This might sometimes be a desirable effect, and sometimes not. If you want every environment variable to be reset when using su, you should give it a dash as argument "su - username".

Planning Groups for a System

Each file on a UNIX system belongs to exactly one user and one group. This ownership dictates who may read and edit the file, and in case the file is an executable file, who might execute it. Directories have similar permissions, which you'll see later.

Ownership information can be seen by using the command ls, if you give it the appropriate set of options:

```
ls -ldg security.html        owner    group
-rw-r--r--   1 blackie  users        12383 Mar 15 10:27
➥security.html
```

In the first column you can see the permissions for the file, in the third column you can see the owner of the file (blackie—that's me), and in the fourth column you can see the group to which the file belongs.

If several people have to work together on a set of files, they do not have to login as the same user. Instead, a group should be created, and the set of files should be placed in this group with appropriate permissions. For example, you would need read and write permissions for the user and the group.

Groups cannot be maintained by an ordinary user, but they must be administered by the super user (root). As an ordinary user,

Finding the names for a file

The second column is the number of names for the given file. This is the number of hardlinks for the given file if it is a plain file. For directories, this is two plus the number of subdirectories: Each subdirectory has a link to the directory with "..", the directory has a reference to itself with ".", and the directory in which it is placed has a reference to it with the name of the directory.

however, you may be in several groups at one time. To see the groups in which you are located, type groups.

Understanding File and Directory Permissions

In the following section, we will use the word *file* to mean both files and directories, and the word *plain file* when to refer to a file (**not** a directory.)

In the previous section, you saw that ls could tell you permission information about files:

```
ls -ldg security.html
-rw-r—r—    1 blackie   users        12383 Mar 15 10:27
➥security.html
```

This permission information is divided into four groups.

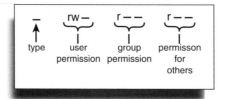

d for directory

a dash for an ordinary file

s for a symbolic link

b for a block special device

c for a character special device

The last two types are most often seen in the /dev directory.

Next comes three blocks of three letters each. The first block governs the permissions for the owner of the file, the second block governs permissions for the people in the same group as the file, and the third block governs permissions for others (that is, not the owner of the file and not the people from the group of the file).

In the three blocks, a dash instead of a letter indicates the absence of the letter that was possible in the given position. This ensures that the output from ls always has the same width, and that the letter in the fourth position always stays the same.

The first of the three letters in each of the three blocks may be the letter r, which indicates read permissions for the file. Read permissions for plain files (that is, not directories) means that the file may be read by the person(s) the block describes.

Read permissions for a directory indicate that the content of the directory may be listed—that is, someone may see which files are in the directory. This does not explicitly mean that the content of the files may be read or that the attributes of the files may be listed.

The second letter in each of the three blocks may be the letter w, which indicates write permission. For plain files, this indicates that the file may be edited. For directories, this means that new files may be created in the directory.

The third letter in each group indicates execute permissions. If it is the letter x, it has the following meaning: For plain files, the file is a program, which may be executed by typing its name on the command line. For directories, you may *get in contact* with it content—that is, you may do the following things when the x permission is on:

- You may read the content of the files (if the files permit this).
- You may go into subdirectories (using cd) if the subdirectory permits this.
- You may get information about the content of the directory (such as the files permission, the date of creation, and sizes).

The third letter may also refer to something else, which the following table shows.

TABLE 11.1 **Additional options for the execute bit**

Type	User	Group	Other
File			
s:	1) The file has x permission for the user.		
	2) The file is a SUID program (see the following section).		
S:	1) The file does not have x permissions for the user.		
	2) The file is a SUID program (see the following section).		
s:		1) The file has x permission for the group.	
		2) The file is a SGID program (see the following section).	
S:		1) The file does not have x permissions for the group.	
		2) The file is a SGID program (see the following section).	
Directory			
s:		1) The directory has x permission for the group.	
		2) New files in this directory will be created with the group ownership as the directory (not the user's default group) (see the section below).	
S:		1) The directory has **not** x permission for the group.	
		2) New files in this directory will be created with the group ownership as the directory (that is, not the user's default group) (see the section below).	
t:			1) The directory has x permissions for others.
			2) Others may create new files in the directory, but they may not delete each other's files (see section below).

Type	User	Group	Other
Directory			
T:			1) The directory has **not** x permissions for others.
			2) Others may create new files in the directory, but they may not delete each other's files (see section below).

SUID/SGID programs

As you saw earlier with the su command, you can change the identity of the shell to another user. However, this requires that you know the password of the other user, unless you are already the root. This restriction is not acceptable in certain specific situations, as the following example shows.

The password file called /etc/passwd is writable only by root (that is, only root may edit this file). When you want to change your password, you must change the content of this file. This is achieved by the passwd program, which is a SUID program (Set User ID). When this program is executed, the identity of the process changes from you to root. This shift of identity happens without querying you for a password.

The passwd program has been made a SUID program by the chmod program.

Likewise, a program may shift group on execution. Such programs are called SGID programs.

Directory Sticky Bit Guards Your Files

Users who have write permission to a directory have effective administrative control over that directory. In addition to creating files, these users can delete and rename files of other users, even if they don't have permission to modify those files.

This may be a problem if you, for example, are an instructor at a university and want to create a directory in which your students can place their assignments. The problem is that if you give the students write permission to the directory, they will also get administrative control over that directory and thus have the capability of removing the assignments of other students!

A solution to this problem is to set the sticky bit on the directory. This gives the student write permissions to the directory but not administrative control over the directory.

In this case, you would set the permissions as follows:

```
chmod u=rwx,og=wxt directory
```

This gives the permission `drwx-wx-wt`. I have on purpose left out the read permission for the group and others. This way, the student cannot see the files in the directory and thus cannot tell who have returned the assignments.

SGID Bit Sets Group on New Files

After you have a group set up for a given assignment, files for this assignment should be created with the group identity of group. This can be achieved in three ways:

1. You could create the files and use the *chgrp* command to change their group identity afterward.

2. You could change the default group in which the new files you create belong. This can be done with the command *newgrp*, but it will only have effect in the shell in which you invoke the *newgrp* command. To change the group this way, just invoke the command `newgrp group`.

3. You could set the `SGID` bit on the directory. With this method, new files created in this directory have the same group identity as the directory; thus, they don't share the group identity of the one who creates them.

To set the `SGID` bit for a directory, type `chmod g+s directory`.

Read and Execute Permission on Directories

Many people get confused by the use of the read permission and the execute permission on directories. Let's take a close look at the following four situations.

- No read permission and no execute permission

  In this case, the directory is closed.

- Read permission and execute permission

  In this case, the directory is open for listing the content of files, listing the content of the directory, and for accessing subdirectories (if the subdirectories allow this).

- Read permission and no execute permission

  This is an odd case that seldom occurs. A user can see the filenames but cannot access them, get information about their attributes, or traverse into subdirectories.

- No read permission and execute permission

  In this situation, a user may not list the content of the directory but may access files, if he knows their names. This is a very convenient permission to set on your home directory, for example. With this permission, people might eventually go into a directory and see your .emacs file (if it has the permission for it), but they may not see any other files you have. In other words, the users may only see the files that you tell them you have and that the users have the permission to see.

Changing Permissions/Owner/Group

Permissions of files and directories can be changed using the command chmod (*ch*ange *mod*e.) This command can either be used with a numerical argument, which state exactly what the permission should be, or with symbolic argument, which may change only part of the permissions (such as only the permissions for the user).

Only the user who owns a given file may change the permissions for this file. (An exception to this rule is, of course, the super user, who may do anything!)

The chmod program changes permission for all files in a directory hierarchy by using the -R options (R stands for recursive)

Setting Permissions by Using Numeric Mode (*chmod*)

The *chmod* command changes the permission for files and directories using a number. This is a very convenient (and fast) way to set the permission.

The idea is that you describe the permission with four numbers, where each number describes a group:

1. The SUID, SGID, and sticky bit

2. Permission for the owner of the file

3. Permission for the group

4. Permission for others

In each group, every option has a number attached to it. The group's is the sum of the permission mumbers. Available options in the first group include the following:

1. The directory sticky bit

2. The SGID bit

3. The SUID bit

Thus, if you want the file to be SUID and SGID, you should use the number 6 (that is, 2+4.) If you do not want any of the three options selected, you should use 0.

Available options in each of three permission blocks include the following:

1. Execute permission

2. Write permission

3. Read permission

Thus, if you want read and write permissions for the user and only read permissions for the group and others on a file called myfile, you should execute this command:

```
chmod 0644 myfile.
```

Leading zeros may be omitted, so the following command is equal to previous one:

```
chmod 644 myfile.
```

Tables 11.2 and 11.3 show the figures for the given options.

Table 11.2 **SUID, SGID, and Sticky bits**

Value	Description
0	-SUID -SGID -Sticky bit
1	-SUID -SGID +Sticky bit
2	-SUID +SGID -Sticky bit
3	-SUID +SGID +Sticky bit
4	+SUID -SGID -Sticky bit
5	+SUID -SGID +Sticky bit
6	+SUID +SGID -Sticky bit
7	+SUID +SGID +Sticky bit

Table 11.3 **Permission figures for the *chmod* command**

Value	Description
0	-r -w -x
1	-r -w +x
2	-r +w -x
3	-r +w +x
4	+r -w -x
5	+r -w +x
6	+r +w -x
7	+r +w +x

Setting Permissions by Using Symbolic Mode (*chmod*)

In the previous section, you saw how to set the permission for files using numerical mode. The major drawback on this is that you do not have the possibility of adding write permission on all files and directories in one try without altering the current mode.

Using symbolic mode, you can alter only part of the permission for files and directories.

The syntax for symbolic mode is in the following form:

`<who> <operator> <permission>`

<who> is zero or more of the characters u, g, o and a:

u - user's permission

g - group's permission

o - other's permission

a - all permission (user, group, and other)

If *<who>* is omitted, it defaults to a, but the value of the file mode creation mask is taken into account (see the following section for information on the file mode creation mask, called umask.)

<operator> is either +, - or =. The choice of characters indicates the following:

+ means add permissions

- means remove permissions

= means set permission absolute for the groups specified by *<who>*

<permission> is one of r, w, x, s, t, u, g, and o:

r - read permission

w - write permission

x - execute permission

X - execute permission if the file is a directory, or if the file has execute permission for one of user, group, or other

s - SUID if *<who>* is u and SGID if *<who>* is g

t - sticky bit if *<who>* is o

u,g,o - indicate that permission is to be taken from the current user, group, or other mode, respectively.

Several permissions may be changed at a time by repeating the *<who>*, *<operator>*, or *<permission>* commands with a comma in between.

A Few Examples

To add read permission for the group and others on a file called myfile, type this line:

```
chmod go+r myfile
```

To add read permission for the group and others on all files and directories in a given directory, type this line:

```
chmod go+r *
```

To add read permission for the group and others on all files and directories in a given directory and on directories below, type this line:

```
chmod -R go+r *
```

To enable users to access files in your home directory only if they know the name of the file they want to access, type this line:

```
chmod go=r /home/user/
```

To be a bit less restrictive and give the group the possibility to see which files you have but to withhold this option from others, type this line:

```
chmod g=rx,o=r /home/user/
```

To open all your files an directory for the group in a given directory, type this line:

```
chmod g+rX *
```

This has the following effects:

- Read permission will be added on all files and directories.

- Execute permission will be added on all directories.

- Execute permission will be added on files that already have execute permission for one of user group or other.

Changing the Group of a File (chgrp)

Using the chgrp command, you can change the group of a file, a directory, or a whole directory hierarchy. The syntax is as follows:

chgrp *<group>* *<file>* - to change the group for a single file or directory

chgrp **-R** *<group>* *<file>* - to change the group for a directory and all the subdirectories.

You must be a member of the group to which you want to change the file(s). To see the groups of which you are a member, use the command groups.

Changing the Owner of a File (*chown*)

In the previous section, we have seen how to change the permission and the group for files—but can the files also change owners?

The answer to this question is yes and no! Yes, you can change the owner of a file with the command *chown*; but, no, an ordinary user (that is, one that's not root) can't do it!

If you really want to give away a file to another person, you have two possibilities:

- Mail it to him as an attachment.
- Give the file read permission (only for a few seconds), let the other person copy the file, and remove your copy of it.

Setting Default Permissions for New Files (*umask*)

With the umask command, you can set up a pattern for the permission of new files. The umask is a number such as the one used for numerical chmod, that consists of three digits between 0 and 7.

The reason for the number is technical and will thus not be described here. The only thing that is important to understand is that when new files are created, they will have the permission described by the umask. In Table 11.4, you can see the permission a given figure describes.

Table 11.4 **Figures for the umask command**

Value	Description
7	-r -w -x
6	-r -w +x
5	-r +w -x
4	-r +w +x
3	+r -w -x
2	+r -w +x
1	+r +w -x
0	+r +w +x

Thus, to give the user full access (rwx) for new files, and to give the group and other only read permission, you should use the command umask 033.

Execute permission will be added only if the file type created is a directory and not for plain files. If you have umask 033, plain files will be created with read and write permission for the user, and read permission for the group and others. Directories will be created with read and execute permission for the user and read permission for the group and others.

Watching the Dangerous *SUID, SGID* Permissions

SUID and SGID files are dangerous because they might give an unauthorized user root access, or at least access to run a program in another user's name.

To make a program SUID root, the user must be root (Remember: you must be the user to which you want to make a program SUID). So if you never mount partitions from other machines, and if you are 100 percent sure that no one can get to the root, you have no problem. However, it is very difficult to be so sure, as hackers may have cracked root's password.

SUID programs are very convenient for hackers, as they might create a back door to the root account, which is still available after root has changed his password to something the hacker does not know.

However, a simple way exists by which to verify that no new SUID program has appeared on your system since last check—use the commands crontab, find, and diff. To use this strategy, you must have a version of the find program, which supports the -perm option. If your version does not support this, you may download one from the gnu archive (URL: http://www.gnu.org/order/ftp.html).

With the command find / -perm ++s, you can recursively traverse the whole file system and search for files that have either SUID or SGID permission. The script in Listing 11.1 does this and saves the output in the file called suid.info. This file is compared with the one from the previous run using diff, and thus only outputs new SUID/SGID programs (or SUID/SGID programs, which have vanished).

Listing 11.1   Program to search for new *SUID/SGID* programs

```
#!/bin/sh
test -e suid.info && mv suid.info suid.info.old
test ! -e suid.info.old && touch suid.info.old
find / -perm ++s suid.info
diff suid.info suid.info.old
```

One change you should make to this program is to give it a full path to where you want it to save the suid.info file.

If you make this little program a cron job, which is executed once each day, you will have set up a system to check for new SUID/SGID files.

You will get an email only as result of the cron job when new SUID/SGID program appears, as it otherwise will not output anything.

SUID/SGID Files, When Mounting File Systems

On some variant of UNIX, the mount command supports a nosuid option. This means that a file system mounted with this option does not give special meanings to SUID/SGID program (that is, they will not be SUID/SGID files). Without this option, mounted file systems may be a problem, as the following example shows.

Imagine that you are a system manager on a UNIX system at an institute on a university campus. One day a system manager from another institute asks if you would be so kind as to mount a file system from his UNIX so that your common students can access their files (located on his hard disk) on your system. What should you answer? Will this affect the security at your system?

It will most definitely affect the security at your system if you do not turn off SUID/SGID with the nosuid option for mount. If the other system manager is hostile, he might create a SUID-root shell on the file system that you mount, and obtain root access to your file system. Even if he is not hostile, you should think about what could happen if the root password on his system is not as well planed as on your system. The answer could be that a hacker cracked the root password and thus gained root access at your system.

Startup, Shutdown, and Managing Jobs

By Steve "Mor" Moritsugu

Bringing up the system

Shutting down the system (root only)

Adding system startup/shutdown jobs (root only)

Running jobs periodically or at a later time (all users)

Checking and changing job priorities (all users)

Starting and killing background jobs (all users)

Suspending and resuming background jobs (all users)

Starting Up the System

Systems vary widely in the steps required to fully bring up UNIX and allow users to log in and do their work. This is because UNIX has been ported to many different types of computers and different processors by different computer companies. In the simplest case, you simply turn the power on, and the UNIX system will come up on its own. The system will be ready for use in a few minutes, or it could take much longer depending on firmware diagnostics, restoring network connections, initializing devices and databases, and so on. Other types of UNIX systems will not come up on their own, and you must enter specific commands to bring them up.

The average user never has to worry about this on most commercial UNIX systems because the system is in a restricted area in the computer room attended by computer operators and administrators. However, there are desktop UNIX systems and home-based UNIX systems where the owner/user is the only operator/administrator. I can't tell you the specific steps required to bring up every UNIX system, but I can tell you the general steps or stages that are involved.

Remove Any Bootable Media

Booting is the process of loading software into memory, which allows a program or an operating system to start running. Most systems can boot from several types of devices. For example, most Intel i86 systems are configured to boot from drive A first (the floppy) and then from drive C (the hard disk) if there is no disk in the floppy drive. Other machines may boot by preference from CD-ROM or tape. Remove such media before bringing up the system because UNIX normally boots from the hard disk.

Power On Auxiliary Subsystems Before the Main Computer

Some systems have external boxes of disk drives, tape drives, or port connections that are connected to the main system by cables. Usually these should be powered up and ready before the main computer is powered up. If you don't do this, the system may not come up at all, or it will be unable to use those devices until the system is rebooted with those devices online.

Power-On Diagnostics

Warning: Improper use can damage the system severely

I can give you general guidelines, but there are always exceptions. So don't bring up a system unless you have been instructed on the proper steps for that specific computer.

Most computers will run some sort of diagnostics when they are first powered on. This could be just a quick memory test. Some computers will run a suite of tests that could take minutes or hours—or could even go forever—unless you know how to end the diagnostics. You should watch the screen output when you first bring up the UNIX system so you get a feel for the typical messages. Then if a hardware problem is detected, you will at least recognize that something is different. Often the bootup will scan for all the devices on your system. If a device takes too long to respond or does not respond at all, you might have a hardware problem.

Loading the UNIX Kernel into Memory

The next step in booting is loading the UNIX kernel file into memory. The kernel contains the driver codes needed to access the disk, monitor, keyboard, and other hardware on the system. On some systems, you will receive a boot prompt from which you can specify boot options or special kernels to load. Sometimes booting requires you to enter a complicated command string that includes the device address of the primary disk containing the kernel file.

SEE ALSO

➤ *For more information on the UNIX kernel, see page 27*

Mounting the Root Disk and Checking It (*fsck*)

The booting process includes a phase of checking to see whether the operating system was shutdown properly the last time. If it was not, there could be damage to the root filesystem, and you may see a message such as this:

```
fsstat: mount failed.  Possibly damaged filesystem.
okay to check the root filesystem (y/n) ?
```

This check is performed by a program called fsck. Sometimes fsck is started automatically without waiting for a response from the user. If you are lucky, fsck will report a tight series of phase messages such as

```
Phase 1: Check Blocks and Sizes
Phase 2: Check Path Names
Phase 3: Check Connectivity
```

and so forth.

If you are unlucky, the phase messages will be strewn with ugly-sounding errors like the following:

```
EXCESSIVE BAD BLOCKS I=1432
POSSIBLE FILE SIZE ERROR I=257
35738 DUP I=138273
DUP/BAD I=374 OWNER=17 MODE=700 SIZE=14328 FILE=/data/
➥maincust
(REMOVE?)
```

Each of these errors indicates possible data corruption or file loss. Sometimes there are thousands of these errors, and the system must be restored from a backup or reloaded from scratch. Some modern UNIX systems offer a journaled filesystem type that makes them much more resistant to such problems as an improper shutdown or system crash. It is also wise to use a UPS (uninterrupted power supply), which contains a battery that will keep the system from crashing in the event of power failure.

Single User Mode

As UNIX is coming up, many systems allow the operator to stop in single user mode, in which the system is only partially initialized and maintenance functions can be performed. On some systems, a special command sequence must be used to get to single user mode. Most systems, for security reasons, require that a user enter the root login password in order to bring the system to single user mode. In single user mode, you are running with root (super-user) privilege. If you type exit from single-user mode, you will not get another login prompt. Instead, the system will exit single user mode and usually start up multi-user mode.

Multi-User Mode

If the system does not stop in single user mode, it goes on to initialize the system and devices for its main run mode, called *multi-user mode*. UNIX is usually quite verbose as it is coming up, giving you startup messages such as the following as each subsystem is activated:

```
Mounting filesystems
cron started, pid=274
Network daemons started: portmap inetd routed
printing subsystem started
```

Again, try to learn your system's bootup messages even if you don't understand what they mean so that you will recognize if something out of the ordinary occurs during bootup. Once all initialization is complete, you should be able to log in to the system on any of the system ports.

System V Run Levels

System V UNIX uses a number from 0 to 6 to indicate how far the system has been initialized. These numbers are called init levels or run levels, and they are outlined in Table 12.1.

TABLE 12.1   **Common UNIX System V run levels**

Run Level	Description
0	Totally shutdown state; ready to power-off
1	Maintenance mode/single user mode
2	Multi-user mode
3	Multi-user mode with filesystems exported (Solaris)
3, 4, 5	Customizable run levels (varies by site)
5	Shutdown and cut power (Solaris)
6	Standard shutdown and reboot

AIX and SCO UNIX normally operate in run level 2. Solaris normally operates in run level 3. Sometimes there is an s or S state for single user mode, which differs from run level 1 only in minor respects. You can display the current run level from the root account by entering the following command:

```
# who -r
.          run-level 2 Feb 18 08:13      2    0    S
#
```

The above example shows that you are currently in run level 2, which you entered on Feb 18 at 08:13. The previous run level was S (single-user mode), which is a state you pass through each time you bring up the system.

Shutting Down the System (*shutdown*)

As we have seen from the previous section, it is vital that UNIX be shut down properly before the power is turned off to prevent file corruption or loss. UNIX offers many commands to shut down the system such as powerdown, reboot, haltsys, or init 0. Beware of such commands. The man pages will tell you that all users must already be logged out, filesystems must be unmounted, and networking must be closed before it is safe to run some of those commands. In general, you should use the shutdown command, which was designed to bring the system down safely.

Shutting down the system

1. Log in as root.

2. Use the who and ps commands to make sure that users or programs are not in the middle of updating important files on the system.

3. Shut down all databases that require a special shutdown before the system itself can be shut down. Follow the proper steps for that database.

4. Enter cd / to verify that you are in the root directory when you shut down the system. If you are in a mounted directory, you could have problems unmounting that directory later.

5. You will encounter two versions of the shutdown command: a System V version (used on SCO UNIX) and a BSD version (used on AIX). Solaris provides both versions, depending on

your PATH variable. Proceed now to either the System V or BSD shutdown procedure described next. If you are not sure which version of shutdown to use, try the System V method first and enter all possible options: -g, -i, and -y. If you should be using the BSD version of shutdown, you will receive an error, but it will not cause any harm.

Running the System V style *shutdown*

1. Make sure you are logged in as root.

2. Enter shutdown, but do not press the Enter key until you're instructed to do so.

3. Enter a space and then -g MIN. This option specifies the grace period. Replace *MIN* with the number of minutes to broadcast messages to all users that the system is going down. (If -g is omitted, the default is to wait one minute.) Enter -g 0 to shut the system down immediately, without waiting. Do a shutdown only if you are very sure no application file updates are in progress (see the appendix, "UNIX Commands" for a definition of *application file*).

4. Enter a space and then -i RLEVEL, where *RLEVEL* is one of the following numbers:

   0 to totally shut down the system (ready for power-off)

   1 to go to maintenance mode/single user mode

   5 to shut down and turn the power off (only on some Solaris systems)

   6 to shut down and automatically reboot

   If no -i option is specified, most systems will go to run level 0 by default; however, some, such as Solaris, will go to run level 1 (single user mode) instead.

5. If you are sure you want to shut the system down, enter a space and then -y.

6. Press the Enter key to execute your command. If you do not include the -y option with shutdown, when the grace period ends, the system will ask if you (still) want to shut the system down. Enter y to proceed with the shutdown command; enter n to abort the shutdown command.

Running the BSD style *shutdown*

1. Make you are logged in as root.

2. Enter shutdown, but do not press the Enter key until you are instructed to do so.

3. Enter a space.

4. If you want to power off the system, enter the -h option.

   If you want to reboot the system, enter the -r option.

5. Enter a space.

6. You now have three options:

   Enter now if you are sure it is okay to shut down the system immediately.

   Enter +MIN, where *MIN* is the number of minutes the system is to wait while shutdown messages are broadcast periodically.

   Enter HH:MM, where *HH* and *MM* are the number of hours and minutes before the system will be shut down.

7. Press the Enter key to execute your command.

Preventing the UPS from damaging the database

Some UPSs will shut down the system in the event of a prolonged power failure. If you have a database that must be shut down before the system is shut down, you must configure your UPS software to properly shut down the database first.

Automating Jobs at Startup or Shutdown

UNIX provides great flexibility in allowing jobs to run automatically, based either on system events or on time and date. Some of these mechanisms are only for the root user (system administrator), but many of them can be used by all users. The following sections describe the most common functions, which can be performed by the root user only.

Automating Jobs at System Startup on System V UNIX (rc2.d)

The root user (only) can customize and add to the jobs that are run automatically at system bootup. Some systems will use the System V method; others (even some SVR4 systems) will use the BSD method.

Look in the directory named /etc. If your system has files called rc, rc0, and rc2, and if it has directories called rc.d, rc0.d, and rc2.d, :it is using the System V type system startup programs or scripts. These are called *rc scripts* (rc stands for "run control") because these scripts control how you enter or leave certain run levels. (Table 12.1 shows the common System V run levels.) rc2 is a script program that is run when the system changes to run level 2 (multi-user mode). The rc2 script program uses files in directory rc2.d, as in this example from SCO UNIX:

```
I01MOUNTFSYS*    P21perf          P90RESERVED*    S85nis*
➥S91manahttp*

P00SYSINIT*      P70uucp*         P93scohttp*     S85tcp*
➥S95psleeper*

P03RECOVERY*     P75cron*         P95calserver*   S88edge*
➥S99apcssd*

P04CLEAN*        P86scologin*     S00MDAC*        S89nfs*
➥messages/

P05RMTMPFILES*   P86sendmail*     S35dlpi         S90atlas*

P15HWDNLOAD*     P86xdlls*        S60sync*        S90fasttrack*

P16KERNINIT*     P87USRDAEMON*    S80lp*          S90iproute*

P20sysetup*      P88USRDEFINE*    S84rpcinit*     S90secure*
```

After the first letter, each script has a number that controls the order in which the scripts will run. Table 12.2 shows what the first letter of each script means:

TABLE 12.2 **System V rc script prefixes**

Prefix Letter	Meaning
K	Kills a process by running this script
S	Starts a process by running this script
P	Runs P numbers in parallel if there are no S or K scripts in that range (SCO UNIX only)

For example, in the previous output listing, you can see that the lp spooling system is started first, and then tcp networking, and then nfs.

Modifying the System V startup scripts

1. In this directory, create your own script whose name begins with S99. This will cause your script to execute after the other initialization scripts. Set the owner, group, and permissions to match the other files in this directory. There can be more than one script that starts with S99.

2. In your S99 script, enter the system commands you want to run when the system goes to multi-user mode. Use full pathnames for each command, directory, and file; for example, you would use /etc/shutdown instead of shutdown.

If in doubt, use the type command to make sure you have the correct full pathname of commands, as in this example:

```
# type shutdown
shutdown is /sbin/shutdown
#
```

3. Do not create backup copies of your script in this rc2.d directory. If you do, S99yourscript.bak (for example) would be executed during every bootup along with S99yourscript because both are in /etc/rc2.d.

4. Use & to run subtasks in the background in order to prevent the possibility of hanging the system and preventing a reboot; for example, the stty command can be used to set the baud rate of a port, but if the device is not ready—if, for example, a modem is waiting for an incoming call—the stty can hang until the device is ready. If this stty command is in your rc script, the system will also hang, and you'll have to reset and go to single user mode to correct the problem. To prevent such a problem, create a script that accesses the desired port and call that script from the rc script in the background, as shown here:

```
/usr/startup/portsetup &
```

5. If your function needs to execute some particular code during system startup and some other code when the system is shut down, you should perform this additional step. Put a copy of your script in /etc/init.d using a name that does not begin with S99. Solaris uses a hard link to do this; SCO

OpenServer 5 uses complex symbolic links. To find out how to do it on your system, look at other scripts in rc2.d and init.d and follow their examples. The idea is to have one script that handles both the startup and shutdown tasks for this function. The script should save $1 as a mode and then, if that mode is started, the script should execute startup code; when that mode is stopped, the script should execute shutdown code. When you finish, link this script into the multi-user startup directory (/etc/rc2.d) or the shutdown directory (/etc/rc0.d) and add S99 for startup or K## for shutdown.

Automating Jobs at System Shutdown on System V UNIX (rc0.d)

On System V type systems, there is a directory called /etc/rc0.d that contains scripts similar to those in /etc/rc2.d. You could add your script to rc0.d to run when the system changes to run level 0 (the totally shutdown state).

Often a better idea—and one that will work in BSD systems also—is to create your own script as described in the following procedure.

Creating your own script to invoke *shutdown*

Note

This procedure will work on both System V and BSD type systems.

1. Enter the command $ `type shutdown` and press Enter. You'll see output something like this:

   ```
   shutdown is /usr/sbin/shutdown
        $
   ```

   This is the full pathname of `shutdown`.

2. Use the `cd` command to change to the directory that `shutdown` is in.

3. Create a text file and name it `shut`. (This is not a standard name, and you can choose a different name for this alternative to the `shutdown` command.)

   Insert the commands you want to run during shutdown. Then end your script with these lines:

   ```
   cd /[sr]
   shutdown OPTS
   ```

Warning

There is a danger that some administrator or system process will use the **shutdown** command directly instead of your **shut** script. If this is a critical issue, add a shutdown script to /etc/rc0.d instead of creating this shut script.

replacing *OPTS* with the options needed by shutdown on your system.

4. Use the chmod, chown, and chgrp commands to give shut the same permissions, owner, and group as shutdown.

5. Now use the shut command instead of shutdown anytime you want to shut down your system.

SEE ALSO

➤ *For more information on writing shell scripts, see page 637*

Automating Jobs at System Startup on BSD UNIX (rc scripts)

If your system uses BSD startup scripts, you will find a number of scripts whose names begin with rc followed by a period, such as rc.net. All these rc scripts will be in the /etc directory. However, not all rc scripts are run during system startup.

If you run the following command on an AIX UNIX system,

```
ls -lu /etc/rc*
```

you will see output similar to this:

```
-r-xr-xr--   1 bin      bin         1786 Aug 21 16:03
➥/etc/rc
-rw-r--r--   1 root     system        48 Feb  4  1996
➥/etc/rc.bak
-r-xr-xr--   1 bin      bin         2502 Feb  4  1996
➥/etc/rc.bsdnet
-r-x------   1 root     system     21187 Feb  4  1996
➥/etc/rc.motpowerfail
-rw-r--r--   1 root     system       571 Feb  4  1996
➥/etc/rc.ncs
-r-xr-xr--   1 bin      bin         7352 Aug 21 16:03
➥/etc/rc.net
-r-xr-xr--   1 bin      bin         4554 Aug 21 16:03
➥/etc/rc.net.serial
-rw-r--r--   1 root     system       982 Feb  4  1996
➥/etc/rc.netls
-rwxr-xr-x   1 root     system      4201 Aug 21 16:04
➥/etc/rc.nfs
-rwx------   1 root     system     29511 Feb  4  1996
➥/etc/rc.powerfail
-rwxrwxr--   1 root     system      4180 Aug 21 16:04
➥/etc/rc.tcpip
```

The -lu option to ls shows you when the rc scripts were last accessed. You can see that only five of the scripts were used in the last reboot on Aug 21 at 16:04. The other rc scripts have not been accessed since 1996.

Here are lines from the /etc/inittab file, which executes some of these rc scripts on startup.

```
brc::sysinit:/sbin/rc.boot 3 >/dev/console 2>&1 # Phase 3 of
➥system boot
powerfail::powerfail:/etc/rc.motpowerfail -t 5 2>&1 | alog
➥-tboot > /dev/console 2>&1 # Power Failure Detection
rc:2:wait:/etc/rc 2>&1 | alog -tboot > /dev/console # Multi-
➥User checks
...
rctcpip:2:wait:/etc/rc.tcpip > /dev/console 2>&1 # Start
➥TCP/IP daemons
rcnfs:2:wait:/etc/rc.nfs > /dev/console 2>&1 # Start NFS
➥Daemons
...
```

To run a job at system startup, you must insert the job within one of the rc scripts that is run at startup. This is a job for an experienced programmer and should not be attempted by a beginner. Errors could prevent your system from booting correctly later.

Automating Jobs by Any User (profile, *cron, at, batch*)

Regular users can automate particular jobs to run when they log in, or at certain times, or on certain days. The system administrator uses similar mechanisms to run system processes periodically.

Automating Jobs When the User Logs In

Two files are executed by every Bourne or Korn shell user during login:

- /etc/profile
- .profile (in the user's own home directory)

Only the root user can modify /etc/profile because changes in that file affect the logins for all users. For security reasons, you should never give write permission for that file to anyone else.

Safety tip: Use two screens when modifying /etc/profile or .profile

If you make errors when changing these files, you could prevent even the root user from logging back in. After you change /etc/profile or .profile, make sure that you can still log in successfully from another screen. If that fails, you are still logged in on your first screen, and you can correct or undo your change.

Users can usually modify their own .profile files to set up their environment preferences on log in. (On some systems, the administrator might allow users read access to .profile but not write access in order to prevent users from making incorrect or undesirable changes to their .profile files.) Execution of the lines in /etc/profile and .profile has the same effect as if the user typed those same lines at the keyboard just after logging in. For example, an exit command from /etc/profile or .profile will put the user back at the login prompt and force a new login.

/etc/profile and .profile are good places to set shell variables such as PATH, CDPATH, TERM, and umask. Preferred stty options for the port can be set automatically also. Changes to /etc/profile affect all users, but those changes can be altered by code in .profile in the user's home directory.

Put df in root's .profile

The system administrator (root) must constantly monitor all filesystems to make sure they are not filling up because that could cause application errors, system errors, and even file corruption. df shows the disk free blocks. Adding df to root's .profile allows root to see how much disk space is available on each root login.

/etc/profile can also be used to add extra security to your system. For example, using standard Bourne shell programming, /etc/profile could check to see if a user is logging in from a modem port and if so, only allow login at restricted times or ask for an extra password. If the /etc/profile code executes the exit command, the user's login will terminate, and he or she will go back to the initial login prompt.

Scheduling Jobs to Re-run Periodically (*cron*)

UNIX maintains a set of tables called *crontabs* (chronological tables), that contain jobs scheduled to run periodically. There is one table or file, usually in /usr/spool/cron/crontabs, for each user who has submitted a cron job. The system runs that job using that user's account.

To see if any cron jobs have been submitted and to view them, you use the -l option (list) with the crontab command. If you are logged in as root, you might see output like this:

```
# crontab -l
17 5 * * 0 /etc/cleanup > /dev/null
```

```
0 2 * * 0,4 /usr/lib/cron/logchecker
3 3 * * * /usr/lib/cleantmp > /dev/null
1 3 * * * /etc/setclk -rd1800 > /dev/null 2>&1
5 18 * * 1-5 /usr/lib/sa/sa2 -s 8:00 -e 18:01 -i 1200 -A
30 1 * * 2,3,4,5,6 /etc/edge.nightly -MB -n root -d
➥/dev/null 1>/dev/null 2>&1
5 4 * * 0 /etc/shutdown -g5 -i6 -y
#
```

Each line in crontabs has six fields separated by one or more spaces or tabs. Table 12.3 describes the six fields and their contents.

Table 12.3   **Fields in crontabs**

Field	Function	Possible range of values
1	minute of the hour	0–59
2	hour of the day	0–23
3	day of the month	1–31
4	month of the year	1–12
5	day of the week	0–6 (0 refers to Sunday)
6	command to run	

You can indicate consecutive ranges with a dash as in 1–5. Multiple values in one field can be specified in any order and should be separated by a comma (and no spaces), such as 1,3,7,2,25.

In Table 12.3, the command to run (in field 6) can be a UNIX command or a shell script. Use a full pathname to reference all files and any commands that are not in /bin or /usr/bin. Any standard output or standard error messages that are not redirected to a file will be mailed to the user who submitted the cron job. If the system was down at the time and day it was scheduled to run the job, that job will be skipped. It will run again at the next scheduled time and day if the system is up then.

Adding/removing/modifying a *cron* job

1. Log in as the user whose cron job you want to modify. (Don't run cron jobs as root unless it is absolutely necessary.) If you have never added a cron job before, use an account other than root, sys, adm, or uucp so you can practice adding and removing a test cron job first.

2. Enter cd to go to your home directory.

3. Unless the command to run via cron is extremely simple, use vi or another editor to create a shell script (called a *cron script* for this procedure). In that cron script, insert the desired command(s) you want to run from cron. You should use a cron script whenever you want to run a sequence of multiple commands from cron. Test your cron script by running it directly from your terminal. Use full pathnames within your cron script for any files to be accessed. Use full pathnames for any system commands that are not in /bin or /usr/bin. If you are using cron for the first time, try using only the date command, which will be mailed to you from cron. Another good first cron script is to create a small result file in your home directory or /tmp, the result of which is shown here:

   ```
   echo cron test `date` > /tmp/fred.cron.tst
   ```

4. At the shell prompt, test your ERASE key as follows. Enter datex but before pressing the Enter key, press the Backspace key or Ctrl+H to erase the x. Then press the Enter key. The current date and time should be displayed. If not, your ERASE key is not working; do not proceed further.

5. Next, enter this command slowly and carefully:

   ```
   crontab -l > cronfile
   ```

   Check your command carefully before you press the Enter key. Use your ERASE key slowly and carefully to correct any errors. If you get an error saying either No such file or Can't open file, you have no current cron jobs. Just ignore this error and continue to the next step.

6. In step 5, if you accidentally omit the -l option, you could delete all your current ongoing cron jobs. If you lose the root user's cron jobs, important system functions will be disabled. The rest of this step discusses how to try to save your cron jobs if you accidentally omit the -l option.

The missing -l option puts your current crontabs in jeopardy. You will then see the PS2 prompt (usually the greater-than sign), which means the shell is waiting for input from the keyboard to replace your current crontabs. Press your INTR key (usually Ctrl+C or DEL) to abort this command. If the INTR key fails, go to another port and run step 5 correctly. Then come back to this port and enter your EOT key (usually Ctrl+D) to wipe out your current crontabs.

To avoid the dreaded PS2 prompt completely, some users use this command instead of that described in step 5:

```
cp /usr/spool/cron/crontabs/MYID cronfile
```

Replace *MYID* in this line with your login id name.

Some users use crontab -e (which automatically invokes the default EDITOR). However, if you forget the -e option, you still face the same problem described in this step.

7. Enter vi cronfile. (You can use any text editor to edit this file.) Now you should see all of your current ongoing cron jobs in the six-field format discussed earlier. For example, you might see the following line:

```
17 5 * * 0 /etc/cleanup > /dev/null
```

If your login account has never submitted a cron job before, this cronfile will be empty. If this cronfile is empty but it is not supposed to be empty (for instance, the root's cronfile should not be empty), go back to step 1 and start over. If you have lost your prior cron entries, you will have to key them all in again.

8. Use the text editor to modify any existing cron jobs and add new ones—in the six-field format—to this file. If you created a cron script in step 3 of this procedure, add a new six-field line to that file, with the full pathname of your cron script in the last field. When you finish editing, save your work and exit from the editor. This cronfile is just a temporary file, so if you don't like your saved results, go back to step 5 and start over.

9. Enter `cat cronfile`.

Make sure that this file contains proper six-field entries for all previous cron jobs to be retained, plus any modified or new cron jobs you've added.

10. Enter `crontab cronfile`.

This will submit your cron changes, replacing all of your previous cron jobs. If you get an error saying that you are not allowed to submit cron jobs, see the later section "Enabling and Disabling cron/at/batch by User."

11. Enter `crontab -l` to display your current crontab entries as submitted. Then review the warnings about this command that appeared earlier in this procedure.

SEE ALSO

➤ *For more information on editing with* vi, *see pages 449 and 471*

➤ *For more information on displaying a file, see page 147*

Using the Asterisk (*) Wildcard in Crontabs

crontab allows an asterisk (*) wildcard to be used as shown in Table 12.4. Note that it is a crontab wildcard, not a Filename Generation Wildcard nor a regular expression wildcard.

Table 12.4   **Using the asterisk (*) wildcard in *crontabs***

crontabs Field	What an Asterisk Means in That Field
1. minute of the hour	Do job every minute, 60 times per hour
2. hour of the day	Do job every hour, 24 times per day
3. day of the month	Ignore this field and use field 5*
4. month of the year	Do job every month, 12 months per year
5. day of the week	Ignore this field and use field 3*

*An asterisk in both fields 3 and 5 means the job is to run every day.

Note

Remember that this file must contain all cron jobs to run for this login. If you delete an entry from this file, you will be deleting it from cron, and it won't run in the future.

Tips on crontab **field 1: the minute of the hour**

If you find an asterisk in field 1 (to run your job 60 times in one hour), it is usually a mistake. Avoid putting a zero in the minute field for every cron job because that could hurt system performance at the start of every hour. Stagger the minute values for those jobs that don't have to start exactly on the hour.

Running Early Morning Weekday Jobs

Here is a typical `crontab` error:

```
30 1 * * 1-5 /u/backup
```

This company works Monday through Friday and wants to execute a backup at 1:30 a.m. after every work day. However, with this command, Friday's work will not be backed up until Monday morning at 1:30 a.m. Because heavy building maintenance work and power problems are more frequent on weekends, this is not good. Here is the corrected entry, which will also run the backup on Saturday morning:

```
30 1 * * 2-6 /u/backup
```

For the same reason, this would not be a good entry for that company:

```
30 1 * * * /u/backup
```

Because no one is in the office on Saturday and Sunday, the tape will not be changed, and Friday night's backup (which really runs early Saturday) will be rewritten Saturday night and Sunday night. A power problem over the weekend could corrupt files, and then those corrupted files would replace the good Friday night backup.

SEE ALSO

➤ *For more information on backups, see page 327*

Scheduling One-Time Jobs at a Specific Date/Time (*at*)

The UNIX at command allows you to schedule a job to run once at a later predetermined time. If you want to run the job more than once (periodically, for example), see the previous section on the `crontab` command.

Scheduling a job using the *at* command

1. Log in as the user whose account will be used to run the job. Use root only if it is absolutely necessary.

2. Enter at, but do not press the Enter key until you are instructed to do so.

3. Enter a space, and then indicate when to run the command using one of these three methods:

- Method 1 is to enter a time only, for example:

3	means 3 a.m.
17	means 5 p.m.
0704	means 7:04 a.m.
7:04pm	means 7:04 p.m.

The job will run within the next 24 hours at the requested time.

- Method 2 is to enter a time and day, for example:

2pm Sat

1923 Aug 24

7:04pm tomorrow

The job will run within the next year at the requested time on the requested day.

- Method 3 is to give an offset, for example:

now + 5 min

now + 2 days

4. Press the Enter key to execute this line. The cursor will go down to the next line that has no prompt character and wait there for more input. If you get an error at this point, see the later section "Enabling and Disabling `crontab/at/batch` by User."

5. Enter the command that you want to run later. Enter it exactly as you would enter it to run it normally. Then press the Enter key to submit the command. You can continue to enter more commands to be executed in sequence. Press the Enter key after each one.

6. When you finish entering commands, the cursor should be at the start of a blank line. Enter your EOT key (usually Ctrl+D), and your normal shell prompt should appear.

You can use the -1 option with the at command to list your current scheduled jobs. You can use the -r option to remove scheduled jobs. The following example illustrates the use of these options. It also shows a quick command you might want to use for testing the at command. It will create a junk file in the current directory in five minutes if you don't remove the job.

```
$ at now + 5 min
date > junk
warning: commands will be executed using /bin/sh
job 888071220.a-9910:0 at Sat Feb 21 06:27:00 1998
$ at -l
888071220.a-9910:0        Sat Feb 21 06:27:00 1998
$ at -r 888071220.a
at: 888071220.a does not exist: No such file or directory
➥(error 2)
$ at -r 888071220.a-9910:0
$ at -l
$
```

In the above example, notice that the -1 option to the at command shows when the job will run, but it does not show which command will be run. Notice the -r option requires that the full job id be entered.

If the system is down at the time and day the at job is supposed to run, the at job will be run as soon as the system is brought up again (unlike cron). You can even write an at job that will queue itself up to run again periodically. You do so by adding a line like this at the end of the at script:

```
echo "sh jobname" | at 2330 sat next week
```

Scheduling One-Time Jobs to Run When the Load Is Light (*batch*)

The batch command can be used to run a job whenever the system feels the load is light enough—which means you can't predict when it will run. If your system is always heavily loaded, batch is not a useful command for you because it will never be able to start your job.

Using the *batch* command

1. Enter batch and press the Enter key. The cursor will go down to the next line with no prompt character, where it will wait for more input. If you get an error at this point, see the later section "Enabling and Disabling crontab/at/batch by User."

2. Enter the command that you want to run later. Enter it exactly as you would enter it to run it normally. Press the Enter key to submit the command. You can continue to enter more commands to be performed in sequence. Press the Enter key after each one.

3. When you finish entering commands, the cursor should be at the start of a blank line. Enter your EOT key (usually Ctrl+D), and your normal shell prompt should appear.

Enabling and Disabling *crontab/at/batch* by User

The root user (system administrator) can modify these two files to allow or deny users to use crontabs:

/usr/lib/cron/cron.allow

/usr/lib/cron/cron.deny

The root user also can modify the following two files to allow/deny users to use the at or batch commands:

/usr/lib/cron/at.allow

/usr/lib/cron/at.deny

If the allow files exist, only users listed in that file can use the command. The deny files are used only if the allow files do not exist. In that case, all users can use the command except those listed in the deny file.

Job Priorities

The following sections cover the commands necessary to view and change the priorities of running processes.

Viewing Jobs and Their Priority (*ps*)

You can use the `-lf` options with `ps` to show each running process (job) and its current priority. For example, take a look at this code:

```
$ ps -lf | pg
  F S     UID   PID  PPID  C PRI NI     ADDR    SZ
➥WCHAN    STIME    TTY         TIME CMD
20 S     mori  9998  9374  6  73 20 fb11e798  132  fb11e798
➥06:54:41 ttyR030    00:00:00 -ksh
20 O     mori 10020  9998  7  48 20 fb11e8f0  160
➥- 06:55:23 ttyR030    00:00:00 ps -lf
30 S     mori 10021  9998  2  78 20 fb11ecf8   72  fb11ecf9
➥06:55:23 ttyR030    00:00:00 pg
```

The column labeled NI shows the process `nice` value (in this case, 20). The higher the `nice` value, the lower its priority to get system resources and time (the nicer it is to everyone else on the system). Table 12.5 outlines typical nice values.

Table 12.5 *nice* **(priority) values**

Type of System	Allowed range for *nice* values	Default value
System V	0 to 39	20
BSD	-20 to +20	0

Starting a Job with Low Priority (*nice*)

Starting a job with low priority (*nice*)

1. Enter `nice`, but do not press the Enter key until you are instructed to do so.

2. Enter a space and then enter -VAL, replacing *VAL* with a number between 1 and 19. The larger the value, the nicer you will be to other users on the system; the slower your job will run. The root user (only) can enter `--VAL` to lower the `nice` value and hence raise his job priority above other users. The root user must be careful, however, not to raise the priority so high that the job takes over and disables all other system functions.

3. Enter a space and then enter the desired command to run. If you enter a pipeline, enter a `nice` command for each stage of the pipeline. (See the next example.) Press the Enter key to execute your command.

Your `nice` or `renice` may differ

Check your man pages on `nice` and `renice`. On some systems, the range of `nice` values and whether to enter them as positive or negative may differ from what's described here.

This example shows that the `nice` command must be explicitly invoked for each command in a pipeline. This command pipes the output of `ps` to `pg`. Note also that `ps` has a `nice` increment of 5, and pg has a `nice` increment of 7. Different values were chosen just to illustrate a point; normally you would use the same value for both.

```
$ nice -5 ps -lf | nice -7 pg
  F S       UID    PID  PPID  C PRI NI      ADDR    SZ
➥WCHAN     STIME      TTY          TIME CMD
20 S      mori 10042  9996  5  73 20 fb11e798  132  fb11e798
➥07:12:35 ttyR029    00:00:00 -ksh
20 O      mori 10066 10042  9  44 25 fb11e8f0  160
➥- 07:13:24 ttyR029    00:00:00 ps -lf
20 S      mori 10067 10042  5  76 27 fb11ecf8   72  f093d7c0
➥07:13:24 ttyR029    00:00:00 pg
$
```

Notice the `pg` command has a `nice` value of 27. That's because `nice -7` means to raise the `nice` value 7 points from the default of 20.

Changing the Priority of an Existing Job (*renice*)

Modern UNIX systems support a `renice` command to allow you to change the `nice` value of a process that has already been started. However, you must first look up the PID value for the desired process using the `ps` command (see the previous `ps` example).

Note

See the glossary for the definition of PID value.

Changing the priority of an existing job (*renice*)

1. Enter the `renice` command, but do not press the Enter key until you are instructed to do so.
2. Enter a space and then the `-n` option.
3. Enter a space and then `VAL`, where *VAL* is a number between 1 and 19. This represents the amount to raise the `nice` value and hence lower the priority of the job.

4. Enter a space followed by the PID number for the process (job) you want to change.

5. Your command should look something like this:

```
renice -n 5 10042
```

Press the Enter key to execute your command.

Background Jobs

UNIX is a multi-tasking operating system. This means that, in general, you can start more than one job, and all will run concurrently. Your station is not tied up waiting for them to finish. You can even specify sequences of jobs so that one job will not start until the previous job has completed.

Starting Background Jobs (&)

To start a job in the background, simply end the UNIX command with a space and then an ampersand (&), as shown in this example:

```
$ make acmesys > acme.log 2>&1 &
27903
$
```

Here's a breakdown of the parts of that command:

make is a command that can take a long time to complete; therefore, you might run it in the background so it does not tie up your station.

> acme.log redirects the output from make into a file called acme.log. This is often a good idea when you're starting background because the output is saved for later review. If you don't redirect the output in this way, it will still go to your screen where it could mix with other output.

2>&1 redirects any error messages from the make command so they will go to the same file as the standard output (so you're saving output and errors from make in the same file).

27903 is the job number, which is also called a process id number or PID. If you save this number, you can use it later to check on this job.

When to use nice, at, **and** batch

Use **nice** or **renice** when you need the job to complete quickly but you want to minimize the impact on other users. Use **at** to make sure the job does not run until the time specified. Use **batch** to make productive use of system idle time, but don't use **batch** on a system that is constantly busy.

Preventing Logoff from Killing Background Jobs (*nohup*)

Logging off the system usually terminates all background jobs. Some shells will warn you that you have stopped jobs. If you then type exit a second time, you will terminate those jobs and log off. The nohup command allows you to start background jobs that will not be killed when you log off.

Starting background jobs using *nohup*

1. At the shell prompt, enter nohup. Do not press the Enter key until you are instructed to do so.

2. Enter a space and then the UNIX command you want to run. Remember to redirect standard output and standard error messages if desired.

3. Enter a space and then the ampersand (&).

4. Press the Enter key to execute your command in the background. Now your logoff will not terminate that background job.

If you do not redirect standard output and standard errors, the nohup command will automatically create a file called nohup.out to save them in.

Killing a Background Job (*kill*)

If you write down the PID that is displayed when you start a background job, it is easy to terminate that job using either of two kill commands. The following procedures shows you how to use both commands.

How to terminate a job by its PID

1. From the shell prompt, enter kill PID, where *PID* is the PID number of the process you want to terminate. Double-check that you have entered the number correctly. Then press the Enter key. This kill command gives the job a

chance to terminate gracefully, closing applications and removing lock files and temporary files. No messages will be displayed.

2. Now enter the command `kill -9 PID`, where *PID* is the same number you used in step 1. Double-check that you have entered the number correctly. Then press Enter. This `kill` will end even uncooperative commands. Although you can execute step 2 immediately after step 1, you might want to wait two seconds to let step 1 wrap up.

3. If step 2 gives the error `No such PID`, ignore that error. It just means that step 1 was enough to end the task, and step 2 was unnecessary but not harmful.

If you don't remember your PID number, you can look it up using the `ps` command.

Using *ps* to find a PID number

1. From the shell prompt, enter these two c⟨

```
ps -ef
ps aux
```

Some systems support both of these comm⟨ times only one gives results.

2. Using the command that works on your sy⟨ initial heading to find the PID column, the⟨ umn, and the command (CMD) column.

3. If necessary, rerun the command and pipe it⟨ `less` to see it a page at a time.

Alternatively, you can pipe the output of the⟨ `grep` to filter out the lines you don't care abo⟨ this will also remove the heading.

4. Locate the command that you want to termin⟨ user column to make sure you started this command.

5. Locate the PID for that command. Then you can follow the procedure for terminating a job by its PID.

Here is an example of a command used to find a background job. However, the output was cut off in mid-process. Because `ps` can show so many processes, the command was aborted using ^C (on Solaris).

```
# ps -ef
    UID   PID  PPID  C    STIME TTY       TIME CMD
    root    0     0  0   Feb 20 ?        0:02 sched
    root    1     0  0   Feb 20 ?        0:15 /etc/init -
    root    2     0  0   Feb 20 ?        0:00 pageout
    root    3     0  0   Feb 20 ?        1:02 fsflush
    root  289     1  0   Feb 20 ?        0:00
  ➥/usr/lib/saf/sac -t 300
```

Suppose you were running the previous command to look for a find command that was started earlier. You could use grep to filter out the lines you don't want, as shown here:

```
# ps -ef|grep find
    root 27961 27955  5 13:53:33 pts/1    0:03 find / -name
  ➥acme -print
    root 27967 27955  0 13:54:19 pts/1    0:00 grep find
#
```

From the CMD field (the last field), you can see that two processes mentioning find were found. Looking at field 2, you see that PID 27961 is the find process you want to terminate. Notice that PID 27967 is the grep process that was looking for find; in other words, grep saw itself while it was looking for find.

Here is a similar example that uses an additional grep -v to remove the extraneous grep process from the output:

```
# ps -ef | grep find | grep -v grep
    root 27961 27955  5 13:53:33 pts/1    0:03 find / -name
  ➥acme -print
#
```

When you know the PID you want to terminate, you can canenter these lines to kill the process:

```
kill 27961
kill -9 27961
```

SEE ALSO

➤ *For more information on* grep, *see page 380*

Extra Job Control Under the Korn Shell

In the previous section, we covered use of background jobs that would apply to all shells, including the Bourne shell. Newer shells have made it much easier to work with background jobs by adding a feature called *job control*. For example, some systems have added job control to the Bourne shell, which can be invoked as jsh. This section describes the other job control commands, which are similar to jsh: They are csh for the C shell and ksh for the Korn shell.

Listing Background Jobs (*jobs*)

To list all background jobs in any shell supporting job control, go to the shell prompt and enter **jobs**.

You will see output like this:

```
$ jobs
[4] + Running              find / -name acme -print >
➥/tmp/acme.find &
[3] - Stopped (SIGTSTP)    man find
[2]   Stopped (SIGTSTP)    bc
[1]   Stopped (SIGTSTP)    vi acmereport
$
```

The job number is given in brackets at the start of each line. The job most recently in the foreground (that was most recently active on your screen) is indicated by a plus sign (+). The second most recent job is indicated by a minus sign (-). Notice that you no longer have to worry about PID numbers.

Suspending and Resuming Jobs (Ctrl+Z, *bg*, *fg*)

One of the most powerful applications of job control is to take a foreground job (one that is tying up your keyboard and screen), suspend it in the background so you can enter other commands, and then retrieve the suspended job later.

In some SCO UNIX operating systems, very few utilities honor the Ctrl+Z method for doing this; in those systems vi is the only command that works. Under Solaris and AIX, however, Ctrl+Z seems to work for every utility. You can use it to move jobs very easily between the foreground and the background. This was true in the Korn shell but not under jsh.

Moving a job to the background and back to the foreground

1. Make sure you are in a shell that supports job control, such as the Korn shell (not the Bourne shell). If you are not sure, invoke the Korn shell with the command `exec ksh`.

   Enter any UNIX command that will take some time to complete. Do not enter a final ampersand (&) to the command, and the job will run in the foreground and tie up your keyboard and screen.

2. To move that job to the background, press Ctrl+Z. You should see an acknowledgment like this, specifying the command you were running:

   ```
   ^Z[1] + Stopped (SIGTSTP)        find / -name acme
   ➡-print
   ```

   If you do not see such a message, either your shell does not support job control or your version of UNIX does not support the use of Ctrl+Z to suspend all jobs.

   You will now have a system prompt, at which you can enter other commands. Your previous job is suspended (it's no longer running).

3. Enter `jobs`, and you will see output like this:

   ```
   [2] + Stopped (SIGTSTP)        find / -name acme -print >
   ➡/tmp/acme.find &
   [1] - Stopped (SIGTSTP)        man find
   ```

4. To allow the job to continue running in the background, at the shell prompt, enter `bg %JOBID`, where *JOBID* is the job number shown by the `jobs` command. If the job is the most recent job—as denoted by the plus sign (+)—you can omit `%JOBID` altogether.

5. Enter `jobs` again. Now you should see output like this, indicating that your job is running:

   ```
   [2] +  Running                  find / -name acme -print >
   ➡/tmp/acme.find &
   [1] - Stopped (SIGTSTP)        man find
   ```

6. To bring your job back to the foreground, at the shell prompt, enter `fg %JOBID`, where *JOBID* is the number of the job you want to bring to the foreground. The command

being run will appear on the screen, and the specified job will again have control of your keyboard and screen.

Killing a Background Job Under the Korn Shell (*kill*)

With job control, it is easy to terminate a background job.

Terminating a background job using job control

1. At the shell prompt, enter `jobs` to determine the job number of the job you want to terminate. This should be small number, no greater than the total number of jobs displayed. This is *not* a PID number.

2. Enter the command `kill %JOBID`, where *JOBID* is the number of the job to be terminated.

Or, to terminate the most recent job, you can enter `kill %%`.

Or, to terminate the second most recent job, you can enter `kill %-`.

Pausing Background Jobs Just Before They Output (*stty*)

Some background jobs will compute for a long time and then display a result. You may want the compute phase to continue in the background but then have the job suspend itself until you are ready for the output.

Suspending jobs just before they output

1. At the shell prompt, enter `stty tostop`. This will cause any new background jobs to suspend just before they start any output. This mode will last until you log off.

2. Enter your desired UNIX command, ending in an ampersand (`&`) so it runs in the background. Press Enter.

3. At the shell prompt, enter `jobs`. From the output of the jobs command, determine whether the background job is running. If the state of the background job is `running`, it is not yet ready to display any output.

4. When the `jobs` command shows that your desired background job is `stopped`, it is ready to provide some output.

Note

You can put the command `stty tostop` in your .profile file if you want it set automatically every time you log in.

Enter `fg %JOBID`, where *JOBID* is the number of the stopped job. This will bring the job to the foreground and start the output so that you can see the output on your screen at a time of your choosing.

Saving and Restoring Files Using *tar* and *cpio*

By Steve "Mor" Moritsugu

Backing Up User Files

Backing up files means to make copies of those files so that the files can be recovered later if needed. The files may be copied to the hard disk, but more often backups are made to tape or diskette so your data is protected if the hard disk is physically damaged. Backups can be done over a network to a tape drive on a different system. *Archiving* is another word for backing up. Files backed up onto tape or diskette are called *archive copies* of your data. These tape or diskette archives can also be used to transfer copies of your data to another system.

This section discusses how a user can back up his own files, either to protect the data or to transfer it to another system. The root user can back up the entire system. This chapter also discusses system backups, which are similar to user backups but with some extra considerations.

If your UNIX system is in a restricted area in the computer operations area, you may not be allowed to go near the actual computer. In that case, you cannot insert a tape or diskette for backup purposes. You may have to put in a request for this back-up and schedule it with your system administrator or computer operations department. The administrator may tell you that all files on the system are backed up periodically so there is no need for you to get your own special backups. If so, find out from them the procedure if you need to restore some files.

Network users can become confused about tape and floppy devices. I have seen Windows users telnet into UNIX, which allows the user to log on and run UNIX commands. Instead, the user puts a diskette into the Windows floppy drive and tries to access UNIX by typing in UNIX commands! This doesn't work because the UNIX commands access the floppy drive on the UNIX system. The magic of networking and telnet allow you to run commands on that distant UNIX system, but any UNIX floppy commands access the floppy on that distant UNIX system, not on your own Windows PC. In this situation, you could use a utility like Windows ftp to bring the UNIX file to your local system and then back it up to your local floppy drive.

This chapter is not for network users, who access UNIX from a remote system. This chapter is for those users who have physical access to the UNIX computer itself. To back up files, put your own floppy disk or tape into the UNIX machine. You then run UNIX commands that are discussed in this chapter to back up the files to that floppy or tape. Finally, remove the floppy or tape and store it in a safe place until you need to restore these backup copies of your files, if ever.

Be careful when you insert a floppy or tape with important files that you want to restore. Another user on the system, even a remote user in a different city, could start a floppy or tape operation that will overwrite your tape. Floppies and tapes usually have a little slider that can be moved to write-protect your media and prevent writing.

SEE ALSO

➤ *For more information on ftp file transfer, see page 583*

UNIX Device Files

In UNIX, there are special files that allow you to access physical devices. These files are called *device files* or *device nodes*. If you redirect output to a special device file, the output goes to that physical device. If you redirect input from a special device file, the input (if any) will come from that physical device. Some devices are more complicated and their device nodes can be accessed only in certain ways or by special programs.

By convention, all the special device files are stored in the /dev directory. This causes the full pathname of the device file to start with /dev/, which indicates that this is not a regular UNIX file. Each device file is a pointer to a driver for that device. A *driver* is a software program that contains subroutines that can be called depending on what device function is desired (for example, read, write, rewind, seek, and so on).

Let us examine some device files on Solaris 2.6. The files that access the floppy happen to contain the word diskette (which is not usually true for other UNIX systems). These files are actually symbolic links to much longer device names so I have added the -L option to 1s to follow the symbolic links and look at the actual device files, as we see here:

```
$ ls -lL /dev/*disket*
brw-rw-rw-   1 root      sys         36,  2 Apr 10 16:57
➥/dev/diskette
brw-rw-rw-   1 root      sys         36,  2 Apr 10 16:57
➥/dev/diskette0
crw-rw-rw-   1 root      sys         36,  2 Apr 27 11:24
➥/dev/rdiskette
crw-rw-rw-   1 root      sys         36,  2 Apr 27 11:24
➥/dev/rdiskette0
$
```

In the preceding example, note that the first character in the line (which stands for the file type) is either the letter b or c. b stands for *block* device file; c stands for *character* device file. A character device is also called a *raw* device. It is a driver that simply passes characters one after the other. This is called *sequential access*. A block driver is used for more complicated situations—in this case, allowing random access to specific blocks of the diskette. Some devices have only a character device and no block device (for example, tape drives allow only sequential access).

In the same example, note that the size of the file is missing. File size is normally listed after the group and before the date of last access. In place of the size, device files have two numbers separated by a comma: a major number and a minor number. In the this example, all the files listed have major number 36 and minor number 2. These device files contain no code or data about the device. In fact, device files are totally empty, which is why no size is listed. The driver code to access all devices on the system is linked together to form one large UNIX kernel. A device file major number indicates which driver in the kernel should be used to access this device. The minor number gives the driver additional information about this device.

Some people mistakenly copy /dev files from one UNIX system to another, thinking they are transferring the driver code to the new system. Since the /dev files are only pointers into the kernel, you can understand why their attempts fail.

Determining What UNIX Device Name to Use

In this chapter, I explain how to use tar and cpio to back up and restore files. You can use these commands on all UNIX systems.

However, you must determine what device name to use. This can differ from system to system.

The best course of action is to contact the system administrator and ask what device names are available for backups and whether there are any special rules that must be followed.

Unfortunately, system documentation often does not cover device names. However there are some man pages that are useful for looking up device names:

Solaris:
for floppy devices: man -s 7D fd
for SCSI tape devices: man st

SCO UNIX OpenServer:
for floppy devices: man fd
for SCSI tape devices: man Stp

SCO UNIX UnixWare 7:
for floppy devices: man 7 fd
for SCSI tape devices: man 7 tape

AIX 4.x:
for floppy devices: man fd
for SCSI tape devices: man rmt

Linux:
for floppy devices: man fd
for SCSI tape devices: man st

On other UNIX systems, if they support man -k to look up man topics by keywords, try these commands to find likely man pages covering devices:

```
man -k flop
man -k disket
man -k tape
man -k scsi
```

On Solaris, use the following command:

```
man -k tape
```

This command produces output that includes these lines:

```
rmt             rmt (1m)          - remote magtape protocol
➥module
```

```
st               st (7d)            - driver for SCSI tape
devices
stli             stli (8)           - Silo Tape Library
Interface
```

On AIX 4.x, there is a useful command:

```
lsdev -C ¦ pg
```

This command shows information about each of the device names
on the system. Here is some example output from that command:

```
hdisk0      Available 04-B0-00-0,0 4.0 GB SCSI Disk Drive
hdisk1      Available 04-B0-00-1,0 4.0 GB SCSI Disk Drive
rmt0        Available 04-B0-00-4,0 Travan TR-4 4GB Tape Drive
cd0         Available 04-B0-00-5,0 CD-ROM Drive
```

There is no easy way to determine on your own the exact device
names to use on an unfamiliar UNIX system. We have looked at
several commands you can use to get some clues as to these device
names. Again the best advice is to ask your system administrator
or anyone on the system who uses a device you want to use.

Tape Drives

The most common type of tape drive found on UNIX systems is a
SCSI tape drive. These require a SCSI controller card to be in your
computer. SCSI disk drives, SCSI tape drives, and SCSI CD-ROM
drives can then be cabled to the SCSI controller. The system
administrator must set up each new SCSI device, although there are
UNIX systems that autosense new SCSI devices upon bootup. Any
administrative setup process will vary from system to system.

Here are some of the most common types of SCSI tape drives:

- Quarter-inch Cartridge (QIC) streamer tape drives—
  Quarter-inch refers to the width of the tape. There are different models of these tape drives. Some hold as little as 250
  MB of data; others hold up to 26 GB of data. Many of the
  larger tape drives can read tapes written on the smaller QIC
  tape drives.

- 4-mm DAT drives—A common model of this drive holds 4
  GB of raw data and up to 8 GB due to compression. Tapes
  come in lengths of 90 meters or 120 meters. Longer tapes
  can hold more data. There are several styles of tapes, such as

DDS or DDS-II, so it is important to get the correct type of tape for your drive.

- 8-mm Exabyte helical scan drives—Two commonly used types of this drive have capacities of 2.3 or 5 GB.

- 9-track half-inch magnetic tape drives—These drives often have settings for Low (800 bpi), Medium (1600 bpi), or High (3200 bpi) density. They are also called *reel to reel* drives. Due to their cost, they are rarely used except to exchange or submit data, especially in government agencies.

New tape drives and changes to this list occur frequently. For example, there are now also Trevan, AIT, and DLT tape drives. If you are going out to purchase a tape cartridge to back up your files, be careful to get the correct type and length of tape for your tape drive. The best way to do this is to write down the brand and model of tapes that are currently being used.

UNIX Tape Device Names

The UNIX driver name for a SCSI tape simply numbers each SCSI tape drive in the order in which it was added to the system. This tape drive number is a logical number that has no relation to any physical values such as SCSI target id number. Here are the SCSI tape device names for some specific types of UNIX systems:

- Solaris—/dev/rmt/0, /dev/rmt/1, /dev/rmt/2, and so on

- SCO UNIX OpenServer—/dev/rStp0, /dev/rStp1, /dev/rStp2, and so on

- SCO UNIX UnixWare 7—/dev/rmt/ctape1, /dev/rmt/ctape2, and so on

- AIX 4.x—/dev/rmt0, /dev/rmt1, /dev/rmt2, and so on

- Linux—/dev/st0, /dev/st1, and so on

The above list shows that to use the first tape drive on a Solaris system, you would use /dev/rmt/0. To use the second tape drive added to a SCO UNIX OpenServer system, you would use /dev/rStp1.

Most systems allow several device names for a given tape drive. Each name has the same major number (since it uses the same kernel driver) but has a different minor number to modify how the tape drive functions. The most common alternative device name is the non-rewinding tape device name. When using the standard tape device name, the UNIX command accessing the tape does not complete until the tape operation has completed and the tape is completely rewound. If you use the non-rewinding tape device instead, then this final rewind operation is not done. This leaves the tape positioned just after the last file accessed so that new files can be read or written at that point, the tape drive hardware supports this.

Following are some alternative names for a SCSI tape device 0:

- Solaris

/dev/rmt/0	standard device name
/dev/rmt/0n	non-rewinding device
/dev/rmt/0l	select low density
/dev/rmt/0m	select medium density
/dev/rmt/0h	select high density
/dev/rmt/0u	select ultra
/dev/rmt/0c	select compressed
/dev/rmt/0b	select BSD behavior

  These options can be combined in combinations.

  Here are the available device files in the directory /dev/rmt:

0	0bn	0cb	0cn	0hb	0hn	0lb	0ln
0b	0c	0cbn	0h	0hbn	0l	0lbn	0m
0mn	0u	0ubn	0n	0ub	0un	0mb	0mbn

- SCO UNIX OpenServer

/dev/rStp0	standard device name
/dev/nrStp0	non-rewinding device
/dev/xStp0	to issue special commands

- SCO UNIX UnixWare 7

  /dev/rmt/ctape1   standard device name

  /dev/rmt/ntape1   non-rewinding device

  /dev/rmt/nrtape1   retention instead of rewinding device

  /dev/rmt/utape1   unload on close

- AIX 4.x

	Low Capacity	**Retention on open**	**Rewind on close**
/dev/rmt0	N	N	Y
/dev/rmt0.1	N	N	N
/dev/rmt0.2	N	Y	Y
/dev/rmt0.3	N	Y	N
/dev/rmt0.4	Y	N	Y
/dev/rmt0.5	Y	N	N
/dev/rmt0.6	Y	Y	Y
/dev/rmt0.7	Y	Y	N

- Linux

  /dev/st0   standard device name

  /dev/nst0   non-rewinding device

Tapes do not have to be formatted before use. Some applications, however, must initialize a tape the first time it is used for that application, but the application should prompt you as needed. Periodically, quarter-inch (QIC) cartridges should be retensioned to ensure smooth tape flow while reading or writing for maximum data reliability. After using the non-rewinding device node, you should issue the rewind command before you remove the tape. The following list gives the complete shell commands to retention or rewind the first tape drive on several types of UNIX systems:

- Solaris 2.x

```
mt -f /dev/rmt/0 retention
mt -f /dev/rmt/0 rewind
```

- SCO UNIX OpenServer

  ```
  tape reten /dev/rStp0
  tape rewind /dev/rStp0
  ```

- SCO UNIX UnixWare 7

  ```
  tape reten /dev/rmt/ctape1
  tape rewind /dev/rmt/ctape1
  ```

- AIX 4.x

  ```
  (no retention command)
  mt -f /dev/rmt0 rewind
  ```

- Linux

  ```
  mt -f /dev/st0 retention
  mt -f /dev/st0 rewind
  ```

Diskette Drives

Floppy diskettes provide a convenient way to back up or transport files or programs, but they hold far less data than a tape backup. The most common floppy diskette drive is the 3.5-inch floppy drive. Each double-sided high-density floppy has a capacity of 1.44 MB. In the past, you could also find boxes of lower-capacity single-sided or low-density floppy diskettes, but these are rare now. Some systems use the older 5.25-inch floppy drives. Double-sided high-density 5.25-inch diskettes could only hold 1.2 MB. 5.25-inch diskettes also used to come in the lower-capacity single-sided or low-density varieties. You might encounter the newer 2.88 MB floppy diskettes, which require special drives to hold that 2.88 MB capacity. Some UNIX systems have no floppy drive at all.

UNIX Diskette Device Names

There are usually a number of floppy device files in the /dev directory to handle these single-sided and low-density diskettes. On SCO UNIX OpenServer, for example, the floppy device names contain phrases such as 48, 96, or 135 to indicate the number of tracks per inch in the floppy diskette; ss or ds to indicate single sided or double sided; and 9, 15, 18, 21, or 36 to indicate the number of sectors per track. The following shows the

various devices files for the A: floppy (floppy drive 0 (fd0) on
SCO UNIX OpenServer):

```
$ cd /dev
$ ls -CF *fd0*
fd0             fd048           fd096ds15       rfd0135ds21
➥rfd048ss8

fd0135ds15      fd048ds8        fd096ds18       rfd0135ds36
➥rfd048ss9

fd0135ds18      fd048ds9        fd096ds9        rfd0135ds9
➥rfd096

fd0135ds21      fd048ss8        rfd0            rfd048
➥rfd096ds15

fd0135ds36      fd048ss9        rfd0135ds15     rfd048ds8
➥rfd096ds18

fd0135ds9       fd096           rfd0135ds18     rfd048ds9
➥rfd096ds9

$
```

We can ignore most of these device names since floppies with
less than 1.44 MB are rarely used anymore. In the following list,
I give the device files for the 1.44 MB 3.5-inch floppy, which is
the most common. I also give the 2.88 MB 3.5-inch floppy
device names, in case you encounter this extended capacity drive.
Most UNIX systems now also provide an autosensing floppy
device file that automatically adjusts to the formatted capacity of
the diskette. You can use these autosensing device files for most
floppy operations, but some UNIX systems do not allow the
autosensing device to be used when formatting. I have also
included the complete shell commands to format a floppy in this
list of floppy device files:

- Solaris

/dev/diskette	autosensing block device file
/dev/rdiskette	autosensing character or raw device file
fdformat /dev/rdiskette	to format a 1.44 MB diskette

  Note that under Solaris, there is a Volume Management
  Daemon (vold) that wants full control of all diskette and
  CD-ROM drives. You cannot access these devices from the
  command line while vold is running.

- SCO UNIX OpenServer

  /dev/fd0   autosensing block device file

  /dev/rfd0   autosensing character or raw
                                    device file

  /dev/fd0135ds36   2.88 MB block device file

  /dev/rfd0135ds36   2.88 MB character or raw
                                    device file

  /dev/fd0135ds18   1.44 MB block device file

  /dev/rfd0135ds18   1.44 MB character or raw
                                    device file

  format /dev/rfd0135ds18   to format a 1.44 MB diskette

- SCO UNIX UnixWare 7

  /dev/dsk/f0t   autosensing block device file

  /dev/rdsk/f0t   autosensing character or raw
                                    device file

  /dev/dsk/f03et   2.88 MB block device file

  /dev/rdsk/f03et   2.88 MB character or raw
                                    device file

  /dev/dsk/f03ht   1.44 MB block device file

  /dev/rdsk/f03ht   1.44 MB character or raw
                                    device file

  format /dev/rdsk/f03ht   to format a 1.44 MB diskette

- AIX 4.x

  /dev/fd0   autosensing block device file

  /dev/rfd0   autosensing character or raw
                                    device file

  /dev/fd0.36   2.88 MB block device file

  /dev/rfd0.36   2.88 MB character or raw
                                    device file

  /dev/fd0.18   1.44 MB block device file

  /dev/rfd0.18   1.44 MB character or raw
                                    device file

  format -d /dev/rfd0   to format a 1.44 MB diskette

- Linux

/dev/fd0	autosensing block device file
(none)	autosensing character or raw device file
/dev/fd0E2880	2.88 MB block device file
(none)	2.88 MB character or raw device file
/dev/fd0H1440	1.44 MB block device file
(none)	1.44 MB character or raw device file
fdformat /dev/fd0H1440	to format a 1.44 MB diskette

Choosing *tar* or *cpio* or Other Backup Programs

tar and cpio are two traditional utilities that are found on all types of UNIX systems, and which allow you to save and restore files. There are many other backup utilities on UNIX systems that do a better job and are easier to use than tar or cpio. They have names like dump, ufsdump, Lone Tar, BackupEdge, bru, mksysb, Solaris Data Backup, ARCserve, Legato Networker, and so on. Some of these are standard utilities on one particular type of UNIX; some are extra-cost software available from third-party vendors. For your own UNIX system, you should survey the backup programs available for your type of UNIX and choose the one that gives you the best features.

Why consider tar or cpio at all if there are better programs available? The answer is that tar and cpio are valuable because you will find them on virtually all UNIX systems. Assume you are going on the road and will visit ten different UNIX systems and want to load a demo program at each site. What type of backup of the demo program will you take with you? If these are unknown systems, your safest bet is to take a tar or cpio backup of the demo. For the same reason, if you need to ship software to many diverse UNIX systems, tar or cpio is a sensible choice.

Warning: Restoring a complete backup is not trivial

You may think that your system is safe because you have a complete backup. However, on many types of UNIX, before you can restore your backup you must completely reinstall and reconfigure the operating system (which can be as difficult as it sounds, if not more so). When evaluating backup programs, give high marks to utilities that can automatically restore your whole system in an emergency.

If you receive software from a vendor who supports several different types of UNIX systems, the software you receive is likely to be in tar or cpio format.

It is valuable for you to learn both tar and cpio because you could receive data in either form. tar is the easier utility to use, however, and many vendors choose this format for sending out their software products. tar is very convenient for backing up specific files or directories. It backs up any directory recursively, which means it backs up all files and subdirectories of that directory, and all files and subdirectories of those subdirectories, and so on.

On the Internet, you will sometimes see download files with the extension .tar, which indicates a tar archive. This means that tar has been used to save a group of files as a single disk file so there is only one file to download instead of many. You may also see the extension .tgz which is a tar archive that has been compressed by gzip so it will be faster to download.

tar has historically had some significant limitations that argue against its use in backing up a complete UNIX system (see the later section "tar Limitations"). cpio offers better flexibility and control in choosing what is backed up, for example. However, this makes cpio more complicated to use. With cpio, you can choose to back up just portions of a directory or choose to exclude portions of a directory, which tar cannot do. cpio also gives you much greater flexibility when selectively restoring files from a backup that tar gives you. cpio allows you to do incremental backups, which means you only back up files that have changed since the last backup; tar does not. cpio, despite its added complexity, is a better choice for doing a complete backup than tar, especially on older UNIX systems.

The following sections discuss the use of tar and cpio in your system backups and restores.

Using *tar* to Back Up and Restore Files

You will find that this section on tar uses much of the same wording as in the following section on cpio. The two commands have similar functionality and only some specific details and examples change the two sections. The tar and cpio sections are complete in themselves without complicated references to one another, but if you read them both, you'll get a strong sense of deja vu.

Backing Up a Directory Subtree

tar stands for *tape archive* utility because typical UNIX backups are done on a tape drive. tar can also back up to a diskette or a disk file. Here is an example of a basic tar command to back up one complete directory:

```
$ cd /usr/fred/projects
$ tar cvf /dev/XXX? .
```

First use cd to change to the directory to back up. tar backs up that directory recursively, automatically including all files and subdirectories and their contents. Following are descriptions of the other elements of this tar command:

$	This represents the shell prompt. Your shell prompt may be different.
tar	A UNIX command to back up files to a tape archive. This tar archive is usually saved on a tape or diskette but can also be saved in a disk file.
cvf	Three separate options for the tar command. tar historically did not allow a dash (-) before the first option but newer versions of tar allow it for compatibility with other UNIX commands. Take a look at each letter separately:

	c	Creates a backup. The first letter in this tar option list must be c, x, or t.
	v	Verbose (shows filenames being backed up).
	f	Allows the specification of the device or file to back up to.

/dev/XXX?	It is very important to replace this with the tape or diskette device name that you want to back up to. (We covered these device names at the

start of this chapter.) You could also specify a disk filename to hold the tar archive.

. A period is a relative pathname indicating that the current directory is the one to back up. Some users mistakenly put an asterisk (*) here rather than the period, but an asterisk does not back up hidden files (files that start with a period) in this directory.

Give tar a valid /dev device name

Don't assume that a valid device name for one system will work on another system. When you enter your tar command, double-check your spelling of the /dev device to back up to. If you use a wrong device name or a misspelled name, tar backs up your files to a disk file, which could use up all available disk blocks and crash your system.

When you run this tar command, you might see output similar to the following:

```
$ cd /usr/fred/projects
$ tar cvf /dev/XXX? .
a ./ 0K
a ./acme/ 0K
a ./acme/report6 1K
a ./pegasus/ 0K
a ./pegasus/1997/ 0K
a ./pegasus/1997/expenses 1K
a ./pegasus/1997/sales 4K
a ./pegasus/1998/ 0K
a ./pegasus/1998/expenses 8K
a ./pegasus/1998/sales 10K
$
```

Because we used the tar v option, we see each directory and file name as it is being backed up, along with the size of the file. The letter a at the start of each line tells us that the file is being archived (saved on the backup diskette or tape). If there is a large amount of data, backups can take hours to complete. Once the tar backup has completed, we can refer to the media that contains the backup as a tar archive. Depending on the type of media, we can also refer to the backup as a tar diskette or tar tape.

If you omit the v option, then no filenames are displayed during the tar backup:

```
$ cd /usr/fred/projects
$ tar cf /dev/XXX? .
$
```

Backing Up Selected Directories or Files

You can specify a list of specific files or directories for tar to back up by using the following command:

```
$ cd /usr/fred/projects
$ tar cvf /dev/XXX? ./acme* ./reports/1997 ./reports/1998
```

./acme* illustrates that shell filename wildcards can be used to generate a list of files—in this case all files and directories that start with acme. ./reports/1997 illustrates that directories can be specified. These are backed up recursively.

The preceding example specifies relative pathnames to back up, which is the recommended procedure.

SEE ALSO

➤ *For more information on the asterisk (*) wildcard, see page 232*

Listing the Table of Contents of a *tar* Archive

Enter the following command to display (to standard output) the contents of a tar archive (the filenames that have been saved on this tar diskette or tape):

```
$ tar tvf /dev/XXX?
```

t shows the table of contents of the backup. The first letter in this tar option list must be c, x, or t. No files are saved or restored by this operation. /dev/XXX? should be replaced with the tar device or backup filename.

When you run this tar command, you might see output such as the following:

```
$ tar tvf /dev/XXX?
drwxr-xr-x 1001/10           0 Apr 28 21:23 1998 ./
dr-xr-x--- 1002/10           0 Apr 28 21:24 1998 ./acme/
-r--r--r-- 1002/10          29 Apr 28 21:24 1998 ./acme/report6
drwxr-xr-x 1001/10           0 Apr 28 21:25 1998 ./pegasus/
drwxr-xr-x 1001/10           0 Apr 28 21:26 1998 ./pegasus/1997/
-rw-r--r-- 1001/10         135 Apr 28 21:26 1998 ./pegasus/1997/
➥expenses
-rw-r--r-- 1001/10        3281 Apr 28 21:27 1998 ./pegasus/1997/
➥sales
```

```
drwxr-xr-x 1001/10         0 Apr 28 21:27 1998 ./pegasus/1998/
-rw-r--r-- 1001/10      7995 Apr 28 21:26 1998 ./pegasus/1998/
➥expenses
-rw-r--r-- 1001/10      9463 Apr 28 21:27 1998 ./pegasus/1998/
➥sales
$
```

Let me pick the third line of this output and explain each field. This line ends in report6.

-r--r--r--	This is the file type and permissions just as ls -l would show them.
1002/10	1002 signifies the owner of this file (the UID number). 10 signifies the group of the file (the GID number).
29	This is the size of the file in bytes.
Apr 28 21:24 1998	This is the date and time of the last modification of the file.
./acme/report6	This is the filename from the backup.

If you omit the v option, only the filenames are displayed:

```
$ tar tf /dev/XXX?
./
./acme/
./acme/report6
./pegasus/
./pegasus/1997/
./pegasus/1997/expenses
./pegasus/1997/sales
./pegasus/1998/
./pegasus/1998/expenses
./pegasus/1998/sales
$
```

Note that it takes as long to list the table of contents as it does to write the tar archive in the first place.

Using *tar* to Restore Archives

In order to use any file from a tar backup, we must first restore the desired file or files from the tar tape or diskette to the hard disk. Before using tar to restore a large tar archive, however, there are several important details to check. The following sections address such concerns as checking for disk free blocks and absolute and relative pathnames, planning where the files are to be restored, working around absolute filename limitations, and changing to the proper directory.

Checking for Disk Free Blocks

It is important to check for disk free blocks in the various filesystems because if any of the UNIX filesystems run out of available disk blocks, application programs may give errors and abort, which could leave databases in a corrupted state. If the root filesystem runs out of blocks, the whole UNIX system could crash.

In the same way, only a limited number of files can be created in any filesystem. df also shows how many more files can be created in each filesystem. Before you restore an archive, check first that the filesystem is not running out of available files.

Here is an example of the df command:

```
$ df
/                       (/dev/dsk/c0t0d0s0 ):   154776 blocks
➥46382 files
/usr                    (/dev/dsk/c0t0d0s6 ):   240348 blocks
➥254137 files
/proc                   (/proc             ):        0 blocks
➥940 files
/dev/fd                 (fd                ):        0 blocks
➥0 files
/export/home            (/dev/dsk/c0t0d0s3 ): 3456112 blocks
➥427351 files
/opt                    (/dev/dsk/c0t0d0s5 ):   382996 blocks
➥268002 files
/tmp                    (swap              ):   198216 blocks
➥9636 files
/export/home/data    (/dev/dsk/c0t0d1s0 ): 8231524 blocks
➥933162 files
$
```

You will see one line in df for each filesystem that exists in your UNIX system. In the above example, there are eight filesystems. Each filesystem is known by the directory at the start of the line.

The /export/home/data filesystem in the above example has the most available blocks (8231524) and the most available files (933162) so that is where you would want to restore any large backups. root (/) has the fewest available blocks (154776) and /tmp has the fewest available files (9636) so you should not restore any large archives to those filesystems. Disregard /proc because it is not a disk filesystem.

You can determine which filesystem a directory is in by finding the longest starting directory in df. For example, /export/home/data/acme is in the /export/home/data filesystem, not the /export/home filesystem because you use the longest df directory that applies.

SEE ALSO

➤ *For more information on* df *and filesystems, see page 74*

Checking for Absolute versus Relative Pathnames

Before you restore any files from a tar backup, list the tar table of contents and check whether the filenames begin with a slash (/). Absolute or full pathnames begin with a slash. Relative pathnames do not begin with a slash.

Take a look at the following example:

```
$ tar tvf /dev/XXX?
drwxr-xr-x 1001/10          0 Apr 28 21:23 1998 /mori/
dr-xr-x--- 1002/10          0 Apr 28 21:24 1998 /mori/acme/
-r--r--r-- 1002/10         29 Apr 28 21:24 1998
➥/mori/acme/report6
drwxr-xr-x$ tar tvf /dev/XXX?   1001/10          0 Apr 28
➥21:25 1998 /mori/pegasus/
drwxr-xr-x 1001/10          0 Apr 28 21:26 1998 /mori/pegasus/
➥1997/
-rw-r--r-- 1001/10        135 Apr 28 21:26 1998 /mori/pegasus/
➥1997/expenses
-rw-r--r-- 1001/10       3281 Apr 28 21:27 1998 /mori/pegasus/
➥1997/sales
drwxr-xr-x 1001/10          0 Apr 28 21:27 1998 /mori/pegasus/
➥1998/
-rw-r--r-- 1001/10       7995 Apr 28 21:26 1998 /mori/pegasus/
➥1998/expenses
-rw-r--r-- 1001/10       9463 Apr 28 21:27 1998 /mori/pegasus/
➥1998/sales
$
```

In this example, all the filenames begin with a slash (for example, /mori/acme/report6). Therefore the above tar backup contains absolute pathnames rather than relative pathnames.

Now consider this example:

```
$ tar tvf /dev/XXX?
dr-xr-x--- 1002/10          0 Apr 28 21:24 1998 ./acme/
-r--r--r-- 1002/10         29 Apr 28 21:24 1998 ./acme/report6
drwxr-xr-x 1001/10          0 Apr 28 21:25 1998 ./pegasus/
drwxr-xr-x 1001/10          0 Apr 28 21:26 1998 ./pegasus/
➥1997/
-rw-r--r-- 1001/10        135 Apr 28 21:26 1998 ./pegasus/
➥1997/expenses
-rw-r--r-- 1001/10       3281 Apr 28 21:27 1998 ./pegasus/
➥1997/sales
drwxr-xr-x 1001/10          0 Apr 28 21:27 1998 ./pegasus/
➥1998/
-rw-r--r-- 1001/10       7995 Apr 28 21:26 1998 ./pegasus/
➥1998/expenses
-rw-r--r-- 1001/10       9463 Apr 28 21:27 1998 ./pegasus/
➥1998/sales
$
```

In the preceding example, all the filenames begin "dot slash" (./). Because they do not start with a slash, they are relative rather than absolute pathnames.

Finally, take a look at this example:

```
$ tar tvf /dev/XXX?
dr-xr-x--- 1002/10          0 Apr 28 21:24 1998 acme/
-r--r--r-- 1002/10         29 Apr 28 21:24 1998 acme/report6
drwxr-xr-x 1001/10          0 Apr 28 21:25 1998 pegasus/
drwxr-xr-x 1001/10          0 Apr 28 21:26 1998 pegasus/1997/
-rw-r--r-- 1001/10        135 Apr 28 21:26 1998 pegasus/
➥1997/expenses
-rw-r--r-- 1001/10       3281 Apr 28 21:27 1998 pegasus/
➥1997/sales
drwxr-xr-x 1001/10          0 Apr 28 21:27 1998 pegasus/1998/
-rw-r--r-- 1001/10       7995 Apr 28 21:26 1998 pegasus/
➥1998/expenses
-rw-r--r-- 1001/10       9463 Apr 28 21:27 1998 pegasus/
➥1998/sales
$
```

In this example, all the filenames again are relative because none begin with a slash.

SEE ALSO

➤ *For more information on relative and absolute pathnames, see page 49*

Planning Where the Files Will Be Restored

In the preceding section, we saw that our tar backup will either contain absolute or relative pathnames. If the pathnames begin with a leading slash, then the pathnames are absolute. This means that we can restore the files from the backup only to the original directory where they came from. This can be dangerous because we would be restoring old versions of each file, wiping out any new versions and losing any updates done since the tar backup was made.

For example, assume we display the tar table of contents and see this line among the output lines:

```
-rw-r--r-- 1001/10      135 Apr 28 21:26 1998 /mori/pegasus/
➥1997/expenses
```

/mori/pegasus/1997/expenses is an absolute pathname. tar can usually restore this file only to that absolute pathname on disk. Before restoring this file, it would be a good idea to copy the current version of that file to ensure that all the new updates are retained.

If the files in the tar archive use relative pathnames, however, we can restore the files to many different directories. This is useful, for example, when we want to look up information in the old file from the tar backup without overwriting the current version of that file. In this case, we would restore the backup file to a temporary working directory, look up the desired information, and then delete the old file when we are done.

Assume we display the tar table of contents and see either filenames that begin with dot slash (./) or filenames that begin with neither dot nor slash, such as the following:

```
-rw-r--r-- 1001/10      135 Apr 28 21:26 1998 ./mori/pegasus/
➥1997/expenses
-rw-r--r-- 1001/10      135 Apr 28 21:26 1998 mori/pegasus/
➥1997/expenses
```

In either case, our backup files are using relative pathnames. You can predict where tar will restore these files by inserting the current directory at the start of the relative pathname to be restored.

For example, if my current directory is /tmp, then tar would restore the expenses file from the previous paragraph to this absolute pathname:

/tmp/mori/pegasus/1997/expenses

In another example, if my current directory is /mori/pegasus, then tar would restore the expenses file from the previous paragraph to this absolute pathname:

/mori/pegasus/mori/pegasus/1997/expenses

Finally, if my current directory is / (the root directory), then tar would restore the expenses file from the previous paragraph to this absolute pathname:

/mori/pegasus/1997/expenses

In summary, if the tar archive contains absolute pathnames, tar restores those files (from tape or diskette) back to their original location. If the archive contains relative pathnames, tar restores the files to pathnames determined by adding the current directory to the tar pathname.

Considering Absolute Filename Work-arounds

If you create your tar archive using absolute filenames, you can restore those files only back to their original location (usually). This is a very great and frustrating limitation of tar. For this reason, the documentation on tar usually advises you to use relative pathnames when doing a tar backup. In the earlier section of this book on using tar to back up a directory subtree, I only document how to back up using relative pathnames.

tar, under Linux/GNU systems, automatically strips the leading slash when the tar backup is created so that the tar archive always uses relative pathnames. However, you can still encounter the frustration of absolute pathnames under Linux/GNU tar in two ways: You can use a special Linux/GNU tar -P option to preserve the leading slash or you might receive a tape from another system written using absolute pathnames.

tar under SCO UNIX has a very nice -A option that suppresses the leading slash on restore. You can then restore absolute pathnames as though they were relative pathnames in the tar archive. You can add the -A option anywhere in the list of tar options as long as it is after the initial x option. I did not find this -A option on AIX, Solaris, or Linux/GNU.

If absolute pathnames in tar is a big problem for you, see whether your system supports the pax command, which should be able to read tar archives and supports an -s option to modify the filenames found.

Changing to the Proper Directory

If the files in the tar archive use absolute pathnames, it makes no difference what directory you change to before doing the tar restore command.

If the files in the tar archive are relative, one of the most crucial and dangerous decisions when restoring relative files using tar is to choose what directory to change to before you start the tar restore. Because you are restoring one or more old archive files, there is a danger of unintentionally overwriting the current version of those files. To determine what directory to change to, compare the pathname on tape with the absolute pathname of the location in which you want to restore the files:

```
Example 1
    pathname on tar archive:
        ./mori/pegasus/1997/expenses
    desired absolute pathname after restore:
        /tmp/restoredata/mori/pegasus/1997/expenses
    directory to change to before doing the tar restore:
        /tmp/restoredata
Example 2
    pathname on tar archive:
        ./mori/pegasus/1997/expenses
    desired absolute pathname after restore:
        /mori/pegasus/1997/expenses
        i.e. we do want to restore the file to its original
➥location
    directory to change to before doing the tar restore:
        /
```

```
Example 3
    pathname on tar archive:
        ./mori/pegasus/1997/expenses
    desired absolute pathname after restore:
        /pegasus/1997/expenses
    directory to change to before doing the tar restore:
        We cannot complete this example by just setting our
►current
        directory. It could be done by more complex procedures
►such as
        creating a subdirectory mori as a symbolic link to
►root (/), or
        by restoring the files to some temporary directory
►and then
        moving them to the desired location.
```

Restoring All Files to the Original Directory

Restoring files can be tricky and dangerous: There is a possibility that you will overwrite the wrong files. I will show you several ways to restore and discuss their good points and bad points.

You probably won't want to use the easiest restore, which is to put all the files back where they came from. If you do this, you destroy your files that have up-to-date information and replace them with files from the backup that have old information. Now you see why I said you probably won't want to do this. This operation is done only rarely. For example, if something goes wrong with a major update operation and all the current files are corrupted, you may want to restore all the files from older but uncorrupted versions from the backup.

To restore all files in the tar backup to their original directory, change to the directory where you originally made your backup. Then issue the tar restore command shown here:

```
$ cd /usr/fred/projects
$ tar xvf /dev/XXX?
```

/usr/fred/projects is just an example directory name. Enter in its place the directory where you made the backup. If the tar archive contains absolute pathnames, it does not matter what directory you change to.

x means to extract files from the backup. The first letter in this tar option list must be c, x, or t. Extracting (restoring) files is always a dangerous option because you must make sure that you do not overwrite the wrong files.

/dev/XXX? should be replaced with the file or device name for your tar archive.

Here is an example showing what the screen looks like when you run this command:

```
$ cd /usr/fred/projects
$ tar xvf /dev/XXX?
x ., 0 bytes, 0 tape blocks
x ./acme, 0 bytes, 0 tape blocks
x ./acme/report6, 29 bytes, 1 tape blocks
x ./pegasus, 0 bytes, 0 tape blocks
x ./pegasus/1997, 0 bytes, 0 tape blocks
x ./pegasus/1997/expenses, 135 bytes, 1 tape blocks
x ./pegasus/1997/sales, 3281 bytes, 7 tape blocks
x ./pegasus/1998, 0 bytes, 0 tape blocks
x ./pegasus/1998/expenses, 7995 bytes, 16 tape blocks
x ./pegasus/1998/sales, 9463 bytes, 19 tape blocks
$
```

Notice each line begins with an x, indicating that the file shown on that line is being extracted from the tar archive to the disk.

Restoring All Files to a Different Directory

Be forewarned that the procedure of restoring all files from a tar archive to a different directory can be used only if there are relative pathnames in the tar archive. Review the earlier sections to check absolute versus relative pathnames, check the disk free blocks, and choose a filesystem that has plenty of available blocks. Then change to the proper directory. Here is an example:

```
$ cd /tmp
$ tar xvf /dev/XXX?
x ., 0 bytes, 0 tape blocks
x ./acme, 0 bytes, 0 tape blocks
x ./acme/report6, 29 bytes, 1 tape blocks
```

```
x ./pegasus, 0 bytes, 0 tape blocks
x ./pegasus/1997, 0 bytes, 0 tape blocks
x ./pegasus/1997/expenses, 135 bytes, 1 tape blocks
x ./pegasus/1997/sales, 3281 bytes, 7 tape blocks
x ./pegasus/1998, 0 bytes, 0 tape blocks
x ./pegasus/1998/expenses, 7995 bytes, 16 tape blocks
x ./pegasus/1998/sales, 9463 bytes, 19 tape blocks
$
```

In this example, the acme and pegasus directories from the tar backup are restored in the /tmp directory. You can choose some directory other than /tmp if another filesystem has enough available disk blocks.

Again, be warned: If the tar archive contains absolute pathnames, your current directory is ignored and the files are restored to their original location, which could be disastrous!

Restoring Only Selected Directories or Files

It is possible to restore only selected directories or files, as this example shows. It is very important to specify the directories or files exactly as they appear in the tar table of contents, including any leading slash (/) or dot slash (./). Any directories are restored recursively.

Consider the following command:

```
$ cd desired-dir
$ tar xvf /dev/XXX? ./acme/report6 ./pegasus/1997
```

desired-dir should be replaced with the desired directory in which you want to issue the tar command.

/dev/XXX? should be replaced with the tar file or device name.

./acme/report6 illustrates how to restore a file.

./pegasus/1997 illustrates how to restore a directory and all of its files and subdirectories.

Note that it takes as long to restore selected files as it takes to write the tar archive in the first place.

Setting and Using the *tar* Table of Backup Devices

Many UNIX systems like Solaris and SCO UNIX allow the common `tar` devices to be placed in a file called `/etc/default/tar`.

Here is an example of that file from Solaris 2.6:

```
#             device           block     size
archive0=/dev/rmt/0            20        0
archive1=/dev/rmt/0n           20        0
archive2=/dev/rmt/1            20        0
archive3=/dev/rmt/1n           20        0
archive4=/dev/rmt/0            126       0
archive5=/dev/rmt/0n           126       0
archive6=/dev/rmt/1            126       0
archive7=/dev/rmt/1n           126       0
```

The system administrator can enter the commonly used `tar` device names in place of the device names shown in this file. This allows entering a single digit to specify the target device in the tar command:

```
$ tar cv2 .
```

In the preceding example, `2` refers to the `archive2` entry in `/etc/default/tar`. Given the `/etc/default/tar` file shown above, the above `tar` command would be equivalent to the following:

```
$ tar cvf /dev/rmt/1 .
```

If no digit is specified, Solaris defaults to the `archive0` device. SCO UNIX looks for a line that starts `archive=`. Use this default case for the most commonly used `tar` device:

```
$ tar cv .
```

Setting the *tar* Blocking Size

tar allows a `b` option to set the block size ranging from 1 to 20 blocks of 512 bytes per tape record. The default value is 20 if no `b` option is specified. `tar` is unique among UNIX commands in that all the option letters are specified first, and then any arguments to those options are listed in the order of the option letters:

```
$ tar cvfb /dev/XXX? 10 .
```

Notice in the preceding command that the f option is specified before the b option, so /dev/XXX? (the argument to the f option) must be specified before the 10 (the argument to the b option).

The only time that the b option should be specified is to try to read a tape that was written with a block size that was not set to the standard default of 20.

tar Limitations

tar historically has had a number of limitations. Newer versions of tar have removed many of these limitations but you should be aware of them and test for them.

Beware of multivolume backups (tar backups that take more than one tape). Older versions of tar did not allow continuation to a second tape or did not handle this reliably. Test this procedure thoroughly before you use it or just back up each group of files onto a single tape.

tar did not back up directories. It creates them as needed on restore, but the owner, group, and permissions are not as they were originally.

tar did not back up empty directories. It only created directories when there were files to restore to that directory.

tar did not back up /dev device files. This made tar a poor choice for a complete system backup.

tar could not salvage files after a bad spot on the tape.

Using *cpio* to Back Up and Restore Files

You will find that this section on cpio uses much of the same wording as in the previous section on tar. The two commands have similar functionality and only some specific details and examples change the two sections. The tar and cpio sections are complete in themselves, without complicated references to one another, but if you read them both, you'll get a strong sense of déjà vu.

Backing Up a Directory Subtree

cpio stands for *copy in/out* and it allows you to back up files to tape, diskette, or a disk file. Here is an example of a basic cpio command to back up one complete directory:

```
$ cd /usr/fred/projects
$ find . -print ¦ cpio -ocvaB > /dev/XXX?
```

First use cd to change the directory to back up. Then use the find command to feed all the pathnames to cpio to back them up. Following are descriptions of the other elements of the cpio command:

$	This represents the shell prompt. Your shell prompt may be different.
find . -print	This find command lists the relative pathname of all files and subdirectories in the current directory.
cpio	A UNIX command to back up files by doing copy in or out. This cpio archive is usually saved on a tape or diskette but can also be saved in a disk file.
-ocvaB	Options for the cpio command. Take a look at each letter individually:

o	Outputs files to the archive. The first option letter to cpio should be either i (input) or o (output).
c	Writes an ASCII header for portability to better read this tape on another system.
v	Verbose (shows filenames being backed up).
a	Resets the last access date of each file that is backed up to what it was before the cpio was run.

B   Sets a tape block size of 5120 bytes. Some tape drives such as DAT tapes or Exabyte tapes require a block size larger than one.

/dev/XXX?   It is very important to replace this with the tape or diskette device name that you want to back up to. (We covered these device names at the start of this chapter.) You could also specify a disk filename to hold the cpio archive.

When you run this cpio command, you might see output like this:

```
$ cd /usr/fred/projects
$ find . -print ¦ cpio -ocvaB > /dev/XXX?
.
acme
acme/report6
pegasus
pegasus/1997
pegasus/1997/expenses
pegasus/1997/sales
pegasus/1998
pegasus/1998/expenses
pegasus/1998/sales
50 blocks
$
```

Because we used the cpio v option, we see each directory and file name as it is being backed up. If there is a large amount of data, backups can take hours to complete. After the cpio backup has completed, we can refer to the media that contains the backup as a cpio archive. Depending on the type of media, we can also refer to the backup as a cpio diskette or cpio tape.

Notice that at the end of the backup, cpio tells you how many blocks the backup took up (50 blocks in this example). It is a good idea to write this on the tape label. If you ever want to restore this entire tape, you will then know how many free blocks you need on the hard disk.

If you omit the v option, then no filenames are displayed during the cpio backup, only the size of the backup at the end:

```
$ cd /usr/fred/projects
$ find . -print ¦ cpio -ocaB > /dev/XXX?
50 blocks
$
```

cpio also allows a V option, which simply prints a dot (.) each time a file is backed up. This allows you to watch the progress of the backup and make sure it is proceeding without displaying so much output that you slow down the backup:

```
$ cd /usr/fred/projects
$ find . -print ¦ cpio -ocaB > /dev/XXX?
..........
50 blocks
$
```

Backing Up Selected Directories or Files

cpio backs up only the filenames that you pipe to it. If you give it a directory name, it backs up only the directory and not its contents. To back up a complete directory, you must use a utility like find to provide all the file pathnames within that directory. We can back up individual selected files like this:

```
$ cd /usr/fred/projects
$ ls ./acme* ./pegasus/report7 ¦ cpio -ocaB > /dev/XXX?
```

ls lists the files to back up by cpio. This does not work on Linux/GNU systems, in which ls can add special indicators to the end of the filenames.

./acme* illustrates that shell filename wildcards can be used to generate a list of files—in this case all files that start with acme.

./pegasus/report7 illustrates another file to be backed up.

The preceding example specifies relative pathnames to back up, which is the recommended procedure.

We can back up multiple directories to cpio as follows:

```
$ cd /usr/fred/projects
$ (
> find ./expenses -print
```

```
> find ./pegasus -print
> ) ¦ cpio -ocaB > /dev/XXX?
```

Parenthesis (()) are used to group multiple find commands and send the combined output to cpio.

The greater than sign (>) at the start of a line is the PS2 prompt. The shell prints this (not the user) to indicate that it is expecting the continuation of a command started on the previous line.

We can back up individual files and complete directories as follows:

```
$ cd /usr/fred/projects
$ (
> echo ./acme* ./pegasus/report7
> find ./expenses -print
> find ./pegasus -print
> ) ¦ cpio -ocaB > /dev/XXX?
```

We can then exclude selected files using grep -v as follows:

```
$ cd /usr/fred/projects
$ (
> echo ./acme* ./pegasus/report7
> find ./expenses -print
> find ./pegasus -print
> ) ¦ grep -v /tmp/ ¦
> grep -v junk ¦
> cpio -ocaB > /dev/XXX?
```

The preceding example backs up the following files:

- All files that start with acme in the current directory
- report7 in the pegasus subdirectory
- All files and directories in the expenses directory
- All files and directories in the pegasus directory
- However, from the preceding files, exclude the following from the backup:

    Any files or directories that contain /tmp/ in their pathname

    Any files or directories that contain junk in their pathname

Listing the Table of Contents of a *cpio* Archive

Enter the following command to display (to standard output) the contents of a cpio archive (the filenames that have been saved on this cpio diskette or tape).

```
$ cpio -itcvB < /dev/XXX?
```

In this command, i is input from an already-made cpio archive. The first letter in this cpio option list must be i or o. t shows the table of contents of the backup. No files are saved or restored by this operation.

On some UNIX systems, cpio autosenses if the tape was written using the c option, so the c option is not needed when reading from the tape. On other UNIX systems, you get an error if you don't use the c option on cpio.

When you run this cpio command, you might see output like this:

```
$ cpio -itcvB < /dev/XXX?
drwxr-xr-x    4 mori     staff        0 Apr 28 21:23 1998, .
dr-xr-x---    2 jane     staff        0 Apr 28 21:24 1998, acme
-r--r--r--    1 jane     staff       29 Apr 28 21:24 1998,
➥acme/report6
drwxr-xr-x    4 mori     staff        0 Apr 28 21:25 1998, pegasus
drwxr-xr-x    2 mori     staff        0 Apr 28 21:26 1998, pegasus/
➥1997
-rw-r--r--    1 mori     staff      135 Apr 28 21:26 1998, pegasus/
➥1997/expenses
-rw-r--r--    1 mori     staff     3281 Apr 28 21:27 1998, pegasus/
➥1997/sales
drwxr-xr-x    2 mori     staff        0 Apr 28 21:27 1998, pegasus/
➥1998
-rw-r--r--    1 mori     staff     7995 Apr 28 21:26 1998, pegasus/
➥1998/expenses
-rw-r--r--    1 mori     staff     9463 Apr 28 21:27 1998, pegasus/
➥1998/sales
50 blocks
$
```

This output contains the same fields as ls -l would display.

If you omit the v option, only the filenames are displayed:

```
$ cpio -itcB < /dev/XXX?
.
acme
acme/report6
pegasus
pegasus/1997
pegasus/1997/expenses
pegasus/1997/sales
pegasus/1998
pegasus/1998/expenses
pegasus/1998/sales
50 blocks
$
```

Note that it takes as long to list the table of contents as it takes to write the cpio archive in the first place.

Using *cpio* to Restore Archives

In order to use any file from a cpio backup, we must first restore the desired file or files from the cpio tape or diskette to the hard disk. Before using cpio to restore a large cpio archive, however, there are several important details to check. The following sections address such concerns as checking for disk free blocks and absolute and relative pathnames, planning where the files are to be restored, working around absolute filename limitations, and changing to the proper directory.

Checking for Disk Free Blocks

It is important to check for disk free blocks in the various filesystems because if any of the UNIX filesystems run out of available disk blocks, application programs may give errors and abort, which could leave databases in a corrupted state. If the root filesystem runs out of blocks, the whole UNIX system could crash.

Review the previous tar section "Checking for Disk Free Blocks." The comments on the df command are applicable to cpio.

One advantage of cpio over tar in this area is that cpio tells you the number of blocks in the full backup, so you know approximately how many available blocks are needed to restore the full backup.

Checking for Absolute versus Relative Pathnames

Before you restore any files from a cpio backup, list the cpio table of contents and check whether the filenames begin with a slash (/). Absolute or full pathnames begin with a slash. Relative pathnames do not begin with a slash.

Consider the following example:

```
/mori/acme/report6
```

This filename is absolute. The following filename is relative:

```
acme/report6
```

cpio removes any leading "dot slash" (./) from the filename, so ./acme/report6 is saved as acme/report6, which is an equivalent form.

Planning Where the Files Will Be Restored

In the preceding sections, we saw that our cpio backup will either contain absolute or relative pathnames. If the pathnames begin with a leading slash, then the pathnames are absolute. This means that cpio can restore the files only from the backup to the original directory where they came from, regardless of the current directory. This can be dangerous because we would be restoring old versions of each file, wiping out the new versions and losing any updates done since the cpio backup was made.

For example, assume we display the cpio table of contents and see this line among the output lines:

```
-rw-r--r--  1 mori   staff 135 Apr 28 21:26 1998, /mori/
➥pegasus/1997/expenses
```

/mori/pegasus/1997/expenses is an absolute pathname. cpio can usually restore this file only to that absolute pathname on disk. Before restoring this file, it would be a good idea to copy the current version of that file so all the new updates are retained.

If the files in the cpio archive use relative pathnames, we can restore the files to many different directories. This is useful, for example, when we want to look up information in the old file from the cpio backup without overwriting the current version of that file. In this case, we would restore the backup file to a temporary working directory, look up the desired information, and then delete the old file when we are done.

Assume we display the cpio table of contents and see filenames that begin with no dot nor slash:

```
-rw-r--r-- 1 mori  staff 135 Apr 28 21:26 1998, mori/pegasus/
➥1997/expenses
```

In this case, our backup files are using relative pathnames. You can predict where cpio will restore these files by inserting the current directory at the start of the relative pathname to be restored.

For example, if my current directory is /tmp, then cpio would restore the expenses file from the previous paragraph to this absolute pathname:

```
/tmp/mori/pegasus/1997/expenses
```

For another example, if my current directory is /mori/pegasus then cpio would restore the expenses file from the previous paragraph to this absolute pathname:

```
/mori/pegasus/mori/pegasus/1997/expenses
```

For another example, if my current directory is / (the root directory) then cpio would restore the expenses file from the previous paragraph to this absolute pathname:

```
/mori/pegasus/1997/expenses
```

In summary, if the cpio archive contains absolute pathnames, cpio restores those files (from tape or diskette) back to their original location. If the archive contains relative pathnames, cpio restores the files to pathnames determined by adding the current directory and to the cpio pathname.

Considering Absolute Filename Work-arounds

If you create your cpio archive using absolute filenames, you can restore those files only back to their original location (usually).

This is a very great and frustrating limitation of `cpio`. For this reason, the documentation on `cpio` usually advises you to use relative pathnames when doing a `cpio` backup. In the earlier section of this book on using `cpio` to backup a directory subtree, I document only how to back up using relative pathnames.

`cpio` under SCO UNIX has a very nice `-A` option that suppresses the leading slash on restore. You can then restore absolute pathnames as though they were relative pathnames in the `cpio` archive. You can add the `-A` option anywhere in the list of `cpio` options as long as it is after the initial `i` option. I did not find this `-A` option on AIX, Solaris, or Linux/GNU.

If absolute pathnames in `cpio` is a big problem for you, see whether your system supports the `pax` command, which should be able to read `cpio` archives and supports an `-s` option to modify any filenames found.

Changing to the Proper Directory

If the files in the `cpio` archive use absolute pathnames, it makes no difference what directory you change to before doing the `cpio restore` command.

If the files in the `cpio` archive are relative, one of the most crucial and dangerous decisions when restoring relative files using `cpio` is to choose what directory to change to before you start the `cpio` restore. Since you are restoring one or more old archive files, there is a danger of unintentionally overwriting the current version of those files. To determine what directory to change to, compare the pathname on tape with the absolute pathname where you want to restore the files, as in the following three examples:

Example 1

Pathname on cpio archive	`mori/pegasus/1997/expenses`
Desired absolute pathname after restore	`/tmp/restoredata/mori/pegasus/1997/expenses`
Directory to change to before doing the cpio restore	`/tmp/restoredata`

Example 2

Pathname on cpio archive	mori/pegasus/1997/expenses
Desired absolute pathname after restore (restore the file to its original location)	/mori/pegasus/1997/expense
Directory to change to before doing the cpio restore	/

Example 3

Pathname on cpio archive	mori/pegasus/1997/expenses
Desired absolute pathname after restore	/pegasus/1997/expenses
Directory to change to before doing the cpio restore	We cannot complete this example by just setting our current directory. It could be done by more complex procedures such as creating a subdirectory mori as a symbolic link to root (/), or by restoring the files to some temporary directory and then moving them to the desired location.

Restoring All Files to the Original Directory

Restoring files can be tricky and dangerous: There is a possibility that you will overwrite the wrong files. I will show you several ways to restore and discuss their good points and bad points.

You probably won't want to use the easiest restore, which is to put all the files back where they came from. If you do this, you destroy your files that have up-to-date information and replace them with files from the backup that have old information. Now you see why I said you probably won't want to do this. This operation is done only rarely. For example, if something goes wrong with a major update operation and all the current files are corrupted, you may want to restore all the files from older but uncorrupted versions from the backup.

To restore all files in the cpio backup to their original directory, change to the directory where you originally made your backup. Then issue the cpio restore command shown here:

```
$ cd /usr/fred/projects
$ cpio -icvdum < /dev/XXX?
```

/usr/fred/projects is just an example directory name. Enter in its place the directory in which you made the backup. If the cpio archive contains absolute pathnames, it does not matter what directory you change to.

I inputs files from the backup. The first letter in this cpio option list must be i or o. Inputting (restoring) files is always a dangerous option because you must make sure that you do not overwrite the wrong files.

We have already looked at c (ASCII header) and v (verbose).

d creates directories as needed. u unconditionally restores—otherwise, an older file from the backup is not allowed to overwrite a newer file on disk.

m preserves the file date and time of the last modification as it was when the file was backed up. Otherwise, this restore operation is a file modification.

/dev/XXX? should be replaced with the file or device name for your cpio archive.

Here is an example showing what the screen looks like when you run this command:

```
$ cd /usr/fred/projects
$ cpio -icvdum < /dev/XXX?
    .
acme
acme/report6
pegasus
pegasus/1997
pegasus/1997/expenses
```

```
pegasus/1997/sales
pegasus/1998
pegasus/1998/expenses
pegasus/1998/sales
50 blocks
$
```

Restoring All Files to a Different Directory

Be forewarned that the procedure of restoring all files from a
cpio archive to a different directory can be used only if there are
relative pathnames in the cpio archive. Review the earlier sections to check absolute versus relative pathnames, check the disk
free blocks, and choose a filesystem that has plenty of available
blocks. Then change to the proper directory:

```
$ cd /tmp
$ cpio -icvdum < /dev/XXX?
.
acme
acme/report6
pegasus
pegasus/1997
pegasus/1997/expenses
pegasus/1997/sales
pegasus/1998
pegasus/1998/expenses
pegasus/1998/sales
50 blocks
$
```

In this example, the acme and pegasus directories from the cpio
backup are restored in the /tmp directory. You can choose a
directory other than /tmp if that filesystem has enough available
disk blocks.

Again, be warned: If the cpio archive contains absolute pathnames, your current directory is ignored and the files are
restored to their original location, which could be disastrous!

Restoring Only Selected Directories or Files

It is possible to restore only selected directories or files, as the
following example shows. It is very important to specify the

directories or files exactly as they appear in the cpio table of contents, including any leading slash (/). Directories are not restored recursively (cpio does not restore the contents of a directory). You must use wildcards if you want to restore a whole directory.

```
$ cd desired-dir
$ cpio -icvdum < /dev/XXX? acme/report6 'pegasus/1997/*'
```

Replace desired-dir with the desired directory where you want to issue the cpio command. Replace /dev/XXX? with the cpio file or device name.

acme/report6 illustrates how to restore a file. 'pegasus/1997/*' illustrates how to restore a directory and all of its files and subdirectories. (Notice the single quotes: We must prevent the shell from manipulating the asterisk (*) as if this were a filename generation wildcard.)

Note that it takes as long to restore selected files as it takes to write the cpio archive in the first place.

Setting the *cpio* Blocking Size

cpio allows a B option to set the block size to 5120 bytes. Larger block sizes can be set by using the -C option instead of -B. Larger block sizes may help performance in backing up to high performance tape drives:

```
$ cd desired-dir
$ find . -print ¦ cpio -ocvaC40960 > /dev/XXX?
```

Notice in the preceding command that -C is used to set a tape block size of 40960 bytes. The same -C value must be used to read this tape:

```
$ cpio -icvdumC40960 < /dev/XXX?
```

SEE ALSO

➤ *For more information on using* cpio *to copy a directory tree from one part of the disk to another, see page 189.*

Managing System Resources

By Sanjiv Guha

Managing disk space

A UNIX system has a number of resources attached to it. The resources are the I/O subsystem (which manages the disk), terminals, CPU, memory, and so on. Here we will concentrate on how to manage the disk space on a UNIX system. The various system resources are managed by the system administrator, who can log on as the root superuser and add, modify, or delete resources. To try to manage resources is inherently dangerous because you may affect one or more users by modifying any or all system resources.

Managing Disk Space

Disk space is managed in terms of filesystem. A *filesystem* consists of one or more directories and subdirectories under it. You can have multiple disk volumes, which make up a filesystem and a directory or file can be anywhere on the filesystem. A file or a directory cannot span across filesystems.

The hierarchy of a disk subsystem follows:

Physical disk
  Partition
    Filesystem
      Directories and files
        Subdirectories and files
          Files

If you have to increase the space for a directory, you must add more space to the partition or filesystem in which the directory resides.

Mounting the Filesystem

Before you can access the directories set up in your UNIX system, the system administrator must mount the filesystem with physical disks. At the system boot time, the system mounts all the true mount points defined in the /etc/filesystem file. At other times, you can mount the filesystem manually.

You can get a list of mounted filesystems by using the following command:

```
mount
```

The system will respond with something like this:

```
node  mounted   mounted    vfs  date          options over
----  -------   --------   ---  -----------   ------- --------
      /dev/hd0  /          jfs  Dec 17 08:04  rw, log =/dev/hd8
      /dev/hd3  /tmp       jfs  Dec 17 08:04  rw, log =/dev/hd8
      /dev/hd1  /home      jfs  Dec 17 08:06  rw, log =/dev/hd8
      /dev/hd2  /usr       jfs  Dec 17 08:06  rw, log =/dev/hd8
```

For each filesystem, the mount command lists the node name, the device name, the name under which it is mounted, the virtual-filesystem type, the date and time it was mounted, and its options. You can use the following options:

rw   Read and write.

ro   Read only.

bg   Enables you to process the mount in background. If the mount fails, the system will keep trying to mount the specified filesystem.

If you want to mount a filesystem called xyz, with the read and write option, you can use the following command:

```
mount -o rw /dev/hd4 /xyz
```

If, on the other hand, you want to mount all the filesystems defined in the /etc/filesytem, you can use the /etc/filesytem. Then you can use the following command:

```
mount -a
```

Unmounting Filesystem

If you want to do any maintenance on a filesystem, you must make the filesystem offline first. You can use the umount command to unmount a file system. If you want to unmount the file system called xyz, for example, you can use the following command:

```
umount xyz
```

You cannot unmount a filesystem, however, if even a single file under that filesystem is in use. The umount will not provide you with any details of which files are in use or who is using it. You can use the -f option to force the unmount with this command:

```
umount -f xyz
```

If you do this, however, the program using the files will not terminate properly and you may lose some of the information.

Space Information

To assess the amount of space available on a filesystem, you can use the df command. If you want to find out about the details of all filesystems, you can use the following command:

```
df
```

The system will respond with this:

```
Filesystem  512-blocks  Free  %Used  Iused  %Iused  Mounted on
/dev/hd0    19368       9976  48%    4714   5%      /
/dev/hd1    24212       4808  80%    5031   19%     /usr
/dev/hd2    9744        9352  4%     1900   4%      /site
/dev/hd3    3868        3856  0%     986    0%      /usr/venus
```

On some systems, the space displays as 512-byte blocks, and you can use a -k flag with df command to display space in 1024-byte blocks. On other systems the space displays in 1024-bytes blocks by default.

If you want to display the space usage of a particular directory, you can use the following command:

```
df .
```

The system will respond with this:

```
Device    512-blocks  free  %used  iused  %iused  Mounted on
/dev/hd4  19368       9976  48%    4714   5%      /
```

Now that you know which filesystem may be running out of space (using the du command), you can use the du command to find out which files are taking up the space. The du command has a number of flags you can use to get different information.

You can use the following command to get the disk usage of the current directory:

```
du -k
```

You will get the following response from the system:

```
240      ./test
8 ./info
16 ./info/lost
 264 .
```

Each line displays the number of 1024-byte block being used by the subdirectory with a total at the end.

If you want to find the size of each and every file in the directory and the subdirectories, you can use the following command:

```
du -k -a
100       ./test/file1
120 ./test/file2
20 ./test/file3
8 ./info/file1
16 ./info/lost/file1
264    .
```

You can use also use the find command to find out the size of files. In addition, find command enables you to list files equal to, less than, or more than a certain specified size.

If you want to find out the list of files in the current directory that are exactly 100000000 bytes in size, you can use the following command:

```
find . -size 100000000c -print
```

If you want to find out the list of files in the current directory that are greater than 100000000 bytes in size, you use the following command:

```
find . -size +100000000c -print
```

If you want to find out the list of files in the current directory that are less than 100000000 bytes in size, you use the following command:

```
find . -size -100000000c -print
```

Limiting Disk Space for Users

As a part of management of disks, you can limit the amount of disk space a user can use or the size of a file a user can create.

You can use the quota command to limit the amount of space that a user can use. You can find out about the current quota of a user with this command:

```
quota -u user1
```

The system will respond with this:

```
User quotas for user user1 (uid 502):
Filesystem blocks quota limit grace Files quota limit  grace
    /u       20    55    60            20    60    65
```

You can get quota for the filesystem User and quotas for user keith (uid 502):

```
Filesystem blocks quota limit grace Files quota limit  grace
    /u       20    55    60            20    60    65
```

You can get a list of quotas for all users for the filesystem /u by using the repquota command as shown here:

```
repquota -u /u
```

The system will respond with this:

```
            Block limits              File limits
User        used  soft  hard  grace   used  soft  hard  grace
root     —  3920     0     0           734     0     0
davec    +-   28     8    30  3 days     3     0     0
keith    —    48     0     0             7     0     0
```

The + printed in the first column next to davec indicates that the user has exceeded established block limits.

You can modify disk quotas for a user by using the edquota command. If you want to make the disk quota of user2 the same as that of user1, you can use the following command:

```
edquota -p user1 user2
```

You can set the maximum file size a process can create. This will help manage the disk space by limiting the size of a file the process can create at a time. You can use the following command to display the file size limit of a process:

```
ulimit -f
```

The system will respond with the following:

```
4194303
```

This means that the maximum file size is 4194303 blocks of 512 bytes.

The system administrator can modify the file size limit by using the following command:

```
ulimit -f 5000000
```

lost+found Directory

The fsck utility creates an entry in the lost+found directory for any file or directory that was not referenced by an entry in the directory. A file may not get deleted properly if the system went down while the delete was in progress; in such a case, an entry may be created in the lost+found directory by fsck utility. The system administrator should look at the files and directories created in the lost+found directories and decide whether to delete them or inform the relevant user to take corrective action.

Some Other Commands for Disk Management

With this in place, you still need some space because the original file is not deleted until it is completely compressed. You can compress a file called xyz in place, then you can use the following command:

```
compress xyz
```

The compressed file will be called xyz.z. The space freed up as a result of compression may vary anywhere starting from 90 percent of the originally occupied space. The actual compression depends on both the data inside the file as well as compression algorithm used.

In some cases, you may be able to archive the offending files to an archive and then remove the files to obtain necessary disk space. The tar command can be used to do so. If you want to archive all the files starting with test from the current directory, you can use the following command:

```
tar cf  test.tar test*
```

This command creates an archive test.tar, which can be later used to retrieve the files. To retrieve files from the archive, you can use the following command:

```
tar xf test.tar
```

UNIX Text Processing

Searching for Lines in a File or Pipeline

By Steve "Mor" Moritsugu

Finding/Displaying Only Lines That Contain a Pattern (*grep*)

To find and display lines in a file that contain a name or pattern, you can use the grep command (I'll tell you where it gets its name later). For example, assume you have an employee file in which each line contains the name and information about one employee. To display just the lines from that file that contain the name "Smith," you would enter:

```
$ grep Smith employee-file
Smith, Carl - 555-6379, hired 3-7-92, dept 6
Smith, Dennis - 555-3291, hired 8-27-96, dept 2
Smithers, Jane - 619/555-1720, hired 4-4-89, dept 2
$
```

In the above output, notice that only lines containing the word "Smith" are displayed. Lines for the other employees are not displayed. Notice in the last line that "Smith" was found as part of the name "Smithers."

Displaying lines from files that contain a pattern

1. At the shell prompt, enter: grep

   Do not press the Enter key until you're instructed to do so.

2. Enter a space, and then enter the pattern you want to look for in the file contents. This pattern can be a name or any sequence of characters.

   The pattern is called a *regular expression* and can include special wildcards (which I will cover later in this chapter). If the pattern contains any punctuation or spaces, you will need to enclose the pattern in single or double quotation marks. (I'll also discuss that further later in this chapter.) In general, a good rule of thumb is to always enclose the pattern in single quotation marks.

3. Enter a space and then enter one or more filenames, separated by spaces. If the files are in the current directory, enter just the basename of each file (see the glossary for a definition of "basename"). If the files are not in the current directory, enter either an absolute or relative pathname for each

file. You can use Filename Generation Wildcard patterns to substitute for one part of the filename that's common among all of the files in the list.

4. Press the Enter key to execute your command.

5. grep displays standard output of any lines that contain the pattern, even if the pattern is contained within a larger word. If you specified more than one file in step 3, grep shows the filenames as well as the lines that contain the pattern, as shown here:

```
$ grep Acme report*
report3:    Acme Enterprises    1,373,383,234  world-wide
report.acme.13:of the four Acme divisions, it is the
➥least
$
```

If you provide grep with a list of files in the command line, it searches those files for the given pattern and displays only the lines that contain the pattern. If you do not provide a list of files, grep reads its input from standard input so grep can be used in a pipeline, as in this example:

```
$ who | grep smith
leesmith       tty3      Mar  6 19:48
smith          ttya03    Mar  6 17:23
$
```

In the above command line, who asks which users are currently logged in. The output from the who command is piped to grep, which looks for lines that contain the name "smith" as either a complete word or part of a larger word. Notice that to use grep in a pipeline, you cannot specify any filenames after the pattern to search for.

grep is the quintessential UNIX filter. Think of a paper filter in a coffee maker. The filter holds the coffee grounds and the hot water. The filter allows the liquid coffee to pass through, but it retains the grounds. The job of a filter is to selectively allow things you want to pass through and to block the things you don't want so they can't get through. This is what grep does, especially when you use it in a pipeline. In the above example, you start with the who command. But because you want to see only the lines that reference "smith," grep passes those lines through. grep blocks all the lines that don't contain "smith"— you could say it filters them out because you don't want to see them. Because some output can contain tens of thousands of lines or more, grep is an extremely important and often used utility under UNIX, filtering out lines you don't want so you can concentrate on just the lines you are interested in.

SEE ALSO

➤ *For more information on file lists, see page 231*

➤ *For more information on filters and piping, see page 31*

Ignoring Upper- and Lowercase When Selecting Lines (*grep -i*)

To ignore case when searching for patterns with grep, you add the -i option to grep, as in the following example:

```
$ grep -i acme report7
The Acme account is currently handled by Linda. It is
once they merged with ACME INDUSTRIES, their stock value
Pauley, Mr. Robert Kacmeth, Ms. Jean Bensen, and other
➥notable
$
```

When you use the -i option with grep, it does not matter if you specify the pattern in uppercase, lowercase, or mixed case characters. In the above example, the -i option instructs grep to find all lines containing the pattern, regardless if the pattern appears in upper-, or lower-, or mixed case. Without the -i option, grep shows a line only if the case of the pattern in the line exactly matches the upper- and lowercase of the pattern.

In older versions of UNIX, use -y instead of -i to ignore case. Some newer versions of UNIX allow -y to ignore case (for backward compatibility), but -i is preferred.

Saving the Selected Lines in a File (*grep*)

You can use redirection (> or >>) to save the output of grep in a file like this:

```
grep 'Acme Shoes' /usr/fred/report* > acme/shoefile
```

In this example, you are looking for the pattern Acme Shoes. Because it contains a space, you must enclose the pattern in single or double quotation marks. The list of files to look in is indicated by a Filename Generation Wildcard pattern that specifies all files in the directory /usr/fred that start with the name report. The command then tells grep to save all the matching lines to a file called shoefile in the acme subdirectory of your current directory. grep does not display the lines onscreen because the output is being redirected.

Here is another similar example:

```
who | grep fredp >> fredplog
```

Here, you are checking to see if the user fredp is currently logged in. If so, you want grep to append his login information— as reported by who—to the fredplog file.

Piping the Selected Lines to Other Commands (*grep*)

grep is often used in a pipeline to filter out unwanted lines so that other commands can process the desired lines. To see how this works, consider the following example:

```
$ who | grep fredp | wc -l
     3
$
```

In this example, who generates a list of every user who is currently logged in. grep cuts down that list to only the lines that mention fredp. wc -l counts the lines that it receives. From the output, you can see that the user fredp is currently logged in simultaneously on three different ports.

This result may be misleading though because grep considers a line to be matching even if the pattern found is part of a larger word. In the example, suppose there is a user named alfredpenn. Notice that the string fredp is found within alfredpenn. What if alfredpenn were logged in on three ports, and fredp was not logged in at all? You would get the same result:

```
$ who | grep fredp | wc -l
      3
$
```

Choosing your Pattern (*grep*)

Much of the skill of using grep comes from wisely choosing what pattern to search for, especially the start of the pattern and the end of the pattern. For example, using the following grep command might not be a very good idea:

```
$ grep ' acme' report*
```

This command requires a space before acme in the pattern, in an effort to avoid words like "Dacmer." However, requiring a starting space is not a good idea because grep will not find acme if it is at the start of a line or if it is in quotation marks (because "acme" does not start with a space).

Assume you have a very large phone-list file containing lines like this:

Bower, Linda 714/555-8182

Decker, Tom 818/714-6192

Mellinger, Fred 714/639-1215

Smith, Will 714/909-3818

Smithson, Charlie 818/603-2194

To quickly look up people with the last name of Smith, you would enter:

```
$ grep Smith, phone-list
Smith, Will 714/909-3818
$
```

Notice that you can add a comma at the end of the grep pattern only because the file contains a comma after the last name. The comma allows you to display Smith while avoiding Smithson. This comma is not a feature of grep; it simply results from how the file is set up.

To count the number of people whose phone number is in area 714, you would enter this command:

```
$ grep 714/ phone-list | wc -1
```

You can specify a slash (/) after 714 only because your file has a slash (/) between the area code and phone number. Using the slash (/) in the pattern allows you to ignore 714 if it is part of the phone number but not if it's the area code. Again the slash (/) is not a feature of the grep command. It is an example of how you can look at the data and wisely choose a pattern that will return the lines you want to see.

Displaying Lines That Don't Contain the Pattern (*grep -v*)

grep is also useful as a reverse filter: You can use it to remove unwanted lines that contain a specified pattern so you can see what is left over. To display lines that don't contain the pattern, use the -v option with grep to make it work as a reverse filter, as in this example:

```
$ who | grep -v guest | wc -1
```

Here, who displays one line for each person logged in to the system. The grep command then uses a reverse filter to exclude lines that contain the word guest so that all other logins will pass through but guest logins will be ignored. The output of grep is then piped to wc -1 which counts the number of logins excluding the guest login.

Adding the Line Number to the Found Lines (*grep -n*)

To make grep show the line number as well as the line that contains the pattern, add the -n option to grep:

```
$ grep -n Acme report8
13: Acme Industries
246:Pacific Acme Ltd
1202:Paul Acmeersch
$
```

As you can see, grep –n displays the line number first, followed by the line that matches the pattern.

If the -n option to display the line number is used with multiple files, the output of grep begins with the filename and then the line number, as shown in the following example:

```
$ grep -n acme report*
report2:25:Acme Enterprises
report8:13: Acme Industries
report8:246:Pacific Acme Ltd
report8:1202:Paul Acmeersch
report.acme:45:whose former name was Acme Inc. until they
➥merged
$
```

Displaying Just Filenames That Contain the Pattern (*grep -l -c*)

Sometimes you just want to know which files reference a particular name or pattern. If the pattern is mentioned on thousands of lines in each file, the normal grep output would be too long to easily analyze. To display just the filenames that contain the pattern, use the -l option with grep to list the filenames and not the lines that contain the pattern:

```
$ grep -l Acme report*
report2
report8
report.acme
$
```

To display each filename and a count of the number of lines in that file that contain the pattern, you can use the -c option with grep, like this:

```
$ grep -c Acme report*
report2:1
report4:0
report8:3
report12:0
report.acme:1
report.pegasus:0
$
```

Finding Lines That Contain Two Patterns (*grep* | *grep*)

You can use grep twice to make a double filter. Lines must then contain two patterns in order to pass through, as shown here:

```
$ grep -i acme report* | grep merge
report7:246:once they merged with ACME INDUSTRIES, their
➥stock value
report.acme:45:whose former name was Acme Inc. until they
➥merged
$
```

In this example, you pipe grep to grep to make a double filter. To pass through the first filter, lines must contain the word acme in either upper- or lowercase. To pass through the second filter, lines must also contain the word merge. The output displays lines that contain both patterns within the line. It does not matter if the second pattern comes before or after the first pattern in the line. Piping grep to grep sets up a logical AND condition, which means that a line must satisfy both conditions to pass through.

Notice that the second grep command must not specify any files so that it will read from standard input and process the output from the first grep command. The following example shows a mistake people sometimes make:

```
$ grep -i acme report* | grep merge report*
```

Don't make this mistake. This example will not generate an error, but it will not do what you intended. Because the second grep command has been given a list of files, it ignores the output from the first grep. What you have here is a failure to communicate. The second grep command is its own single filter, which only looks for lines that contain merge and displays them—even if they don't contain acme. The first grep command does all that work for nothing because its output is ignored.

You can also combine a regular filter with a reverse filter, as in this example:

```
$ grep -i Acme report* | grep -vi Dacmer
```

> **grep -c counts lines, not occurrences**
>
> When looking at grep -c output, people often make the common mistake of thinking that the number next to the filename is the number of times the pattern occurs in the file. Note, however, that grep -c counts the number of lines, not occurrences. If the pattern occurs 10 times but all on one line, grep -c will show a result of 1, not 10.

Which filter should come first?

If you have a double filter, you will get the same result no matter what order you apply the filters in. For better efficiency, however, the first filter should be the one that eliminates the most lines. Then the second filter will have less work to do.

Here, you first use a regular filter to find lines that contain acme in either upper- or lowercase. Note, however, that the first filter also finds lines that contain Dacmer because Dacmer contains acme. The second grep is a reverse filter that removes lines from the first filter. The end result is lines that contain Acme but do not contain Dacmer. However, there is still one potential problem here: Any lines that contain both Acme and Dacmer will be removed by the reverse filter. Later you will see how perl can filter out whole words by ignoring patterns within other words.

Wildcard Pattern Matching in Lines (Regular Expressions)

One of the things that makes UNIX very powerful is the way that patterns can be used to specify what you are looking for in a general way. You saw this with Filename Generation Wildcards, which allow you to form a list of files based on a pattern. In this section, you will meet a totally different form of UNIX wildcard that I call a Regular Expression Wildcard. UNIX neophytes often confuse Filename Generation Wildcards with regular expression wildcards and then wonder why things do not work as they expect.

A regular expression is a string of characters that you want to search for. Short regular expressions can be combined together to make one larger regular expression. A regular expression then can be either a complete pattern or a single element of a pattern. Regular expressions can contain special characters or metacharacters that have special pattern-matching capabilities. I will refer to these special characters as regular expression wildcards to differentiate them from Filename Generation Wildcards.

In this chapter, you will see how to use regular expressions to find desired lines in a file or pipeline. In the following chapter, you will learn how to use regular expressions to modify a file or pipeline. Although regular expressions are complex, it's important that you know about them because they are a basic tool of UNIX that gives it much of its power and elegance.

SEE ALSO

➤ *For more information on Filename Generation Wildcards, see page 232*

Selecting Lines That Contain a Pattern (grep)

Here is a typical grep command:

```
grep acme report7
```

If you enter this command, grep will search the contents of the file report7 and display all lines that contain the string acme even if acme is part of a larger word. Note that the pattern acme can be positioned anywhere in the line, and grep will display that line.

Selecting Lines That Start with a Pattern (^)

What if you only want to see lines if they start with acme? You can specify this by adding a regular expression wildcard. You add the circumflex (^), also called the caret, to the start of your pattern as shown here:

```
grep '^acme' report7
```

Notice the single quotation marks around the search pattern. It is generally a good idea to put single quotation marks around the pattern (but there is one case in which you should use double quotation marks; you'll learn about that later). As you might recall, you usually put single quotation marks around the pattern if the pattern contains any punctuation or spaces. But it doesn't hurt to use single quotation marks even if there are no punctuation or spaces.

In the above example, the circumflex (^) is a regular expression wildcard that stands for the start of the line. Thus, only lines that begin with acme will match the pattern. In its output, grep will display those lines, including any text that follows acme on the lines.

The circumflex (^) is not a wildcard character unless it occurs at the start of the pattern. For example, consider this command:

```
grep '2^4' mathproblems
```

Here, grep will display all lines that contain 2^4 anywhere within the line. The circumflex (^) is just another character to search for because it does not occur at the start of the pattern.

To search for lines that begin with a circumflex (^), you would have to enter a command like this:

```
grep '^^' filename
```

In the above example, the first circumflex (^) is a regular expression wildcard indicating the start of the line. The second circumflex (^) is not a wildcard; it indicates a literal circumflex (^) character.

To specify that a leading circumflex (^) is a literal circumflex (^) and does not indicate the start of the line, you can precede it with a backslash (\):

```
grep '\^acme' report7
```

In this example, grep searches for and displays all lines that contain ^acme anywhere within the line.

Note that every line has a beginning. Therefore, the following command would match every line in the file:

```
grep '^' report7
```

Selecting Lines That End with a Pattern ($)

What if you only want to see lines that end with acme? You can do this by adding another regular expression wildcard, the dollar sign ($), to the end of your pattern:

```
grep 'acme$' report7
```

Here, the dollar sign ($) is a regular expression wildcard that stands for the end of the line. Thus, only lines that end with acme will match the pattern. grep then displays those lines, including any text that precedes acme on the lines.

The dollar sign ($) is only a wildcard if it occurs at the end of the pattern; otherwise, it indicates a literal dollar sign ($) character. To indicate that you want to search for a literal dollar sign ($) as the last character of a pattern, precede the dollar sign ($) with a backslash (\) so it will not indicate the end of a line.

UNIX documentation avoids the term wildcard

In cards, a wildcard is usually a special card that can be used as whatever card you need. You can see that it is a stretch to call the circumflex (^) and dollar sign ($) wildcards. Therefore, UNIX documentation usually calls them special characters or *metacharacters*. I believe that people understand the word wildcard better, though. Besides, I've played a card game where you got to draw an extra card if you got a red 4, and we even called that a wildcard.

Specifying the Contents of the Entire Line (^$)

To specify that you want to search for an entire line, you can use the leading circumflex (^) and the trailing dollar sign ($) wildcards in the same pattern, as in this example:

```
grep '^acme$' report7
```

To understand the above example, you must know that regular expressions are compared character-by-character from left to right with each line of the file or pipeline. For a line to match the pattern in the given example, it must have these elements in this order:

- the start of the line

- the word acme

- the end of the line

For example, this line does not match the pattern previously specified:

```
acme acme
```

Even though the line starts with acme and ends with acme, it does not match. If you compare the regular expression ^acme$ with the line acme acme left-to-right, it's easy to see that the regular expression allows for only one acme in the line.

Here is another example of using the circumflex and dollar sign characters together:

```
grep '^$' report7
```

Given this command, grep searches for and displays all empty lines—lines in which the end of line immediately follows the start of line.

Now consider this other example:

```
grep '$^' report7
```

Here, the circumflex (^) is not a wildcard because it does not occur at the start of the pattern. Similarly the dollar sign ($) is not a wildcard. Thus, this grep command searches for and displays all lines in the file report7 that contain a dollar sign ($) followed by a circumflex (^) anywhere within the line.

Where does grep get its name?

ed is a text editor that was commonly used before vi was available. In the ed editor, g/re/p is a command used to globally search for the regular expression enclosed in slashes (/) and then to print each line containing the pattern. When a separate utility was developed to do the same thing, it kept the ed command name without the slashes.

Including Shell Variables in Regular Expressions

You can use shell variables within your regular expressions, as shown here:

```
who | grep $LOGNAME
```

In this example, $LOGNAME usually contains a user id name. who displays all logins, and grep filters out unwanted lines, to show only those lines where the user is logged in.

If shell variables are adjacent to other pattern elements, enclose them in curly braces {} like this:

```
grep "${prefix}acme${SUFFIX} Inc" report7
```

For this example, suppose $prefix contains g4 and $SUFFIX contains UK. The example would then execute the following command:

```
grep "g4acme-UK Inc" report7
```

Because the pattern contains a space, you must enclose it in double quotation marks. See the later section on quoting regular expressions for more information.

SEE ALSO
➤ *For more information on shell variables, see page 30*

Including Command Substitution in Regular Expressions

Regular expressions can also contain elements that you specify using shell command substitution indicated by backquotes (`) or $(). For example, take a look at the following command:

```
grep "report`date '+%Y'`" report7
```

In this example, the regular expression is made up of two elements:

1. the word report

2. this command in backquotes: `date '+%Y'`

Within the second element, '+%Y' is an option to the date command telling it to display the current year in four-digit format. The backquotes (` and `) take the output of the enclosed command, substitute it into the current command line, and remove the backquoted command.

Therefore, if the current year is 1998, the previous grep command is equivalent to this:

```
grep "report1998" report7
```

When you use command substitution, a regular expression can contain elements generated by any other UNIX command or pipeline.

SEE ALSO

➤ *For more information on command substitution, see page 245*

Quoting Regular Expressions to Prevent Problems

If your regular expression doesn't contain punctuation characters or spaces, you do not have to put it in any type of quotation marks. However, you can use double or single quotation marks around the pattern.

If your regular expression does contain punctuation characters or spaces but does not use any shell variables or command substitutions (as described previously), you should enclose the whole regular expression in single quotation marks. This ensures that the shell will not try to interpret some of the punctuation as shell directives, filename wildcards, and so on. If your regular expression contains any backslashes (\), put an extra backslash (\) before each one.

There is one exception to these rules, however. If your regular expression contains one or more single quotation marks ('), put a backslash (\) in front of each punctuation character and space in your regular expression and do *not* enclose it in any quotation marks. For example, suppose you want to search for the following exact string that contains single quotation marks:

```
item '73' corneil
```

To do so, you would use this grep command:

```
grep item\ \'73\'\ corneil filename
```

However, if your regular expression uses shell variables or command substitution, you would enclose the whole regular expression in double quotation marks. Then put a backslash in front of any of the following characters that appear in your regular expression:

- a dollar sign ($) if it's not the beginning of a shell variable
- a backquote (`) if it's not enclosing command substitution
- a double quotation mark (") inside your regular expression

You must also change any individual backslashes (\) in your regular expression to four backslashes (\\\\). (This is because the shell will remove two of them, and the actual backslash must be preceded by one backslash in order for grep to work properly.)

For example, suppose that $cost is a shell variable containing an amount, and you want to find all lines in report7 that contain the following pattern:

```
"honest" abe's \ $$cost
```

You would use this grep command:

```
grep "\"honest\" abe's \\\\ \$$cost" report7
```

Alternatively, you could use a combination of single and double quotation marks around regions of the regular expression as shown here:

```
grep '"honest" abe'\''s \\ $'"$cost" report7
```

Note, however, that things can become complicated if $cost contains punctuation.

SEE ALSO

➤ *For more information, see page 104*

UNIX Commands That Allow Regular Expressions

Only the following UNIX commands allow the use of regular expressions:

```
grep, egrep, fgrep
```

```
sed
```

```
awk
```

```
perl
```

`vi` (when searching and substituting)

`ed` (when searching and substituting)

Comparing Filename Wildcards with Regular Expression Wildcards

Sometimes people are confused about when to use regular expressions and when to use Filename Generation Wildcard patterns. The following guidelines should alleviate some of the confusion:

- Use regular expressions when you want to search the contents of files or pipelines for patterns. Only a handful of commands support the use of regular expressions; see the previous section.

- Use Filename Generation Wildcard patterns when you want to create a list of filenames based on a pattern. Many UNIX commands will accept a list of files on the command line.

Allowing Any Characters in Certain Pattern Positions (.)

The period (.) is a regular expression wildcard. It represents any single character, which enables you to specify exactly how many character positions to allow before, after, or between other pattern elements. The following command shows an example of the period character in use:

```
grep 'dog.bone' report7
```

Given this command, `grep` would display all lines that contain dog, followed by any single character, followed by bone. For example, it might return lines that contain the following strings:

dog-bone

dog bone

dog/bone

dogEbone

It would not, however, display a line containing dogbone because there is no character separating dog and bone in that case.

To specify that you want to match an actual period (.) in a regular expression, you precede the period with a backslash (\) like this:

```
grep '5\.25' report7
```

This command would display any lines containing 5.25. The backslash (\) is needed before the period to prevent grep from thinking the period is a regular expression wildcard that matches any character.

Specifying Allowed Characters in Pattern Positions ([...])

Square brackets allow you to specify a set of alternatives for the character in that position within a regular expression, as shown in the following example:

```
grep 'dog[- EZ1-3]bone' report7
```

Given this command, grep would display lines that contain any of the following strings:

dog-bone

dog bone

dogEbone

dogZbone

dog1bone

dog2bone

dog3bone

Note, however, that unless other allowed dog bone references were included in the lines, grep would not display lines that contain the following strings:

dog4bone (because 4 is not an allowed alternative)

dogEZbone (because the square brackets represent only a single character within the pattern) dogbone (because there is no single character between dog and bone)

Inside the brackets [], a dash (-) between two letters or digits indicates an inclusive range. To indicate a literal dash (-) as a character in the list, you must place it first or last in the list. To indicate a right bracket (]) as a character in the list, place it as the first list element as in []abc]. A period (.), asterisk (*), left bracket ([), or backslash (\) inside the brackets is treated as a literal character without special meaning. Consider, then, the following command:

```
grep '[0-9][0-9][0-9]' report7
```

Here, grep displays any lines containing three (or more) consecutive digits. Even if you are only searching for three digits, grep might find more than three digits because the pattern does not prohibit more digits before or after the three digits.

Here is another example:

```
grep '^[A-Z]' report7
```

Given this command, grep will display all lines that begin with a capital letter.

Specifying Disallowed Characters in Pattern Positions ([^ ...])

If the list in square brackets begins with a circumflex (^), it will match any single character except for the ones in the list. For example, given the following command

```
grep 'acme[^0-9]' report7
```

grep will display all lines containing acme followed by one character, as long as that character is not a digit. It will not display lines that end with acme because there must be one character following acme in this pattern.

Here is another example:

```
grep '^[^a-zA-Z]' report7
```

This command will display all lines that start with some character other than a letter. It will not display empty lines, however, because some non-letter character must be present.

Specifying Number of Occurrences of a Regular Expression Element ({})

When specifying regular expressions, you can use a shorthand method of specifying the number of occurrences of the previous regular expression element. This shorthand method uses escaped braces: \{ and \}. Here's an example of a command with escaped braces:

```
grep '2[0-9]\{10\}000' report7
```

In this command, the regular expression tells grep to look for a 2, followed by exactly 10 digits, followed by 000. grep does *not* read this as a 2, followed by any digit, followed by 10 more digits. It reads this as a 2, followed by 10 occurrences of a digit (not 11 occurrences), followed by 000.

Specifying number of occurrences of an element

1. At the shell prompt, enter your desired command containing a regular expression. Enter the pattern element that is to be repeated. This pattern element can be a simple letter, a digit, or a regular expression wildcard such as a period (.) or brackets []. Do not press the Enter key until you're instructed to do so.

2. Enter \{. (Do not enter any spaces unless you're instructed to do so.)

3. Enter the desired number of occurrences of the previous pattern element.

4. If that number is a minimum number and you want to allow the pattern to be repeated more times than that, enter a comma (,).

5. If there is a maximum number of times you want to allow the pattern element to be repeated, enter that number now.

6. Enter \}.

Have we seen this before?

The square brackets in Filename Generation Wildcards are very similar to regular expression wildcards. However, to disallow the characters in brackets, Filename Generation Wildcards put an exclamation point (!) as the first character while regular expression wildcards put a circumflex (^) as the first character.

7. Now complete the rest of your regular expression and the command. When you finish, press Enter to execute your command.

Consider the following example:

```
grep '$[0-9]\{3,5\}\.' report7
```

Given this command, grep would display all lines that contain a dollar sign ($), followed by at least three digits but not more than five digits, followed by a period (.) Note that because the period is escaped, it is not a wildcard.

Here's another example:

```
grep '[a-zA-Z]\{20,\}' report7
```

This command would display all lines that contain words of 20 or more upper- or lowercase letters. Note that the comma is superfluous here; you'll learn why in the section on unbounded "or more" wildcards.

Specifying Zero or More Occurrences of a Regular Expression Element (*)

The asterisk is a regular expression wildcard that you can use as a shorthand method for this expression:

```
\{0,\}
```

The asterisk (*) tells grep to allow zero or more occurrences of the previous regular expression element. Don't confuse this with the asterisk (*) Filename Generation Wildcard, which means something different and is used in a totally different context.

The following command shows you how to use the asterisk regular expression wildcard:

```
grep 'ab*c' report7
```

In this command, b* indicates that grep should allow zero or more b's. Given this command, grep would display lines that contain any of the following strings:

ac (0 occurrences of b)

abc (1 occurrence of b)

abbc (2 occurrences of b)

abbbc (3 occurrences of b)

abbbbc (4 occurrences of b)

and so on, including
abbbbbbbbbbbbbbbbbbbbbbbbbbbbbbbbbbbbbbbbbbbbbbc

To indicate zero or more occurrences of any character, you can use the period and the asterisk together (.*), as in this example:

```
grep 'dog.*bone' report7
```

This command would display lines that contain the following strings:

dogbone

dog-bone

doggy bone

My dog has a bone.

My dog is named Rover. Please add a soup bone to the grocery list.

The above command would not display cases where dog is on one line and bone is on the next. The whole regular expression must be on one line.

As another example, this command

```
grep '[0-9]*' report7
```

would display all lines that contain zero or more digits. Every line of the file would be displayed because every line of the file will contain zero or more digits. (Count the digits in each line and you will see that I am right.)

```
grep '[0-9][0-9]*' report7
```

This command displays any line containing one digit followed by zero or more digits. Essentially, this finds and displays all lines with one or more digits.

```
grep '$[0-9][0-9]*\.' report7
```

Why do UNIX scripts contain [ ]

Because there are spaces or tabs at the left margin, some `grep` commands can contain a pattern like '^[ ]*acme'. The characters within the square brackets are one space and one tab. This pattern looks for acme immediately after the left margin of zero or more spaces or tabs.

Given this command, grep displays any lines that contain a dollar sign ($), followed by one or more digits, followed by a period (.). The previous command is also equivalent to this one:

```
grep '$[0-9]\{1,\}\.' report7
```

Anytime you see two consecutive occurrences of a regular expression element followed by an asterisk (*), remember that you can find one or more of that element by using a command such as this:

```
grep 'abb*c' report7
```

This command tells grep to display any lines that contain a, followed by one or more b's, followed by a c.

Dropping Unbounded "or more" Regular Expression Wildcards

UNIX offers several ways for you to indicate that an element is to be used a certain number of times "or more." For example, you could use any of the following expressions:

```
a\{6,\}        (6 or more of the letter a)
b*             (0 or more of the letter b)
cc*            (1 or more of the letter c)
ddd*           (2 or more of the letter d)
```

Compare these two commands:

```
grep '[0-9]\{3,\}' report7
grep '[0-9]\{3\}' report7
```

The first of these commands will display lines that contain three or more digits. The second command will display lines that contain three digits. However the second command does not specify limitations on what characters may come after those three digits. Thus the second command will allow more digits after the three digits. In other words, it will also display lines containing three or more digits. In other words, the two commands will both display the exact same output even though you specified "or more" in the first command but not in the second.

The same is true for these two commands:

```
grep 'abb*' report7
grep 'ab' report7
```

The first command will display lines containing a, followed by one or more b's. The second command will display lines containing ab. The two commands are equivalent, however, because any line that contains a, followed by one or more b's also contains a, followed by one b (and vice versa). The command without the "or more" is better, though, because it is more efficient and easier to understand, and you can predict the results.

I call these unbounded "or more" situations because you are not specifying pattern elements before and after the "or more" element. If the "or more" element is unbounded, either before or after the element, omit the "or more" part from your grep command. This will make the grep command more efficient, and you will better understand what lines your grep command will output.

Here are some bounded "or more" situations:

```
grep "abb*c" report7
grep '^[0-9]*$' report7
grep '$[0-9]\{5,\}\.' report7
```

In each of these commands, pattern elements have been specified both before and after the "or more" wildcards. Here the "or more" is significant, however; if you leave it out, you will change the output from the command.

Extra Regular Expression Wildcards Available in *egrep*

The egrep command is an extended version of grep that allows some regular expression wildcards grep doesn't allow. However, egrep does not support the braces {} wildcard to specify the number of occurrences. Sometimes the set of egrep regular expression wildcards are called *extended regular expressions* or *full regular expressions*. The syntax for egrep is the same as that for grep.

Specifying One Or More Occurrences of an Element with egrep (+)

To specify that the previous pattern element is to be used one or more times, you use the plus sign (+) wildcard with egrep, as shown here:

```
egrep 'ab+c' report7
```

This command would display lines that contain a, followed by one or more b's, followed by c. The plus sign (+) wildcard is not supported by grep.

Using a Regular Expression Element Zero or More Times with *egrep* (?)

To specify zero or one occurrence of an element, you can use the question mark (?) with egrep:

```
egrep 'Mrs?. Smith' report7
```

The above command would display lines that contain strings such as these:

Mr. Smith

Mrs. Smith

However, it would not display lines with Mrss. Smith. The question mark (?) must be preceded by a backslash (\) or enclosed in double or single quotation marks (as shown). The question mark (?) wildcard is not supported by grep.

Searching for One of Several Patterns (|)

Using egrep, you can search for and display lines that contain one of several patterns. You separate those patterns with the vertical bar (|), which is also used as the pipe sign (|). Here's an example:

```
egrep 'acme|pegasus|apollo' report7
```

This command will display lines that contain acme or pegasus or apollo. The vertical bar (|) must be preceded by a backslash (\) or enclosed in double or single quotation marks (as shown).

Parentheses () can be used to group the vertical bar (|) choices, as shown here:

```
egrep 'project (acme|pegasus|apollo)' report7
```

This command will display lines that contain project acme or project pegasus or apollo.

Extra Regular Expression Wildcards Available Only in *perl*

perl is a complete programming language that runs under UNIX and Windows. While it usually does not come with any commercial UNIX distribution, it is readily available via the Internet for most UNIX systems. If perl is available on your system, you can use it as a grep-like command-line utility that provides search and display capabilities not available in grep or egrep.

Using *perl* to find lines with patterns

1. If you are going to use perl in a pipeline, enter the UNIX command sequence that will generate the output for perl to process. End this sequence with a pipe sign (|). Do not press Enter until you're instructed to do so.

2. Enter perl -ne 'print if /.

   The -e option to perl allows you to enter a line of perl code on the command line. The -n option allows perl to process each line of standard input or any files specified on the command line. Do not press Enter until you're instructed to do so.

3. Enter the pattern to search for. You can include any of the regular expressions for grep and also those for egrep. Braces {} to indicate a repeat count should not be preceded by a backslash (\) as they are with grep.

4. Enter /.

5. If you want to ignore case in the pattern, enter i.

6. If you want to ignore spaces in the pattern, enter x.

7. Enter a single quotation mark (').

8. If you are not piping to perl, enter a space and then enter one or more filenames to search.

9. Press the Enter key to execute your command.

Here is a complete example:

```
perl -ne 'print if /^acme [0-9] {3,} \ /ix' report7 report8
```

This command illustrates that complex regular expressions are easier to read using perl. The regular expression is found between the slashes (/) in the command. If you use the perl x option after the closing slash (/), spaces are ignored in the regular expression unless they are escaped—preceded by a backslash (\). Think of the x as allowing you to expand the pattern, using spaces freely to make it more readable. The other perl feature that improves readability is that backslashes (\) are not used before braces {} indicating repeat counts.

Finding Words That Are Not Parts of Larger Words (*b*)

Using perl, you can search for words that are not part of larger words. This is difficult or impossible using grep or egrep.

To specify a word boundary, enter \b in the regular expression for perl. With perl, a word can contain upper- or lowercase letters, digits, or the underscore character (_).

```
perl -ne 'print if /\b in \b/ix' report7
```

In this example, the regular expression is placed within slashes (/). Again, you use the x option following the final slash (/) so that spaces can be inserted in the regular expression to improve readability. This command will display any lines in report7 that contain the word in. By placing \b before and after the word in, you can specify that the word in cannot be part of a larger word.

Therefore, the output will not display lines that contain the words tin, bin, dinner, or into, for example. However, it will display the word in if it is at the start of a line, at the end of a line, or has punctuation around it.

In this command

```
perl -ne 'print if /\b in /ix' report7
```

the \b occurs only before the word in. The command will display all lines that contain words that start with in, including larger words such as into or intend.

To specify that a position not be on a word boundary, you use \B, as in this example:

```
perl -ne 'print if / in \B /ix' report7
```

This command will display all lines that contain the string in as part of a longer word such as inn or into or dinner. However the words tin and bin would not match the pattern because they have a word boundary after the word in.

SEE ALSO

➤ *For more information on* perl, *see page* 717

Turning Off Regular Expression Wildcards (\,*fgrep*)

To turn off the special nature of a regular expression wildcard, precede it with a backslash (\) as in this example:

```
grep '2\*3' mathreport
```

Here, you are looking for the string 2*3, so you have to turn off the special meaning of the asterisk (*).

If you have a large number of wildcards to turn off, you can use the fgrep command, which does not allow any regular expression wildcards. All characters are regular characters to fgrep. Therefore, with this command

```
fgrep '*****' report7
```

you can look for all lines with five or more asterisks (*). You don't have to precede each one with a backslash, though, because you used the fgrep command instead of grep.

fgrep is also useful for ignoring wildcards in the contents of shell variables, as in this example:

```
fgrep "$USERINPUT" report7
```

Checking Only Specific Fields to Select a Line (*awk*)

awk is an extensive programming language that is available on all commercial UNIX systems. You can use a subset of it as a grep-like command-line utility that provides search and display capabilities not available in grep or egrep.

SEE ALSO

➤ *For more information on* awk, *see page 671*

Displaying a Line If Exact Match in One Field (*awk*)

grep checks the whole line for a match. If you want to check only a specific field of the line, you can do that using awk.

Displaying a line based on exact match in one field

1. If you are going to use awk in a pipeline, enter the UNIX command sequence that will generate the output for awk to process. End this sequence with a pipe sign (|). Do not press the Enter key until you're instructed to do so.

2. Enter awk '$FNUM ==.

   Replace *FNUM* with the field number you want to check. For awk, you separate the fields with one or more spaces or tabs. The first field is 1. The last field can be indicated by replacing *FNUM* with NF (as in awk '$NF ==). Do not press the Enter key until you're instructed to do so.

3. Enter a space, and then enter the pattern to search for surrounded by double quotation marks. No wildcards are allowed. (See the next section if you want to use wildcards.)

Two reasons to avoid fgrep

fgrep is supposed to be the fast grep because it does not have to handle regular expressions. However it is often the slowest of the grep commands. The X/Open (Ver 2) spec calls fgrep obsolete and prefers the equivalent command grep -F.

4. Enter a single quote (').

5. If you are not piping to awk, enter a space and then enter one or more filenames to search.

6. Press Enter to execute your command.

Here is an example:

```
awk '$3 == "acme"' report7
```

This command will display lines of report7 in which field 3 of the line contains only the word acme.

Displaying a Line Based on Numeric Value in One Field (*awk*)

You can use the same format to display a line if a particular field contains a numeric value. No quotation marks are required around the numeric value. You can make the following tests:

```
==    equal to
!=    not equal to
>     greater than
>=    greater than or equal to
<     less than
<=    less than or equal to
```

```
awk '$1 > 3.6' yearend.rpt
```

The previous command will display all lines in yearend.rpt in which the first field of the line contains a number larger than 3.6. If the field starts with a letter (i.e., it is not numeric), awk treats it as an impossibly large numeric value.

Displaying a Line If There Is a Regular Expression Match in One Field (*awk*)

To use regular expressions when checking for a matching string, change the test from == to tilde (~) and put slashes (/) around the regular expressions, as shown here:

```
awk '$3 ~ /^acme[0-9]/' report7
```

This command will display all lines from report7 in which field 3 starts with acme, followed by a digit.

awk allows the same regular expression wildcards as egrep, which include the following:

+	for one or more occurrences of previous element
?	for zero or one occurrences of previous element
|	for allowed alternative patterns
()	for grouping patterns

awk, like egrep, does not allow the use of \{ \} to specify the number of occurrences.

Displaying a Line Based on Multiple Conditions (&&,||)

To check for two conditions before displaying a line, use && to indicate a logical AND. For example, in this command:

```
ls -l | awk '$3 == "fred" && $5 > 2300'
```

awk is checking field 3 from ls –l, which is the owner of each file. It is also checking field 5, which is the size of the file in bytes. This command will display only files owned by fred which are larger than 2300 bytes.

To check for one condition or another being true, use || to indicate a logical OR, as in this example:

```
ls -l | awk '$3 == "fred" || $5 > 2300'
```

This command will display all files that are either owned by fred or are greater than 2300 bytes.

To group conditions, use parentheses () like this:

```
ls -l | awk '( $3 == "fred" || $3 == "jane") && $5 > 2300'
```

This command will display files owned by either fred or jane providing the size is greater than 2300 bytes.

Replacing or Removing Text from a File or Pipeline

By Steve "Mor" Moritsugu

Replacing or Removing Strings (Using Regular Expression)

The preceding chapter showed how to use regular expression wildcards to find lines containing a pattern within a file or pipeline. That chapter also showed that regular expression wildcards can look similar to Filename Generation Wildcards, but these are two different sets of wildcards used for totally different purposes even though they use some of the same wildcard characters. This section teaches you how to replace a substring within a line and how to use regular expression patterns to define the string to be replaced.

SEE ALSO

➤ *For more information on regular expression wildcards see page 388*

Replacing One String with Another (*sed*, regular expression)

To replace one string with another when displaying the output of a file, use the sed command like this:

```
sed 's/Mr. Smith/Ms. Wilson/g' report7
```

sed	is the stream editor. It makes any editing changes we specify as it processes the data stream one line at a time.
's/Mr. Smith/Ms. Wilson/g'	is the editing command we are giving to sed. This command is usually enclosed in single quotation marks to protect the punctuation inside from shell interpretation. Use double quotation marks rather than single quotation marks if you want to include any shell variables as part of the editing command.

`'s/Pattern/Repl/g'`   is the general format of the sed substitute command. `Pattern` is the string for which to search and `Repl` is the string with which to replace it. `Pattern` may contain regular expression wildcards, but `Repl` may not. Our example searches for the string `Mr. Smith` and replaces all occurrences of it with the string `Ms. Wilson`. This is true even if the `Pattern` is part of a larger word—for example, Mr. Smithson would become Ms. Wilsonson. We will see later in this chapter how Perl can prevent this problem.

`report7`   is the file for sed to process. You can also specify a list of files, and sed will display the contents of each of them, making the substitution indicated. Filename Generation Wildcards can be used to generate the list of files.

Note that sed displays the changed output to standard output; it does not modify the file itself. The output from this command can then be piped to another command or it can be redirected to a file.

Here is the same sed command used in a pipeline situation:

```
cat report* ¦ sed 's/Mr. Smith/Ms. Wilson/g' ¦ pg
```

report* is not a regular expression wildcard. It is a Filename Generation Wildcard that generates a list of all files that start with the word *report*. The cat command will output these files on the standard output that is piped to the same sed command that we just analyzed. The output from sed will then be displayed one page at a time onscreen.

Using Regular Expression Wildcards in the *sed* Search String

The preceding chapter discussed regular expression (R.E.) wildcards. See the appendix under "wildcard" for a quick reference of all the special symbols. Here is an example sed command that uses R.E. wildcards in the search string.

```
sed 's/JPC[^A-Za-z]*SPR/JPC-SPR/g' report7
```

In this example,
```
[^A-Za-z]
```

is a regular expression wildcard that indicates any one character that is not an uppercase or lowercase letter.
```
[^A-Za-z]*
```

is an regular expression wildcard that indicates zero or more occurrences of any non-letter character.
```
JPC[^A-Za-z]*SPR
```

is the pattern to search for in the preceding sed command. It is looking for JPC followed by SPR with zero or more of any non-letter characters in between. That pattern can be found in each of the following lines except for the last line:

```
The JPCSPR company
long history of JPC-SPR relations
many JPC/SPR employees
JPC*SPR company president
four JPC(-)SPR votes
negotiate JPC SPR contracts
two companies, JPC and SPR, merged
```

In these lines, the writer has not been consistent in referring to the company name, but we can use an R.E. wildcard pattern to match all the different references and replace them with one consistent reference. The following shows how the preceding lines would be displayed after running our example sed command, which is repeated here:

```
sed 's/JPC[^A-Za-z]*SPR/JPC-SPR/g' report7

The JPC-SPR company
long history of JPC-SPR relations
many JPC-SPR employees
JPC-SPR company president
four JPC-SPR votes
negotiate JPC-SPR contracts
two companies, JPC and SPR, merged
```

Notice the last line did not match the R.E. pattern, and so no replacement was made in that line.

Saving the Replaced Output in the Original File (*sed*)

sed displays the replaced lines to standard output. If you want to replace the contents of a file, you must use two UNIX commands and a temporary file. For example:

```
sed 's/pattern/repl/g' report7 > /tmp/sed$$ mv /tmp/sed$$
➥report7
```

This technique was explained in Chapter 4.

SEE ALSO
➤ *For more information on saving output in the original file, see page 114*

Making the Replacement Only Once per Line (*sed*)

Remove the g flag from the substitute command to make the replacement a maximum of once per line. Without the g flag, we will still make the replacement once on every line where the pattern occurs, but never more than once on any given line. For example:

```
sed 's/IBW/MCC/' partslist
```

Assume that the file partslist, mentioned in the preceding command, contains lines like this:

```
402     IBW-10    IBW(4),IBW(5)
403-6   IBW-11-6  IBW(3),MNT(16)
527     GRV-6     GRV(13,MNT(14)
```

The preceding sed command would replace those lines as follows:

416

```
402      MCC-10      IBW(4),IBW(5)
403-6    MCC-11-6    IBW(3),MNT(16)
527      GRV-6       GRV(13,MNT(14)
```

Notice that only the first occurrence of IBW on each line has been replaced.

You should omit the g flag whenever you use the circumflex (^) R.E. wildcard or the dollar sign ($) R.E. wildcard (see appendix under "wildcard"). For example:

```
sed 's/^[    ]*Chapter/Section/' book3
```

In this example,

```
[    ]
```

is an R.E. wildcard that indicates either a space or tab. There is a space and a tab character within the square brackets.

```
^[    ]*
```

indicates zero or more spaces or tabs at the start of a line.

```
^[    ]*Chapter
```

indicates the word *Chapter* on the left margin—that is, it can be indented and still match the pattern.

The preceding sed command will replace the word *Chapter* with *Section* but only if *Chapter* is the first word on the line, ignoring any leading spaces. The replacement word *Section* will not be indented even if *Chapter* was indented. We will see in the next section how to preserve what wildcards matched, which would allow the replacement to have the same indentation.

Your command will still work if you include the g flag with the circumflex (^) or dollar sign ($) R.E. wildcards. The g flag is just unnecessary and slightly inefficient because there cannot be more than one match per line when you use either of these two R.E. wildcards.

Changing the Delimiter (*sed*)

The character immediately following

```
sed 's
```

is the delimiter that marks the start and end of the search pattern and replacement string. Slash (/), colon (:), and percent sign (%) are the most commonly used delimiters. These three commands all do the same thing:

```
sed 's/xxx/yyy/g' report7      # delimiter is slash (/)
sed 's:xxx:yyy:g' report7      # delimiter is colon (:)
sed 's%xxx%yyy%g' report7      # delimiter is percent sign (%)
```

Choose a delimiter that is not a character in the search pattern or the replacement string. To change all occurrences of /usr/fred to /usr/jane, for example, I would choose a delimiter other than slash (/). For example:

```
sed 's:/usr/fred:/usr/jane:g' report7
```

Some UNIX systems freely allow any character to be used as the delimiter besides the three common ones that I have mentioned. Alternatively you can put a backslash (\) before the delimiter character to use it within the source or destination string if you don't want to change the delimiter. The following line is equivalent to the preceding example, but more difficult to read:

```
sed 's/\/usr\/fred/\/usr\/jane/g' report7
```

Removing (Deleting) a String from a Line (*sed*, R.E.)

To remove or delete a string, use the sed replacement command and specify an empty replacement string. For example:

```
sed 's/ (LPX)//g' report
```

This example searches for a space followed by LPX in parentheses and will delete those six characters wherever found.

Selective Replacement or Deletion

We can limit which lines sed acts on to do replacement or deletion. One way to do that is to specify a starting and ending line number. For example:

```
sed '14,253 s/Mr. Smith/Ms. Wilson/g' report7
```

14   specifies the starting line number for sed to start making replacements. Line 1 is the first line of the file or pipeline.

253   specifies the last line number for sed replacements.

Use a dollar sign ($) to specify the last line of the file, as follows:

```
sed '14,$ s/Mr. Smith/Ms. Wilson/g' report7
```

This command is useful when you want to process most of a file, but it has a header section that you don't want to process.

Another way to selectively replace or delete a pattern is to specify a qualifying pattern that must appear on the lines to be processed. For example:

```
sed '/Acme/ s/Mr. Smith/Ms. Wilson/g' report7
```

In the preceding example, the replacement will only occur on lines that contain the qualifying string Acme. Instead of Acme, we could also have specified a qualifying pattern containing R.E. wildcards. If the qualifying pattern contains a slash (/), precede it with a backslash (\), as follows:

```
sed '/\/usr\/fred/ s/Mr. Smith/Ms. Wilson/g' report7
```

In this example, the replacement will only occur on lines that contain the qualifying string /usr/fred. You can also use an initial \x to select any character x as the delimiter for the qualifying pattern. For example:

```
sed '\:/usr/fred: s/Mr. Smith/Ms. Wilson/g' report7
```

In the preceding example, the replacement will only occur on lines that contain the qualifying string /usr/fred.

If you want to process a section of consecutive lines but don't know the starting and ending line number, you can use patterns to specify start and end, as follows:

```
sed '/^ *Chapter 2/,/^ *Chapter 3/ s/Mr. Smith/Ms. Wilson/g'
➥report7
```

In this example, the replacement will occur on all output lines in the section of report7 whose first line has the words *Chapter 2*, which may come after some leading spaces. The section for replacement ends on the line that contains *Chapter 3* (again leading spaces are allowed). Notice both patterns are in slashes (/) and separated by a comma (,).

Using Special Characters

To search for a literal asterisk (*) or period (.) in the search pattern, precede that character with a backslash (\) so that sed will not take it as a wildcard. For example:

```
sed 's/321\.43/421.43/g' report7
```

In the preceding example, the backslash (\) indicates that the following period is not a wildcard, so sed will search for 321.43 and replace all occurrences of that exact string with 421.43.

There is no way to search for a pattern that begins on one line and ends on the next line. You cannot use \n in either the search pattern or the replacement string. You can use an escaped newline to start a newline in the replacement string, as follows:

```
$ date ¦ sed 's/ /\
>/g'
Sun
Mar
22
11:38:09
PST
1998
$
```

In this example, you are changing each space in the output to a newline. Notice we put a backslash before pressing the Enter key for the newline in the sed replacement string. We then get our PS2 prompt (>), which tells us we are still entering part of a previous command. We then enter the rest of the sed command.

To include a literal single quotation mark (') in cither the search or replacement strings, you cannot use single quotation marks to enclose the strings as in previous examples. Also using a preceding backslash to quote the internal single quotation mark (') does not help. You must change to double quotation marks around the sed command, as follows:

```
sed "s/it's/it is/g" report7
```

See the following section for other issues when using sed with double quotation marks rather than single quotation marks.

Using Shell Variables in the Search or Replacement String

If there is a phrase that you use often in the search or replacement string, you can save it in a shell variable for easy re-use, as follows:

```
CO="Acme"
```

To use shell variables in your sed command, use double quotation marks rather than single quotation marks, as follows:

```
sed "s/president of $CO/chairman of $CO/g" report7
```

This command searches for president of Acme and changes those words to chairman of Acme.

If a shell variable is adjacent to other letters or digits or underscore, enclose the variable in curly braces {}, as follows:

```
sed "s/president of ${CO}Ltd/chairman of ${CO}Ltd/g" report7
```

The preceding command searches for president of AcmeLtd and change those words to chairman of AcmeLtd.

When using double quotation marks rather than single quotation marks, you must also put a backslash (\) before the following:

A dollar sign ($), if not beginning a shell variable

A backquote (`), if not enclosing command substitution

A double quotation mark inside your string

You must also change any literal backslashes (\) in your search or replacement string into four backslashes (\). (This is because the shell will remove two of them, and the backslash must be preceded by a backslash to indicate a literal backslash.)

SEE ALSO

➤ *For more information on shell variables see page 30*

Don't Replace 0 or More Occurrences (*sed*)

Assume that report7 contains these lines:

```
five trucks XXX
three XX cars
```

Assume that we want to replace any group of X's with a question mark (?). Here is the wrong way to do that:

```
sed 's/X*/?/g' report7          # wrong way
```

Here is the output from the preceding command:

```
?f?i?v?e? ?t?r?u?c?k?s? ??
?t?h?r?e?e? ?? ?c?a?r?s?
```

The reason we see the replacement string so many times is because there are always zero occurrences of any character between any two other characters. If I have the letters *ab*, for example, there are zero occurrences of the letter *X* between those two characters. To correct the preceding sed command, we should specify one or more *X*'s, not zero or more *X*'s.

Here is the correct sed command to use:

```
sed 's/XX*/?/g' report7         # correct way
```

XX* specifies one *X* followed by zero or more *X*'s, which is equivalent to one or more *X*'s. Here is the output from that command:

```
five trucks ?
three ? cars
```

Using, in the Replacement String, What a Wildcard Matched (*sed*)

If you enclose part or all of the R.E. pattern in escaped parentheses, sed will remember the exact characters that matched that part of the pattern. You can then use the remembered string in the replacement pattern as \1. Use \2 for a second remembered pattern, and so on. Here is an example we analyzed previously in this chapter:

```
sed 's/^[    ]*Chapter/Section/' book3
```

It changes *Chapter* to *Section* but, as we saw, the replacement string loses the left margin it had previously. We can correct that as follows:

```
sed 's/^\([    ]*\)Chapter/\1Section/' book3
```

`\(  \)`	are the escaped parentheses.
`\([    ]*\)`	uses escaped parentheses to remember how many spaces or tabs were found at the left margin before the word *Chapter*.
`\1`	in the destination string restores the remembered string.

Here is a different example. Assume that report7 contains lines that contain numbers up to six digits. For example:

```
12345 cartons and 534723 sets
73293 boxes of 24 items
1837 containers of 144 packages
```

We can use sed to put a comma in the numbers to make them more readable, as follows:

```
sed 's/\([0-9]\{1,3\}\)\([0-9]\{3\}\)/\1,\2/g' report7
```

`\( [0-9] \{ 1,3 \} \)`	is the first part of the pattern to search for. It matches one, two, or three consecutive digits. These are wildcards discussed in the preceding chapter. Also see the appendix under "wildcard." I have added spaces so that you can see the elements within the pattern, but spaces are not allowed in the actual command. The actual digits matched are remembered as the first remembered string (`\1`).
`\( [0-9] \{ 3 \} \)`	is the second part of the pattern to search for. It matches three consecutive digits. These must immediately follow the first part of the pattern. Putting the two patterns together causes our command to

look for (and replace) any occurrences of four to six consecutive digits. The actual digits matched by this R.E. pattern are remembered as the second remembered string.

\1,\2   is the replacement string. It consists of the first remembered string, then a comma (,), and then the second remembered string. Thus we are putting back the original numbers with a comma in between.

Here is the output of that command:

```
12,345 cartons and 534,723 sets
73,293 boxes of 24 items
1,837 containers of 144 packages
```

sed can use lots of punctuation

When I first started using UNIX, I automatically ignored any **sed** commands with lots of punctuation. This is a prime example of where UNIX can seem to be cryptic. I wish someone had shown me then how to break such patterns down into simple elements. Pattern matching on the command line is one of the things that gives UNIX its elegance and power.

Eliminating All but the Search Pattern (*sed*)

Assume that report7 contains lines like this:

```
Income in Jan 52384 as reported in accounting report.
Income in Feb 63283 as reported in accounting report.
Income in Mar 61966 as reported in accounting report.
```

Assume that we only want to display the month and the amount, and we want to delete the rest of the text on the line. Rather than try to form a pattern for the rest of the text to delete, we also have the option to form a pattern for the text to keep, if that is easier. We can then eliminate all but the search pattern by remembering the text found as the search pattern, as follows:

```
sed 's/.*\([A-Z][a-z][a-z] [0-9]\{5\}\).*/\1/' report7
```

.*   begins and ends our search pattern. This specifies zero or more characters before and after our pattern, so the whole line will be replaced.

\(... \)   will remember the characters that match our pattern, so we can use them in the replacement.

`[A-Z][a-z][a-z]`	match the three-letter month that begins with a capital letter.
`[0-9]\{5\}`	matches five consecutive digits.
`\1`	in the replacement string puts back only the matched month and amount in place of the entire line.

Here is the output from that `sed` command:

```
Jan 52384
Feb 63283
Mar 61966
```

This technique is also useful when setting shell variables with values from some UNIX commands. We can use `sed` to extract just the pattern we want and save it in the variable, as discussed in the next section.

Rule: R.E. Wildcards Match the Longest Possible Span

Here is the output from the UNIX `id` command:

```
$ id
uid=501(mori) gid=100(users) groups=100(users),11(floppy)
$
```

We can use `sed` to extract our current logon name from the `id` output, which is given in the first set of parentheses. Here is wrong way to do that:

```
$ id ¦ sed 's/.*\(\(.*\)\).*/\1/'        # wrong way
floppy
$
```

`.*`	begins and ends our pattern so that we can replace the whole line as discussed in the preceding section.
`( ... )`	tells `sed` we are looking for text within parentheses.
`\(.*\)`	tells `sed` to remember all the actual characters found within the parentheses.
`\1`	in the replacement string tells `sed` the replacement is to only consist of what was found inside parentheses.

The preceding command found the word inside the last parentheses because of the rule that R.E. wildcards always match the longest possible span. At the start of the pattern to search for, we have `.*` (which indicates zero or more characters before a parenthesis. This could match everything in the line up to the first parenthesis, or the second parenthesis, … or the last parenthesis. We can come closer to the correct result by replacing the first `.*` with `[^(]*`, which indicates zero of more of any character except for a left parenthesis. For example:

```
$ id ¦ sed 's/[^(]*(\(.*\)).*/\1/'        # still wrong
mori) gid=100(users) groups=100(users),11(floppy
$
```

Now the problem is that the middle `.*` matches all characters from the first left parenthesis to the last right parenthesis because of the longest span rule. We can correct that problem by replacing the middle `.*` with `[^)]*`, which indicates zero or more of any character except for a right parenthesis, as follows:

```
$ id ¦ sed 's/[^(]*(\(([^)]*\)).*/\1/'        # correct
mori
$
```

Now we have extracted the contents of the first parenthesis. We can use the same construction to place the result in a shell variable, as follows:

```
MYLOGIN=`id ¦ sed 's/[^(]*(\(([^)]*\)).*/\1/'` # extract 1st
➥parenthesis
```

> **R.E. wildcards are greedy**
>
> We can use the technical term "greedy" to describe wildcards that match the longest possible string of characters in the line.

Using Perl to Replace or Delete Strings

Perl is a complete programming language that runs under both UNIX and Windows. Although it usually does not come packaged with any commercial UNIX distribution, it is readily available via the Internet for most UNIX systems. If Perl is available on your system, you can also use it as a simple command-line utility which provides replacement capabilities not available in sed.

For simple replacement, `perl` is just like sed if you use the `-pe` option to `perl`. The following two commands are equivalent:

```
     sed 's/Mr. Smith/Ms. Wilson/g' report7
perl -pe 's/Mr. Smith/Ms. Wilson/g' report7
```

Earlier this chapter discussed the g flag for sed. It means the same thing to perl: process all patterns on the line, not just the first occurrence on a line. As in sed, you can omit the g flag to perl, as follows:

```
perl -pe 's/Mr. Smith/Ms. Wilson/' report7
```

The preceding command will only replace Mr. Smith the first time it is found on a line. Any other occurrences of Mr. Smith on the same line will not be replaced.

perl does not use backslashes (\) before braces {} for repeat counts or before parentheses () for remembered strings as sed, grep, and awk do. You must then use preceding backslashes in perl if you want to indicate parentheses as literal characters in the pattern. Preceding backslashes are only needed before literal braces if they take the form {n}, {n,}, or {n,m}, which could be confused with R.E. wildcards.

Although perl can accomplish a large number of things, I am just going to look in this section at command-line replacement capabilities in perl that can't be done in sed.

SEE ALSO

➤ *For more information on R.E. wildcards and Perl see page 30*

➤ *For more information on Perl programming see page 717*

How to Match the Shortest Possible Span (*perl*)

One of the wildcards supported in perl but not in sed is the question mark (?). Use this after another wildcard (for example, * or +) to limit the scope of that wildcard to the shortest possible span. Now we can solve the id extraction problem from the preceding section much more easily. For example:

```
$ id ¦ perl -pe 's/.*?\((.*?)\).*/\1/'
mori
$
```

.*?\(indicates zero or more characters before a left
                    parenthesis. The ? says to match the shortest possi-
                    ble span, so the pattern matches everything up to
                    and including the first parenthesis on the line.

(. . .)   remembers the actual characters matched. `perl` does not use backslashes (\) here.

\(.*?\)   indicates the shortest span between a left and right parenthesis. This limits us to the contents of one set of parentheses.

Expanding Patterns for Readability (*perl*)

The x flag (only available in perl) allows spaces to be put into the search pattern so that the elements can be separated for readability. All spaces in the pattern are ignored unless preceded by a backslash (\). We can apply this to the id extraction command in the preceding section:

```
$ id ¦ perl -pe 's/.*?\((.*?)\).*/\1/'
```

Here is the same command with the x flag and spaces for readability:

```
$ id ¦ perl -pe 's/.*?  \( ( .*? ) \)   .*/\1/x'
```

Replacing Words That Are Not in Larger Words (*perl*)

Earlier in this chapter we looked at this command:

```
sed 's/Mr. Smith/Ms. Wilson/g' report7
```

We saw that it would also change Mr. Smithson to Ms. Wilsonson. We can avoid that if perl is on your UNIX system by using the \b wildcard that matches a word boundary in perl, as follows:

```
perl -pe 's/Mr. Smith\b/Ms. Wilson/g' report7
```

Mr. Smith matches the pattern and will be replaced. Mr. Smithson does not match the pattern and so will not be replaced. If Mr. Smith is followed by punctuation or the end of the line, it still satisfies the \b (word boundary) condition and so would be replaced. Multiple \b wildcards can be used at the start, end, and inside one search pattern.

SEE ALSO

➤ *For more information on the* \b perl *wildcard, see page 405*

Replacing One String or Another (*perl*)

Use the vertical bar (¦) to separate one alternative from another in the search pattern, as follows:

```
perl -pe 's/cars|trains|planes/vehicles/g' report7
```

The preceding command will search for the words *cars*, *trains*, or *planes* and replace each of them with the word *vehicles*.

We can use parentheses for grouping alternatives, as follows:

```
perl -pe 's/in (two¦four) (cars¦trains)/by freight/g'
➥report7
```

The preceding command would look for the following phrases:

```
in two cars
in four cars
in two trains
in four trains
```

It would replace all occurrences of those four phrases with the words *by freight*.

These parentheses also remember the actual text that matches the pattern that can be referenced as \1 or \2. Use (?:...¦...) if you don't want to remember the pattern, as follows:

```
perl -pe 's/in (?:two¦four) (cars¦trains)/in three \1/g'
➥report7
```

(?:two¦four)	allows either the word *two* or *four* here. It does not remember what was matched.
(cars¦trains)	allows either the word cars or trains here and does remember what was matched.
\1	allows us to put the remembered string (cars or trains) in the replacement.

Ignoring Case When Matching the R.E. Pattern

It is very cumbersome to ignore upper/lowercase when using sed to make replacements. For example:

```
sed 's/[aA][cC][mM][eE] [cC][oO][rR][pP]\./Acme Inc./g'
➥report7
```

The /i flag causes perl to ignore case and enables us to write the equivalent command like this:

```
perl -pe 's/acme corp\./Acme Inc./gi' report7
```

Selective Replacement or Deletion

We can add a qualifying R.E. using the format if /Q.R.E./ to do selective replacement or deletion in perl, where Q.R.E. is my abbreviation for qualifying R.E.

```
perl -pe 's/Mr. Smith/Ms. Wilson/g if /acme/' report7
```

In the preceding example,

```
if /acme/
```

sets acme the Q.R.E. so that the replacement of Ms. Wilson for Mr. Smith will only occur on lines that contain acme somewhere in that line.

Using *awk* to Replace or Delete Strings

awk is an extensive programming language available on all commercial UNIX systems. As discussed in the preceding chapter, awk can be used in a simple command-line form when we want to selectively process lines based on the contents of specific fields.

SEE ALSO
➤ *For more information on displaying lines using* awk, *see page 407*

➤ *For more information on* awk *programming, see page 671*

Replacement or Deletion Based on Fields

In the a previous chapter, we saw how to display lines from a file if a specific field was equal to a specified value. For example:

```
awk '$3 == "acme"' report7
```

In this example, lines from report7 will only be displayed if the complete field 3 of that line exactly matches the word acme. We can modify that command to search for and replace a regular expression (R.E.) pattern on lines where field 3 exactly matches the word acme, as follows:

```
awk '$3 == "acme" { gsub ("R.E.","repl") } {print}' report7
```

$3	is the field number to check. $1 is the first field. $NF would indicate the last field in any line. Each field is separated by one or more spaces or tabs.
acme	is an example string to check for. It may not contain any R.E. wildcards because of the ==.
R.E.	is the pattern to search for that may contain R.E. wildcards.
repl	is the string that is to replace the search pattern everywhere it is found on the line. An & in this repl string will be replaced with the characters that matched the whole R.E. pattern.
report7	is an example file to process. A list of files could also be specified here including filename generation wildcards. If no files are given, awk will read from standard input, so you can pipe to it from other commands.

No spaces are required inside the single quotation marks. I have added them because they are permitted for readability.

If you want to delete the R.E. pattern on just the selected lines, change the repl string to the empty string, as follows:

```
awk '$3 == "acme" { gsub ("R.E.","") } {print}' report7
```

To only make the replacement on the first occurrence in a line but not replace other occurrences on that same line, use sub rather than gsub, as follows:

```
awk '$3 == "acme" { sub ("R.E.","") } {print}' report7
```

As we saw with grep in the previous chapter, we can test numeric values in fields using ==, !=, >, >=, <, or <=, and so on.

```
awk '$3 > 6.7 { gsub ("R.E.","repl") } {print}' report7
```

In the preceding command, the replacement will only occur if field 3 contains a numeric value larger than 6.7. We can also limit the replacement to lines that contain a regular expression pattern in a particular field, as follows:

```
awk '$3 ~ /Q.R.E./ { gsub ("R.E.","repl") } {print}' report7
```

Q.R.E. is my abbreviation for a qualifying R.E.—that is, an R.E. that must be present somewhere in the line for the replacement to occur. We can combine several conditions using ¦¦ for "OR" and && for "AND", as follows:

```
awk '$2 <= 3.14 && $3 ~ /acme/ { gsub ("R.E.","repl") }
➥{print}' report7
```

In the preceding example, the replacement will not occur unless both conditions are true: field 2 is less than or equal to 3.14 and field 3 equals or contains acme, which is the pattern specified as the Q.R.E.

Displaying Only Selected Fields (*awk*)

I frequently use awk when I want to only display selected fields from a line. Use { print $n } to display just field *n* from the output, as follows:

```
$ ls -l report7
-rw-r--r--   1 mori      users         2966 Mar 22 15:08
➥report7
$ ls -l report7 ¦ awk '{print $5}'
2966
$
```

In the preceding example, we used awk to print just field 5 from ls -l, which gives us the size in bytes of the report7 file. We can use the same command to save the size in a variable, as follows:

```
$ SIZE=`ls -l report7 ¦ awk '{print $5}'`
```

In the preceding command, we use backquotes to save the size of report7 in variable SIZE. We can display both the name from field 9 and the size from field 5 as in this example:

```
$ ls -l ¦ awk '{print $9, $5}'
acme 17263
report7 2966
report8 34238
$
```

We can specify literal strings in the output in double quotation marks. We can also use tabs to make the columns line up better. In the following example, I have specified a tab as the sole character in the double quotation marks between $9 and $5:

```
$ ls -l ¦ awk '{print "file: " $9 "    " $5}'
file:
file: acme      17263
file: report7   2966
file: report8   34238
$
```

Here is another example. In the output of ls -l, field 3 is the file owner. We have already seen how to cause awk to only process fields based on the contents of a particular field. For example:

```
$ ls -l ¦ awk '$3 == "root" {print "file: " $9 "    " $5}'
```

In this example, we will only display the filename and size if the owner of the file is root. In the next example, we are checking field 2 to see whether the link count for the file is greater than 4, as follows:

```
$ ls -l ¦ awk '$2 > 4 {print "file: " $9 "    " $5}'
```

In the next example, we will only display information about the file if field 4, the group name, contains an R.E. pattern. For example:

```
$ ls -l ¦ awk '$4 ~ /^work/ {print "file: " $9 "    " $5}'
```

In the preceding example, we will only display the filename and size if field 4, the group of the file, starts with the word work. Also as we have seen before with awk, we can use ¦¦ as an "OR" condition and && and as an "AND" condition, as follows:

```
$ ls -l ¦ awk '$2 > 4 && $4 ~ /^work/ {print "file: " $9 "
➡" $5}'
```

Conditionally Replacing a Particular Field Value (*awk*)

We can conditionally replace the value of a field of output by adding an awk action with this format:

```
{if (condition) $n = value} {print action}
```

Often this is used to modify a field if it is either below or above a certain threshold.

```
$ ls -l ¦ awk '{if ($5 > 20000) $5=20000} {print "file: " $9
➥"      " $5}'
file:
file: acme      17263
file: report7  2966
file: report8  20000
$
```

In the preceding example, report8 had a value larger than 20000, but we used the awk command to set the largest reported value at 20000. We could also set the value to some word in double quotation marks, as follows:

```
$ ls -l ¦ awk '{if ($5 > 20000) $5="overflow"} {print "file: "
➥$9 "      " $5}'
file:
file: acme      17263
file: report7  2966
file: report8  overflow
$
```

Formatting Fields into Straight Columns (*awk*)

awk has many features of the C language, including the printf function. For example:

```
$ ls -l ¦
> tail +2 ¦
> awk '{ printf("Name: %16s, Size: %5d, Blocks: %6.2f\n",
➥$9, $5, $5/512)}'
Name:             acme, Size: 17263, Blocks:  33.72
Name:          report7, Size:  2966, Blocks:   5.79
Name:          report8, Size: 34238, Blocks:  66.87
$
```

```
ls -l ¦
```
is the first line of our example. Notice that shell pipelines may be split after the pipe sign (¦), to be continued on the next line.

`tail +2 |`	enables us to ignore the first line of the `ls -l` output, which is a heading that contains the total number of blocks before the file information begins.
`printf("format string", v1, v2, ...)`	is the general form of the `printf` function. The format string can contain literal words like `Name:` in our example. It should end in `\n`, which indicates a newline.
`%16s`	in our example, this indicates that the first variable listed following the format string should be displayed using at least 16 character positions. The `s` after the 16 says to display the value as a string. This specification is used to display the filename in our example.
`%5d`	indicates the next variable or value following the format string should be displayed using at least five character positions. The `d` after

the 5 says to display the value as a decimal integer—that is, a whole number without a fractional part. This specification is used to display the size in bytes in our example.

%6.2f   indicates the next value following the format string should be displayed using at least six character positions. The f after the 6.2 says to display the values as a floating-point number—that is, a number with a decimal fraction. The .2 says to display two decimal places to the right of the decimal point. This specification is used to display the calculated size in blocks in our example.

$5/512   is a calculation we are doing for the size in blocks. $5 is the size in bytes, so $5/512 is the size in blocks.

We can enter a minus sign (-) after the percent sign (%) to cause printf to left justify the output in the field, as follows:

```
$ ls -l |
> tail +2 |
> awk '{ printf("Name: %-16s, Size: %-5d, Blocks: %-6.2f\n",
➥$9, $5, $5/512)}'
Name: acme             , Size: 17263, Blocks: 33.72
Name: report7          , Size: 2966 , Blocks: 5.79
Name: report8          , Size: 34238, Blocks: 66.87
$
```

When left justifying the output in the fields, it no longer looks
nice to follow the field with a comma, so we can remove the
commas from the format string, as follows:

```
$ ls -l |
> tail +2 |
> awk '{ printf("Name: %-16s  Size: %-5d  Blocks: %-6.2f\n",
➥$9, $5, $5/512)}'
Name: acme              Size: 17263  Blocks: 33.72
Name: report7           Size: 2966   Blocks: 5.79
Name: report8           Size: 34238  Blocks: 66.87
$
```

Numbers are easier to compare when they are right justified,
which will cause the decimal points to line up again down the
column. Let's go back to right justifying the two numeric fields
and put back the comma after the second field, as follows:

```
$ ls -l |
> tail +2 |
> awk '{ printf("Name: %-16s  Size: %5d, Blocks: %6.2f\n",
➥$9, $5, $5/512)}'
Name: acme              Size: 17263, Blocks:  33.72
Name: report7           Size:  2966, Blocks:   5.79
Name: report8           Size: 34238, Blocks:  66.87
$
```

Yes, now note that the columns of numbers are easier to compare. If any of the values are longer than the size we specified,
the full value will be displayed and the other columns will be
offset, as follows:

```
$ ls -l |
> tail +2 |
> awk '{ printf("Name: %-16s  Size: %5d, Blocks: %6.2f\n",
➥$9, $5, $5/512)}'
```

```
Name: acme              Size: 17263, Blocks:   33.72
Name: long-long-long-filename  Size: 1993126, Blocks: 3892.82
Name: report7           Size:  2966, Blocks:    5.79
Name: report8           Size: 34238, Blocks:   66.87
$
```

Removing Characters by Column Positions (*cut*)

We can use the UNIX cut command to remove selected column positions from a list of files or a pipeline and display the results. The -c option to cut enables us to specify a range of column positions. The way to think about this command is that we are going to cut this range out of the output and keep it in the output and the rest gets thrown away, as follows:

```
$ date
Sun Mar 22 17:58:40 PST 1998
$ date | cut -c5-10
Mar 22
$
```

In the preceding example, -c5-10 specifies that we want to keep columns 5 through 10 and throw the rest away. We can specify more than one range, separated by a comma, as follows:

```
$ date | cut -c5-10,24-28
Mar 22 1998
$
```

Leave off the ending number in the range to allow that range to go to the end of the line, as follows:

```
$ date | cut -c5-10,24-
Mar 22 1998
$
```

The -f option to cut can be used to specify a field number if a tab character separates each field, as follows:

```
$ cat data2
acme      1978      24.6
saturn    1953       8.3
```

```
wondra   1981      16.7
$ cut -f1,3 data2
acme     24.6
saturn   8.3
wondra   16.7
$
```

In this example, -f1,3 tells cut to cut out and keep fields 1 and 3.

If some character other than a tab is used as the field separator, you can use the -d option to specify that field separator character, as follows:

```
$ cat data3
acme:1978:24.6
saturn:1953:8.3
wondra:1981:16.7
$ cut -d: -f1,3 data3
acme:24.6
saturn:8.3
wondra:16.7
$
```

Although it is possible to set the -d field separator to a space, this is not useful in most situations because cut does not allow multiple spaces to be regarded as a single field separator. For example:

```
$ cat data4
xxx  yyy   zzz
$ cut -d' ' -f1,3 data4
xxx yyy
$
```

In the preceding example, two spaces appear between xxx and yyy in the data file. There are three spaces between yyy and zzz. cut therefore considers the file data4 to have this content:

```
field 1: xxx
field 2: empty
field 3: yyy
field 4: empty
field 5: empty
field 6: zzz
```

If you have trouble understanding that, picture the spaces as colons (:) instead, as follows:

```
xxx::yyy:::zzz
```

Wherever two colons (really two spaces) are together, there is an empty field between them, like this:

```
xxx:<empty>:yyy:<empty>:<empty>:zzz
  1     2     3     4        5      6
```

We normally expect a group of spaces to be one field separator. Therefore awk is more useful for displaying whitespace separated fields than cut. For example:

```
$ cat data4
xxx  yyy    zzz
$ awk '{print $1, $3}' data4
xxx zzz
$
```

Extracting Fields from UNIX Commands

If you want to extract a field from the output of a UNIX command, should you use awk to extract by field number or use cut to extract by column positions? Many commands allow fields to be extracted by either method. Take, for example, ls -1:

```
$ ls -l
-rw-r--r--   1 mori      users        2966 Mar 22 15:08
➡report7
$
```

The filename is the field in this output where you find the most variation in size of the field, so it is fortunate that it is the last field. If it were the first field, very long filenames would move all the other fields out and change their column positions.

In the /dev directory, the number of fields in ls -1 changes, as follows:

```
$ ls -l /dev ¦ head -5
total 13
crw-------   1 root      root       10, 134 Jan 20  1997
apm_bios
crw-------   1 root      sys        16,   1 Feb 18  1994 arp
```

```
crw-rw-rw-   1 root      sys          10,   3 Jul 17   1994
➥atibm
crw-rw-rw-   1 root      sys          14,   4 Jul 18   1994
➥audio
$
```

In this directory, files don't have a size in field 5. Rather they have two values, separated by comma and space(s). This puts the filename in field 10 rather than 9 as in other directories. Therefore to write a program to extract the filename from ls -l output which includes the /dev directory, it would be better to use cut than awk. Then again on some systems, you may encounter very long group names or very large file sizes, which causes you to have to adjust the column positions that you use.

```
-rwxr-xr-x   1 root      bin         2688 Oct 15   1995
➥arch
-rwxr-xr-x   1 root      bin        61201 Aug  6   1995 ash
-rw-rw----   1 mori      group       1828 Mar 19 14:56
➥Main.dt
-rw-rw----   1 mori      group        231 Feb 19 19:04
➥Personal.dt
```

In the preceding example, you see ls -l output from two different systems. The first two lines are from a Linux system. The second two are from SCO UNIX. Notice that the column positions for ls -l are different between these two versions of UNIX. If I wanted to write one program to extract the filename from ls -l, and I wanted it to work on both Linux and SCO UNIX, I would use awk to extract field 9 (so long as the program does not have to work with ls -l from the /dev directory).

It is very common to find programs that extract information from fields in UNIX command output. Some will use awk, and some will use cut. Problems can develop when values in the fields get very large or when you want to run the same program on a different system. As long as you are aware of these troublespots, you can often quickly find the problem and solve it by modifying the extraction code. You might have to change the column positions being used in a cut command, for example, or change the field number used in an awk command.

Replacing/Removing Characters in a File or Pipeline (*tr*)

The tr command enables us to translate every occurrence of one specific character into a different character. It also enables us to delete every occurrence of a specific character. tr does not allow any files on the command line, so you must pipe any data for tr to translate.

Determining Which Type of *tr* Is on Your UNIX System

Unfortunately, there are two different versions of tr. They differ in whether they require brackets [] around ranges of characters. Some versions of UNIX have one type of tr; other versions have a different type of tr.

Here is how the non-bracket version of tr works:

```
$ echo abcdefaabbcc ¦ tr 'a-c' '1-3'
123def112233
$
```

In this command, echo sends the letters abcdefaabbcc to the tr command. tr looks up each letter in its first list. If found, it translates it to the corresponding character in its second list. If the character is not found in the first list, it is passed "as is" to the output.

The bracket version of tr works the same way, except that it requires square brackets around any ranges, as follows:

```
$ echo abcdefaabbcc ¦ tr '[a-c]' '[1-3]'
123def112233
$
```

The following versions of UNIX require brackets for tr ranges:

- HP-UX
- SCO UNIX 3.2v4
- Solaris 2.x (SunOS 5.x)

The following versions of UNIX do not require brackets:

- SCO UNIX 3.v5 (OpenServer 5)
- Linux (Slackware 3.0.0)
- IBM AIX 4.x

Here is a simple test you can run on your system to see which type of tr command you have:

```
echo abc[] ¦ tr '[a-c]' '12345'
```

If tr requires brackets, you will see this output:

```
123[]
```

The square brackets in "[a-c]" just enclose a range and are not part of the list. Therefore tr maps abc to 123 and passes the input square brackets as is. If your version of tr does not require brackets, the same command line will give this output:

```
23415
```

Because brackets are not required around ranges, their presence in the list is treated just as any other character; therefore [will map to 1, a will map to 2, b to 3, c to 4, and] to 5.

Changing Upper- to Lowercase or Vice Versa (*tr*)

One of the most common uses of tr is to map (that is, translate) all uppercase characters to lowercase, as follows:

```
$ echo ABCdef[] ¦ tr "[A-Z]" "[a-z]"
abcdef[]
$
```

Use the square brackets in the preceding example even if your version of tr does not require brackets. If your version does require brackets, 26 characters in the first list map to the 26 corresponding elements in the second list. If your version does not require brackets, 28 characters in the first list map to the 28 characters of the second list. In both cases, the left bracket ([) will be passed as a left bracket ([), and the same is true for the right bracket (]).

Don't use tr to replace strings

```
tr 'wilson' 'smith'
```
will translate all w's to s's, all i's to m's, and so on. Use **sed** when you want to replace strings, as follows:

```
sed 's/wilson/smith/g'
```

We can convert lowercase to uppercase as follows:

```
$ echo ABCdef[] ¦ tr "[a-z]" "[A-Z]"
ABCDEF[]
$
```

Setting/Zeroing Eighth Bit of Each Character (*tr*)

Text files normally have the eighth bit of each character set to zero. This is also called the most significant bit. If set to one, it changes the meaning of the character to some extended character set, which can cause strange symbols to appear or even lock up your terminal. When downloading a file, you may end up with a file that you can't display because it has some characters with the eighth bit on—that is, set to one. We can use tr to turn the eighth bit off, as follows:

```
$ tr "[\201-\376]\377" "[\001-\176]\177" < file1 > file2
```

file1   is the file where some characters have the eighth
                 bit on.

file2   will be created by the tr command, which is a
                 copy of file1, but the eighth bit will be off on all
                 characters.

Use the brackets even if your version of tr does not require them because then the same command will work on all UNIX systems. Most UNIX systems will let us include \377 in the range, but SCO UNIX 3.2v5 will not. Therefore I have specified \377 separately from the range in brackets in the preceding command so that the command will work on all types of UNIX systems, including SCO UNIX 3.2v5.

We can use a similar command if you need to turn the eighth bit on all characters:

```
$ tr "[\001-\176]\177" "[\201-\376]\377" < file1 > file2
```

Removing Selected Characters (*tr*)

You can use the -d option with a single list to remove selected characters from the pipeline, as follows:

```
tr -d '!@#$%^&*()' < file1 > file2
```

This command removes the selected punctuation characters from file1 and saves the result in file2.

Control characters can cause problems if they occur within data or text files. End users can accidentally input control characters into the data by using the arrow keys in applications that do not support the arrow keys. The next tr example shows how to remove all control characters except for tab and newline:

```
$ tr -d '[\001-\010][\013-\037]\177' < file1 > file2
```

The preceding command should be used on systems where tr requires brackets. If used on the other type of system, it will also remove brackets from the output that is not what we want. For systems that do not require brackets, here is the same command to remove all control characters except for tab and newline:

```
tr -d '\001-\010\013-\037\177' < file1 > file2
```

Translating Most Control Characters into One Error Character (*tr*)

Rather than deleting all control characters, you may want to translate them into some character as an error indication that something has been modified. Use '[X*]' as the second string to translate all characters in the first list to character X, as follows:

```
tr '[\001-\010][\013-\037]\177' '[^*]' < file1 > file2
```

The preceding command translates all control characters except for tab and newline to a circumflex (^). If your system does not require brackets, use this form of the tr command:

```
tr '\001-\010\013-\037\177' '[^*]' < file1 > file2
```

Notice that brackets are required around [^*] even in the second case where brackets are not used around ranges.

Replacing/Removing Whole Lines

There are several ways in which you can replace or remove whole lines.

Replacing Whole Lines (*sed*)

To completely replace any line that contains a pattern, you can use the sed command like this:

```
sed 's/.*acme.*/   ***canceled***   /'
```

acme   represents the pattern to look for. You can replace this with any desired R.E. pattern.

.*acme.*   matches the whole line that contains acme, so the whole line will be replaced.

Removing Lines Containing an R.E. Pattern (*grep*)

To totally remove any lines containing a pattern, use the -v option to grep, as follows:

```
grep -v 'R.E.'
```

The -v option to grep reverses the sense of grep. Instead of showing lines that contain the pattern, grep will then show only lines that do not contain the pattern, effectively removing any lines from the output which do contain the pattern.

SEE ALSO

➤ *For more information on the* grep *command, see page 380*

Removing Repeated Lines (*uniq*)

Use the uniq command to remove from the output any lines that exactly match the preceding line. Assume that we have a file called cars, which contains different brands of automobiles, as follows:

```
$ cat cars
ford
ford
pontiac
BMW
ford
pontiac
$
```

Here is the output from the `uniq` command on that file:

```
$ uniq cars
ford
pontiac
BMW
ford
pontiac
$
```

In the preceding file, only line 2 exactly matches the preceding line, so it was removed. You can see there are other matching lines in this file, but `uniq` does not remove them because they are not adjacent. Notice that the `sort` command does put identical lines adjacent to each other, as follows:

```
$ sort cars
BMW
ford
ford
ford
pontiac
pontiac
$ sort cars ¦ uniq
BMW
ford
pontiac
$
```

In this example, we have made `uniq` work more effectively by first sorting the lines. We can count the number of different cars in the file by piping the output from the preceding command to `wc -l` to count the lines, as follows:

```
$ sort cars ¦ uniq ¦ wc -l
      3
$
```

The `-u` option to `uniq` displays just the lines that are unique— that is, that have no adjacent matching lines. For example:

```
$ sort cars ¦ uniq -u
BMW
$
```

The -d option shows just the duplicated lines, as follows:

```
$ sort cars ¦ uniq -d
ford
pontiac
$
```

The -c option counts the number of duplicates for each line, as follows:

```
$ sort cars ¦ uniq -c
      1   BMW
      3   ford
      2   pontiac
$
```

SEE ALSO

➤ *For more information on the* sort *command, see page 202*

Using *vi* to Edit a Text File

By Steve "Mor" Moritsugu

Introducing the *vi* Text Editor

A text editor enables you to create and modify text documents that contain just the letters and characters that you can type in on your keyboard. A word processor, on the other hand, not only allows text editing but also allows changing the presentation of that text by selecting the font size and style. Simple text files are extremely important under UNIX. All UNIX system administration, with few exceptions, is ultimately done by editing text files that customize the system and control how it operates. Shell scripts and C programs are keyed in as text files by a programmer. Even Internet Web pages are simple text files with fonts, colors, and graphics indicated as textual directives to the Web browser.

vi is the one text editor that is available on all UNIX systems. Don't look for font choices in vi because it is not a word processor. Some UNIX users do not like vi because you have to memorize all the commands. There are no drop-down menus to help you cut and paste or replace text. There is no help facility inside vi (but I will show you how to fix that).

Some types of UNIX systems do provide alternatives to vi, such as emacs, pico, or WordPerfect for UNIX. Some users edit text under Windows and then download it to UNIX. If you work on only one UNIX system and can guarantee that you will never have to work on a different one, choose any text editor that is available on your system. If you work with more than one type of commercial UNIX system, however, you may find that porting your favorite editor to each one is a losing battle. In that case, follow me through this chapter on vi and I will make it easy for you learn the basics. vi is like UNIX: It is difficult to get started, but after you do, you can do powerful things that make it worth the effort.

How to Start *vi*

How to start and end *vi*

1. At the shell prompt, enter vi.

   (Don't press Enter until directed.)

2. Enter a space, and then the name of the file you want to edit. (Don't press Enter until directed.) If the file does not already exist, vi will create it for you. If the file is in another directory, enter its pathname. If you just want to practice with vi, see the following procedure. More advanced users can omit the filename at this point; this enables you to enter vi, but you must then remember to save your work to a file before you exit vi.

3. Press Enter. vi will start and show you the current contents of your file. Because vi is a full-screen editor, it will put a tilde (~) at the start of screen lines that are beyond the end of the file. If you are editing a new file, all the lines on the screen will therefore start with a tilde until you insert text into those lines.

4. Note that all of your changes are being made in vi's work-space, not in the file itself. If you don't save your work before you exit vi, all your editing will be lost.

5. When done editing, press Esc and then enter the following:

:wq (to save your work and exit vi), or enter:

:q! (to abort [that is, throw away] your changes and exit vi)

Press Enter to complete this step.

Creating a File for *vi* Practice

If you are new to UNIX, you probably don't have any files that are safe for you to edit yet; therefore follow this procedure to create a scratch file that you can use to practice vi.

How to Practice with *vi*

1. Log on to UNIX.

2. At the shell prompt, enter cal 1998 > cal-junk.

Press Enter to execute this line. I use the word *junk* in any filenames that are just for practice and can be killed later. This step will create a text file that contains a calendar that you can practice editing.

3. When you want to practice with vi, at the shell prompt, enter vi cal-junk.

Press Enter to execute this line.

452

4. When done practicing with vi, press Esc and then enter the following:

:wq   (to save your work and exit vi) or enter:

:q!   (to abort [that is, throw away] your changes and exit vi)

Press the Enter key to complete this step.

To remove this practice file, enter the following:

```
rm cal-junk
```

Press Enter to execute this line. It is good manners to clean up after yourself, but you may delay deleting this file for several days or weeks while you practice with vi.

Edit Anything with Just 10 *vi* Commands

There are more than 75 separate letter and punctuation commands to learn in vi. Where should you start? Here are the first 10 vi commands to learn, and they will enable you to edit anything. If you are new to vi, follow the preceding procedure to create a cal-junk practice file so that you don't accidentally change an important file.

Moving Around Using *h,j,k,l*

In vi, you can move the cursor by entering the commands listed in Table 17.1.

Never practice on /etc/
passwd

This is a critical system file that you should not play with, especially if you are logged on as root. Actually don't practice on any files in /etc. Don't practice as root.

TABLE 17.1   **Moving around using *h,j,k,l***

vi Command	Description	Mnemonic	Alternative key
h	Move left	Leftmost char	Left-arrow key
j	Move down	j goes below line	Down-arrow key
k	Move up	k loops up	Up-arrow key
l	Move right	Rightmost char	Right-arrow key

These four keys—h,j,k,l—occur next to each other on your keyboard. The mnemonic in the table will help you remember which key does what. A lowercase j goes below the line to remind you of down, for example.

Don't depend too much on the arrow key alternatives. Sometimes you will find that everything will work in vi except for the arrow keys because they require that the terminal settings, the keyboard, and certain system files (such as termcap or terminfo) all be properly coordinated. Even if the arrow keys work most of the time, they can become unreliable over a slow connection or on a heavily loaded system or network. Learning to use h,j,k, and l rather than the arrow keys will also help you later with mapping sequences to keys and command-line editing in the Korn shell—a very useful feature.

When you enter h,j,k, or l in vi, it should not echo to the screen. Instead, the cursor should just move in the desired direction. You do not have to press Enter to execute the command. If the h,j,k, or l appear onscreen, somehow you have gotten into Insert mode and have inserted those characters into your workspace. Press Esc to end Insert mode; now h,j,k,l should work correctly.

vi will not let you move to a position on the screen unless there is text in the workspace at that position. You cannot move past the end of a line. You cannot move down from the last line. If you edit an empty file, you will not be able to move at all until you enter some text.

SEE ALSO

➤ *For more information on command-line editing, see page 497*

vi Beeps on Error

If you try to do an illegal command in vi (such as moving down from the last line), vi will beep to signal an error. It is possible to turn this off (:set noerrorbells), but vi beginners should listen for the error beeps and learn from these mistakes.

> **Beware of Caps Lock when using the J key**
>
> If you accidentally leave your Caps Lock key on and use h,k, or l to move around, it is harmless. A j to go down, however, would become J to join lines as we shall see. Multiple J's will join many lines and before you know it, you have a mess. In the next chapter on mapping a key, I show a way to prevent this.

Using a Repeat Count

You can put a repeat count directly before most vi commands. 50h will move left 50 characters. 999j will move down 999 lines. With a repeat count, it is easy to move up or down large distances, which is a necessity in huge files.

If the repeat count given for the cursor movement is too large, you will get differing results depending on which type of UNIX you are on. If vi beeps, the cursor will not move at all because you cannot move beyond the end of the line or down past the last line. If there is no beep, vi on that system has moved you as far as possible and stopped at the last character or last line in the workspace.

If h,j,k, and l move the cursor, how do you enter those characters into the document? Read on....

Using *i* to Insert

Here is the fifth vi command to learn. Enter i to turn on Insert mode. In Insert mode, all the text that you type is entered at the current cursor position into the workspace. Press Esc to turn off Insert mode; this puts you back into vi Command mode. You can input multiple lines in one insert by pressing Enter after each line.

Using *x* and *dd* to Delete

Tip: Beware of arrow keys in Insert mode

If you try to use the arrow keys while in Insert mode, it may not produce the changes you expect on some systems. Before moving the cursor, press Esc to end Insert mode. Then move the cursor to the next section and enter **i** to re-enter Insert mode.

Here is the sixth vi command to learn. Enter x to delete one character where the cursor is. 25x will delete 25 characters. vi will reduce any repeat count larger than the rest of the line so that the rest of the current line is deleted but the following lines are not affected.

Here is the seventh vi command to learn. Enter dd to delete the current line. You can be anywhere in the line when you enter dd. 25dd will delete 25 lines, including all of the current line.

Using *J* to Join Lines

Here is the eighth vi command to learn. Unlike some editors, vi has no end-of-line character that you can delete to join two lines. The only way to join two lines is to use the J command. 5J will join 5 lines. J, 1J, and 2J all do the same thing: they join two lines. Any leading spaces in the second line will be reduced to a single space.

Using *:wq* to Save and Exit

Here is the ninth vi command to learn. So far all of your changes have modified the vi workspace, which is a temporary file. To save your work and exit, enter the following:

:wq

The leading colon will cause the cursor to go down to the last line where the w and q will echo onscreen. Press Enter to complete this command and any other vi command that starts with a colon (:).

Using *:q!* to Abort Changes

Here is the 10th vi command to learn. If you don't like your changes, you can exit vi without saving them back to the original file by entering the following:

:q!

This returns you to the shell prompt and throws away all the editing you have done. Be aware that after you throw away your editing changes by :q!, you cannot change your mind later and get them back again.

This completes the 10 commands you need to use vi. You can now edit anything. Practice with these 10 for a while. Then read the following section in this chapter to see the next group of vi commands you should master.

Where does dd gets its name?

There is a convention in vi that a double-letter command operates on the whole line. cc changes the whole line; yy yanks the whole line; and dd deletes the whole line.

Tip: Use backspaces to abort a Colon (:) command

If you type in a colon (:) command such as :q!, and then change your mind, do *not* press Esc because this will execute the :q! command and throw away all of your changes. To abort a colon command, press the Backspace key or Ctrl+H repeatedly until the cursor has left the last line. The left-arrow key will not work for this.

Adding a Help Facility to *vi*

There is no help facility within vi, which makes vi difficult to use—especially if you only use it occasionally. Here is a way to add a help facility to use while you are in vi.

Adding a help facility to *vi*

1. Use vi to create a text file, /tmp/vihelp,

   with these contents:

```
echo "
(You may put repeat count BEFORE most commands.)
:q!        -- abort vi without saving
cW         -- change word(s) until ESC
x    dd    -- delete char(s) or line(s)
G          -- go to end of file
1G         -- go to line one of file
i          -- insert text until ESC
A          -- insert at end of line until ESC
J          -- join lines
h,j,k,l -- move left,down,up,right
Ctrl+L Ctrl+R   -- repaint the screen
r          -- replace one char
:wq        -- save and exit vi
:f         -- show filename, current line, size
u          -- undo"
```

2. Make sure you included the quotation marks (") in the first and last lines.

3. Log on as root or ask your system administrator to do the next steps.

4. Enter ls -l /usr/bin/vihelp.

   We want to see the message No such file.

   If this file already exists, do *not* continue with this procedure.

5. Enter these commands:
```
cd /usr/bin
mv /tmp/vihelp vihelp
chmod 755 vihelp
```

6. Now exit and log back on as a nonroot user.

7. Enter vi to edit any test file and check out the new help
facility by entering the following:
```
:!vihelp
```

8. Press Enter when you are done reading the help and are
ready to resume vi editing.

9. You can use vi to expand the help message in file
/usr/bin/vihelp as desired. Make sure the final quotation
marks occur at the end of the last line.

Learn These Eight *vi* Commands Next

Press *Ctrl+L Ctrl+R* to Repaint the Screen

Sometimes over a modem line or slow network, garbage may
appear on your screen or the cursor will end up on a different
line than vi thinks it is. If the cursor is on the wrong line, you
will see characters from a different line appear at the cursor
when you space to the right. To clear up this problem, press
these two control characters, Ctrl+L Ctrl+R, to repaint your
screen to match the workspace.

Undo Changes Using *u*

vi remembers the last insert, delete, or modification done. If you
want to undo it, enter the **u** command in vi Command mode.
You do not have to be near the line where the change was made
when issuing the u command. Commands to move the cursor are
ignored by the u command and cannot be undone. (Actually
many cursor motion commands can be undone by entering backquote backquote [``].) A second u command will undo the undo
command, reinstating the last change again. A third u command
will toggle the undo and remove the last change. A fourth u
command will reinstate the last change, and so on.

If you join five lines with the 5J command, a u command will
separate them into their original lines. A second u will join them
again. You can watch the lines magically join together and then
separate each time you enter the u command. This is a great way
to learn about more complex vi commands.

The Real Repaint command

Actually some terminals require
only Ctrl+R, and some require
only Ctrl+L to repaint the
screen. If you use them both
(in any order), however, it
works for all cases!

Using the *u* command if something goes wrong

1. Sometimes an accidental control character or line noise will cause garbage on the vi screen. Press Ctrl+L Ctrl+R to repaint the current screen and remove the garbage.

2. Enter the u command to undo the last change. The cursor will move to the location of that change.

3. Enter u several times to watch the change toggle. If the change is an undesirable side-effect of the accident, enter u one or two more times to undo the bad change.

Using *A* to Append Text at the End of Line

The capital A command first moves the cursor to the end of the current line. It then enables you to start inserting text after the last character on the line. Press Esc to end Insert mode.

Using *:w* to Save Your Work Periodically

If you are making a lot of changes in your vi session, it is prudent to save your work periodically. Enter :w to write the current workspace to the disk file. Then if you accidentally hit the wrong keystroke or your system connection dies, you can log back on and your disk file will have the last-saved contents.

Using *:w* File to Save in a Different File

You can save your work to a different file than you are editing by entering the following:

```
:w newfile
```

If I am editing a critical document, for example, I might enter the following:

```
:w doc1
```

After more editing, I might enter this:

```
:w doc2
```

In this way, I can save many versions of this one file. This gives me more chances to recover information in case I accidentally delete some text and then save the file without that text.

Handling Write Permission Failure

When trying to save your work, vi may return an error such as Permission Denied, or Read Only.

Handling errors saving a file in *vi*

1. Try saving the file using this command:
   :w!

2. If that fails, save your work temporarily like this:
   :w /tmp/cantwrite
   :q

3. Now you can move your changes in /tmp/cantwrite to your desired filename or directory.

Using *r* to Replace One Character

Enter r to replace one character. The next character typed will appear onscreen, replacing the character that was at that cursor position. Then you will be back in Command mode, ready to enter new vi commands.

Using *cW* to Change Words

Using *cW* to change words

1. Move the cursor to the start of the desired word or words to change.

2. If you want to change more than one word, enter the number of words to change. Do not press Enter.

3. Enter cW.

   A dollar sign ($) will appear at the end of the last word to change. Do not press Enter.

4. Start typing your replacement text. It can be shorter or longer than the words being changed. It can have fewer or more words. You may use the Enter key to input multiple lines. If the new text is longer, the remainder of the line will move to the right to accommodate it as you type.

5. Press Esc after you have entered all the replacement text. If the new text is shorter than the words being replaced, the

remainder of the line will move to the left to fill up the gap automatically.

6. Here is an example command:

```
3cWacmeESC
```

The preceding command will change (replace) three words (including the word where your cursor is). It will replace those three words with the single word *acme*.

Using *1G/G* to Go to Start/End of File

Enter a number and then capital *G* to go to that line number—for example, 1475G will move the cursor to line 1,475 of the workspace. If the file does not have that many lines, it will give an error beep. Moving quickly to a specific line number in a file can be useful for a C programmer because the compiler often reports the line number in the source where an error occurs.

The two most common uses of the G command are 1G to go to the start of the file and G to go to the end of the file.

Using *:f* to See the Filename, Size, and Where You Are

Enter :f to see the name of the file you are currently editing, what line you are on, and how many lines are in the file. For example:

```
"report7" [Modified] line 43 of 335 --12%--
```

Tips to Help You Use *vi*

Here are the third group of vi commands to learn.

Restoring the Whole Line Using *U*

In vi Command mode, capital U will undo all changes on the current line since you moved to it. After you leave a line, you lose the ability to restore it back to its original state.

Using *spell* to Find Misspelled Word

Standard UNIX has only minimal spell checking capability. The following steps demonstrate how to use it.

How to find misspelled words

1. From the shell prompt, enter `spell < filename ¦ pg`.

(Filename is the file to spell check.)

Replace `pg` with your preferred utility to view results one page at a time.

2. All unknown words will be displayed onscreen, one per line. The context (that is, the complete line) in which the misspelled words appear is not shown.

3. Mentally flag any misspelled words, and then manually use `vi` to find and correct them in the file, one by one.

Formatting Paragraphs

If you are using standard English paragraphs, one of the frustrating limitations of `vi` occurs when you have to lengthen or shorten an internal line in the paragraph. An odd-sized line looks out of place in the middle of the paragraph. You can fix the odd line by moving text to or pulling text from the next line; but now the next line has an odd size. You then have to hand-adjust each line to the end of the paragraph.

Here are two easier ways to handle that situation.

How to format paragraphs using *fmt*

1. At the shell prompt, enter the following:
`type fmt`

If you get the error `Not found`, `fmt` is not supported on your version of UNIX. Skip this procedure and use the following procedure to format if `fmt` is not found. `fmt` was not available on SCO UNIX OpenServer 5, but it is on Solaris 2.x, AIX 4.x, and Linux.

2. To format a paragraph in `vi`, move your cursor to the start of the paragraph. Enter the following:
`!}fmt`

This should adjust the rest of the lines of your paragraph so that no lines are too long or too short. If this does not work, enter u to undo that change and follow the next procedure instead.

3. The fmt command assumes that the left margin is correct for the paragraph. If the left margin also needs to be adjusted, enter this:

```
!}fmt -c
```

Here is a procedure to format paragraphs that works well even if fmt is not on your system and if there are no tabs in the line.

How to format paragraphs

1. Enter cd to go to your home directory.

2. Enter cp .exrc .exrcbak to back up your current .exrc file. Ignore any cp errors that .exrc does not exist. (In that case, there is no need to back it up.)

3. Enter vi .exrc.

4. Look at the full contents of this file and make sure there is no line that starts with map g.

If there is such a line, do *not* continue with this procedure.

5. Make sure there is a line that starts with set wrapmargin=, or that starts with set wm=.

If you do not find such a line, enter this line at the end of the file:

```
set wm=10
```

6. Press Esc and then Q.

The cursor will go to the last line and a colon will appear.

7. Enter map g 0721Bi.

Do not press Enter.

8. Press Ctrl+M

Press Esc.

Press Ctrl+V.

Press Esc.

Now press Enter.

9. Enter vi.

   The word *vi* should echo on the bottom line of the screen. Press Enter.

10. Enter :wq to save your changes to .exrc and exit vi.

11. Check that all went well by entering cat -v .exrc.

    At the end of the file, you should see this line:
    ```
    map g 0721Bi^M^[
    ```

    If something went wrong, use vi to correct that line. If necessary, restore .exrc from the backup and start over.

12. The preceding steps prepare the .exrc file and only need to be done once for each logon user. Now use vi to edit a test file with a paragraph that needs to be formatted. Make sure the file is backed up in case something goes wrong. Move the cursor to the start of the paragraph that needs to be formatted.

13. Count the number of lines in the paragraph. Enter that number followed by J to join all the lines of the paragraph into one long line.

14. Enter g repeatedly until all the lines of the paragraph have been formatted correctly.

Recovering a Lost Edit

If vi ever terminates abnormally, there is a chance you can recover some or all of the text you were editing, even if you didn't save it to disk.

Recovering a lost edit
```
From the shell prompt, enter vi -r.
```

1. You will see a list of files that vi has preserved because it aborted abnormally while editing them. These are actually the vi workspace files that may contain some edits that had not been saved to the disk file.

2. If you see a file you want to look at, enter the following:
   ```
   vi -r filename
   ```

   Filename must appear exactly as shown in the list—that is, type in any preceding directory names exactly as shown.

3. After looking at the text with vi, if you decide you want to keep this information, enter this:

```
:w absfile
```

absfile represents the full pathname of the file you want to save it as.

4. Exit from vi as follows:

```
:q
```

5. After you recover a file in this way and exit vi, that file is removed from the preserved list and you cannot try to recover it again. It is a good idea to check your preserved files periodically and recover and save or discard them to prevent vi preserve files from accumulating in the preserve areas.

Starting *vi* in Read-Only Mode

To edit a file in Read-only mode, substitute the view command for vi in your command line. view starts vi in Read-only mode. If you try to write the file, view will give an error saying that the file is read-only. This is a good precaution for those cases where you are just looking at the contents and don't intend to make any changes. I especially advise root (that is, system administrator) users to use view when just looking at system configuration files.

You can override view's Read-only mode and save changes, as follows:

```
:w!
```

Table of Text Insertion Commands in *vi*

TABLE 17.2 **Text insertion commands in *vi***

vi Command	Description
i	Insert text just before cursor until Esc
I	Insert text at start of line until Esc
a	Insert text just after cursor until Esc

vi Command	Description
A	Insert text at end of line until Esc
o	Open a new line above the current line, insert until Esc
O	Open a new line below the current line, insert until Esc

Moving Around in *vi*

Many cursor commands in vi enable us to move to different parts of the screen or the file we are editing. First we need to go over how to count words—which is useful for moving, deletion, and replacement.

Using Separated Words Versus Contained Words Versus Non-Words

Separated words (or space delimited/delineated words) are any groups of characters separated by one or more spaces, tabs, or end of line. Contained words are any groups of letters or digits separated by punctuation, spaces, tabs, or end of line. Hudson--on--the--Bay is one separated word, but four contained words. Each double dash (--) is a non-word. Therefore Hudson--on--the--Bay has seven contained words and non-words. The next table shows that the w command enables us to move forward by contained words and non-words. The next chapter shows how differentiating separated words versus contained words can be useful.

Table of Motion Comands in *vi*

TABLE 17.3   **Table of motion comands in *vi***

vi Command	Description
h j k l	Move left/down/up/right
0	Move to start of current line
^	Move to start of first word on current line

continues…

TABLE 17.3 Continued

vi Command	Description
$	Move to last character of current line
w b	Move forward/backward one contained word or non-word
W B	Move forward/backward one separated word
e E	Move to end of current contained/separated word
L M H	Move to lowest/middle/highest line on screen
{ }	Move to start of preceding/next paragraph
Ctrl+F Ctrl+B	Move forward/backward one full screen
Ctrl+D Ctrl+U	Move down/up one half screen
nG	Go to line *n*
1G G	Go to first/last line

Moving by Searching for a String

Moving the cursor to a pattern

1. In vi Command mode, enter / to search forward in the workspace. Enter ? to search backward in the workspace. The cursor will move to the last line of the screen and echo the / or ?. Do not press Enter until instructed.

2. Enter the pattern to search for. Press Enter to execute. The cursor will move to next occurrence of the pattern. Your pattern may contain regular expression wildcard patterns as described in Chapter 15.

3. If the pattern is not found in the rest of the file, vi will wrap around and start searching at the other end of the file. If vi has to wrap around, this message usually appears: Wrapped. If the pattern does not exist anywhere within the whole file, the cursor will remain where it was and this message will appear: Not found.

4. To repeat the last search, enter n.

   This will find the next occurrence of the same pattern.

To repeat the last search but in the opposite direction, enter N.

If you were previously searching forward in the file, N will find the next occurrence backward in the file.

Moving in the Line to a Specific Character

If you are logged on to a UNIX system over the Internet, you may find responses to your vi keystrokes have almost incapacitating delays. Rather than counting how many characters or words to move, I often use the vi f command when I have to move right to a desired character in one command.

Moving in the line to a specific character

1. Determine the letter or digit I want to move to. I usually avoid vowels because they are too common in the line.

2. Enter f followed by the desired letter or digit.

3. The cursor will move to the next occurrence of that character.

4. Enter semicolon (;) to move to the next occurrence of that same character.

Finding a Matching Enclosure Symbol

If you are a programmer, you may need to enter complicated formulas using nested enclosure symbols such as: ({ [ ] }). For example:

```
{ printf("%d",tbsz(r7y[4])) }
```

vi understands such nesting and can automatically find the matching closing or opening parenthesis, bracket, or brace even if it is on a different line. Place the cursor on the desired enclosure symbol and press % to move the cursor to the matching enclosure symbol at that nesting level.

Setting a Mark So That You Can Return There

vi offers great facility for dealing with huge text files. vi can mark and return to up to 26 different places within the file.

Setting a mark and returning to the marked spot

1. Move the cursor to a desired spot in the file and enter ma. m is the vi command to mark this spot, and a is the name or label we can use to refer to this spot later. We can use any letter of the alphabet; therefore we can set up to 26 marks.

2. To return to that spot later, enter: 'a or `a.

3. Apostrophe (') a ('a) says to go to the start of the line containing mark a.

   Backquote (`) a (`a) says to go to the exact character we were on when we set the mark.

Table of *vi* Commands for Deleting Text

In the following table, notice how vi delete commands are based on the cursor motion commands.

You may precede most of these commands with a repeat count.

TABLE 17.4   Text deletion commands in *vi*

vi Command	Description
x dd	Delete character(s)/whole line(s)
D	Delete from cursor to end of line
dw dW	Delete forward to next contained/separated word
db dB	Delete backward to next contained/separated word
de dE	Delete to end of current contained/separated word
d0 d$	Delete to start/end of current line
dh dl	Delete character(s) to left/right
d{ d}	Delete to start of previous/next paragraph
d'a	Delete to start of line containing mark a
d`a	Delete to exact character containing mark a

Recovering Deleted Text

vi automatically saves the previous nine deletions in numbered buffers. If you delete the wrong thing, you may be able to get it back if you realize it soon enough. Note that many UNIX systems save only text deleted by the d command, not the x command.

Recovering deleted text from numbered buffers

1. Move the cursor to some empty lines where you can easily see any text that might be recovered.

2. Enter "1p.

   The most recently deleted text will be inserted at the cursor.

3. If this is not what you are looking for, enter u to undo the insert and remove the unwanted text.

4. Enter a period (.). This will insert text from the next most recent deletion.

5. If this is not what you are looking for, enter u to undo the insert and remove the unwanted text.

6. Continue entering these two characters, period (.) and u.

   This enables you to view all nine of the numbered delete buffers to see whether your desired text can be recovered.

Table of *vi* Commands for Changing Text

The following table shows how much text will be changed by the c command. A dollar sign ($) sign will appear at the end of the region to be changed. Enter the new replacement text and press Esc when done. The remaining text on the line will move left or right as needed.

If the dollar sign showing the end of the region to change is not where you expect, press Esc and the whole region will disappear. Then immediately press u and the line will be restored to its original text.

In the following table, notice how vi change commands are based on the cursor motion commands.

You can precede most of these commands with a repeat count.

TABLE 17.5 **Table of _vi_ commands for changing text**

_vi_ Command	Description
cc	Change whole line(s)
C	Change from cursor to end of line
cw cW	Change forward to next contained/separated word
cb cB	Change backward to next contained/separated word
ce cE	Change to end of current contained/separated word
c0 c$	Change to start/end of current line
ch cl	Change character(s) to left/right
c{ c}	Change to start of preceding/next paragraph
c'a	Change to start of line containing mark a
c`a	Change to exact character containing mark a

Replacing Text

Enter r to replace one character. Enter the new desired character. vi will then be ready for a new command. Do not press Esc.

Enter R to go into Replacement mode. Now anything you type will replace the current text. Press Esc to end this mode.

Letting the *vi* Editor Work for You

by Steve "Mor" Moritsugu

Zipping Through Repetitive Editing

The preceding chapter covered the mechanics of using vi. This chapter shows how vi uses the tools from that chapter to automate almost any situation where, in other editors, we would have to manually enter the same set of keystrokes (or worse, mouse drags) over and over again.

Using . to Repeat an Edit

The period (.) command repeats the last insert, delete, or modification, but applies it to the current cursor position. The catch is, it only repeats the very last change. Assume, for example, that you are composing a letter and want to change a three-word company name (like Acme Computer Products) to some other name over and over again. If you first delete the old three-word name, and then insert the new name, and then replace one character that you mistyped; then the last change that you made is to replace one character. The period command can now repeat this last change over and over again, but replacing that one character would not be a useful thing to repeat.

The period command is one of the vi power tools. To use it, you must be able to first accomplish your change by using a single vi command. You can precede that command with a repeat count. Then the period command can repeat that useful command as needed. In the preceding example, we wanted to replace three words, so we should have used the following:

3cw

The 3 is a repeat count because we want to change three words. The c command enables us to type in new input of any length to replace the indicated text until we press Esc. The w indicates contained words, which means that any punctuation following the third word would not be changed. We covered separated words versus contained words in the preceding chapter. 3cW would change three separated or space-delineated words, which would also change any following punctuation.

Having successfully executed 3cw once, we can now find the next occurrence of any three words that we want to change and move the cursor there. Press the period (.) key and the current three contained words will be replaced by the same text we typed in previously. Move the cursor to the next occurrence and press period to replace all the three-word sequences throughout the document as needed. This is selective replacement because you can look at each occurrence and either press the period there or not, as desired. Avoid the temptation to do other editing as you move along, because that will cause the period command to forget your three-word change and remember a new change. The next section shows you how to automate this selective find and replace even more. But first a couple more points.

Notice that 3cw is a syntactic command that does not specify the original contents—that is, the period (.) command can then be used on any desired three words. If there are several three-word company names, the period command can change any of them to our new text. Just move the cursor to any three-word pattern and press period.

Sometimes the text to be changed may contain a variable number of words, but it always fits into the same number of characters—for example, an entry in a table. Assume our table entry is 15 characters long and we want to type in the same new entry to replace several different entries. The key to successfully using the period command is to construct a single vi command to repeat. In this case, our first command could be either of the following:

```
15cl
R
```

15cl uses the l command to move right, so 15cl changes 15 characters to the right of the cursor, including the current character. Because this is a table, we would need to type in exactly 15 characters so that the new text exactly fits the table size. We can also use the R command to replace exactly 15 characters in one command.

Using *n* and . to Search and Selectively Repeat an Edit

We can combine the n command to repeat the last search with the period command to really zip through repetitious editing chores.

Note that this procedure is useful when you want to view each line to decide whether you should change it. If you don't need to view each occurrence, use the procedure for global or partial text substitution as discussed later in this chapter.

Two-finger editing

1. Invoke vi to edit the document where you want to selectively replace some text.

2. Enter 1G to make sure you are at the start of the document.

3. Enter /pattern, where pattern is the word(s) that you want to selectively replace. This moves the cursor to the first occurrence of that pattern.

4. Decide whether you want to retain any punctuation immediately following the pattern, such as period (.) or quotation marks ("). If so, you use contained words. If not, you use separated words. (This is discussed more in the preceding section on the period command.)

5. Count the number of words to replace. For separated words, each word is separated by spaces or tabs. For contained words, count the number of words and non-words to be replaced. Enter that count now. Do not press Enter.

6. Enter the letter c.

   Do not press Enter.

7. For contained words, enter w.

   For separated words, enter W.

   A dollar sign ($) should appear showing you the end of the text to change.

8. If the dollar sign ($) does not appear in the correct place, press Esc, and then enter u.

This restores the original text. Go back to step 4 and try again.

9. Type in the new replacement text. It can be longer or shorter than the original text. Press Esc when done.

10. Press the letter *n* to go to the next occurrence of the pattern to replace. Look it over and decide whether you want to make the replacement there.

11. If you want to make the replacement, enter a period (.).

Your new text replaces the pattern.

12. Now for real editing speed, place one index finger on the period key and the other index finger on the *n* key. Press *n* to go to the next occurrence of the pattern and look it over. Press period only if you want to replace it. With this two-finger editing, you can literally selectively replace hundreds of occurrences in a few minutes.

SEE ALSO

➤ *For more information on contained versus separated words, see page 465*

Mapping a Key to a Commonly Used Command Sequence

The period (.) command is limited in that it can only repeat the very last insert, delete, or modify editing command that you performed. There will be times when repetitive editing cannot be accomplished by the n command and the period command because several editing commands and/or motion commands must be done for each repetition.

We can handle this situation by mapping an unused command key to a sequence of vi editing commands and/or motion commands in sequence. In the preceding chapter on vi, you saw how to map the letter *g* to a sequence of commands that can format a paragraph. After a letter has been mapped, position the cursor and press that letter. Then the commands mapped to that letter will be executed.

Before you can map a key, however, you must find out whether your terminal supports Ctrl+V in Visual mode. The Ctrl+V is important for mapping because it enables you to enter control

Don't forget you can undo a mistake

As you are doing your two-finger editing, you may press the period when you meant to press the *n* key. The period will cause your last change to be applied again. To correct this mistake, just enter u to undo the last change.

characters as part of the sequence to be mapped. Some terminals require a special sequence to use Ctrl+V, so you need to check that first.

Checking whether Ctrl+V is supported in Visual mode

1. At the shell prompt, enter vi.

   Press Enter to execute this command. Note that no filename is to be specified.

2. When in vi, enter a colon (:). The cursor should go to the bottom line and a colon (:) should appear there.

3. Press Ctrl+V as you would any control character.

4. Look at your screen. If the bottom line looks like this:

   :^

   and the cursor is directly under the circumflex (^), your terminal supports Ctrl+V in Visual mode. If your screen has any other result, such as a blank line at the bottom, your terminal does not support Ctrl+V in Visual mode.

5. Press Esc twice.

6. Enter a colon (:).

7. Enter q!, and then press Enter. You should now be back at the shell prompt.

Now we are ready to map a character. Here is an example mapping to give you a feel for what mapping can do. Let's say that I want to map the available *v* key so that every time I enter a v in Command mode, it does the following:

```
Go down to next line: j
Go to the start of the line: 0
Move right 15 characters: 15l
Replace the next 10 characters with acme: 10clacmeESC
      10cl says change the next 10 characters to the right
          with whatever I type in until I press ESC
Go to the end of the line and insert a dash (-): A-
      Notice we use the capital A command to insert at the
        ➥end of line.
Then insert Dept 2 and terminate the insert: Dept 2ESC
```

Here is the map command that will accomplish all of this:

```
:map v j015l10clacme^[A-Dept 2^[
```

In the preceding command, notice the following:

- Multiple vi commands can be strung together to form our mapping. Do put any spaces between the commands.

- The Esc character appears above as ^[. Control characters often appear preceded by a circumflex (^). If you insert the Enter key within a mapping, it will appear as ^M. You must press Ctrl+V before each control character or Enter key that is part of your mapping command. Pressing Ctrl+V causes vi to display a circumflex (^) to alert you that the very next character input, if it is a control character, will be treated as just another data character in the line.

Now you are ready to actually set up a mapping.

How to map a key to a sequence of commands

1. From vi's Command mode (that is, not Insert mode), enter a colon (:). The cursor should go down to the last line on the screen and a colon (:) prompt will appear there. Do not press Enter until instructed.

2. In the preceding procedure, you determined whether your terminal supports Ctrl+V in Visual mode. If your terminal does not support Ctrl+V in Visual mode (or if you are not sure), from vi Command mode enter Q.

   Notice that this is a capital *Q*. Do not press Enter. The cursor will go to the bottom of the screen and a colon (:) prompt will appear. You have now left Visual mode. This step is not needed, but is harmless if your terminal does support Ctrl+V in Visual mode.

3. Enter map.

   Do not press Enter until instructed.

4. Enter a space, and then enter the desired command letter to map. You should avoid any letter that is a vi command because you will not be able to do that command any more after that letter is mapped. Actually only five upper- or lowercase letters are not vi commands: *g K q v V*. I usually map

g to format paragraphs, as shown in the preceding chapter. I recommend against mapping capital *K* because *h*, *j*, *k*, and *l* are used to move the cursor, and we don't want usage of those cursor motion letters disturbing our text if the Caps Lock has been accidentally left on. Therefore I recommend that you use lowercase *v* or uppercase *V* as the desired command letter to map.

5. Enter a space, and then enter the vi command sequence to enter every time the mapped letter is pressed. As you saw earlier, enter a Ctrl+V before any control characters or Esc or the Enter key in your command sequence. The Ctrl+V will cause a circumflex (^) to appear before your control character.

6. Now press Enter to complete your map command. Because you did not precede it with a Ctrl+V, this Enter key terminates the map command.

7. If your terminal does not support Ctrl+V, you will still be on the last line with a colon (:) prompt.

   Enter vi, and then press Enter. This returns you to Visual mode.

8. Your cursor should now have left the bottom line and you are in vi Command mode ready to enter vi commands, including the new command letter that you just mapped.

When you have hundreds of repetitive editing changes to make, the best way to speed this up is to set up two-finger editing—as discussed earlier—using the n command to search for the next pattern to change and the period (.) command to repeat the last change. If the last change is too complicated to be done by a single command, set up a mapping so that the whole command sequence can be done by a single letter like the *v* key. Use the slash (/) command to find the first occurrence to change. Now put one index finger on the *n* key and the other index finger on the *v* key. Press *n* to find the next occurrence to change. Press *v* only if you want to change it.

You will lose your mapping when you exit from vi. In the preceding chapter on vi, in the section on formatting paragraphs, you saw how to put the letter *g* mapping into a file called .exrc in your home directory. Notice that in this file, you put the complete map command but you do not put a colon (:) before the word *map*. Any mapping set up in .exrc in your home directory is available to you every time you use vi.

Preventing *J* from Turning Your Text to Mush

If you use h, j, k, and l to move the cursor instead of the arrow keys, you will discover that, if the Caps Lock is accidentally on, it is harmless to enter H, K, and L:

H moves the cursor to the highest line on the screen.

K is not a command (as long you don't map this character).

L moves the cursor to the lowest line on the screen.

If you wanted to go down 10 lines and so pressed the j key 10 times, but did not notice that your Caps Lock was on, you would now find that you have joined 10 lines together. You will have created one long line that probably takes up more than one line and it looks like mush. To fix it, you must painstakingly insert the missing Enter key at the end of each of the original lines. The J command also trims any leading spaces in the line, so you would have to re-enter any leading spaces. After you have made this mistake a couple of times, you may wish there was a way to prevent this problem. There is, and I will show you how I do it.

Preventing problems with accidental Js

1. Put this mapping in your .exrc file in your home directory:
   map J J:

2. Having done that, if you enter several capital *J*s by mistake, the first *J* will join two lines and then go into Colon (:) mode on the bottom line. The rest of the *J*s will harmlessly appear on the bottom line. After you realize your mistake, just press Backspace or Ctrl+H until you have moved all the way to the left and are off the last line.

3. Enter **u** if you want to undo the effect of the single J command that was executed. You have now fully recovered from your mistake.

Why is Ctrl+V a problem on some terminals?

If your TERM is set to tvi925, a down-arrow sends a Ctrl+V. If you press Ctrl+V while in vi on that terminal, vi will think that a down-arrow key has been pressed, so vi gets confused. We can eliminate the problem by using Q to exit from Visual mode temporarily. Alternatively you will not have problems with Ctrl+V if you set your TERM to vt100 or ANSI.

Don't map the K key

Of the four cursor motion commands: h, j, k, and l, only j is a problem if the Caps Lock is accidentally left on. If you map the *K* key, however, you could have two problem keys.

If you do want to join several lines together, you can still do so by preceding the *J* with a repeat count. This will join the requested number of lines and then go into Colon mode on the bottom line. Just press Backspace or Esc to leave the bottom line and continue your other editing.

Global and Partial Text Substitution

vi has a built-in colon command g to globally search for and replace all occurrences of one pattern with another. Because you just learned how to use sed and awk in the previous chapters, however, I am going to show you how to use other UNIX commands, like sed and awk, to modify your whole file or any part of your file. After you learn this technique, you can do much more than the global g command can do.

Substituting R.E. Patterns Throughout the File

How to globally replace a pattern in your document

1. In vi Command mode, enter a colon (:). This should move the cursor to the last line where a colon prompt is waiting.

2. Enter the following:

```
%! sed 's/R.E./newstring/g'
```

%! tells vi to apply the following UNIX command to all lines of your file.

sed is the stream editor that we looked at in a previous chapter.

s is the sed command to substitute one string for another.

R.E. stands for regular expression. Enter the string to search for which may include R.E. wildcards.

newstring stands for the replacement string to be put wherever the R.E. string is found.

g tells sed to do this substitution as many times as the source string is found. You may leave off the g to tell sed to only

    replace the first occurrence of the source string on
    ➥any line but

    not subsequent occurrences on the same line.

3. Press Enter to execute your command.

4. The changes will be made to all lines and you should now be back in vi Command mode. On some types of UNIX systems, you may be prompted to press Enter or Return to continue.

5. Check the lines of your file to see whether you are happy with the changes made. If not, you can remove all the changes by entering the u command to undo them. Remember the u command can only undo the preceding change, so check the file immediately after doing these replacements.

SEE ALSO
➤ *For more information on R.E. patterns, see page 388*

Substituting R.E. Patterns in a Portion of the File

Using the technique in the preceding section, you can also do the replacement only in a section of the file (which is not possible with the global g command that was not covered). The following procedure uses the fact that you can set marks in the file to reference that line, as you saw in an earlier chapter on vi.

How to substitute strings in a section of the file

1. In vi, move the cursor to the start of the section where the text substitution is desired.

2. Enter ma.

This will set mark a at that line. If mark a is already in use to mark another line of the file, you can choose any other letter for your mark. You can have up to 26 marks set.

3. Move the cursor to the last line of the section to be modified.

4. Enter ! 'a.

Do not press the Enter key until instructed. Change the letter *a* in the preceding example if you are using a different mark. Notice that the quotation mark is a single quotation

---

Why not use built-in vi replacement commands?

vi supports two built-in colon commands, **g** (global) and **s** (substitution, which I don't cover in this book because calling the external **sed** command fills the same function as both of these built-in commands. This gives you more practice with **sed**, which is an important UNIX command and shows you how to call other external UNIX commands to manipulate your text (as you shall see).

mark, not a backquote. This should take the cursor to the last line and a bang sign (!) prompt should appear there.

5. Enter the following:

```
sed 's/R.E./newstring/g'
```

This is the same sed command that we analyzed in the preceding step-by-step procedure.

6. Press Enter to execute your command.

7. The changes will be made to the section of your file and you should now be back in vi Command mode. On some types of UNIX systems, you may be prompted to press Enter or Return to continue.

Check the lines of your file to see whether you are happy with the changes made. If not, you can remove all the changes by entering the u command to undo them. Remember the u command can only undo the preceding change, so check the file immediately after doing these replacements.

To summarize:

```
:%! sed ...    replaces throughout the file
!'a sed ...    replaces back to or forward to mark a
```

SEE ALSO

➤ *For more information on setting marks in vi, see page 467*

Conditionally Substituting Text in vi

We can replace the sed command in the preceding section with other sed commands or other different commands entirely to give us great control over how text is substituted in vi.

```
:%! sed '/R.E.1/ s/R.E.2/newstring/g'          # general
➥form
:%! sed '/acme$/ s/^president/chairperson/g'   # example
```

The first line shows the general form of a modified sed command that we can also use in vi to conditionally substitute text. In this form of the sed command, sed will search for R.E.2 and replace it with newstring, but only in lines that contain R.E.1. In the second line, you can see an example using this form of sed.

In that example, if president occurs at the start of a line, we will replace it with chairperson, but only if the line ends in the word acme.

```
:%! awk '$n == "sstring" {gsub("R.E.2","newstring")}
➥{print}' # general form
:%! awk '$3 == "K6697" {gsub("D...","M46253")} {print}'
➥# example
```

The first line shows the general form of an awk command that we can also use in vi to conditionally substitute text. Using awk, we can check a particular field to decide whether we should do the text substitution in that line. In this form of the awk command, awk searches for all occurrences of R.E.2 and replaces them with newstring, but only in lines where field n exactly matches sstring. In the second line, you can see an example using this form of awk. In that example, any time that D is followed by three characters, the D and those three characters will be replaced with M46253, but only if field 3 of the line contains K6697.

```
:%! awk '$n >= numval {gsub("R.E.2","newstring")} {print}' #
➥general form
:%! awk '$3 >= 16.2 {gsub("D...","M46253")} {print}'        #
➥example
```

This example shows the general form and an example which is similar to the preceding awk command. Use this awk form when you want to do a substitution, but only if a particular field contains a value greater than or equal to numval. We can replace >= with the following:

```
>=   (greater than or equal)
<=   (less than or equal)
==   (equal to)
!=   (not equal to)
>    (greater than)
<    (less than)
```

```
:%! awk '$n ~ /R.E.1/ {gsub("R.E.2","newstring")} {print}' #
➥general form
:%! awk '$3 ~ /P[0-9]$/ {gsub("D...","M46253")} {print}'    #
➥example
```

The preceding example again shows the general form and an example that is similar to the two previous awk commands. Use the preceding awk form when you want to do a substitution, but only if a particular field contains an R.E. pattern. In the specific example here, any time that D is followed by three characters, the D and those three characters will be replaced with M46253, but only if field 3 of the line ends with a P followed by a digit.

Changing the Indentation of Your Lines

You can change the indentation by using the sed command to either add spaces to the left margin or remove them.

```
:%! sed 's/^ *//'
```

The preceding sed command removes all leading spaces for all lines of the file.

```
!'a sed 's/^ *//'
```

This sed command removes all leading spaces from the current line to mark a.

```
:%! sed 's/^/   /'
```

The preceding sed command adds three leading spaces to each line of the file.

```
!'a sed 's/^/   /'
```

This sed command adds three leading spaces to the lines starting from the current line to mark a.

Moving/Copying Sections of Text in vi

Moving and copying sections of text can by done in several ways. I will show you how to use marks to do this because I think it gives you the best control and the most successful results.

Moving/Copying Text in the Same File

Moving/copying text in the same file

1. In vi, move the cursor to the start of the text to move or copy.

2. Enter ma.

   This command executes without pressing Enter. It sets mark a at that line. If mark a is already in use to mark another line of the file, you can choose any other letter for your mark. You can have up to 26 marks set.

3. Move the cursor to the last line of the section to be moved or copied.

4. To move the text, enter d'a.

   This command executes without pressing Enter. It deletes all text from the current line to and including mark a, and saves it in what is called an unnamed buffer.

5. To copy the text, enter y'a.

   This command executes without pressing Enter. It yanks—that is, copies—all text from the current line to and including mark a and saves it in what is called an unnamed buffer.

6. Move the cursor to the line just above the desired place to put the moved or copied text. If you want to move or copy text to the beginning of the file, you must insert a blank line at the start of the file, so you can be in the line just above where you want to do the insert.

7. Enter p.

   This command executes without pressing Enter. It will paste—that is, insert—all text saved in the unnamed buffer by the previous steps 4 or 5.

Moving/Copying Text Between Different Files

Moving/copying text between different files

1. Use vi to edit the source file—that is, the file that contains the text to be moved or copied.

2. Move the cursor to the start of the text to move or copy.

3. Enter ma.

This command executes without pressing Enter. It sets mark a at that line. If mark a is already in use to mark another line of the file, you can choose any other letter for your mark. You can have up to 26 marks set.

4. Move the cursor to the last line of the section to be moved or copied.

5. To move the text, enter "bd'a.

This command executes without pressing Enter. It deletes all text from the current line to and including mark a and saves it in buffer b. If buffer b is already in use saving other text, you can choose any other letter for your buffer. You can save text in up to 26 buffers, named for each letter of the alphabet and hence they are also called "named buffers." Named buffers are always preceded by double quotation marks ("). The letter of mark used and the letter of the named buffer do not have to be the same.

6. To copy the text, enter "by'a.

This command executes without pressing Enter. It yanks—that is, copies—all text from the current line to and including mark a and saves it in buffer b. If buffer b is already in use saving other text, you can choose any other letter for your buffer. You can save text in up to 26 buffers, named for each letter of the alphabet and hence called named buffers. Named buffers are always preceded by double quotation marks ("). The letter of mark used and the letter of the named buffer do not have to be the same.

7. If you have done any text modifications in this file that you want to preserve, save your changes now.

Enter :w.

The preceding vi command writes the vi workspace to the file. Do not exit from vi at this point because that would clear all of vi's unnamed and named buffers.

8. Enter :e file2.

Colon (:) e changes the file you are editing while preserving the text in named buffers. Replace file2 in the preceding command with the name of the file to which you want to move or copy the saved text.

9. In this new file, move the cursor to the line just above the desired place in this file to put the moved or copied text. If you want to move or copy text to the beginning of this file, you must insert a blank line at the start of the file, so you can be in the line just above where you want to do the insert.

10. Enter "bp.

This command executes without pressing Enter. It pastes—that is, inserts—all text saved in the buffer b by the previous steps 5 or 6.

Setting Options for Inserting Text

In vi, the set command enables you to turn on or off various modes in vi. This section looks at modes that enhance text input.

Setting vi to Always Show the Input Mode

Sometimes people have trouble in vi because they lose track of whether they are in Insert mode or Command mode. I have seen files created by beginners that contain lines like this:

```
:wq
:w!q
:wq!
wq
q
:q
```

vi has a mode that tells you in the bottom right-hand corner of the screen if you are in Insert mode, Replace mode, Append mode, and so on. To turn on this mode, enter the following:

```
:set showmode
```

To turn off this mode, enter this:

```
:set noshowmode
```

Turning on Autowrap at End of Line

vi has a mode that will check whether you are near the end of line when inserting text. If so, it takes the current word and moves it to the start of the next line as though you had pressed the Enter key just before the start of this word. With this mode on, you never have to press Enter. vi autowraps the line for you. To turn this mode on, enter the following:

```
:set wrapmargin=10
```

The preceding command causes any word that gets within 10 characters of the end of the line to autowrap to the start of the next line. You can set a larger or smaller number than 10 to determine where you want to wrap the end of line.

To turn off this mode, enter this:

```
:set wrapmargin=0
```

This command may be abbreviated as wm, as follows:

```
:set wm=10
```

Turning on Autoindent at Start of Line

If you are using vi in a document with an indented left margin, it will be useful for you to turn on Autoindent mode. Anytime you advance to the next line while in Insert, Append, or Replace mode, vi automatically enters the same number of spaces as on the preceding line.

To turn off this mode, enter the following:

```
:set noautoindent
```

You can abbreviate this command as ai, as follows:

```
:set ai
:set noai
```

Using Abbreviations for Long Strings

If you have a long phrase to enter frequently, you can set up an input abbreviation that vi will expand for you as soon as you insert the abbreviation.

Setting up and using vi abbreviations

1. In vi, enter colon (:), and then enter `abbrev`.

   Do not press Enter until instructed.

2. Enter a space, and then enter the abbreviation you want to use to signal that the long phrase is really to be inserted at the cursor.

3. Enter a space, and then enter the long phrase itself.

4. Press Enter to set up this abbreviation.

5. To make use of the abbreviation that has been set up, from vi, go into Insert mode and start inserting text. As part of the text you enter, insert the abbreviation from step 2. You should see that the abbreviation text is immediately expanded by vi to the longer phrase.

Number Lines

In vi, there is a mode to show line numbers before each line of a file. These line numbers are not inserted into the file itself, but are just displayed to the screen. This can be useful if you compile a C language program and the compiler tells you that you have an error at line 1453.

To turn on vi line numbering, enter the following:

```
:set number
```

To turn off this mode, enter this:

```
:set nonumber
```

This command can be abbreviated as `nu`, as follows:

```
:set nu
:set nonu
```

Ignoring Case When Searching Using / or *?*

To ignore case when searching ahead for strings using slash (/) or searching backward using question mark (?), enter the following:

```
:set ignorecase
```

To turn off this mode, enter this:

```
:set noignorecase
```

You can abbreviate this command as ic, as follows:

```
:set ic
:set noic
```

Saving Your Options in *.exrc*

If you have :set options that you want to use every time you enter vi, you can create a file called .exrc in your home directory. It can contain set options, map commands, and abbreviations, as follows:

```
set autoindent
set ignorecase
set showmode
set wm=10
map g 0721Bi^M^[
map J J:
abbrev SVR4 UNIX, System V, Release 4
```

Notice that each line in this file does *not* start with a colon (:).

SEE ALSO

➤ *For more information on home directories, see page 44*

Harnessing Other UNIX Commands to Work in vi

Earlier you saw how to apply sed to some or all of the lines of the file. You can use that same technique to use other UNIX commands to manipulate lines in vi.

Checking Other UNIX Commands While in vi

While you are editing in vi, you might want to look up some information by running other UNIX commands or pipelines. You can do this from vi Command mode, by entering this:

```
:! cmd
```

Replace cmd in the preceding command with the desired UNIX command or pipeline you want to run. The output from that command will appear on your screen. At the end, it will prompt you to press the Enter key. Then you will be back in vi Command mode ready to do more editing of your file. You saw this process in the preceding chapter on vi when you wrote a script that displayed a help message for vi. In that exercise, we used the colon bang (:!) to run the vihelp script so that we could see the help message and then resume editing.

```
:! cal 1998 ¦ pg
```

The preceding example displays a calendar of the year 1998, one page at a time. You can now use pg to go back and forth in the calendar for 1998 to look up what day a particular date falls on. After you end this cal 1998 pipeline, you will automatically resume your editing in vi with the current screen completely refreshed.

Inserting the Output of Other UNIX Commands into Your File

You can insert the output from any UNIX command or pipeline into your file by moving the cursor to a blank line. Then enter this:

```
!! cmd
```

Replace cmd in the preceding command with the desired UNIX command or pipeline you want to run. Bang-bang (!!) causes the current line you are on to be provided as standard input to the cmd you enter. The output from that command will be inserted in your file in place of the current line.

```
!! cal 1999
```

This example inserts a calendar of the year 1999 into your file in place of the current line. Hint: I usually enter this type of command on a blank line.

```
!! cat ffile
```

The preceding vi command inserts the contents of `ffile` in place of the current line. `ffile` can be specified as a basename, or as an absolute or relative pathname. Alternatively, you can use the built-in vi command :r ffile to insert the contents of `ffile` at the current cursor position.

Sorting All or Part of the File

In vi, you can sort all the lines of your file by entering the following:

```
:%! sort
```

You can enter any desired `sort` options (see Appendix A). All lines of the file will be passed to the `sort` command. The output of the `sort` command will replace the current contents of the file. If you don't like the results, you can enter u to undo that last modification.

How to sort a section of your file

1. Move the cursor to the start of the section to sort.

2. Enter ma.

   This command executes without pressing Enter. It sets mark a at that line. If mark a is already in use to mark another line of the file, you can choose any other letter for your mark. You can have up to 26 marks set.

3. Move the cursor to the last line of the section to be sorted.

4. Enter !'a sort.

   Enter any desired options after `sort` (see Appendix A). Press the Enter key to execute this command.

5. Now the lines in the section will be sorted.

SEE ALSO

➤ *For more information on the* sort *command, see page 202*

Deleting Lines That Match a Pattern

In vi, you can delete all the lines of your file that contain an R.E. pattern by entering the following:

```
:%! grep -v 'R.E.'
```

You can enter any desired grep options (see Appendix A). All lines of the file will be passed to the grep command. The output of the grep command will replace the current contents of the file. If you don't like the results, you can enter **u** to undo that last modification.

Deleting lines with a pattern from a section

1. Move the cursor to the start of the section where you want to delete lines that contain a pattern.

2. Enter ma.

   This command executes without pressing Enter. It sets mark a at that line. If mark a is already in use to mark another line of the file, you can choose any other letter for your mark. You can have up to 26 marks set.

3. Move the cursor to the last line of the section.

4. Enter !'a grep -v R.E..

   Enter any desired options after grep (see Appendix A). Follow the standard rules for grep, including any needed quotation marks around the R.E. pattern. Press Enter to execute this command.

5. Now the lines in the section that contain the R.E. pattern will be removed.

SEE ALSO

➤ *For more information on the* grep *command, see page 380*

Encrypting/Decrypting All or Part of Your File

If your UNIX system supports the crypt command, you can apply the technique in the preceding section to crypt also.

```
:%! crypt
```

The preceding vi command will ask you for a key. It will then use that key to encrypt or decrypt the whole file. Safeguard your key carefully because you cannot decrypt the text without it.

```
!'a crypt
```

The preceding vi command will encrypt or decrypt a section of the file from the current line to mark a.

SEE ALSO

➤ *For more information on the* crypt *command, see page 217*

Inserting a Banner Headline into Your Document

You can use the UNIX banner command to change a line so that each character is about 10 characters tall, as follows:

```
!! banner
```

This vi command pipes the current line of the file to banner and replaces that line with the output from banner.

SEE ALSO

➤ *For more information on the* banner *command, see page 167*

Printing a Section of Your File

Printing a section of your file from vi

1. In vi Command mode, enter the following:
   ```
   :w
   ```

   This vi command writes the file to disk, which is important to do before the rest of these steps.

2. Set mark a at the start of the section to print.

3. Move to the end of the section to print and enter:
   ```
   !'a lp
   ```

   You can use either lp or lpr, depending on which one your system supports. You can add any desired options, such as selecting the destination printer or number of copies.

4. The preceding command deletes all the lines to be printed from your file. Enter u to undo the deletion and restore those lines to your file. It is very important that the u command be run immediately after step 3.

SEE ALSO

➤ *For more information on printing, see page 169*

Counting Number of Lines/Words/Characters in Part of Your File

Printing a section of your file from vi

1. In vi Command mode, enter the following:

   ```
   :w
   ```

   This vi command writes the file to disk, which is important to do before the rest of these steps.

2. Set mark a at the start of the section to be counted, as follows:

   ```
   ma
   ```

3. Move to the end of the section to be counted, and enter this:

   ```
   !'a wc
   ```

4. The preceding command deletes all the lines to be counted and replaces them with three numbers:

   Number of lines in that section

   Number of words in that section

   Number of characters in that section

   Write down any of these numbers if you need them.

5. Enter **u** to undo the deletion and restore those lines to your file. It is very important that the u command be run immediately after step 3.

Editing Multiple Files

You can give vi a list of files to edit, as follows:

```
vi report*
```

When you finish editing one file, save it (:w) and use :n to start editing the next file in the list.

Command-Line Editing in the Korn Shell

By Sanjiv Guha

While working with UNIX or, for that matter, any other operating system, you must correct key entry errors by using the available keys on the terminal. However, not all keyboards have the same layout and, furthermore, may not have the same keys. Because of this, you may not be able to correct keying errors and may find yourself retyping whole command strings.

Korn shell provides two different ways of editing commands in the command line. You can either use keys used by the source editor vi or you can use the source editor emacs. Depending on which editor you are familiar with, you can invoke either of these options for command line editing.

You must explicitly invoke either the vi or emacs command-line editing option. If you do not do so in your .profile file, then by default you get the Korn Shell line-editing options, which are minimal.

Invoking Command-Line Edit Options

If you are familiar with vi, then you can use the following command on the command line or have it in the .profile file (which gets executed at logon) to use **vi** command for command-line editing:

```
set -o vi
```

On the other hand, if you are familiar with emacs editor, use the following command:

```
set -o emacs
```

You can have only one of these active at any time. The most recent command is in effect.

History of Commands

Korn shell keeps a history of the commands across the session. That is, even if you log out, you can still obtain the commands you entered in the previous session by using the Korn shell command fc. The history is, by default, stored in the

$HOME/.sh_history file, where $HOME is the home directory for the user. If you want to modify the filename for the history file, you can modify the filename specified in the system variable HISTFILE. You can include the following command in the .profile file to modify the history file name.

```
export HISTFILE=$HOME/myhistoryfile
```

If you want to get a list of the last few commands, enter the following:

```
fc -l
```

The system responds as follows:

```
116  ls -l
117  ls
118  find . -print
119  vi test.c
120  rm test.c
```

The numbers on the left are the line numbers of the commands in the history file. A higher number indicates a more recent command than one with a lower number.

If you want to obtain a list of commands within a specified number of lines, use the following command:

```
fc -l 117 119
```

This command lists the command numbers 117 through 119 in the history file:

```
117  ls
118  find . -print
119  vi test.c
```

You can also use *relative number* to list the commands. The following command lists all commands starting with the second to last command from the most recent command:

```
fc -l -2
```

The system response is as follows:

```
118  find . -print
119  vi test.c
120  rm test.c
```

If you want to obtain the list of commands in reverse order, you can use the following command:

```
fc -l -r -2
```

The system response is as follows:

```
117   rm test.c
118   vi test.c
118   find . -print
```

You can also execute just one of the commands in the history file using the -s flag with fc command. If you want to execute the most recent command only, use the following command:

```
fc -s
```

If you want to execute the command at line 118, for example, you can use the following command:

```
fc -s 118
```

vi Command Edit Mode

The vi command-line editor, like the source editor, has two modes:

- Entry mode
- Command mode

In the *entry mode*, you enter the command and press Enter to signal the entry of the command so that the command is executed. You can use the Esc key at any time while in entry mode to switch to command mode. In the command mode, you can navigate to any part of the command you have entered so far and modify it, including inserting new strings in the middle of the command.

In the *command mode*, you can use one or more letters to activate different editing commands of vi. While in the command mode, if you press a key that does not translate to a vi command, then you usually hear a beep sound from the terminal. In vi command mode, lowercase letters have different meanings from the uppercase letters.

Korn shell keeps a history of the previous commands you have entered. You can use the command-line editing commands to recall these commands and modify or add to them before executing them.

Now take a look at some details of the command-line editing commands when set -o vi has been used to set vi as the command-line editor. The commands are discussed in alphabetic order:

a	Invokes insert mode so that text can be entered after the current cursor position.
A	Invokes insert mode so that text can be entered at the end of current line.
b	Allows cursor to move back one character at a time. You can prefix it with a number *n* to repeat it *n* times.
B	Allows cursor to be moved back to the previous word (blank, delimited text). You can prefix it with a number *n* to repeat it *n* times.
C	Deletes all the characters from the current position to end of the line and allows you to enter new characters.
dd	Deletes complete line of text.
D	Deletes to the end of the line from the current cursor position.
e	Moves the cursor to the end of the current word. You can prefix it with a number *n* to repeat it *n* times.
E	Moves the cursor to the end of the blank, delimited word. You can prefix it with a number *n* to repeat it *n* times.

f followed by a character	Moves the cursor to the next occurrence of the specified character. You can prefix it with a number n to repeat it n times.
F followed by a character	Moves the cursor to the previous occurrence of the specified character. You can prefix it with a number n to repeat it n times.
G	Brings up the earliest command in the command history file. You can prefix it with a number n to position the command number n in the command history file.
h	Moves cursor to the left by one character. You can prefix it with a number n to repeat it n times.
i	Puts you in insert mode before the current position of the cursor to enter text.
I	Puts you in insert mode before the first non-blank character in the line.
j	Brings up the next command from the command history file. You can prefix it with a number n to repeat it n times.
k	Brings up the previous command from the command history file. You can prefix it with a number n to repeat it n times.
l	Moves cursor to the right by one character. You can prefix it with a number n to repeat it n times.
n	Repeats the last search of the command history file. The direction of the search is from most recent command to least recent command.

N	Repeats the last search of the command history file. The direction of the search is from least recent command to most recent command.
p	Inserts the text from the delete or yank buffer after the cursor position. You can prefix it with a number *n* to repeat it *n* times.
P	Inserts the text from the delete or yank buffer before the cursor position. You can prefix it with a number *n* to repeat it *n* times.
r followed by a character	Replaces the character at the current cursor position by the specified character. You can prefix it with a number *n* to repeat it *n* times.
R	Puts you in replace mode, in which you can override all characters from the current cursor position. You can go past the current last character. You can end the replace mode by pressing the Esc key.
s	Deletes the command line and puts you in insert mode for entering text.
t followed by a character	Moves cursor to the next occurrence of the specified character on the current command line.
T followed by a character	Moves cursor to the previous occurrence of the specified character on the current command line.
u	Undoes the last change made to the command line. If you repeat the u command, you toggle between the changed version of the command line and the non-modified version of the command line.

U	Restores the original text in the command line by undoing all modifications.
v	Puts you in vi editor with the content of the current command line. You can then use standard vi commands to edit it. On exiting vi with :wq, each line is executed as a command one after the other. You can prefix it with a number *n* to edit the line number *n* in the command history file.
w	Moves the cursor to the next word on the command line. You can prefix it with a number *n* to repeat it *n* times.
W	Moves the cursor to the next space-delimited word on the command line. You can prefix it with a number *n* to repeat it *n* times.
x	Deletes the character at the cursor position and keep it in the delete buffer. You can prefix it with a number *n* to repeat it *n* times.
X	Deletes the character before the cursor position and keeps it in the delete buffer. You can prefix it with a number *n* to repeat it *n* times.
yy	Yanks the current command line and keeps it in the yank buffer.
Y	Yanks the text from current cursor position to the end of the line and keeps it in the yank buffer.
0 (zero)	Moves cursor to the first non-space, non-tab character on the current command line.

$	Moves cursor to the last character on the command line.
-	Same as j. You can prefix it with a number *n* to repeat it *n* times.
+	Same as k. You can prefix it with a number *n* to repeat it *n* times.
¦	Moves cursor to the first character in the command line. If you prefix it with a number *n*, the cursor moves to the character position *n* on the command line.
/ followed by a string and ending with Enter key	Searches the command history file for the specified string anywhere in the command in the direction from most recent command to the least recent command.
/ followed by ^ and a string, and ending with Enter key	Searches the command history file for the specified string at the beginning of the command in the direction from most recent command to the least recent command.
? followed by a string and ending with Enter key	Searches the command history file for the specified string anywhere in the command in the direction from least recent command to the most recent command.
? followed by ^ and a string, and ending with Enter key	Searches the command history file for the specified string at the beginning of the command in the direction from least recent command to the most recent command.
~	Modifies a lowercase letter to an uppercase letter, or vice versa.

#	Inserts a pound sign (#) at the beginning of the command line and executes it so that it goes to the command history file. The command is not actually executed because the # sign in the beginning means that Korn shell treats it as a comment.
=	Displays the file name, which matches the current word.
*	Replaces the current word with a list file and directory names starting with names matching the current word.
Space	Same as 1.
Enter	Executes the current command.
Control key followed by the letter 1	Redraws the current line.

Alias

You can use the alias command to define a shortcut for a command string. There are two types of aliases: regular alias and tracked alias. A *tracked* alias shows you the complete path of the command.

You can use the alias command by itself to generate a list of all aliases set up in the current environment. If you use the -t command as follows then you will get a list of all tracked aliases:

```
alias -t
```

You can use the alias command to define an alias for a command or for a number of commands. In the following example, an alias is set up for ls command as ls command but with the -l option.

```
alias ls="ls -l"
```

Introducing the emacs Editor

By Jesper Pedersen

A text editor enables you to create and modify text documents that contain the letters and characters that you can type on your keyboard. With a word processor, on the other hand, you can not only edit text, you can also change the presentation of that text by selecting the font size and style.

This chapter introduces you to the most advanced text editor available: emacs. A common saying about emacs is this: *If it can't be done in emacs, it ain't worth doing at all.* The following list of some of emac's basic features gives you an idea about what this means:

- An extremely useful undo facility.
- Autosaving files every 300 characters, or approximately every 30 seconds. This guarantees that you lose only a minimal amount of your work in case of program/power/human failure.
- A lot of online help through the Info System (a hypertext format similar to the one used on the World Wide Web).
- Modes for different assignments, including functions and keyboard bindings to speed your work (for example, modes for writing HTML documents, C programs, LaTeX documents).
- Spelling facilities (the ispell program, for example).
- Powerful macros that may speed up your work considerably.
- Incremental searches.
- Search and replace, using regular expression.
- Binding keys on your keyboard to your specific needs.

emacs enables you to do almost anything (and everything ... on your computer). The following list presents just some of the tasks worth doing in emacs:

- Diffing files using ediff
- Finding differences in text files
- Reading/composing mail
- Editing files on other file systems

Most important of all, emacs is extremely configurable. You can customize it to whatever your needs might be! (This chapter presents a number of customization examples for your review.)

Technical Terms

To "really" explain emacs to you, it is necessary to introduce a few technical terms. The subject will become easier and more accessible when you understand these terms. A good understanding of these terms will also serve as a solid foundation on which to further build your knowledge about emacs. Armed with an understanding of the following rudimentary terms, you can start searching constructively for information in the emacs info pages:

- *Buffer.* A buffer is the basic editing unit in emacs. One buffer corresponds to one text file being edited. Although you can have several buffers, you edit only one at a time. You can, however, have several buffers visible simultaneously. Most often a buffer contains the text of a file you are editing.

- *Point.* The point refers to the place where text would appear if you inserted it into a given buffer. Each buffer has exactly one point.

- *Region.* The region is the text selected. Numerous functions may work either on the whole buffer, or only on the region (for example, spell checking).

- *Ctrl+X.* This is what Control+X means: You press the Ctrl key and keep it down while you press x; then you release both.

- *M+X.* This is what Meta+X means: You press the key labeled Meta (or Alt if no keys are labeled Meta), and keep it down while you press X; then you release both. If your keyboard does not have a Meta key, or if you are logged on using Telnet (where the Meta key might not work), you can use an alternative key sequence: *Esc+X.* You press the Escape key (often labeled Esc), release it, and then press X.

The emacs menu bar

One difference between running emacs with and without X is the presence of a menu bar at the top of the window. In newer versions of emacs, however, you may find a menu bar when running in non-X mode (also called Text mode).

If your version of emacs is earlier than 19.22, you should consider updating your emacs installation. The newer versions have many features that make the upgrade worthwhile.

Starting emacs

emacs can run both with and without the presence of X windows. This chapter assumes that you have X windows. Don't worry if you don't have X windows, however; the following information doesn't require that you have it.

To start emacs, just type emacs. This brings up a window that looks like the one in Figure 20.1.

The toolbar is at the top of the window. You can use this toolbar just like a toolbar in Microsoft Windows. Its content changes depending on what you are doing.

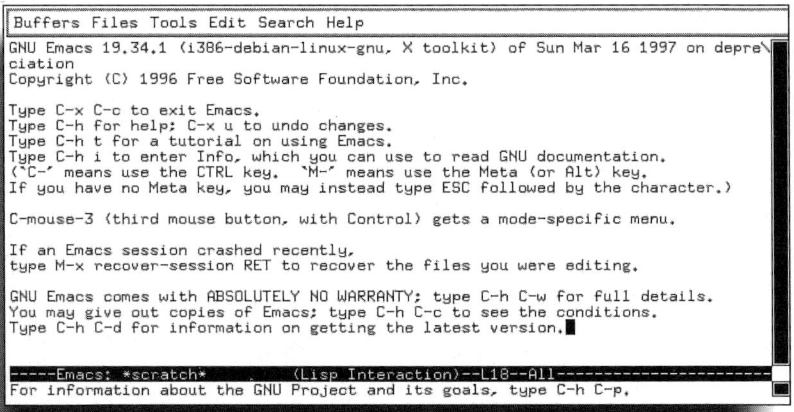

FIGURE 20.1

The emacs startup window.

```
 Buffers Files Tools Edit Search Help
 GNU Emacs 19.34.1 (i386-debian-linux-gnu, X toolkit) of Sun Mar 16 1997 on depre\
 ciation
 Copyright (C) 1996 Free Software Foundation, Inc.

 Type C-x C-c to exit Emacs.
 Type C-h for help; C-x u to undo changes.
 Type C-h t for a tutorial on using Emacs.
 Type C-h i to enter Info, which you can use to read GNU documentation.
 (`C-' means use the CTRL key.  `M-' means use the Meta (or Alt) key.
 If you have no Meta key, you may instead type ESC followed by the character.)

 C-mouse-3 (third mouse button, with Control) gets a mode-specific menu.

 If an Emacs session crashed recently,
 type M-x recover-session RET to recover the files you were editing.

 GNU Emacs comes with ABSOLUTELY NO WARRANTY; type C-h C-w for full details.
 You may give out copies of Emacs; type C-h C-c to see the conditions.
 Type C-h C-d for information on getting the latest version.█

-----Emacs: *scratch*        (Lisp Interaction)--L18--All----------------------
For information about the GNU Project and its goals, type C-h C-p.
```

Below the toolbar is the buffer. At first, it contains some startup information. As you start to type, however, the buffer's content is replaced with your text.

At the bottom of the window is the status line, in reversed video. At the beginning of an emacs session, this status bar contains the following information:

- To the left of the text emacs: are five dashes. This indicates that the buffer is synchronized with the file on disk (that is, the content of the buffer is the same as the content of the file on disk). If the content of the buffer is changed, the five dashes will be replaced with the text --**-.

- Next to the text emacs: is the name of the buffer. Because you haven't loaded any file yet, the buffer is just a dummy buffer named *scratch*. When you open a file, the filename will be located here.

- Next is information about which mode you have started (the text Fundamental). This could have been HTML, for example, if you had loaded the HTML mode.

- Next is the number of the line at which the point is located (the text L1).

- Finally, you see information about which part of the buffer you are looking at. All indicates that all the buffer is visible. Alternatives are: Bot—at the bottom of the text; Top—at the top of the text; and 8%—8% down in the buffer.

Below the status line is an empty line. This line is used to interact with you when emacs wants information from you.

Opening/Saving Files and Exiting emacs

How to open a file using the mouse

1. From the Files menu, choose Open File.

2. Type the name of the file you wish to edit. (If you type a name of a file that does not exist, a new one will be created; then this new file will be opened.)

Now the file is loaded into a buffer, and you can edit it to your heart's content. To move around within the buffer, you use the cursor keys.

When you choose an item in the menu bar, you should be very attentive to the shortcut listed next to the item. If you learn these shortcuts, your interaction with emacs will be substantially faster, and thus you will get more work done.

How to open a file without using the mouse

1. Press Ctrl+x, Ctrl+f.

2. Type the name of the file you wish to edit.

Entering commands and inserting text

In contrast to vi, emacs does not have an Editing mode and a Command mode. In emacs, you enter commands by using the Ctrl key and the Meta key; you insert text by just typing it.

After you are finished editing your file, you can save it by pressing Ctrl+x, Ctrl+s, or by choosing Files, Save Buffer from the menu bar.

To exit emacs, choose Exit Emacs from the Files menu, or use the shortcut Ctrl+x, Ctrl+c.

Using the Undo Facility

emacs has a very powerful undo mechanism that can help you when you regret a modification. To undo a modification, go to the Edit menu and choose Undo. (Bound to Ctrl+_; this is Control and then underscore.) If you perform several undo actions in succession, you will undo just as many corrections. Note that emacs may collect several text insertion commands into one entity. This means that one undo command may remove several words.

A very important point to note about the Undo facility is that the undo actions may be undone too! (That is, undo and redo are the same function.) An example may clarify the matter.

Example of an undo command

1. Start emacs.
2. Type 1 2 3 4 on four separate lines.
3. Now undo until you have removed 3 and 4.
4. Type 5.
5. Now start undoing, and observe.

You will see that 5 is removed, and then 3 and 4 are inserted again. If you continue undoing, you will see that 4, 3, 2, and finally 1 will be removed.

Cut and Paste

A capability that makes the computer so much better than an ordinary typewriter is cut and paste—the possibility to move text around in your documents, copy text into several places, and so forth. To mark a section of the text, you can use either the mouse or the keyboard.

Copying/cutting text using the mouse

1. Place the mouse over the beginning of the text you want to mark.

2. Press the left mouse button. While you keep the mouse button pressed, drag to the location where the selection should end.

3. Release the mouse button.

4a. If you want to copy the text to the clipboard (and don't want to delete it from the buffer), select the Edit menu and choose Copy.

4b. If you want to cut the text to the clipboard (and delete it from the buffer), select the Edit menu and choose Cut.

Copying/cutting text using the keyboard

1. Place the point (the insertion cursor, remember) at the start of the text you want to select.

2. Press Ctrl+spacebar (that is, the Control key and the spacebar). At the bottom of the buffer, the text Mark set should appear.

3. Go to the location where you want the selection to end.

4a. If you want to copy the text to the clipboard, press M+w. (M is the Meta key.)

4b. If you want to cut the text to the clipboard, press Ctrl+w.

Although remembering the key bindings may seem difficult, you should try very hard to do so; it will make your interaction with emacs much faster. You won't need to grab the mouse, for example, when you want to cut and paste.

Pasting the most recent selection into the buffer using the mouse

1. Place the mouse over the point where you want to paste the text.

2. Press the middle mouse button.

Using the mouse

You can only use the mouse in emacs, Xemacs, or emacs in one of its newer versions under X.

Pasting the most recent selection into the buffer using the keyboard

1. Place the point at the location to which you want to paste.

2. Press Ctrl+y.

Remember that emacs saves more than one step of undo information. The same is true regarding selections: You can paste a selection that is not the most recent one.

Pasting what is not the most recent selection into the buffer using the mouse

1. Place the point where you want to paste the text (either by moving with the cursor keys, or by pressing the left mouse button at the location).

2. From the Edit menu, choose Select and Paste, and then choose the selection that you want to paste.

Pasting what is not the most recent selection into the buffer using the keyboard

1. Place the point at the location to which you want to paste.

2. Press Ctrl+y to paste the most recent selection.

3. Now you may go through the list of older selections by pressing M+y until you reach the selection you want.

Automatic Backups

emacs saves your buffers once in a while to disk, to ensure that if by accident you should not save a buffer before exiting, it is not lost forever. When emacs opens a file for which the backup file is newer, it suggests that you recover data from the autosaved file.

If you get the backup notification message, it might be a good idea to see what the difference is between the original file and the autosaved file, using the diff command. (The autosaved file has the same name as the original, except that the autosaved file has a pound sign (#) character at the beginning and at the end of its name.)

Recovering an autosaved file

1. Press M+x.

2. Type `recover-file` and press Enter.

3. Type the filename and press Enter.

4. Emacs asks whether you really mean it. If you still do, type yes and press Enter.

Binding Keys

You probably have three important questions on your mind right now:

1. Why are the bindings so difficult and so nonintuitive?

2. Is there any chance that I will ever learn all these strange bindings?

3. Can I change the binding so that undo is bound to Ctrl+backspace, for example?

The short answers: 1) Don't you have more important things to worry about? 2) Yes; 3) Yes.

The more detailed answers follow.

To the first question, whether you will ever learn all these different bindings, I can answer in the affirmative. It will come with time, if you just force yourself not to use the mouse when alternatives are available.

The reason for the bindings is not very clear, but a good guess might be that it is because emacs was not designed from scratch, but rather is a result of years of development. Because of backward-compatibility issues, the bindings are the way they are. There seems to be a general plan, however:

- All letters, numbers, and symbols on the keyboard insert the label given on the key, if pressed without either the Control or Meta key.

- A function that is used very often is available with either the Control or Meta key pressed. (For example, *go to end of line* is bound to Ctrl+e, *undo* is bound to Ctrl+_ (that is, Control and underscore), and *paste* is bound to Ctrl+y.)

- If the Control prefix is bound to a function that works on characters for a given key, the Meta prefix works on words (if this gives any meaning for the given function). Likewise, if the Control prefix works on lines, the Meta prefix will work on sentences. Examples of this include the following: Ctrl+t transposes two characters; M+t transposes two words; Ctrl+e moves the point to the end of the line; and M+e moves the point to the end of the sentence.

- Functions that are used more seldom are bound with a prefix Ctrl+x. Examples of this include the following: Ctrl+x, Ctrl+c exits emacs; Ctrl+x 2 splits the window in two, with a buffer in each one.

- Function, which is specific to a given mode, is prefixed with Ctrl+C.

- Function, which is very seldom used, or which it would not be a good idea to have bound on the keyboard, is not bound at all, but is accessible by pressing M+x and typing the name of the function.

How to see a list of all keyboard bindings

1. Press Ctrl+h, Ctrl+B. This should split the window. In one of the windows, a description of all bindings should appear.

2. Press Ctrl+x, o. This moves the selection to the window that contains the description.

3. Browse through the text with the arrow keys.

4. When you are finished, press Ctrl+x, 0 (zero) to bury the help buffer.

When you have found a function that sounds interesting, you can get more information about it:

How to see the description of a given function

1. Press Ctrl+h, f.

2. Type the function name that you want more information about (for example, open-line).

3. Press Ctrl+x, 1 to bury the window after you finish. (It is Ctrl+x, 1 this time because the selection is in the window, which you want to keep.)

Now we're almost ready to rebind the keyboard to your personal preference. Before we do that, however, it is very useful to know which binding already exists for a given key. This information is retrieved by pressing Ctrl+h, c, and then pressing the key in mind. This action displays the function name for the function bound to this key. To get more information about the function, follow the previous instructions.

How to rebind a key

1. Press M+x.

2. Type global-set-key to bind the key in all buffers, or type local-set-key to bind only the key in the given buffer.

3. Press Enter.

4. Press the key that you want to rebind.

5. Type the function name you want to bind to the given key.

Now you can bind the keyboard just the way you want it. One thing you still need to learn, however, is how to save the bindings from session to session.

The file called .emacs located in your home directory is a setup file for emacs. Information in this file is read each time emacs starts. The file is writing in a language called *emacs LISP* or *elisp* for short.

The following description applies only to global key bindings. It is much more difficult to bind local keys because some sort of description of which buffers they apply to is needed. This is beyond the scope of this book.

How to save a key binding into the *.emacs* file

1. Create the key binding as previously described.

2. Press M+x.

3. Type `repeat-complex-command` and press Enter.

4. Browse through the history list either with the up/down-arrow keys, or press M+p and M+n until you get to a line that starts with `(global-set-key`.

5. Copy this line into the clipboard.

6. Press Ctrl+g. (This will give a beep in your speaker, and the buffer should disappear.)

7. Open the file .emacs in your home directory.

8. Go to an appropriate location in this file, and paste. This should insert the text `(global-set-key`.

9. Save the file.

Key binding with Control+Shift

Different modes may rebind keys in defiance of that to which you have already bound them. This might be avoided by using Control+Shift as a prefix for your own key bindings.

Defining Macros

One of the main things that computers are much better at than humans are is trivial, repetitive work. emacs has macros that help you to do such tasks. A *macro* is a facility that enables you to record a sequence of keystrokes for later playback.

How to record a macro

1. Press Ctrl+x).(This starts the recording.)

2. Make the keystrokes that you wish to record.

3. Press Ctrl+x). (This ends the recording.)

If you want to keep several macros defined at the same time, you need to name them.

How to name a keyboard macro

1. Press M+x.

2. Type `name-last-kbd-macro` and press Enter.

3. Type a name for the newly defined macro.

You can invoke the last defined keyboard macro (named or not) by pressing Ctrl+x, e. You can invoke a named keyboard macro by pressing M+X and typing its and then pressing Enter.

If you name a macro, you can bind it to a key (as described in the preceding section).

Macros survive only as long as emacs. When you close emacs, all the defined macros disappear unless you save them in the .emacs file.

How to save a macro into the *.emacs* file

1. Define the macro as outlined previously.

2. Name the defined macro as outlined previously.

3. If you want to bind the macro to a key, do so as outlined in the preceding section.

4. Open your .emacs file and go to an appropriate location in it.

5. Press Ctrl+1, M+x.

6. Type `insert-kbd-macro` and press Enter.

7. Type the name of the defined macro and press Enter.

Repeating Macros

When you have defined a macro, you want to use it often (maybe even a hundred times). To do this, you can use emacs' repeating facility. If you press Control and type a number (while keeping Control pressed), the following command executes that many times. (This is not 100 percent correct, but in most cases it is so.) Thus, if you want to repeat a macro 20 times, press Ctrl+2 Ctrl+0 Ctrl+x, e. (This is Control 20, and the keyboard prefix for executing a macro.)

Often, you will want to execute a macro on several lines. An example of this could be to insert > at the beginning of every line in a region of the text.

Selecting with the mouse

You can also complete steps 2–4 by using the mouse to select the region.

Using repeated macros to insert at the start of every line in a region

1. Record a macro that inserts > at the beginning of the line.

2. Go to the starting line of the region.

3. Press Ctrl+*the key you have bound for this macro* (Control+spacebar, for example).

4. Go to the end of the region.

5. Press M+x.

6. Type `apply-macro-to-region-lines` and press Enter.

If you need to create a macro that involves inserting numbers (increasing or decreasing), go to `ftp://archive.cis.ohio-state.edu/pub/gnu/emacs/elisp-archive/functions/counter.el.Z`. It will not be described further here because it is not part of the standard emacs distribution. It is really easy to install, however, and it proves extremely useful. If the preceding site is busy, try the mirror site at `ftp://src.doc.ic.ac.uk/gnu/emacsBits/elisp-archive/`.

If you ever catch yourself in a situation where the sound from the keyboard goes Tik taak tik tik ... Tik taak tik tik ... Tik taak tik tik, it might be worth considering creating a macro!

Searching and Replacing Text

When you are writing programs or documents, you may often want to search for a given text in your document. emacs has several functions for searching for text. This section describes these functions.

Another task that you often find yourself doing is replacing some text with another. There are three kinds of searches:

- *Ordinary searches*. In this kind of search, you type the text that you want to search for; emacs will go to the first occurrence of this text. You can then ask it to go to the second occurrence, the third, and so on.

- *Incremental searches.* In this kind of search, emacs starts the search as soon as you type the first letter. As you type more letters, emacs searches further on in your document, to reflect the increased level of information about what you are searching for.

- *Regular searches.* In this kind of search, you can add wildcards, just like you do in the shell (although the wildcards are formed in a different way—called *regular expressions*).

There are two ways to replace text:

- *Ordinary search and replace.* In this strategy, you type the text that you want to replace and the text you want it substituted with. Then for each match, emacs asks whether you want to replace this match.

- *Regular search and replace.* In regular search and replace, you can replace text by using regular expression. This way you can replace \printf{...} with write ..., for example.

Incremental Searches

The search type most often used is the *incremental search.* Therefore, let's start out with that one.

To search forward using incremental search, press Ctrl+s. To search backward, press Ctrl+r.

After you have pressed either Ctrl+s or Ctrl+r, you can type the letters for which you are searching. Each time you add a new letter, emacs tests whether the words found match (by searching using the previous letters). If this is not the case, emacs searches further in your document. When you have added as many letters as you wish, you can press Ctrl+s or Ctrl+r to search further on with the letters typed so far. This way you can switch between typing letters and pressing either Ctrl+s or Ctrl+r.

Incremental search is much faster than ordinary search because you do not need to type the whole word. If you are searching for the word *miscellaneous*, for example, it might be enough just to type misc. If you do that using ordinary search and find that misc also matches the word *miscalculation*, which occurs several times in your document, you may have to start all over again in your ordinary search. In incremental search, however, all you have to do is type the letter e, which will make you search for *misce* (which doesn't match the word *miscalculation*).

Ordinary Searches

In one situation, an ordinary search is preferable to an incremental search—namely, when you have the word to search for on your clipboard.

How to search using an ordinary search

1. Press Ctrl+s or Ctrl+r twice for an ordinary search forward; respective ordinary search backward.

2. Type the letters you wish to search for. Or, in the case that the letters are located on the clipboard, press Ctrl+y.

Ordinary Search and Replace

emacs has a function for replacing one sequence of letters with another. This function replaces text from the current position in the buffer through to the end of the buffer.

How to search and replace

1. Press M+%. (This is the function `query-replace`.)

2. Type the text that you want to replace, and press Enter.

3. Type the text that you want to insert, and press Enter.

emacs will now go to the first occurrence of the text and ask what you want to do. You have the following possibilities:

- Press y to replace the occurrence and go to the next one.

- Press n to skip the occurrence and go to the next one.

- Press ! to replace the occurrence and all the following matches too.

- Press q to stop the replacing.

- Press the comma key (,) to replace the current occurrence, but not move the cursor point immediately. (To restart replacement, press y.)

Regular Search and Replace

Two functions exist for regular expression incremental searches, bound to Ctrl+M+s and Ctrl+M+s for forward respective backward searching. A function called query-replace-regexp (not bound to any key) exists for search and replace with regular expressions.

Regular expression is beyond the scope of this book. Therefore, instead of explaining all the details, I will show you an example of its power. For further information, you should look it up in the info pages.

Example: Replacing printf("…") with write …

Imagine that you want to replace all the occurrences of the pattern printf("…") with write …

The text represented by the three dots shall be the same after write as it is between the quotation marks. That is, printf("Hello world") should be replaced with write Hello world. Ordinary replacement would not do here because you might expect the pattern ") to occur several places where it does not match printf(".

First, we have to create the regular expression, which matches printf("…"), where the three dots could be anything. This is done with the regular expression \bprintf("\([^)]*\)")\b. Okay, let's take that step by step:

1. \b matches a word boundary. This way our replacement will not replace, for example, sprintf("…") because of the s at the beginning.

2. This is just ordinary text to be matched.

3. This starts a regular grouping. This is necessary, if we wish to refer to the text between the brackets in the replacement.

4. The square brackets signal a list of characters to match. The ^ character at the beginning of this list says that the list should be negated. (That is, it is a list of characters that should not be matched.) All in all, this element says that a single character, different from a closing bracket, may be matched.

5. A star says that the preceding element may be matched any number of times. Together with the square bracket, this says that any number of characters may be read, as long as it is not an ending bracket.

6. This ends the group started in part 3.

7. Ordinary text to match.

8. This matches a word boundary (see part 1).

Regular expressions try to match as much as possible. Therefore, if part 4 had not said that an ending bracket was illegal, it would have read from the first printf to the very last one (any characters may be matched with a single dot).

Now we are ready to do the replacement.

Replacing *printf*... with *write*...

1. Press M+x.

2. Type query-replace-regexp and press Enter.

3. Type \bprintf("\([^)]*\)")\b and press Enter.

4. Type write \1 and press Enter.

Now emacs will ask you for permission to replace the first occurrences of printf... Note the \1 in the replacement string. It will be expanded to the text matched in between the brackets in the text that is replaced.

Compiling a List of Matches

Sometimes you want to see the whole list of lines that match a given text search. This may be done with the function list-matching-lines. It is not bound to any key; to access it, therefore, you need to use M+X. If this function is given a numeric prefix (which is given just like the repeating count, previously described—pressing Control, and while holding it typing the number), that many lines will be shown as context.

How to get a list of all matches

1. If you want to see a context (that is, lines around the matching line), press Control, and while holding it down, press the number of lines to show as context.

2. Press M+x.

3. Type `list-matching-lines` and press Enter.

4. Type the text you are searching for. (Technically speaking, this is in fact a regular expression. So long as you are not searching for +,*,\(,\),\|, however, you will never notice.)

emacs will now split the window in two, where you will see the list in one of the windows. By pressing the middle mouse button on one of the matches, the other window will update its view to show this match.

When you are finished, you can close the window with the list of matches by pressing either Ctrl+x, 1 (if you are located in the window you want to keep), or Ctrl+x, 0 (if you are located in the window you want to remove.)

Figure 20.2 shows an example of such a list that was created with a context of 1.

Case in Searches

emacs is very configurable. You have already seen how the keyboard can be bound to your personal preferences. The built-in functions can be controlled using variables that instruct them how to work.

There is a variable that tells emacs whether searches should be case-sensitive or not case-sensitive. If its value is set to t (True in elisp), searches will be not case-sensitive. If, however, it is set to nil (False in elisp), searches will be case-sensitive.

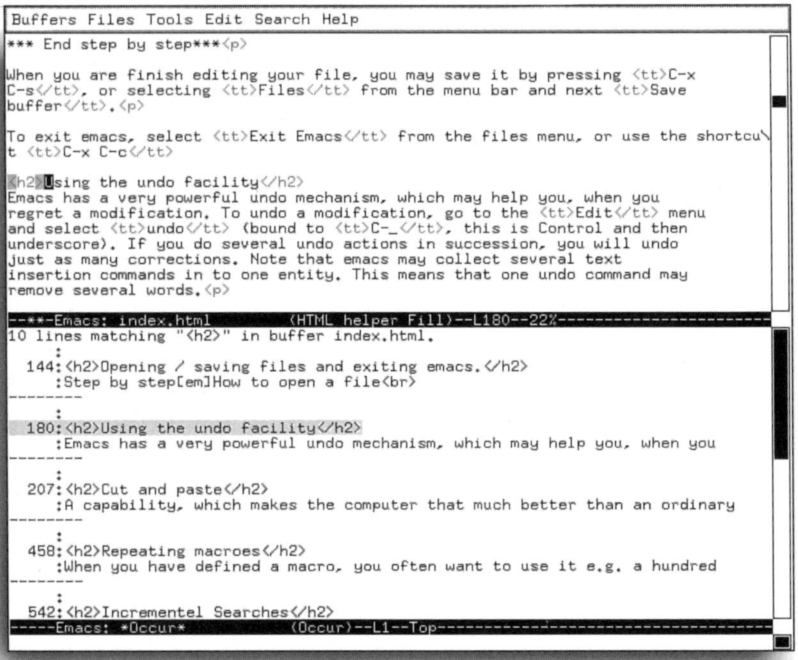

FIGURE 20.2

Showing a list of matches using *list-matching-lines*.

```
Buffers Files Tools Edit Search Help
*** End step by step***<p>

When you are finish editing your file, you may save it by pressing <tt>C-x
C-s</tt>, or selecting <tt>Files</tt> from the menu bar and next <tt>Save
buffer</tt>.<p>

To exit emacs, select <tt>Exit Emacs</tt> from the files menu, or use the shortcu\
t <tt>C-x C-c</tt>

<h2>Using the undo facility</h2>
Emacs has a very powerful undo mechanism, which may help you, when you
regret a modification. To undo a modification, go to the <tt>Edit</tt> menu
and select <tt>undo</tt> (bound to <tt>C-_</tt>, this is Control and then
underscore). If you do several undo actions in succession, you will undo
just as many corrections. Note that emacs may collect several text
insertion commands in to one entity. This means that one undo command may
remove several words.<p>
--**-Emacs: index.html        (HTML helper Fill)--L180--22%---------------------
10 lines matching "<h2>" in buffer index.html.
       :
   144:<h2>Opening / saving files and exiting emacs.</h2>
       :Step by step[em]How to open a file<br>
--------
       :
   180:<h2>Using the undo facility</h2>
       :Emacs has a very powerful undo mechanism, which may help you, when you
--------
       :
   207:<h2>Cut and paste</h2>
       :A capability, which makes the computer that much better than an ordinary
--------
       :
   458:<h2>Repeating macroes</h2>
       :When you have defined a macro, you often want to use it e.g. a hundred
--------
       :
   542:<h2>Incrementel Searches</h2>
----Emacs: *Occur*            (Occur)--L1--Top--------------------------------
```

Enabling caseless searches

1. Press M+x.
2. Type set-variable and press Enter.
3. Type case-fold-search.
4. Type t to enable caseless searches, or nil to get cases in searches.
5. Press Enter.

Spell Checking Documents

emacs has a very useful interface called ispell: a spell checker. If you don't have ispell installed on your system, you can download it via FTP from ftp://ftp.gnu.org/pub/gnu/.

Basically, emacs offers three functions: ispell-word (bound to M+$), ispell-region, and ispell-buffer.

To start ispell, press M+x and type the name of one of the functions (you have seen this process before, remember?). Now emacs will start spell checking. If you spell check only a single word, and the word is correct, it will say `miscellaneous is cor-rect`. If you spell check a region or the whole buffer, emacs will say `Spell-checking done` when it is finished with your buffer.

In case of spelling errors, emacs highlights the word that it failed to find in its dictionary and gives you a list of possibilities. You can select the correct word from this list by pressing the number listed next to the word, as shown in Figure 20.3.

FIGURE 20.3
Spell checking with emacs.

If emacs doesn't guess the correct word, you can type it yourself by pressing *r* (*r* for *r*eplace), typing the word, and finally pressing Enter. If the word is likely to be misspelled many times throughout the document, it might be a better idea to press a capital *R*, which will ask for a replacement, and afterward do a query-replace. This way you do not have to type the replacement string for each occurrence of the misspelled word.

If, on the other hand, the word is a new technical expression that is spelled correctly, you can either press the spacebar to accept the word this time, press *a* to accept the word throughout the lifetime of the buffer, or press *i* (i for *i*nsert) to insert the word into your personal dictionary.

There are a few extra options when using ispell. To see these, press Ctrl+h, f and type `ispell-help`.

Major and Minor Modes

When you are writing HTML documents, you will find that you want emacs to be configured in one way. You will want it to be configured in quite a different way when you are writing C++ programs or ordinary letters (that is, such as ones that you send to your mother on her birthday).

Examples of differences between the two configurations include the following:

- The way text is indented. (In C++ mode, the indentation level should increase on opening braces, and decrease on closing ones.)
- The set of functions bound to the Ctrl+c key prefix.
- The content of the menus. (C++ mode adds a menu entry called C++.)

All such configurations are saved in packages called *modes*. Modes exist for most programming languages; for example, C, C++, Java, Python, TCL, Assembler, HTML, LISP, TeX, AmsTeX, LaTeX, and many more.

Modes for a given *language* are called *major modes*. Another sort of modes (called *minor modes*) are those that add minor changes to the behavior of emacs. You can have only one major mode loaded at a time, whereas you may have many minor modes loaded simultaneously. The set of minor modes that you want to have loaded might be the same in different major modes.

Examples of minor modes include the following:

- *Auto-fill mode*. When this minor mode is turned on, emacs automatically inserts line breaks. You can configure at which column line breaks should occur by moving the cursor to that column and pressing Ctrl+x, f.

- *Mouse-avoidance mode*. When this minor mode is loaded, the cursor moves away if the point is getting to close.

- *Font-lock mode*. When Font-lock mode is enabled, text is fontified as you type it.

- *Auto-compress mode*. When this minor mode is active, emacs automatically compresses and decompresses files.

- *Column-number mode*. When this minor mode is enabled, the column number appears in the status line.

To see a list of major modes, refer to the section titled "Getting Help About emacs."

Loading Minor Modes

You can toggle a minor mode on and off by pressing M+X and typing its name.

There are two types of minor modes: those that are independent of the buffer, and those that are buffer dependent. In the preceding list, Mouse-avoidance mode, Auto-compress mode, and Column-number mode are buffer independent; Auto-fill mode and Font-lock mode are buffer dependent.

Buffer-independent minor modes that you want available by default can be started in the .emacs file by typing the mode's name in brackets. Consider the following:

```
; semicolon starts a comment in the .emacs file
(mouse-avoidance-mode) ; start mouse-avoidance-mode in its
➥default setup

; an alternative way of starting it, this time with an
➥argument, which
; describes how it should be started. Only one of these
➥commands should
; be used.
mouse-avoidance-mode 'exile)
```

Some of the minor modes may have an optional argument (like Mouse-avoidance mode just described). To see whether a given mode has any options, you should see the description of the function with the name of the mode (using Ctrl+f, f).

The buffer-dependent minor mode is a bit harder to start by default. There is a general way to start a minor mode when a major mode is started, namely using *hooks*. Hooks are additional functions that can be invoked when a major mode is started. Each major mode has such a hook called *mode-name*-hook. The code needed in the .emacs file to start Auto-fill-mode when using the major mode Text mode is as follows:

```
(add-hook 'text-mode-hook
  (function
    (lambda ()
      (auto-fill-mode 1))))
```

Loading Major Modes

You can still select the major mode for a given buffer by pressing M+X and typing its name. You cannot, however, turn it off that way (because a buffer always should have exactly one major mode). Therefore, to turn off a major mode, you have to turn on another. (One major mode with almost no functionality exists, and is called Fundamental mode. You may switch to this one to turn off a given mode.)

You can tell emacs to start a given major mode when loading a file by placing a special pattern on the first line of the file, which looks like this:

```
-*-Mode name-*-
```

To start C++ mode for a given file, you can insert the text:

```
// -*- c++-mode -*-
```

Note the two slashes at the beginning of the line, which tells the C++ compiler that this line is just a comment. This way the C++ compiler will not try to compile the instruction to emacs.

Another way to get emacs to start a major mode automatically is to tell it which mode to start, depending on the filename. This way you can tell emacs that files ending in .c should be started in

Ctrl+*mode*, files ending in .pas should be started in Pascal mode, and files ending in .doc should be started in Text mode. This is done by setting the variable to `auto-mode-alist`. You might use the following example as a template for this:

```
(setq auto-mode-alist (append (list
     '("\\.html"  . html-helper-mode)
     '("Makefile"   . makefile-mode))
   auto-mode-alist))
```

The second line states that files ending in .html should be edited in the major mode called `html-helper-mode`, and the third line says that files called Makefile should be edited in `makefile-mode`.

Before you start defining a lot of patterns this way, it might be worthwhile to inspect the variable `auto-mode-alist` first, because many mode specifiers are defined by default. Check this out by pressing Ctrl+h, v, typing `auto-mode-alist`, and then pressing Enter.

Getting Help About emacs

emacs has a lot of help available online, ranging from descriptions of key bindings to a general introduction to emacs. Common to it all is that it is available with the key prefix Ctrl+h. In the following list, you can get an overview of the available information:

- *Ctrl+h*, *Ctrl+h* (describe help). This is the most important key binding for you to remember. This is the entrance to an index of all the key bindings.
- *Ctrl+h*, *f* (describe function). Given a function name, this gives you documentation about that function. (We have already seen numerous examples of this.)
- *Ctrl+h*, *v* (describe variable). Given a variable name, this function will describe the variable. Variables are used to configure how emacs works in different situations.
- *Ctrl+h*, *c* (describe key). With this function, you may find out what a given key does.

- *Ctrl+h*, *w* (where is command). When you have found a function that you like, you may want to find out whether it is bound to a key, and if, where. This function helps you with this task.

- *Ctrl+h*, *a* (apropos). This function proves very useful when you are searching for a function that will do a specific job. It enables you to type part of a command name, and then it will give you a list of all matches.

- *Ctrl+h*, *p* (find packages). This function enables you to search for packages and modes based on categories. This is a very good way to find enhancements to your emacs setup.

- *Ctrl+h*, *i* (load info). This loads the info pages. See the following section.

Info Pages

If you press Ctrl+h, i, you will get into a huge world of information, namely the *info pages*. The info pages are much like HTML pages used on the Web, with hyper-references between the different documents. If you start this journey by pressing the question mark key (?), you will get to a page that contains the key bindings in the info system. The following are the four most important ones:

- If you press Enter on top of a reference, you will get to the document it refers to. (References are bold face.) You can also follow a hyperlink by pressing the middle mouse button on top of the reference, if you have such a mouse.

- When you have followed a hyper-reference, you can go back to the document you came from by pressing *l*. (This is the alphabetic letter *el*.)

- The info pages are organized like a book, with sequential pages (in contrast to HTML documents, where there are several pages possible as the next page for a given one). This way, you can read the info pages one by one. You can go to the next page by pressing *n*, and to the previous one by pressing *p*.

- If you press *i*, you will be asked for a word to look up in the index of the given info page set. Next, the page that describes this word will be loaded.

Figure 20.4 shows an example of an info page. At the first line, you can see references to the previous page (in page order) and to the page above. Note that there is no *Next* page; this is the last one in the given section.

The text `Entering emacs` is a hypertext reference, which is highlighted because the mouse was placed over the text when the screenshot was done. At the bottom of the window are four references to subsections.

```
Buffers Files Tools Edit Search Help
File: emacs,  Node: Init File,  Prev: Syntax,  Up: Customization

The Init File, `~/.emacs'

   When Emacs is started, it normally loads a Lisp program from the file
`.emacs' in your home directory.  We call this file your "init file"
because it specifies how to initialize Emacs for you.  You can use the
command line switches `-q' and `-u' to tell Emacs whether to load an
init file, and which one (*note Entering Emacs::.).

   There can also be a "default init file", which is the library named
`default.el', found via the standard search path for libraries.  The
Emacs distribution contains no such library; your site may create one
for local customizations.  If this library exists, it is loaded
whenever you start Emacs (except when you specify `-q').  But your init
file, if any, is loaded first; if it sets `inhibit-default-init'
non-`nil', then `default' is not loaded.

   Your site may also have a "site startup file"; this is named
`site-start.el', if it exists.  Emacs loads this library before it
loads your init file.  To inhibit loading of this library, use the
option `-no-site-file'.

   If you have a large amount of code in your `.emacs' file, you should
move it into another file such as `~/SOMETHING.el', byte-compile it,
and make your `.emacs' file load it with `(load "~/SOMETHING")'.  *Note
Byte Compilation: (elisp)Byte Compilation, for more information about
compiling Emacs Lisp programs.

* Menu:

* Init Syntax::      Syntax of constants in Emacs Lisp.
* Init Examples::    How to do some things with an init file.
* Terminal Init::    Each terminal type can have an init file.
* Find Init::        How Emacs finds the init file.
--%%-Info: (emacs)Init File     (Info Narrow)--L1--All------------------
```

FIGURE 20.4
An info page.

Carrying on with emacs

On the Web, you can find a reference card for emacs at
`http://www.imada.ou.dk/Technical/Refcards/`, which may help you with all the different key bindings. I (Jesper K. Pedersen)

have written a program that I believe is very valuable for beginners to emacs. It is called The Dotfile Generator, and is a configuration tool that helps you set up many of emacs' variables. The Dotfile Generator can be downloaded from its home page, `http://www.imada.ou.dk/~blackie/dotfile`.

At `ftp://ftp.gnu.org/pub/gnu/` you can find two manuals about elisp: a reference manual called `elisp-manual` and an introduction called `emacs-lisp-introduction`. (The introduction is for newcomers to programming!)

Extra emacs Packages

You have already seen many of the features of emacs. However, one of its most powerful features is still to be explored. Namely, emacs has the capability to be extended with user code. In one of the earlier sections, you saw how you could save your key bindings and macros in the .emacs file from session to session. You can also write entirely new functions, which may be accessible using M+X and another bound key.

This capability is shared by users, literally. Many people have developed extra functions to be used with emacs, and many of these functions are already shipped along with emacs. On the Web, you can find over a thousand packages for use with emacs. Check out the following address: `ftp://archive.cis.ohio-state.edu/pub/gnu/emacs/elisp-archive`. These packages include major modes, minor modes, and a lot of user functions.

A List of Useful emacs Functions Not Mentioned in the Text

Table 20.1 lists emacs functions (very useful, I believe).

TABLE 20.1   **Useful emacs commands**

Function	Bound to Which Key	Description
downcase-word	M+l	Changes all the letters from the starting point to the end of the word to lowercase.
capitalize-word	M+c	Makes the first letter upper-case, with the rest of the word in lowercase.
upcase-word	M+u	Changes all the letters from the cursor point to end of the word to uppercase.
beginning-of-line	Ctrl+a	Moves the cursor point to the beginning of the line.
end-of-line	Ctrl+e	Moves the cursor point to the end of the line.
goto-line	unbound	Queries the user for a line number and goes to that line.
kill-line	Ctrl+k	Moves the text to the end of the line if the point isn't at the end of line; otherwise, removes the line break.
kill-buffer	Ctrl+x, k	Removes the current buffer.
TX fill-paragraph	M+q	Rearranges the given paragraph so that all lines will be filled up.

Communicating with Other Users and Systems

Accessing Other UNIX Systems by Modem

By James Edwards

Overview of modem communications

Controlling UNIX serial devices

Testing configurations with the cu program

Configuring dial-in and dial-out communications

Transferring files with the cu program

Transferring files and executing programs with uucp

Extending the network through the PPP

This chapter is concerned with the "how-to" of accessing other UNIX systems over modems. I will provide step-by-step instructions to guide you through the more common tasks associated with this form of intersystem communications.

But first, some basics need to be covered. Remember, UNIX is a multiuser operating environment, and as such, it needs to implement some fundamental controls over the available (and shared) system resources. Before you can successfully make use of these resources, you must have a basic understanding of how they have been configured.

This chapter starts with some basic concepts. We will begin by looking at some of the generic features and functionality of modem communications and some typical configuration requirements. After that, we will focus directly on how you need to configure your systems. We will finish up with some specifics as to how you can make use of these resources.

An Overview of Modem Communications

Modems are telephones for computers. Like any standard telephone, they can handle both incoming and outgoing data to and from any location. Modems speak their own language, which computers understand but humans don't. As such, when a modem dials a number, the call must be answered by another modem in order for any meaningful communication to occur. But telephones are like this too. After all, what would be the point of making a telephone call to somebody who doesn't speak the same language as you?

Once two modems are connected, it becomes possible to enable effective communication between the two remote hosts operating the modems. Typically, this communication enables such things as file and printer resource sharing and the execution of remote applications.

Figure 21.1 summarizes the events involved in establishing a connection between two remote hosts. This provides a useful guide for determining what devices are involved at each step of the connection process.

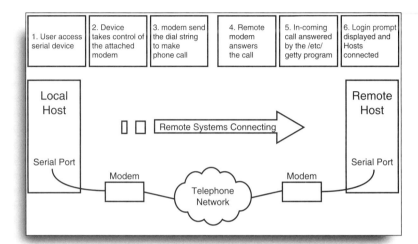

FIGURE 21.1

Connecting remote UNIX hosts.

UNIX Serial Devices

UNIX systems use special files known as *devices* to give users access to system hardware. These devices are commonly stored in the /dev subdirectory, with one or more files providing access to a specific piece of hardware.

The exact number and names of serial ports on any particular system depends on both the hardware configuration and the version of UNIX. Luckily, there are some common standard implementations we can refer to as a guide.

Typically, most hardware platforms have four serial ports, referred to as COM1, COM2, COM3, and COM4. The corresponding UNIX device files for these ports are commonly called /dev/ttyS0, /dev/ttyS1, /dev/ttyS2, and /dev/ttyS3. The exact names of these devices might vary slightly, depending on the flavor of UNIX you are running.

Thinking back to Figure 21.1, you will need to be able to configure UNIX to handle both dial-in and dial-out modem services. UNIX provides separate device files, depending on which service you want to use—and you should try to remember to use the right device. Devices providing dial-out devices are typically called /dev/cua1, /dev/cua2, /dev/cua3, and /dev/cua4. The corresponding /dev/ttyS1 through /dev/ttyS4 devices are normally reserved for dial-in purposes.

Because your modem is physically attached to a serial port, your only access to it is through the corresponding device file. It's important to understand which ports are configured and available on your UNIX system. The tasks outlined in the next section help you check which serial device drivers are present.

Checking Serial Device Files

It's important to know which devices are available on your UNIX system.

Finding the available serial devices

1. Type ls -1 /dev/ttyS? and press Enter.

2. A list of devices similar to the following appears:

```
crw--w--w-  1 root   root   4, 64 Mar 14 20:56
➥/dev/ttyS0

crw--w--w-  1 root   root   4, 65 Mar 14 20:56
➥/dev/ttyS1

crw--w--w-  1 root   root   4, 66 Mar 14 20:56
➥/dev/ttyS2

crw--w--w-  1 root   root   4, 67 Mar 14 20:56
➥/dev/ttyS3
```

3. Type ls -1 /dev/cua? and press Enter.

4. A list of devices similar to the following appears:

```
crw--w--w-  1 root   uucp   5, 64 Mar 14 20:56
➥/dev/cua0

crw--w--w-  1 root   uucp   5, 65 Mar 14 20:56
➥/dev/cua1

crw--w--w-  1 root   uucp   5, 66 Mar 14 20:56
➥/dev/cua2

crw--w--w-  1 root   uucp   5, 67 Mar 14 20:56
➥/dev/cua3
```

The exact names of these device files might be different, depending on the UNIX version and flavor. For example, under most SCO UNIX and Linux implementations, the serial device files for dial-out lines are called /dev/ttyna and are called /dev/ttynA for dial-in lines, where *n* represents the serial port number.

Serial Communication Configuration

Now that we have identified the devices that our UNIX hosts can make use of, we have some service configuration tasks to complete. These configuration tasks depend on whether we will be enabling dial-in or dial-out devices or a mixture of the two. One very important consideration is enabling effective access control. We need to ensure that once one user has grabbed a serial device, no other user can access that device until the connection has been dropped and the call has been completed.

Serial Communication Dial-In Configurations

When a user dials in to your host, you want to present him with the standard login prompt, giving him system access following the supply of a valid username and password. UNIX systems achieve this through the interaction of four separate programs—init, getty, login, and shell. Figure 21.2 illustrates the cyclical relationship that exists between these four programs.

The init process is the first real process to be run whenever you start the UNIX operating system. As such, it is an essential part of the operation of any UNIX system. UNIX relies on the init process to act as a launching pad for all other programs and to control all system devices. In reality, init is pretty dumb. It relies on a special configuration file called /etc/inittab to tell it what to do.

Listing 21.1 is an excerpt from the /etc/inittab file on my UNIX system. It serves as an example of how the init process exercises its power over the available serial devices.

FIGURE 21.2

The circle of serial device life:
init, getty, login, and shell.

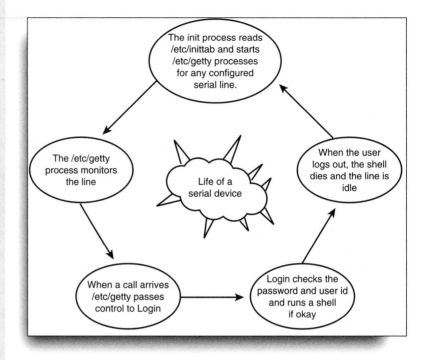

LISTING 21.1   A sample /etc/inittab file

```
# Serial lines
s1:45:respawn:/sbin/getty 19200 ttyS0
s2:45:respawn:/sbin/getty 19200 ttyS1
s3:45:respawn:/sbin/getty 19200 ttyS2
s4:45:respawn:/sbin/getty 19200 ttyS3
```

The syntax of any entry within the /etc/inittab file is fairly straightforward. Each entry consists of four distinct parts (*fields*) separated by a colon (:). The first field is called a *tag* and is simply an arbitrary value that provides an index within the /etc/inittab file. Listing 21.1 has separate tags labeled s1, s2, s3, and s4, each corresponding to the four available serial devices.

The second field tells the init process at which run level to execute that particular file entry. All the entries in Listing 21.1 are for run levels 4 and 5. The third field tells init what to do when the program indicated in the fourth field has finished. In Listing 21.1, this field contains the word "respawn," which means "restart the program after it terminates." The fourth field is the most interesting, because it contains the name of the program you want init to run. In our example, this is a program called /etc/getty. This program is run with two options. The first is the maximum bit rate of the attached modem, and the second is a serial device file /dev/ttyS1 through /dev/ttyS4.

/etc/getty is a monitoring program. It reads the file called /etc/gettydefs, which is used to store configuration settings for any attached modems, including such things as the modem's supported data rate, flow control, and parity settings. The /etc/getty process reads /etc/gettydefs and waits for the modem to receive a call. When an incoming call arrives, /etc/getty fires up a login process, displays a login prompt to the user who is dialing in, and then terminates.

Having init assign /etc/getty to any of your serial device files provides an effective method of servicing dial-in user requests. When a call has been completed, the shell program terminates, and the init process "respawns" another /etc/getty process to watch for the next incoming call. In this manner, the circle of life for your serial devices continues.

Serial Configuration for Dial-Out

To be able to dial out of your UNIX system, you need to be able to get control of a serial device from the /etc/getty process. This can be best achieved by editing the /etc/inittab entry for a particular serial device, changing the respawn setting in the third field to off:

```
S3:45:off:/etc/getty 19200 ttyS3
```

What if you want to make both outgoing and incoming calls? With the configuration just shown, you have no option but to install two modems and two telephone lines—one inbound and the other outbound. There is an alternative, however. It makes use of lock files that record when a serial device is in use, for either an inbound or outbound call, preventing any other access to that device until the call has been completed. This alternative approach uses a program called /etc/uugetty and its associated configuration file, /etc/conf.uugetty.

Configuring a single serial device for both inbound and outbound access

1. Edit the /etc/inittab file using the vi command by typing vi /etc/inittab and pressing Enter.

2. Scroll through /etc/inittab to locate the existing entry for the serial device controlling the attached modem.

3. Place a # character at the start of the line to comment out the entry. The resulting line should look like this:

   ```
   #s2:45:respawn:/etc/getty 19200 ttyS2
   ```

4. Enter o to start a new line using the vi editor, and then enter the following text:

   ```
   S2:456:respawn:/etc/uugetty ttyS2 19200
   ```

5. Save the /etc/inittab file and exit the vi program by pressing the Esc key and then Shift+ZZ.

6. After you have finished editing the /etc/inittab file, you need to instruct the init process to read your new configurations. To do this, enter the following command at the shell prompt:

   ```
   kill -HUP 1
   ```

The preceding procedure demonstrated how, through the use of the /etc/uugetty program, you can configure your UNIX system to accept and answer dial-in requests. It's important to note that, by running the /etc/uugetty program against any of your serial devices, that device will no longer be available for dialing out of your system. In the example, by running /etc/uugetty against the /dev/ttyS2 device, you effectively reserved that device to handle dial-in requests only. If you have only one modem and telephone line, handling both dial-in and dial-out requests could prove tricky.

All is not lost, however. UNIX provides another set of serial device files that you can use for dial-out purposes. Under Linux and SCO UNIX systems, these files are called /dev/cua#, where # refers to the port number. For example, in the preceding procedure, you configured the /dev/ttyS2 device to accept dial-in calls. To use the same modem and telephone line for dial-out requests, you could use the corresponding dial-out device,

/dev/cua2. As long as no one is dialing into the system at the same time, you can make an outbound call using the /dev/cua2 device and still leave /etc/uugetty free to monitor the connection for incoming calls.

Logging in Using the cu Program

Now that you have configured /etc/getty to watch for incoming calls, let's try to dial in to the system. Most flavors of UNIX provide a standard communication program called *cu*, which stands for "call UNIX." The cu program is very rudimentary and doesn't have all the bells and whistles associated with many commercially available communication packages. However, cu is fully functional. This section will explore how you can make use of this program to complete simple host-to-host communications. Administrators commonly reserve the use of the cu program as a troubleshooting tool, because it provides a simple and effective way to test the configuration of serial devices, control files, and modems.

Before we investigate the advanced features of cu, let's begin by checking your configurations.

Using cu to log in to another UNIX system

1. Start the cu program from the shell prompt by typing cu and pressing Enter. The program will return the following syntax statement:

```
Usage: cu [options] [system or phone number]
```

2. My modem is attached to my COM3 port, so I would need to instruct cu to use the device /dev/cua2. At the shell prompt, I would type cu -l /dev/cua2 to start cu using this serial device. You should type the same command, substituting the device name you are using.

3. If everything has been configured correctly, the cu program will echo the word Connected and will await further instructions. If cu echoes a message similar to this one, you have a problem:

```
cu: open (/dev/ttyS2): Permission denied
cu: /dev/ttyS2: line in use
```

Keep init informed

You can use any of the /dev/ttyS1 through /dev/ttyS4 devices, but if you do, you need to tell init not to run /etc/getty or /etc/uugetty against that device.

A message similar to this one means that something else is using that particular serial line. That something else is probably the init process, which will likely be running /etc/getty.

4. Open the /etc/inittab file using the vi program and ensure that the entry for that serial line has been commented out. Remember, if you change the /etc/inittab file, you will need to tell the init process to reread the file. This can be done in one of two ways: Either type `init q` and press Enter, or type `kill -HUP 1` and press Enter.

5. If the cu program responds by initially echoing `Connected` but then immediately echoes an error message stating `cu: Got hangup signal`, you are connecting to a serial line without a modem attached. Determine which line your modem is connected to and rerun cu using the correct device.

6. If you were successful in connecting cu to the modem, type `at`. You might not see the characters as you type them, but you should see the word `OK` echoed to your screen. This message comes from your modem, which is telling you that it is alive and working.

7. Type `ate1` and press Enter. The modem will echo `OK` to your screen. Now everything you type will be displayed.

8. Now let's try to connect to your remote host. Enter `atdt` followed by the telephone number of your remote host's modem. The modem will ignore any spaces. If you are dialing through a PBX, you might need to dial a 9 first in order to access an outside circuit. You can type a comma to indicate a pause, allowing the switch some additional time to allocate the circuit.

9. The modem will dial the number and connect to the remote modem. At the remote host, the /etc/getty or /etc/uugetty program will notice the incoming call and issue a login prompt that will be echoed to your screen. Log in using your username and password.

10. To disconnect, type `exit` to quit the remote shell program. Then enter ~. The system will respond by echoing the system name in parentheses. Ignore this and press ".". The cu program will echo `Disconnected` and return you to the shell prompt.

Configuring cu

It's possible to configure the cu program to place a call to a remote system without having to specify which particular device to use and without having to directly attach to the modem in order to dial the remote system's telephone number. In such a way, you can configure your system with one or more dial-out lines and ask the cu program to grab the first available line and automatically dial the telephone number you need.

The cu program uses four configuration files associated with the uucp suite of programs. These configuration files normally reside in the subdirectory /usr/lib/uucp/ and are called Devices, Dialers, Systems, and Permissions.

Change to the /usr/lib/uucp/ subdirectory and type `ls -l` to display the files within the subdirectory. Look for the presence of your uucp configuration files. If no files exist, you can create them from scratch. It is important to remember that these four configuration files are interrelated and must cross-reference each other in order to work successfully. The following procedure will walk you through a sample configuration of these files.

Configuring cu files

1. Enter `vi Devices` (note the capital D in the filename). In this file you need to define which serial ports you want to make available and set up references to these ports that can be used by the /usr/lib/uucp/Systems and /usr/lib/uucp/Dialers configuration files. The following code illustrates the syntax of entries within the Devices file:

```
# /usr/lib/uucp/Devices
#add a definition for each serial device that will be
➥used for dial out
modem   cua1    -    19200   hayes
modem   cua2    -    19200   hayes
modem   cua3    -    19200   hayes
modem   cua1    -    19200   hayes
```

Each line in the Devices file refers to a defined dial-out device within /dev. You identify the modem and the highest available modem speed, as well as a key word to identify the type of device attached to this port. Notice that all the entries use the same keyword, modem,. In this way, a dial-out request will be able to simply grab the first available port rather than waiting for a specific device to become free.

2. Enter a new line within the /usr/lib/uucp/Devices file by typing o and then modem device - 19200 hayes (replacing the word *device* with the name of your dial-out device file). Press Esc and then press Shift+ZZ to exit and save the /usr/lib/uucp/Devices file.

3. Now edit the /usr/lib/uucp/Dialers file by entering vi Dialers (again, note the uppercase D in the filename). In this file you need to define the initialization settings that you want the cu or uucp program to send the modem. Here's an example:

```
# /usr/lib/uucp/Dialers
#add a definition for each modem defined in the
➥Drivers file
hayes  =W-,    ""ATZ OK ATDT\T CONNECT
```

4. You need to make a reference to the hayes keyword you placed in the /usr/lib/uucp/Devices file. Enter a new line by pressing o and the enter the following line:

```
hayes  =W-,    "" ATZ OK ATDT\T CONNECT
```

The ATZ command resets the modem, with the expected return of OK from the modem. The ATDT command should be familiar from the section "Logging in Using the cu Program." The \T refers to the telephone number that is defined for the specified system and passed from the /usr/lib/uucp/Systems file.

5. Save and exit the /usr/lib/uucp/Dialers file by pressing Esc and then entering ZZ.

6. The /usr/lib/uucp/Systems file defines the name of the system to dial, the type of port that should be used, a schedule for allowing unattended connection (specifically, for uucp program use), the telephone number to dial, and some script commands to allow for automatic login once connected. Here's an example:

```
# /usr/lib/uucp/Systems
```

```
#add a definition for each remote system that users
➥will wish to access.
Horse MoTuWe0800-1700 modem 19200 123456 "" \n login:
➥-login: name word:pass
Jupiter Any modem 19200 123456 "" \n ogin:-ogin:
➥username word:password
Remote Any  modem 19200 12345678
```

7. Enter vi /usr/lib/uucp/Systems to edit this file. Press **o** to enter a new line, and type

```
remote  Any  modem  19200 12345678
```

This defines an entry for the cu program to use to connect to your remote UNIX system at any time of day, using any device of type modem, as indicated in the /usr/lib/uucp/ Devices file. In addition, you specify the bit rate at which to connect and the telephone number to dial. Save and exit the file by pressing Esc and zz.

8. On the remote UNIX system you need to configure the /usr/lib/uucp/Permissions file to enable yourself to remotely log in and to define given read and write privileges that you want to make available. Open or create the /usr/lib/uucp/ Permissions file, and add the following lines:

```
LOGNAME=local_machine MACHINE=local_machine
SENDFILES=yes
```

The /usr/lib/uucp/Permissions file is critical when you are allowing unattended uucp access to your UNIX host. In those circumstances, an entry for all hosts that you will allow access to should be defined within the file, and entries should be provided against the following keywords:

MACHINE	The system name
LOGNAME	The system name as it will appear in the logfiles
CALLBACK	A number to call back on once a connection has been made at a given number
REQUEST	Specifies whether a remote system can request files

SENDFILES	Specifies whether a remote system can send files
READ	Specifies which directories a remote system can read
WRITE	Specifies the directories a remote system can write to
COMMANDS	Specifies commands that uux can execute

9. Save the Permissions file and exit to the shell prompt by pressing Esc and then `ZZ`.

Using the cu Program

You can now make use of your new configuration files to improve the operation of the cu program. In addition, you can explore some other cu functionality, such as transferring files.

Using cu to transfer a file

1. Log in to UNIX and type `cu -z remote` (where *remote* is the system name you specified within the /usr/lib/uucp/Systems file). The cu program will automatically connect to the remote system and return the login prompt for your username and password.

2. Log in to the remote system. Then enter the command ~?. The cu program will display a list of available commands.

3. Enter `~%put` to transfer a file to the remote host.

4. The cu program will prompt you for the local file to transfer to the remote system. Enter a local filename.

5. The cu program will prompt you for the name to call the file once it has been transferred to the remote system. You can use the same name by simply pressing Enter.

6. The cu program will indicate when the transfer has been completed.

7. Enter ~. to disconnect and return to the shell prompt.

Listing 21.2 illustrates the execution of the preceding steps, showing the transfer of the file /home/report to a remotely attached system. Note that it is also possible to use other escape sequences to transfer files. Enter the ~? command to list the available commands within your own implementation of the cu program.

LISTING 21.2 Transferring a file using *cu*

```
~[local_host]?
[Escape sequences]
[~. hangup]                      [~!CMD run shell]
[~$CMD stdout to remote]         [~¦CMD stdin from remote]
[~+CMD stdin and stdout to remote]
[~# send break]                  [~cDIR change directory]
[~> send file]                   [~< receive file]
[~pFROM TO send to Unix]         [~tFROM TO receive from Unix]
[~sVAR VAL set variable]         [~sVAR set boolean]
[~s!VAR unset boolean]           [~v list variables]
[~z suspend]
[~%break send break]             [~%cd DIR change directory]
[~%put FROM TO send file]        [~%take FROM TO receive file]
[~%nostop no XON/XOFF]           [~%stop use XON/XOFF]
[connected]
~%put
file to send: /home/report
Remote file name [report]:
...
[file transfer complete]
[connected]
~.
Disconnected.
```

Running commands on the local system

1. Log in to UNIX and connect to a remote host using cu -z remote (where *remote* is the host name of the remote system you configured within the /usr/lib/uucp/Systems file). After you're connected to the remote host, log in with a valid userid and password.

2. Create a new file called /home/cu_remote_file on the remote host by typing vi /home/cu_remote_file at a shell

prompt. Press o and enter This is a test of the cu program. Press the Esc key and then ZZ to save the file and return to the shell prompt.

3. Enter the command sum cu_remote_file. The sum program will output two numbers: a 16-bit checksum of the file cu_remote_file, and an approximation of the size of the file. Write down both of these values.

4. Enter ~%take /home/cu_remote_file /home/cu_local_file to transfer the file to the local UNIX host, and save it using the same filename.

   When cu indicates that the transfer is complete, you can check that the file has been transferred without errors by running the sum command on the transferred copy of the file.

5. Enter ~! /bin/sh to run a shell on the local system from within the cu program. At the shell prompt, type sum cu_local_file and then press Enter. As before, the sum program will output two numbers. Check these against those generated in step 3. If the transfer occurred with no errors, these numbers will be the same.

6. Type exit to return to the cu program. Log out of your remote connection and press ~. to exit the cu program.

After you have configured your files for cu operation, you can also run uucp commands.

Transferring Files Via uucp

UUCP stands for UNIX-to-UNIX Copy Program. It is not just one program, but a suite of utilities that provide a way to transfer files and execute applications across physically distributed UNIX platforms. The uucp suite is most often employed for unattended file transfers—particularly for the moving of email between systems. However, it is possible for users to use these programs for their own file transfer requirements.

Creating a file transfer program

1. Log in to UNIX and create a test file called uucp_data.

2. At the shell prompt, enter
    ```
    uucp uucp_data remote\!/home/uucp_data
    ```

3. Use vi to edit the /usr/lib/uucp/Systems file and add the following command to the entry you created for the host remote. After the telephone number, add the following test:
    ```
    " "" \r gin:-gin: <userid> word: <password>
    ```

    Replace <userid> and <password> with a valid username and password on host remote.

4. The uucp command will reference the /usr/lib/uucp/ Systems file and locate the entry for host remote. When it finds the reference, a connection will be made to the remote host, and uucp will automatically log in using the username and password pair specified. Once login is complete, the file uucp_data will be transferred, and uucp will terminate the connection.

5. The uucp program expects a number of parameters that offer useful additional functionality. It is possible to use th -m switch to force the system to return an email informing you when a transfer has been completed. Enter the following command at the shell prompt:
    ```
    uucp -m uucp_data remote\!/home/uucp_data
    ```

    and then press Enter.

6. Similarly, if you were copying a file to a remote system, you might want to inform a user on that system when the file arrives. You can do this through the -n switch. Use the following command to send an email to user Lauren located on the remote system when the file transfer has been completed:
    ```
    uucp -nlauren uucp_data remote\!/home/uucp_data
    ```

Restrict where users place files

The /usr/lib/uucp/Permissions file needs to be edited to allow you to transfer your file to the specified location. In the preceding example, that was the case. However, it's good practice to restrict where on the remote system users are allowed to place files. Normally this will be /usr/spool/uucp or /usr/spool/uucppublic.

Running Remote Commands

The uux program is part of the uucp suite. It allows users with the proper permission to execute commands on remote UNIX hosts. Again, the execution of this command is controlled via the /usr/lib/uucp/Permissions file.

Running remote commands

1. Log in to UNIX and issue the command uux remote\!date.

2. The program will execute the date command on the remote host and return the result to your shell.

Typically, the uux command will not be executed directly by users but will be used as part of applications such as email and network news servers. For this reason, most systems will limit execution of rmail and rnews programs within the /usr/lib/uucp/Permissions file.

Checking on the Status of uucp Tasks

Users can check the status of any outstanding uucp file transfer request through the use of the uustat program.

Running uustat

1. Log in to UNIX, and at the shell prompt, type uustat.

2. A list of currently queued jobs will be displayed. Here's an example:
   ```
   jupiter  02/14 - 20:45:00 (POLL)
   mars     02/14 - 20:53 S jupiter filename.txt 48871
   ➥/home/james/docs/sams/uucp/filename.txt
   catfish  02/23 - 10:25:00 (POLL)
   ```

3. By default, uustat will display only those jobs queued by the user issuing the uustat command. To display all the jobs currently scheduled, type uustat -all.

You can run the uustat program with some optional parameters to find out additional information about the performance of the individual uucp programs.

Running uustat with parameters

1. Type uustat -e and press Enter. This will provide a list of all currently queued program execution requests.

2. Type uustat -m and press Enter. This command will generate a summary of the status of making connections to remote hosts. Here's an example:

```
remote          05/23 - 10:15      CALLER SCRIPT FAILED
dtcg02          05/30 - 11:30      LOGIN FAILED
jupiter          05/30 - 11:30     CONN FAILED (CALLER
➡SCRIPT FAILED)
```

The preceding code illustrates failed uucp connections to three hosts; remote, dtcg02, and jupiter.

Canceling a uucp Request

You can use the uustat program to cancel an outstanding uucp file transfer or program execution request.

Using uustat to cancel a uucp request

1. Log in to UNIX. At the shell prompt, edit the /usr/lib/uucp/Systems file by typing
```
vi /usr/lib/uucp/Systems
```

2. Press the o key to add a new line, and then type the following text:
```
nohost Never modem 19200 123456
```

This defines a new system called nohost that will never be called by the uucp programs.

3. Put a message into the uucp queue by issuing a transfer request to nohost that you know will never be sent. Enter the following and then press Enter:
```
uucp /home/uucp_data nohost\!/home/uucp_data
```

4. Type uustat. You will see a code line similar to the following:
```
nohostN001 nohost root 03-15 02:25 Sending
➡/home/uucp_data (1864 bytes) to /home/uucp_data
```

Watch Caps Lock when canceling with uustat

The command uustat -K (with an uppercase K) will remove all currently queued uucp requests. When canceling jobs with uustat, make sure that the Caps Lock key hasn't been accidentally set.

5. To remove the transfer request, enter the following command:

```
uustat -k nohostN001
```

Extending the Network by Modem (PPP)

Point-to-point protocol (PPP) provides a way to transmit IP packets over a modem-to-modem connection. A PPP connection between two remote UNIX hosts provides a way for all remote users and applications to access one another over a single modem link rather than restricting communication to individual users at any one time.

In such a way, it is possible to use PPP to extend a network such that remote hosts can interoperate as if they were located on the same local LAN. However, it should be noted that the speed of communication between two systems connected over a dial-up line will be an order of magnitude slower than if they were connected by a LAN.

Configuring a Simple PPP Connection

There are three distinct parts to configuring the operation of PPP upon any UNIX host: creating a PPP user account on the remote system (on the system accepting the incoming call), developing the Chat script, and executing the PPP daemon. Let's examine each in turn.

Creating a PPP user account

1. It is advisable to set up and dedicate a special user account to controlling the execution of the PPP. Log in to UNIX as the root user on the remote system and create a new account. Then edit the /etc/passwd file such that it looks similar to the following:

```
ppp_user:e9prWE5B4fs:501:202:ppp execution account:
➥/tmp:/usr/lib/ppp/ppp-on
```

It should be noted that the GID and UID values will be system-specific, as will the password you create in the second field. The startup program is indicated as being the file /usr/lib/ppp/ppp-on, which is a configuration script that will turn ppp services on.

2. Before you can turn on PPP services, you need to establish connectivity between your modems. This is similar to when you were looking at logging in remotely using the cu program: Before you could enter a username and password on the remote system, you had to connect to get the local modem to dial the telephone number of the remote host. The chat program gives you an effective way to do this for PPP.

   Enter the following to create a new PPP chat script:
   ```
   vi /usr/lib/ppp/ppp-chat
   ```

   and then press Enter.

3. Enter o to add the following line, substituting the correct username (typically ppp or ppp_user), password, and telephone number for your system:
   ```
   ATZ OK ATDT12345678 CONNECT ogin: ppp word: <password>
   ```

   Notice that the syntax employed by the chat program is very similar to the entries you made within the /usr/lib/uucp/ Systems configuration files. The first entry resets the modem, and the modem sends out an OK. Then the chat script dials the telephone number of your remote host. Once the CONNECT message and login prompt have been received, the chat script sends the username and again the password at the subsequent password prompt.

   Save and exit the new /usr/lib/ppp/ppp-chat file by pressing Esc and then zz.

4. Create the shell script that will start the PPP connection by entering the following command:
   ```
   vi /usr/lib/ppp/ppp-on
   ```

   and edit the file to contain the following entries:
   ```
   #!/bin/sh
   #script to activate ppp connection
   pppd connect "chat -f /usr/lib/ppp/ppp-chat"
   ➥/dev/cua2 19200
   ➥-detach 130.100.0.5:130.200.0.20 defaultroute
   ```

Notice that in this example I have set the dial-out device for PPP to be /dev/cua2 and the local and remote IP addresses as 130.100.0.5 and 130.200.0.20. You should amend this to reflect your system's configuration. When you have finished, press the Esc key and then ZZ to save the file and return to the shell prompt.

5. You need to set permissions on this file to allow the root user to execute the script and activate the PPP connection. To do this, enter

```
chmod 744 /usr/lib/ppp/ppp-on
```

6. Establish the PPP link by running the shell script.

Stopping the PPP Connection

Removing an existing PPP connection is achieved by sending a hangup signal to the pppd process ID (PID).

The pppd process will store its PID in the device lock file it creates in the subdirectory /var/lock. This file will have a name relating to the serial device name. For my PPP configuration, I used the serial device /dev/cua2, so my lock file is called /var/lock/LCK..cua2.

Removing a PPP connection

1. Log in to UNIX as the root user and enter cat /var/lock/ LCK..cua2. This will echo to the screen a number that is the PID of the pppd currently using the /dev/cua2 serial device.

2. Tell the pppd to terminate by sending it the hangup signal using the kill command kill -HUP PID, where *PID* is the number returned in step 1.

A Final Note

This chapter explained how you can gain access to the modems connected to your UNIX system. However, it is worth remembering that among the many flavors of UNIX, the filenames of some system devices might have some slight differences.

Note

Many flavors of UNIX provide basic shell scripts to turn PPP connections on and off. Although these files are commonly called ppp-on and ppp-off, their directory location can vary considerably between UNIX flavors. Type find / -name ppp-o* -print in order to locate these files on your system, and then press Enter.

It should be noted that over the past few years, other more efficient and effective methods for transferring files between UNIX hosts have steadily replaced the use of UUCP. It would be fair to say that it has become fairly uncommon to find a UNIX host that relies on UUCP as a file-transfer mechanism. Much of the downfall of UUCP can be attributed to the increased adoption of the use of the Sendmail program to transfer email messages. But the increased ubiquity of the hosts being permanently connected to the Internet hasn't helped its cause. If hosts are to be continuously connected through the Internet, there is value in adopting a batched file transfer method.

In part, UUCP's loss has been PPP's gain, with the adoption of PPP-enabled connections as the favored way of providing connectivity to the Internet. This chapter illustrated how you might configure a UNIX host in order to establish an ephemeral PPP connection. However, it should be noted that most PPP connections are established as permanent connections and that the ppp-off script is never run.

Accessing Other UNIX Systems on the Network or Internet

By James Edwards

The TCP/IP suite of protocols is at the very heart of networking UNIX systems. This chapter addresses the operation of these protocols. Although this one chapter won't turn you into a TCP/IP guru, you will get sufficient information and guidance that will enable you to sufficiently use the protocols and connect into a network.

Some Important Networking Concepts

Before you begin, you need to cover some basics. Networking involves a number of hardware and software components that need to be installed and configured. Figure 22.1 provides a useful starting point, illustrating how these components fit together to provide network connectivity.

FIGURE 22.1

Components of network connectivity.

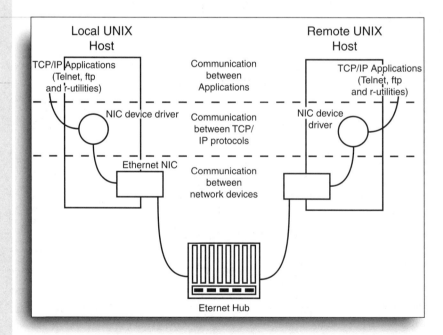

Figure 22.1 illustrates a UNIX host connecting to an Ethernet network and using the TCP/IP protocols to communicate with a neighboring host. How does all this fit together? Well, the Ethernet network provides us with a foundation for

communication—a way for our hosts to be physically connected. After our hosts are connected, they can communicate; through the TCP/IP protocols. These protocols provide the hosts with a way to "do things" to each other such as execute remote programs, share resources, and transfer files.

Ethernet is by far the most common form of physical network transport. Other forms do exist, however, including token ring, FDDI, and Asynchronous Transfer Mode (ATM), some of which may sound familiar. Although each of these network types employ distinct features and functionality, and all require very different configuration, some similarities do exist. In fact, the same general connectivity components outlined in Figure 22.1 hold true across all these physical network types. This chapter examines Ethernet in detail because it is the most likely network form you will need to interface with.

Checking Your Network Connections

You begin by physically attaching your system to the network. This is accomplished through the use of a network interface card, or NIC (pronounced *nick*). The NIC will need to be physically installed within your UNIX system. A number of connection points off the system's motherboard—referred to as *slots*—are specifically reserved for the purpose. In fact, many UNIX systems are commonly shipped from the manufacturer with a NIC already installed.

After the NIC has been physically installed within your system, you need to "tell" UNIX how to identify and communicate with it. In UNIX, all communication to system hardware is handled through special files called devices. These devices need to be configured within the UNIX kernel. Therefore when you add a new NIC, you need to ensure that a corresponding device file has been made available to the kernel.

More often than not, your system will automatically detect the existence and current configuration of an installed NIC upon system boot. With some UNIX flavors, however, it is necessary to run a standard configuration program to tell the system about a freshly added NIC and how to communicate with it.

The configuration program that you will need to run depends on the flavor of UNIX that you are using. These programs are more often than not menu-driven and guide the user through the configuration of a new device.

A relatively simple way to ensure that a new device entry has been recognized by the UNIX kernel is to look at the messages displayed as the system boots. The following tasks illustrate how this might be achieved on a PC-based UNIX system.

As any UNIX system boots, it echoes device configuration and initialization messages to the console. These messages may flash by quickly, making examination very difficult. Thankfully, however, these messages are also written to a special log that can be displayed using the dmesg command.

1. Type the command dmesg | more and look for references to the Ethernet devices.

2. Depending on your system's boot process, it is possible that the dmesg is too big and unwieldy to leaf through looking for a reference to an Ethernet driver.

   If so, type dmesg | grep eth to pinpoint any defined device. Listing 22.1 illustrates the result of this command on my dmesg file.

LISTING 22.1   Searching for an Ethernet card

```
# dmesg | grep eth
eth0: WD80x3 at 0x300, 00 00 C0 FE 55 28, IRQ 5, 0xca000
#
```

3. The output from dmesg displays the current configuration of the installed NIC. In the Listing 22.1 example, the UNIX device eth0 corresponds to the NIC installed using IRQ 5, at memory address ca000 and using I/O channel 300. These values were the default ones the manufacturer provided. If I want to change any of these values, I must follow the NIC manufacturer's instructions for doing so.

4. Now that you know how the UNIX system refers to the installed NIC, you can configure it for operation—through the use of the interface configuration program called ifconfig (pronounced *i f config*). Many, but not all, flavors of UNIX provide us with a way to confirm the presence of a defined device through the netstat command. Type netstat -i and press Enter. This command displays the status of all system interfaces—any unconfigured interfaces will have an asterisk next to their device name.

Checking IP Addresses

Each NIC needs to be allocated a unique address for the TCP/IP protocols to work. An assigned IP address is taken from an available 32-bit binary address space. For simplicity and ease of use, however, you can reference this address space using a concept referred to as Decimal Dot Notation.

The operation of Decimal Dot Notation calls for a 32-bit IP address to be divided into four equal parts, each part being 8 bits long. Each of these 8-bit values can then be represented as a decimal number value, with each decimal number separated from the next by a "dot." Listing 22.2 illustrates this point; notice how it becomes far easier to refer to an address as it is divided and then represented as decimal numbers.

LISTING 22.2   Representing binary IP addresses through decimal dot notation

```
00000110000000110000000010000000001       - 32 bit binary value
00000110 00000110 00000010 00000001       - Divided into 4 equal parts
10      .   10   .    2   .    1  - Represent each as a decima value
```

Remember that you use TCP/IP protocols to move data between different hosts within networks. To successfully achieve this, each host needs a unique IP addresses. In fact, a network host can have more than one IP address—one for each NIC installed. You can use a standard program called ifconfig to assign an IP address to NIC. The following task list provides a quick example:

1. Log on to UNIX as root (only the root user can execute the `ifconfig` command).

2. Type the following commands at the com mand line: `ifconfig eth0 130.100.10.1`, replacing the entry `eth0` with the installed and configured NIC device name and `130.100.10.1` with the IP address that you want to assign to this interface.

3. You can also run the `ifconfig` command to report the configuration of any installed interface. To do this, type `ifconfig -a`.

The use of the `-a` switch tells `ifconfig` to report the configuration for all installed interfaces. Listing 22.3 provides an example.

LISTING 22.3 *ifconfig* **configuration details**

```
#ifconfig -a
le0:flags=63<UP, BROADCAST, NOTRAILERS, RUNNING>
    inet 10.252.10.66 netmask ffffffe0 broadcast 10.252.10.95
eth0: flags=63<UP, BROADCAST, NOTRAILERS, RUNNING>
    inet  130.100.10.1  netmask  ffff0000 broadcast  130.100.255.255
eth1: flags=63<UP, BROADCAST, NOTRAILERS, RUNNING>
    inet  10.252.10.33  netmask  ffffffe0 broadcast  10.252.10.63
```

Notice in Listing 22.3 that `ifconfig` reports back that interface `eth0` has an IP address of `130.100.10.1` and a netmask value of `130.100.255.255`. To understand IP addresses, you need to be aware that the address identifies both a host address and a network address. The `netmask` value is used to tell UNIX which part of the IP address is the host part and which is the network part.

A `netmask` is constructed to cover the network part of the address with binary 1s, which equals a value of 255 for each of the decimal numbers within our Decimal Dot Notation. If we apply the provided netmask value to any IP address, it will reveal both the host and network portion of an address. The following example in Listing 22.4 provides an example of how a mask might be used.

LISTING 22.4   Examining the netmask value

```
00000110 00000110 00000010 00000001   - Divided into 4 equal parts
   10  .   10   .   2  .   1       - Represent each as a decimal value

  255  .  255   .   0  .   0       - the decimal mask value
11111111 11111111 00000000 00000000   - the binary mask value

masked  . masked .   2  .   1       - the mask covers the first two decimal
                                     numbers leaving the host address

  10   .   10   .  host.  host    - the mask covers the network
                                     portion of our address
```

Overall, the IP address space is divided into three main groups, referred to as address classes. Each of these classes provides an address space that is suited to a specific type of network. Table 22.1 details the break down of these classes, indicating the address range and the typical network use.

TABLE 22.1   Understanding the entire IP address space

Address Classes	Address Range	Default Mask	Typical Use and Function
Class A	1.0.0.0 127.255.255. 255	255.0.0.0	Class A addresses contain a small number of network addresses, but each network can address more than 16 million hosts.
Class B	128.0.0.0 191.255.255. 255	255.255.0.0	The Class B address space provides for a large number of medium-size networks that each contain over 64 thousand hosts each.
Class C	192.0.0.0 223.255.255. 255	255.255.255.0	The Class C address space provides for millions of small-scale networks each holding a maximum of 254 hosts in each network.
			The address space above the Class C limit of 223.255.255.255 is reserved and should be ignored.

Table 22.1 indicates that you can tell the class that an IP address belongs to just by looking at the first decimal number of the address; by using the default mask value, you can automatically determine both the network number and the host address.

When you configure IP addresses, you can optionally use the default mask value or alternatively specify your own mask, enabling the capability to refer to more networks, each containing fewer hosts. These additional networks are referred to as subnetworks because they are a subset of the address class, and the netmask is now referred to as a subnet mask. You can use the ifconfig program to define subnet mask values.

1. Log on to UNIX as the root administrator. Type ifconfig a to report the current configuration of all the interfaces installed in your system. Select one interface. I will use the interface eth0. You should substitute references to that interface with your own.

2. Type ifconfig eth0 130.100.10.1, and then press Enter.

3. Type ifconfig eth0 and notice that the netmask value is set to the Class B default of 255.255.0.0 or, if your system displays this only in hexadecimal, ffffffff0000.

4. Type ifconfig eth0 130.100.10.1 netmask 255.255.255.0, and then press Enter.

5. Type ifconfig eth0 and now notice that the netmask value is set to a value of 255.255.255.0 or, if your system displays this only in hexadecimal, ffffffffffff00.

The ifconfig program has a number of additional options that enable a user to make changes to the way the TCP/IP protocols operate over a given interface. The details of these settings are beyond the scope of this chapter. For a more detailed breakdown of functions, refer to the UNIX man pages. Before leaving the ifconfig program, it is useful to make one last change: to set the broadcast value.

In the development of TCP/IP protocols, two schools of thought developed relating to how an interface should send a packet to all the hosts on any network. Remember from our discussion, an IP address consists of both a host and network portion. Both approaches agreed that the network portion of the IP address would need to be identified, but one approach decided that all hosts within this network would be identified using all 1s in the host portion of the address while the other specified all 0s. Over time the all-1s broadcast won dominance. By far it is now the most commonly found setting; because the option exists, however, it is important that you check your interface configurations to ensure that you are using the correct setting.

Make a task list to illustrate the use of the ifconfig program to report interface configuration and note broadcast of all 0s and then to change this to all 1s. The list also illustrates the complete use of the ifconfig command to include the IP address, the subnet mask, and the broadcast address.

1. Log on to UNIX as the root administrator, and type the following command (substituting the specified values to match your own configurations and address requirements): ifconfig eth0 130.100.10.1 netmask 255.255.255.0 broadcast 130.100.10.0. Then press Enter.

2. Type ifconfig eth0 and notice that the broadcast address for this interface has been set to 130.100.10.0.

3. Now configure the interface for an all-1s broadcast (remember that this is the most commonly used setting). To do this, type the following commands: ifconfig eth0 130.100.10.1 netmask 255.255.255.0 broadcast 130.100.10.255, and then press Enter.

4. Type ifconfig eth0 and notice that the broadcast address for this interface has been set to 130.100.10.255.

Naming a UNIX Host

Referring to UNIX hosts through IP addresses can and will prove to be somewhat cumbersome; you can make things easier by giving your host a name. To do this, you provide an entry in the hosts /etc/hosts file:

1. Log on to UNIX as the root administrator (changing the hostname is one of those things that only root can do).

2. The /etc/hosts file is used to associate a hostname with the IP address of our system. When we refer to this hostname, the system will reference the /etc/hosts file to determine the corresponding IP address. The /etc/hosts file can be extended to include references to other hosts that we need access to.

3. Now edit the /etc/hosts file. Type in the following commands: vi /etc/hosts, and then press Enter. Listing 22.5 provides an example of a /etc/hosts file. Notice how entries are arranged within this file.

4. Each line in the /etc/hosts file provides a hostname to IP address mapping. Multiple hostnames, known as aliases, can be provided to any individual IP address. Press o to add a new line to the /etc/hosts file. Enter the IP address of one of the interfaces in your host, press the Tab key and enter a hostname.

5. In the example outlined in Listing 22.5, I added a host entry for IP address 130.100.50.1 of fin.sales.catfish.com. Save and exit the /etc/hosts file by pressing the Esc key and then Shift ZZ.

Listing 22.5 provides a sample of a /etc/hosts file. Each entry relates an IP address to a given hostname.

LISTING 22.5   Example */etc/hosts* file

```
#
# include and entry for the loopback interface
127.0.0.1                   localhost

# include entries for host machines here
# IP address              hostname               alternative names
#
130.100.10.1              www.catfish.com        web
130.100.10.10             man.catfish.com        manhost       loghost
130.100.50.1              fin.sales.catfish.com
10.10.4.2                 mars.catfish.com       mars
#
# corporate nameserver
10.193.10.1               dns.catfish.com        dns           namessrv
```

Notice in Listing 22.5 that the entry for IP address `130.100.10.1` contained two hostname entries: `www.catfish.com` and `web`. It is possible to associate multiple names to the same IP address; these alternative names are referred to as aliases. Let's edit our `/etc/hosts` file and add an alias to this file. In my example, I will add alias to the host `130.100.50.1` currently called `fin.sales.catfish.com`.

1. Log on to UNIX as root and type the command `vi /etc/hosts`. Then press Enter.

2. Scroll down to the line you need to add an entry for within the `/etc/hosts` file. You can either do this by pressing the *j* key or the down-arrow key. In my example, I move down to the 130.100.50.1 entry, and move to the end of the line.

3. Press *a* to add to this line, and add the new alias. Type the new hostname `accounts`.

Testing a Connection with Ping

The `ping` program is easily the most commonly used utility within TCP/IP networks. The `ping` program is used to test network connectivity between hosts. This is accomplished through the operation of something called the Internet Control Message Protocol—or more simply, ICMP.

The `ping` program works by sending an ICMP `ECHO REQUEST` packet to a remote host. When this host receives the packet, it will return an ICMP `ECHO_RESPONSE` packet. In such a way, we can use the `ping` utility for two purposes: to confirm the end-to-end connectivity between hosts, and to provide a measure of the round trip delay or how quickly we can reach any remote host.

1. Log on to UNIX. It doesn't have to be as the root account—anyone can run the `ping` command.

2. Let's ping the new interface we just added. Type in the following commands (replacing my IP address for the one you used): `ping 130.100.10.1`, and then press Enter. The `ping` command should respond with output similar to that in Listing 22.6.

LISTING 22.6   An example of the *ping* program

```
#   ping 130.100.10.1

ping   130.100.10.1(130.100.10.1):   56 data bytes
64 bytes from 130.100.10.1: icmp_seq=0. ttl=252 time=215. ms
64 bytes from 130.100.10.1: icmp_seq=1. ttl=252 time=216. ms
64 bytes from 130.100.10.1: icmp_seq=2. ttl=252 time=217. ms
64 bytes from 130.100.10.1: icmp_seq=3. ttl=252 time=216. ms
64 bytes from 130.100.10.1: icmp_seq=4. ttl=252 time=216. ms
^c
---PING STATISTICS-------------------------------
5 packets transmitted, 5 packets received, 0% packet loss
round-trip min/avg/max = 215/216/217
#
#
```

Depending on the UNIX version, aix, sco, and linux all
work as in Listing 22.6. In addition, TCP/IP implementation on other PC OS works in this manner. However, the
version of ping found with Solaris works as you outline. (I
address this fact in the note that follows the task list.)

3. Listing 22.6 illustrates the use of ping being used to test the
connectivity to the IP address 130.100.10.1.

4. It is possible to instruct ping as to how many ICMP packets
it should send to the remote destination; in our examples,
we didn't indicate any amounts, so the command needed to
be terminated with a control-break. By default, a data packet
is 56 bytes in length; to this is added an 8-byte ICMP header. The remote host returns ECHO_RESPONSE packets. For each
of these packets, the ping utility will display an increasing
sequence number, a time-to-live (ttl) value (which is decre-
mented for every gateway the packet passes through), and a
round trip delay recorded in milliseconds.

5. It is also possible to specify a hostname rather than an IP
address. If this is done, ping will need to first look up the
hostname before executing the connectivity test. Type in the
following command: ping mars.catfish.com, and then press
Enter.

LISTING 22.7   Another example of the *ping* program

```
#  ping mars.catfish.com

ping  mars.catfish.com(130.100.10.1) :  56 data bytes
64 bytes from 130.100.10.1: icmp_seq=0. ttl=252 time=215. ms
64 bytes from 130.100.10.1: icmp_seq=1. ttl=252 time=216. ms
64 bytes from 130.100.10.1: icmp_seq=2. ttl=252 time=217. ms
64 bytes from 130.100.10.1: icmp_seq=3. ttl=252 time=216. ms
64 bytes from 130.100.10.1: icmp_seq=4. ttl=252 time=216. ms
^c
---PING STATISTICS-----------------------------
5 packets transmitted, 5 packets received, 0% packet loss
round-trip min/avg/max = 215/216/217
#
#
```

Checking Whether Domain Name Services Are Running

In the preceding section, I outlined the operation of the /etc/hosts file and indicated how this file provides a convenient way to map between IP addresses and hostnames. One of the limitations of using the /etc/hosts file is that you need to ensure that all hosts within the network have the same address mappings. This obviously raises some potentially huge maintenance issues as the number of hosts of our networks increase. More importantly, imagine how ineffective Internet access would be if we had to create an entry in our /etc/hosts file containing the IP addresses of any host we wanted to access!

Obviously, an alternative approach is called for. That alternative is the domain name system—or, more simply, DNS. The DNS provides hostname-to-IP-address mapping through a collection of hierarchical databases.

With the aid of DNS, it is possible to query a single host, the domain name server, and locate any networked host. Now a domain name server will track IP addresses and hostnames within its own network, but will know how to and where to forward requests for hostnames outside of its own network or domain. In such a way it becomes possible for us to locate and maintain the

Note

The implementation of the ping program can differ somewhat between UNIX implementations, requiring different switch settings to be used to enable certain functionality. If you type ping mars.catfish.com on a Sun workstation, for example, you would expect the response mars.catfish. com is alive. If you wanted to obtain similar statistics as displayed in Listings 22.6 and 22.7, you would need to use the -s switch and specify both the packet data size and the number of ECHO_REQUEST packets that you wanted to send. The command ping -s mars.catfish.com 56 5, for example, would tell ping to send 56 bytes of data in five separate request packets to the remote host mars.catfish.com.

IP-to-hostname mappings of all network hosts—even one as large as the Internet.

So, two questions: 1. How do we know whether our host has been configured to use DNS, and 2. How do we tell our TCP/IP programs to access this configuration? Well, all TCP/IP programs will in fact function if they are supplied with either an IP address or alternatively a hostname. If a hostname is supplied, however, the program will first need to resolve that name into the host's IP address. This resolution process is standard—first a check to find a local DNS configuration file is made; if this fails, the program will try to find a matching entry in the /etc/hosts file; and if this fails, it will post the error message unknown host.

1. Create a resolver file on your UNIX host. Type vi /etc/resolv.conf, and then press Enter. If a resolv.conf file didn't already exist, one will be created when you use vi.

2. Press the *o* key to start a new line, and type domain catfish.com. Then press Enter.

3. You need to include the IP address of the DNS server within your configuration file. To do this, type in the keyword nameserver followed by a space and the IP address of the your network's DNS server. Save the file and exit the vi program by pressing the Esc followed by Shift ZZ.

4. Listing 22.8 illustrates my /etc/resolv.conf file, which includes references for two DNS servers—a primary and a secondary, or backup, server.

LISTING 22.8   An example */etc/resolv.conf* file

```
#   /etc/resolv.conf
#
#   default domain setting
domain              catfish.com

#available nameservers, primary and secondary
nameserver          130.100.10.10
nameserver          130.100.20.50
#
#   end of file
```

5. Now you have completed your resolver configuration; let's test it out. Run the `ping` program. Instead of specifying an IP address, however, enter a hostname. For example, `telnet www.catfish.com`.

6. If everything works, the `catfish.com` Web server should respond to the ping request.

Checking Whether You Are Connected to the Internet

Many companies will connect their networks to the Internet. This means that after you are able to access your local network hosts you may, by default, also be able to access the entire Internet.

Use could use the `ping` program to check whether you have Internet access. Type in `ping ds.internic.com`. If you get a response, you are connected!

If you still cannot access the Internet, the reason might be because you need to gain access through a proxy service. A *proxy* provides application services on behalf of a user by a secured third party. This third party is called a proxy server and is often, but not always, integrated within the Internet firewall server. The use of a proxy means that individual users are shielded from having to conduct direct communication with external devices, which increases network security.

If your site is using proxies, you need to ensure your application programs—Telnet, FTP, and Web browser—have been configured to use the proxy service. This configuration involves entering the IP address of the host running the proxy, as well as the port number the application is running on. Figure 22.2 illustrates the configuration of proxy servers and ports for my Web browser program.

Note

Importantly, the `ping` program does not always accurately reflect whether you have Internet connectivity. This is because some companies restrict the type of application traffic that they allow in from the Internet. If your `ping` program failed with an error message of `host unreachable`, try connecting to a major Internet site using your Web browser.

FIGURE 22.2

Configuring a Web browser for using proxy services.

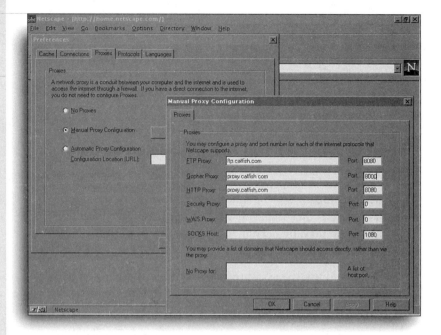

Logging on to UNIX over the Network

After connectivity has been established, you can start to execute some applications over the network. The following section examines the execution of a number of application programs, illustrating what functionality can be achieved.

Using Telnet to Log On

1. The Telnet program provides us with the ability to log on and access resources on a remote host. The Telnet program takes the remote hostname or IP address as an argument and will attempt to open a connection to the specified host. Type in the following commands, replacing the specified host-name with the name of your own host: Telnet www.catfish.com. Then press Enter.

2. The Telnet program will first try to resolve the hostname www.catfish.com. Notice in Listing 22.9 how it does this and then uses the IP address to connect to the remote server. Once connected, a logon prompt displays.

LISTING 22.9 An example Telnet connection

```
#
# telnet www.catfish.com.
Trying 130.100.10.1…
Connected to www.catfish.com.
Escape character is '^]'.


(www.catfish.com.) (ttyp12)


login:
```

3. Log on to the remote host by entering a valid username and password. Once logged on, type who to see who else is logged on to this host. To exit, type exit and press Enter.

4. The Telnet program can work in Interactive mode as well. To demonstrate this, type Telnet and then press Enter.

When Is *rlogin* Preferred over *Telnet*

The rlogin program is one of a number of r-utilities (the *r* stands for "remote") developed to run over TCP/IP networks. This program is very similar to the Telnet program in that it enables a user to operate a terminal session on a remote host. Different from Telnet, however, the rlogin program does not require us to provide a userid and a password.

The r-utility programs make reference to two configuration files: /etc/hosts.equiv, and a file optionally stored in a user's home directory called .rhosts. Imagine we have two hosts in our network—one called jupiter, the other called mars—both of which are in the catfish.com domain.

All network users have an account on each host with a similarly constructed username (both usernames are of the form first initial and surname, such as jedwards). By configuring the /etc/hosts.equiv file, we could allow all users to access either machine by only logging on once to their local machine and then using the rlogin program. The following task list illustrates how to achieve this:

1. Log on to UNIX as the root administrator and type vi /etc/hosts.equiv and press Enter.

2. Add a new line to the /etc/hosts.equiv file by pressing *o* and then Enter. On this new line, add an entry for the host you want to provide equivalent user access to. In my example, I would enter the hostname jupiter.catfish.com. Save and exit the /etc/hosts.equiv file.

3. Log off as the root user, and then log back on to the jupiter.catfish.com server using another user account. At the shell prompt, enter the following command: rlogin mars.catfish.com. Then press Enter. The rlogin command will forward a logon request to the remote host. The server checks for equivalency by looking for the user's local hostname within its own /etc/hosts.equiv. If a match is found, the logon is allowed and a shell program will be launched on the remote host.

We can enable similar functionality by this time creating a .rhosts file in a specific user's home directory. Consider the same host configuration as before. Imagine now, however, that we have not configured a /etc/hosts.equiv file, but require to give equivalence access between our hosts to one user account.

1. Log on as a user on the host mars.catfish.com. Use the vi program to create a new file called .rhosts in the user's home directory. This will be similar to the following:
   vi $HOME/.rhosts

2. Press *o* to start a new line and add the following entry, jupiter.catfish.com   jedwards, the first entry being the remote hostname; the second being the logon account name on the host to which we will be giving equivalence. Once complete, save the file and exit vi.

3. Log off the `mars.catfish.com` host and log on to `jupiter.cat-fish.com`, using the userid `jedwards`. Now, at the UNIX shell prompt, issue the following command: `rlogin mars`. Then press Enter. Again, because we have created equivalence between the hosts, you will be automatically logged on to the mars server without having to supply either a username or a password.

From these examples, you should be able to see that the configuration of either `/etc/hosts.equiv` or `.rhosts` has the potential to be a very powerful asset, but at the same time raises some serious security concerns. An unscrupulous user could make a change within either of these files and then gain access to any host account. The following points provide some guidelines for limiting the abuse of providing host equivalence:

- Set effective file permissions on the `/etc/hosts.equiv` file.

- The `/etc/hosts.equiv` file should be set with permissions that enable it to be edited only by `root`. Other users of the system require read access, but it is advisable not to enable the file as readable by the world.

- Never include a plus sign (+) within the `/etc/hosts.equiv` file.

- A plus sign on its own provides equivalency to any and all hosts, meaning that access to any like-named accounts is granted from all networked hosts. All unscrupulous users would need to do to access a remote host account is create a similarly named account on their local machine.

- Include only the names of specific hosts, not individual accounts.

- Refrain from allowing users to create `.rhosts` files. In general, the same security rules examined earlier for the `/etc/ hosts.equiv` file need to be applied to `.rhosts` files. Because any user can create a `.rhosts` file within his own home directory, however, it would be an administrative nightmare to ensure the syntax within each of the files. It is recommended that any required equivalence between accounts be set through the `/etc/hosts.equiv` file and that `.rhosts` files not be used. Where equivalence between accounts of dissimilar names is required, an account username and password should always be provided.

Transferring Files Across the Network

The Telnet and rlogin commands provide a way for a remote user to access system resources, but not an effective way to transfer files across the network. These deficiencies are alleviated through the operation of the file transfer protocol (or more simply, FTP).

The following section examines the operation of FTP and illustrates how it can be used to transfer files between UNIX hosts. FTP can operate both from the command line and interactively. Let's start by looking at using it interactively.

1. Log on to UNIX as any user, but not to the root account. At a shell prompt, enter the command ftp and press Enter.

2. The ftp program will drop into command mode and offer the prompt ftp>. Type in the word open and press Enter.

3. FTP will prompt for the name of the remote host you want to open a connection to. At this prompt, I entered in the hostname ftp.catfish.com to access my FTP host machine. Enter the hostname of another UNIX system within your network.

4. If successful, the remote server prompts you to enter a user name and then a password. On your system, enter this information. FTP will inform you when you are successful and return you to the ftp> prompt. We are now connected to the remote server and can transfer files. Listing 22.10 provides an illustration of these tasks.

LISTING 22.10   Accessing a remote host using *ftp*

```
# ftp
ftp> open
(to) ftp.catfish.com.
Connected to ftp.catfish.com.
220 ftp server (Monday, March 30 12:12:22 EST 1998) ready.
     .
Name (ftp.catfish.com. james
331 password required for james.
Password: *******
230 Guest login ok, access restrictions apply.
ftp>
```

5. The ftp program enables you to display remote files and to move around the file systems contained on the remote server. Type in the command ls -l and then press Enter. FTP will transfer a listing of the current directory on the remote machine. The following listing provides a summary of the files on the host ftp.catfish.com.

LISTING 22.11   Using *ftp* to list files

```
ftp> ls -l
200 Okay
150- ftp server ready
150 Opening data connection for /bin/ls
total 6
-rw-rw-r-x  1 root     system      1634     Apr 4  1996   cu_mor
-rw-r--rwx  1 root     system      424      Apr 4  1996    source.c
-rw-rw-r--  1 root     system      3234     Apr 4  1996    fames.c
-rw-rwxr--  1 root     system      634      Apr 4  1996    pigsou.c
-rw-rw-r-x  1 root     system      1634     Apr 4  1996    cracko.4
-rw-r-xrwx  1 root     system      234      Apr 4  1996    seventen
226 Transfer complete.
ftp>
```

6. Let's transfer the file source.c from ftp.catfish.com to our local host. Before we do this, let's change to our home directory on our local host; we do this through the ftp command lcd. Type the following, replacing the file reference with your own home directory: lcd /home/james.

7. To transfer the file, type get source.c, and then press Enter. The ftp program will then transfer the file, indicating when the transfer has completed.

Transferring Multiple Files with FTP

1. The ftp program can also transfer multiple files in one go. Let's try this out by transferring all the files in the remote directory on ftp.catfish.com. Before we can do this, however, we need to make a couple of adjustments to our current FTP session.

2. Notice in Listing 22.11 that some of the files contained in the remote subdirectory are in fact executable files. As such we need to tell ftp to transfer these programs in Binary mode rather than Text mode. This can be done by typing in the word binary and pressing Enter.

3. Also, instead of transferring files one at a time, we can use the mget command to transfer multiple files in one go. By default, however, the mget program will work in Interactive mode, prompting us for each file. We can overcome this by turning the FTP Interactive mode off. Do this by typing in the word prompt.

4. Now we are ready to transfer all the files from the remote host. Type in the command mget and press Enter. The ftp program will prompt for the files to be fetched. Type in *.* to transfer all files. FTP will transfer the files one by one, indicating when each transfer is completed as well as performance statistics such as the transfer time and number of bytes copied between systems.

5. Listing 22.12 provides a summary of these tasks. Notice how I also added the FTP command hash. This causes FTP to print a hash mark (#) to the screen for every 1024 bytes it transfers. This can prove very useful, especially if large files need to be transferred. You should note that the number of bytes between hash marks may differ slightly between different UNIX flavors.

LISTING 22.12   Transferring multiple files using FTP

```
ftp>
ftp> binary
200 type set to I.
ftp> prompt
Interactive mode off
ftp> hash
Hash mark printing on
ftp> mget
(remote-files) *.*
local: cu_mar remote: cu_mar
200 Okay
```

```
150 Opening data connection for XXX (XXX bytes).
226 Transfer complete.
local: source.c remote: source.c
200 Okay
150 Opening data connection for XXX (XXX bytes).
####
226 Transfer complete.
4560 bytes received in 0.00467 secs (9.5e+02 Kbytes/sec)
local: frames.c remote: frames.c
200 Okay
150 Opening data connection for XXX (XXX bytes).

################################################################
➥##############
###############################
226 Transfer complete.
115695 bytes received in 0.347 secs (3.3e+02 Kbytes/sec)
local: pigsou.c remote: pigsou.c
200 Okay
150 Opening data connection for XXX (XXX bytes).

################################################################
➥################################################################
################################################################
➥###############################
226 Transfer complete.
1570 bytes sent in 0.01432 secs (1.9e+02 Kbytes/sec)
local: cracko.4 remote: cracko.4
200 Okay
150 Opening data connection for XXX (XXX bytes).
#
226 Transfer complete.
240 bytes sent in 0.00299 secs (1.9e+02 Kbytes/sec)
```

Using *rcp* to Transfer Files

Just as rlogin provided us with an alternative to using Telnet,
another of the r-utilities—rcp—provides us with an alternative to
using FTP for file transfers. The use of rcp requires the configuration of a .rhosts file in the user's home directory. The following examples leads us through the necessary .rhosts
configuration before illustrating the operation of this utility.

Note

All the available FTP commands can be displayed by
pressing the question mark (?)
key at the ftp prompt. In
addition, remember that when
setting commands—such as
prompt, hash, binary—
these are all toggle commands
that can be reset by entering
the command again.

The ftp utility can be used to
transfer files from the local host
to a remote host. This is
accomplished in a similar way
to that outlined earlier. Instead
of using the commands get
and mget, however, use the
commands put and mput.

1. Log on to the remote, not as the root user, using an ordinary account. Enter the following commands to create a new .rhosts file in the account's home directory: vi $HOME/ .rhosts. Then press Enter.

2. Open a new line in this file by pressing *o*, and enter the name of your local host and the account name on that host to whom you want to grant access. My local host is jupiter.catfish.com, for example, and my account name on that host is jedwards. Therefore I make the following entry within the .rhosts file on the remote host:

jupiter.catfish.com   jedwards.

3. Save the .rhosts file, exit from vi, and log off of the remote host. Now you are ready to execute any of the r-utilities.

4. Log on to your local host (the one you added an entry for in step 2). Type the following command to create a new file that you can use for testing the rcp utility: touch testfile. Then press Enter. Run the rcp utility to place a copy of this file in the home directory on the remote server mars.cat-fish.com by typing the following;

rcp testfile mars.catfish.com/home/jedwards/testfile.

5. After the transfer has completed, log on to the remote host and check that the file has been copied. To do this, type in rlogin mars.catfish.com, and then type in ls -l $HOME/ testfile

6. One advantage of using the rcp program to transfer files over and above the ftp program is a capability to perform recursive coping of entire directory structures. The following command provides an example of this;

rsh -r catfish.com:/usr/lib/source   /backup/source

This command copies the subdirectory /usr/lib/source and all the underlying subdirectories and files to the local subdi-rectory /backup/source. The only way to achieve a similar functionality using FTP is to tar all the files under /usr/lib/source and then transfer that one file. Obviously rcp provides us with a lot more flexibility.

Executing Commands on Another System in the Network

The rsh program (sometimes pronounced *rush* or alternatively r-s-h) provides a method to execute commands on remote hosts without having to log on beforehand. As the program's name suggests, it is another of the r-utilities. As such, the /etc/hosts.equiv and .rhosts configuration covered in previous sections of this chapter need to be applied before we can use the command.

1. Create an entry for your local UNIX host in the .rhosts file of the remote host. In my case, I would do this by logging on the host mars.catfish.com (my remote host) and typing vi $HOME/.rhosts, then adding the entry jupiter.catfish.com before saving and exiting the file.

2. Log off the remote host and log on to the local host. Execute the rsh command to execute the /bin/ls program against the remote host by typing the following command line: rsh mars.catfish.com /bin/ls. Then press Enter.

3. The rsh command will produce a file listing of the $HOME directory on the remote host. Try executing some other executables on the remote host. The following are some interesting examples.

4. Enter the command line rsh mars.catfish.com /bin/sh to start up a UNIX shell on the remote host.

5. The command rsh mars.catfish.com who displays the users currently logged on to the remote host.

6. Executing the rsh command without specifying a command to execute on the remote host will result in the user being logged on the remote host, the same result as if we had used the rlogin command. To try this, enter the command line rsh mars.catfish.com.

A Final Note

The tasks outlined in this chapter enable you to get your hosts networked. This will provide a basis for you to be able to run all the most common network applications—and access remote systems.

It is worth remembering that with nearly 30 different flavors of UNIX commercially available, some differences in program operation and syntax will be evident. I have tried to adopt an approach to cover the approaches adopted by most of the major UNIX flavors; as always, it is worthwhile referring to your system's man pages for version-specific options of the commands and programs covered throughout this chapter.

Accessing UNIX from Windows

By James Edwards

Windows and TCP/IP

Dial-up networking

Most users operate one of the Windows family of operating systems on their PCs—the majority making use of the Windows 95 version. It's likely that these same users will need to communicate with UNIX hosts—either located within their own network, or in public networks such as the Internet. In this chapter we address the issues of providing Windows 95 users with access to UNIX hosts.

The Windows operating system prides itself on its Plug-and-Play configuration capabilities. What does this mean? Well, when a new device such as a modem is added to a PC, Windows automatically attempts to recognize and configure it. If any additional configuration information is required, Windows automatically starts a simple program to guide and prompt the user for the information needed to complete the configuration.

By and large, the operating system accomplishes these tasks very favorably, especially in comparison to any flavor of UNIX! However, there are a number of "gotchas" that you should be aware of—this chapter helps to identify some of those things.

Windows and TCP/IP

The TCP/IP protocols are very much the de facto standard for networking. Windows offers native support for these protocols, along with a simple program, called a *wizard*, for guiding users through the necessary installation and configuration processes.

To enable effective TCP/IP networking support for LAN connections under Windows, the configuration of three separate components is required: the Microsoft Client for Networking, a Network Interface Card (NIC) adapter, and the TCP/IP protocols. All of these configuration steps rely on the Network icon located in the Windows Control Panel; the following task guides you through the necessary steps required to enable TCP/IP networking within Windows.

Enabling TCP/IP networking

1. Open the Control Panel. This can be done by clicking the Start button located on the Task Bar. Then highlight

Settings and click the option Control Panel. When the Control Panel has opened, double-click on the Network icon.

2. Within the Network window, click the Configuration tab. Examine the displayed list of components appearing in the window below the words The Following Network Components Are Installed. To connect to a network you must ensure that three entries are present: Client for Microsoft Networks, NIC Adapter, and TCP/IP Network Adapter.

3. If any of these entries are not present within your configurations, they can be added by first clicking the Add button. You are presented with four options: to add a client, protocol, adapter, or service. Let's step through adding the networking client first.

4. Select Client in the Component Type option box, and then click the Add button. Select Microsoft as the manufacturer, and under the Network Clients window select the option Client for Microsoft Networking. Confirm this selection by clicking OK.

5. Add the NIC Adapter in a similar fashion: Click on the Add button, select the option Adapter, and click the Add button. Highlight the manufacturer for the NIC that you have installed in your PC; if your exact NIC is not displayed, click on the Have Disk button and follow the instructions for loading the NIC vendors device drivers from diskette. Click on the Add button and then the OK button to confirm and complete the operation.

6. Next, have Windows load the TCP/IP protocols, and configure them for use over the installed NIC. Do this by clicking on the Add button, this time selecting the option Protocol. Click on the Add button, and select Microsoft under the list of available manufacturers. Specify TCP/IP as the network protocols to add, and complete the operation by clicking on the OK button.

Associating protocols with adapters

When more than one network adapter has been installed, Windows 95 makes use of an arrow to associate a network protocol with a specific network adapter. If only a single network adapter has been configured, Windows does not provide this association, but instead simply states the protocol name within the Network window.

7. At this stage we have all the networking components loaded, but we haven't configured any of them. First, configure the NIC. In the option window under The Following Network Components Are Installed, click once on the entry for your NIC Adapter.

8. Click on the Properties button and then click on Driver type. Choose the Enhanced Mode (32 bit and 16 bit) NDIS Driver option. Click on the Bindings tab, and check the box for TCP/IP *NIC* Adapter (where *NIC* will reflect your NIC manufacturer). Click on the OK button to complete this configuration.

9. Now configure the TCP/IP protocols. Under the title bar The Following Network Components Are Installed window, click once on TCP/IP NIC Adapter and then click the Properties button.

10. Click on the IP address tab. If you have been allocated an IP address, click once on the option button Specify and IP Address and then enter your IP address and the corresponding netmask. If you will be allocated an IP address through a DHCP server, check the option button Obtain an IP Address Automatically.

11. Click on the Bindings tab, and check the Microsoft Client option box. Click the OK button to save this change.

12. All the remaining settings are purely optional. However, one other important option is the configuration of DNS. If you plan to use DNS (for example, to be able to connect to the Internet), then click once on the Enable DNS option button. In the configuration boxes provided add the hostname you want to call your PC as well as its domain name. I called my host pcclient and my domain catfish.com. Figure 23.1 outlines this configuration.

13. You must also add the IP address of DNS server under the window DNS Server Search Order. Click the Add button to add the DNS reference, and then click the OK button once to save these settings. Again, Figure 23.1 illustrates this configuration.

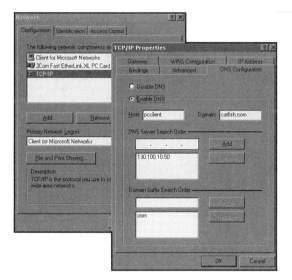

FIGURE 23.1
Configuring DNS under
Windows 95.

Testing the Connection with Ping

The *ping* tool ships as part of the standard Windows operating system and provides an excellent tool for both confirming our PC configuration and troubleshooting network connectivity. Unfortunately, the version of ping that ships with Windows is a DOS program, and as such must run in a Windows DOS box. The following task illustrates how we can make use of this command.

Using the ping tool

1. Bring up your Windows taskbar and click once on the Start button. Move the cursor to highlight the Run option and click once. The Run option box appears. Type the following command line at the Open prompt: ping 130.100.10.2 (replace my IP address with the IP address you used in your own interface configuration).

2. The ping program executes but, because it is a DOS-based program, it first opens a DOS window. Ping sends a request packet to the specified interface asking it for an immediate response. If you have correctly configured your PC, you should see a response similar to the one outlined in Figure 23.2.

Using the hosts file instead of DNS

Windows supports the use of a hosts file as an alternative to using DNS. This file is located in the Windows subdirectory and its syntax is exactly the same as that used on a UNIX host, with individual IP addresses mapping to specified host names. If you don't have access to a DNS server, and don't want to refer to your hosts using IP addresses, the \Windows\hosts file provides a useful alternative.

FIGURE 23.2
Pinging a local interface to check network connectivity.

3. If you configured a \Windows\hosts file or have access to a DNS server, you can use a hostname in place of the IP address. To test this, activate a DOS box and type ping hostname (replace *hostname* with the name of your remote host).

Viewing Local TCP/IP Settings

Pinging the IP address

It is important to remember that if you use a hostname, the ping program must resolve this hostname before ping can test host connectivity. If for some reason the name you specify cannot be resolved, ping cannot report whether the host is reachable. For this reason it is preferable to specify a host's IP address rather than its hostname when using ping.

Windows provides a utility that allows us to view detailed information about our current network configurations. This utility is called winipcfg.exe and is located in the \Windows subdirectory. Let's view some of the functionality provided through this utility.

Using the *winipcfg* utility

1. Bring up your taskbar and click once on the Start button, and then click on the Run menu option. This brings up a dialog box; type in \Windows\winipcfg as the program you wish to open and press Enter.

2. The winipcfg program starts and displays a window similar to the one shown in Figure 23.3.

As Figure 23.3 illustrates, the winipcfg program displays useful configuration information that can be used to help troubleshoot network connectivity problems.

FIGURE 23.3
TCP/IP configuration information with `winipcfg`.

3. The example in Figure 23.3 illustrates the TCP/IP configuration for my Ethernet connection; it is also possible to discover the configuration for other configured interfaces. If
you have configured your PC for dial-up networking, click
on the down arrow to activate the drop-down list and select
the option PPP Adapter. `winipcfg` displays the configuration
for that interface.

4. Click on the More Info button; `winipcfg` expands to include
a lot of additional information relating to your current connection. Figure 23.4 provides an illustration for my PPP
Adapter configuration.

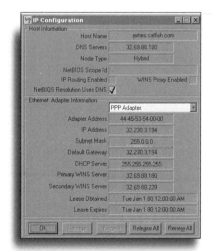

FIGURE 23.4

Using `winipcfg` to display
TCP/IP connectivity details.

Troubleshooting with `winipcfg`

The use of `winipcfg` can prove especially useful if your IP address is allocated to you automatically through DHCP. Once you know your IP address, you can troubleshoot more effectively. Also notice on the `winipcfg` display two additional buttons: Release All and Renew All. If your interface did get its IP address through DHCP then these buttons would provide you with a way to release or renew the IP address you are using.

Transferring Files to and from UNIX with ftp

Windows provides a standard implementation of the ftp program for file transfer. Like the Windows version of the ping and telnet programs, ftp is made available only as a DOS program. However, it is still a useful and effective way to transfer files between Windows and UNIX hosts.

Using ftp to transfer files

1. In order to use ftp to transfer a file from a remote host, you must ensure that the host is able to accept your ftp request. To do this the host must be running an ftp server process. To confirm this, log on to the remote host and type the following commands: `cat inetd.conf ¦ grep ftp`. If the server can handle inbound ftp client requests, a response similar to the following should be displayed:

LISTING 23.1   Checking whether the ftp server is running on the remote UNIX host

```
# cat /etc/inetd.conf ¦ grep ftp
ftp      stream  tcp     nowait  root    /usr/sbin/tcpd
    /usr/sbin/wu.ftpd
#
```

2. To activate the ftp program, move the cursor to the taskbar and click the Start button. Click once on the Run menu option, and a dialog box appears, requesting the name of the program you wish to execute. Type in `ftp` and press Enter.

3. A DOS window appears, along with the ftp command prompt `ftp>`.

4. Type in `?` to display a list of the available commands. You must first open a connection to the remote host. In the following example, I open a connection to my ftp server called `ftp.catfish.com`. Type the following commands, replacing the indicated hostname with the name of your remote UNIX server: open `ftp.catfish.com` and then press Enter.

5. If successful, the remote server prompts you to enter a user name and then a password. Enter this information; ftp

informs you when you are successful and returns you to the ftp> prompt. You are now connected to the remote server and able to transfer files. Figure 23.5 illustrates these tasks.

FIGURE 23.5
Accessing a remote UNIX host using ftp.

6. The ftp program allows you to display remote files and to move around the file systems contained on the remote server. Type in the command dir and then press Enter. ftp displays a listing of the current directory on the remote host.

7. To transfer a file from the remote host to your Windows PC, type the command get filename (where *filename* is the name of the file on the remote host), then press Enter. The ftp program transfers the file and indicates when the transfer has completed.

8. Similarly, you can transfer a file from your Windows PC to the remote UNIX host. To do this, type put filename (where *filename* is the name of the file to transfer). This time when ftp reports that the transfer is complete, type dir and press Enter. The resulting directory listing should now also include your freshly transferred file.

Logging On to UNIX with telnet

If you want to log on to any UNIX host across a TCP/IP connection, you must use the telnet program. This program, which ships as part of the Windows operating system, provides terminal emulation facilities for TCP/IP networks.

Windows versus UNIX ftp

The standard Windows version of the ftp program is identical to the UNIX version of the program, which is illustrated in Chapter 22, "Accessing Other UNIX Systems on the Network or Internet." The additional features and functions outlined in Chapter 22 can also be applied to the Windows version of the ftp program.

Logging on to a UNIX host with telnet

1. To start telnet, click on the Start button and select the Run menu option. In the Run program dialog box type `telnet` and click the OK button to start the program.

2. To connect to a remote host, click on the Connect menu option and then on the Remote System option.

3. A Connect option box is displayed. Enter the hostname or IP address of your remote UNIX host. Remember, if you enter a hostname, you must either have DNS configured or have an entry for the host in your `\Windows\hosts` file. Figure 23.6 provides an illustration.

FIGURE 23.6

Using telnet to log on across a TCP/IP connection.

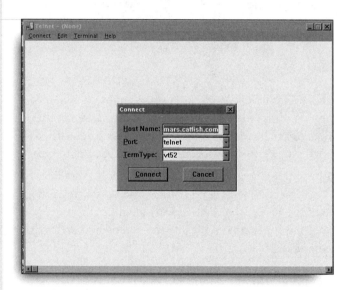

4. Click on the Connect button to activate the connection. The remote host's logon screen should be displayed for you to provide your username and password.

5. To disconnect from the host, click on the Connect menu item and select the Disconnect option.

Dial-up Networking

Windows provides you with two options for accessing UNIX hosts over dial-up connections. One option is to configure your Windows PC to be able to operate the TCP/IP protocols over a modem connection. This option enables you to run any one of the TCP/IP–based applications outlined so far within this chapter and is typically the route chosen in providing a PC with a connection into the Internet.

An alternative approach is to configure Windows to enable a user with the ability to log on to a remote host. This option allows you to access files and resources on the remote host; however, this option is limited in that it provides access to only a single remote host at any one time. The following sections examine both of these approaches

Accessing UNIX Hosts via the Internet

To access hosts over the Internet you must complete four tasks: install and configure your modem, configure the modem's physical port, configure the networking devices and protocols, and configure a connection script that will dial your Internet service provider's telephone number and initiate communication over your configured devices.

The following task list provides a simple guide through this process, beginning with the installation and configuration of your modem.

Accessing UNIX hosts over the Internet

1. Click the Start button located on the taskbar. Move the cursor to the Settings menu option and then right click the Control Panel option. When the Control Panel folder opens, double-click on the Modems icon. If you already have a modem installed, the Modems Properties dialog box appears. If this is the case, right-click the Add button before proceeding.

2. The Install a New Modem window opens. Click on the Next button to run the Installation Wizard and have

Windows guide you through the installation process. Click on the Next button to continue with this process.

3. You will be asked if you want Windows to search for the newly installed hardware; select the NO option button and click on Next. From the displayed Device Type list, select Modem and click Next.

4. Check the option Don't Detect My Modem, I Will Select It from a List and click the Next button. A new window opens; select both your modem's manufacturer and model under the provided options.

5. Click on the Next button to continue the installation, and select the COM port the modem will use. Windows attempts to install your modem—the screen may blank for a few seconds as it completes the process. Upon completion a window is displayed, reporting the success of the installation process; click the Finish button to exit the Installation Wizard.

6. Pressing the Finish button brings up the Modem Properties window. To effectively complete the installation process, you must define how Windows is to use the modem; this is done by clicking on the Dialing Properties button found within this window.

7. The Dialing Properties screen prompts you to enter your local dialing area code and whether you need to dial a special number before being able to dial any location. This might be the case if your modem line connects via a PBX and requires a 9 to be dialed in order to access an outside telephone line. Make any changes to the Dialing Properties screen required for your own environments.

8. Click the OK button to save and exit the Dialing Properties screen, and again to exit the Modem Properties screen.

The next step is to ensure that your COM port settings correspond to those you configured for your modem during its installation. This is achieved through accessing the System icon, again located within the Control Panel. The following tasks summarize the settings we need to make.

Configuring COM port settings

1. To open the Control Panel, click the Start button located on the taskbar. Move the cursor to the Settings menu option and then right-click the Control Panel option. The Control Panel folder opens; double-click on the System icon.

2. The System Properties window opens; click on the Device Manager tab and then double-click the COM port to which you connected your modem. Click on the Port Settings tab to adjust the displayed values so that they correspond to the ones you configured for your modem.

3. Click OK to save the settings and return to the System Properties window, then click OK to close this window and return to the Control Panel folder.

After you have installed your modem and communication port, you must set up and configure the TCP/IP protocols to be able to communicate over these devices. This is achieved by the completion of the following steps.

Configuring TCP/IP protocols

1. Open the Windows Control Panel by clicking on the Start button, then choosing Settings, and then Control Panel. Double-click on the Network icon.

2. Click on the Configuration tab and examine the list of currently configured components. In order for you to configure dial-up networking, the following two entries must be present: Dial-up Adapter and TCP/IP Dial-up Adapter.

   If either of these items is not present, it must be added. If you need to add an item, click on the Add button. You are presented with four options of things you can add: a client, a protocol, an adapter, and a service.

   If you need to add a dial-up adapter, click on the adapter option and click the Add button. Select Microsoft as the manufacturer, and select Dial-up Adapter under the Network Protocols window. Click the OK button to confirm the operation.

If you need to add the TCP/IP protocol Dial-up Adapter option, click the Add button, click the protocol option, and then again click the Add button. Select Microsoft as the manufacturer and select TCP/IP as the network protocol. Complete the operation by clicking the OK button.

3. Now for TCP/IP protocol configuration: In the The Following Network Components Are Installed window, click on Dial-up Adapter. Click on the Properties button, and then click on the Driver Type option and choose Enhanced Mode (32 bit and 16 bit) NDIS Driver. Click on the Bindings tab and then check the box for TCP/IP Dial-up Adapter. Click on the OK button to complete this operation.

4. In the The Following Network Components Are Installed window, click on TCP/IP Dial-up Adapter and then click on the Properties button. This screen then provides a place to configure the TCP/IP protocol parameters. Figure 23.7 provides an example.

FIGURE 23.7

Configuring TCP/IP parameters.

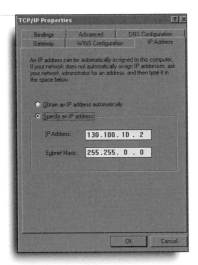

5. The essential item to configure is the IP address of the Windows PC. To do this, click on the IP Address tab. If you have been allocated an IP address to use, click on the Specify an IP Address option button and then enter your IP address

and associated netmask. If you have not been allocated an IP address, click on the Obtain an IP Address Automatically option.

6. If your PC is able to make use of DNS, click on the DNS Configuration tab. Next, check the Enable DNS option button, and then add your PC's hostname and domain name. Then add the IP address of DNS server in the DNS Server Search Order window and click the Add button.

7. Finally, click the OK button to save the configuration and exit.

Your modem is configured and your device port and the protocol configuration set up. Now you must instruct Windows how to establish a connection; this is achieved via the Dial-up Networking option. The following task illustrates the necessary configuration steps.

Configuring dial-up networking

1. Double-click on the My Computer icon, the Dial-Up Networking folder, and the Make New Connection icon. This starts a wizard program to guide you through the setup of a new dial-up networking session.

2. Enter a name to describe the session and select the modem that the wizard should use. Click the Next button to continue.

3. Enter the telephone number of the server you are dialing, including country and area codes as appropriate. Click on the Next button and the wizard informs you that your session configuration is complete. Click on the Finish button to save and exit.

4. Your session is saved in the Dial-up Networking folder. Select this icon, and right-click, then select the Properties option and then the Server Type option button. The screen shown in Figure 23.8 is displayed.

5. This dialog box allows us to specify which protocols are able to operate across the established connection. Click on the TCP/IP Settings button and enter TCP/IP configuration information for this specific connection, which overrides the values specified in the Control Panel. This allows you to configure TCP/IP differently for any particular connections you might make.

FIGURE 23.8

Specifying the server type for dial-up networking.

6. To activate this session, double-click on the Session icon in the Dial-up Networking folder. A dialog box appears, prompting for your user name and password, as well as the telephone number that is to be dialed. Enter your user name and password and click on the Connect button.

7. Windows dials the specified telephone number, and attempts to connect using your user name and password. After a connection has been established, you can use any of the TCP/IP programs to access remote servers across this connection.

Accessing a UNIX Host over a Terminal Connection

Chapter 21, "Accessing Other UNIX Systems by Modem," illustrated how a UNIX host can provide remote logon support through the use of modems and dial-up lines. Windows provides comparable functionality through its HyperTerminal program. This program allows a PC to be configured to be able to establish a terminal connection with a remote host.

Configuring HyperTerminal to access a UNIX host

1. To configure a connection using HyperTerminal, click on the Start button and move the cursor to the Programs menu option. Windows displays the available program groups on your PC. Select Accessories, and then HyperTerminal.

2. In the HyperTerminal folder, double-click on the program called Hypertrm.exe. This starts the HyperTerminal configuration program, which guides you through the rest of the necessary configuration steps.

3. Enter a name for the new connection, and select an icon for this connection from the available list. Click OK to continue.

4. HyperTerminal prompts you for the telephone number of the remote host you want to connect to. To complete this information, add the country and area code information by selecting the drop-down box. HyperTerminal helps you to complete these steps.

5. Click on the down arrow at the end of the Connect Using window and select the modem you want HyperTerminal to use. When you have finished entering this information, click on the OK button to continue.

6. HyperTerminal displays the number you want to dial, as well as the location you are dialing from within the Connect dialog box. An example of this is illustrated in Figure 23.9.

7. If you must change the configured telephone number of your remote host you can do so by clicking on the Modify button. This action displays the Properties window for your connection (see Figure 23.10).

8. Clicking on the Phone Number tab allows you to change the telephone number, including the country and area code, of the remote host. This tab also provides you with the ability to change connections modem configuration by clicking on the Configure button.

9. Click on the Settings tab. The options available on this screen allow you to change the look and feel of the terminal session. You shouldn't need to make changes to any of these settings as long as you ensure that the Emulation option is set to Auto detect. Click on the OK button to return to the Connect dialog box.

FIGURE 23.9

Accessing the HyperTerminal Connect dialog box.

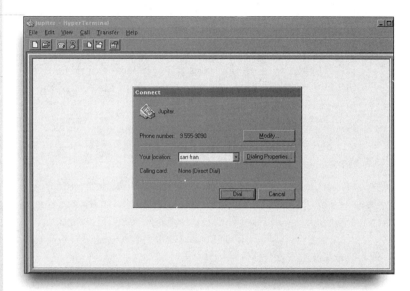

FIGURE 23.10

Changing the dial-in properties of a HyperTerminal connection.

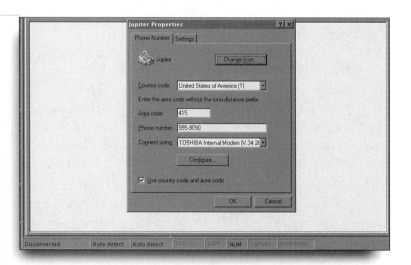

10. Click on the Dialing Properties button to tell HyperTerminal which location you are dialing from. This option is particularly useful if you travel and need to access a remote host from many different locations. Click the OK button to return to the Connect dialog box.

11. After you are happy with your connection configuration settings, click the Dial button to make the remote connection. When a connection is made, the remote UNIX host presents you with a logon screen in which to enter your user name and password.

Transferring Files to and from the Remote Host

After you have logged on to a remote host, HyperTerminal provides you with a simple and effective way to transfer files to and from a remote host. To achieve this, the host must employ a method of downloading files across dial-in connections through the use of communication server software such as Kermit. The following steps illustrate how a HyperTerminal user can transfer files using this software.

Transferring files with HyperTerminal

1. Connect to your remote UNIX host by using HyperTerminal as previously described, and log on with a valid username and password.

2. On the remote host, start up the kermit file transfer program by typing `kermit`. Inform the remote host that you want to upload a binary file from your PC by typing `set file type binary` and pressing Enter, then type `receive` to place the host in the correct mode to receive your file. Press Alt+X to escape back to the HyperTerminal program.

3. Click on the Transfer menu option in the HyperTerminal program, and then on the Send Files option. A dialog box appears in which you type the name of the file to transfer, or click on the Browse button to locate the file. When you have selected the file, click on the Send button to start the transfer.

4. HyperTerminal can also be used to receive files from the remote system. This can be set up by selecting the Receive Files option under the Transfer menu. Use the Browse button to indicate where transferred files are to be placed, and then use the Transfer program on your remote host to send files to your HyperTerminal session.

Reading and Sending UNIX Email via Netscape on Windows

The Netscape Communicator application suite is primarily an Internet browser; however, it also offers Internet email capabilities. The operation of the Netscape application requires a TCP/IP connection from the Windows PC into the Internet. This can be provided though a network connection made via a NIC or a modem.

Configuring Netscape Communicator for email

1. Launch the Netscape Navigator by clicking on the Start button, selecting the Programs option, scrolling to the Netscape folder, and clicking on the Netscape Navigator icon. Alternatively, if you have created a shortcut to this application you can launch it by simply double-clicking on the shortcut icon.

2. On the Netscape option bar select Window and then Netscape Mail. Netscape displays the email client and prompts for a user id and a password to access your remote email account. After it is connected, the email window should look similar to the one in Figure 23.11.

3. New email messages are automatically placed in your Inbox folder. Click on the Inbox folder in the top right window; Netscape indicates the number of unread messages.

4. A summary line for each message within your Inbox appears to the right of this window. You can open any of these messages by clicking on it, with the message then appearing in the window at the bottom of the Netscape email client.

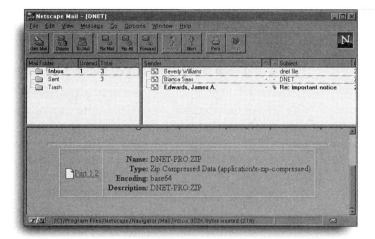

FIGURE 23.11
Netscape email client.

5. Move the mouse arrow to any one of the dividers between these three windows—as you do, notice that the cursor changes shape. Click and hold down the mouse button—as you move the mouse, the individual window sizes change.

6. To send a message, click on File then on the New Mail Message menu option. Alternatively, use the shortcut of pressing Ctrl+M.

7. A Message Composition dialog box appears; enter the email address of the recipient or alternatively click on the Mail To button and the Address book appears. Figure 23.12 provides an illustration.

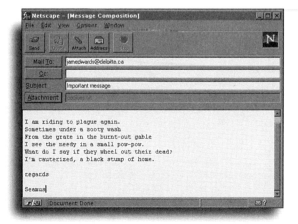

FIGURE 23.12
Creating a new email message using Netscape Navigator.

8. Attach a file to your email message by clicking on the Attachment button. Click on the Attach File button in order to locate the file, click the Open button to select a highlighted file, and then click on OK to continue.

9. Click on the Send button. If you didn't enter anything on the subject line, Netscape again prompts you for a message subject. Enter a subject if you want and then press OK to continue.

UNIX and the Internet

By Gordon Marler

Surfing the Internet from UNIX

Some of the first machines that could access the World Wide Web were running UNIX. The first Web browser to be widely used was Mosaic, an X-Windows application developed by the National Center for Supercomputing Applications (NCSA) at the University of Illinois. It runs on several flavors of UNIX, and is still available today, even though it does not have some of the nicer features of the latest generation of browsers.

Browsers such as Netscape Navigator/Communicator, Sun's HotJava, and Lynx appeared later. If your flavor of UNIX doesn't have X-Windows, or you don't have the proper hardware to run it, you can still run Lynx because it only requires a dumb terminal.

TABLE 24.1   **Web browsers that run on UNIX and where to get them**

Netscape Navigator/ Communicator	`http://home.netscape.com/`
NCSA Mosaic	`ftp://ftp.ncsa.uiuc.edu/Mosaic/Unix/binaries/2.6/`
Lynx	`ftp://www.slcc.edu/pub/lynx/release2-8/`
Sun HotJava	`http://www.javasoft.com/products/hotjava/` `➡index.html`

The locations mentioned in Table 24.1 are probably a format that you're familiar with because many companies today put Uniform Resource Locators (URLs) in their advertisements; these look something like this: `http://www.somecompany.com/`. The *http* portion of these URLs tells your Web browser which *protocol* to use when talking with the Web server you specify after `http://`.

To help you become more familiar with these protocols and when you might want to use them, Table 24.2 lists and describes a lot of the more common ones.

TABLE 24.2   **URL protocol specifiers and their purpose**

`http://`	Used to specify a Web page
`https://`	Used to specify a secure Web page, which will be encrypted as it is sent to you
`ftp://`	Specifies the use of the file transfer protocol to upload/download files
`news://`	Specifies a host that will be used as a Network News (Usenet) server
`file:/<pathname>`	Enables you to load a local file into your browser (note only *one* slash after the colon in this protocol)
`gopher://`	Designates a host offering Gopher services

It's good to remember that many Web servers on the Internet can provide one, some, or all the services listed in Table 24.2 for different parts of their Web site. Many will at least provide the first three.

Usually, if you want to find a company's Web site, you can assume that the URL for it will be very close to http:// www.*companyname*.com—unless some other company with a similar name is already using it.

You will find out pretty quickly that the World Wide Web is not very centrally organized, and information is spread out over a vast area. If you're looking for something in particular, you either have to know where it is already, or you need help finding it. Web *search engines* can help you out with that.

These engines are generally extremely large UNIX servers that send out *spiders* or *robots*. These seek out, examine, and catalog every Web page on every Web server they can find. I list a few of the ones currently available in Table 24.3. You can look them over and pick one that suits you best. Each has its own way of letting you specify what you want to search for in its respective catalogs. Some of these services have better catalogs than others, but that changes over time. Each one has a handy help feature that will help you make basic searches. The advanced search features take about a page to explain each server type.

Finding the right site

If you're trying to guess a company's Web site address, and you end up on some other company's Web site, you will usually find a link to the place you really want to go. Here's an example:

You want to go to the homepage of Diamond Multimedia, the manufacturer of PC video cards. You try `http://www.diamond.com`, but discover that this is the Web site for SI Diamond Technology, Inc. But look! There's a link to the Diamond Multimedia Web site: `http://www.diamondmm.com`.

These links usually come about because the Webmaster of the site you originally ended up on is tired of receiving email asking how to get to the Web sites of companies with names similar to his company.

TABLE 24.3   **A few Web search engines**

AltaVista	`http://www.altavista.digital.com/`
Yahoo!	`http://www.yahoo.com/`
Lycos	`http://www.lycos.com/`

Depending on where your UNIX machine is, you may have a *firewall* between your machine and the Internet. If you access the Internet from work, and your company is of any size at all, this is probably the case. If you access the Internet through an Internet service provider from home, you probably don't have to worry about it.

If you do have a firewall, your system or network administrator has probably set up a *proxy server*, and you're going to have to take some special steps to get your browser to use the proxy server rather than try to go through the firewall directly and fail. The firewall protects your network from intrusion from the Internet, but it also keeps you from getting out. The workaround is to have a proxy server built, which is the only machine allowed direct access to or from the Internet through the firewall. In effect, your browser will ask the proxy to go get a Web page, and then the proxy will hand it to your browser when it arrives. Don't worry that this will be slow; the proxy server usually gets information off the Web faster than you could directly anyway, and it's a lot safer.

All you have to know is the name of the proxy server and the port that it's listening to. Then you tell your browser, and away you go! The only tricky part might be that it is possible that every single protocol listed in Table 24.1 could have its own separate proxy server! This is only common at sites that have an incredible amount of network traffic coming through. An example from when I set up the Lynx browser is shown later.

Automatic proxies

At some sites, the system administrator will not give you the name of your proxy server, but will instead give you a URL that points to an automatic proxy file, which you will have to enter into your browser's Automatic Proxy Configuration. This file contains a script that loads automatically every time you start your browser and programs your browser to intelligently pick the right proxy server for any request you make.

This facility is used at sites that have more than one proxy server, so that you don't have to worry about which proxy to point your browser at all the time. You have to use a browser that supports this facility, however. Netscape Communicator definitely supports it now. Others are following suit.

Downloading Software from the Internet

You already learned how to download files via FTP from the UNIX command line in Chapter 24, but you can also use your Web browser to do the same thing. With the browser, it's much easier because all you need to do is point and click.

Most Internet sites that have software you want will enable you to use *anonymous ftp* to download the files you want. It is the convention in anonymous FTP to use anonymous as your username and then give your email address as your password. Some browsers, such as Netscape Navigator, enable you to select a preference that automatically sends anonymous as your username and your email address as your password if you don't specify a username in your URL.

If you don't have a browser that enables you to set preferences for anonymous FTP—or if you are trying to get FTP access to a site that requires you use a specific username and password—you can explicitly enter your username and password for an FTP session through the browser. The syntax of the URL is this:

```
ftp://username:password@the.ftp.site.com/
```

SEE ALSO

➤ *For information on transferring files via ftp, see page 596*

Downloading Lynx

For this example, I'm assuming that you don't have a browser yet. Therefore you will want to use the UNIX command line to do the FTP transfers.

The source code for Lynx is available for FTP at www.slcc.edu in the directory /pub/lynx/release2-8/.

Because the Lynx source code is distributed as a tarred, zipped file (not compressed or gzipped), you also need to get an unzip utility from the Internet; UNIX doesn't come with one by default. You can find a free one already compiled for almost all flavors of UNIX at ftp.cdrom.com in the /pub/infozip/UNIX/ directory.

Reading and writing zip files

I know that we shouldn't have to talk about compression in this chapter, but the compression tool that the Lynx developers used to compress their source code actually derives from the PC PKZIP utility. Therefore the tool is not a part of UNIX, and wasn't discussed in the chapter that covers compression on UNIX. This also means that the standard UNIX compression tools can't read these PKZIP files.

As is often the case with UNIX, however, someone has taken the time to write a utility to read/write these PKZIP files, and has made it freely available to you. You just have to get it and install it yourself, or ask your system administrator to do it for you.

I have stripped out the part of the FTP output that was not especially helpful. Note that these messages on the FTP server can change at any time and frequently do.

```
% ftp -i ftp.cdrom.com

Connected to wcarchive.cdrom.com.
220 wcarchive.cdrom.com FTP server (Version DG-2.0.12 Tue
➥Mar 24 18:34:00 PST 1998) ready.
Name (ftp.cdrom.com:gmarler): anonymous
331 Guest login ok, send your complete e-mail address as
➥password.
Password: username@host.com
230-Welcome to wcarchive - home ftp site for Walnut Creek
➥CDROM.
230-There are currently 3000 users out of 3000 possible.
230-


        ….

230-Please send mail to ftp-bugs@ftp.cdrom.com if you
➥experience any problems.
230-Please also let us know if there is something we don't
➥have that you think
230-we should!
230-
230 Guest login ok, access restrictions apply.
ftp> binary
200 Type set to I.
ftp> hash
Hash mark printing on (8192 bytes/hash mark).
ftp> cd /pub/infozip/UNIX/
250-This directory contains executables for UNIX systems
➥that generally do not
250-ship with a C compiler.
250-
250-    AIX/                    executables for IBM AIX on
➥RS/6000
250-    CLIX/                   executables for Intergraph
➥CLIX
250-    CONVEX/                 executables for ConvexOS
250-    DEC/                    executables for DEC
➥Digital UNIX (OSF/1) and Ultrix
250-    FREEBSD/                executables for FreeBSD 2.x
➥on Intel
```

```
250-    HP/                        executables for HP/UX
250-    LINUX/                     executables for Linux on
➥Intel
250-    QNX/                       executables for QNX on
➥Intel
250-    SCO/                       executables for SCO UNIX
➥on Intel
250-    SGI/                       executables for Silicon
➥Graphics Irix
250-    SUN/                       executables for SunOS and
➥Solaris 2.x on SPARC
250-
250-Send problem reports on Zip and UnZip to:
➥Zip- Bugs@lists.wku.edu
250-
250-Last updated:  1 December 1997
250-
250 CWD command successful.
ftp> cd SUN
250-This directory contains SunOS and Solaris executables
➥for SPARC and Intel x86
250-hardware.
250-
250-   1856 Dec  4 1997   README              what you're
➥reading right now
250-240193 Jun  3 1996   gzip124x.tar.Z     gzip 1.2.4, SunOS
➥exes/docs, tar archive
250-195440 Feb 10 1994   gzip124x.zip       gzip 1.2.4,
➥SunOS exes/docs, zipfile
250-208685 Nov  8 1997   unz532x-41x.tar.Z  UnZip 5.32, SunOS
➥4.x exes/docs, tarball
250-162289 Nov  8 1997   unz532x-41x.zip    UnZip 5.32, SunOS
➥4.x exes/docs, zipfile
250-207751 Nov  8 1997   unz532x-sol.tar.Z  UnZip 5.32,
➥Solaris/SPARC 2.x exes/docs
250-161083 Nov  8 1997   unz532x-sol.zip    UnZip 5.32,
➥Solaris/SPARC 2.x exes/docs
250-204513 Nov  5 1997   unz532x-x86.tar.Z  UnZip 5.32,
➥Solaris/x86 2.x exes/docs
250-152404 Nov  5 1997   unz532x-x86.zip    UnZip 5.32,
➥Solaris/x86 2.x exes/docs
94295 Nov  8 1997   zip22x-41x.zip     Zip 2.2, SunOS 4.x
➥exes (no encryption)
250- 91733 Nov  8 1997   zip22x-sol.zip     Zip 2.2,
➥Solaris/SPARC exes (no encrypt.)
250-
```

```
250-Binaries with encryption support are available from
250-ftp://ftp.icce.rug.nl/infozip/UNIX/SUN/ :
250-
250-129862 Nov  9 1997  zcr22x-41x.zip      Zip 2.2, SunOS
➥4.x exes (with encryption)
250-127574 Nov 15 1997  zcr22x-sol.zip      Zip 2.2,
➥Solaris/SPARC exes (w/encrypt.)
250-103685 Nov  8 1997  zcr22x-x86.zip      Zip 2.2,
➥Solaris/x86 exes (w/encryption)
250-
250-The SunOS 4.x executables have been tested under SunOS
➥4.1.4 and Solaris 2.5.1
250-and are virtually indistinguishable in speed from native
➥Solaris 2.x binaries.
250-There have been reports that they don't work well under
➥Solaris 2.4, however,
250-so both flavors are provided.
250-
250-The x86 binaries were compiled under Solaris 2.4 with SC
➥2.0.1.
250-
250-All Info-ZIP packages contain documentation.  The
➥sources are in ../../src .
250-
250-Send problem reports on Zip and UnZip to:  Zip-
➥Bugs@lists.wku.edu
250-Send problem reports on gzip to:
➥gzip@prep.ai.mit.edu
250-
250-Last updated:  4 December 1997
250-
250 CWD command successful.
ftp> get unz532x-sol.tar.Z
200 PORT command successful.
150 Opening BINARY mode data connection for unz532x-
➥sol.tar.Z (207751 bytes).
#########################
226 Transfer complete.
local: unz532x-sol.tar.Z remote: unz532x-sol.tar.Z
207751 bytes received in 3.4 seconds (60 Kbytes/s)
```

Now that you have the unzip utility, you can pipe it through GNU's gzip utility to decompress it, and then extract the information from the enclosed tar file. After you have done this, you will probably want to copy the binaries to /usr/local/bin and the man pages to /usr/local/man/man1, or have your system administrator do it for you.

```
% cat unz532x-sol.tar.Z ¦ gzip -d ¦ tar xvf -
x ., 0 bytes, 0 tape blocks
x COPYING, 11259 bytes, 22 tape blocks
x README, 9901 bytes, 20 tape blocks
x WHERE, 16717 bytes, 33 tape blocks
x unzip, 106844 bytes, 209 tape blocks
x unzip.1, 37276 bytes, 73 tape blocks
x unzip.doc, 44561 bytes, 88 tape blocks
x unzipsfx, 54984 bytes, 108 tape blocks
x unzipsfx.1, 13119 bytes, 24 tape blocks
x unzipsfx.doc, 13657 bytes, 27 tape blocks
x zipinfo symbolic link to unzip
x zipinfo.1, 22013 bytes, 43 tape blocks
x zipinfo.doc, 23897 bytes, 47 tape blocks
x zipgrep, 1157 bytes, 3 tape blocks
x zipgrep.1, 3868 bytes, 8 tape blocks
x zipgrep.doc, 3550 bytes, 7 tape blocks
x funzip, 21196 bytes, 42 tape blocks
x funzip.1, 4649 bytes, 10 tape blocks
x funzip.doc, 3914 bytes, 8 tape blocks
```

After you have all the necessary utilities in place, you can go ahead and download the source code for Lynx.

```
% ftp -i www.slcc.edu
Connected to SOL.SLCC.EDU.
220 sol.slcc.edu FTP server (UNIX(r) System V Release 4.0)
➥ready.
Name (www.slcc.edu:gmarler): anonymous
331 Guest login ok, send ident as password.
Password: username@host.com
230 Guest login ok, access restrictions apply.
ftp> cd /pub/lynx/release2-8
250 CWD command successful.
ftp> dir
200 PORT command successful.
150 ASCII data connection for /bin/ls (205.172.10.173,48147)
➥(0 bytes).
total 3786
```

```
-r--r--r--   1 163      14            204102 Mar 10 10:54
CHANGES
-r--r--r--   1 163      14              2514 Mar 10 04:45 fea-
tures.html
-r--r--r--   1 163      14              2281 Mar 10 12:14 fea-
tures.txt
-r--r--r--   1 163      14              3285 Mar 10 04:25
index.html
-r--r--r--   1 163      14              3060 Mar 10 12:14
index.txt
drwxr-xr-x   9 163      14              1024 Mar 10 12:19
lynx2-8
-r--r--r--   1 163      14           1669681 Mar 10 12:07
lynx2-8.zip
-r--r--r--   1 163      14             25671 Mar 10 12:07
lynx2-8.zip-lst
-r--r--r--   1 163      14              2085 Mar 14 19:28
ssl.html
-r--r--r--   1 163      14              1786 Mar 14 19:42
ssl.txt
226 ASCII Transfer complete.
671 bytes received in 0.034 seconds (19 Kbytes/s)
ftp> binary
200 Type set to I.
ftp> hash
Hash mark printing on (8192 bytes/hash mark).
ftp> get lynx2-8.zip
200 PORT command successful.
150 Binary data connection for lynx2-8.zip
➥(205.172.10.173,48148) (1669681 bytes).
##############################################################
➥##############################################################
##############################################################
➥#####################
226 Binary Transfer complete.
local: lynx2-8.zip remote: lynx2-8.zip
1669681 bytes received in 67 seconds (24 Kbytes/s)
```

The source code for Lynx is in a zip archive, so just run the
unzip utility on it. This creates the Lynx source directory and
drops all the source code in it.

```
% unzip lynx2-8.zip
Archive:  lynx2-8.zip
   creating: lynx2-8/
```

```
inflating:  lynx2-8/COPYHEADER
inflating:  lynx2-8/COPYING
inflating:  lynx2-8/INSTALLATION
inflating:  lynx2-8/LYMessages_en.h
```

.....

Running *make* on Lynx

A couple of assumptions are made for this section:

- You own the C Compiler suite for your flavor of UNIX or you have installed the GNU C compiler. For most purposes, the GNU compiler is preferred because it is actually better than most commercial compilers. Pretty nice, especially because it's free.

- You have the make utility that comes with your C Compiler suite or you have installed the GNU make utility. Neither one is preferred over the other.

As with many current UNIX source distributions, Lynx is packaged with GNU's autoconfig utility, which will analyze your flavor of UNIX and make sure that all the proper settings are made to enable you to compile Lynx without trouble. Any package like this will have a configure script in its top-level source tree. All you need to do is run configure, and it will create the proper Makefile for your machine.

```
% cd lynx2-8
% ./configure
creating cache ./config.cache
checking host system type... sparc-sun-solaris2.5.1
checking for gcc... gcc
checking whether the C compiler (gcc  ) works... yes
checking whether the C compiler (gcc  ) is a cross-compiler
➥... no
checking whether we are using GNU C... yes
```

.....

```
updating cache ./config.cache
creating ./config.status
```

> **GNU (and free!) software**
>
> To find out more about GNU software products such as the GNU C Compiler, and GNU make, you can go to the Free Software Foundation web site: http://www.gnu.org.
>
> You will find documentation and source code for all the GNU products. Not only are they freely available, but they often work better than the tools that came standard with your flavor of UNIX.

```
creating makefile
creating WWW/Library/unix/makefile
creating src/makefile
creating src/chrtrans/makefile
creating lynx_cfg.h
```

Now that you have configured the Lynx source for your platform, you can have the make utility compile it for you:

```
% make
```

If Lynx compiles successfully, you can install it by typing the following:

```
# make install
```

You will need to have root access to /usr/local/ on your system, or have your system administrator install Lynx for you.

Using a Character-Based Browser (Lynx)

Now that you have gone to all that trouble to build a binary for Lynx that runs on your machine, you actually get to use it!

1. First, if your site is behind a firewall, you need to make sure that you are set up to use the appropriate proxy server if available. Check with your system administrator to find out what your proxy server's name is, and what port it talks on. If you are not behind a firewall, go to step 3.

2. After you know your proxy server's name and port number (for this example, let's call the server relay.mycompany. com, and the port it talks on 8080), you need to set a few environment variables before you can run Lynx. Assume for simplicity that your proxy server is a proxy for all the following protocols: HTTP, HTTPS, and FTP. If it is not, your system administrator can tell you.

   If you are using the C Shell, put the following in your logon scripts:

```
setenv http_proxy      http://relay.mycompany.com:8080/"
setenv https_proxy     http://relay.mycompany.com:8080/"
setenv ftp_proxy       ftp://relay.mycompany.com:8080/"
```

If you are using the Bourne/Korn Shell, put the following in your logon scripts:

```
http_proxy=http://relay.mycompany.com:8080/; export
➥http_proxy

https_proxy=http://relay.mycompany.com:8080/; export
➥https_proxy

ftp_proxy=http://relay.mycompany.com:8080/; export
➥ftp_proxy
```

3. Now you can run Lynx. At the command line, type `lynx`.

Using Lynx is pretty straightforward. Here is a table of the most frequently used commands.

TABLE 24.4   Brief Lynx command summary

g	Go to a URL, enables you to type in a URL to go to.
/pattern	Search for a pattern in the current Web page.
Up arrow	Move up through the hyperlinks in the current Web page.
Down arrow	Move down through the hyperlinks in the current Web page.
Return	Go to the currently selected hyperlink.

UNIX Vendor Web Sites

Most of the UNIX vendors keep a presence on the Web, and allow varying degrees of access to the Web site's technical support contents based on how much you have paid them for support. Several of the vendors keep a separate site for a main entry point into their Web and another for UNIX support.

TABLE 24.5   Web sites of UNIX vendors

Sun Microsystems (SunOS, Solaris)	main entry point: http://www.sun.com UNIX support: http://sunsolve1.sun.com

continues...

Finding support

I have included the main entry points to each vendor's Web site because these never change. If you find that the UNIX support pages in Table 24.5 change, you can always be sure that if you go to the main entry point for that vendor, you can find a link to the new UNIX support page.

TABLE 24.5   **Continued**

Hewlett-Packard (HP-UX)	Main entry point:
	`http://www.hp.com`
	UNIX support:
	`http://us-support.external.hp.com/`

IBM (AIX)	Main entry point:
	`http://www.ibm.com`
	UNIX support:
	`http://www.rs6000.ibm.com/support/`

Silicon Graphics (IRIX)	Main entry point:
	`http://www.sgi.com`
	UNIX support:
	`http://www.sgi.com/software/`

Accessing UNIX Technical Support

Several kinds of technical support are available from each UNIX vendor. Some are provided free of charge, but most require that you have a support contract with the vendor. This section reviews each type of support and how you can obtain it. Although each vendor deals with support in a slightly different way, Sun's support system is used as an example.

When you purchase your UNIX system(s), you are usually given the option to purchase support for both the hardware and the software, which could include the operating system, bundled software tools, and additionally, any unbundled tools that you elect to buy, such as special compilers or applications. You generally have the option to purchase one of several levels of service, ranging from assistance five days a week, during business hours, to seven days a week, 24 hours a day. Sun calls these service plans SunSpectrum, and they lay out how their plans work at `http://www.sun.com/service/support/sunspectrum/` `index.htm`. Most vendors have something very similar.

Recently, vendors have started to offer software support separately from hardware support. Sun calls this Software Only, or Software Subscription service. They discuss the exact components of this offering at `http://www.sun.com/service/`

support/sw_only/index.html. This kind of service will probably become more and more common as time goes on, because many people and businesses just want to purchase support for software, and take care of hardware problems as they come up.

Direct support for reporting problems with the operating system or the tools that are bundled with it is reserved for customers with support contracts. To report a problem, you generally make a phone call to the vendor's 800 number, give them your contract number, and you will be asked to briefly describe your problem. You will be given a service order number for the problem, and an engineer will get back to you within a time frame specified in your contract. Generally you will find that the problem you're experiencing has already been dealt with, and the engineer will point you to a patch or other workaround.

Another method of reporting such problems is through electronic mail or the vendor's support Web site, mentioned in the preceding section.

Speaking of Web sites, vendors are making more and more of their support capabilities available through their support Web sites. If you go to Sun's, you will see that some support is available free of charge, such as patches, Frequently Asked Questions, and documentation.

Some portions of the Web site are restricted to customers having support contracts. The services provided here are the capability to use a search engine on the patch database to help you find the problem that happens to bother your exact hardware and software combination, and point you to the patch that will fix it for you. (More on patches a couple of sections from now.) Other contract services include the capability to download special system diagnostic tools and examine online documentation such as white papers, problem symptom and resolution reports, and information on how to transition from one version of the operating system to another, among others.

A final method of getting technical support is often the most useful, and it's free! We're going to talk about using Usenet at the end of this chapter, but it's good to mention that there is a

Escalating a service call

Here's something most vendors don't tell you when you get a service contract, but you should know it anyway. If a problem you have found is severely impacting you, the technical support people aren't calling you back in a timely manner, or they seem to be overly inexperienced, you can *escalate* the call. You do this by calling the tech support center back, give them your service order number, and ask to speak to the escalation manager. You can explain the poor service to him and ask to have the call escalated in priority. You will only want to do this in cases of extreme emergency, or when a software support engineer just won't call you back. I generally only have to do it once a year or so.

set of newsgroups for virtually every computer type and operating system that ever existed. Often you will find that experts frequent these newsgroups and they are usually only too happy to provide you with any help you need. *However*, it is often the case that any question you may have, especially if you're a beginner, has already been asked hundreds of times. If so, it will generally be included in a *Frequently Asked Questions* (*FAQ*) message sent out on each newsgroup once a month or so. This is a single message consisting of every support question that has been asked and answered for a specific newsgroup topic since it was created. You will be saving yourself a lot of trouble (and hate email) by reading this message before asking everyone in the newsgroup about your particular problem. More about the specific names of such newsgroups at the end of this chapter.

Accessing Free (Non-Supported) Software

All vendors provide some internally developed software for monitoring your system free of charge. They are free because they are not supported officially. If you want to report a problem with them, you have to take it up with the original author of the tools, who may or may not be able to do anything, depending on their current workload.

An example of such a tool for Suns is SymbEL, originally known as Virtual Adrian, available from `http://www.sun.com/sun-on-net/performance/se3/`. It enables you to analyze the inner workings of the operating system *kernel*, and reports modifications you could make to get better performance out of it. You will notice that it is explicitly stated that the package is not officially supported, but that they would appreciate feedback via email and will consider any requests for enhancement.

Such tools actually work quite well. The problem is *finding* them, because non-supported applications are not given prominent exposure. If you know the names of the tools that you want, it's a pretty easy process of feeding these names into a Web search engine and coming up with at least a hint of where to obtain the latest copies of them. It's also worthy of note that not all such programs are created or provided by the vendor. Some are written by experienced programmers who want to share them with everybody.

Usenet is another location to look for or hear about such tools. The groups you should monitor for your particular vendor are discussed later in this chapter.

Checking Patches/Updates

As mentioned earlier, vendors make certain critical patches available free on their Web sites. The freely provided patches are also usually available in *patch clusters*, which are a group of patches targeted at a specific release of the operating system. Periodically checking the vendor's Web site for new releases of individual patches or patch clusters is a good idea, because this will keep you up to date on issues that might otherwise bite you unexpectedly.

If you have a support contract with your UNIX vendor, you are in a much better position because you can mark certain patches or patch clusters on their Web site so that you are notified immediately via email when updates to them are released. You also have the option of using sophisticated search engines to locate patches that affect your exact hardware/software/operating system version configuration.

You also have access to a very nice tool on Sun's Web site to help you determine the right patches to apply to your system (and probably similar tools on other platforms) if you have software support. The tool is called patchdiag, and it compares the patches currently loaded on your system with the patches that Sun currently recommends that you have loaded. It then produces a report telling you what you have loaded, and what you should have loaded. It even has a separate section describing patches that affect operating system/applications, and another section that describes the patches that affect security. Very nice.

One word about patches on UNIX machines. Many vendors are rightfully paranoid about permanently removing any files replaced by a patch application. So they take the files that are to be replaced and tuck them away, just in case you ever want to back the patch out. Just be aware that you may lose a bit of disk space because of this.

As different patches for the same problem are updated, applying one patch on top of the other takes more and more disk space. If you have the time but not the disk space to spare, you can remove the old patch before applying the new one. Usually when you upgrade your operating system, such patch remnants are removed completely anyway, so you can reclaim the space.

Checking Security Bulletins

Security Bulletins for your particular flavor of UNIX are generally displayed very prominently on your vendor's Web site. An archive of past security alerts is also usually available free of charge. Each bulletin describes a part of the operating system that can be compromised by people with the right information. It also describes the patches or actions necessary to block the threat.

Patches for security holes are almost always freely available. You may choose to manually check occasionally for new security bulletins, or you can get on a mailing list that is prominently mentioned in each individual security bulletin. You will be notified when a bulletin is issued for your particular platform automatically after that.

Checking Year 2000 Issues

Unless you have been asleep for the past couple of years, you have heard of all the problems the year 2000 will bring to the computing world in general. Most of these issues have to do with the fact that many applications and some operating systems were written with the first two digits of the year (that's the 19 in the year 1999) hard-coded everywhere. Only the last two digits of the year actually changed in databases, and other files where dates were stored. Therefore when the year 2000 arrives, these applications will change the last two digits of the year to 00, and the year will appear to be 1900 to them.

As you might imagine, this will cause programs that depend on the date moving *forward* as time progresses to get a little confused, and do some nasty things to the data that they have control over. Things such as bank records, billing programs, and others may be affected unless such programs are discovered and repaired prior to December 31, 1999.

This whole thing came about because people working on these applications and operating systems had no idea that anyone would still be using *their* applications or even the same computers when the year 2000 arrived. And some developers are still in the bad habit of coding programs that handle date-sensitive information in the same way.

Most UNIX vendors are very conscious of this issue and have spent a great deal of effort to go through their system administration and general system programs to make sure that all of them are year 2000-compliant. If you are running older versions of their operating systems, they probably have patches that you can apply to fix these problems today. The newer versions of UNIX claim complete year 2000 compliance. If you have a support contract with your UNIX vendor, these patches are prominently displayed on their support Web sites, and can be downloaded directly to your system for application. If you have not purchased a support contract with your UNIX vendor, most of them will still provide their year 2000 patches via the free services section of their support Web pages, because they are critical to keeping you up and running.

Of course, patching your UNIX operating system and the tools that your vendor ships with it may not be enough. You probably have applications that you purchased from other vendors, and you will need to either check with them directly or visit their Web sites. As with the UNIX vendors, most application vendors prominently claim fixes to the year 2000 problem on the first page of their support Web site.

Reading the Network News on UNIX

One of the oldest activities on the Internet is reading the Network News, otherwise known as Usenet. Usenet is essentially a gigantic collection of individual discussion topics that range from job offerings (misc.jobs.offered) to how to administer your Sun computer (comp.sys.sun.admin) to how to care for your African Grey parrot (alt.pets.parrots.african-grey). Often you can speak with experts in the particular topic, or offer advice if you are an expert in this field. Each newsgroup is very specific in its content, but this is only enforced if the newsgroup is moderated. A moderated newsgroup has an assigned moderator who reads every incoming message to the newsgroup to verify that it belongs there. If it doesn't, he rejects it. An unmoderated newsgroup is usually a free-for-all, but people generally are polite enough to stick to the topic at hand. If the group gets completely out of control, it can be dropped from all news servers throughout Usenet.

Newsgroups are arranged in a hierarchy, where the first word in the newsgroup name is the least specific, and as you proceed into the newsgroup name it becomes more specific. Table 24.4 lists and explains this convention.

TABLE 24.6   **Top level of several Usenet newsgroup hierarchies**

comp.*	Computer related newsgroups (for example, comp.sys.sun, comp.sys.hp)
rec.*	Recreational newsgroups (for example, rec.humor, rec.gardens.roses)
sci.*	Science-related newsgroups (for example, sci.math, sci.archaeology)
alt.*	Alternative newsgroups (for example, alt.binaries.startrek)
misc.*	Miscellaneous topics that don't fit anywhere else

When you select a newsgroup to read/write to, it is called *subscribing* to the newsgroup. When you send a message to be included in a newgroup, it is called *posting* to the newsgroup. When you do this, it will take a day or so to filter out to all the news servers in the world, and then people will very likely reply to what you have written. It used to be that you had to scan the newsgroup each day, manually looking for any reply to your original question/remark. Thankfully, most news readers today provide a facility called *threading*, which finds original postings and places any responses to them in chronological order immediately following them. You will find that trn (**t**hreaded **r**ead-**n**ews) and Netscape provide this feature, although Netscape calls newsgroups "discussion groups," and calls the portion of their browser which you use to read news "Collabra Discussions."

Having a news reader client is not enough to enable you to read and post to Usenet. You need to have access to a news server. If you are at a large site, your system administrator has probably set up a news server, or has arranged with another site to provide this service. In any case, your system administrator can tell you the name of this server so that you can connect to it. If your UNIX machine is standalone, and you are accessing the Internet through an Internet service provider, you can ask them what the name of their news server is. After you know the name of the news server, set the environment variable NNTPSERVER so that it points to it. Most news reader clients look for this environment variable when they start up and use it to identify the news server they should connect to.

1. You want to use trn to read Network News. First, make sure that trn is available. If not, ask your system administrator to install it (or something equivalent) for you; or, if you're on your own, you can download the source code for it and compile it yourself. After it is installed, you can proceed to the next step.

2. Find out what the name of your news server is from your system administrator or Internet service provider and set your NNTPSERVER environment variable accordingly. For this example, assume the name of the news server is *news.mycompany.com*.

   For Bourne, Bash, and Korn Shell users
   ```
   NNTPSERVER=news.mycompany.com; export NNTPSERVER
   ```

   For C Shell Users
   ```
   setenv NNTPSERVER news.mycompany.com
   ```

3. Now run trn and subscribe to all the comp.sys.sun.* newsgroups. At the command line, type trn. (The bolded terms at the end of the lines in the following output reflect what you type in as response.)

NNTP

NNTPSERVER stands for Network News Transfer Protocol SERVER.

```
To add new group use a pattern or "g newsgroup.name". To
➡get rid of newsgroups you aren't interested in, use
➡the 'u' command.
No unread news in subscribed-to newsgroups. To subscribe
➡to a new newsgroup use the g<newsgroup> command.
***End of newsgroups -- what next? [qnp] a comp.sys.sun

Newsgroup comp.sys.sun.admin not in .newsrc -- subscribe?
➡[ynYN] y
Put newsgroup where? [$^Lq] $

 . . .

====== 456 unread articles in comp.sys.sun.admin -- read
➡now? [+ynq] y
```

4. When you typed a comp.sys.sun, you instructed trn to search the entire list of newsgroups for any that had comp.sys.sun in their title and ask you whether you want to subscribe to each one in turn. If you said yes, it would ask you where you wanted to put this new newsgroup in your current list of subscribed newsgroups. Pressing the dollar sign ($) puts this newsgroup at the end of your current list. After you have added all your new newsgroups, you are given the opportunity to read the messages in each one.

5. If you would like to post a message to any newsgroup, you do so from anywhere within trn by typing !Pnews. You will be asked what newsgroup you want to send a message to. You can specify more than one newsgroup at once if you like, by separating the newsgroup names with commas.

6. Pressing the *h* key at any time in trn will give you the Help menu.

As discussed earlier, newsgroups deal with specific flavors of UNIX. Reading the ones specific to your flavor can be very helpful, and even more helpful when you need to ask a question, because you are speaking in a forum that deals only with that topic. But you need to know what the newsgroups are. The good news is that the name of the newsgroups follow a specific pattern. Table 24.7 shows the major Sun newsgroups and their purposes.

TABLE 24.7   **Sun-specific newsgroups**

comp.sys.sun.announce	Major announcements of interest to people that use Sun computers
comp.sys.sun.admin	Information on system administration of Sun computers
comp.sys.sun.apps	Information on applications that run on Sun computers
comp.sys.sun.hardware	Information on Sun computer hardware
comp.sys.sun.misc	Miscellaneous information on Sun computers that doesn't fit into any other newsgroup
comp.sys.sun.wanted	Usually requests for Sun hardware, but sometimes software too

If you are using Hewlett-Packard's HP-UX, don't give up hope. Just replace "sun" in the preceding table with "hp." and you have the same newsgroups for your platform. Other flavors of UNIX have newsgroups named similarly.

Shell Programming

Writing Bourne Shell Scripts

By Gordon Marler

Writing/executing a simple script

Creating/using your own variables

Interacting with the user

Supplying script input on the command line (*$1*)

Executing code based on test results (*if*)

Performing arithmetic calculations (*expr/bc*)

Special shell variables

Ending the script and setting completion status (*exit*)

The Bourne shell is the standard shell and can be found on every flavor of UNIX that has ever existed. Although it can be considered a subset of the Korn shell, many people still write scripts in the Bourne shell because it's guaranteed to be portable among different versions of UNIX.

You have already seen that the shell can be used as a command line interface to UNIX, but it also contains programming constructs that enable you take repetitive command sequences and automate them in a script. An example of this would be finding all the programs you currently have running in the system and reporting them to you. You can also have a script interact with you and make decisions based on your input. An example of this would be a script that asks you for a particular user's name, and then finds all the programs in the system that belong to that user and reports them to you.

One simple rule before we jump in: The pound sign (#) character signifies that the rest of the characters following it are part of a comment and will not be interpreted by the shell unless the # is the first character on the first line. You will see why in a second.

Writing/Executing a Simple Script

You can begin by creating a very simple Bourne shell script that prints Hello World and then exits.

1. First, you need to create the empty file where you will put your script. Call this file testscript. Enter touch testscript.

2. To make sure this file is seen as containing an executable script, you must turn on execute permission for the file. Enter chmod +x testscript.

3. Now you need to put something in the file to let UNIX know that this is a Bourne shell script. Most versions of UNIX understand the #! notation. If the first two characters in a file are #!, UNIX will take everything else on the first line of the file to be the command interpreter (usually a shell) that will be used to execute the contents of the file. In

this case, we want the Bourne shell to execute the contents of our file, so we will use vi or some other editor to enter the first line of the testscript file: `#!/bin/sh`.

4. Printing `"Hello World"` is accomplished by entering the second line of the file: `echo "Hello World."`

5. You can test your script by running it:

```
$ ./testscript
Hello World
$
```

6. Your finished script should look like this:

```
#!/bin/sh
echo "Hello World"
```

SEE ALSO

➤ *For more information on working with scripts, see page 288*

Creating/Using Your Own Variables

You will often find it convenient to store the output of a command you run in your script for use later in the script. Or, you might want to hard-code some information such as a long directory path, but you don't want to type the whole path in every time you need to use it in the script. And if this directory path ever needs to be changed, it would be nice to be able to change it in only one place in the script, and yet have it take effect throughout the script. To do this, you must create a variable. A shell variable begins with any letter or underscore (_) character, followed by zero or more numbers, letters, or underscores.

To assign a value to the variable, you use the equals sign (=) and then the value you want to assign to the variable. Note that you can't use a space before or after the equals sign. Study these examples:

`LocalBinaries=/usr/local/bin`	Valid
`TMP=/tmp`	Valid
`_mybinaries=/home/gmarler/bin`	Valid
`rocket_0=apollo`	Valid

`0_rocket=mercury`	Invalid—First character cannot be a number
`myvar = myvalue`	Invalid—Spaces around = sign

To retrieve the value stored in a variable, you place a dollar sign ($) in front of the variable name. This can also be done by surrounding the variable name with curly braces ({...}) and putting a dollar sign ($) in front of the whole thing. You will see when this would be necessary a little later.

Let's write a script that sets a variable, and then prints its value out:

1. Follow steps 1–3 of the section "Writing/Executing a Simple Script," but call the filename `testscript2`.

2. On the second line of the script, set the variable named `tmp_dir` to `/tmp`. Enter: `tmp_dir=/tmp`.

3. On the next line, print the value of the variable `tmp_dir`. Enter: `echo " Variable tmp_dir contains: $tmp_dir."`

4. Save your script file. It should now contain the following:
   ```
   #!/bin/sh
   tmp_dir=/tmp
   echo "Variable tmp_dir contains: $tmp_dir"
   ```

5. Test your script:
   ```
   $ ./testscript2
   Variable tmp_dir contains: /tmp
   ```

I said that it might be necessary to use the `${variablename}` syntax when you want to retrieve the value stored in a variable. This is true whenever you are going to use the value of a variable in a manner similar to this:

```
mv $filename ${filename}OLD
```

Here our intention is to use the name of a file kept in variable `filename` twice: The first time to refer to the original filename, and the second time to create a new name for the original file, with OLD tacked on the end of it. You might make the mistake of trying to write the same thing like this:

```
mv $filename $filenameOLD
```

This attempts to move the file referenced in variable `filename` to the name referenced by the variable `filenameOLD`, which doesn't even exist. From this example, you can probably see that it would be good to get into the habit of always using the `${variablename}` form of referencing the contents of a variable because it always works.

Using Backquotes to Set a Variable

Rather than manually setting the values of all your variables, you can run a program and store its output in a variable. You run the command you wish to capture the output of by surrounding it with backquotes (`` ` ``). This is also known as command substitution, because the shell takes the command you type in backquotes, runs it as a separate program as though you had typed it in on the command line, and then takes the output and substitutes it for the entire backquoted expression. The backquote is on the same key as the tilde (~) on your keyboard.

You can test this facility by writing a script that collects your username, the name of the computer you are running the script on, and the current date to print an informational message.

Testing the backquote method for setting a variable

1. Follow steps 1–3 of the section "Writing/Executing a Simple Script," but name the file `system_info`.

2. Store the output of the date program in the variable today. Enter ``today=`date` ``.

3. Find out who you are logged on as by running `whoami` and store this in the variable identity. Enter ``identity=`whoami` ``.

4. Find out what the name of the machine is and store it in the variable machine. Enter ``machine=`hostname` ``.

5. Print this information out in a nice format. Enter `echo`
   `"Hello, today is $date. I am logged in as $identity on`
   `machine $machine."`

6. Save your script. It should look like this:
   ```
   #!/bin/sh
   today=`date`
   identity=`whoami`
   ```

```
machine=`hostname`
echo "Hello, today is $date. I am logged in as $identity
➥on machine $machine"
```

7. Test the script:

```
$ ./system_info
Hello, today is Thu Mar 12 01:03:27 PST 1998. I am
➥logged in as gmarler on machine proteon
```

You need to make sure that the commands you want to execute by using the backquotes can actually be found by your shell script. You do this by explicitly setting the PATH environment variable within your script. You want to do this because scripts that don't have this variable set will inherit the PATH of the user who runs the script. If that user doesn't have the same path as you, the author of the script, it may mysteriously fail to run for that user.

SEE ALSO

➤ *For more information on setting your path and finding the actual path to programs you want to run, see page 97 and page 100*

You want to write a script that runs the whoami and hostname commands, and you would like to make very sure that the script will actually find these two commands no matter who runs them. Here's how:

Using *whoami* and *hostname*

1. Find out which directories these commands are located in. On Solaris, whoami is located in /usr/ucb/whoami, and date is located in /usr/bin/hostname.

2. Now you know that you need to create a line in your script (preferably the first line) that specifies that you want /usr/ucb and /usr/bin in your PATH. That line should look like this: PATH=/usr/ucb:/usr/bin

3. Here's an example of the entire script:

```
#!/bin/sh
PATH=/usr/ucb:/usr/bin
myhost=`hostname`
myidentity=`whoami`
echo "My username is $myidentity, and my machine name is
➥$myhost"
```

Using quotation marks

If the command in backquotes is going to produce multiple lines of output, you need to make sure that you enclose the backquoted command in double quotation marks. Otherwise, the new lines in the output will be stripped out, and you will get one very long, ugly line! Double quotation marks are also necessary if you intend to echo the output from such a command after it has been stored in a variable.

Interacting with the User

The following section further demonstrates some of the script commands discussed earlier in this chapter, and adds some new ones to your skill set.

Displaying Headings and Prompts (*echo*)

You have already used the echo command to output the results of a script's actions. You also use it, however, to print pretty much any output you want the user to see. By default, echo prints the information you give it plus a new line so that you are forced to go to the next line unless you specify otherwise.

The echo command allows for the following formatting escape characters that help you create headings, titles, and prompts.

\c	Prints the text up to this point without going to the next line. Useful for prompts.
\n	New line. Useful for forcing text after this to be printed on the next line
\t	Tab. Useful for formatting headings and prompts.
\\	Useful for inserting the backslash character in the line.
\0xx	Useful for inserting unprintable control characters. 0xx is an octal representation of an ASCII character. The zero is required.

Using what you know to print information about the user

1. First, print a header for your table of information. Use a couple of tabs in front of the header to more-or-less center it, and put an extra blank line after it to distance it from the rest of the table. Because echo already forces you to the next line, you just need to add another new line to the end:

```
echo "\t\tCURRENT USER INFORMATION\n."
```

2. You need the username of the person running the script for a command used later; so you will save it in a variable:

```
identity=`whoami`.
```

3. Now you will print some information about the user. Notice that backquoted commands are used right inside the line to be output. These commands are run, and their output is substituted in the text before it is printed:

```
echo "My Unix username is: `whoami`"
echo "My Unix machine name is: `hostname`"
echo "My current directory is: `pwd`"
```

4. Finally, you print a list of all the programs currently being run in the system by the person running this script. Note the new line (\n) in the middle of the line. This forces the rest of the output of this echo command to appear beginning on the next line. The rest of the line is a backquoted command that gets a list of all the programs running in the system (ps -ef) and passes that output into the grep command, searching for all the programs being run by the person running the script. Note that double quotation marks had to be used here; otherwise the multi-line output of the backquoted command would have shown up as one big line.

```
echo "Programs I am currently running: \n `ps -ef ¦ grep
➥$identity`"
```

5. Here's the whole script:

```
#!/bin/sh
echo "\t\tCURRENT USER INFORMATION\n"
identity=`whoami`
echo "My Unix username is: `whoami`"
echo "My Unix machine name is: `hostname`"
echo "My current directory is: `pwd`"
echo "Programs I am currently running: \n `ps -ef ¦ grep
➥$identity`"
```

Usually, you will also want to use echo to let the user know that you expect some kind of input. When you do this, you can either print your prompt on one line and let the user type his response on the next line, or you can allow the response to be typed on the same line as the prompt.

This line of code will print "Please enter your password", and then move the cursor to the next line.

```
echo "Please enter your password"
```

This line of code will print "Please tell me your name:", a space, and then leave the cursor after the space. As you can see, the \c formatting character prevents the cursor from going to the next line.

```
echo "Please tell me your name: \c"
```

Now that you have printed a prompt, let's go to the next section to see how to read the user's response.

Getting User Input into a Shell Variable (*read*)

Now that you know how to output information from your script to the user, it's time to learn how to accept input from the user and use it in your script.

The read function serves this purpose. The thing to remember about this function is that it only takes a single type of input: any amount of text (usually up to 1,024 characters) that must be followed by a return. Until the Return key is pressed, the read function won't actually do anything with what the user types in.

The following steps show you how to ask the user for any username and then report the programs currently being run in the system by that username.

Reporting on currently running programs

1. First, prompt the user to type in a UNIX username, leaving the cursor on the same line: echo "Please enter a username: \c."

2. Now, read the response into a variable named username:

   ```
   read username.
   ```

3. Now print a nicely formatted header, and use the username variable to find all the programs being run by that username. We store that information in the variable programs:

   ```
   echo "\n\t\tCURRENT USER INFORMATION\n"
   programs="`ps -ef | grep $username`"
   ```

4. We now print a line using the username variable again, followed by two carriage returns and the contents of the program variable:

   ```
   echo "User $username is running the following programs:
   ➡\n\n $programs"
   ```

5. Here's the whole script:

```
#!/bin/sh
echo "Please enter a username: \c"
read username
echo "\n\t\tCURRENT USER INFORMATION\n"
programs="`ps -ef | grep $username`"
echo "User $username is running the following programs:
➥\n\n $programs"
```

Another thing to remember about read is that it can be used to read values into more than one variable.

```
echo "Please enter your firstname, lastname, age and weight"
read firstname lastname age weight
```

If the user enters more values than the number of variables you read into, however, the last variable in your read command will receive all the extra values. In the following example, if the user were to type John Smith 20 160 in response to the prompt, the variable firstname would contain "John", and the variable lastname would contain "Smith 20 160". Probably not what you want.

```
echo "Please tell me your first and last name"
read firstname lastname
```

Supplying Script Input on the Command Line (*$1*)

So far, we have created scripts that either don't need any input from the user at all, or that have to interact directly with the user every time you run them. You will often find it convenient to give a script all the information it needs when you start it so that it won't have to ask you any questions while it runs. This is especially true if you're going to run the script in the background, because you don't have the chance to give any extra input to such a script because running it in the background disconnects it from the terminal. It is also useful when another script is going to be running your script and passing it information.

When you run a script and pass it arguments like this:

```
myscript arg1 arg2 arg3 …
```

Inside your script, the special variables $1, $2, and $3 get set to arg1, arg2, and arg3, respectively. This works all the way up to $9. If you need to handle more than nine arguments, you need to use another method that entails the use of the for directive. That directive is discussed a few sections from now.

It is also handy to note that $0 gets set to the actual name of your script (myscript, in this case). You may find that handy when you want to print information messages and want to include the name of your script in them.

Executing Code Based on Test Results (*if*)

All programming languages have some way of deciding whether to execute code based on whether a condition is true or not. The shell provides this to you as the if statement. The full format of the if statement is as follows:

```
if  conditional
then
    command
    …
elif conditional
then
    command
    …
else
    command
    …
fi
```

Here's how it works: the *conditional* in all cases is any command that you can execute. If the exit status of the command is zero (0)—which means that it was successful—then the commands immediately following the *conditional* are executed, up to the next else, elif, or fi. If the exit status of the command is anything but zero—which means that the command failed in some way—then the commands after the `conditional` are skipped up to the next `else`, `elif`, or `fi`.

The `elif` statement, if present, stands for `else if`, and enables you to test another conditional before falling through to the `else` statement, or out of the whole `if` statement. This part of the statement is not required, and is provided in case you need to use it.

The `else` statement, if present, is executed only if the previous `if` conditional was not true. This part of the statement is also not required.

If you don't like putting the keyword `then` on a line by itself, you can put it on the same line as the `if` or `elif` keywords as long as you use a semicolon to separate it from the `conditional`.

```
if conditional; then
```

```
elif conditional; then
```

You'll notice that we said the `conditional` can be any command, but it is often the `test` command. Let's look at a few examples to see how this works.

Checking File Type, Size, or Permissions

One of the things the `test` command enables you to do is examine several qualities of any `filesystem` object (file or directory) and make decisions in your script based on them. The following table is not a complete list of the options `test` can use for a `filesystem` object, but it does cover the most commonly used ones.

Table 25.1   **Options to test used on *filesystem* objects**

`-d file`	Is the file a directory?
`-f file`	Is the file a normal file?
`-r file`	Is the file readable by this script?

-w file	Is the file writable by this script?
-x file	Is the file executable by this script?
-s file	Does the file have a length greater than zero?

Using the *test* command

1. Let's create a file and run several tests on it from a script called testif1. First, let's make it a zero length file, and set the permissions on it.
   ```
   touch /tmp/testfile
   chmod 775 /tmp/testfile
   ```

2. Now we can write our script. Let's start by using a couple of separate if statements:
   ```
   MYFILE="/tmp/testfile"
   if test -d $MYFILE
   then
      echo "My file is a directory!"
   fi
   if test -f $MYFILE
   then
      echo "My file is an ordinary file!"
   fi
   ```

   If you save and run this script as is, you should get the following output:
   ```
   % ./testif
   My file is an ordinary file!
   ```

   This is what you would expect.

3. Now let's create a new script called testif2. We'll use the elif and else statements here:
   ```
   MYFILE="/tmp/testfile"
   if test -d $MYFILE
   then
      echo "My file is a directory!"
   elif test -f $MYFILE
   then
      echo "My file is an ordinary file!"
      if test -w $MYFILE
      then
   ```

```
        echo "This file is writeable too!"
    else
        echo "This file is not writeable"
    fi
    if test -r $MYFILE
    then
        echo "This file is readable!"

    else
        echo "This file is not readable"
    fi
fi
```

Notice that you can put an `if` statement inside another `if` statement. With the current file permissions, this script should output the following:

```
% ./testif2
My file is an ordinary file!
This file is writeable too!
This file is readable!
```

4. Now let's modify the permissions on the file slightly, by turning off the ability to write to it so that we can test the script.

```
chmod -w /tmp/testfile
```

5. Now run the script again:

```
% ./testif2
My file is an ordinary file!
This file is not writeable
This file is readable!
```

SEE ALSO

➤ *For related information, see page 286*

It's worth noting that you don't have to have a separate `if` statement for every condition that you want to test for. You can combine several `test` commands on one line if you like, or if it happens to be convenient for what you're trying to accomplish. In the following table, `exp` stands for any option of the `test` command.

Table 25.2   **Operators for combining multiple test commands**

test exp$_1$ && test exp$_2$	If exp$_1$ *and* exp$_2$ are true, the whole command is true.
test exp$_1$ || test exp$_2$	If exp$_1$ OR exp$_2$ are true, the whole command is true.
test ! exp$_1$	If exp$_1$ turns out to be true, it is now false, and vice-versa.

Another example of the *test* command

1. We can now write a script that's a bit shorter called testif3. Let's change the permissions of our file back for a second.
   ```
   chmod +w /tmp/testfile
   ```

2. We will test to see whether the file is an ordinary file and writable, and readable:
   ```
   MYFILE="/tmp/testfile"
   if test -f $MYFILE && test -w $MYFILE && test -r $MYFILE
   then
       echo "My file is an ordinary file, and it is writeable
       ➥and readable!"
   fi
   ```

3. Now if the file has nothing in it, it wouldn't make sense to try to run it as a program, even if the execute bit was on, would it? Let's have the script test for this scenario and tell us about it. Notice that the -s test returns true (0) only if the file has a size greater than zero, and false (1) if the file size is exactly zero. Therefore we reverse the sense of the test by using the ! operator on it. This makes the logic of the statement read as follows: If the file is executable *and* if the file has zero length, print the message.
   ```
   if test -x $MYFILE && test ! -s $MYFILE
   then
       echo "This file is empty!  Why would you try to
       ➥execute it?"
   fi
   ```

4. Let's look at the output of the script:

```
% ./testif3
My file is an ordinary file, and it is writeable and
➥readable!
This file is empty! Why would you try to execute it?
```

There is a another way to write the test command that makes it much more readable in your scripts, and uses the square brackets ([...]):

[-x *file*] is equivalent to test -x *file*.

From this point on, we will be using the [...] syntax for the test command.

Don't forget the space

When you use this form of **test** in your scripts, you have to make certain that you put a space *after* the opening square bracket ([) and a space *before* the closing square bracket (]). If you don't, it's a syntax error.

Checking Variable Contents

In addition to checking file attributes, you can use test to see what's in your variables and make decisions based on their contents. There are separate operators for testing variables you want to interpret as strings, and those you want to interpret as integers.

Table 25.3   String operators for test

-n *string*	Return true if *string* has a value (is not null)
-z *string*	Return true if *string* has no value (is null)
string1 = *string2*	Return true if *string1* is identical to *string2*
string1 != *string2*	Return true if *string1* is not identical to *string2*

A few examples should clarify how these work. You can use any of these statements as the conditional portion of an if statement in your script. You should remember that any variable you pass to test should be surrounded by double quotation marks.

First we can check to see whether a variable has any value at all.

```
myvar=
if [ -z "$myvar" ]; then
    echo "This variable has no value"
fi
```

That last example can actually bite you, however, if the variable `myvar` contains certain non-alphanumeric characters such as the equals sign (=), because `test` will think that you're trying to assign a value to a variable! To make sure this never happens to you, you can use another construct, which you will find is extremely common in shell scripts.

```
myvar=
if [ X = X"$myvar" ]; then
    echo "This variable has no value"
fi
```

Did you see how that works? If `myvar` has no value, the statement boils down to this: Does x equal x? Which is, of course, true.

Now let's do some comparisons between string variables.

```
animal1="pig"
animal2="cow"
if [ $animal1 = $animal2 ]; then
    echo "These animals are the same"
elif [ $animal1 != $animal2 ]; then
    echo "These animals are different"
fi
```

If the strings stored in your variables are numeric, you need to use another set of operators to treat them as if they were numbers. You need to make this distinction, as you will see from the following examples. Remember that these operators work only on integers. They do not understand numbers with a decimal place in them.

Table 25.4 **Integer operators for test**

`int1 -eq int2`	`int1` is equal to `int2`
`int1 -ne int2`	`int1` is not equal to `int2`
`int1 -gt int2`	`int1` is greater than `int2`
`int1 -ge int2`	`int1` is greater than or equal to `int2`
`int1 -lt int2`	`int1` is less than `int2`
`int1 -le int2`	`int1` is less than or equal to `int2`

```
value1="6 "
value2="00005"
if [ "$value1" -ne "$value2" ]; then
    echo "These values are not equal"
fi
if [ "$value1" -eq 6 ]; then
    echo "value1 is equal to 6"
fi
if [ "$value2" -eq 5 ]; then
    echo "value2 is equal to 5"
fi
```

Now, if you had used the string operator = rather than the integer operator -eq in the last two tests, you would not have received output from either one of them. That's because there is a space after the 6 in value1, and four zeros before the 5 in value2, and the string operators are looking for an exact character match, rather than a numerical match.

Checking Command Results

I know that I said the *conditional* part of an if statement is usually a form of the test command, but you can use any command or program that returns a zero (0) if it completes successfully, and any other number if it doesn't.

An example of this would be if you wanted to find out if anyone was running the vi text editor on the system. Actually, this script will locate any vi program running in the system, as well as anything else generated by ps -ef that has the word "vi" in it.

```
if ps -ef | grep "vi"; then
    echo "Yep, someone is running vi"
else
    echo "No one is running vi at this time"
fi
```

Notice that we ran ps -ef, piped the output into grep, and told it to look for any line that ended with the last two characters *vi*. If grep is successful in that search, it will return a status code of zero, and the line acknowledging that vi is running somewhere in the system will be returned. Notice that only the status code of the last command that ran in the *conditional* is examined for success or failure. The status code of ps is ignored.

SEE ALSO

➤ *For more information on running searches and piping results, see page 380 and page 388*

Let's take a look at the output of the preceding program:

```
% ./vitest
gmarler 16145 16128  0 17:49:02 pts/10   0:00 vi
Yep, vi is running
```

What happened? Well, the first line of output was produced by running ps -ef | grep "vi$". The second line was produced by your script. If you don't want the output of the *conditional* program to be seen by the person running your script, you can redirect the output of such programs to /dev/null. The modified line would look like this.

```
if ps -ef | grep "vi$" > /dev/null; then

...
```

That's fine as long as the programs you run in a *conditional* send any information to *standard output*. If they also send any informational messages or errors to *standard error*, however, you will have to change the line to send both of them to /dev/null if you don't want to see these messages interspersed with yours. In that case, the line would change to this:

```
if ps -ef | grep "vi$" > /dev/null 2>&1; then
...
```

You don't actually even have to use if to get these results. You can use the && and || operators to connect a series of commands that you want to execute under certain conditions. First, let's examine how to look at these operators. You can think of

```
command1 && command2
```

as meaning "If and only if *command1* executed successfully, execute *command2*." You can think of:

```
command1 || command2
```

as meaning "If *command1* did not execute successfully, execute *command2*."

You can connect as many commands as you think necessary with these operators. Here's an example of the common task of copying a log file to another location to preserve it for future examination before emptying the current log file. You don't want to allow the current log file to be emptied before you are sure that the copy to another location was successful.

```
cp ${logfile} ${logfile}.1 && cp /dev/null ${logfile}
```

You could rewrite this to give a nice little message notifying someone that the script could not make a copy of the log file. The parentheses are used to make sure that the commands connected by && are fully evaluated before the echo could possibly have a chance to run. If both of the first two commands are successful, the echo will never run.

```
( cp ${logfile} ${logfile}.1 && cp /dev/null ${logfile} ) ||
➥echo "Could not copy ${logfile} to ${logfile}.1"
```

This is a bit shorter (but not as easy to read) than writing the equivalent:

```
if cp ${logfile} ${logfile}.1; then
    cp /dev/null ${logfile}
else
    echo "Could not copy ${logfile} to ${logfile}.1"
fi
```

Performing Arithmetic Calculations (*expr/bc*)

You have probably noticed that all the examples worked with so far have dealt strictly with text, with no mention of how to deal with numeric calculations. That's because the shell thinks that everything *is* text; it only sees numbers as ASCII characters. If you need to perform any kind of numeric calculations, you have to use programs outside the shell to do them for you via the backquote operator. The output of these programs can be assigned to a variable or printed directly from the echo command.

If all you need to perform are integer calculations, you can use the expression evaluator program, expr.

Table 25.5 **Mathematic operations used in *expr***

`result=`expr 5 + 4``	Addition: Stores "9" in variable result.
`result=`expr 5 - 4``	Subtraction: Stores "1" in variable result.
`result=`expr 5 * 4``	Multiplication: Stores "20" in variable result. Note that the asterisk (*) has to be escaped with a backslash.
`result=`expr 4 / 2``	Division: Stores "2" in variable result.
`result=`expr 5 % 4``	Remainder (Modulus): Stores "1" in variable result. That is, 5 divided by 4 leaves a remainder of 1.
`result=`expr 5 / 4``	Division: Stores "1" in variable result. Remember, expr can't do anything except integer calculations.

If you need to use floating point math in your script, you can use bc to do your calculations. You will have to be sure to specify the number of decimal places of accuracy to bc each time you use it.

Using the *bc* command

1. You want to write a script that will take the number of kilobytes of disk space a user has and convert it into megabytes, with an accuracy of two decimal places. To make it simple, we will provide the amount of disk space inside the script. We will see how to pass it into the script later:

```
$diskspace_kb=1808071.
```

2. To get an accuracy of two decimal places, we must use the scale directive to bc; and to get the number of megabytes, we divide the number of kilobytes by 1,024. Notice that we run echo external to the script and pipe the commands to bc. The double quotation marks are necessary to protect the commands from being interpreted by the shell before they get to bc:

```
diskspace_mb=`echo "scale=2; $diskspace_kb/1024" | bc`
echo $diskspace_mb
```

3. In this case, you should get the following output:

```
1765.69
```

> **Escaping the expr command**
>
> Multiplication in `expr` uses the asterisk (*), but you have to escape it with a backslash. Why? Because `expr` is a backquoted command, which is run just like you had typed it in on the command line. If you did that, the asterisk would have been interpreted as a wildcard and would have been converted into the list of all files in the current directory. Not what you want.

Special Shell Variables

For your convenience, the shell predefines several variables, some of which change as your script runs, and others that are permanently set for the life of the script.

Checking the Number of Command-Line Arguments Given ($#)

When someone runs your script, it is always good to make sure that he or she passed the correct number of arguments to it. When your script is run, the shell sets $# to that number. You can check it by using the integer comparison operators already discussed.

If you know that you have to have three options passed to your script, for example, here's how you could check:

```
if [ "$#" -ne 3 ]
then
    echo "Sorry, you did not pass the necessary 3 arguments
    ➥to this script"
fi
```

You will normally perform this test before any others in your scripts.

Checking the Status of the Last Command ($?)

After running a command, it is a very good idea to make sure that it executed properly and act accordingly. Whenever a command is executed on UNIX, it returns an exit status code when it stops running. The shell captures the value of this exit status code and stores it in the special $? variable. You have to examine this variable immediately, however, because it will be reset as soon as the next command is executed. Also, don't try to run a test on the $? variable; doing so resets its value! Save it in a temporary variable first, unless you just want to echo it to the user.

Usually the value of the variable will be zero (0) if the command executed successfully, and any number other than zero (usually 1) if it did not.

In the first example, we will try to copy a log file to another location before setting the original log file to zero length and compressing the copy:

```
cd /var/adm
cp messages messages.1
STATUS=$?
if [ "$STATUS" -eq 0 ]; then
    compress messages.1 &    # Run the compress in the
    ➥background
else
    echo "Could not make a copy of the original log file"
fi
```

If the cp command in the preceding example fails, it is because something went terribly wrong—like your filesystem is full, or something is actually wrong with the disk it is on. Not all commands return values other than zero on this kind of failure. As you have seen, the test comparison commands return zero or one based on whether the comparison is valid.

```
firstname="john"
lastname="smith"
[ "$firstname" = "$lastname" ]
echo $?    # This would print 1, since they are NOT equal
[ "$firstname" = "john" ]
echo $?    # This would print 0, since they ARE equal
```

Using Non-Conflicting Temporary Files ($$)

If you write a script that many people find useful, it is possible that many of them will be running it simultaneously. If this script needs to open temporary files while it runs, you need to take steps to prevent one copy of the script from clobbering the temporary files of another copy of it that is running at the same time. Thankfully, the $$ variable enables you to do this. Whenever you run a script, $$ is set to that script's process ID (PID).

SEE ALSO

➤ *For related information, see page* 77

This makes it unlikely that the $$ variable of one script will be the same as any other copy of the same script running in the same system. Therefore you can use this variable as part of any temporary filename that this script needs to create.

Assume that you want to write a script that will take a file, number all the lines in it with the nl command, save this modified version of the file temporarily, and then print the contents of the temporary file to the screen:

```
if [ "$#" -ne 1 ]; then
    echo "This script wants 1 argument"
    exit
else
    nl $1 >/tmp/nm$$     # Run the Unix nl command on the file
    ➥named in $1
    cat /tmp/nm$$     # Print the contents of the temp file to
    ➥the screen
fi
```

Passing All Arguments to Another Command ($*)

Now you know how to count the number of arguments that were passed into your script by using $#, but how do you get the actual list of arguments themselves? The special variable $* contains that list.

If you want a script to perform a long listing of any files that you specify on the command line with ls, you could write it this way:

```
if [ "$#" -eq 0 ]; then
    echo "This script takes at least one argument"
    exit
fi
listing="`ls -l $*`"
echo "$listing"
```

As you can see, ls gets all the command-line arguments that you passed into the script. Therefore if the script is called lister, and you run it like this:

```
./lister core /tmp/test
```

It would be the same as typing the following:

```
ls -l core /tmp/test
```

Ending the Script and Setting Completion Status (*exit*)

When your script has done its job and is about to terminate, it is a good idea to return an exit status explicitly instead of letting the shell guess what the exit status ought to be. This is especially true if you are exiting because of an error condition, because you would like to give notice of it to any script that might be calling *your* script. And it is generally nice to give an exit status of zero (0) if your script exits normally so that any script that might be calling yours can check your exit status and feel confident that everything is okay.

We have used the exit command in a few previous examples, but never with an argument. Any argument you give exit will be the exit status of your script. Here's a quick example that shows how to exit your script happily and unhappily, depending on the result of a couple of tests.

```
if cp ${filename} ${filename}.1; then
    echo "Compressing ${filename}.1"
    compress ${filename}.1
    cp /dev/null ${filename}
    exit 0         # Ahh! Exiting happily, mission accomplished
else
    echo "Could not copy ${filename} to ${filename}.1"
    exit 1         # Ack! Exiting unhappily
fi
```

Giving Proper UNIX Usage Errors

You have probably noticed that when you run a UNIX command with the wrong number or wrong type of arguments, you get a quick little message from the command letting you know the correct number and order of arguments that it wants.

So far in the examples, we have just printed a message saying that the information entered was wrong. We did not give the user a clue as to what he should have typed.

Here's an example of what you should put as the first test in each of your scripts. In this example, we have the first part of a script that will copy files to an archive location, compress the archived files, and then destroy the originals. It requires that you give it at least one filename to perform this action on.

```
if [ $# -eq 0 ]; then
    echo "Usage: $0 filename …"                 # If no arguments
    ↪were
    echo "Please enter filename(s) to be archived"     #
    ↪given, print this kindly
    exit 1                                   # usage message and exit
fi

…
```

Looping Through Each Command-Line Argument (*for*)

You will often have a list of items in your script that will each need to have a particular action performed on them. The for loop construct can help with this. It's general form is as follows:

```
for variable in list-of-items…
do
    command
    …
done
```

Where *variable* gets set to each value in the *list-of-items*, and *command* is run each time *variable* changes.

Remember that when we discussed the $1, $2, … $9 variables, we stated that you could only reference the first nine arguments to a program with them. Using the for loop, you can access any number. You just learned what the $* variable was for, so let's use a for loop to print all the command-line arguments passed into a script that was run like this:

```
myscript dog cat mouse horse
```

So now $* should contain dog cat mouse horse. Inside myscript the code looks like this:

```
for arg in $*
do
    echo $arg
done
```

Therefore the output from the script is each command-line argument printed on a separate line:

```
dog
cat
mouse
horse
```

Let's use the same idea to write a script that takes all the filenames given on the command line and compresses them (if they exist).

```
if [ "$#" -eq 0 ]; then
    echo "This command requires at least one argument"
    echo "$0: filename-to-compress …"
    exit 1
fi
for FILE in $*
do
    if [ -f "$FILE" ]; then      # Does this file even exist?
        echo "Compressing file $FILE now"
        compress $FILE
    else
        echo "Sorry, filename $FILE does not exist"
    fi
done
```

Debugging Your Script

If a script doesn't do what you expect, or if a variable doesn't seem to have the value you think it should, you can do a couple of things to debug the problem. The easiest is to use the -x option to the Bourne shell. You can do this by modifying the first line of your script to look like this:

```
#!/bin/sh -x
```

Or, you can run the shell directly on your script with the -x option like this:

```
sh -x scriptname
```

Both methods accomplish the same thing; the shell is instructed to print each line in the script one by one, expanding any variables to show the values they contain, and running any backquoted commands, showing their results. After each line is printed this way, it is actually executed. Here's an example script, which we will run with debugging turned on:

```
#!/bin/sh
1.machine=`hostname`
2.identity=`whoami`
3.date=`date`
4.echo "Hello, today is $date"
5.echo "I am logged in as user $identity on machine
➥$machine"
```

Running "info" with debugging turned on:

```
% sh -x ./info
1.+ hostname
2.machine=proteon
3.+ whoami
4.identity=gmarler
5.+ date
6.date=Sat Mar 21 19:22:28 PST 1998
7.+ echo Hello, today is Sat Mar 21 19:22:28 PST 1998
8.Hello, today is Sat Mar 21 19:22:28 PST 1998
9.+ echo I am logged in as user gmarler on machine proteon
10.I am logged in as user gmarler on machine proteon
```

Debugging a script

1. Line one of the script is represented by lines 1 and 2 of the debugging output. Notice that the backquoted hostname command is marked with a plus sign (+) on line 1 to let you know that it was an externally executed command. Line 2 shows you the result. Variable machine now has the value proteon, the name of the machine.

2. Line 2 of the script is executed in lines 3 and 4 of the debugging output. Line 3 shows the external command

whoami being executed, and line 4 shows the output of that command being assigned to the variable identity.

3. Line 3 of the script is shown in lines 5 and 6 of the debugging output. Line 5 shows the external command date being executed, and line 6 shows its output being assigned to variable date.

4. Line 4 of the script is shown in lines 7 and 8 of the debugging output. Note that line 7 expands the date variable. Line 8 is the output that you would see normally even if you didn't run the script in debugging mode.

5. Line 5 of the script is shown in lines 9 and 10 of the debugging output. Line 9 expands the values of the identity and machine variables, and line 10 prints the output that you would normally see from this script.

You can also use the -xv option, which produces an even more verbose debugging output from the script.

A more difficult, or at least more tedious method of debugging is to use echo a great deal, printing out the values of variables that you didn't set in your script, such as command-line arguments that get passed into your script, just to make sure that you're getting the information that you think you ought to.

Looping Through a List of Items (*for*)

You can manually type in the entire list of items you want to loop through using for.

```
for x in 1 2 3 4 5
do
    echo $x
done
```

You can also create the list of items you want to loop through by doing so directly in your script, or have an external program do it for you via the backquote operator.

Processing All Files in a Directory

In a previous example, we wrote a script that compressed the files you specified when you ran the script. You can also write a script that will take all the files in a directory and do "something" to all them, like compress them, so that you don't have to specify anything on the command line at all, unless it is the directories that contain the files. Let's try this:

```
if [ "$#" -eq 0 ]; then
    echo "This command requires at least one argument"
    echo "$0: directory-containing-files-to-compress …"
    exit 1
fi
for DIR in $*
do
    if [ ! -d "$DIR" ]; then
        echo "Sorry, directory $DIR does not exist"
        exit 1
    fi
    for FILE in `ls $DIR`
    do
        if [ -d "$FILE" ]; then
            echo "Yikes!, this is a directory"
        else
            echo "Compressing $FILE now"
            compress $FILE
        fi
    done
done
```

As you can see, we did not need to test whether the files existed because the script generated the list of files. We only had to make sure that the specified directories actually existed. We also had to check to see whether our directory contained other directories as well as files.

Processing All Files in a Directory Tree

Now that we have processed all the files in a directory, what if the directory itself contains another directory, and so on? We will probably want to process all the files in all the subdirectories too. Here's an example of how we can handle this situation.

Processing files

1. As always, start your script by making sure that the proper number of arguments has been entered. In this case, just one is sufficient, but required.

```
if [ "$#" -eq 0 ]; then
    echo "This command requires at least one argument"
    echo "$0: directory-containing-files-to-compress …"
    exit 1
fi
```

2. Now take each directory mentioned on the command line and make sure that it actually exists.

```
for DIR in $*
do
    if [ ! -d "$DIR" ]; then
        echo "Sorry, directory $DIR does not exist"
        exit 1
    fi
```

3. We use the find command to generate the entire list of files under each directory. We can then check each line returned from find to see whether it describes a file (it could be describing a subdirectory, symbolic link, or a pipe), and compress it if it is a file.

```
    for FILE in `find $DIR -print`
    do
        if [ -f "$FILE" ]; then
            echo "Compressing $FILE now"
            compress $FILE
        else
            echo "Yikes, This is not a file"
        fi
    done
done
```

Selecting from a Menu of Items (*case*)

If you want your script to give someone a set menu of options, and then want to act on his or her responses, the case statement is a convenient way to do it. It takes the following form:

```
case value in
    pattern1 )      command

        …
        command;;
    pattern2 )      command

            …
            command;;

    …

    patternx )      command

        …
        command;;
    esac
```

Where *value* is any text string that will be compared with the patterns *pattern₁, pattern₂, …, patternₓ*. The *command* list following the first pattern that matches *value* will be executed. Usually a catch-all pattern (like *) will be used as the last pattern to catch anything that you weren't expecting, or that the user mistyped. Note the required double semicolons (;;) after the last command in each pattern section. Don't forget these; otherwise, you will end up executing several more commands than you were intending to!

The following example covers a script that enables you to compress, to perform a long listing on, or to delete a file.

Compressing, listing, or deleting a file

1. First, you need to print out the menu for the user to pick from. Note the use of the \c control character to ensure that the new line is suppressed and the cursor will remain just after the colon, waiting for input.

```
echo "What would you like to do:

1.      Compress a file
2.      Do a long listing of a file
```

```
3.          Delete a file

Please select one of the above (1-3): \c"
```

2. Now you can read the user's selection after he types it in, and pass it into the `case` statement.

```
read selection
case "$selection" in
```

3. Now that you have his selection, the `case` statement will cover each contingency. The first one is the selection of a file to compress. You will prompt for the file, check to make sure it really exists, and then compress it if it does.

```
1)    echo "Enter filename to compress: \c"
      read filename
      if [ -f "$filename" ]; then
          compress $filename
      else
          echo "Bad filename"
      fi;;
```

4. The second possible selection is for a file to perform a long listing on. Again you prompt for the filename, make sure it exists, and then perform the listing.

```
2)    echo "Enter filename to list: \c"
      read filename
      if [ -f "$filename" ]; then
          ls -l $filename
      else
          echo "Bad filename"
      fi;;
```

5. Now for the third scenario—a filename to be deleted. You prompt for the filename, make sure that it exists, and then delete it.

```
3)    echo "Enter filename to delete: \c"\
      read filename
      if [ -f "$filename" ]; then
          rm $filename
      else
          echo "Bad filename"
      fi;;
```

6. Finally, you want to perform your catch-all, and report it as a bad selection from the menu. Then you end the **case** statement.

```
    *)     echo "Incorrect selection";;
esac
```

Writing *awk* Scripts

by David B. Horvath, CCP

awk is the generic name for the programming language created for UNIX by Alfred V. Aho, Peter J. Weinberger, and Brian W. Kernighan in 1977. The name awk comes from the initials of the creators' last names. Kernighan was also involved with the creation of the C programming language and UNIX; Aho and Weinberger were involved with the development of UNIX. Because of their backgrounds, you will see many similarities between awk and C.

There are several versions of awk: the original awk, nawk, POSIX awk, and gawk (GNU awk). nawk was created in 1985 and is the version described in *The awk Programming Language* (see the complete reference to this book later in the chapter in the section titled "Summary"). POSIX awk is defined in the *IEEE Standard for Information Technology*, *Portable Operating System Interface, Part 2: Shell and Utilities Volume 2*, ANSI-approved April 5, 1993 (IEEE is the Institute of Electrical and Electronics Engineers, Inc.). GNU awk is based on POSIX awk.

The acronym GNU stands for "GNU is Not UNIX." It is the name of a series of useful software packages commonly found in UNIX environments that are being distributed by the GNU project at MIT. The packages are generally free and available at various locations on the Internet (you are charged if you want a copy on a physical medium such as a floppy or tape). The development of the packages is a cooperative process with the work being done by many volunteers. This effort is largely led by Richard M. Stallman (one of the developers of the emacs editor).

GNU

Yes, the GNU acronym is self refer-encing. But it was created that way on purpose. This type of naming has a history in products related to, but not covered by the trademark of, UNIX. A noncommercial operat-ing system similar to UNIX was known as XINU: "XINU is Not UNIX."

The awk language (in all of its versions) is a pattern-matching and processing language with a lot of power. It will search a file (or multiple files) searching for records that match a specified pattern. When a match is found, a specified action is performed. As a programmer, you do not have to worry about opening, looping through the file reading each record, handling end-of-file, or closing it when done. These details are handled automat-ically for you.

It is easy to create short awk programs because of this functionality—many of the details are handled by the language automatically. There are also many functions and built-in features to handle many of the tasks of processing files.

When to Use *awk*

There are many possible uses for awk, including extracting data from a file, counting occurrences within a file, and creating reports.

The basic syntax of the awk language matches the C programming language; if you already know C, you know most of awk. In many ways, awk is an easier version of C because of the way it handles strings and arrays (dynamically). If you do not know C yet, learning awk will make learning C a little easier.

awk is also very useful for rapid prototyping or trying out an idea that will be implemented in another language such as C. Instead of your having to worry about some of the minute details, the built-in automation takes care of them. You worry about the basic functionality.

Features of *awk*

As is the UNIX environment, awk is flexible, contains predefined variables, automates many of the programming tasks, provides the conventional variables, supports the C-formatted output, and is easy to use. awk enables you to combine the best of shell scripts and C programming.

Of course, the "normal" C programming constructs such as if/else, do/while, for, and while are supported. awk doesn't support the switch/case construct. It supports C's printf() for formatted output and also has a print command for simpler output.

awk Fundamentals

Unlike some of the other UNIX tools (shell, grep, and so on), awk requires a program (known as an "awk script"). This program can be as simple as one line or as complex as several thousand lines. (I once developed an awk program that summarized data at several levels with multiple control breaks; it was just short of 1,000 lines.)

When not to use awk

awk works with text files, not binary. Because binary data can contain values that look like record terminators (newline characters)—or not have any at all—**awk** will get confused. If you need to process binary files, look into Perl or use a traditional programming language like C.

Variables within awk

There are usually many different ways to perform the same task within **awk**. Programmers get to decide which method is best suited to their applications. With the built-in variables and functions, many of the normal programming tasks are automatically performed. **awk** will automatically read each record, split it up into fields, and perform type conversions whenever needed. The way a variable is used determines its type—there is no need (or method) to declare variables of any type.

The awk program can be entered a number of ways—on the command line or in a program file. awk can accept input from a file, piped in from another program, or even directly from the keyboard. Output normally goes to the standard output device, but that can be redirected to a file or piped into another program. Output can also be sent directly to a file rather than standard output.

Using *awk* from the Command Line

The simplest way to use awk is to code the program on the command line, accept input from the standard input device (keyboard), and send output to the standard output device (screen). Listing 26.1 shows this in its simplest form; it prints the number of fields in the input record along with that record.

Listing 26.1   Simplest use of *awk*

```
     $ awk '{print NF ": " $0}'
Now is the time for all
6: Now is the time for all
Good Americans to come to the Aid
7: Good Americans to come to the Aid
of Their Country.
3: of Their Country.
Ask not what you can do for awk, but rather what awk can do for you.
16: Ask not what you can do for awk, but rather what awk can do for
    you.
Ctrl+d
$ _
```

NF is a predefined variable set to the number of fields on each record. $0 is that record. The individual fields can be referenced as $1, $2, and so on.

You can also store your awk script in a file and specify that filename on the command line by using the -f flag. If you do that, you don't have to contain the program within single quotation marks.

Some notes about Listing 26.1 and others

Ctrl+D is one way of showing that you should press (and hold) the Ctrl (or Control) key and then press the *D* key. This is the default end-of-file key for UNIX. If this doesn't work on your system, use stty -a to determine which key to press. Another way this action or key is shown on the screen is ^d.

The entire **awk** script is contained within single quotation marks (') to prevent the shell from interpreting its contents. This is a requirement of the operating system or shell, not the **awk** language.

How to run examples in this chapter

All examples will show the use of **awk** as the UNIX command that implements the **awk** language. Your machine may have both **awk** and **nawk**, just the **awk** command (implementing old **awk**, **nawk**, POSIX **awk**, or even **gawk**), or **gawk**. You will have to use the command appropriate to your machine.

You can use the normal UNIX shell redirection or just specify the filename on the command line to accept the input from a file rather than the keyboard:

```
awk '{print NF ": " $0}' < inputs
awk '{print NF ": " $0}' inputs
```

Multiple files can be specified by just listing them on the command line as shown in the second form—they will be processed in the order specified. Output can be redirected through the normal UNIX shell facilities to send it to a file or pipe it into another program:

```
awk '{print NF ": " $0}' > outputs
awk '{print NF ": " $0}' ¦ more
```

Of course, both input and output can be redirected at the same time.

One of the ways I use awk most commonly is to process the output of another command by piping its output into awk. If I wanted to create a custom listing of files that contained the filename and then the permissions only, I would execute a command like this:

```
ls -l ¦ awk '{print $NF, " ", $1}'
```

$NF is the last field (which is the filename—I am lazy—I didn't want to count the fields to figure out its number). $1 is the first field. The output of ls -l is piped into awk, which processes it for me.

If I put the awk script into a file (named lser.awk) and redirected the output to the printer, I would have a command that looks like this:

```
ls -l ¦ awk -f lser.awk ¦ lp
```

See the section titled "Commands On-the-Fly" later in this chapter for more examples of using awk scripts to process piped data.

awk **Processing (Patterns and Actions)**

Each awk statement consists of two parts: the pattern and the action. The pattern decides when the action is executed and, of

---

Running multiple scripts simultaneously

gawk and other versions of awk that meet the POSIX standard support the specification of multiple programs through the use of multiple -f options. This enables you to execute multiple awk programs on the same input. Personally, I tend to avoid this just because it gets a bit confusing.

Script naming

I tend to save my awk scripts with the file type (suffix) of .awk just to make it obvious when I am looking through a directory listing. If the program is longer than about 30 characters, I make a point of saving it because there is no such thing as a "one-time only" program, user request, or personal need.

Use caution when entering the awk command

If you forget the -f option before a program filename, your program will be treated as if it were data.

If you code your awk program on the command line but place it after the name of your data file, it will also be treated as if it were data.

course, the action is what the programmer wants to occur. Without a pattern, the action is always executed (the pattern can be said to "default to true").

There are two special patterns (also known as blocks): BEGIN and END. The BEGIN code is executed before the first record is read from the file and is used to initialize variables and set up things like control breaks. The END code is executed after end-of-file is reached and is used for any cleanup required (like printing final totals on a report). The other patterns are tested for each record read from the file.

The general program format is to put the BEGIN block at the top, any pattern/action pairs, and finally, the END block at the end. This is not a language requirement—it is just the way most people do it (mostly for readability reasons).

The action is contained within curly braces ({ }) and can consist of one or many statements. If you omit the pattern portion, it defaults to true, which causes the action to be executed for every line in the file. If you omit the action, it defaults to print $0 (print the entire record).

The pattern is specified before the action. It can be a regular expression (contained within a pair of slashes (/ /)) that matches part of the input record or an expression that contains comparison operators. It can also be compound or complex patterns that consist of expressions and regular expressions combined or a range of patterns.

Regular Expression Patterns

The regular expressions used by awk are similar to those used by grep, egrep, and the UNIX editors ed, ex, and vi. They are the notation used to specify and match strings. A regular expression consists of characters (such as the letter *A*, *B*, or *c*—that match themselves in the input) and metacharacters. Metacharacters are characters that have special (meta) meaning; they do not match to themselves but perform some special function.

Table 26.1 shows the metacharacters and their behavior.

Tips on using BEGIN and END

BEGIN and END blocks are optional; if you use them, you should have a maximum of one each. Don't code two BEGIN blocks, and don't code two END blocks.

Table 26.1 **Regular expression metacharacters in *awk***

Metacharacter	Meaning
\	Escape sequence (next character has special meaning, \n is the newline character and \t is the tab). Any escaped metacharacter will match to that character (as if it were not a metacharacter).
^	Starts match at beginning of string.
$	Matches at end of string.
.	Matches any single character.
[ABC]	Matches any one of A, B, or C.
[A-Ca-c]	Matches any one of A, B, C, a, b, or c (ranges).
[^ABC]	Matches any character other than A, B, and C.
Desk¦Chair	Matches any one of Desk or Chair.
[ABC][DEF]	Concatenation. Matches any one of A, B, or C that is followed by any one of D, E, or F.
*	[ABC]* matches zero or more occurrences of A, B, or C.
+	[ABC]+ matches one or more occurrences of A, B, or C.
?	[ABC]? matches to an empty string or any one of A, B, or C.
()	Combines regular expressions. For example, (Blue¦Black)berry matches to Blueberry or Blackberry.

Typical search strings can be used to search for specific strings (such as Report Date), strings in different formats (such as the month of May spelled different ways such as may, MAY, May), or as groups of characters (any combination of upper- and lowercase characters that spell out the month of May). These look like the following:

```
/Report Date/   { print "do something" }
/(may)¦(MAY)¦(May)/ { print "do something else" }
/[Mm][Aa][Yy]/ { print "do something completely different" }
```

Try combining

All of these patterns can be combined to form complex search strings.

Comparison Operators and Patterns

The comparison operators used by awk are similar to those used by C and the UNIX shells. They are the notation used to specify and compare values (including strings). A regular expression alone will match to any portion of the input record. By combining a comparison with a regular expression, specific fields can be tested.

Table 26.2 shows the comparison operators and their behavior.

Table 26.2   **Comparison operators in *awk***

Operator	Meaning
==	Is equal to
<	Less than
>	Greater than
<=	Less than or equal to
>=	Greater than or equal to
!=	Not equal to
~	Matched by regular expression
!~	Not matched by regular expression

Using comparison operators

Comparison operators enable you to perform specific comparisons on fields rather than the entire record. Remember that you can also perform them on the entire record by using $0 rather than a specific field.

Typical search strings can be used to search for a name in the first field (Bob) and compare specific fields with regular expressions:

```
$1 == "Bob"    { print "Bob stuff" }
$2 ~ /(may)|(MAY)|(May)/ { print "May stuff" }
$3 !~ /[Mm][Aa][Yy]/ { print "other May stuff" }
```

Compound Pattern Operators

The compound pattern operators used by awk are similar to those used by C and the UNIX shells. They are the notation used to combine other patterns (expressions or regular expressions) into a complex form of logic.

Table 26.3 shows the compound pattern operators and their behavior.

Table 26.3   **Compound pattern operators in *awk***

Operator	Meaning
&&	Logical AND
¦¦	Logical OR
!	Logical NOT
()	Parentheses—used to group compound statements

If you wanted to execute some action (print a special message, for instance), if the first field contained the value "Bob" and the fourth field contained the value "Street", you could use a compound pattern that looks like this:

```
$1 == "Bob" && $4 == "Street" {print"some message"}
```

Range Pattern Operators

The range pattern is slightly more complex than the other types—it is set true when the first pattern is matched and remains true until the second pattern becomes true. The catch is that the file needs to be sorted on the fields that the range pattern matches. Otherwise, it might be set true prematurely or end early.

The individual patterns in a range pattern are separated by a comma (,). If you have 26 files in your directory with the names A to Z, you can show a range of the files as shown in Listing 26.2.

Listing 26.2   Range pattern example

```
$ ls ¦ awk '{$1 == "B", $1 == "D"}'
B
C
D
$ ls ¦ awk '{$1 == "B", $1 <= "D"}'
B
```

continues…

Listing 26.2 **Continued**

```
$ ls | awk '{$1 == "B", $1 > "D"}'
B
C
D
E
$ _
```

The first example is obvious—all the records between B and D are shown. The other examples are less intuitive, but the key to remember is that the pattern is done when the second condition is true. The second awk command shows only the B because C is less than or equal to D (making the second condition true). The third awk shows B through E because E is the first one that is greater than D (making the second condition true).

Handling Input

As each record is read by awk, it breaks it down into fields and then searches for matching patterns and the related actions to perform. It assumes that each record occupies a single line (the newline character, by definition, ends a record). Lines that are just blanks or are empty (just the newline) count as records, just with very few fields (usually zero).

You can force awk to read the next record in a file (cease searching for pattern matches) by using the next statement. next is similar to the C continue command—control returns to the outermost loop. In awk, the outermost loop is the automatic read of the file. If you decide you need to break out of your program completely, you can use the exit statement. exit will act like the end-of-file was reached and pass control to the END block (if one exists). If exit is in the END block, the program will immediately exit.

By default, fields are separated by spaces. It doesn't matter to awk whether there is one or many spaces—the next field begins when the first nonspace character is found. You can change the field separator by setting the variable FS to that character. To set your field separator to the colon (:), which is the separator in /etc/passwd, code the following:

```
BEGIN { FS = ":" }
```

The general format of the file looks something like the following:

```
david:!:207:1017:David B Horvath,CCP:/u/david:/bin/ksh
```

If you want to list the names of everyone on the system, use the following:

```
gawk —field-separator=: '{ print $5 }' /etc/passwd
```

You will then see a list of everyone's name. In this example, I set the field separator variable (FS) from the command line using the gawk format command-line options (--field-separator=:). I could also use -F :, which is supported by all versions of awk.

The first field is $1, the second is $2, and so on. The entire record is contained in $0. You can get the last field (if you are lazy like me and don't want to count) by referencing $NF. NF is the number of fields in a record.

Coding Your Program

The nice thing about awk is that, with a few exceptions, it is free format—like the C language. Blank lines are ignored. Statements can be placed on the same line or split up in any form you like. awk recognizes whitespace, much like C does. The following two lines are essentially the same:

```
$1=="Bob"{print"Bob stuff"}
$1     ==     "Bob"        {      print     "Bob stuff"       }
```

Spaces within quotation marks are significant because they will appear in the output or are used in a comparison for matching. The other spaces are not. You can also split up the action (but you must have the opening curly brace on the same line as the pattern):

```
$1     ==     "Bob"        {
                              print     "Bob stuff"
                           }
```

You can have multiple statements within an action. If you place them on the same line, you need to use semicolons (;) to separate them (so awk can tell when one ends and the next begins).

Printing multiple lines looks like the following:

```
$1    ==    "Bob"       {
                            print    "Bob stuff"; print "more
                            ➥stuff";  print    "last stuff";
                        }
```

You can also put the statements on separate lines. When you do that, you don't need to code the semicolons, and the code looks like the following:

```
$1    ==    "Bob"       {
                            print    "Bob stuff"
                            print    "more stuff"
                            print    "last stuff"
                        }
```

Make extensive use of comments

Anything on a line after the pound sign or octothorpe (#) is ignored by awk. These are notes designed for the programmer to read and aid in the understanding of the program code. In general, the more comments you place in a program, the easier it is to maintain.

Personally, I am in the habit of coding the semicolon after each statement because that is the way I have to do it in C. To awk, the following example is just like the preceding one (but you can see the semicolons):

```
$1    ==    "Bob"       {
                            print    "Bob stuff";
                            print    "more stuff";
                            print    "last stuff";
                        }
```

Actions

The actions of your program are the part that tells awk what to do when a pattern is matched. If there is no pattern, it defaults to true. A pattern without an action defaults to {print $0}.

All actions are enclosed within curly braces ({ }). The open brace should appear on the same line as the pattern; other than that, there are no restrictions. An action will consist of one or many actions.

Variables

Except for simple find-and-print types of programs, you are going to need to save data. That is done through the use of variables. Within awk, there are three types of variables: field, predefined, and user-defined. You have already seen examples of the first two—$1 is the field variable that contains the first field in the input record, and FS is the predefined variable that contains the field separator.

User-defined variables are ones that you create. Unlike many other languages, awk doesn't require you to define or declare your variables before using them. In C, you must declare the type of data contained in a variable (such as int—integer, float—floating-point number, char—character data, and so on). In awk, you just use the variable. awk attempts to determine the data in the variable by how it is used. If you put character data in the variable, it is treated as a string; if you put a number in, it is treated as numeric.

awk will also perform conversions between the data types. If you put the string "123" in a variable and later perform a calculation on it, it will be treated as a number. The danger of this is, what happens when you perform a calculation on the string "abc"? awk will attempt to convert the string to a number, get a conversion error, and treat the value as a numeric zero! This type of logic error can be difficult to debug.

```
BEGIN {total = 0.0; loop = 0; first_time = "yes"; }
```

Like the C language, awk requires that variables begin with an alphabetic character or an underscore. The alphabetic character can be upper- or lowercase. The remainder of the variable name can consist of letters, numbers, or underscores. It would be nice (for yourself and anyone else who has to maintain your code after you are gone) to make the variable names meaningful. Make them descriptive.

Although you can make your variable names all uppercase letters, that is a bad practice because the predefined variables (such as NF or FS) are in uppercase. It is a common error to type the predefined variables in lowercase (such as nf or fs)—you will not get any errors from awk, and this mistake can be difficult to debug. The variables won't behave like the proper, uppercase spelling, and you won't get the results you expect.

Don't forget to initialize

You should initialize all your variables in a **BEGIN** action like this:

Predefined Variables

awk provides you with a number of predefined (also known as built-in) variables. These are used to provide useful data to your program; they can also be used to change the default behavior of the awk (by setting them to a specific value).

Table 26.4 summarizes the predefined variables in awk. Earlier versions of awk don't support all these variables.

Table 26.4 *awk* **predefined variables**

V	Variable	Meaning	Default Value (if any)
N	ARGC	The number of command-line arguments	
G	ARGIND	The index within ARGV of the current file being processed	
N	ARGV	An array of command-line arguments	
G	CONVFMT	The conversion format for numbers	%.6g
P	ENVIRON	The UNIX environmental variables	
N	ERRNO	The UNIX system error message	
G	FIELDWIDTHS	A whitespace separated string of the width of input fields	
A	FILENAME	The name of the current input file	
P	FNR	The current record number	
A	FS	The input field separator	Space
G	IGNORECASE	Controls the case-sensitivity	0 (case-sensitive)
A	NF	The number of fields in the current record	
A	NR	The number of records already read	

V	Variable	Meaning	Default Value (if any)
A	OFMT	The output format for numbers	%.6g
A	OFS	The output field separator	Space
A	ORS	The output record separator	Newline
A	RS	Input record separator	Newline
N	RSTART	Start of string matched by match function	
N	RLENGTH	Length of string matched by match function	
N	SUBSEP	Subscript separator	"\034"

V is the first implementation that supports a variable. A = awk, N = nawk, P = POSIX awk, and G = gawk.

The ARGC variable contains the number of command-line arguments passed to your program. ARGV is an array of ARGC elements that contains the command-line arguments themselves. The first one is ARGV[0], and the last one is ARGV[ARGC-1]. ARGV[0] contains the name of the command being executed (awk). The awk command-line options won't appear in ARGV—they are interpreted by awk itself. ARGIND is the index within ARGV of the current file being processed.

The default conversion (input) format for numbers is stored in CONVFMT (conversion format) and defaults to the format string "%.6g". See the section titled "printf" for more information on the meaning of the format string.

The ENVIRON variable is an array that contains the environmental variables defined to your UNIX session. The subscript is the name of the environmental variable for which you want to get the value.

If you want your program to perform specific code depending on the value in an environmental variable, you can use the following:

```
ENVIRON["TERM"] == "vt100"   {print "Working on a Video
➡Tube!"}
```

If you are using a VT100 terminal, you will get the message Working on a Video Tube! Note that you put quotation marks around the environmental variable only if you are using a literal. If you have a variable (named TERM) that contains the string "TERM", you would leave the double quotation marks off.

The ERRNO variable contains the UNIX system error message if a system error occurs during redirection, read, or close.

The FIELDWIDTHS variable provides a facility for fixed-length fields instead of using field separators. To specify the size of fields, you set FIELDWIDTHS to a string that contains the width of each field separated by a space or tab character. After this variable is set, gawk will split up the input record based on the specified widths. To revert to using a field separator character, you assign a new value to FS.

The variable FILENAME contains the name of the current input file. Because different (or even multiple files) can be specified on the command line, this provides you a means of determining which input file is being processed.

The FNR variable contains the number of the current record within the current input file. It is reset for each file that is specified on the command line. It always contains a value that is less than or equal to the variable NR.

The character used to separate fields is stored in the variable FS with a default value of space. You can change this variable with a command-line option or within your program. If you know that your file will have some character other than a space as the field separator (like the /etc/passwd file in earlier examples, which uses the colon), you can specify it in your program with the BEGIN pattern.

You can control the case-sensitivity of gawk regular expressions with the IGNORECASE variable. When set to the default, zero, pattern matching checks the case in regular expressions. If you set it to a nonzero value, case is ignored. (The letter A will match to the letter a.)

The variable NF is set after each record is read and contains the number of fields. The fields are determined by the FS or FIELD-WIDTHS variables.

The variable NR contains the total number of records read. It is never less than FNR, which is reset to zero for each file.

The default output format for numbers is stored in OFMT and defaults to the format string `"%.6g"`. See the section titled "`printf`" for more information on the meaning of the format string.

The output field separator is contained in OFS with a default of space. This is the character or string that is output whenever you use a comma with the print statement, such as the following:

```
{print $1, $2, $3;}
```

This statement prints the first three fields of a file separated by spaces. If you want to separate them by colons (like the /etc/passwd file), you just set OFS to a new value: OFS=":".

You can change the output record separator by setting ORS to a new value. ORS defaults to the newline character (\n).

The length of any string matched by the match() function call is stored in RLENGTH. This is used in conjunction with the RSTART predefined variable to extract the matched string.

You can change the input record separator by setting RS to a new value. RS defaults to the newline character (\n).

The starting position of any string matched by the match() function call is stored in RSTART. This is used in conjunction with the RLENGTH predefined variable to extract the matched string.

The SUBSEP variable contains the value used to separate subscripts for multidimension arrays. The default value is `"\034"`, which is the double quotation mark character (").

Changing input fields change the entire record

If you change a field ($1, $2, and so on) or the input record ($0), you will cause other predefined variables to change. If your original input record had two fields and you set $3=`"third one"`, then NF would be changed from 2 to 3.

Strings

awk supports two general types of variables: numeric (which can consist of the characters 0 through 9, + or -, and the decimal [.]) and character (which can contain any character). Variables that contain characters are generally referred to as strings. A character string can contain a valid number, text such as words, or even a formatted phone number. If the string contains a valid number, awk can automatically convert and use it as if it were a numeric variable; if you attempt to use a string that contains a formatted phone number as a numeric variable, awk will attempt to convert and use it as it were a numeric variable—that contains the value zero.

String Constants

Using string constants in comparisons

You have already seen string constants used earlier in this chapter—with comparisons and the print statement.

A string constant is always enclosed within the double quotation marks (" ") and can be from zero (an *empty* string) to many characters long. The exact maximum varies by UNIX version; personally, I have never hit the maximum. The double quotation marks aren't stored in memory. A typical string constant might look like the following:

```
"Using UNIX"
```

String Operators

There is really only one string operator and that is concatenation. You can combine multiple strings (constants or variables in any combination) by just putting them together. Listing 26.1 does this with the print statement where the string ": " is prepended to the input record ($0).

Listing 26.3 shows a couple ways to concatenate strings.

Listing 26.3   Concatenating strings example

```
awk 'BEGIN{x="abc""def"; y="ghi"; z=x y; z2 = "A"x"B"y"C"; print x,
    y, z, z2}'
abcdef ghi abcdefghi AabcdefBghiC
```

Variable x is set to two concatenated strings; it prints as abcdef. Variable y is set to one string for use with the variable z. Variable z is the concatenation of two string variables printing as abcdefghi. Finally, the variable z2 shows the concatenation of string constants and string variables printing as AabcdefBghiC.

If you leave the comma out of the print statement, all the strings will be concatenated together and will look like the following:

```
abcdefghiabcdefghiAabcdefBghiC
```

Built-In String Functions

In addition to the one string operation (concatenation), awk pro-vides a number of functions for processing strings.

Table 26.5 summarizes the built-in string functions in awk. Earlier versions of awk don't support all these functions.

Table 26.5 *awk* **built-in string functions**

V	Function	Purpose
N	gsub(*reg*, *string*, *target*)	Substitutes *string* in *target* string every time the regular expression *reg* is matched
N	index(*search*, *string*)	Returns the position of the *search* string in *string*
A	length(*string*)	The number of characters in *string*
N	match(*string*, *reg*)	Returns the position in *string* that matches the regular expression *reg*
A	printf(*format*, *variables*)	Writes formatted data based on *format*; *variables* is the data you want printed
N	split(*string*, *store*, *delim*)	Splits *string* into array elements of *store* based on the delimiter *delim*
A	sprintf(*format*, *variables*)	Returns a string containing formatted data based on *format*; *variables* is the data you want placed in the string
G	strftime(*format*, *timestamp*)	Returns a formatted date or time string based on *format*; *timestamp* is the time returned by the systime() function
N	sub(*reg*, *string*, *target*)	Substitutes string in target string the first time the regular expression reg is matched

continues...

Table 26.5   **Continued**

V	Function	Purpose
A	substr(*string*, *position*, *len*)	Returns a substring beginning at *position* for *len* number of characters
P	tolower(*string*)	Returns the characters in *string* as their lowercase equivalent
P	toupper(*string*)	Returns the characters in *string* as their uppercase equivalent

V is the first implementation that supports a variable. A = awk, N = nawk, P = POSIX awk, and G = gawk.

The gsub(*reg*, *string*, *target*) function enables you to globally substitute one set of characters for another (defined in the form of the regular expression *reg*) within *string*. The number of substitutions is returned by the function. If *target* is omitted, the input record, $0, is the target. This is patterned after the substitute command in the ed text editor.

The index(*search*, *string*) function returns the first position (counting from the left) of the *search* string within *string*. If *string* is omitted, 0 is returned.

The length(*string*) function returns a count of the number of characters in *string*. awk keeps track of the length of strings internally.

The match(*string*, *reg*) function determines whether *string* contains the set of characters defined by *reg*. If there is a match, the position is returned, and the variables RSTART and RLENGTH are set.

The printf(*format*, *variables*) function writes formatted data converting *variables* based on the *format* string. This function is very similar to the C printf() function. More information about this function and the formatting strings is provided in the section titled "printf " later in this chapter.

The split(*string, store, delim*) function splits *string* into elements of the array *store* based on the *delim* string. The number of elements in *store* is returned. If you omit the *delim* string, FS is used. To split a slash (/) delimited date into its component parts, code the following:

```
split("08/12/1962", results, "/");
```

After the function call, results[1] contains 08, results[2] contains 12, and results[3] contains 1962. When used with the split function, the array begins with the element one. This will also work with strings that contain text.

The sprintf(*format, variables*) function behaves like the printf function except that it returns the result string instead of writing output. It produces formatted data converting *variables* based on the *format* string. This function is very similar to the C sprintf() function. More information about this function and the formatting strings is provided in the section titled "printf" later in this chapter.

The strftime(*format, timestamp*) function returns a formatted date or time based on the *format* string; *timestamp* is the number of seconds since midnight on January 1, 1970. The systime function returns a value in this form. The format is the same as the C strftime() function.

The sub(*reg, string, target*) function enables you to substitute the one set of characters for the first occurrence of another (defined in the form of the regular expression *reg*) within *string*. The number of substitutions is returned by the function. If *target* is omitted, the input record, $0, is the target. This is patterned after the substitute command in the ed text editor.

The substr(*string, position, len*) function enables you to extract a substring based on a starting *position* and *length*. If you omit the *len* parameter, the remaining string is returned.

The tolower(*string*) function returns the uppercase alphabetic characters in *string* converted to lowercase. Any other characters are returned without any conversion.

The toupper(*string*) function returns the lowercase alphabetic characters in *string* converted to uppercase. Any other characters are returned without any conversion.

Special String Constants

awk supports special string constants that cannot be entered from the keyboard or have special meaning. If you wanted to have a double quotation mark (") character as a string constant (x = """), how would you prevent awk from thinking the second one (the one you really want) is the end of the string? The answer is by escaping, or telling awk that the next character has special meaning. This is done through the backslash (\) character, as in the rest of UNIX.

Table 26.6 shows most of the constants that awk supports.

Table 26.6 ***awk* special string constants**

Expression	Meaning
\\	The means of including a backslash
\a	The alert or bell character
\b	Backspace
\f	Formfeed
\n	Newline
\r	Carriage return
\t	Tab
\v	Vertical tab
\"	Double quotation mark
\xNN	Indicates that NN is a hexadecimal number
\0NNN	Indicates that NNN is an octal number

Arrays

When you have more than one related piece of data, you have two choices: You can create multiple variables, or you can use an array. An array enables you to keep a collection of related data together.

You access individual elements within an array by enclosing the subscript within square brackets ([ ]). In general, you can use an array element any place you can use a regular variable.

Arrays in awk have special capabilities lacking in most other languages: They are dynamic; they are sparse; and the subscript is actually a string. You don't have to declare a variable to be an array, and you don't have to define the maximum number of elements—when you use an element for the first time, it is created dynamically. Because of this, a block of memory is not initially allocated; in normal programming practice, if you want to accumulate sales for each month in a year, 12 elements will be allocated, even if you are only processing December at the moment. awk arrays are sparse; if you are working with December, only that element will exist, not the other 11 (empty) months.

In my experience, the last capability is the most useful—the subscript being a string. In most programming languages, if you want to accumulate data based on a string (like totaling sales by state or country), you need to have two arrays—the state or country name (a string) and the numeric sales array. You search the state or country name for a match and then use the same element of the sales array. awk performs this for you. You create an element in the sales array with the state or country name as the subscript and address it directly like the following:

```
total_sales["Pennsylvania"] = 10.15
```

awk does not, however, directly support multidimension arrays.

Array Functions

Versions of awk starting with nawk provide a couple of functions specifically for use with arrays: in and delete. The in function tests for membership in an array. The delete function removes elements from an array.

If you have an array with a subscript of states and want to determine whether a specific state is in the list, you put the following within a conditional test (more about conditional tests in the section titled "Conditional Flow"):

```
"Delaware" in total_sales
```

You can also use the in function within a loop to step through the elements in an array (especially if the array is sparse or associative). This is a special case of the for loop, and is described in the for statement section.

To delete an array element, (the state of Delaware, for example), you code the following:

```
delete total_sales["Delaware"]
```

It is always good practice to delete elements in an array, or entire arrays, when you are done with them. Although memory is cheap and large quantities are available (especially with virtual memory), you will eventually run out if you don't clean up.

Multidimension Arrays

Although awk doesn't directly support multidimension arrays, it does provide a facility to simulate them. The distinction is fairly trivial to you as a programmer. You can specify multiple dimensions in the subscript (within the square brackets) in a form familiar to C programmers:

```
array[5, 3] = "Mary"
```

This is stored in a single-dimension array with the subscript actually stored in the form 5 SUBSEP 3. The predefined variable SUBSEP contains the value of the separator of the subscript components. It defaults to the double quotation mark (" or \034) because it is unlikely that the double quotation mark will appear in the subscript itself. Remember that the double quotation marks are used to contain a string; they are not stored as part of the string itself. You can always change SUBSEP if you need to have the double quotation mark character in your multidimension array subscript.

If you want to calculate total sales by city and state (or country), you will use a two-dimension array:

```
total_sales["Philadelphia", "Pennsylvania"] = 10.15
```

You can use the in function within a conditional:

```
("Wilmington", "Delaware") in total_sales
```

You can also use the in function within a loop to step through the various cities.

Be careful deleting array elements

When an array element is deleted, it has been removed from memory. The data is no longer available.

Deleting elements in an array

You cannot delete all elements in an array with one statement.

You must loop through all loop elements and delete each one. You cannot delete an entire array directly; the following is not valid:

```
delete total_sales
```

Built-In Numeric Functions

awk provides a number of numeric functions to calculate special values.

Table 26.7 summarizes the built-in numeric functions in awk. Earlier versions of awk don't support all these functions.

Table 26.7 *awk* **built-in numeric functions**

V	Function	Purpose
A	atan2(x, y)	Returns the arctangent of y/x in radians
N	cos(x)	Returns the cosine of x in radians
A	exp(x)	Returns e raised to the x power
A	int(x)	Returns the value of x truncated to an integer
A	log(x)	Returns the natural log of x
N	rand()	Returns a random number between 0 and 1
N	sin(x)	Returns the sine of x in radians
A	sqrt(x)	Returns the square root of x
A	srand(x)	Initializes (seeds) the random number generator; systime() is used if x is omitted
G	systime()	Returns the current time in seconds since midnight, January 1, 1970

V is the first implementation that supports a variable. A = awk, N = nawk, P = POSIX awk, and G = gawk.

Arithmetic Operators

awk supports a wide variety of math operations. Table 26.8 summarizes these operators.

Table 26.8 *awk* **arithmetic operators**

Operator	Purpose
x^y	Raises x to the y power
x**y	Raises x to the y power (same as x^y)

continues...

Table 26.8   Continued

Operator	Purpose
x%y	Calculates the remainder (modulo/modulus) of x/y
x+y	Adds x to y
x-y	Subtracts y from x
x*y	Multiplies x times y
x/y	Divides x by y
-y	Negates y (switches the sign of y); also known as the unary minus
++y	Increments y by 1 and uses value (prefix increment)
y++	Uses value of y and then increments by 1 (postfix increment)
—y	Decrements y by 1 and uses value (prefix decrement)
y—	Uses value of y and then decrements by 1 (postfix decrement)
x=y	Assigns value of y to x. awk also supports operator-assignment operators (+=, -=, *=, /=, %=, ^=, and **=)

awk and floating point

All math in **awk** uses floating point (even if you treat the number as an integer).

Conditional Flow

By its very nature, an action within a awk program is conditional. It is executed if its pattern is true. You can also have conditional programs flow within the action through the use of an if statement.

The general flow of an if statement is as follows:

```
if (condition)
    statement to execute when true
else
    statement to execute when false
```

condition can be any valid combination of patterns shown in Tables 26.2 and 26.3. else is optional. If you have more than one statement to execute, you need to enclose the statements within curly braces ({ }), just as in the C syntax.

You can also stack if and else statements as necessary:

```
if ("Pennsylvania" in total_sales)
    print "We have Pennsylvania data"
```

```
else if ("Delaware" in total_sales)
   print "We have Delaware data"
else if (current_year < 2010)
   print "Uranus is still a planet"
else
   print "none of the conditions were met."
```

The Null Statement

By definition, if requires one (or more) statements to execute; in some cases, the logic might be straightforward when coded so that the code you want executed occurs when the condition is false. I have used this when it would be difficult or ugly to reverse the logic to execute the code when the condition is true.

The solution to this problem is easy: Just use the null statement, the semicolon (;). The null statement satisfies the syntax requirement that if requires statements to execute; it just does nothing.

Your code will look something like the following:

```
if (($1 <= 5 && $2 > 3) || ($1 > 7 && $2 < 2))
   ;           # The Null Statement
else
   the code I really want to execute
```

The Conditional Operator

awk has one operator that actually has three parameters: the conditional operator. This operator enables you to apply an if-test anywhere in your code.

The general format of the conditional statement is as follows:

```
condition ? true-result : false-result
```

Although this might seem like duplication of the if statement, it can make your code easier to read. If you have a data file that consists of an employee name and the number of sick days taken, you can use the following:

```
{ print $1, "has taken", $2, "day" $2 != 1 ? "s" : "", "of
➥sick time" }
```

This prints day if the employee only took one day of sick time and prints days if the employee took zero or more than one day of sick time. The resulting sentence is more readable. To code the same example using an if statement would be more complex and look like the following:

```
if ($2 != 1)
    print $1, "has taken", $2, "days of sick time"
else
    print $1, "has taken", $2, "day of sick time"
```

Looping

Pay attention to block statements (curly braces)

Forgetting the curly braces around multiple statements is a common programming error with conditional and looping statements.

By their very nature, awk programs are one big loop—reading each record in the input file and processing the appropriate patterns and actions. Within an action, the need for repetition often occurs. awk supports loops through the do, for, and while statements that are similar to those found in C.

As with the if statement, if you want to execute multiple statements within a loop, you must contain them in curly braces.

The *do* Statement

do versus do while

The do statement is sometimes referred to as the do while statement.

The do statement provides a looping construct that will be executed at least once. The condition or test occurs after the contents of the loop have been executed.

The do statement takes the following form:

```
do
    statement
while (condition)
```

In the loop

In general, you must change the value of the variable in the condition within the loop. If you don't, you will have a loop forever condition because the test result (*condition*) would never change (and become false).

statement can be one statement or multiple statements enclosed in curly braces. condition is any valid test like those used with the if statement or the pattern used to trigger actions.

Loop Control (*break* and *continue*)

You can exit a loop early if you need to (without assigning some bogus value to the variable in the condition). awk provides two facilities to do this: break and continue.

break causes the current (innermost) loop to be exited. It behaves as if the conditional test was performed immediately with a false result. None of the remaining code in the loop (after the break statement) executes, and the loop ends. This is useful when you need to handle some error or early end condition.

continue causes the current loop to return to the conditional test. None of the remaining code in the loop (after the continue statement) is executed, and the test is immediately executed. This is most useful when there is code you want to skip (within the loop) temporarily. The continue is different from the break because the loop is not forced to end.

The *for* Statement

The for statement provides a looping construct that modifies values within the loop. It is good for counting through a specific number of items.

The for statement has two general forms, as follows:

```
for (loop = 0; loop < 10; loop++)
    statement
```

and

```
for (subscript in array)
    statement
```

The first form initializes the variable (loop = 0), performs the test (loop < 10), and then performs the loop contents (*statement*). Then it modifies the variable (loop++) and tests again. As long as the test is true, *statement* will execute.

In the second form, *statement* is executed with subscript being set to each of the subscripts in *array*. This enables you to loop through an array even if you don't know the values of the subscripts. This works well for multidimension arrays.

statement can be one statement or multiple statements enclosed in curly braces. The condition (loop < 10) is any valid test like those used with the if statement or the pattern used to trigger actions.

Modifying the loop control variable

You can modify the loop control variable using many different methods. The increment operator (loop++) is shown here because it is the most commonly used operator (to step through an array, for example). Any valid operation can be used here, even something like this: loop = loop * 2 + another_variable.

A word of caution

In general, you don't want to change the loop control variable (`loop` or `subscript`) within the loop body. Let the `for` statement do that for you, or you might get behavior that is difficult to debug.

Postfix or prefix?

This example showed the postfix increment. It doesn't matter whether you use the postfix (`loop++`) or prefix (`++loop`) increment—the results will be the same. Just be consistent.

Changing the value of the condition

In general, you must change the value of the variable in the condition within the loop. If you don't, you will have a loop forever condition because the test result (*condition*) would never change (and become false).

For the first form, the modification of the variable can be any valid operation (including calls to functions). In most cases, it is an increment or decrement.

The `for` loop is a good method of looping through data of an unknown size:

```
for (i=1; i<=NF; i++)
    print $i
```

Each field on the current record will be printed on its own line. As a programmer, I don't know how many fields are on a particular record when I write the code. The variable NF lets me know as the program runs.

The *while* Statement

The final loop structure is the `while` loop. It is the most general because it executes while the condition is true. The general form is as follows:

```
while(condition)
    statement
```

statement can be one statement or multiple statements enclosed in curly braces. *condition* is any valid test like those used with the `if` statement or the pattern used to trigger actions.

If the condition is false before the `while` is encountered, the contents of the loop will not be executed. This is different from `do`, which always executes the loop contents at least once.

Advanced Input and Output

In addition to the simple input and output facilities provided by awk, you can take advantage of a number of advanced features for more complicated processing.

By default, awk automatically reads and loops through your program; you can alter this behavior. You can force input to come from a different file, cause the loop to recycle early (read the next record without performing any more actions), or even just read the next record. You can even get data from the output of other commands.

On the output side, you can format the output and send it to a file (other than the standard output device) or as input to another command.

Input

You don't have to program the normal input loop process in awk. It reads a record and then searches for pattern matches and the corresponding actions to execute. If multiple files are specified on the command line, they are processed in order. It is only if you want to change this behavior that you have to do any special programming.

next and *exit*

The next command causes awk to read the next record and perform the pattern match and corresponding action execution immediately. Normally, it executes all your code in any actions with matching patterns. next causes any additional matching patterns to be ignored for this record.

The exit command in any action except for END behaves as if the end of file was reached. Code execution in all pattern/actions is ceased, and the actions within the END pattern are executed. exit appearing in the END pattern is a special case—it causes the program to end.

getline

The getline statement is used to explicitly read a record. This is especially useful if you have a data record that looks like two physical records. It performs the normal field splitting (setting $0, the field variables, FNR, NF, and NR). It returns the value 1 if the read was successful and zero if it failed (end of file was reached). If you want to explicitly read through a file, you can code something like the following:

```
{ while (getline == 1)
  {
      # process the inputted fields
  }
}
```

You can also have `getline` store the input data in a field instead of taking advantage of the normal field processing by using the form `getline` *variable*. When used this way, NF is set to zero, and FNR and NR are incremented.

Input from a File

It won't change

If you use `getline < "file-name"` to read data into your program, neither **FNR** nor **NR** is changed.

You can use `getline` to input data from a specific file rather than the ones listed on the command line. The general form is `get-line < "filename"`. When coded this way, `getline` performs the normal field splitting (setting $0, the field variables, and NF). If the file doesn't exist, `getline` returns –1; it returns 1 on success, and 0 on failure.

You can read the data from the specified file into a variable. You can also replace *filename* with stdin or a variable that contains the filename.

Input from a Command

Another way of using the `getline` statement is to accept input from a UNIX command. If you want to perform some processing for each person signed on the system (send him or her a message, for instance), you can code something like the following:

```
{ while ("who -u" ¦ getline)
  {
      # process each line from the who command
  }
}
```

The who command is executed once, and each of its output lines is processed by `getline`. You could also use the form `"command" ¦ getline variable`.

Ending Input from a File or Command

Whenever you use `getline` to get input from a specified file or command, you should close it when you are done processing the data. There is a maximum number of open files allowed to awk; this number varies with operating system version or individual account configuration (a command output pipe counts as a file). By closing files when you are done with them, you reduce the chances of hitting the limit.

The syntax to close a file is just this:

```
close ("filename")
```

filename is the one specified on the `getline` (which could also be `stdin`, a variable that contains the filename, or the exact command used with `getline`).

Output

There are a few advanced features for output: pretty formatting, sending output to files, and piping output as input to other commands. The `printf` command is used for pretty formatting—instead of seeing the output in whatever default format `awk` decides to use (which is often ugly), you can specify how it looks.

Pretty Formatting (*printf*)

The `print` statement produces simple output for you. If you want to be able to format the data (producing fixed columns, for instance), you need to use `printf`. The nice thing about `awk` `printf` is that it uses syntax that is very similar to the `printf()` function in C.

The general format of the `awk` `printf` is as follows (the parentheses are only required if a relational expression is included):

```
printf format-specifier, variable1,variable2,
➥variable3,..variablen
printf(format-specifier, variable1,variable2,
➥variable3,..variablen)
```

The variables are optional, but *format-specifier* is mandatory. Often you will have `printf` statements that only include *format-specifier* (to print messages that contain no variables):

```
printf ("Program Starting\n")
printf ("\f")          # new page in output
```

format-specifier can consist of text, escaped characters, or actual print specifiers. A print specifier begins with the percent sign (%),

A matter of habit

Personally, I use the second form because I am so used to coding in C.

followed by an optional numeric value that specifies the size of the field, and then the format type follows (which describes the type of variable or output format). If you want to print a percent sign in your output, you use %%.

The field size can consist of two numbers separated by a decimal point (.). For floating-point numbers, the first number is the size of the entire field (including the decimal point); the second number is the number of digits to the right of the decimal. For other types of fields, the first number is the minimum field size and the second number is the maximum field size (number of characters to actually print); if you omit the first number, it takes the value of the maximum field size.

The print specifiers determine how the variable is printed; there are also modifiers that change the behavior of the specifiers. Table 26.9 shows the print format specifiers.

Table 26.9   **Format specifiers for *awk***

Format	Meaning
%c	ASCII character
%d	An integer (decimal number)
%i	An integer, just like %d
%e	A floating-point number using scientific notation (1.00000E+01)
%f	A floating-point number (10.43)
%g	awk chooses between %e or %f display format (whichever is shorter) suppressing nonsignificant zeros
%o	An unsigned octal (base 8) number (integer)
%s	A string of characters
%x	An unsigned hexadecimal (base 16) number (integer)
%X	Same as %x but using ABCDEF instead of abcdef

Printing with %c

If you attempt to print a numeric value or variable using %c, it will be printed as a character. (The ASCII character for that value will print.)

The format modifiers change the default behavior of the format specifiers. Listing 26.4 shows the use of various specifiers and modifiers.

Listing 26.4   *printf* format specifiers and modifiers

```
printf("%d %3.3d %03.3d %.3d %-.3d %3d %-3d\n", 64, 64, 64, 64, 64,
➡64, 64)
printf("%c %c %2.2c %-2.2c %2c %-2c\n", 64, "abc", "abc", "abc",
➡"abc", "abc")
printf("%s %2s %-2s %2.2s %-2.2s %.2s %-.2s\n",
        "abc", "abc", "abc", "abc", "abc", "abc", "abc")
printf("%f %6.1f %06.1f %.1f %-.1f %6f\n",
        123.456, 123.456, 123.456, 123.456, 123.456, 123.456)


64 064 064 064 064  64 64
@ a  a a   a a
abc abc abc ab ab ab ab
123.456000   123.5 0123.5 123.5 123.5 123.456000
```

When using the integer or decimal (%d) specifier, the field size defaults to the size of the value being printed (two digits for the value 64). If you specify a field maximum size larger than that, you automatically get the field zero filled. All numeric fields are right-justified unless you use the minus sign (-) modifier, which causes them to be left-justified. If you specify only the field minimum size and want the rest of the field zero filled, you have to use the zero modifier (before the field minimum size).

When using the character (%c) specifier, only one character prints from the input no matter what size you use for the field minimum or maximum sizes and no matter how many characters are in the value being printed. Note that the value 64 printed as a character shows up as @.

When using the string (%s) specifier, the entire string prints unless you specify the field maximum size. By default, strings are left-justified unless you use the minus sign (-) modifier, which causes them to be right-justified.

When using the floating (%f) specifier, the field size defaults .6 (as many digits to the left of the decimal and 6 digits to the right). If you specify a number after the decimal in the format, that many digits will print to the right of the decimal and awk will round the number. All numeric fields are right-justified unless you use the minus sign (-) modifier, which causes them to be left-justified. If you want the field zero filled, you have to use the zero modifier (before the field minimum size).

The best way to determine printing results is to work with it. Try out the various modifiers and see what makes your output look best.

Output to a File

You can send your output (from `print` or `printf`) to a file. The following creates a new (or empties out an existing) file containing the printed message:

```
printf ("hello world\n") > "datafile"
```

If you execute this statement multiple times or other statements that redirect output to *datafile*, the output will remain in the file. The file creation/emptying out only occurs the first time the file is used in the program.

To append data to an existing file, you use the following:

```
printf ("hello world\n") >> "datafile"
```

Output to a Command

In addition to redirecting your output to a file, you can send the output from your program to act as input for another command. You can code something like the following:

```
printf ("hello world\n") ¦ "sort -t`,`"
```

Any other output statements that pipe data into the same command will specify exactly the same command after the pipe character (¦) because that is how awk keeps track of which command is receiving which output from your program.

Closing an Output File or Pipe

Whenever you send output to a file or pipe, you should close it when you are done processing the data. There is a maximum number of open files allowed to awk. This number varies with operating system version or individual account configuration (a pipe counts as a file). By closing files when you are done with them, you reduce the chances of hitting the limit.

The syntax to close a file is just this:

```
close ("filename")
```

filename is the one specified on the output statement (which can also be stdout, a variable that contains the filename, or the exact command used with a pipe).

Functions

In addition to the built-in functions (such as gsub or srand), you can write your own. User-defined functions are a means of creating a block of code that is accessed in multiple places in your code. They can also be used to build a library of commonly used routines so that you do not have to recode the same algorithms repeatedly.

There are two parts to using a function: the definition and the call. The function definition contains the code to be executed (the function itself), and the call temporarily transfers from the main code to the function. Command execution is transferred two ways back to the main code: implicit and explicit returns. When awk reaches the end of a function (the close curly brace [}]), it automatically (implicitly) returns control to the calling routine. If you want to leave your function before the bottom, you can explicitly use the return statement to exit early.

Function Definition

The general form of an awk function definition looks like the following:

```
function functionname(parameter list) {
    the function body
}
```

You code your function just as if it were any other set of action statements and can place it anywhere you would put a pattern/action set. If you think about it, the function *function-name(parameter list)* portion of the definition could be considered a pattern, and *the function body* could be considered the action.

A late addition

User-defined functions are not a part of the original awk—they were added to nawk and are supported by more recent versions.

function versus func

gawk supports another form of function definition where the `function` keyword is abbreviated to `func`. The remaining syntax is the same.

Use caution with user-defined variables

When working with user-defined functions, you must place the parentheses that contain the parameter list immediately after the function name when calling that function. When you use the built-in functions, this is not a requirement.

```
func functionname(parameter list) {
    the function body
}
```

Listing 26.5 shows the defining and calling of a function.

Listing 26.5   Defining and calling functions

```
BEGIN { print_header() }

function print_header( ) {
    printf("This is the header\n");
    printf("this is a second line of the header\n");
}

This is the header
this is a second line of the header
```

The code inside the function is executed only once—when the function is called from within the BEGIN action. This function uses the implicit return method.

Function Parameters

Like C, awk passes parameters to functions by value. In other words, a copy of the original value is made and that copy is passed to the called function. The original is untouched, even if the function changes the value.

Any parameters are listed in the function definition separated by commas. If you have no parameters, you can leave the parameter list (contained in the parentheses) empty.

Listing 26.6 is an expanded version of Listing 26.5; it shows the pass-by-value nature of awk function parameters.

Listing 26.6   Passing parameters

```
BEGIN { pageno = 0;
        print_header(pageno);
        printf("the page number is now %d\n", pageno);
}
```

```
function print_header(page ) {
   page++;
   printf("This is the header for page %d\n", page);
   printf("this is a second line of the header\n");
}


This is the header for page 1
this is a second line of the header
the page number is now 0
```

awk does not perform parameter validation

When you call a function, you can list more or fewer parameters than the function expects. Any extra parameters are ignored, and any missing ones default to zero or empty strings (depending on how they are used).

Take advantage of it

You can take advantage of the lack of function parameter validation. It can be used to create local variables within the called function—just list more variables in the function definition than you use in the function call. I strongly suggest that you comment the fact that the extra parameters are really being used as local variables.

The page number is initialized before the first call to the print_header function and incremented in the function. When it is printed after the function call, however, it remains at the original value.

A called function has several ways to change variables in the calling routines—through explicit return or by using the variables in the calling routine directly (those variables are normally global anyway).

Explicit Returns from Functions (*return* Statement)

If you want to return a value or leave a function early, you need to code a return statement. If you don't code one, the function will end with the close curly brace (}). Personally, I prefer to code them at the bottom.

If the calling code expects a returned value from your function, you must code the return statement in the following form:

```
return variable
```

Expanding on Listing 26.6 to let the function change the page number, Listing 26.7 shows the use of the return statement.

Listing 26.7   Returning values

```
BEGIN { pageno = 0;
        pageno = print_header(pageno);
        printf("the page number is now %d\n", pageno);
}
```

continues…

Listing 26.7   Continued

```
function print_header(page ) {
    page++;
    printf("This is the header for page %d\n", page);
    printf("this is a second line of the header\n");
    return page;
}


This is the header for page 1
this is a second line of the header
the page number is now 1
```

The return Statement

The **return** statement enables you to return only one value back to the calling routine.

The updated page number is returned to the code that called the function.

Writing Reports

Generating a report in awk entails a sequence of steps, with each step producing the input for the next step. Report writing is usually a three-step process: pick the data, sort the data, and make the output pretty.

Complex Reports

Using awk, it is possible to quickly create complex reports. It is much easier to perform string comparisons, build arrays on-the-fly, and take advantage of associative arrays than to code in another language (such as C). Instead of having to search through an array for a match with a text key, that key can be used as the array subscript.

I have produced reports using awk with three levels of control breaks, multiple sections of reports in the same control break, and multiple totaling pages. The totaling pages were for each level of control break plus a final page; if the control break did not have a particular type of data, the total page did not have it either. If there was only one member of a control break, the total page for that level wasn't created. (This saved a lot of paper when there was really only one level of control break—the highest.)

This report ended up being more than 1,000 lines of awk (nawk, to be specific) code. It takes a little longer to run than the equivalent C program, but it took a lot less programmer time to create. Because it was easy to create and modify, it was developed using prototypes. The users briefly described what they wanted, and I produced a report. They decided they needed more control breaks, and I added them; then they realized a lot of paper was wasted on total pages, so the report was modified as described.

Being responsive to user changes

Being easy to develop incrementally without knowing the final result made it easier and more fun for me. By my being responsive to user changes, the users were made happy!

Extracting Data

As mentioned earlier in this chapter, many systems don't produce data in the desired format. When working with data stored in relational databases, there are two main ways to get data out: use a query tool with SQL, or write a program to get the data from the database and output it in the desired form. SQL query tools have limited formatting capability, but can provide quick and easy access to the data.

One technique I have found very useful is to extract the data from the database into a file that is then manipulated by an awk script to produce the exact format required. When required, an awk script can even create the SQL statements used to query the database (specifying the key values for the rows to select).

The following example is used when the query tool places a space before a numeric field that must be removed for a program that will use the data in another system (mainframe COBOL):

```
{   printf("%s%s%-25.25s\n", $1, $2, $3);   }
```

awk automatically removes the field separator (the space character) when splitting the input record into individual fields and the formatting %s string format specifiers in the printf are contiguous (do not have any spaces between them).

Commands On-the-Fly

The capability to pipe the output of a command into another is very powerful because the output from the first becomes the input that the second can manipulate. A frequent use of one-line awk programs is the creation of commands based on a list.

The find command can be used to produce a list of files that match its conditions, or it can execute a single command that takes a single command-line argument. You can see files in a directory (and subdirectories) that match specific conditions with the following:

```
$ find . -name "*.prn" -print
./exam2.prn
./exam1.prn
./exam3.prn
```

Or you can print the contents of those files with the following:

```
find . -name "*.prn" -exec lp {} \;
```

The find command inserts the individual filenames that it locates in place of the {} and executes the lp command. If you wanted to execute a command that required two arguments (to copy files to a new name) or execute multiple commands simultaneously, however, you couldn't do it with find alone. You could create a shell script that would accept the single argument and use it in multiple places, or you could create an awk single-line program:

```
$ find . -name "*.prn" -print ¦ awk '{print "echo bak" $1;
➡print "cp " $1 " " $1".bak";}'
echo bak./exam2.prn
cp ./exam2.prn ./exam2.prn.bak
echo bak./exam1.prn
cp ./exam1.prn ./exam1.prn.bak
echo bak./exam3.prn
cp ./exam3.prn ./exam3.prn.bak
```

To get the commands to actually execute, you need to pipe the commands into one of the shells. The following example uses the Korn shell; you can use the one you prefer:

```
$ find . -name "*.prn" -print ¦
    awk '{print "echo bak" $1; print "cp " $1 " "
    ➡$1".bak";}' ¦
    ksh
bak./exam2.prn
bak./exam1.prn
bak./exam3.prn
```

Before each copy takes place, the message is shown. This is also handy if you want to search for a string (using the grep command) in the files of multiple subdirectories. Many versions of the grep command don't show the name of the file searched unless you use wildcards (or specify multiple filenames on the command line). The following uses find to search for C source files, awk to create grep commands to look for an error message, and the shell echo command to show the file being searched:

```
$ find . -name "*.c" -print |
    awk '{print "echo " $1; print "grep error-message "
    ➡$1;}' |
    ksh
```

The same technique can be used to perform lint checks on source code in a series of subdirectories. I execute the following in a shell script periodically to check all C code:

```
$ find . -name "*.c" -print |
    awk '{print "lint " $1 " > " $1".lint"}' |
    ksh
```

The lint version on one system prints the code error as a heading line and then the parts of code in question as a list below. grep shows the heading, but not the detail lines. The awk script prints all lines from the heading until the first blank line (end of the lint section).

When in doubt...

When in doubt, pipe the output into **more** or **pg** to view the created commands before you pipe them into a shell for execution.

One Last Built-In Function: *system*

There is one more built-in function that doesn't fit in the character or numeric categories: system. The system function executes the string passed to it as an argument. This enables you to execute commands or scripts on-the-fly when your awk code has the need.

You can code a report to automatically print to paper when it is complete. The code looks something like that shown in Listing 26.8.

Listing 26.8   Using the *system* function

```
BEGIN { pageno = 0;
        pageno = print_header(pageno);
        printf("the page number is now %d\n", pageno);
}


# The production of the report would be coded here


END { close ("report.txt");
      system ("lpr -Pmyprinter report.txt");
}


function print_header(page ) {
   page++;
   printf("This is the header for page %d\n", page) > "report.txt";
   printf("this is a second line of the header\n")  > "report.txt";
}


This is the header for page 1
this is a second line of the header
the page number is now 0
```

The output is the same as that of Listing 26.6, except that the output shows up on the printer rather than the screen. Before printing the file, you must close it.

Some Final Words

This chapter introduced the awk programming language in its various implementations. It is a very powerful and useful language that enables you to search for data, extract data from files, create commands on-the-fly, or even create entire programs.

It is very useful as a prototyping language—you can create reports very quickly. After showing them to the user, changes can be made quickly also. Although it is less efficient than the comparable program written in C, it is not so inefficient that you cannot create production programs. If efficiency is a concern with an awk program, it can be converted into C.

For further information, see the following:

Aho, Alfred V., Brian W. Kernighan and Peter J. Weinberger. *The awk Programming Language*. Reading, Mass.: Addison-Wesley, 1988 (copyright AT&T Bell Lab).

See also the man pages for awk, nawk, or gawk on your system.

Writing Perl Programs

By David Pitts

This chapter gives you an introduction to writing Perl scripts. It was written using Perl version 5. Some of the things mentioned in this chapter will not work with version 4 of Perl. It is meant to give enough information for a Perl novice to begin writing his own programs to enhance his performance in the real world. This chapter basically deals with three areas: user input, processing, and output, with an emphasis on user input and processing. Basic output is covered in the form of writing output to standard out (the monitor) and to files.

First, however, what is Perl? Perl is a programming language that is best for almost everything. The author of Perl, Larry Wall, says that it stands for "Pathologically Eclectic Rubbish Lister." After you have had the opportunity of using Perl for a while, I think that you will agree that a better definition is "Practical Extraction and Reporting Language." Those of you who are used to C will find the syntax similar, but better. You will also find that without the compiling associated with C, the designing and changing of tools becomes quick and easy. That is correct; Perl is not compiled. Perl is an interpreted language of sorts. Perl is compiled at runtime, so the speed is almost that of a compiled C program, but it is as easy to write code in as you would a shell program. For those who are used to awk or sed, Perl takes advantage of regular expressions for providing pattern matching. Basically, Perl has become a replacement to C, shell scripting, TCL, and other programming languages and techniques normally associated with system administration.

Fortunately, Perl does not end there. It is a complete language, ready to handle the complex needs of the programming community. Perl has been used in the genome project for mapping DNA; and Majordomo, the most popular mailing list manager, is written in Perl. Perl is being used for thousands (literally) of other projects. For more information on how Perl is being used, see the Comprehensive Perl Archive Network (www.perl.com).

Writing/Executing a Simple Perl Script

Every programming course I have ever taken begins with designing a "Hello World" program. This chapter is no exception. We can begin by running a Perl script explicitly from the command line. Assuming the location of the Perl executable is in your path, the following program

```
perl -e 'print "Hello world!\n";'
```

prints the following output:

```
Hello world!
```

The -e tells Perl to execute what is following explicitly. This method is limited to 80 characters. If you need something longer than 80 characters, you need to put the lines in a text file. This file will do two things. First it tells the computer what to do (call the Perl interpreter) and second, it tells the Perl interpreter what to interpret.

How is this done you might ask? As you may know from your experience with shell scripting, if you have any, you use the first line of a script to tell the computer what program to call. If I were calling a ksh program, for example, my first line would look like this:

```
#!/bin/ksh
```

In Perl, it is similar. You have pound (#) bang (!) followed by the location of the interpreter. Therefore, your first line of your new program should look something like this:

```
#!/site/bin/perl
```

Everything that follows this line is sent to the program (in this case Perl) as an argument. Therefore, the "Hello World" program could be a file that looks like this:

```
#!/site/bin/perl
print "Hello World!\n";
```

Admittedly, this is not much of a program. However, it is sufficient for making sure that Perl runs and that you have the correct permissions on the file. For Perl to read and execute the script, the script must have read and execute set for the person running the program. (-r-x------ would allow the owner of the script to run the Perl program and -------r-x would allow anyone to run the program.)

A Quick Note on Termination

Each line of code must end with some form of termination. There are two types of termination in Perl. The first is the semicolon (;). It is used to terminate a line of code. The second is the right curly bracket (}). It is used to terminate a block of code. Many beginners (and experts, too) forget their terminators.

What happens when you forget your terminator? The program tries to compile anyway, but almost always errors out on the line following the one missing the semicolon, or at the end of the program for a missing right curly bracket.

Why is a terminator so important? A terminator is used to tell Perl when a line or block of code is done so that it knows what to do with that code. To Perl, a hard return means nothing. For example, the following two sets of code are the same from Perl's perspective. The second is just easier for us mere humans to read.

```
$first_name="David; $last_name="Pitts; $work="Best
➡Consulting";
```

```
$first_name="David;
$last_name="Pitts;
$work="Best Consulting";
```

Therefore, the motto goes, "terminate, or be terminated!"

Interacting with the User

Having a program that prints something is okay. The next step in the process would be to allow the program to interact with the user. There are several different ways of allowing this interaction; parameters can be passed to the program or input can come from the command line.

Before we go on, let me take a moment and point out the main data types used in Perl. They are literals, variables—including strings, arrays, and hashes—code references, filehandles, and here-is's. Each of these is given brief descriptions and examples in the following sections.

Literals

Literals are actual values. Literals are literally what they are. There are numeric literals—for example, 1, 2, 3, 4, and so on. There are string literals: abc, xyz, Fred, Sylvia, and so on. Some characters are not literals, but are metacharacters. These characters match something other than themselves. These metacharacters are \ | ( ) [ ] { } ^ $ * + ?.

There is not room in one chapter to go through what all these mean. Most of them should be familiar to you if you have any experience with regular expressions. An important one to understand is the backslash. A backslash (\) turns a metacharacter into a literal character. It also turns some literal characters into metacharacters; for example, a \n is a new line, a \t is a tab character.

Variables

Variables are named storage locations used to hold a value. That value could be a number, a character, a string of numbers and characters, or anything else that the program sees fit. Here are some examples of variables.

$var	A simple scalar variable.
@var	The entire array; in a scalar context, the number of elements in the array.
$var[4]	The fifth element of the array @var (as with most counting with computers, the first element of an array is the 0th element, not the first).
$d = \@var	$d is a reference to the array @var.
$$d[4]	The fifth element of the array referenced by $d.
$var[-1]	The last element of array @var.
$var[$x][$y]	$yth element of the $xth element of the array @var.
$#var	Last index of array @var.

`%var`	The entire hash; in a scalar context, true if the hash has elements. (A hash is also called an associative array.)
`$var{'Name'}`	A value from the hash array `%var`.
`$d = \%var`	Now `$d` is a reference to the hash `%var`.
`$$d{'Name'}`	A value from the hash array referenced by `$d`.
`@var{'x','y'}`	A slice of `%var`; same as (`$var{'x'}`,`$var{'y'}`).

By default, all variables are global variables. This means that if you use a variable in one part of a program or subroutine, and then use it in another part, it is still pointing to the same location and any changes made to it in one location affects it in the other location as well. There are two ways of declaring a local variable. I will not discuss their differences here, with one exception. A locally declared variable will carry its value to another subroutine called from within the current subroutine, where a `my` will not. The two ways of making a variable local to a subroutine is with the `my` and the `local` identification. This means that the subroutine gets its own copies of these variables, and any manipulation of these variables does not affect identically named variables outside of that subroutine. The following example shows how to use the `my` and `local` identification.

```perl
my $name = "David";
local @brothers_family = ("John", "Kathy", "Pat", "Emily");
my ($John, $Kathy, $Pat, $Emily) = @brothers_family;
```

Note that the following is not the correct way of initializing the variables `$x` and `$y` to be local variables:

```perl
my $x, $y = 1;
```

This is the same as writing this:

```perl
my $x;
$y = 1;
```

This initializes `$x` as a local variable, and sets `$y` (globally) to be equal to 1.

Code References

Code references are subroutines. A subroutine is a snippet of code that can be invoked from a different location in the program to handle some portion of the goal of the program. If the subroutine returns a meaningful value, it is also called a function. There are two parts to a subroutine. First, there is the actual snippet of code; and second, there is the thing that invokes the code.

A subroutine is defined using the reserve word sub followed by a space, and then the name of the subroutine. The entire subroutine is enclosed in begin and end brackets ({}), as the following subroutine shows.

A pound sign (#) is used to start a comment.

Comments extend from where the pound sign starts until the end of the line. Therefore, if you want three lines of comments, you must place a pound sign at the beginning of each line.

```
sub weekday {
# determine day of week
$y=$year;
$d=$mday;
$m=$month;
@d= (0,3,2,5,0,3,5,1,4,6,2,4);
@day=(Sunday, Monday, Tuesday, Wednesday, Thursday, Friday,
➥Saturday);
$y-- if $m < 3;
$weekday = $day[($y+int($y/4)-int($y/100)+int($y/400)+$d[$m-
➥1]+$d) % 7];
}   # end of sub weekday
```

To call a subroutine, you place an ampersand (&) sign in front of the name of the subroutine. To call the subroutine weekday, for example, you do this:

```
&weekday;
```

Parameters can also be passed with subroutines by placing them inside of parentheses.

```
&subroutine(list);
```

This is the same as passing a list of arguments to the program. Therefore, I will defer a discussion about this to the section titled "Supplying Script Input as a Parameter" later in this chapter.

Filehandles

A *filehandle* is a symbolic name that you give to a file, pipe, socket, or device. You use the filehandle rather than the actual name when performing operations on file, pipe, socket, or device. The following example shows a common use of a filehandle.

```
open (FILE, "$filename");
@file = <FILE>;
close FILE;
```

The first line is opening the file associated with the variable $filename. That file will now be referred to using the filehandle FILE. (It could have been anything; I use FILE to remind me that it is a file; likewise, I would have used DIR if I were opening a directory listing.) The second line is saving the entire file as an array called @file. Finally, the third line closed the file associated with the variable $filename by closing the filehandle.

Table 27.1 shows how to open files for different purposes.

TABLE 27.1   Commands for opening files

Command	What It Does
`open (FILE, "filename");`	Read from an existing file
`open (DAVID, "<filename");`	Opens a file explicitly (same as above)
`open (church,">filename");`	Creates a file and opens it to be written to (overwrites an existing file)
`open (log,">>filename");`	Appends to a file (does not overwrite an existing file)
`open(file, "| output-pipe-command");`	Sets up an output filter
`open(file, "input-pipe-command |");`	Sets up an input filter

As you can see, the filehandle can be named anything. After it is opened, the filehandle can be used to access a file or pipe until it is either explicitly closed, or until a new file or pipe is opened with the same filehandle.

Here-Is's

Here-is's are a line-oriented form of quoting. Typically, it is used for printing multiple lines of text. It is quicker to use one print statement with a here-is reference than to print each line individually. Referencing a here-is is done by using two less-than signs (<<) followed by a string used to close the quoted material (no space between the less-than signs and the string). Don't forget to put a semicolon at the end of the statement so that Perl will know where the statement ends. The following is an example of using here-is's to print multiple lines of code.

```
print <<"Print_to_here"
My name is $f_name $l_name

I live at:    $street
    $city, $state  $zip

Print_to_here
;
```

If a space is put in after the two less-than signs or if no string is used to close the quoted material, the print statement will print until it comes to a blank line. Therefore, had I put a space between the << and the " in the first line, all that would have printed would have been the first line rather than the whole thing.

Special Perl Variables

Perl has several special built-in variables. These variables have a certain value, or take on a specific value without having to be "told" by the program. Table 27.2 lists and describes these special variables.

TABLE 27.2   **Special Perl variables**

Variable	Purpose or Function
$_	The default input and pattern-searching space.
$.	The line number associated with the current line of the last filehandle read.
$/	The input record separator.
$,	The output field separator for the print operation.
$"	The separator that joins elements of arrays interpolated in strings.
$\	The output record separator for the print operator.
$#	The output format for printed numbers.
$*	Set to 1 to do multi-line matching within strings.
$?	The status returned by the last `...` command, close, pipe, or system operator.
$]	The Perl version number.
$[	The index of the first element of an array, and of the first character in a substring.
$;	The subscript operator for multi-dimensional array emulation.
$@	The error message returned from the last eval or do command.
$!	If used in a string context, yields the corresponding error string; in a numeric context, yields the current value of errno.
$:	The set of characters after which a string may be broken to fill continuation fields in a format.
$0	The filename of the Perl script being executed.
$$	The process ID of the Perl interpreter running the current script.
$<	The real user ID of the current Perl process.
$>	The effective user ID of the current Perl process.
$(	The real group ID of the current Perl process.

Variable	Purpose or Function
$)	The effective group ID of the current Perl process.
$^A	The accumulator for formline and write operations.
$^D	The debug flags as passed to Perl using -d.
$^F	The highest system file descriptor.
$^I	Inplace edit extension as passed to Perl using -i.
$^L	Form-feed character used in formats.
$^P	Internal debugging flag.
$^T	The time when the current Perl program started.
$^W	The value of the -w option as passed to Perl.
$^X	The name by which this Perl interpreter was invoked.
$%	The current page number of the currently selected output channel.
$=	The page length of the current output channel.
$-	The number of lines remaining in the current page.
$~	The name of the current report format.
$^	The name of the current top-of-page format.
$|	If set to nonzero (default is 0), it forces a flush after every print or write on the currently selected output channel.
$ARGV	The name of the current file when reading from < >.
$&	The string matched by the last successful pattern match.
$'	The string preceding the last successful pattern match.
$`	The string following the last successful pattern match.

continues…

TABLE 27.2 **Continued**

Variable	Purpose or Function
$+	The last bracket matched by the last search pattern.
$1..$9..	Contains the subpatterns from the corresponding sets of parentheses in the last pattern successfully matched.
@_	Parameter array for subroutines; also used by split if not an array context. Similar to $_ with strings.
@ARGV	Contains the command-line arguments for the script.
@EXPORT	Names the methods a package exports by default.
@EXPORT_OK	Names the methods a package can export if explicitly requested.
@INC	Contains the list of places to look for Perl scripts to be evaluated by the do and require commands.
@ISA	List of base classes of a package.
%ENV	The current environment variables.
%INC	List of files that have been included with do, require, and use.
%OVERLOAD	Can be used to overload operators in a package.
%SIG	Used to set signal handlers for various signs.

Supplying Script Input as a Parameter

Many programs allow parameters to be passed when the programs are instantiated. The programs must be smart enough to know what to do with these parameters. The same is true for any routine called in Perl. Fortunately, Perl has a built-in array that captures any parameters passed to it from the command line. That array is the @argv array. As in any language, the elements of the array are numbered starting with zero (0). Therefore, if two parameters were passed to the program, the first value would be the 0th element of the array, and the second parameter would be the first element of the array.

The @argv array is the default array. There are several ways of getting the information out of the array. The elements can be referred to, as alluded to earlier. If this method is used, the values stay in the array. Another way of getting the information out of the array is to shift it off of the array. Using the shift command, we can remove elements off of an array one at a time, moving all other elements in the array down one spot.

For example, assume that you have the following array.

```
@argv = (1,2,3,4);
```

You can set the value of the first element of the array to a variable like this.

```
$number = $argv[0];
```

This sets $number to have the value of "1", and @argv has the value of (1,2,3,4). The following example sets $number to the value of "1", but @argv will now have the value of (2,3,4).

```
$number = shift @argv;     # this is equivalent to $number =
➥shift; for the @argv array only.
```

Supplying Script Input on the Command Line

It is not necessary to pass variables to a program when the program is instantiated. It is also possible to read input from the command line. This is done with the use of the angle operator. The angle operator uses a special filehandle called STDIN. By placing the input filehandle between less-than and greater-than signs, we can get input from a command line. The value must be assigned to a variable and does include the hard return used when inputting the data. The following line takes standard input, and saves it to the variable $input.

```
$input = <STDIN>;
chomp($input);
```

The second line removes the ending hard return from the string.

Control Structures

Control structures provide programs with the capability to make decisions, to perform actions based on criteria. Perl has basically two types of control structures: conditionals and interactives. Conditionals are based on the concept that if something is true, perform some action once. Interactives (also known as loops) are based on the concept that if something is true, perform some action until that something is no longer true. This brings us to the question, what is truth?

What Is Truth?

This is a question that has plagued philosophers for thousands of years. Fortunately, we are programmers, not philosophers, and we know what truth is. Truth can be broken down into two types. The first way of looking at truth is a simple value check. If that value is equal to nil or zero, it is false; otherwise, it is true. Therefore, in the preceding example, if $value was anything other than nil or zero (that is, it has some value), it is printed; otherwise, it is not. Here are some examples, using this basic format, showing the difference between true and false.

```
$value = "";
if ($value) { print $value }
```

Nothing gets printed, because $value is nil.

```
$value = "David";
if ($value) { print $value }
```

David is printed, because "David" is not nil or zero.

The other way of looking at truth is with truth tables—looking at how one value compares with another value. To look at these truth tables, we must first have an understanding of how comparisons are done in Perl. They are done differently depending on whether they are comparing stings or numbers. Table 27.3 shows the relational operators for numbers and strings as well as what they mean.

TABLE 27.3   Relational operators for numbers and strings

Numeric	String	Meaning
>	gt	Greater than (returns " " if false, and 1 if true).
>=	ge	Greater than or equal to (returns " " if false, and 1 if true).

Numeric	String	Meaning
<	lt	Less than (returns " " if false, and 1 if true).
<=	le	Less than or equal to (returns " " if false, and 1 if true).
==	eq	Equal to (returns " " if false, and 1 if true).
!=	ne	Not equal to (returns " " if false, and 1 if true).
<=>	cmp	Comparison (returns -1 if left is less than right, 0 if equal, and 1 if left is greater than right).

Using the preceding table, we can then come up with some more complex if commands.

```
if ($value == 24) { print $value }
if ($value == 24 && $name eq "David") {print $name}
if ($value == 24 || $name eq "David") {print $value}
```

The first line is probably fairly understandable: If the value of $value is 24, then print the value of $value. The next two lines use a logical operator to allow a complex set of checking to determine truthfulness. The double ampersand sign (&&) is a logical AND, and a double pipe (||) is a logical OR. With the logical AND, the values on both sides of the && must be true for the entire statement to be true. With the logical OR, only one side has to be true. They use the following basic truth table.

Comparison	Value
True && True	True
True && False	False
False && False	False
False && True	False
True || True	True
True || False	True
False || False	False
False || True	True

Executing Code Based on Test Results (*if*)

Now that we have input, either from the command line or from standard input, we can do something with it. The most common thing to do with input is to test the results and do something if the results are a certain thing. This test result is done with the `if` command. The syntax of the `if` command is the verb *if* followed by a truth statement. After the truth statement, a block of code gets executed if the truth statement evaluates to true; otherwise, it skips that section of code. A simple *if* statement, then, would look something like this.

```
if ($value) { print $value }
```

Decision Making (*if-else*)

Having the capability to check on the truthfulness of something is okay, but with many processes, the desire is to take it one step further: To say "If something is true, do one thing; if it is not true, do something else." This can easily be done in Perl with the `if-else` statement.

```
if ($value eq "True") { do something }
else { do something else }
```

This is about as basic as it gets; a simple yes or no question, with each receiving a separate set of instructions. Of course, with the `elsif` verb, it is possible to have a hierarchy of work performed based upon certain conditions (that is, if the first condition is false, check the next condition). The following example shows that if the value is true, then it does something; if it is false, it then checks another value, and depending on its value, does one of several things.

```
if ($value eq "True") { do something }
    elsif { if ($range <= 22) { do something }
    elsif (($range > 22 ) && ($range <= 44)) { do something }
    elsif (($range > 44) && ( $range <= 70)) { do something }
    else {do something }
}   # end else
```

As you can see, with a combination of ifs, elsifs, and elses, it is possible to create any conditional type statement that may be necessary.

Looping Through Each Command-Line Argument (*for*)

The if statement helps to identify what to do when there is a choice. The for command is used when you want to loop through a series of code a certain number of times. Say, for example, that you want to perform a task until a certain variable (such as a counter) reaches a certain value. In English what you would do might look something like this:

> Initialize the counter to zero. If the counter is less than or equal to 10, run the series of commands. After the counter is greater than 10, go on to the rest of the program.

Perl uses the same syntax for the for loop as C does. The format is as follows.

```
for (initial value;while true value; change value) { do
➡stuff }
```

Here is an example with actual variables that may help shed some light on what was just said.

```
for ($counter=0; $counter <= 10; $counter++) { do stuff }
```

Notice that the for loop has three parts. First, you have the initial state of the for loop ($counter = 0). Next you have under what conditions you are going to execute the code (while the counter is less than or equal to 10). Finally, you have an expression to modify the state of the loop (increment $counter). As long as the truth condition is true ($counter <= 10), the loop will continue to execute.

You will probably recognize that the for loop is identical in nature to the while loop. The syntax is different, but the concept is the same. Just for completeness, however, here is the same loop as a while loop so that you can see the difference:

```
while ($counter <=10) {do stuff }
```

The main difference between the two is that there must exist in the "do stuff" code a change to the state variable or you will wind up with an endless loop.

Looping Through Something in Its Entirety (*foreach*)

Similar to the `for` loop is the `foreach` loop. The `foreach` loop is used to perform a set of instructions on an entire scalar quantity, such as an array. The syntax is quite simple; I will again give it in plain English and then in Perl.

In plain English, you would say "for each entity in my set, perform these instructions." Sound simple? Well, it is. The following is the Perl version of the foreach command:

```
foreach $value (@array) { do stuff }
```

In the preceding example, each element of the array, @array, is assigned to the variable $value. Then, the block of code is executed. It is not necessary to have the variable there ($value). If it is missing, the special variable $_ will contain the value of each element as the loop is executed. Here is a real-world example that may help to shed some light on this.

For example, suppose that you want to open a file, save its contents to an array, and check each line for a \n and replace it with a <br>. This is a good example of looping. The key that this is a looping function is the "check each line" statement. Such a program could look like this.

```
#!/site/bin/perl
open (FILE,"filename")  ¦¦ die "File not found:  $!\n";
@file=<FILE>;
close(FILE);
foreach (@file) {
    $_ =~ s/\\n/<br>/g;
    push (@temp, $_);
} # end of foreach  (@file)
open (FILE< ">filename");
print FILE @temp;
close FILE;
```

Commonly Used Functions in Perl

Although it would take a hundred pages or more to give a brief description of all the functions of Perl, it is adequate to list some of the common functions dealing with arrays, lists, and scalars; giving the novice the ability to make some very powerful and complex tools. Therefore, this section gives a brief description and provides examples for some of the most commonly used functions. Before this occurs, a few points need to be made about functions in general.

Functions can be used as terms in an expression. Some of these functions take on a *list* as an argument. Such a list can be any combination of scalar and list values, but the entire list will be treated as a single dimensional list value. Elements in a list must be separated by a comma, or by a =>; which is a shorthand version of a comma.

Functions do not have to have parentheses around their arguments. Many programmers use parentheses around the arguments to help distinguish them from the function name, and to help indicate that they are arguments. Caution must be taken, however, because parentheses in the wrong location can give varying, and many times, unexpected results. The following example will help to make this more clear:

```
print 1+1+1;      # prints "3"
print (1+1)  + 1;      # prints "2"
print (1+1)+1;      # prints "2"
print +(1+1)+1;      # prints "3"
print ((1+1)+1);      # prints "3"
```

As you can see, spacing has little or no effect, but the parentheses have a lot of effect on the output.

The functions we are going to look at fall into the following categories: array, file, hash, system, and variable manipulation. The functions can be broken down into these categories—realizing that some do fit into multiple categories—like this:

```
Array Manipulation:    pop, push, shift, unshift, splice
File Manipulation:     open, close
Hash Manipulation:     each, keys, values
```

```
System Manipulation:    time, localtime, system
Variable Manipulation:    ++, --, ., chomp, split, join
```

An accurate observer would note that some of these are not actually functions (., ++, --), but are important enough to be included anyway.

Array Manipulation

Arrays can be treated as stacks. Therefore, things can be added or removed from either end of the stack. With the ability to add and remove things from the beginning and ending of an array, we can perform first-in-first-out and last-in-first-out functionality. Things can also be removed from the middle of a stack. With this in mind, we look at the following five functions.

Pop and Push

My wife told me that if I pushed her too far, she would pop me (or it). This is not a reflection on our relationship, but a reminder of what push and pop do. Obviously she already had a lot to deal with, and I was adding to the end of her list. If I continued to do that, she would remove those things back off her list. Push and pop, therefore, add and remove things from the end of an array. The syntax and an example of these follow.

```
push ARRAY, LIST
```

The following example uses a foreach statement to read each line of an array. Each line is then subjected to a search and replace routine, and the result of that line is pushed on to an array called @temp.

```
foreach $line (@ARGV)
        { $line =~ s/$search/$replace/g ;
          push (@temp, $line);
} # end of foreach $line (@stuff)
print @stuff,"\n\n",@temp;
```

The pop function works similarly, as seen here:

```
pop ARRAY
pop
```

If ARRAY is omitted, the function pops @ARGV or @_. The following example pops each element off an array, performs the same search and replace routine as the preceding example, and the result is pushed on to a second array.

```
while (@ARGV) {
    $argument = pop;
    $argument =~ s/$search/$replace/g ;
    push (@temp, $argument);
} # end while (@ARGV)
    print @temp, "\n\n\", @ARGV;
```

What is the difference between these two examples? There are two differences. Let us look at the output of the print statements. In both examples, $search = "David" and $replace = "John", and the arguments passed were "David was here." Output of the push example looks like this:

```
Johnwashere.
```

```
Johnwashere.
```

And output of the pop example looks like this:

```
here.wasJohn
```

The differences are that in the pop example, @ARGV loses all of its values because they are popped off the list (removed), and in the second, each of them are just addressed. The second difference is that in the pop example, the output is the opposite of the input. Can you figure out why?

Shift and Unshift

Shift and unshift are just like push and pop, except they work on the other side of the array. Push and pop add and remove items from the end of the array, and unshift and shift add and remove items from the beginning of an array. We will use examples similar to push and pop, and see what the differences are. First, however, here is their syntax:

```
unshift ARRAY, LIST
```

Remember, unshift prepends items to an array—that means it adds them to the beginning of the array.

```
foreach $line (@ARGV)
        { $line =~ s/$search/$replace/g ;
          unshift (@temp, $line);
} # end of foreach $line (@stuff)
print @temp,"\n\n",@ARGV;
```

Example's output:

```
here.wasJohn


Johnwashere.



Notice, that @temp is  backwards of the input parameters,
➥"David was here.".


shift ARRAY
shift
```

Just like its counterpart, pop, shift removes items from @ARGV or @_ if no ARRAY is given.

```
while (@ARGV) {
        $argument=shift;
        $argument =~ s/$search/$replace/g;
        unshift (@temp, $argument);
} # end while (@ARGV)


print @temp, "\n\n", @ARGV;
```

Example's output:

```
here.wasJohn
```

Notice that even though it took the items from the beginning of the stack first, it also put them back in the beginning first. Therefore, the new array, @temp, now contains all the arguments in reverse order.

Splice

Sometimes, we want to take a bigger piece of an array, or we want to take something out of the middle. That is what the splice is for. As a matter of fact, we can use splice as a replacement for shift, unshift, pop, and push. The syntax of splice looks like this:

```
splice ARRAY, OFFSET, LENGTH, LIST
splice ARRAY, OFFSET, LENGTH
splice ARRAY, OFFSET
```

This function removes elements designated by OFFSET and LENGTH from an array, and replaces them with the elements of LIST, if there are any. Splice returns the elements removed from the array. If the LENGTH is omitted, shift removes everything after the OFFSET.

The following table shows how to use splice rather than push, pop, shift, and unshift, to remove a piece from the middle of the array.

Splice	Equivalent
splice(@array, $#array+1, 0, $x, $y);	push (@array, $x, $y);
splice(@array,(@array, -1);	pop (@array);
splice(@array, 0, 1);	shift (@array)
splice(@array, 0, 0, $x, $y);	unshift (@array, $x, $y);
splice(@array, $x, 1, $y);	$array[$x] = $y;

Did you see that special looking variable $#array? That value returns the index of the last element in the array. By adding one to it, we get the OFFSET value (arrays start counting at 0; OFFSET starts counting at 1).

File Manipulation

The two most common things you will do with a file is open and close it. Closing a file is very simple, and is discussed first. Opening a file depends on what you are going to do with the file, so a little extra time is spent explaining it.

Close

Closing a filehandle is not a necessary step up through version 5 of Perl. A file is automatically closed when the program ends, or when a new file is opened with the same FILEHANDLE name. There is no guarantee that this will hold true in future versions of Perl, and it is also good programming etiquette to close any files that you open. If you do not remember what filehandles are, see the previous section that discusses them. The syntax is simple:

```
close FILEHANDLE;
```

I give you an example here, but it should be obvious:

```
open (FILE, $file);
$file=<FILE>;
close FILE;
```

Open

Opening a file is done by opening the file and giving it a file-handle. The filehandle is then referred to in the program. Files can be opened for various reasons: to be read from, to be written to, and to be concatenated to. The following table shows the different ways of opening a file.

Command	What It Does
`open (FILE, "filename");`	Reads from an existing file
`open (DAVID, "<filename");`	Opens a file explicitly (same as above)
`open (church,">filename");`	Creates a file and opens it to be written to (overwrites an existing file)
`open (log,">>filename");`	Appends to a file (does not overwrite an existing file)
`open(file, "| output-pipe-command");`	Sets up an output filter
`open(file, "input-pipe-command |");`	Sets up an input filter

As you can see, it is important to know what you are going to do with the file; otherwise, you can accidentally delete an existing file or append to a file that you meant to overwrite.

Hash Manipulation

Hash arrays are different from a regular array. A hash array is an associative array. Where a normal array is an indexed list, with each item referred to by its index number, a hash is a list of value pairs. A value pair is where the first item (key) refers to the second item (value); and when the first item is referred to, the second item is the value returned. This can be easily thought with the following small hash array for the days of the week:

```
%day_of_the_week =
( 0, Sunday, 1, Monday, 2, Tuesday, 3, Wednesday, 4,
➥Thursday, 5, Friday, 6, Saturday);
```

The hash can also be defined this way:

```
%day_of_the_week=  (
     0 => 'Sunday',
     1 => 'Monday',
     2 => 'Tuesday',
     3 => 'Wednesday',
     4 => 'Thursday',
     5 => 'Friday',
     6 => 'Saturday',
);
```

Note, the comma after the last key/value pair *must be there*.

Now that we have a hash defined, we can look at the three functions: each, keys, and values; and see how they relate to our %day_of_the_week hash.

each

```
each %hash
```

The each function returns a two-element list consisting of the key and value for the next value of a hash. The each function is unique in that you can use successive calls to each to iterate over the entire hash. You should not add elements to a hash while you are iterating it, but you can delete from it.

keys

```
keys %hash
```

This function returns all the keys of the hash.

values

```
values %hash
```

This function returns all the values of the hash.

This example shows listing out each of the values of our %day_of_the_week hash.

```
while (($key, $value) = each %day_of_the_week) {
        print "$key has value $value\n";
}
```

The result of this program is as follows:

```
0 has value Sunday
1 has value Monday
2 has value Tuesday
3 has value Wednesday
4 has value Thursday
5 has value Friday
6 has value Saturday
```

System Manipulation

System manipulation is really not a good term for these functions. Basically, it is reading something from the system, or performing a system call. We could also include others here (such as exec, fork, kill, and times), but these are the basic ones.

time

time returns the number of seconds since the birth of UNIX, January 1, 1970 Universal Time. It can be used to determine how long it has been since a file was accessed, or how long it takes to complete a task. A common function of time is to use it as a parameter of localtime. An example on how to use this function is shown with the localtime function section.

localtime

This function returns a nine-element list with the time corrected for the current time zone. The nine elements are shown in the following table, along with their possible values.

Element	Possible Values
seconds	0..59
minutes	0..59
hour	0..23
month day	1..31
month	0..11
year	current year minus 1900
day of the week	0..6
day of the year	0..364
whether it is daylight savings time	0..1

The following example takes the current date and prints the time, date, day of the week, day of the year, and whether it is daylight savings time. You will notice some modifications to the variables to deal with certain values starting with zero. Also, the daylight savings time is changed to "True" or "False".

```perl
#!/usr/bin/perl
($sec, $min, $hour, $mday, $mon, $year, $wday, $yday,
➥$isdst) = localtime(time);
$year+=1900;
$yday++;
if ($sec < 10) { $sec = "0".$sec }
if ($min < 10) { $min = "0".$min }
if ($hour < 10) { $hour = "0".$hour }
if ($isdst) {$isdst = "True" } else { $isdst = "False" }
%tday = (
        0 => 'Sunday',
        1 => 'Monday',
        2 => 'Tuesday',
        3 => 'Wednesday',
        4 => 'Thursday',
        5 => 'Friday',
        6 => 'Saturday',
```

```
) ;

%tmonth = (
            0  => 'January',
            1  => 'February',
            2  => 'March',
            3  => 'April',
            4  => 'May',
            5  => 'June',
            6  => 'July',
            7  => 'August',
            8  => 'September',
            9  => 'October',
            10 => 'November',
            11 => 'December',
);

print "Time:   $hour:$min:$sec\n";
print "Today:   $tmonth{$mon} $mday, $year\n";
print "Day of the week:   $tday{$wday}\n";
print "Day of the year:   $yday\n";
print "Daylight Savings time?:   $isdst\n";
```

The result of this file is the following output:

```
Time:   20:09:46
Today:   March 24, 1998
Day of the week:   Tuesday
Day of the year:   83
Daylight Savings time?:   False
```

As you can imagine, the time and `localtime` functions are great for such things as logs, reports, and other applications where it is handy to know when something happened.

system (` `)

The `system` command allows a Perl program to have access to the system. There are two ways of calling the system. The first is with the `system` command; the second is by placing the command between back-tics. The problem with making system calls is that it greatly limits the portability of your code. One of the nice things about the system command is that it blocks SIGINT and SIGQUIT, and keeps it from killing the program. Also, the result of a program called with system can be saved with a variable, allowing the program to examine the results and perform any necessary steps from the results. A very simple example is listed here. Fortunately, there are ways within Perl to perform this task; therefore, you can keep your programs portable.

```
$cur_dir = `ls`;
```

Actually calling the system command looks like this.

```
$cur_dir = system (ls);   # parentheses not necessary.
```

Perl assumes that you know what you are doing, and, therefore, lets you do whatever you want. A command such as $remove = `rm -r \`; can just kill a system!

Variable Manipulation

Variable manipulation is grouped into a couple of different groups. First there are the increment and decrement symbols (++ and - -), the dot (.), and then split and join. Finally, there is the chomp command. It is in this order that we discuss these topics.

++, - -

These two symbols increment and decrement the value of a variable by one. The following example shows incrementing the variable $penny by one, and then decrementing it by one.

```
$penny++;
$penny--;
```

You will find this much quicker and easier than the following:

```
$penny += 1;
or
$penny = $penny -1;
```

.

The dot (.) is used to concatenate strings. Given the following two strings,

```
$string1 = "University of Kentucky Wildcats";
$string2 = "are the best basketball players ever!";
```

These strings can be concatenated into one string by using the dot.

```
$string3=$string1.$string2;
```

This produces the following output when printed:

```
University of Kentucky Wildcatsare the best basketball players
➥ever!
```

The concatenation did not put a space between the strings; therefore, we must add it. This can be done like this:

```
$string3=$string1." ".$string2;
```

This produces the following result when printed:

```
University of Kentucky Wildcats are the best basketball
➥players ever!
```

If a string of numbers are concatenated, they are put together just like text is; it is not manipulated. For example, the following lines produce the output 123456:

```
$a=123;
$b=456;
$c=$a.$b;
print $c;
```

split

split is used to turn a delimited string into a list.

```
split /PATTERN/, EXPR, LIMIT;
split /PATTERN/, EXPR;
split /PATTERN/;
split;
```

This function scans a string given by EXPR for delimiters indicated with /PATTERN/. It then splits that string into a set of substrings. If the LIMIT is set to a non-zero, positive number, the string is split into no more than that number of substrings. In the process, the /PATTERN/ being matched goes away.

The following example is how you could split up the /etc/passwd file into its seven different fields. The account lines are colon delimited, so we search on the pattern of the colon.

```
($user,$password,$uid,$gid,$gcos,$home,$init_prog) = split
➥(/:/, @passwd);
```

The split, then, breaks up big strings into smaller strings. The join function takes small strings and joins them together into big strings.

join

```
join EXPR, LIST;
```

join takes strings and joins them into a single string with the EXPR delimiting them. This is the opposite of the split function. The following example takes the seven elements associated with a password entry and joins them together with a colon as the EXPR.

```
$entry = join (':', $user,$password,$uid,$gid,$gcos,$home,$init_prog);
```

chomp

```
chomp VARIABLE;
chomp LIST;
chomp;
```

chomp is used to remove trailing newlines from the selected string(s). If VARIABLE or LIST is omitted, it chomps $_. One common use for chomp is to remove the input coming from the keyboard.

```
print "Spell out the answer to this math problem:  2 + 2=
➥Answer:  ";
$answer = <STDIN>;
chomp $answer;
if ($answer eq "four" ¦¦ $answer eq "Four") { print "Right!
➥The answer is four (4)" }
else { print "Sorry! The answer is four (4)" }
```

If you comment out the chomp $answer line, then no matter what answer you put in there, it will be false, because our if statement is looking for either "four" or "Four", and there is not a newline in either of these strings.

Debugging Your Script (*-d*)

The Perl debugger is not a separate program. Instead you invoke Perl with the -d option, and you are in Debug mode. While in Debug mode, you have the ability to examine source code, set breakpoints, dump out your function call stack, change the values of variables, and so forth. This section does not go through all the functionality of the debugger, nor does it give you all the available commands. What this section does do is introduce you to the basic debugging commands, and shows you how to find out more. Specifically, the things that you are shown here are how to set, list, and remove breakpoints; how to step through a program; how to check and change the value of a variable; and how to get help.

I will be using the following short program as a basis for describing the debugger. This program is called rep.pl and is used to search and replace strings in a file. You will notice that I added the -d option so that Perl would run in Debug mode.

```perl
#!/usr/bin/perl -d
#
#   Open file, replace every occurrence of a string.
#   Usage:  rep string1 string2 file
$file = @ARGV[2];
$search = @ARGV[0];
$replace = @ARGV[1];

if ($file eq "") {
print "Usage: rep.pl [search] [replace] [file name]\n\n";   }

else     {
open (FILE, "$file") || die "File not found: $! ";
@stuff = <FILE>;
close FILE;

foreach $line (@stuff)
        { $line =~ s/$search/$replace/g ;
          push (@temp, $line); }

open (FILE, ">$file");
```

```
print FILE @temp;
close FILE;


}
```

When I run this program, Perl comes up in Debug mode. This means that the code does get compiled. If there are compilation errors (such as missing semicolons), the debugger will not run. Assuming there are no compilation errors, the debugger should come up, and look something like this.

```
Loading DB routines from perl5db.pl version 1
Emacs support available.


Enter h or `h h' for help.


main::(./rep.pl:6):       $file = @ARGV[2];
  DB<1>
```

By the way, I ran the program with the following command:

```
rep.pl david
```

This will be important as we look at the values of some of the strings, as well as the final output of the program itself.

Listing Code (*l*)

The first thing I want to do is list my code. To list code you type the letter l. This produces the following results:

```
DB<1> l
6==>     $file = @argv[2];
7:      $search = @ARGV[0];
8:      $replace = @ARGV[1];
9:
10:     if ($file eq "") {
11:     print "Usage: rep.pl [search] [replace] [file
        ➥name]\n\n";   }
12:
13:     else    {
14:     open (FILE, "$file") || die "File not found: $! ";
15:     @stuff = <FILE>;
DB<1>
```

The debugger indicates my current line with the ==> pointing to the line (line 6). You will notice that it skipped right over the comments at the beginning of the program and went straight to line 6. By default, the debugger lists 10 lines of code. You can specify any range you wish by placing a starting line number and then a dash followed by the number of lines you want to print. Therefore, if I told it I wanted it to print the first three lines of the program, it would look like this:

```
DB<2> l 1-3
1           #!/usr/bin/perl -d
2           #
3           #  Open file, replace every occurance of a string.
```

Execute a Line of Code (*n*)

After I have listed my code, I now want to execute the first line. I execute the first line by typing the letter n. This tells the debugger to execute the line and go to the next line. That produced the following results:

```
main::(./rep.pl:7):     $search = @ARGV[0];
  DB<3>
```

Printing Values of Variables

At this point, I told it to execute the next two lines of code. This gives me something else to work with. I now want to know the value of the variables $_, $ARGV[0], $ARGV[1], and $ARGV[2].

```
DB<3> print $_

  DB<4> print $ARGV[0]
david
  DB<5> print $ARGV[1]

  DB<6> print $ARGV[2]

  DB<7>
```

As I suspected, the value of $_ is nothing. The value of $ARGV[0] is "david", and $ARGV[1] and $ARGV[2] is also nothing. I think I want to change the value of $ARGV[1] to "David" rather than nothing. I do this by telling the variable what it should be, as follows:

```
DB<7> $ARGV[1]="David"

  DB<8> print $ARGV[1]
David
  DB<9>
```

As a matter of fact, you can execute any Perl command from the debugger command line, and it will affect the program that you are running. The only limitation is that you are limited to one line per prompt, and you do not place a semicolon after the command.

Breakpoints

You can use breakpoints to set up one or more stopping points in your program. A breakpoint, once set, tells the debugger to stop on this line, if it reaches it. In our example, I want to set a breakpoint on the 10th line. I want the program to stop at the if statement so that I can figure out what the values are. To set a breakpoint, you use a letter b followed by line number. Optionally, you can place a condition on there as well. If a condition is placed, the breakpoint will only stop the execution of the program if it reaches the line and the condition is true. Therefore, what I want to do is set a breakpoint that stops the program if $file equals "". That command would look like this:

```
DB<5> b 10 $file eq ""
  DB<6> l 6-15
6==>       $file = @ARGV[2];
7:         $search = @ARGV[0];
8:         $replace = @ARGV[1];
9
10:b       if ($file eq "") {
11:        print "Usage: rep.pl [search] [replace] [file
           ➥name]\n\n";    }
12
13         else    {
14:        open (FILE, "$file") || die "File not found ";
15:        @stuff = <FILE>;
```

Did you notice that line 10 looks different? It has a b next to the line number. This is how the debugger indicates a breakpoint. Now I want the debugger to run until it gets to the breakpoint. I do this by issuing a letter c. I follow the c with a w so that I can see a window of code around my current line.

```
DB<7> c
main::(./rep.pl:10):     if ($file eq "") {
  DB<7> w
7:        $search = @ARGV[0];
8:        $replace = @ARGV[1];
9
10==>b    if ($file eq "") {
11:       print "Usage: rep.pl [search] [replace] [file
          ➥name]\n\n";   }
12
13        else    {
14:       open (FILE, "$file") || die "File not found ";
15:       @stuff = <FILE>;
16:       close FILE;
  DB<7>
```

Now I want to take another look at my variables $ARGV[0] and $ARGV1], so I type in the following command:

```
DB<7> print $ARGV[0] $ARGV[1]
```

Remember, I said only one command per line. Here I did two commands. I told it to print out two different values. Here is the result of the command:

```
Scalar found where operator expected at (eval 5) line 2, at
➥end of line
        eval '($@, $!, $,, $/, $\\, $^W) = @saved;package
        ➥main; $^D = $^D | $DB:
:db_stop;
print $ARGV[0] $ARGV[1];

;' called at /usr/lib/perl5/perl5db.pl line 1153
        DB::eval called at /usr/lib/perl5/perl5db.pl line
        ➥1062
        DB::DB called at ./rep.pl line 10
        (Missing operator before ?)
        eval '($@, $!, $,, $/, $\\, $^W) = @saved;package
        ➥main; $^D = $^D | $DB:
```

```
:db_stop;
print $ARGV[0] $ARGV[1];

;' called at /usr/lib/perl5/perl5db.pl line 1153
        DB::eval called at /usr/lib/perl5/perl5db.pl line
        ➥1062
        DB::DB called at ./rep.pl line 10
Segmentation fault
```

Well, this told me two things. First of all, use one command per
line. Second, it tells me that if there is an error, a segmentation
fault will occur, and the Perl program will bomb. So, I restart
and try again. I added my breakpoint back so that I had the same
conditions as before. I realize that now, however, I don't need
that breakpoint. I now need to delete it. To delete a breakpoint,
you enter a lowercase d. If a line number follows the d, the
breakpoint is removed from that line. An uppercase D will delete
all installed breakpoints.

```
DB<2> d 10
6:      $file = @ARGV[2];
7:      $search = @ARGV[0];
8:      $replace = @ARGV[1];
9
10==>   if ($file eq "") {
11:     print "Usage: rep.pl [search] [replace] [file
        ➥name]\n\n";   }
12
13      else    {
14:     open (FILE, "$file") || die "File not found ";
15:     @stuff = <FILE>;
  DB<4>
```

My breakpoint at line 10 is now gone. I have added some more
breakpoints, and now I want to list them out. I do that with a
capital L, as follows:

```
DB<7> L
./rep.pl:
 6:     $file = @ARGV[2];
   break if (1)
 11:    print "Usage: rep.pl [search] [replace] [file
        ➥name]\n\n";   }
   break if (1)
```

```
15:      @stuff = <FILE>;
  break if (1)
 DB<7>
```

It seems I have three breakpoints set: lines 6, 11, and 15. A capital D will delete them all, and I will be ready to go.

```
DB<7> D
Deleting all breakpoints...
  DB<7>
```

There is a lot more that can be done with the debugger. It would take an entire chapter to go into all the functionality that is there. So, before we close the book on the debugger, let me point you to a source of further understanding with the debugger. That source is the help facility built in to the debugger itself. If you just type an h by itself, you will get a long listing of all the possible command options available. If you are like me, you cannot read fast enough to catch it as it is scrolling off the screen. Therefore, if you type h h, it will give the same list in a different format. This one will be in a two columned list that should fit on a single screen. Following each command is a very short description on what that command does. I see the v shows versions of modules, for example:

```
DB<10> v
'Term/ReadLine.pm' => '/usr/lib/perl5/Term/ReadLine.pm'
'dumpvar.pl' => '/usr/lib/perl5/dumpvar.pl'
'perl5db.pl' => '1 from /usr/lib/perl5/perl5db.pl'
  DB<10>
```

Finally, when you are done, a simple "q" will quit you out of the program.

Some Final Words

Perl is a fully functioning powerful language that is easy to use. It brings together the power of C and the ease of shell programming. Perl does not stop there, however. Perl does object orienting. Perl can be combined with other languages, including C, TK, and Java. It is easy to use, and has some great support behind it.

For further information on Perl, check out the Perl Web site at www.perl.com. There you will find the latest versions of Perl, along with the Comprehensive Perl Archive Network (CPAN), which has tons of code, most of which falls under the same copyright license as Perl itself. You will also find FAQs there. If you get stuck, you can also go to the comp.lang.perl.misc newsgroup and post questions there as well.

UNIX Commands

NOTE: [brackets] indicate optional fields.

= - Set shell variable

Usage: `variable=new-contents`

Std input: Not used

Std output: Not used

SEE ALSO

➤ *For more information, see page 54*

apropos - Same as man -k

at - Run command a specified date/time

Std input: Used to input one or more commands terminated with EOT key (usually Ctrl+D)

Std output: Not used

SEE ALSO

➤ *For more information, see page 313*

Notes: To prevent Usage, edit /usr/lib/cron/at.allow and at.deny

awk - Aho, Weinberger, and Kernighan's C-like programming language

Std input: Only used if no list-of-files is given

Std output: Used to display results

Note: On some systems, use nawk (new awk) or gawk (GNU awk).

Using awk from the command-line to display selected lines:

```
awk '$n == "string"' [list-of-files]
     (display line if field n equals string)
awk '$n > 3.5' [list-of-files]
     (display line if field n is greater than
     ↪value.
       can also test ==, !=, >, <, >=, <=)
awk '$n ~ /R.E./' [list-of-files]
     (display line if field n contain R.E.)
```

SEE ALSO

➤ *For more information, see page 407*

Using awk to display selected fields:

```
awk '{print $1, $5, $0}' [list-of-files]
awk '{if ($5 > 20000) $5=20000} {print "file: " $9
↪"        " $5}'
awk '{ printf("Name: %16s, Size: %5d, Blocks:
↪%6.2f\n", $9, $5, $5/512)}'
```

Using awk from the command-line to replace strings:

```
awk '$3 == "acme" { gsub ("R.E.","repl") }
↪{print}' [list-of-files]
awk '$n > 3.5 { gsub ("R.E.","repl") } {print}'
↪[list-of-files]
awk '$n ~ /R.E./ { gsub ("R.E.","repl") }
↪{print}' [list-of-files]
```

SEE ALSO

➤ *For more information, see page 429*

Using awk from the command-line to remove strings:

```
awk '$3 == "acme" { gsub ("R.E.","") } {print}'
↪[list-of-files]
```

SEE ALSO

➤ *For more information, see page 429*

banner – Display words in banner header size

Usage: banner [words to display]

Std input: Used only if no words supplied on command line

Std output: Used to display results

SEE ALSO
➤ *For more information, see page 167*

Notes: Puts separate words on separate lines unless spaces are escaped or quoted. Truncates each line at 10 characters.

`batch` - run command when system is Not busy

Usage: `batch`

Std input: Used to input one or more commands

Terminated with EOT key (usually Ctrl+D)

Std output: Not used

SEE ALSO
➤ *For more information, see page 315*

Notes: To prevent Usage, edit /usr/lib/cron/at.allow and at.deny

`bc` - Business calculator

Can do infinite precision arithmetic.

For two decimal places, enter `scale=2`.

To quit, enter `quit`.

`bg` - Start suspended job running in the background

Usage: `bg %JOBID`

SEE ALSO
➤ *For more information, see page 322*

Useful options: Same as `kill` (Korn shell) under `%JOBID`

Bourne shell (See `sh`)

C shell (See `csh`)

`cal` - Display a calendar

Usage: `cal [year]`

Std input: Not used

Std output: Used to display results

Notes: 98 is Not the same year as 1998

`cancel` - Cancel print job

Usage: `cancel JOBID`

Std input: Not used

Std output: Not used

cat - Display/concatenate files or pipeline

Usage: `cat [list-of-files]`

Std input: Only used if no list of files is given

Std output: Used to display results

SEE ALSO

➤ *For more information, see page 223*

Useful options: `-n` means include line numbers in the output

SEE ALSO

➤ *For more information, see page 164*

`-nb` means number only non-blank lines

`-v` means display control chars as printable chars

cd - Change directory

Usage: `cd dirname`

Std input: Not used

Std output: Not used except for CDPATH (see following Notes)

SEE ALSO

➤ *For more information, see page 42*

Notes: If no dirname given, takes you to your home directory. If a dirname is a basename, `cd` will check whether dirname is a subdirectory of any parent directory in CDPATH. If so, `cd` will change to that directory and output its full pathname to Std output.

chgrp - Change the group of a file

Usage: `chgrp newgroup list-of-files`

Std input: Not used

Std output: Not used

Can only be done by the file owner or root.

chmod - Change the mode (permissions) of a file

Usage: `chmod perms list-of-files`

Std input: Not used

Std output: Not used

Can only be done by the file owner or root.

Perms can be specified in two ways:

Symbolic: `[ugoa][+-=][rwxst]`

Absolute or numeric:

`read=4 + write=2 + execute=1`

`owner * 100 + group * 10 + other`

`4000=SUID, 2000=SGID, 1000=sticky`

chown - Change the owner of a file

Usage: `chgrp newowner list-of-files`

Std input: Not used

Std output: Not used

Can only be done by the file owner or root.

cmp - Compare two files of any type

Usage: `cmp file1 file2`

Std input: Not used

Std output: Used to display results

Notes: `cmp` stops after finding the first difference. No output means the files are identical.

SEE ALSO

➤ *For more information, see page 267*

Useful options: `-l` means list all the differences

col - Filter control characters from pipeline

Usage: `col options`

Std input: Provides input to col

Std output: Used to display results

SEE ALSO

➤ *For more information, see pages 167-168*

Useful options: -b means filter out backspaces (^H)

-x means do not convert consecutive spaces to tabs

comm - Show common and unique lines between two sorted files

Usage: `comm file1 file2`

Std input: Only used if file1 or file2 is a dash (-)

Std output: Used to display results

Notes: `col 1` shows lines only in file1.

`col 2` shows lines only in file2.

`col 3` shows lines in common.

SEE ALSO

➤ *For more information, see page 266*

Useful options:

-1 means suppress `col 1` (lines only in file1).

-2 means suppress `col 2` (lines only in file2).

-3 means suppress `col 3` (common lines).

compress - Compress a file

Usage: `compress filename`

Std input: Not used

Std output: Not used

SEE ALSO

➤ *For more information, see page 219*

Notes: Adds .Z to compressed filename

Useful options:

-H allows better compression on SCO UNIX.

copy - Special file copy command

Not available on all UNIX systems

Usage: Copy options source dest

Useful options:

`-m` means set destination last mod and last access to match the source.

`-o` means set owner and group to match the source.

`-r` means copy directories recursively, so all subdirectories are copied.

cp - Copy files

Usage: `cp file1 file2`

`cp list-of-files dest-dir/.`

Std input: Not used

Std ouput: Not used

SEE ALSO

➤ *For more information, see page 181*

Useful options:

`-i` means interact with user and ask permission before overwriting an existing file (not available on older UNIX).

`-p` means preserve owner, group, permissions, especially from root account (not available on all UNIX systems).

`-r` means copy directories recursively, so all subdirectories are also copied (not avail on all UNIX systems).

cpio - Copy file in/out, especially to tape

Usage: `generate file names ¦ cpio options`

Std input: Used to supply a list of pathnames to `cpio`

Std ouput: Usually redirected to tape device

SEE ALSO

➤ *For more information, see page 355*

Major options: (One of these must be the first option.)

-o means write (save) files on cpio archive.

-it means list files on tape without restoring them.

-i means restore files from cpio archive.

-p means pass a subdirectory subtree to another directory.

SEE ALSO

➤ *For more information, see page 189*

Options for backup using cpio:

-a means reset date/time of last access for each disk file to what it was before cpio accessed the file.

-B means block the output 10 blocks (5,120 bytes) per record.

-c means write character header for greater portability to other UNIX systems. May not be used with -H odc.

-C XX means set tape blocks size to XX bytes.

-H odc means SVR4 systems will write a cpio tape that pre-SVR4 systems can read. May not be used with -c option.

-L means follow symbolic links (not on AIX).

-v means verbose output, which lists each file as it is copied.

-V means just show a period as each file is backed up.

Options for restore using cpio:

-A means suppress leading slash so that absolute files can be restored to other directories (SCO).

-c means look for character header for greater portability to other UNIX systems. Some UNIX systems will autosense whether archive file or tape was written with this option. On other systems, you must include -c on restore if tape was written with -c.

-d means create destination directories as needed.

-k means skip past corrupted spot on tape and try to resume reading files.

-m means keep the same date/time of last modification for each file as in the source directory.

-t means don't restore any files; just display the table of contents of the tape.

-u means unconditionally overwrite any existing destination files or else an older file will not overwrite a newer one.

-v means verbose output, which lists each file as it is copied.

-V means just show a period as each file is backed up.

SEE ALSO

➤ *For more information, see page 189*

Options for passing files using cpio:

-a means reset date/time of last access for each file to what it was before cpio accessed the file. May not be used if -m option is included.

-d means create destination directories as needed.

-L means follow soft links (see next section) so that the pointed to file is copied rather than the pointer file.

-m means keep the same date/time of last modification for each destination file as in the source directory. May not be used if -a option is included.

-u means unconditionally overwrite any existing destination files or else an older file will not overwrite a newer one.

-v means verbose output, which lists each file as it is copied.

-V means just show a period as each file is backed up.

crontab - Submit a whole new cron table for this user

Usage: crontab NEWTABLE   # submit new table

crontab -l # list current table

Std input: Not used

Std output: Used to display output for -l option

SEE ALSO

➤ *For more information, see page 308*

Notes: To prevent usage, edit /usr/lib/cron/cron.allow and cron.deny.

Useful options:

-l means list the current table.

crypt - Encrypt or decrypt file or pipeline

Usage: crypt < filename

Std input: Redirect this from file or pipeline

Std output: Used to display results

SEE ALSO

➤ *For more information, see page 217*

Notes: To decrypt requires the same key that was used to encrypt.

csh - Run the C shell

csplit - Split file into smaller files by context

Usage: csplit options filename [prefix]

Smaller files will be prefix00, prefix01, prefix02,

Default prefix is xx.

Std input: Not used

Std output: Not used

SEE ALSO

➤ *For more information, see page 227*

Useful options:

-k preserves created files in spite of errors such as using 99 as a repeat count.

Examples:

```
csplit -k filename '/Chapter/' '{99}'
csplit filename '/boundaryword/' '/boundaryword/'
➥'/boundaryword/'
```

cut - Cut and keep columns or fields of output

Usage: cut options [list-of-files]

Std input: Only used if no list-of-files is given

Std output: Used to display results

Useful options:

-c5-16,42- means specify columns to keep in output.

-dX means set char X as the field delimiter.

-fn means cut and keep field n.

SEE ALSO

➤ *For more information, see page 437*

date - Display the system date and time

Usage: Date format

Std input: Not used

Std output: Used to display results

Format has the form "+%X" where X can be:

S second (0–59)

M minute (0–59)

I hour (1–12)

p am or pm

H hour (0–23)

T time (hh:mm:ss)

Z time zone

A complete weekday name

a weekday (three letter)

w day of the week (0–6)

d day of the month (1–31)

j day of the year (1–366)

U week of the year (0–53)

m month (1–12)

b month (three letter)

h month (three letter)

B complete month

y year (two digits)

Y year (four digits)

D MM/DD/YY

c date/time

df - Shows disk free blocks

SEE ALSO

➤ *For information, see page 340*

diff - Show differences between two text files

Usage: `diff file1 file2`

Std input: Only used if file1 or file2 is a dash (-)

Std output: Used to display results

Notes: Output beginning with < sign are from the first file. Lines beginning with > sign are from the second file. No output means the files are identical.

SEE ALSO

➤ *For more information, see page 262*

Useful options:

-b means ignore trailing blanks and treat strings of blanks as a single blank.

SEE ALSO

➤ *For more information, see page 262*

diff3 - Compare 3 text files

Usage: `diff3 file1 file2 file3`

Std input: Not used

Std output: Used to display results

Notes: In results, `===` means all three files differ as shown. `===n` means file n (1, 2, or 3) differs from the others as shown.

SEE ALSO

➤ *For more information, see page 264*

du - Show disk Usage

echo - Display text

To suppress the newline at end of line

```
echo -n some text      # on some UNIX systems

echo "some text\c"     # on other UNIX systems
```

egrep - Like grep, but supports additional R.E. wildcards

See grep. See wildcards, regular expressions

expr - Evaluate simple calculations

For example: CNT=`expr $CNT + 1`

```
VALUE=`expr $VALUE \* 2`
```

fg - Bring background job to foreground

Usage: fg %JOBID

SEE ALSO

➤ *For more information, see page 322*

Useful options:

Same as kill (Korn shell) under %JOBID

fgrep - Like grep, but does not support any R.E. wildcards

See grep

file - Show the type of contents of a file

Usage: file list-of-files

Std input: Not used

Std output: Used to display results

Notes: If there is no magic number, it makes its best guess as to the contents based on the beginning of the file.

SEE ALSO

➤ *For more information, see page 150*

filename generation wildcard: see wildcard

find - **Find files based on search options**

Usage: find `start-dir options actions`

Std input: Not used

Std output: Used to display results

Notes: Find searches all subdirectories of the start directory.

SEE ALSO

➤ *For more information, see page 153*

Useful options:

`-atime [+-]ndays` means select only files last accessed `ndays` ago. `option` + means more than ndays, - means less than `ndays`, else means exactly `ndays` ago.

SEE ALSO

➤ *For more information, see page 252*

`-ctime [+-]ndays` means select only files whose inode was modified `ndays` ago. `option` + means more than `ndays`, - means less than `ndays`, else means exactly `ndays` ago.

SEE ALSO

➤ *For more information, see page 252*

`-depth` means list the contents of a directory before the directory itself. Sometimes useful when restoring from non-root account.

`-group GROUP` means select only files whose group is GROUP.

`-inum NUM` means select only files whose inode number is NUM.

SEE ALSO

➤ *For more information, see page 195*

`-mount` means select only files in the same filesystem as the starting directory.

`-mtime [+-]ndays` means select only files last modified `ndays` ago. `option` + means more than `ndays`, - means less than `ndays`, else means exactly `ndays` ago.

SEE ALSO

➤ *For more information, see page 252*

`-name FNAME` means select only files with basename FNAME.

FNAME may contain filename generation wildcards, but then must be in single quotation marks.

-newer filename means select only files newer than given file (that is, modified more recently)

SEE ALSO

➤ *For more information, see page 252*

-perm DDD selects only files whose octal permissions are DDD.

-perm -DDDD selects only files who have the same permissions turned on as in DDDD. It ignores permissions that are off in DDDD.

-size [+-]nblocks means select only files of size nblocks. option + means more than nblocks. - means less than nblocks, else means exactly nblocks in size.

SEE ALSO

➤ *For more information, see page 259*

-type TYPE means select only files of type TYPE where TYPE can be:

f for regular file

d for directory

c for character special device node

b for block special device node

-user USER means select only files owned by USER.

Option logical grouping:

If you specify two options, both must be true to select file

-o means logical OR.

\(\) can be used for grouping.

! means reverse test (negation).

Useful actions:

-print means display the names selected. Some UNIX systems do this as the default if no action is specified.

SEE ALSO

➤ *For more information, see pages 252, 259*

-exec means execute the following UNIX command for each file selected. {} in the command indicates where to place the filename. The command must end in \;.

SEE ALSO

➤ *For more information, see pages 252, 259*

finger - Display information about one user or all who are logged on

fsck - Filesystem check

SEE ALSO

➤ *For more information, see page 296*

Useful options:

-b means reboot if checking root filesystem made significant mods on disk (important).

-s means reconstruct the free list unconditionally.

grep - Globally find R.E. patterns and print (display) that line

Usage: grep R.E.pattern [list-of-files]

Std input: Only used if no list-of-files is given

Std output: Used to display results

SEE ALSO

➤ *For more information, see page 380*

Useful options:

-c means to display just filenames and count of lines that contain the pattern.

SEE ALSO

➤ *For more information, see page 386*

Pattern (grep)

-i means to ignore upper/lowercase.

SEE ALSO

➤ *For more information, see page 382*

-l means just list the filenames that contain the pattern.

SEE ALSO

➤ *For more information, see page 386*

Pattern (grep)

-n means to include the line number with each line displayed.

SEE ALSO

➤ *For more information, see page 385*

-v means to reverse the test, show lines that do not contain the pattern.

SEE ALSO

➤ *For more information, see page 385*

-y same as -i, but only on older UNIX systems.

gzip - Compress a file

Usage: gzip filename

Std input: Not used

Std output: Not used

SEE ALSO

➤ *For more information, see page 219*

Notes: Adds .gz to compressed filename

head - Display initial lines of a file or pipeline

Usage: head options [list-of-files]

Std input: Only used if no list-of-files is given

Std output: Used to display results

SEE ALSO

➤ *For more information, see page 215*

Useful options:

-n means display just n lines.

id - Display your user logon and group

`jobs` (Korn shell) - Display your background jobs

Std input: Not used

Std output: Used to display the results

SEE ALSO
➤ *For more information, see page 322*

`join` - Join lines from two files based on a join field

Usage: `join options file1 file2`

Std input: Only used if file is given as a dash (-)

Std output: Used to display the results

SEE ALSO
➤ *For more information, see page 224*

Useful options:

`-a`N means include all lines in file N.

`-j`N means use field N rather than 1 as the join field.

`-j`N M means use field M in file N as the join field.

`-o` A.B means display field B from file A.

`-t` means set the field separator to the following character.

`kill` (Bourne shell) - Terminate a UNIX process

Usage: `kill -SIG PID`

Std input: Not used

Std output: Not used

SEE ALSO
➤ *For more information, see page 320*

Useful options:

`-SIG` means send signal SIG to the process. If omitted, send SIGTERM signal (terminate) or replace SIG with 15.

Other useful signals to send via `kill`:

SIGHUP (SIG = 1) line disconnect or parent terminated

SIGINT (SIG = 2) intr key pressed (Ctrl+C or Del)

SIGQUIT (SIG = 3) quit key pressed

SIGKILL (SIG = 9) force termination

kill (Korn shell) - Terminate a background process

Usage: kill -SIG PID   (as in kill [Bourne shell] earlier)

or kill %JOBID

Std input: Not used

Std output: Display process info line

SEE ALSO

➤ *For more information, see page 325*

Useful options:

%JOBID means job whose number is JOBID.

%+ means job most recently put in background.

%% means same as %+.

%- means job second most recently put in background.

%CMD means job whose command starts with CMD.

%?CMD means all jobs whose command contains CMD.

ksh (Korn shell)- Redirection

>| filename - means override noclobber and redirect to existing file shell options.

noclobber - prevent redirect over existing files

Noclobber Option in the Korn Shell

shell startup runs /etc/profile, then .profile in user's home directory.

less - Display a file or pipeline one screen at a time

Usage: less [list-of-files]

Std input: Only used if no list-of-files is given

Std output: Used to display results

SEE ALSO

➤ *For more information, see page 160*

Notes: Not available on most commercial UNIX systems.

Prompt at end of each screen is line XXX.

Useful commands after you are in less:

h displays a help menu.

space or f or Ctrl+f goes to next page.

b or Ctrl+b goes to preceding page.

G goes to last page.

1G goes to the first page.

nf goes forward n pages.

nb goes backward n pages.

nG goes to line n.

/string goes to next occurrence of that string.

n repeats the preceding search.

d or Ctrl+D goes down a half screen.

r or Ctrl+R or Ctrl+L redisplay the current page.

!CMD to execute UNIX CMD as a subshell, resumes less when done.

ln - **Create soft/symbolic or hard link**

Usage: ln [-s] existing-file link-file

Std input: Not used

Std output: Not used

SEE ALSO

➤ *For more information, see page 193*

Useful options:

-s means create a soft/symbolic link rather than a hard link.

SEE ALSO
➤ *For more information, see page 197*

lp (System V) - Print a file or pipeline

Usage: lp options [list-of-files]

Std input: Only used if no list-of-files is given

Std output: Not used

SEE ALSO
➤ *For more information, see page 172*

Useful options:

-n NUM means print NUM copies.

-d PTR means print output on printer PTR. If -d not given, print on system default printer. If no default, give error.

lpr (BSD) - Print a file or pipeline

Usage: lpr options [list-of-files]

Std input: Only used if no list-of-files is given

Std output: Not used

SEE ALSO
➤ *For more information, see page 172*

Useful options:

-# NUM means print NUM copies.

-P PTR means print output on printer PTR. If -P not given, print on system default printer. If no default, give error.

lpstat - Display print spooling status

Usage: lpstat options

Std input: Not used

Std output: Used to display results

SEE ALSO
➤ *For more information, see page 171*

Notes: If no options given, shows pending print requests in queue.

-p -D means show what printers are available and their description, if any.

ls - List files in a directory

Usage: ls options [list-of-files-or-directories]

Std input: Not used

Std output: Used to display results

Notes: If no directory is specified, it lists your current directory.

Useful options:

-a means show all files, hidden, non-hidden, and dot-dot (..).

-b means show any control chars in filenames.

-c means if long format, show date/time inode was last changed.

-C means list output in columns.

SEE ALSO

➤ *For more information, see page 46*

-d means show any directory names rather than the contents of those directories.

SEE ALSO

➤ *For more information, see page 148*

-F means show the file type by adding slash (/) to directories, asterisk (*) to executables, and at sign (@) to symbolic links.

SEE ALSO

➤ *For more information, see page 46*

-i means include the file's inode number as the first field in each output line.

SEE ALSO

➤ *For more information, see page 195*

-l means list files in long format, includes date/time of last mod.

SEE ALSO

➤ *For more information, see page 252*

-L means follow symbolic link and show info for the pointed-to file.

-r means list files in reverse of normal order.

SEE ALSO

➤ *For more information, see page 252*

-R means recursively list subdirectories.

-t means list files in order of time/date rather than by name.

SEE ALSO

➤ *For more information, see page 252*

-u means if long format, show date/time of last Usage (last access).

SEE ALSO

➤ *For more information, see page 252*

mail/mailx - Read and send email

man - Display online manual page

Usage: man unixcmd

Std input: Not used

Std output: Used to display results

SEE ALSO

➤ *For more information, see page 89*

Useful options:

-a means show all sections containing this command, not just the first.

-k WORD means show command names whose description contains WORD.

mkdir - Make new directory

Usage: mkdir dirname

Std input: Not used

Std output: Not used

SEE ALSO

➤ *For more information, see page 51*

Useful options:

-p means create any parent directories needed to create dirname.

more - **Display a file or pipeline one screen at a time**

Usage: more [list-of-files]

Std input: Only used if no list-of-files is given

Std output: Used to display results

SEE ALSO

➤ *For more information, see page 160*

Notes: Prompt at end of each screen is --More--.

Useful commands after you are in more:

h displays a help menu.

space or f goes to next page.

Some of the following commands are not available under the more command in some versions of UNIX, especially if piping to the more command.

Ctrl+B goes to preceding page.

G goes to last page.

1G goes to the first page.

nf goes forward n pages.

nb goes backward n pages.

nG goes to line n.

/string goes to next occurrence of that string.

n repeats the preceding search.

d goes down a half screen.

Ctrl+L redisplays the current page.

!CMD to execute UNIX CMD as a subshell, resumes more when done.

mt - Issue magnetic tape commands

Usage: `mt -f /dev/XXX? cmd`

Std input: Not used

Std ouput: Not used

See the `tape` command.

SEE ALSO
➤ *For more information, see page 336*

Useful commands:

`rewind`

`retention`

mv - Move/rename files

Usage: `mv file1 file2`

`mv list-of-files dest-dir/.`

`mv dir1 dir2`

Std input: Not used

Std ouput: Not used

SEE ALSO
➤ *For more information, see page 181*

Useful options:

`-f` means force the move without a confirmation request if you don't have write permission to the file but do have write permission to the directory.

`-i` means interact with user and ask permission before overwriting an existing file.

nice - Start a job with a low priority

Usage: `nice -VAL UNIXCMD`

Std input: Not used

Std output: Used as UNIXCMD uses them

SEE ALSO

➤ *For more information, see page 317*

Useful options:

-VAL means lower priority by VAL points.

--VAL means raise priority by VAL points (root only).

nl - **Number lines in file output or pipeline**

Usage: nl [list-of-files]

Std input: Only used if no list-of-files is given

Std output: Used to display results

SEE ALSO

➤ *For more information, see page 164*

Useful options:

-ba means number all lines including blank lines.

nohup - **Start background that won't terminate on logoff**

Usage: nohup UNIXCMD &

Std input: Not used

Std output: Used as UNIXCMD uses them

SEE ALSO

➤ *For more information, see page 320*

od - **Display contents as an octal dump**

Usage: od [list-of-files]

Std input: Only used if no list-of-files is given

Std output: Used to display results

SEE ALSO

➤ *For more information, see page 165*

Useful options:

-b means show output as bytes, not words.

-c means show any printable characters.

-d means show output in decimal.

-x means show output in hexadecimal.

passwd - Change your password

paste - Display files side-by-side on each line

Usage: `paste list-of-files`

Std input: Only used if dash (-) is given as a filename

Std output: Used to display results

SEE ALSO

➤ *For more information, see page 223*

perl - Practical extraction and report language

Std input: Only used if no list-of-files is given

Std output: Used to display results

Using `perl` from the command line to display selected lines:

```
perl -ne 'print if /R.E./xi' [list-of-files]
```

/x means ignore spaces in R.E. for better readability.

/i means ignore upper/lowercase.

SEE ALSO

➤ *For more information, see page 404*

Using perl from the command line for replacement or deletion:

```
perl -pe 's/R.E./repl/gx' [list-of-files]
perl -pe 's/R.E./repl/gx if /acme/' [list-of-files]
```

Preceding example: Only do replacement if acme R.E. pattern is found in the line.

/x means ignore spaces in R.E. for better readability.

/g means make change globally, not just once per line.

SEE ALSO

➤ *For more information, see page 425*

Useful options:

-e means Perl script is on command line.

SEE ALSO

➤ *For more information, see page 404*

-n means process each line of std input or files specified, but do not display the lines unless directed.

SEE ALSO

➤ *For more information, see page 404*

-p means process each line of std input or files specified and display each line after processing it.

SEE ALSO

➤ *For more information, see page 425*

pg - Display a file or pipeline one screen at a time

Usage: pg [list-of-files]

Std input: Only used if no list-of-files is given

Std output: Used to display results

SEE ALSO

➤ *For more information, see page 160*

Notes: Prompt at end of each screen is a colon (:).

Useful commands after you are in pg:

h displays a help menu.

Enter goes to next page.

- goes to preceding page.

$ goes to last page (can crash the system on huge pipeline!).

1 goes to the first page.

+n goes forward n pages.

-n goes backward n pages.

nl goes to line n.

/string goes to next occurrence of that string.

/ repeats the preceding search.

/string/b put found string on bottom so that you catch all occurrences.

d goes down a half screen.

Redisplay the current page.

!CMD to execute UNIX CMD as a subshell, resumes pg when done.

pr - Format output for printing

Usage: pr options [list-of-files]

Std input: Only used if no list-of-files is given

Std output: Used to display results

SEE ALSO

➤ *For more information, see page 175*

Useful options:

-COLS means use number in COLS as number of columns to create on the page for output. Truncate any lines longer than column size.

-eSIZ means expand tabs to spaces. If SIZ given, use that as number of char positions per tab, else use 8.

-f means insert form feed at end of each page.

-h "HEAD LINE" means use this heading rather than filename at top of page.

-l LINES means format number of lines per page as LINES.

-nSIZ means number each line in body of output. If SIZ is given, use that many chars in number, right justified, else use 5 chars in number.

-p means beep and wait for Enter key after each page.

ps - Show process status

Std input: Not used

Std output: Used to display status

SEE ALSO

➤ *For more information, see page 317*

pwd - Print working directory

Usage: `pwd`

Std input: Not used

Std output: Used to display results

SEE ALSO

➤ *For more information, see page 43*

qcan - Cancel print job on AIX

Usage: `qcan options`

Std input: Not used

Std output: Not used

SEE ALSO

➤ *For more information, see page 174*

Useful options:

`-P PTR -x JOBID` means cancel job ID for printer PTR.

Regular expression wildcard: see Wildcard

renice - Lower the priority of a running job

Usage: `renice -VAL PID`

Std input: Not used

Std output: Not used

SEE ALSO

➤ *For more information, see page 318*

Useful options:

`-VAL` means lower priority by VAL points.

`--VAL` means raise priority by VAL points (root only).

rm - Remove file(s)

Usage: `rm list-of-files`

Std input: Not used

Std output: Not used

Notes: Will give an error if list-of-files contains a directory unless `-r` option is given.

SEE ALSO

➤ *For more information, see page 191*

Useful options:

-f means force delete when file is not writable without asking confirmation.

SEE ALSO

➤ *For more information, see pages 53, 191*

-i means Interactive mode, ask confirmation before each file.

SEE ALSO

➤ *For more information, see page 53*

-r means that if list-of-files contains a directory, recursively delete that directory and all of its subdirectories and files. WARNING: This is dangerous! There is no undelete in case of mistakes!

SEE ALSO

➤ *For more information, see page 53*

`rmdir` - **Remove a directory**

The directory to remove must be empty except for dot (.) and dot dot (..).

`sed` - **Stream editor**

Usage: sed cmd [list-of-files]

Std input: Only used if no list-of-files is given

Std output: Used to display results

Useful sed commands:

q means quit.

SEE ALSO

➤ *For more information, see page 215*

s means substitute.

SEE ALSO

➤ *For more information, see page 412*

Using sed from the command line to replace strings in output:

```
sed 's/R.E./repl/g' [list-of-files]
```

```
sed 's:R.E.:repl:g' [list-of-files] # can change delimiter
sed '5,23 s/R.E./repl/g' [list-of-files]
    ➥only change lines 5 thru 23, $ means end of line
sed '/acme/ s/R.E./repl/g' [list-of-files]
    ➥only change lines that contain acme
sed '/s1/,/s2/ s/R.E./repl/g' [list-of-files]
    ➥only changes lines from first occurrence of s1
    ➥thru next occurrence of s2
sed 's/.*acme.*/    *** canceled ***    /'
    ➥replace whole line
```

SEE ALSO

➤ *For more information, see page 412*

Using sed from the command line to delete strings in output:

```
sed 's/R.E.//g' [list-of-files]
```

SEE ALSO

➤ *For more information, see page 412*

sh - **Run the Bourne shell**

Command substitution uses backquotes (`).

SEE ALSO

➤ *For more information, see page 245*

Comments are introduced by space, then the pound (#) sign.

SEE ALSO

➤ *For more information, see page 86*

Filename Generation Wildcards: See Wildcards

Redirection:

> file or 1> file means redirect standard output.

2> file means redirect standard error.

>> file or 2>> file means append output or error.

2>&1 means redirect std error to wherever std output is going.

See tee pipe.

Shell startup runs /etc/profile, and then .profile in user's home directory.

Special shell variables:

CDPATH - Chosen list of parent directories of most commonly accessed directories.

SEE ALSO

➤ *For more information, see page 54*

PATH - List of directories to use when searching for commands.

SEE ALSO

➤ *For more information, see page 97*

shutdown (BSD version) - Shut down the UNIX system

Std input: Not used

Std output: Not used

SEE ALSO

➤ *For more information, see page 300*

Notes: Requires root privilege

Useful options:

-h means halt the system.

-r means shut down and reboot.

now means don't wait to shut down.

+MIN means wait MIN minutes before shutting down.

shutdown (System V version) - Shut down the UNIX system

Std input: Not used

Std output: Not used

SEE ALSO

➤ *For more information, see page 300*

Notes: Requires root privilege

Useful options:

-g MIN means broadcast warning and wait MIN minutes grace period before shutdown.

-i STATE means go to run-level STATE.

-y means don't ask user to confirm shutdown after grace period.

sleep - Pause program for n seconds

sort - Sort file or pipeline

Usage: sort options [list-of-files]

Multiple files are merged before sorting.

Std input: Only used if dash (-) is in the list-of-files or no list-of-files is given

Std output: Used to display results

SEE ALSO

➤ *For more information, see pages 202, 223, and 259*

Useful options:

Initial options apply to all sort keys. Options following a sort key apply only to that key.

-b means ignore leading blanks in sort field.

SEE ALSO

➤ *For more information, see page 204*

-d means ignore leading punctuation.

SEE ALSO

➤ *For more information, see page 208*

-f means fold upper/lowercase together.

SEE ALSO

➤ *For more information, see page 207*

-k means define sort keys using new method: -k m opts, n.

SEE ALSO

➤ *For more information, see page 210*

-n means sort numbers by magnitude.

SEE ALSO

➤ *For more information, see page 204*

-o means save output in following filename.

SEE ALSO

➤ *For more information, see page 206*

-r means sort in reverse order.

SEE ALSO

➤ *For more information, see pages 207, 259*

+m means skip m fields per line and then start sorting.

SEE ALSO

➤ *For more information, see pages 209, 259*

+m options -n defines sort keys within the line.

SEE ALSO

➤ *For more information, see page 210*

split - Split file into smaller files of equal lines

Usage: split options [filename] [prefix]

Smaller files will be prefixaa, prefixab, prefixac, and so on.

Std input: Only used if no filename given or dash (-) given as filename

Std output: Not used

SEE ALSO

➤ *For more information, see page 226*

Useful options:

-N creates smaller files of N lines each (except the last one). The default is 1000.

strings - Show printable strings within any type of file

Usage: strings options [list-of-files]

Std input: Only used if no list-of-files is given

Std output: Used to display results

SEE ALSO

➤ *For more information, see page 165*

Useful options:

-n LEN means set min LEN printable sequence to report.

stty - Set/display terminal characteristics

Useful command options:

-a means show all stty options, precede with minus sign (-) if turned off.

Useful stty options:

erase means set/show the erase key.

SEE ALSO

➤ *For more information, see page 103*

intr means set/show the interrupt key.

SEE ALSO

➤ *For more information, see page 111*

tostop means suspend running background jobs when they start any output.

SEE ALSO

➤ *For more information, see page 325*

su - Become superuser or another user

sum - Compute checksum on file or pipeline

Usage: sum options [list-of-files]

Std input: Only used if no list-of-files is given

Std output: Used to display results

Notes: Matching checksum indicates a high probability that the data is the same.

SEE ALSO

➤ *For more information, see pages 267, 269*

Useful options:

-r means compute rotating checksum that can detect differences in order as well as contents.

SEE ALSO

➤ *For more information, see pages 267, 269*

tail - Display the last lines of a file or pipeline

Usage: tail options [filename]

Std input: Only used if no filename is given

Std output: Used to display results

SEE ALSO

➤ *For more information, see page 216*

Useful options:

-f means follow—that is, continuously display any data append-ed to file until Enter key is pressed.

-n means display just n lines. (Warning: Large values of n can be ignored.)

+n means display from line n to end of file.

tape - Issue magnetic tape commands

Usage: `tape cmd /dev/XXX?`

Std input: Not used

Std ouput: Not used

See the `mt` command.

SEE ALSO

➤ *For more information, see page 336*

Useful commands:

`rewind`

`reten`

tar - Tape archive

SEE ALSO

➤ *For more information, see page 340*

Useful options when backing up:

c means create backup (must be the first option).

b means set tape block size.

f means specify the backup device or file.

h means follow symbolic links (AIX).

L means follow symbolic links (SCO).

v means verbose.

Useful options when restoring:

x means extract files from backup (must be the first option).

A means suppress leading slash in filenames (SCO).

m means set date of last modification to when restore was done, else set last mod of original tape files.

v means verbose.

tee - Save Std input to file and send same information out std output

Usage: `cmd ¦ tee filename`

Std input: Used to read input

Std output: Used to display current output

SEE ALSO

➤ *For more information, see page 116*

Useful options:

-a means append to file, not overwrite.

test - Evaluate condition as true or false

Usage: `test condition`

or:

`[ condition ]`

File tests:

-f name means is name a regular file?

-d name means is name a directory?

-r name means is name readable?

-w name means is name writable?

-x name means is name executable?

-c name means is name a char device file?

-b name means is name a block device file?

-s name means is name a file with size > zero?

-h or -L name means is name a symbolic link?

String tests:

"string" means is string not empty?

-z string means is string empty (zero size)?

s1 = s2 means are the two strings the same?

s1 != s2 means are the two strings not the same?

Numeric tests:

v1 -eq v2 means is v1 equal to v2?

We can also test -ne, -gt, -ge, -lt, -le.

Combining tests:

-a means logical AND.

-o means logical OR.

touch - **Update file last access and last modification date/time**

Will create an empty file if it does not exist, but won't affect the contents of an already existing file.

tr - **Translate characters**

Usage: tr "list1" "list2" < file1 > file 2

Std input: Always used, will not accept filenames

Std output: Used to display results

Notes: If char is found in list1, replace it with corresponding char in list2.

SEE ALSO

➤ *For more information, see page 441*

Useful options:

-d means delete the chars found in list 1.

Useful examples:

```
tr "[A-Z]" "[a-z]" # convert upper to lower case
tr "[\201-\376]\377" "[\001-\176]\177" < file1 > file2
```

```
                    # turn off 8th bit
tr '\001-\010\013-\037\177' '[^*]' < file1 > file2
                    # translate most control chars to ^
```

type - Show full pathname of command

Usage: `type unixcmd`

Std input: Not used

Std output: Used to display results

SEE ALSO

➤ *For more information, see page 100*

Notes: Works in both the Bourne shell and Korn shell

tty - Display your current system tty port name

umask - Show your current file creation permission mask

uname - Display the system type and name

uniq - Remove non-uniq lines

Usage: `uniq options [list-of-files]`

Std input: Only used if no list-of-files is given

Std output: Used to display results

SEE ALSO

➤ *For more information, see page 445*

Useful options:

-d means show only duplicated lines.

-u means show only unique lines.

-c means show count for each line of number of duplicates.

uucp - UNIX to UNIX copy over serial lines and modems

uuencode/uudecode - Transform/restore file to/from printable text

Usage: `uuencode binaryfile destname > textfile`

Std input: Only used if binary file not given

Std output: Used to display results

Usage: `uudecode textfile`

Std input: Not used

Std output: Not used

SEE ALSO

➤ *For more information, see page 221*

`vi` - Visual editor

SEE ALSO

➤ *For more information, see pages 449, 471*

Starting vi:

`vi -r` means display files that can be restored.

`view file` means run vi in read-only mode.

Colon commands:

`:abbrev word` means new phrase.

`:!cmd` means run UNIX `cmd` in subshell, and then resume vi.

`:f` means show current line number and filename.

`:map c string` means map char c to string.

`:q!` means quit without saving.

`:w` means write changes to disk.

`:w file` means save in file.

`:wq` means write (save changes) and quit.

Colon set modes, abbreviation, and how to put it back:

`:set autoindent, :set ai, :set noai`

`:set ignorecase, :set ic, :set noic`

`:set number, :set nu, :set nonu`

`:set showmode, :set noshowmode`

`:set wrapmargin=10,` turn off by setting to zero

Replacing in Colon mode:

`!!` cmd means replace current line with output of UNIX cmd.

`!'a` cmd means apply UNIX command from cursor to mark a.

`!'a` sed `'s/st1/st2/g'` means replace string st1 with string st2 where found from cursor to mark a.

`:%!` sed `'s/st1/st2/g'` means replace st1 throughout the file. st1 may contain regular expression wildcards.

Copy and paste, and delete and paste:

`y'a` means yank to start of line that contains mark a.

`y`a` means yank to mark a.

`y...` means follow y with a motion command to indicate how much text to yank and save.

`"ay...` means yank and save in named buffer a.

`p` means paste unnamed buffer at the current cursor.

`"ap` means paste named buffer at the current cursor.

`"np` means paste what you deleted n times ago.

Delete text commands:

`dd` means delete line.

`x` means delete character.

`D` means delete to end of line.

`d'a` means delete to start of line that contains mark a.

`d`a` means delete to mark a.

`d...` means follow d with a motion command to indicate what to delete.

`"ad...` means delete and save in named buffer a.

Insert text commnds:

`i` means insert at or left of cursor until Esc.

`I` means insert at start of line until Esc.

`a` means insert after cursor until Esc.

A means insert at end of line until Esc.

o means open line below and insert until Esc.

O means open line above and insert until Esc.

Miscellaneous commands:

J means join lines; nJ joins n lines.

Most vi commands allow a preceding repeat count.

u means undo last insert/delete/modify.

U means restore line to when you first got there.

. means repeat last insert/delete/change.

Modifying text:

C means change to end of line with input until Esc.

CC means change current line until Esc.

r means replace character.

R means replace until Esc.

Moving the cursor

0,^,$ mean start of line, first printable char, end of line.

h,j,k,l mean same as left, down, up, right arrow.

H,M,L mean move high, medium, low on the current screen.

Gn means go to line n; G means go to end of file.

Ctrl+F/Ctrl+B forward/backward one full screen.

Ctrl+D/Ctrl+U down/up one half screen.

W,B,E mean move a word ahead, back, or to end of word.

w,b,e same as preceding explanation, but go to next contained word or non-word.

mc means set mark c.

'c means go to start of line containing mark c.

`c means go to mark c.

Searching:

/string means move ahead to next occurrence of string.

?string means move back to string.

Regular Expressions are allowed.

/ or ? without a string repeat last search.

n or N also repeat preceding search.

fc means move to character c.

; means repeat preceding f command.

% means find matching closure symbol—for example [{( )}].

whence - **Show full pathname of command**

Usage: whence unixcmd

Std input: Not used

Std output: Used to display results

SEE ALSO

➤ *For more information, see page 100*

Notes: Works in the Korn shell, but not Bourne shell.

which - **Show full pathname of command**

Usage: which unixcmd

Std input: Not used

Std output: Used to display results

SEE ALSO

➤ *For more information, see page 100*

Notes: Works in the Bourne shell, but not Korn shell.

who - **Display who is on the system and other system information**

Usage: who options

Std input: Not used

Std output: Used to display results

Useful options:

-b means show date/time of last system reboot.

-r means show current run-level and when entered.

SEE ALSO

➤ *For more information, see page 299*

wildcard - Filename generation

SEE ALSO

➤ *For more information, see page 232*

* means zero or more of any character except slash (/) and leading period.

SEE ALSO

➤ *For more information, see page 232*

Contain a Pattern (*)

? means exactly one of any character except slash (/) and leading period.

SEE ALSO

➤ *For more information, see page 239*

Positions (?)

[...] means exactly one of the alternatives listed except (/) and leading period.

SEE ALSO

➤ *For more information, see page 241*

[!...] means any one character except for the alternatives listed, cannot match a slash (/) or leading period.

SEE ALSO

➤ *For more information, see page 243*

Positions ([!...])

wildcard - Regular expressions (R.E.)

SEE ALSO

➤ *For more information, see page 388*

^ if at start of pattern indicates start of line.

SEE ALSO

➤ *For more information, see page 389*

$ if at end of pattern indicates end of line.

SEE ALSO

➤ *For more information, see page 390*

. means exactly one of any character.

SEE ALSO

➤ *For more information, see page 395*

[...] means exactly one of the alternatives listed.

SEE ALSO

➤ *For more information, see page 396*

[^...] means any one character except for the alternatives listed.

SEE ALSO

➤ *For more information, see page 397*

\{n\} means exactly n occurrences of preceding element (supported in grep and sed, not supported in egrep or awk—use {n} for Perl).

SEE ALSO

➤ *For more information, see page 398*

\{n,\} means n or more occurences of preceding element (supported in grep and sed, not supported in egrep or awk—use {n,} for Perl).

SEE ALSO

➤ *For more information, see page 398*

\{n,m\} means between n and m (inclusive) occurences of preceding element (supported in grep and sed, not supported in egrep or awk—use {n,m} for Perl).

SEE ALSO

➤ *For more information, see page 398*

* means 0 or more occurrences of preceding element.

SEE ALSO

➤ *For more information, see page 399*

It matches longest possible span.

SEE ALSO

➤ *For more information, see page 424*

*? matches shortest posssible span (perl only).

SEE ALSO

➤ *For more information, see page 426*

.* means 0 or more occurrences of any character.

This is just one example of the * wildcard.

+ means 1 or more occurrences of preceding element (supported in egrep, perl, and awk, not supported in grep and sed).

SEE ALSO

➤ *For more information, see page 403*

Matches longest possible span.

SEE ALSO

➤ *For more information, see page 424*

+? matches shortest posssible span (perl only).

SEE ALSO

➤ *For more information, see page 426*

? means 0 or 1 occurences of preceding element (supported in egrep, perl, and awk, not supported in grep and sed).

SEE ALSO

➤ *For more information, see page 403*

¦ allows specifying alternative patterns to search for (supported in egrep, perl, and awk, not supported in grep and sed).

SEE ALSO

➤ *For more information, see page 403*

( ) allows grouping alternatives (supported in egrep, perl, and awk, not supported in grep and sed).

SEE ALSO

➤ *For more information, see page 403*

\(\) remembers what characters matched the enclosed pattern (supported in grep and sed, not supported in egrep or awk—use ( ) for perl).

\1, \2 refers to remembered string 1 or 2. See \(\).

\b indicates word boundary (perl only).

SEE ALSO

➤ *For more information, see page 405*

\B indicates non-word boundary (perl only).

SEE ALSO

➤ *For more information, see page 405*

\x put backslash (\) before any wildcard X to use it as a literal character in the string.

xargs - Execute another UNIX command with passed arguments

Usage: xargs cmd [opts]

Std input: Used to pass a list of arguments for cmd

Std output: However cmd uses it

SEE ALSO

➤ *For more information, see page 247*

Useful options:

-n NUMB means limit number of arguments put on each tovalue specified as NUMB.

Glossary

[] Brackets.

{} Braces.

$HOME Environment variable that points to your logon directory.

$PATH The shell environment variable that contains a set of directories to be searched for UNIX commands.

.bmp Bitmap graphics file.

.c C source file.

.gif GIF graphics file.

.gz File compressed using the GNU gzip utility.

.h C header file.

.htm HTML document.

.html HTML document.

.o Compiled object file.

.ps PostScript file

.tgz Gzipped tar file.

.tif TIFF graphics file.

.txt Text document.

.Z File compressed using the compress command.

/ Root directory.

/dev/null file The place to send output that you are not interesting in seeing; also the place to get input from when you have none (but the program or command requires something). This is also known as the bit bucket (where old bits go to die).

/dev Device directory.

/etc/group file This file contains information about groups, the users they contain, and passwords required for access by other users. The password might actually be in another file, the shadow group file, to protect it from attacks.

/etc/inittab file The file that contains a list of active terminal ports for which UNIX will issue the logon prompt. This also contains a list of background processes for UNIX to initialize. Some versions of UNIX use other files, such as /etc/tty.

/etc/motd file Message of the day file; usually contains information the system administrator feels is important for you to know. This file displays when the user signs on to the system.

/etc/passwd file Contains user information and password. The password might actually be in another file, the shadow password file, to protect it from attacks.

/etc/profile The file containing shell environment characteristics common to all users of the Bourne and Korn shells.

/usr/local Locally developed public executables directory.

/var/spool Various spool directories.

Absolute pathname is a method of referring to a file where all directories from the root directory to that file are specified. An absolute pathname always starts with a slash, indicating it is starting from root (for example, /reports/abc refers to the abc file in the reports subdirectory of root).

Administrative control of a directory Users who have write permission to a directory have effective administrative control over that directory. In addition to creating files, they can delete and rename files of other users, even if they don't have permission to modify those files. If the directory sticky bit is set, having write permission does not give administrative control of the directory.

ANSI American National Standards Institute.

API Application Program Interface. The specific method prescribed by a computer operating system, application, or third-party tool by which a programmer writing an application program can make requests of the operating system. Also known as Application Programmer's Interface.

Application data file A file, usually one of many, that contains data for that application.

Application program A software program, usually one of a great many, that provides part of the programming for an application.

Application One or more software programs that provide a capability, such as an accounting application.

Arguments See *parameters*.

ARPA See *DARPA*.

ASCII American Standard Code for Information Interchange. Used to represent characters in memory for most computers.

AT&T UNIX Original version of UNIX developed at AT&T Bell Labs, later known as UNIX Systems Laboratories. Many current versions of UNIX are descendants; even BSD UNIX was derived from early AT&T UNIX.

awk Programming language developed by A.V. Aho, P.J. Weinberger, and Brian W. Kernighan. The language is built on C syntax, includes the regular expression search facilities of grep, and adds in the advanced string and array handling features missing from the C language. nawk, gawk, and POSIX awk are versions of this language.

Background job is a job that you initiated but is running independently of your keyboard and screen so that you can do other things. Many important UNIX system processes run as background jobs, waiting for user requests or other events. (These are often called system daemons.) See *Foreground job*.

Backup The process of storing the UNIX system, applications, and data files on removable media for future retrieval.

Basename The longest right-hand part of a pathname that contains no slashes (/) (for example, in `/usr/fred/reports/acme`, `acme` is the basename of that pathname). A basename can be any type of file including a directory. Also basename, as used in this book, can refer to a filename that has no slashes and no directory portion.

Bash Stands for GNU Bourne Again Shell and contains most Bourne shell, sh, and Korn shell, ksh, enhancements.

Boot or boot up The process of starting the operating system (UNIX).

Bourne shell A standard shell on all UNIX systems that supports basic programming but few user keyboard conveniences.

BSD UNIX Version of UNIX developed by Berkeley Software Distribution and written at University of California, Berkeley.

BSD Berkeley Software Distribution.

C shell A user interface for UNIX written by Bill Joy at Berkeley. It features C programming-like syntax.

C Programming language developed by Brian W. Kernighan and Dennis M. Ritchie. The C language is highly portable and available on many platforms including mainframes, PCs, and, of course, UNIX systems.

CAD Computer-aided design.

Cast Programming construct to force type conversion.

CD-ROM Compact disc-read only memory. Computer-readable data stored on the same physical form as a musical CD. Large capacity, inexpensive, slower than a hard disk, and limited to reading. There are versions that are writable (CD-R, CD Recordable) and other formats that can be written to once or many times.

CGI Common gateway interface. A means of transmitting data between Web pages and programs or scripts executing on the server. Those programs can then process the data and send the results back to the user's browser through dynamically creating HTML.

Character special A device file used to communicate with character-oriented I/O devices such as terminals, printers, or network communications lines. All I/O access is treated as a series of bytes (characters).

Characters, alphabetic The letters *A* through *Z* and *a* through *z*.

Characters, alphanumeric The letters *A* through *Z* and *a* through *z*, the numbers 0 through 9.

Characters, control Any nonprintable characters. The characters are used to control devices, separate records, and eject pages on printers.

Characters, digits The numbers 0 through 9.

Characters, numeric The numbers 0 through 9.

Checksum A numeric value produced by summing all the characters within a file. This sum enables you to do a quick check that the file matches another file. By comparing the checksums, you can quickly check whether two files (are likely to) contain the same contents or whether a file still has the same contents it had when the checksum was last computed. Often the sum is shifted or rotated after each character is added (think of multiplying by two). This is then called a rotating checksum, which can detect file differences where the data is the same but in a different order. The goal of the checksum is that a small difference between two files should generate a large difference between the checksums. If two files have the same checksum, there is a high probability that they contain the same contents. If their checksums differ, the two files are definitely not the same.

Child directory Same as a subdirectory.

Child process A process or job started by another process or job which is called the parent process.

Child process See *Subprocess*.

Child shell See *Subshell*.

Class A model of objects that have attributes (data) and behavior (code or functions). It is also viewed as a collection of objects in their abstracted form.

Command substitution A shell feature that allows backquotes (`) containing another UNIX command to substitute the output of that command as words in the current command.

Command-line editing UNIX shells support the capability to recall a previously entered command, modify it, and then execute the new version. The command history can remain between sessions. (The commands you did yesterday can be available for you when you log on today.) Some shells support a command-line editing mode that uses a subset of the vi, emacs, or gmacs editor commands for command recall and modification.

Command-line history See *Command-line editing*.

Command-line parameters Used to specify parameters to pass to the execute program or procedure. Also known as command-line arguments.

Comment Explanatory words meant for a human reader. Usually comments have special starting characters so that the computer will ignore them. In UNIX shell programming, use a pound sign (#) to start a comment. Other programming languages can use other starting characters for comments.

Configuration files Collections of information used to initialize and set up the environment for specific commands and programs. Shell configuration files set up the user's environment.

Contained words In vi, contained words are any groups of letters and digits. They are separated from other contained words by punctuation, spaces, tabs, and end of line. For example, abc—·def=3 contains three contained words: abc, def, and 3. See *Separated words* and *Non-words*.

CPU Central processing unit. The primary "brain" of the computer—the calculation engine and logic controller.

Current directory The directory that is assumed as the base for any relative pathnames. Many UNIX commands will assume this directory if no directory is specifically given. Use the cd command to change your current directory.

Daemon A system-related background process that often runs with the permissions of root and services requests from other processes.

DARPA (U.S. Department of) Defense Advanced Research Projects Agency. Funded development of TCP/IP and ARPAnet (predecessor of the Internet).

Database server See *Server, database*.

Default directory Same as current directory.

Device file File used to implement access to a physical device. This provides a consistent approach to access of storage media under UNIX; data files and devices (such as tapes and communication facilities) are implemented as files. To the programmer, there is no real difference.

Device node A type of file used to access hardware devices such as tape drives or floppy disks.

Digit One of the characters 0 through 9. A digit is always a single character. One or more digits make up a number.

Directory A means of organizing and collecting files together. The directory itself is a file that consists of a list of files contained within it. The root (/) directory is the top level and every other directory is contained in it (directly or indirectly). A directory might contain other directories, known as subdirectories.

Directory navigation The process of moving through directories is known as navigation. Your current directory is known as the current working directory. Your logon directory is known as the default or home directory. Using the cd command, you can move up and down through the tree structure of directories.

Dirname the part of a pathname from the start to the last internal slash (/)—for example, in /usr/fred/reports/acme, /usr/fred/reports is the dirname. If there is no slash (/) in the pathname, its dirname is represented by a period (.), which indicates the current directory. See *Basename*.

DNS Domain name server. Used to convert between the name of a machine on the Internet (**name.domain.com**) to the numeric IP address (**123.45.111.123**).

DOS Disk operating system. Operating system based on the use of disks for the storage of commands. It is also a generic name for MS-DOS and PC-DOS on the personal computer. MS-DOS is the version Microsoft sells, PC-DOS the version IBM sells. Both are based on Microsoft code.

Double Double-precision floating point.

dpi Dots per inch.

Email Messages sent through an electronic medium rather than through the local postal service. There are many proprietary email systems designed to handle mail within a LAN environment; most of these can also send over the Internet. Most Internet (open) email systems make use of MIME to handle attached data (which can be binary).

EBCDIC Extended Binary Coded Decimal Interchange Code. The code used to represent characters in memory for mainframe computers.

Ed A common tool used for line-oriented text editing.

Elm Interactive mail program.

emacs A freely available editor now part of the GNU software distribution. Originally written by Richard M. Stallman at MIT in the late 1970s, it is available for many platforms. It is extremely extensible and has its own programming language; the name stands for editing with macros.

Encapsulation The process of combining data (attributes) and functions (behavior in the form of code) into an object. The data and functions are closely coupled within an object. Instead of all programmers being able to access the data in a structure their own way, they have to use the code connected with that data. This promotes code reuse and standardized methods of working with the data.

Environment variables See *Variables, environmental.*

Escaped characters Characters preceded by a backslash (\). Usually you escape a character to take away its special meaning, but sometimes you escape a normal character to give it special meaning.

Ethernet A networking method where the systems are connected to a single shared bus and all traffic is available to every machine. The data packets contain an identifier of the recipient, and that is the only machine that should process that packet.

Expression A constant, variable, or operands and operators combined. Used to set a value, perform a calculation, or set the pattern for a comparison (regular expressions).

FIFO First In, First Out. See *Pipe, named.*

File compression The process of applying mathematical formulas to data, typically resulting in a form of the data that occupies less space. A compressed file can be uncompressed, resulting in the original file.

File, indexed A file based on a file structure where data can be retrieved based on specific keys (name, employee number, and so on) or sequentially. The keys are stored in an index. This is not directly supported by the UNIX operating system; usually implemented by the programmer or by using tools from an ISV. A typical form is known as ISAM.

File, line sequential See *File, text.*

File, sequential This phrase can mean either a file that can only be accessed sequentially (not randomly), or a file without record separators (typically fixed length, but UNIX does not know what that length is and does not care).

File Collection of bytes stored on a device (typically a disk or tape). Can be source code, executable binaries or scripts, or data.

File, text A file with record separators. Can be fixed or variable length; UNIX tools can handle these files because the tools can tell when the record ends (by the separator).

Filename The name used to identify a collection of data (a file). Without a pathname, it is assumed to be in the current directory.

Filename Generation Wildcards Special characters that can be used in pattern words in command lines. The shell will replace pattern words with a list of existing files that match the pattern. Don't confuse these wildcards with regular expression wildcards.

Filename, fully qualified The name used to identify a collection of data (a file) and its location. It includes both the path and name of the file; typically, the pathname is fully specified (absolute). See *Pathname* and *Pathname, absolute*.

Filesystem A hierarchical directory system built in a section of a disk drive or disk structure such as RAID. Non-root filesystems must be mounted on a directory (sometimes at the root) before they can be accessed. All accesses to the mount point directory access the section of the disk where the filesystem resides. This is in contrast to the DOS convention of specifying disk sections as D: or E:. Filesystems usually cannot grow, hence some directories on your system can be full while others still have available unused disk blocks. Filesystems are stored in a disk partition and are sometimes referred to as being the disk partition. See *Mount* and *Mount point*.

Finger User information lookup program.

Firewall A system used to provide a controlled entry point to the internal network from the outside (usually the Internet). This is used to prevent outside or unauthorized systems from accessing systems on your internal network. The capability depends on the individual software package, but the features typically include filter packets and filter datagrams, system (name or IP address) aliasing, and rejecting packets from certain IP addresses. In theory, it provides protection from malicious programs or people on the outside. It can also prevent internal systems from accessing the Internet on the outside. The name comes from the physical barrier between connected buildings or within a single building that is supposed to prevent fire from spreading from one to another.

Flags See *Options*.

Float Single-precision floating point.

Foreground job A job that is running on and tying up your keyboard and screen. See *Background job*.

FSF Free Software Foundation.

FTP File Transfer Protocol or File Transfer Program. A system-independent means of transferring files between systems connected via TCP/IP. Ensures that the file is transferred correctly, even if there are errors during transmission. Can usually handle character-set conversions (ASCII/EBCDIC) and record terminator resolution (linefeed for UNIX, carriage return and linefeed for MS/PC-DOS).

Full pathname Same as absolute pathname.

Gateway A combination of hardware, software, and network connections that provides a link between one architecture and another. Typically, a gateway is used to connect a LAN or UNIX server with a mainframe (that uses SNA for networking, resulting in the name SNA gateway). A gateway can also be the connection between the internal and external network (often referred to as a firewall). See *Firewall*.

GID Group ID number.

Globbing See *Filename generation*.

GNU GNU stands for GNU's Not UNIX, and is the name of free useful software packages commonly found in UNIX environments that are being distributed by the GNU project at MIT, largely through the efforts of Richard Stallman. The circular acronym name ("GNU" containing the acronym GNU as one of the words) is a joke on Richard Stallman's part. One of the textbooks on operating system design is titled: "XINU: XINU is not UNIX," and GNU follows in that path.

GPL GNU General Public License.

grep A common tool used to search a file for a pattern. egrep allows the use of extended (hence the *e* prefix) regular expressions; fgrep uses limited expressions for a faster (hence the *f* prefix) searches.

GUI Graphical user interface.

Here document The << redirection operator, known as here document, allows keyboard input (stdin) for the program to be included in the script.

Hidden file A file or directory whose filename begins with a leading period (.). Some utilities will not process hidden files by default (for example, ls and filename generation wildcards). Hidden files are usually system and configuration files that should not be included when you process data files.

HTML Hypertext Markup Language. Describes World Wide Web pages. It is the document language used to define the pages available on the Internet through the use of tags. A browser interprets the HTML to display the desired information.

I-node Used to describe a file and its storage. The directory contains a cross-reference between the i-node and pathname/filename combination. Also known as inode. A file's entry in disk data structure (ls -i).

ICMP Internet Control Message Protocol. Part of TCP/IP that provides network layer management and control.

Inheritance A method of object-oriented software reuse in which new classes are developed based on existing ones by using the existing attributes and behavior and adding on to them. If the base object is automobiles (with attributes of engine and four wheels and tires; behavior of acceleration, turning, deceleration), a sports car would modify the attributes: engine might be larger or have more horsepower than the default, the four wheels might include alloy wheels and high-speed–rated tires; the behavior would also be modified: faster acceleration, tighter turning radius, faster deceleration.

Init level Same as run level.

Inode number The entry number of a given file in the inode table. See *Inode*. Each filesystem has its own inode table, so two different files could have the same inode number if they reside in different filesystems on the same system. See *Filesystem*.

Inode table See *Inode*.

Inode A table entry where all information about a file is stored except for the filename and the actual file data itself. The inode contains such fields as the file owner, group, permissions, date/time of last access/modification. Each UNIX filesystem contains an inode table that keeps track of all the files in that section of the disk. See *Filesystem*. There is also an inode table in memory that keeps track of all files currently being referenced.

Int Integer.

Internet service provider Companies that specialize in connecting you to the Internet.

Internet A collection of different networks that provide the capability to move data between them. It is built on the TCP/IP communications protocol. Originally developed by DARPA, it was taken over by NSF, and has now been released from governmental control.

IRC Internet relay chat. A server-based application that enables groups of people to communicate simultaneously through text-based conversations. IRC is similar to Citizen Band radio or the chat rooms on some bulletin boards. Some chats can be private (between invited people only) or public (where anyone can join in). IRC now also supports sound files as well as text; it can also be useful for file exchange.

ISAM Indexed Sequential Access Method. On UNIX and other systems, ISAM refers to a method for accessing data in a keyed or sequential way. The UNIX operating system does not directly support ISAM files; they are typically add-on products.

ISO International Standards Organization.

ISP See *Internet service provider*.

ISV Independent software vendor. Generic name for software vendors other than your hardware vendor.

K&R Kernighan and Ritchie.

Kernel The core of the operating system that handles tasks such as memory allocation, device input and output, process allocation, security, and user access. UNIX tends to have a small kernel when compared to other operating systems.

Keys, control These are keys that cause some function to be performed instead of displaying a character. These functions have names: The end-of-file key tells UNIX that there is no more input; it is usually the Ctrl+D (^D) key.

Keys, special See *Keys, control*.

Korn shell A user interface for UNIX with extensive scripting (programming) support. Written by David G. Korn. The shell features command-line editing and will also accept scripts written for the Bourne shell.

LAN Local area network. A collection of networking hardware, software, desktop computers, servers, and hosts all directly connected together. A LAN could be an entire college campus.

Limits See *Quota*.

LISP List Processing Language.

Logon The process with which a user gains access to a UNIX system. This can also refer to the user ID that is typed at the logon prompt.

lp Line printer.

lpc Line printer control program.

lpd Line printer daemon.

lpq Printer spool queue examination program.

lprm Printer spool queue job removal program.

ls List directory(s) command.

Magic number A number embedded in some files that allows the system to determine type of contents of that file by looking up the number in a table of magic numbers.

Man page The output from the man command that displays pages from the UNIX online manual that tells you how to use most UNIX commands and what options are available for that command.

Memory, real The amount of storage that is being used within the system (silicon; it used to be magnetic cores).

Metacharacter A printing character that has special meaning to the shell or another command. It is converted into something else by the shell or command; the asterisk (*) Filename Generation Wildcard is converted by the shell to a list of all files in the current directory, for example.

MIME Multipurpose Internet Mail Extensions. A set of protocols or methods of attaching binary data (executable programs, images, sound files, and so on) or additional text to email messages.

motd Message of the day.

Mount The act of making a predefined disk drive or section on a disk subsystem (for example, RAID) available to the system. The system maintains an internal mount table of currently mounted filesystems.

Mount commands are normally run automatically when the system is started. See filesystem and Mount point and Unmount.

Mount directory Same as a mount point.

Mount point This a standard UNIX directory (which should not, but may contain files and subdirectories) used by a mount command to become the access point for a filesystem in another disk drive or section of a disk subsystem (for example, RAID). The files and directories in the mount point directory disappear after it is mounted. Instead the files and directories of the mounted filesystem appear to be in the mount point directory. Any accesses or changes within the mount point directory actually occur in the mounted filesystem. See *Filesystem* and *Mount*.

Multitasking operating system One that supports multiple jobs running concurrently, especially when a single user can initiate multiple jobs running concurrently.

Multi-user operating system One that supports multiple users connected to the system running diverse applications simultaneously.

mwm Motif window manager.

Netnews This is a loosely controlled collection of discussion groups. A message (similar to an email) is posted in a specific area and then people can comment on it, publicly replying to the same place (posting a response) for others to see. A collection of messages along the same theme is referred to as a thread. Some of the groups are moderated, which means that nothing is posted without the approval of the owner. Most are not, and the title of the group is no guarantee that the discussion will be related. The official term for this is Usenet news.

NFS Network file system. Means of connecting disks that are mounted to a remote system to the local system as if they were physically connected.

NNTP Netnews Transport Protocol. Used to transmit Netnews or Usenet messages over top of TCP/IP. See *Netnews* for more information on the messages transmitted.

Non-words In vi, non-words are any groups of punctuation. For example, `abc---def=3` contains two non-words: `---` and `=`. See *Contained words* and *Separated words*.

Object An object in the truest sense of the word is something that has physical properties, like automobiles, rubber balls, and clouds. These things have attributes and behavior. They can be abstracted into data (attribute) and code (behavior). Instead of just writing functions to work on data, they are encapsulated into a package that is known as an object.

Operator Metacharacter that performs a function on values or variables. The plus sign (+) is an operator that adds two integers.

Options Program- or command-specific indicators that control behavior of that program. Sometimes called flags. The `-a` option to the `ls` command shows the files that begin with . (such as `.profile`, `.kshrc`, and so on). Without it, these files would not be shown, no matter what wildcards were used. These are used on the command line. See also *Parameters*.

OSF Open Software Foundation.

Parameters Data passed to a command or program through the command line. These can be options (see Options) that control the command or arguments that the command works on. Some have special meaning based on their position on the command line.

Parent directory A directory that contains another directory is said to be the parent directory of that subdirectory.

Parent process A process or job that creates or spawns a subtask also called a child process.

Parent shell Shell (typically the logon shell) that controls another, often referred to as the child shell or subshell. See *Shell*.

Password The secure code that is used in combination with a user ID to gain access to a UNIX system.

Pathname A method of referring to a file that contains a slash—that is, the directory containing the file is indicated. See *Relative* and *Absolute pathnames*.

Perl Programming language developed by Larry Wall. (Perl stands for Practical Extraction and Report Language or Pathologically Eclectic Rubbish Language; both are equally valid). The language provides the capabilities of shell programming, awk and sed, and many enhancements. It is often used to program CGI Web scripts for both UNIX and Windows.

Permissions When applied to files, they are the attributes that control access to a file. There are three levels of access: owner (the file creator), group (people belonging to a related group as determined by the system administrator), and other (everyone else). The permissions are usually r for read, w for write, and x for execute. The execute permissions flag is also used to control who may search a directory.

PGP Pretty Good Privacy encryption system.

PID Process ID Number: Every job or process under UNIX is listed in a table called the process table. The job's entry number in that table is its ID number or PID.

Pine Interactive mail program.

Pipe A method or the action of redirecting the output of one UNIX command to feed the input to a second UNIX command. This eliminates the need to use a file to store temporary results. The pipe self-regulates its flow so that it uses much less disk space than a temporary file would require.

Pipe file See *Pipe, named*.

Pipe sign A vertical bar character (|).

Pipe, named An expanded function of a regular pipe (redirecting the output of one program to become the input of another). Instead of connecting `stdout` to `stdin`, the output of one program is sent to the named pipe and another program reads data from the same file. This is implemented through a special file known as a pipe file or FIFO. The operating system ensures the proper sequencing of the data. Little or no data is actually stored in the pipe file; it just acts as a connection between the two.

Pipeline A sequence of UNIX commands each linking through a pipe. See *Pipe*.

Piping The action of using a pipe. See *Pipe*.

POSIX Portable Operating System Interface, UNIX. POSIX is the name for a family of open system standards based on UNIX. The name has been credited to Richard Stallman. The POSIX Shell and Utilities standard developed by IEEE Working Group 1003.2 (POSIX.2) concentrates on the command interpreter interface and utility programs.

PostScript Adobe Systems, Inc. printer language.

PPID Parent PID: The PID (see PID) of the process or job which started the current process or job being considered.

PPP Point-to-Point Protocol. Internet protocol over serial link (modem).

pppd Point-to-Point-Protocol daemon.

Present directory Same as current directory.

Printcap Printer capability database.

Process A discrete running program under UNIX. The user's interactive session is a process. A process can invoke (run) and control another program that is then referred to as a subprocess. Ultimately, everything a user does is a subprocess of the operating system.

Process identifier Shown in the heading of the `ps` command as PID. The unique number assigned to every process running in the system.

pwd Print working directory command.

Quota General description of a system-imposed limitation on a user or process. It can apply to disk space, memory usage, CPU usage, maximum number of open files, and many other resources.

Quoting The use of single and double quotation marks to negate the normal command interpretation and concatenate all words and whitespace within the quotation marks as a single piece of text.

R.E. pattern My abbreviation for regular expression pattern. This phrase is technically redundant because a regular expression is a pattern. More advanced UNIX users should drop the word pattern and just refer to a regular expression. See *Regular expression*.

R.E. wildcard My abbreviation for regular expression wildcard. See *Regular expression*.

RAID Redundant array of inexpensive/ independent disks. A RAID subsystem enables you to combine several disks into one larger disk structure providing striping (for better performance by equalizing the disk load), mirroring (to protect against media or drive failures), or parity (to provide redundancy protection without having to double the number of data disk drives).

RCS Revision control system.

Recursively processing Recursively processing a directory means that all of its subdirectories are also processed, as are all subdirectories of those subdirectories, and so on. It means that all subdirectories will be processed, no matter how many levels removed from the starting directory.

Redirection The process of directing a data flow from the default. Input can be redirected to get data from a file or the output of another program. Normal output can be sent to another program or a file. Errors can be sent to another program or a file.

Regular expression A pattern that may contain one or more regular expression wildcards. Also a name for a subpattern element of a larger regular expression. See *Regular expression wildcard*.

Regular expression wildcard These are special characters that enable us to specify patterns in a general way within files and pipelines. These wildcard patterns are used by utilities such as grep, sed, awk, and Perl to find desired text to display or modify. Don't confuse these with Filename Generation Wildcards.

Regular file A UNIX file that contains user or system data, text, programming, and so on, as distinguished from a directory, device node, named pipe, semaphore, or shared memory file. This is the most common type of file on a UNIX system.

Relative pathname A method of referring to a file where the directory portion of the filename is indicated as a relative path from the current directory. A relative pathname never starts with a slash— for example, reports/abc refers to the abc file in the reports subdirectory of your current directory. See *Relative path*.

Remark Same thing as comment.

RFC Request For Comment. Document used for creation of Internet- and TCP/IP-related standards.

rlogin Remote login. Gives the same functionality as Telnet, with the added functionality of not requiring a password from trusted clients, which can also create security concerns. See *Telnet*.

Root directory The main system directory that contains all the other directories and files. It is denoted by a single slash (/).

Root user The user who is the UNIX system administrator, also called superuser. Root is regarded as the co-owner of all files, and hence has permission to access all files on the system.

Routing The process of moving network traffic between two different physical networks; also decides which path to take when there are multiple connections between the two machines. It might also send traffic around transmission interruptions.

RPC Remote Procedural Call. Provides the capability to call functions or subroutines that run on a remote system from the local one.

RPM Red Hat Package Manager.

Run level In System V, a number from 0 to 6 that describes the system state.

SCRIPT A program written for a UNIX utility including shells, awk, Perl, sed, and others. See *Shell scripts*.

SCSI Small computer system interface.

sed A common tool used for stream text editing, having ed-like syntax.

Separated words In vi, separated words are any group of characters, separated by spaces, tabs, newlines, or formfeeds. Separated words are also called space delineated/delimited words. See *Contained words* and *Non-words*.

Server, database A system designated to run database software (typically a relational database such as Oracle, SQL Server, Sybase, or others). Other systems connect to this one to get the data (client applications).

SGID Set group ID.

Shell The part of UNIX that handles user input and invokes other programs to run commands. Includes a programming language (for example, Bourne shell, C shell, Korn shell, tcsh, and bash).

Shell environment The shell program (Bourne, Korn, C, tcsh, or bash) invocation options and preset variables that define the characteristics, features, and functionality of the UNIX command-line and program execution interface.

Shell or command prompt The single character or set of characters that the UNIX shell displays for which a user can enter a command or set of commands.

Shell scripts A program written using a shell programming language like those supported by Bourne, Korn, or C shells.

Signal A special flag or interrupt used to communicate special events to programs by the operating system and other programs.

Sit in a directory Informal way to refer to your current directory or changing to a directory. (It will be easier to access these files if you sit in /tmp, for example.)

SLIP Serial Line Internet Protocol. Internet over a serial line (modem). The protocol frames and controls the transmission of TCP/IP packets of the line. PPP is usually preferable to SLIP.

SNA System Network Architecture. IBM networking architecture.

Special files Same as device nodes.

Spool files Temporary copies of files queued up for printing held until they are done printing. This term can also apply to many temporary files held by other system processes such as uucp.

stderr The normal error output for a program that is sent to the screen by default. Can be redirected to a file.

stdin The normal input for a program, taken from the keyboard by default. Can be redirected to get input from a file or the output of another program.

stdout The normal output for a program that is sent to the screen by default. Can be redirected to a file or to the input of another program.

Stream A sequential collection of data. All files are streams to the UNIX operating system. To it, there is no structure to a file; that is something imposed by application programs or special tools (ISAM packages or relational databases).

Subdirectory A directory contained within another directory. If you refer to all subdirectories of a given directory, you are referring not only to its immediate subdirectories but also to every subdirectory of its subdirectories. See *Directory*.

Subnet A portion of a network that shares a common IP address component. Used for security and performance reasons.

Subprocess Process running under the control of another, often referred to as the parent process. See *Process*.

Subshell Shell running under the control of another, often referred to as the parent shell (typically the logon shell). See *Shell*.

Subtree A portion of the UNIX directory tree formed by a directory and each of its files and subdirectories and each of their files and subdirectories, going on like this as far as possible.

SUID Set user ID.

Superuser Usually the root operator.

System administrator The person who takes care of the operating system and user administrative issues on UNIX systems. Also called a system manager, although that term is much more common in DEC VAX installations.

System manager See *System administrator*.

tar Tape archiving utility.

TCP Transmission Control Protocol.

TCP/IP Transport Control Protocol/ Internet Protocol. The pair of protocols and also generic name for suite of tools and protocols that forms the basis for the Internet. Originally developed to connect systems to the ARPAnet.

tcsh A C shell-like user interface featuring command-line editing.

Telnet Protocol for interactive (character user interface) terminal access to remote systems. The terminal emulator that uses the Telnet protocol is often known as telnet or tnvt100.

telnet Remote logon program.

Termcap Terminal capability database.

Terminal A hardware device, normally containing a cathode ray tube (screen) and keyboard for human interaction with a computer system. Does not support graphics or images.

Text processing languages A way of developing documents in text editors with embedded commands that handle formatting. The file is fed through a processor that executes the embedded commands, producing a formatted document. These include roff, nroff, troff, RUNOFF, TeX, LaTeX, and even the mainframe SCRIPT.

TFTP Trivial File Transfer Protocol or Trivial File Transfer Program. A system-independent means of transferring files between systems connected via TCP/IP. It is different from FTP in that it does not ensure that the file is transferred correctly, does not authenticate users, and is missing a lot of functionality (such as the `ls` command).

Tin Interactive news reader.

Truncate To remove/discard the ending portion, whatever exceeds some limit (for example, truncate names to 14 characters).

UDP User Datagram Protocol. Part of TCP/IP used for control messages and data transmission where the delivery acknowledgment is not needed. The application program must ensure data transmission in this case.

UID User ID: Each logon user has an identifying user number called the UID as listed in `/etc/passwd`. See *User ID number*.

UIL Motif User Interface Language.

umount The command that does an unmount. See *Unmount*.

Unmount The act of removing a filesystem from the system mount table, which makes its contents no longer accessible to the system (until it is mounted again). This also transforms the mount point directory back to a normal directory with its old contents now available. See *Filesystem*, *Mount*, and *Mount point*.

URL Uniform resource locator. The method of specifying the protocol, format, logon (usually omitted), and location of materials on the Internet.

Usenet See *Netnews*.

UUCP UNIX-to-UNIX copy program. Used to build an early, informal network for the transmission of files, email, and Netnews.

Variables, attributes The modifiers that set the variable type. A variable can be string or integer, left- or right-justified, read-only or changeable, and other attributes.

Variables, environmental A place to store data and values (strings and integers) in the area controlled by the shell so that they are available to the current and subprocesses. They can just be local to the current shell or available to a subshell (exported).

WAN Wide area network. A network where some of the network connections involve the phone company (for example, digital lines, ISDN, or T1).

Web See *World Wide Web*.

Whitespace One or more spaces and tabs that are normally interpreted to delineate commands and arguments to commands (for example, filenames unless contained within quotation marks).

World Wide Web A collection of servers and services on the Internet that run software and communicate using a common protocol (HTTP). Instead of the users' having to remember the location of these resources, links are provided from one Web page to another through the use of URLs.

Working directory Same as current directory

WWW See *World Wide Web*.

WYSIWYG What You See Is What You Get.

X Window System A windowing and graphics system developed by MIT, to be used in client/server environments.

X11 See *X Window System*.

X See *X Window System*.

yacc Yet another compiler.

Index

commands

directories